MySocLab®

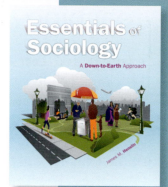

WE BELIEVE IN LEARNING. That's why the **new MySocLab** combines proven learning applications with powerful assessment to engage your students, assess their learning, and help them succeed.

The **new MySocLab** delivers proven results in helping students succeed, provides engaging experiences that personalize learning, and comes from a trusted partner with educational expertise and a deep commitment to helping students and instructors achieve their goals.

Engage

The **new MySocLab** provides innovative materials for student success, including:

Social Explorer Activities: Social Explorer activities allow students to interact with data and draw conclusions based on what they've learned.

Documentary Video Clips: New documentary film clips highlight current local and global issues.

"Sociology Focus" blog: A new blog features sociological voices on contemporary issues **www.sociologyfocus.com.**

The Pearson eText lets students access their textbook anytime, anywhere, and any way they want—including listening online or downloading to iPad.

Assess

Assessment tied to every video, application, and chapter enables both instructors and students to track progress and get immediate feedback. With results feeding into a powerful gradebook, the assessment program helps instructors identify student challenges early—and find the best resources with which to help students.

Succeed

A **personalized study plan** for each student, based on Bloom's Taxonomy, arranges content from less complex thinking–like remembering and understanding–to more complex critical thinking– like applying and analyzing. This layered approach promotes better critical-thinking skills and helps students succeed in the course and beyond.

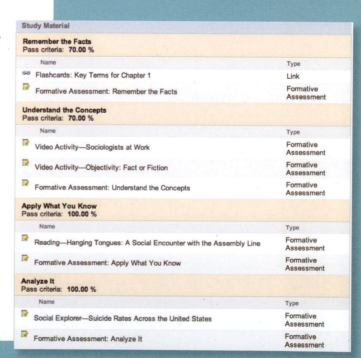

Teaching Tool Highlights

- **Integrated Test Bank**—The new Test Bank is fully integrated with the new learning architecture in the book and MySocLab program. Each question is tagged to Bloom's Taxonomy and to the Chapter-Specific Learning Objectives. The Test Bank is available in MySocLab; Pearson's MyTest and TestGen platforms; and a variety of Learning Management Systems including Blackboard and WebCT.

- **MySocLab Instructor's Manual**—The MySocLab instructor's manual provides advice for utilizing MySocLab in a variety of ways. From introducing short video clips during lecture to fully integrating MySocLab into your course, the MySocLab Instructor's Manual provides everything you need to know to use MySocLab effectively. The manual also includes a complete table of contents for readings in MySocLibrary as well as a complete listing of the media assets available in the lab.

- **ClassPrep**—ClassPrep makes lecture preparation simpler and less time consuming. It collects the very best class presentation resources—art and figures from our leading texts, videos, lecture activities, classroom activities, demonstrations, and much more—in one convenient online destination. You may search through ClassPrep's extensive database of tools by content topic (arranged by standard topics within the sociology curriculum) or by content type (video, audio, simulation, Word documents, etc.). You can select resources appropriate for your lecture, many of which can be downloaded directly, or you may build your own folder of resources and present from within ClassPrep.

- New activities and assessment in **MySocLab** engage students and help them succeed.

- The **outstanding supplements package** supports a wide range of instructional settings including small discussion groups, large lecture halls, and online or Web-based courses.

- **Create a Custom Text**—For enrollments of at least 25, create your own textbook by combining chapters from best-selling Pearson textbooks and/or reading selections in the sequence you want. To begin building your custom text, visit www.pearsoncustomlibrary.com. You may also work with a dedicated Pearson Custom editor to create your ideal text - publishing your own original content or mixing and matching Pearson content. Contact your Pearson Publisher's Representative to get started.

Why do you need this new edition?

6 good reasons why you should buy this new edition of
Essentials of Sociology: A Down-to-Earth Approach

1. **Personalized Learning**—The new MySocLab delivers proven results in helping you succeed, provides engaging experiences that personalize learning, and comes from a trusted partner with educational expertise and a deep commitment to helping students and instructors achieve their goals.

2. **New Media Activities**—MySocLab now features video, reading, and interactive map activities for each chapter that bring the content to life.

3. **Improve Critical Thinking**—Learning objectives have been added to every chapter, which help readers build critical thinking and study skills.

4. **New Design**—*Essentials of Sociology: A Down-to-Earth Approach* has been redesigned for a new generation of learners to help you see sociology come alive!

5. **Living Data**—New Living Data activities in MySocLab allows you to interact with charts and graphs from the text to explore data on a deeper level.

6. **Pearson Choices**—We know you want greater value, innovation, and flexibility in products. You can choose from a variety of text and media formats to match your learning style and your budget.

For specific details on the many changes in this edition, see page xxxiii.

PEARSON

Essentials of Sociology

TENTH EDITION

Essentials of Sociology

A Down-to-Earth Approach

James M. Henslin

Southern Illinois University, Edwardsville

PEARSON

Boston   Columbus   Indianapolis   New York   San Francisco   Upper Saddle River
Amsterdam   Cape Town   Dubai   London   Madrid   Milan   Munich   Paris   Montréal   Toronto
Delhi   Mexico City   São Paulo   Sydney   Hong Kong   Seoul   Singapore   Taipei   Tokyo

Planet Friendly Publishing
✔ Made in the United States
✔ Printed on Recycled Paper
Text: 10%   Cover: 10%
Learn more: www.greenedition.org

At Pearson we're committed to producing books in an Earth-friendly manner and to helping our customers make greener choices. Manufacturing books in the United States ensures compliance with strict environmental laws and eliminates the need for international freight shipping, a major contributor to global air pollution.

Printing on recycled paper helps minimize our consumption of trees, water, and fossil fuels. The text of *Essentials of Sociology,* Tenth Edition, was printed on paper made with 10% post-consumer waste, and the cover was printed on paper made with 10% post-consumer waste. According to The Environmental Paper Network's Paper Calculator, by using this innovative paper instead of conventional papers, we achieved the following environmental benefits:

Trees Saved: 167 • Air Emissions Eliminated: 25,476 pounds
Water Saved: 68,920 gallons • Solid Waste Eliminated: 6,936 pounds

Editorial Director: Craig Campanella
Editor in Chief: Dickson Musslewhite
Senior Acquisitions Editor: Brita Mess
Editorial Assistant: Zoe Lubitz
Director of Marketing: Brandy Dawson
Executive Marketing Manager: Kelly May
Marketing Assistant: Frank Alacron
Managing Editor: Denise Forlow
Project Manager: Marianne Peters-Riordan
Senior Manufacturing and Operations Manager for Arts & Sciences: Mary Fischer
Operations Specialist: Alan Fischer
Design Manager: John Christiana

Art Director: Anne Bonanno Nieglos
Interior Designer: Laura Gardner
Cover Illustrator: Patrick Fagan/Creative Circle
Cover Designer: Wanda Espana, Wee Design Group
Director, Digital Media: Brian Hyland
Digital Media Editor: Rachel Comerford
Assistant Editor: Seanna Breen
Development Editor: Jennifer Auvil
Production Development: Dusty Friedman
Full Service Project Management and Composition: PreMediaGlobal
Printer/Binder and Cover Printer: Courier Companies, Inc.
Text Font: ITC Galliard Std

Credits and acknowledgments borrowed from other sources and reproduced, with permission, in this textbook appear on appropriate page within text (or on page CR1).

Many of the designations by manufacturers and seller to distinguish their products are claimed as trademarks. Where those designations appear in this book, and the publisher was aware of a trademark claim, the designations have been printed in initial caps or all caps.

Library of Congress Cataloging-in-Publication Data

Henslin, James M.
    Essentials of sociology : a down-to-earth approach / James M. Henslin. — 10th ed.
        p. cm.
    ISBN 978-0-205-89847-3
1. Sociology.   I. Title.
    HM586.H43 2012
    301—dc23

2012014783

10 9 8 7 6 5 4 3 2

Student Edition:
ISBN 10: 0-205-89847-5
ISBN 13: 978-0-205-89847-3

Instructor's Review Copy:
ISBN 10: 0-205-90657-5
ISBN 13: 978-0-205-90657-4

Books á la carte:
ISBN 10: 0-205-90007-0
ISBN 13: 978-0-205-90007-7

To my fellow sociologists, who do such creative research on social life and who communicate the sociological imagination to generations of students. With my sincere admiration and appreciation,

Jim Henslin

Brief Contents

Contents

Chapter 2   Culture   38

Chapter 3   Socialization   64

Chapter 4   Social Structure and Social Interaction   92

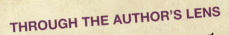

THROUGH THE AUTHOR'S LENS

Vienna: Social Structure and Social Interaction in a Vibrant City

One of the most difficult sociological concepts to grasp is social structure. The concreteness of the photos helps capture this concept, changing it from abstract to part of everyday life. Students have no problem understanding *social interaction*, of course, and in this photo essay they can see how social structure provides the contours for social interaction. (pages 108–109)

THROUGH THE AUTHOR'S LENS

When a Tornado Strikes: Social Organization Following a Natural Disaster

As I was watching television on March 20, 2003, I heard a report that a tornado had hit Camilla, Georgia. "Like a big lawn mower," the report said, it had cut a path of destruction through this little town. In its fury, the tornado had left behind six dead and about 200 injured. (pages 120–121)

Chapter 5   Social Groups and Formal Organizations   124

THROUGH THE AUTHOR'S LENS

Helping a Stranger

Serendipity sometimes accompanies sociologists as they do their work, which was certainly the case here. The entire episode took no more than three minutes, and I was fortunate to capture it with my camera. Real life sometimes differs sharply from that portrayed in research laboratories. (page 144)

Chapter 6   Deviance and Social Control   152

Part III   Social Inequality

Chapter 7   Global Stratification   182

THROUGH THE AUTHOR'S LENS

The Dump People: Working and Living and Playing in the City Dump of Phnom Penh, Cambodia

I went to Phnom Penh, the capital of Cambodia, to inspect orphanages, to see how well the children were being cared for. While there, I was told about people who live in the city dump. *Live* there? I could hardly believe my ears. I knew that people made their living by picking scraps from the city dump, but I didn't know they actually lived among the garbage. This I had to see for myself. (pages 202–203)

Chapter 8   Social Class in the United States   210

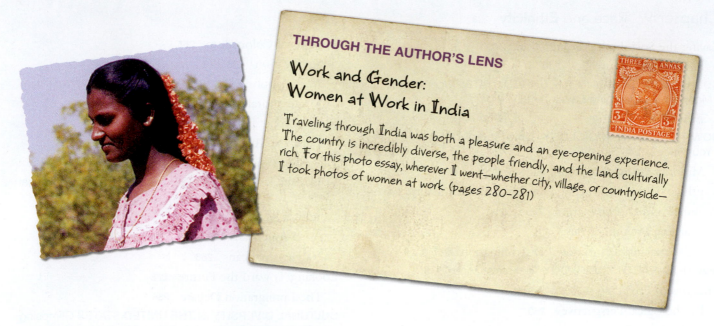

THROUGH THE AUTHOR'S LENS

Work and Gender: Women at Work in India

Traveling through India was both a pleasure and an eye-opening experience. The country is incredibly diverse, the people friendly, and the land culturally rich. For this photo essay, wherever I went—whether city, village, or countryside—I took photos of women at work. (pages 280–281)

Part IV   **Social Institutions**

Chapter 11   Politics and the Economy 314

THROUGH THE AUTHOR'S LENS

Small Town USA
Stuggling to Survive

All across the nation, small towns are struggling to survive. Parents and town officials are concerned because so few young adults remain in their home town. There is little to keep them there, and when they graduate from high school, most move to the city. With young people leaving and old ones dying, the small towns are shriveling. I took most of these photos in the South. (pages 340–341)

Chapter 12   Marriage and Family   350

Chapter 13   Education and Religion   380

THROUGH THE AUTHOR'S LENS

Holy Week in Spain

Religious groups develop rituals designed to evoke memories, create awe, inspire reverence, and stimulate social solidarity. One of the primary means by which groups, religious and secular, accomplish these goals is through the display of symbols.

I took these photos during Holy Week in Spain—in Malaga and Almuñecar. Throughout Spain, elaborate processions feature tronos that depict the biblical account of Jesus' suffering, death, and resurrection. During the processions in Malaga, the participants walk slowly for about two minutes; then because of the weight of the tronos, they rest for about two minutes. They repeat this process for about six hours a day. (pages 402–403)

Part V   Social Change

Chapter 14   Population and Urbanization 414

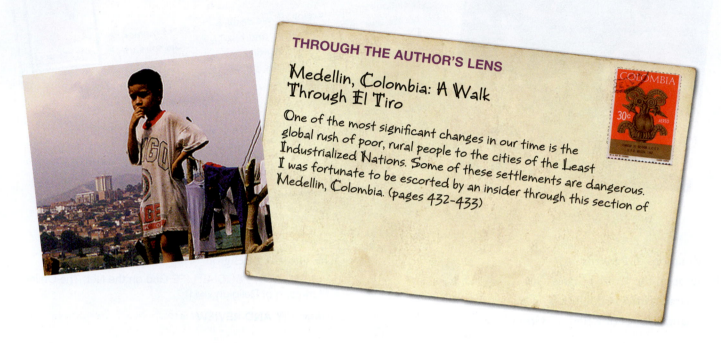

THROUGH THE AUTHOR'S LENS

Medellin, Colombia: A Walk Through El Tiro

One of the most significant changes in our time is the global rush of poor, rural people to the cities of the Least Industrialized Nations. Some of these settlements are dangerous. I was fortunate to be escorted by an insider through this section of Medellin, Colombia. (pages 432–433)

Chapter 15 Social Change and the Environment 448

Special Features

Cultural Diversity around the World

Mass Media in Social Life

THINKING CRITICALLY

Sociology and the New Technology

Guide to Social Maps

WELCOME TO SOCIOLOGY! I've loved sociology since I was in my teens, and I hope you enjoy it, too. Sociology is fascinating because it is about human behavior, and many of us find that it holds the key to understanding social life.

If you like to watch people and try to figure out why they do what they do, you will like sociology. Sociology pries open the doors of society so you can see what goes on behind them. *Essentials of Sociology: A Down-to-Earth Approach* stresses how profoundly our society and the groups to which we belong influence us. Social class, for example, sets us on a particular path in life. For some, the path leads to more education, more interesting jobs, higher income, and better health, but for others it leads to dropping out of school, dead-end jobs, poverty, and even a higher risk of illness and disease. These paths are so significant that they affect our chances of making it to our first birthday, as well as of getting in trouble with the police. They even influence our satisfaction in marriage, the number of children we will have—and whether or not we will read this book in the first place.

When I took my first course in sociology, I was "hooked." Seeing how marvelously my life had been affected by these larger social influences opened my eyes to a new world, one that has been fascinating to explore. I hope that you will have this experience, too.

From how people become homeless to how they become presidents, from why people commit suicide to why women are discriminated against in every society around the world—all are part of sociology. This breadth, in fact, is what makes sociology so intriguing. We can place the sociological lens on broad features of society, such as social class, gender, and race–ethnicity, and then immediately turn our focus on the smaller, more intimate level. If we look at two people interacting—whether quarreling or kissing—we see how these broad features of society are being played out in their lives.

We aren't born with instincts. Nor do we come into this world with preconceived notions of what life should be like. At birth, we have no concepts of race–ethnicity, gender, age, or social class. We have no idea, for example, that people "ought" to act in certain ways because they are male or female. Yet we all learn such things as we grow up in our society. Uncovering the "hows" and the "whys" of this process is also part of what makes sociology so fascinating.

One of sociology's many pleasures is that as we study life in groups (which can be taken as a definition of sociology), whether those groups are in some far-off part of the world or in some nearby corner of our own society, we gain new insights into who we are and how we got that way. As we see how *their* customs affect *them,* the effects of our own society on us become more visible.

This book, then, can be part of an intellectual adventure, for it can lead you to a new way of looking at your social world—and, in the process, help you to better understand both society and yourself.

I wish you the very best in college—and in your career afterward. It is my sincere desire that *Essentials of Sociology: A Down-to-Earth Approach* will contribute to that success.

James M. Henslin
Department of Sociology
Southern Illinois University, Edwardsville

P.S. I enjoy communicating with students, so feel free to comment on your experiences with this text. You can reach me by e-mail: henslin@aol.com

To the Instructor ... from the Author

Remember when you first got "hooked" on sociology, how the windows of perception opened as you began to see life-in-society through the sociological perspective? For most of us, this was an eye-opening experience. This text is designed to open those windows onto social life, so students can see clearly the vital effects of group membership on their lives. Although few students will get into what Peter Berger calls "the passion of sociology," we at least can provide them the opportunity.

To study sociology is to embark on a fascinating process of discovery. We can compare sociology to a huge jigsaw puzzle. Only gradually do we see how the intricate pieces fit together. As we begin to see these interconnections, our perspective changes as we shift our eyes from the many small, disjointed pieces to the whole that is being formed. Of all the endeavors we could have entered, we chose sociology because of the ways in which it joins the "pieces" of society together and the challenges it poses to "ordinary" thinking. To share with students this process of awareness and discovery called the sociological perspective is our privilege.

As instructors of sociology, we have set ambitious goals for ourselves: to teach both social structure and social interaction and to introduce students to the sociological literature—both the classic theorists and contemporary research. As we accomplish this, we would also like to enliven the classroom, encourage critical thinking, and stimulate our students' sociological imagination. Although formidable, these goals are attainable, and this book is designed to help you reach them. Based on many years of frontline (classroom) experience, its subtitle, *A Down-to-Earth Approach,* was not proposed lightly. My goal is to share the fascination of sociology with students and thereby make your teaching more rewarding.

Over the years, I have found the introductory course especially enjoyable. It is singularly satisfying to see students' faces light up as they begin to see how separate pieces of their world fit together. It is a pleasure to watch them gain insight into how their social experiences give shape to even their innermost desires. This is precisely what this text is designed to do—to stimulate your students' sociological imagination so they can better perceive how the "pieces" of society fit together—and what this means for their own lives.

Filled with examples from around the world as well as from our own society, this text helps to make today's multicultural, global society come alive for students. From learning how the international elite carve up global markets to studying the intimacy of friendship and marriage, students can see how sociology is the key to explaining contemporary life—and their own place in it.

In short, this text is designed to make your teaching easier. There simply is no justification for students to have to wade through cumbersome approaches to sociology. I am firmly convinced that the introduction to sociology should be enjoyable and that the introductory textbook can be an essential tool in sharing the discovery of sociology with students.

The Organization of This Text

This text is laid out in five parts. Part I focuses on the sociological perspective, which is introduced in the first chapter. We then look at how culture influences us (Chapter 2), examine socialization (Chapter 3), and compare macrosociology and microsociology (Chapter 4).

Part II, which focuses on social groups and social control, adds to the students' understanding of how far-reaching society's influence is—how group membership penetrates even our thinking, attitudes, and orientations to life. We first examine the different types of groups that have such profound influences on us and then look

at the fascinating area of group dynamics (Chapter 5). After this, we focus on how groups "keep us in line" and sanction those who violate their norms (Chapter 6).

In Part III, we turn our focus on social inequality, examining how it pervades society and its impact on our own lives. Because social stratification is so significant, I have written two chapters on this topic. The first (Chapter 7), with its global focus, presents an overview of the principles of stratification. The second (Chapter 8), with its emphasis on social class, focuses on stratification in U.S. society. After establishing this broader context of social stratification, we examine inequalities of race and ethnicity (Chapter 9) and then those of gender and age (Chapter 10).

Part IV helps students become more aware of how social institutions encompass their lives. We first look at politics and the economy, our overarching social institutions (Chapter 11). After examining the family (Chapter 12), we then turn our focus on education and religion (Chapter 13). One of the emphases in this part of the book is how our social institutions are changing and how their changes, in turn, influence our orientations and decisions.

With its focus on broad social change, Part V provides an appropriate conclusion for the book. Here we examine why our world is changing so rapidly, as well as catch a glimpse of what is yet to come. We first analyze trends in population and urbanization, those sweeping forces that affect our lives so significantly but that ordinarily remain below our level of awareness (Chapter 14). We conclude the book with an analysis of technology, social movements, and the environment (Chapter 15), which takes us to the cutting edge of the vital changes that engulf us all.

Themes and Features

Six central themes run throughout this text: down-to-earth sociology, globalization, cultural diversity, critical thinking, the new technology, and the influence of the mass media on our lives. For each of these themes, except globalization, which is incorporated in several of the others, I have written a series of boxes. These boxed features are one of my favorite components of the book. They are especially useful for introducing the controversial topics that make sociology such a lively activity.

Let's look at these six themes.

DOWN-TO-EARTH SOCIOLOGY

As many years of teaching have shown me, all too often textbooks are written to appeal to the adopters of texts rather than to the students who must learn from them. Therefore, a central concern in writing this book has been to present sociology in a way that not only facilitates understanding but also shares its excitement. During the course of writing other texts, I often have been told that my explanations and writing style are "down-to-earth," or accessible and inviting to students—so much so that I chose this phrase as the book's subtitle. The term is also featured in my introductory reader, *Down-to-Earth Sociology: Introductory Readings,* now in its 15th edition (New York: The Free Press, 2012).

This first theme is highlighted by a series of boxed features that explore sociological processes that underlie everyday life. The topics that we review in these *Down-to-Earth Sociology* boxes are highly diverse. Here are some of them.

- How a sociologist became a gang leader (for a day) (Chapter 1)
- The experiences of W. E. B. Du Bois, an early sociologist, in studying U.S. race relations (Chapter 1)
- 2-D, a new subculture and a different kind of love (Chapter 2)
- The relationship of heredity and the environment (Chapter 3)
- Boot camp as a total institution (Chapter 3)
- How football can help us understand social structure (Chapter 4)
- How beauty influences our interaction (Chapter 4)
- The McDonaldization of society (Chapter 5)

- Serial killers (Chapter 6)
- Urban gangs (Chapter 6)
- What life is like after hitting it big in the lottery (Chapter 8)
- How the super-rich live (Chapter 8)
- Stealth racism in the rental market (Chapter 9)
- How a man became a live exhibit in a New York zoo (Chapter 9)
- Feisty to the end: the elderly maintaining their gender roles (Chapter 10)
- Greedy surgeons and their women victims (Chapter 10)
- Testing stereotypes by looking at the background of suicide terrorists (Chapter 11)

- Child soldiers (Chapter 11)
- Our chances of getting divorced (Chapter 12)
- The meanings of cohabitation (Chapter 12)
- How tsunamis can help us to understand world population growth (Chapter 14)
- The gentrification of Harlem (Chapter 14)
- Deception and persuasion in propaganda (Chapter 15)

This first theme is actually a hallmark of the text, as my goal is to make sociology "down to earth." To help students grasp the fascination of sociology, I continuously stress sociology's relevance to their lives. To reinforce this theme, I avoid unnecessary jargon and use concise explanations and clear and simple (but not reductive) language. I also use student-relevant examples to illustrate key concepts, and I base several of the chapters' opening vignettes on my own experiences in exploring social life. That this goal of sharing sociology's fascination is being reached is evident from the many comments I receive from instructors and students alike that the text helps make sociology "come alive."

GLOBALIZATION

In the second theme, *globalization*, we explore the impact of global issues on our lives and on the lives of people around the world. All of us are feeling the effects of an increasingly powerful and encompassing global economy, one that intertwines the fates of nations. The globalization of capitalism influences the kinds of skills and knowledge we need, the types of work available to us—and whether work is available at all. Globalization also underlies the costs of the goods and services we consume and whether our country is at war or peace—or, as we seem to be, in some uncharted middle ground between the two. In addition to the strong emphasis on global issues that runs throughout this text, I have written a separate chapter on global stratification (Chapter 7). I also feature global issues in the chapters on social institutions and the final chapters on social change: population, urbanization, social movements, and the environment.

What occurs in Russia, Germany, and China, as well as in much smaller nations such as Afghanistan and Iraq, has far-reaching consequences on our own lives. Consequently, in addition to the global focus that runs throughout the text, the next theme, cultural diversity, also has a strong global emphasis.

CULTURAL DIVERSITY AROUND THE WORLD AND IN THE UNITED STATES

The third theme, *cultural diversity*, has two primary emphases. The first is cultural diversity around the world. Gaining an understanding of how social life is "done" in other parts of the world often challenges our taken-for-granted assumptions about social life. At times, when we learn about other cultures, we gain an appreciation for the life of other peoples. At other times, we may be shocked or even disgusted at some aspect of another group's way of life (such as female circumcision) and come away with a renewed appreciation of our own customs.

To highlight this first subtheme, I have written a series of boxes called **Cultural Diversity around the World.** Among the topics with this subtheme are

- food customs that shock people from different cultures (Chapter 2)
- where and why people dance with the dead (Chapter 2)
- how women become men in Albania (Chapter 3)
- human sexuality in Mexico and Kenya (Chapter 6)
- female circumcision (Chapter 10)
- where young children are workers (Chapter 11)
- the new capitalism in China (Chapter 11)
- female infanticide in India and China (Chapter 14)
- urbanization in the Least Industrialized Nations (Chapter 14)
- the destruction of the rain forests and indigenous peoples of Brazil (Chapter 15)

In the second subtheme, **Cultural Diversity in the United States,** we examine groups that make up the fascinating array of people who form the U.S. population. The boxes I have written with this subtheme review such topics as

- how studying job discrimination turned into public sociology (Chapter 1)
- the controversy over the use of Spanish or English (Chapter 2)
- the terms that people choose to refer to their own race–ethnicity (Chapter 2)
- how education can be a conflict for immigrants (Chapter 3)
- how the Amish resist social change (Chapter 4)
- how our own social networks perpetuate inequality (Chapter 5)
- the upward social mobility of African Americans (Chapter 8)
- how Tiger Woods represents a significant change in racial–ethnic identity (Chapter 9)
- the author's travels with a Mexican who transports undocumented workers to the U.S. border (Chapter 9)
- how human heads and animal blood challenge religious tolerance (Chapter 13)

Seeing that there are so many ways of "doing" social life can remove some of our cultural smugness, making us more aware of how arbitrary our own customs are—and how our taken-for-granted ways of thinking are rooted in culture. The stimulating contexts of these contrasts can help students develop their sociological imagination. They encourage students to see connections among key sociological concepts such as culture, socialization, norms, race–ethnicity, gender, and social class. As your students' sociological imagination grows, they can attain a new perspective on their experiences in their own corners of life—and a better understanding of the social structure of U.S. society.

CRITICAL THINKING

In our fourth theme, *critical thinking,* we focus on controversial social issues, inviting students to examine various sides of those issues. In these sections, titled **Thinking Critically,** I present objective, fair portrayals of positions and do not take a side—although occasionally I do play the "devil's advocate" in the questions that close each of the topics. Like the boxed features, these sections can enliven your classroom with a vibrant exchange of ideas. Among the issues addressed are

- managing diversity in the workplace (Chapter 5)
- our tendency to conform to evil authority, as uncovered by the Milgram experiments (Chapter 5)
- sexting (Chapter 6)
- unintended consequences of the three-strike laws (Chapter 6)
- bounties paid to kill homeless children in Brazil (Chapter 7)

- *maquiladoras* on the Mexican–U.S. border (Chapter 7)
- social class inequality in the treatment of mental and physical illness (Chapter 8)
- cyber war (Chapter 15)
- ecosabotage (Chapter 15)

These *Thinking Critically* sections are based on controversial social issues that either affect the student's own life or focus on topics that have intrinsic interest for students. Because of their controversial nature, these sections stimulate both critical thinking and lively class discussions. These sections also provide provocative topics for in-class debates and small discussion groups, effective ways to enliven a class and present sociological ideas. In the Instructor's Manual, I describe the nuts and bolts of using small groups in the classroom.

SOCIOLOGY AND THE NEW TECHNOLOGY

The fifth theme, *sociology and the new technology,* explores an aspect of social life that has come to be central in our lives. We welcome our many new technological tools, for they help us to be more efficient at performing our daily tasks, from making a living to communicating with others—whether those people are nearby or on the other side of the globe. The significance of our new technology, however, extends far beyond the tools and the ease and efficiency they bring to our lives. The new technology is better envisioned as a social revolution that will leave few aspects of our lives untouched. Its effects are so profound that it even changes the ways we view life.

This theme is introduced in Chapter 2, where technology is defined and presented as an essential aspect of culture. The impact of technology is then discussed throughout the text. Examples include how technology is related to cultural change (Chapter 2), fantasy life (Chapter 4), the control of workers (Chapter 5), and the maintenance of global stratification (Chapter 7). We also examine how technology led to social inequality in early human history and how it now may lead to world peace—and to Big Brother's net thrown over us all (Chapter 11). The final chapter, (Chapter 15) "Social Change and the Environment," concludes the book with a focus on this theme.

To highlight this theme, I have written a series of boxes titled **Sociology and the New Technology.** In these boxes, we explore how technology affects our lives as it changes society. We examine, for example, how technology

- is blurring the line between fantasy and reality (Chapter 4)
- is changing the way people find mates (Chapter 12)
- by allowing "designer babies," might change society (Chapter 12)
- is likely to lead to real "star wars" (Chapter 15)

THE MASS MEDIA AND SOCIAL LIFE

In the sixth theme, we stress how the *mass media* influence our behavior and permeate our thinking. We consider how they penetrate our consciousness to such a degree that they even influence how we perceive our own bodies. As your students consider this theme, they may begin to grasp how the mass media shape their attitudes. If so, they will come to view the mass media in a different light, which should further stimulate their sociological imagination.

To make this theme more prominent for students, I have written a series of boxed features called **Mass Media in Social Life.** In these boxes, we consider

- the influence of computer games on images of gender (Chapter 3)
- the worship of thinness—and how this affects our own body images (Chapter 4)
- the reemergence of slavery in today's world (Chapter 7)
- how the mass media underlie changing gender relations in Iran (Chapter 10)

- how the mass media shape our perceptions of the elderly (Chapter 10)
- the myth of increasing school shootings (Chapter 13)

- the Internet marketing of religion (Chapter 13)

NEW TOPICS

It is always a goal—and a challenge—to keep *Essentials of Sociology* current with cutting–edge sociological research and to incorporate into the analyses national and global changes that affect our lives. For a chapter-by-chapter listing of some of this edition's numerous new topics, see "What's New In This Edition" on the next page.

As is discussed in the next section, some of the most interesting—and even fascinating—topics are presented in a visual form.

New and Expanded Features

VISUAL PRESENTATIONS OF SOCIOLOGY

Showing Changes Over Time   In presenting social data, many of the figures and tables show how these data change over time. This feature allows students to see trends in social life and to make predictions of how these trends, if they continue, might affect their own lives. Examples include Figure 1.5, *U.S. Marriage, U.S. Divorce* (Chapter 1) Figure 8.3, *The More Things Change, the More They Stay the Same: Dividing the Nation's Income* (Chapter 8); Figure 10.2, *Changes in College Enrollment, by Sex* (Chapter 10); Figure 10.17, *Trends in Poverty* (Chapter 10); Figure 12.4, *The Number of Children Americans Think Are Ideal* (Chapter 12), and Figure 12.11, *Cohabitation in the United States* (Chapter 12).

This hallmark feature of the text is reinforced by a visual presentation that appears at the end of most chapters: **By the Numbers.** By the Numbers pulls key data and statistics from the text, tables, and figures in the chapter, and presents the data in paired comparisons. These comparisons represent some of the key changes occurring in our society and around the world.

Through the Author's Lens   Using this format, students are able to look over my shoulder as I experience other cultures or explore aspects of this one. These eight photo essays (including two new ones) should expand your students' sociological imagination and open their minds to other ways of doing social life, as well as stimulate thought-provoking class discussion.

Vienna: Social Structure and Social Interaction, which appears in Chapter 4, is new to this edition. The photos I took in this city illustrate how social structure surrounds us, setting the scene for our interactions, limiting and directing them.

When a Tornado Strikes: Social Organization Following a Natural Disaster When a tornado hit a small town just hours from where I lived, I photographed the aftermath of the disaster. The police let me in to view the neighborhood where the tornado had struck, destroying homes and killing several people. I was impressed by how quickly people were putting their lives back together, the topic of this photo essay (Chapter 4).

Helping a Stranger Occasionally, maybe rarely, when doing sociological research, everything falls into place. This photo essay could carry the subtitle *Serendipity in Research.* The propitious (for me) accident in Vienna, which I was able to photograph, casts doubt on classic laboratory research regarding the willingness of people to help a stranger based on the number of people present (Chapter 5).

The Dump People: Working and Living and Playing in the City Dump of Phnom Penh, Cambodia Among the culture shocks I experienced in Cambodia was not to discover that people scavenge at Phnom Penh's huge city dump—this I knew

WHAT'S NEW IN THIS EDITION?

CHAPTER 1 THE SOCIOLOGICAL PERSPECTIVE
Topic: The use of Facebook to document the race-ethnicity of friendships of college students
Topic: How applied sociology relates to *Dora the Explorer*

CHAPTER 2 CULTURE
Cultural Diversity Box: Cultural Diversity around the World Box: Dancing with the Dead

CHAPTER 3 SOCIALIZATION
Topic: Advertising as a source of gender messages in the mass media
Topic: Movies as a source of gender messages in the mass media
Topic: How the effects of day care follow children (NICHD research; latest testing at age 15)
Topic: The facial expressions of people blind since birth, upon learning they had won or lost at the Paralympics, were the same as those of sighted people
Topic: The average number of commercials Americans are exposed to has jumped to 200,000 a year

CHAPTER 4 SOCIAL STRUCTURE AND SOCIAL INTERACTION
Topic: The U.S. army is trying to apply body language to alert soldiers to danger when interacting with civilians in a military zone
Topic: Perhaps coming soon: Snap-together BioBricks to produce your own life forms
Sociology and the New Technology Box: "So, You Want to Be Yourself?" Cloning and the Future of Society
Through the Author's Lens: Social Structure and Social Interaction in the City

CHAPTER 5 SOCIAL GROUPS AND FORMAL ORGANIZATIONS
Through the Author's Lens: Helping a Stranger (which shows limitations to Darley and Latane's laboratory research on the diffusion of responsibility)
Cultural Diversity Box: How Your Social Networks Perpetuate Social Inequality
Sociology and the New Technology Box: Cyberloafers and Cybersleuths: Surfing at Work
Topic: Technology and the control of workers— toward a maximum-security society
Topic: To receive prizes on a fake game show, 80 percent of contestants gave victims what they thought were near-lethal 450 volt shocks
Topic: The most effective way to increase employee diversity of a work force is to set goals for increasing diversity and make managers accountable for reaching them
Topic: Research on millions confirms Milgram's 6 degrees of separation

CHAPTER 6 DEVIANCE AND SOCIAL CONTROL
Topic: How genetic explanations are being used to explain crime
Topic: Unemployment increases but crime stays at lower levels
Down-to-Earth Sociology Box: "The Naked Pumpkin Runners and the Naked Bike Riders: Deviance or Freedom of Self-Expression?"
Cultural Diversity around the World Box: "'Dogging' in England"
Thinking Critically: Sexting

Topic: A corporate decision leads to the deaths of 600 miners in West Virginia
Topic: Courts fine Northrop Gruman $325 million for a white collar crime–and the federal government then awards the company $325 million
Topic: Anthony Sowell of Cleveland added to the list of serial killers

CHAPTER 7 GLOBAL STRATIFICATION
Topic: Defense Department buys and destroys 9,500 copies of a book critical of its handling of 9/11

CHAPTER 8 SOCIAL CLASS IN THE UNITED STATES
Topic: Waiting lists for preschools that cost $37,000 a year
Topic: Upper middle-class parents who pay $1,000 to train their 4-year olds in test-taking skills so they can get into public kindergartens for gifted students
Topic: Microsoft co-founder Paul Allen's 414-foot yacht has two helicopters, a swimming pool, and a submarine
Topic: The top fifth of the U.S. population now receives 50.3% of the nation's income
Topic: *10 percent* of the nation's families now own *75 percent* of the nation's wealth
Topic: Status inconsistent men are twice as likely to have heart attacks as status consistent men, but status inconsistent women do not have a higher risk of heart attacks
Topic: With migration and the economic crisis, most of the poor now live in the suburbs
Topic: Poverty has increased, and now 21 million U.S. children are poor
Topic: *Poverty triggers:* events that propel people into poverty
Topic: Over a four-year period, *one-third* (32 percent) of Americans experience poverty for at least two months.
Topic: Census Bureau is using alternative poverty lines
Topic: public kindergartens for gifted students

CHAPTER 9 RACE AND ETHNICITY
Down-to-Earth Sociology Box: "Can a Plane Ride Change Your Race?"
Topic: Construction of the fence along the Mexican border cancelled
Topic: With the economic crisis, net immigration from Mexico is now zero
Topic: Arabs added to Figure 9.5 U.S. Racial-Ethnic Groups
Topic: Michael Kimmel's research on Neo-Nazi skinheads in Sweden
Topic: Susana Martinez elected as the first Latina governor (New Mexico)
Topic: Countrywide pays $335 million to settle lawsuit for discriminatory lending against Latinos and African Americans

CHAPTER 10 GENDER AND AGE
Down-to-Earth Sociology Box: "Women and Smoking: Let's Count the Reasons"
Down-to-Earth Sociology Box: "Feisty to the End: Gender Roles among the Elderly"
Topic: Disagreement among feminists regarding "erotic capital"
Topic: Health workers have developed a strategy to get entire villages to renounce female circumcision

Topic: With our economic crisis, children's poverty is now higher than it was in 1967—and all the years in between
Table 10.1 Age of Rape Victims

CHAPTER 11 POLITICS AND ECONOMY
Topic: Supreme Court's 2010 decision, *Citizens United v. Federal Election Commission*, which opened the floodgates for corporations to bankroll politicians

CHAPTER 12 MARRIAGE AND FAMILY
Topic: The transfer of authority in Cuba as an example of Weber's routinization of charisma
Topic: China's new capitalism has lifted a *half billion people* out of poverty
Topic: Number of new billionaires in China
Topic: New opening vignette
Topic: Adoption by gay and lesbian couples
Topic: Feelings of romantic love light up the same area of the brain as does craving for cocaine
Topic: Single women who give birth are taking longer to get married
Topic: On average, the children of cohabiting parents aren't as healthy as the children of married parents
Topic: Of the recently married, the divorce rate of those who did and did not cohabit before marriage is about the same
Topic: Gender equality in the initiation of marital violence indicates the need to direct anti-violence socialization to both males and females
Topic: New research on 13,000 cases of sibling incest
Illustration: Table 12.4 Fathers' Contact with Their Children After Divorce
Sociology and the New Technology Box: What Color Eyes? How Tall? Designer Babies on the Way

CHAPTER 13 EDUCATION AND RELIGION
Down-to-Earth Sociology Box: How I Became a Fairy: Education and the Perpetuation of Social Inequality
Topic: *juku* (cram schools) in Japan
Topic: Trend for community colleges to become four-year colleges
Topic: In Russia, officials have begun to check the content of history books for their "degree of patriotism"
Topic: In Japan, teachers must visit each student's home once a year

CHAPTER 14 POPULATION AND URBANIZATION
Illustration: Figure 14.11 How the World Is Urbanizing
Topic: India government offers $106 cash bonuses for newlywed women who wait two years before getting pregnant
Topic: 5,000 year old city buried under sand discovered in Norway
Topic: Urbanization has accelerated and by 2050 two-thirds of the world's population will live in cities
Topic: World population reached seven billion in 2011

CHAPTER 15 SOCIAL CHANGE AND THE ENVIRONMENT
Topic: New opening vignette
Thinking Critically: Cyber War and Cyber Defense
Topic: Car and truck engines that burn natural gas will become common

about—but that they also live there. With the aid of an interpreter, I was able to interview these people, as well as photograph them as they went about their everyday lives. An entire community lives in the city dump, complete with restaurants amidst the smoke and piles of garbage. This photo essay reveals not just these people's activities but also their social organization (Chapter 7).

Work and Gender: Women at Work in India As I traveled in India, I took photos of women at work in public places. The more I traveled in this country and the more photos I took, the more insight I gained into gender relations. Despite the general submissiveness of women to men in India, women's worlds are far from limited to family and home. Not only are women found at work throughout the society, but what is even more remarkable is how vastly different "women's work" is in India than it is in the United States. This, too, is an intellectually provocative photo essay (Chapter 10).

Small Town USA: Struggling to Survive To take the photos for this essay, I went off the beaten path. On a road trip from California to Florida, instead of following the interstates, I followed those "little black lines" on the map. They took me to out-of-the-way places that the national transportation system has bypassed. Many of these little towns are putting on a valiant face as they struggle to survive, but, as the photos show, the struggle is apparent, and, in some cases, so are the scars (Chapter 11).

Holy Week in Spain I was fortunate to be able to photograph religious processions in two cities, Malaga, a provincial capital, and Almuñecar, a smaller city of Granada. Spain has a Roman Catholic heritage so deep that some of its city streets are named Conception, Piety, Humility, Calvary, Crucifixion, The Blessed Virgin, etc. In large and small towns throughout Spain, elaborate processions during Holy Week feature *tronos* that depict the biblical account of Jesus' suffering, death, and resurrection. As you will see in this photo essay, these events have a decidedly Spanish flavor.

I was also allowed to photograph the preparations for a procession, so this photo essay also includes some "behind-the-scenes" photos. During the processions in Malaga, the participants walk slowly for one or two minutes, then because of the weight of the *tronos,* they rest for one or two minutes. Except for Saturdays, this process repeats for about six hours each day during Holy Week, with different *tronos* featured and different bands and organizations participating. As you will see, some of the most interesting activities occur during the rest periods (Chapter 13).

A Walk Through El Tiro in Medellín, Colombia One of the most significant social changes in the world is taking place in the Least Industrialized Nations. There, in the search for a better life, people are abandoning rural areas. Fleeing poverty, they are flocking to the cities, only to find even more poverty. Some of these settlements of the new urban poor are dangerous. I was fortunate to be escorted by an insider through a section of Medellín, Colombia, that is controlled by gangs (Chapter 14).

Other Photos by the Author

Sprinkled throughout the text are photos that I took in Austria, Cambodia, India, Latvia, Spain, and the United States. These photos illustrate sociological principles and topics better than photos available from commercial sources. As an example, while in the United States, I received a report about a feral child who had been discovered living with monkeys and who had been taken to an orphanage in Cambodia. The possibility of photographing and interviewing that child was one of the reasons that I went to Cambodia. That particular photo is on page 67. Another of my favorites is on page 154.

Photo Essay on Subcultures

To help students better understand subcultures, I have retained the photo essay on subcultures in Chapter 2. Because this photo essay consists of photos taken by others, it is not a part of the series, *Through the Author's*

Lens. The variety of subcultures featured in this photo essay, however, should be instructive to your students.

Photo Collages   Because sociology lends itself so well to photographic illustrations, this text also includes photo collages. I am very pleased with the one in Chapter 1 that features some of the many women who became sociologists in earlier generations, as these women have largely gone unacknowledged as sociologists. In Chapter 2, students can catch a glimpse of the fascinating variety that goes into the cultural relativity of beauty. The collage in Chapter 5 illustrates categories, aggregates, and primary and secondary groups, concepts that students sometimes wrestle to distinguish. The photo collage in Chapter 10 lets students see how differently gender is portrayed in different cultures.

Other Special Pedagogical Features

In addition to chapter summaries and reviews, key terms, and a comprehensive glossary, I have included several other features to aid students in learning sociology. **In Sum** sections help students review important points within the chapter before going on to new materials. I have also developed a series of **Social Maps,** which illustrate how social conditions vary by geography (see page xxiii).

Learning Objectives   New to this edition are *learning objectives*. These are located at the foot of the chapter's pages. Rather than saying "The learning objective is this or that" or "You should know this or that," I have put most learning objectives in a question format. This format is designed not only to alert the students to what they should learn but also to help them think about what they are reading. You might also find these learning objectives useful in your classroom interaction, as they are handy "jumping off" places for class discussions and for reinforcing the students' learning.

Chapter-Opening Vignettes   These accounts feature down-to-earth illustrations of a major aspect of each chapter's content. Some are based on my research with the homeless, the time I spent with them on the streets and slept in their shelters (Chapters 1 and 8). Others recount my travels in Africa (Chapters 2 and 10) and Mexico (Chapters 12 and 14). I also share my experiences when I spent a night with street people at Dupont Circle in Washington, D.C. (Chapter 4). For other vignettes, I use current and historical events (Chapters 7, 9, 13, and 15), classic studies in the social sciences (Chapters 3 and 6), and even scenes from novels (Chapters 5 and 11). Students have often told me that they find the vignettes compelling, that they stimulate interest in the chapter.

Thinking Critically About the Chapters   I close each chapter with critical thinking questions. Each question focuses on a major feature of the chapter, asking students to consider some issue. Many of the questions ask the students to apply sociological findings and principles to their own lives.

On Sources   Sociological data are found in an amazingly wide variety of sources, and this text reflects that variety. Cited throughout this text are standard journals such as the *American Journal of Sociology, Social Problems, American Sociological Review,* and *Journal of Marriage and the Family,* as well as more esoteric journals such as the *Bulletin of the History of Medicine, Chronobiology International,* and *Western Journal of Black Studies.* I have also drawn heavily from standard news sources, especially the *New York Times* and the *Wall Street Journal,* as well as more unusual sources such as *El País.* In addition, I cite unpublished papers by sociologists.

Acknowledgments

The gratifying response to earlier editions indicates that my efforts at making sociology down to earth have succeeded. The years that have gone into writing this text are a culmination of the many more years that preceded its writing—from graduate school to that equally demanding endeavor known as classroom teaching. No text, of course, comes solely from its author. Although I am responsible for the final words on the printed page, I have received excellent feedback from instructors who used the first nine editions. I am especially grateful to

Reviewers

Sandra L. Albrecht, *University of Kansas*

David Allen, *Georgia Southern University*

Angelo A. Alonzo, *Ohio State University*

Kenneth Ambrose, *Marshall University*

Alberto Arroyo, *Baldwin–Wallace College*

Karren Baird-Olsen, *Kansas State University*

Linda Barbera-Stein, *University of Illinois*

Richard J. Biesanz, *Corning Community College*

Charles A. Brawner III, *Heartland Community College*

Shelly Breitenstein, *Western Wisconsin Technical College*

Richard D. Bucher, *Baltimore City Community College*

Richard D. Clark, *John Carroll University*

John K. Cochran, *University of Oklahoma*

Matthew Crist, *Moberly Area Community College*

Russell L. Curtis, *University of Houston*

William Danaher, College of Charleston

John Darling, *University of Pittsburgh–Johnstown*

Ray Darville, *Stephen F. Austin State University*

Nanette J. Davis, *Portland State University*

Tom DeDen, *Foothill College*

Paul Devereux, *University of Nevada*

Lynda Dodgen, *North Harris Community College*

James W. Dorsey, *College of Lake County*

Helen R. Ebaugh, *University of Houston*

Obi N. Ebbe, *State University of New York–Brockport*

Margaret C. Figgins-Hill, *University of Massachusetts–Lowell*

Robin Franck, *Southwestern College*

David O. Friedrichs, *University of Scranton*

Richard A. Garnett, *Marshall University*

George W. Glann, Jr., *Fayetteville Technical Community College*

Norman Goodman, *State University of New York–Stony Brook*

Anne S. Graham, *Salt Lake Community College*

Donald W. Hastings, *The University of Tennessee–Knoxville*

Penelope E. Herideen, *Holyoke Community College*

Michael Hoover, *Missouri Western State College*

Hua-Lun Huang, *University of Louisiana*

Charles E. Hurst, *The College of Wooster*

Dick Jobst, *Pacific Lutheran University*

Mark Kassop, *Bergen Community College*

Alice Abel Kemp, *University of New Orleans*

Dianna Kendall, *Austin Community College*

Gary Kiger, *Utah State University*

Ross Koppel, *University of Pennsylvania*

Jenifer Kunz, *West Texas A&M University*

David Kyle, *University of California–Davis*

Patricia A. Larson, *Cleveland State University*

Abraham Levine, *El Camino Community College*

Mike Lindner, *Gloucester County College*

Fr. Jeremiah Lowney, *Carroll College*

Cecile Lycan, *Spokane Community College*

John J. Malarky, *Wilmington College*

Patricia Masters, *George Mason University*

Bonita Sessing Matcha, *Hudson Valley Community College*

Ron Matson, *Wichita State University*

Armaund L. Mauss, *Washington State University*

Roger McVannan, *Broome Community College*

Evelyn Mercer, *Southwest Baptist University*

Robert Meyer, *Arkansas State University*

Richard B. Miller, *Missouri Southern State College*

Beth Mintz, *University of Vermont–Burlington*

Meryl G. Nason, *University of Texas, Dallas*

Craig J. Nauman, *Madison Area Technical College*

W. Lawrence Neuman, *University of Wisconsin–Whitewater*

Charles Norman, *Indiana State University*

Laura O'Toole, *University of Delaware*

Mike Pate, *Western Oklahoma State College*

William Patterson, *Clemson University*

Phil Piket, *Joliet Junior College*

Annette Prosterman, *Our Lady of the Lake University*

Adrian Rapp, *North Harris Community College*

Nancy Reeves, *Gloucester County College*

Donald D. Ricker, *Mott Community College*

Howard Robboy, *Trenton State College*

Terina Roberson, *Central Piedmont Community College*

Alden E. Roberts, *Texas Tech University*

Sybil Rosado, *Benedict College*

Kent Sandstrom, *University of Northern Iowa*

Don Shamblin, *Ohio University*

Walt Shirley, *Sinclair Community College*

Laura Siebuhr, *Centralia College*

Marc Silver, *Hofstra University*

Michael C. Smith, *Milwaukee Area Technical College*

Roberto E. Socas, *Essex County College*

Sherry Sperman, *Kansas State University*

Susan Sprecher, *Illinois State University*

Randolph G. Ston, *Oakland Community College*

Kathleen Tiemann, *University of North Dakota*

Tracy Tolbert, *California State University*

Suzanne Tuthill, *Delaware Technical Community College*

Lisa Waldner, *University of Houston–Downtown*

Larry Weiss, *University of Alaska*

Douglas White, *Henry Ford Community College*

Stephen R. Wilson, *Temple University*

Stuart Wright, *Lamar University*

Meifang Zhang, *Midlands Technical College*

I couldn't ask for a more outstanding team than the one that I have the pleasure to work with at Pearson. I want to thank Brita Mess for keeping things on schedule and for working so diligently on the design; Jenn Auvil for coordinating the many processes that this edition required; Dusty Friedman, who gave up other projects to work on this book, and for always encouraging me to reach farther; Jenn Albanese, whose pursuit of countless research leads has been an ongoing help in this formidable task of keeping up with the sociological literature and abreast of social change; Kate Cebik, whose eye for photo composition and willingness to "keep on looking" for the "exact" photo have enhanced the visual appeal of this edition.

I do so appreciate this team. It is difficult to heap too much praise on such fine, capable, and creative people. Often going "beyond the call of duty" as we faced nonstop deadlines, their untiring efforts coalesced with mine to produce this text. Students, whom we constantly kept in mind as we prepared this edition and exchanged hundreds of emails, are the beneficiaries of this intricate teamwork.

I would also like to thank those who prepared the many supplements that go with *Essentials of Sociology*. Their efforts, so often unacknowledged, are important in our goal of introducing students to sociology and awakening their sociological imagination. The Instructor's Manual/Test Bank for this edition of *Essentials of Sociology* was prepared by Jessica Herrmeyer.

Since this text is based on the contributions of many, I would count it a privilege if you would share with me your teaching experiences with this book, including any suggestions for improving the text. Both positive and negative comments are welcome. It is in this way that I continue to learn.

I wish you the very best in your teaching. It is my sincere desire that *Essentials of Sociology: A Down-to-Earh Approach* contributes to your classroom success.

James M. Henslin,
Professor Emeritus
Department of Sociology
Southern Illinois University, Edwardsville

I welcome your correspondence. E-mail is the best way to reach me: henslin@aol.com

About the Author

JIM HENSLIN was born in Minnesota, graduated from high school and junior college in California and from college in Indiana. Awarded scholarships, he earned his master's and doctorate degrees in sociology at Washington University in St. Louis, Missouri. After this, he won a postdoctoral fellowship from the National Institute of Mental Health and spent a year studying how people adjust to the suicide of a family member. His primary interests in sociology are the sociology of everyday life, deviance, and international relations. Among his many books are *Down-to-Earth Sociology: Introductory Readings* (Free Press), now in its 15th edition, and *Social Problems* (Allyn and Bacon), now in its 10th edition. He has also published widely in sociology journals, including *Social Problems* and *American Journal of Sociology*.

While a graduate student, Jim taught at the University of Missouri at St. Louis. After completing his doctorate, he joined the faculty at Southern Illinois University, Edwardsville, where he is Professor Emeritus of Sociology. He says, "I've always found the introductory course enjoyable to teach. I love to see students' faces light up when they first glimpse the sociological perspective and begin to see how society has become an essential part of how they view the world."

Jim enjoys reading and fishing, and he also does a bit of kayaking and weight lifting. His two favorite activities are writing and traveling. He especially enjoys visiting and living in other cultures, for this brings him face to face with behaviors and ways of thinking that challenge his perspectives and "make sociological principles come alive." A special pleasure has been the preparation of the photo essays that appear in this text.

Jim moved to Latvia, an Eastern European country formerly dominated by the Soviet Union, where he had the experience of becoming an immigrant. There he observed firsthand how people struggle to adjust to capitalism. While there, he happened to be present at a historical event. See the lower photo on page 633. He also interviewed aged political prisoners who had survived the Soviet gulag. He then moved to Spain, where he was able to observe how people adjust to a declining economy and the immigration of people from contrasting cultures. (Of course, for this he didn't need to leave the United States.) To better round out his cultural experiences, Jim is making plans for extended stays in India and South America, where he expects to do more photo essays to reflect their fascinating cultures. He is grateful to be able to live in such exciting social, technological, and geopolitical times—and to have access to portable broadband Internet while he pursues his sociological imagination.

The author at work—sometimes getting a little too close to "the action" (preparing the "Through the Author's Lens" photo essay on pages 402–403.)

Anita Henslin

Essentials
of Sociology

The Sociological Perspective

The Sociological Perspective

Even from the glow of the faded red-and-white exit sign, its faint light barely illuminating the upper bunk, I could see that the sheet was filthy. Resigned to another night of fitful sleep, I reluctantly crawled into bed.

I kept my clothes on.

The next morning, I joined the long line of disheveled men leaning against the chain-link fence. Their faces were as downcast as their clothes were dirty. Not a glimmer of hope among them.

No one spoke as the line slowly inched forward.

When my turn came, I was handed a cup of coffee, a white plastic spoon, and a bowl of semiliquid that I couldn't identify. It didn't look like any food I had seen before. Nor did it taste like anything I had ever eaten.

My stomach fought the foul taste, every spoonful a battle. But I was determined. "I will experience what they experience," I kept telling myself. My stomach reluctantly gave in and accepted its morning nourishment.

The room was strangely silent. Hundreds of men were eating, each one immersed in his own private hell, his mind awash with disappointment, remorse, bitterness.

> The room was strangely silent. Hundreds of men were eating, each immersed in his own private hell . . .

As I stared at the Styrofoam cup that held my coffee, grateful for at least this small pleasure, I noticed what looked like teeth marks. I shrugged off the thought, telling myself that my long weeks as a sociological observer of the homeless were finally getting to me. "It must be some sort of crease from handling," I concluded.

I joined the silent ranks of men turning in their bowls and cups. When I saw the man behind the counter swishing out Styrofoam cups in a washtub of murky water, I began to feel sick to my stomach. I knew then that the jagged marks on my cup really had come from another person's mouth.

How much longer did this research have to last? I felt a deep longing to return to my family—to a welcome world of clean sheets, healthy food, and "normal" conversations.

Australia

The Sociological Perspective

Why were these men so silent? Why did they receive such despicable treatment? What was I doing in that homeless shelter? After all, I hold a respectable, professional position, and I have a home and family.

You are in for an exciting and eye-opening experience. Sociology offers a fascinating view of social life. The *sociological perspective* (or imagination) opens a window onto unfamiliar worlds—and offers a fresh look at familiar ones. In this text, you will find yourself in the midst of Nazis in Germany and warriors in South America. Sociology is broad, and your journey will even take you to a group that lives in a city dump. (If you want to jump ahead, you can see the photos I took of the people who live—and work and play—in a dump in Cambodia on pages 202–203.) You will also find yourself looking at your own world in a different light. As you view other worlds—or your own—the sociological perspective enables you to gain a new perception of social life. In fact, this is what many find appealing about sociology.

The sociological perspective has been a motivating force in my own life. Ever since I took my introductory course in sociology as a freshman in college, I have been enchanted by the perspective that sociology offers. I have enjoyed both observing other groups and questioning my own assumptions about life. I sincerely hope the same happens to you.

Seeing the Broader Social Context

The **sociological perspective** stresses the social contexts in which people live. It examines how these contexts influence people's lives. At the center of the sociological perspective is the question of how groups influence people, especially how people are influenced by their **society**—a group of people who share a culture and a territory.

To find out why people do what they do, sociologists look at **social location,** the corners in life that people occupy because of where they are located in a society. Sociologists look at how jobs, income, education, gender, race–ethnicity, and age affect people's ideas and behavior. Consider, for example, how being identified with a group called *females* or with a group called *males* when you were growing up has shaped *your* ideas of who you are. Growing up as a female or a male has influenced not only how you feel about yourself but also your ideas of what you should attain in life and how you relate to others.

Sociologist C. Wright Mills (1959) put it this way: "The sociological imagination [perspective] enables us to grasp the connection between history and biography." By *history,* Mills meant that each society is located in a broad stream of events. This gives each society specific characteristics—such as its ideas about the proper roles of men and women. By *biography,* Mills referred to our experiences within these historical settings, which give us our orientations to life. In short, people don't do what they do because they inherited some internal mechanism, such as instincts. Rather, *external* influences— our experiences—become part of our thinking and motivation. In short, the society in which we grow up, and our particular location in that society, lie at the center of what we do and how we think.

Consider a newborn baby. As you know, if we were to take the baby away from its U.S. parents and place it with the Yanomamö Indians in the jungles of South America, when the child began to speak, his or her words would not be in English. You also know that the child would not think like an American. The child would not grow up wanting credit cards, for example, or a car, a cell phone, an iPod, and video games. He or she would take his or her place in Yanomamö society—perhaps as a food gatherer or a hunter—and would not even know about the world left behind at birth. And, whether male or female, the child would grow up assuming that it is natural to want many children, not debating whether to have one, two, or three children.

Read

Invitation to Sociology
by Peter Berger
on **mysoclab.com**

Can you explain how history and biography are both essential elements of the *sociological perspective?*

If you have been thinking along with me—and I hope you have—you should be thinking about how *your* social groups have shaped *your* ideas and desires. Over and over in this text, you will see that the way you look at the world is the result of your exposure to specific human groups. I think you will enjoy the process of self-discovery that sociology offers.

The Global Context—and the Local

How life has changed! Our predecessors lived on isolated farms and in small towns. They grew their own food and made their own clothing. They bought only sugar, coffee, and a few other items that they couldn't produce. Beyond the borders of their small communities lay a world they perceived only dimly. The labels on our clothing (from Hong Kong to Italy), in contrast, as well as the many other imported products that have become part of our daily lives shout that our world has shrunk into a global village.

Even though we can pick up a telephone or use the Internet to communicate instantly with people anywhere on the planet, we continue to occupy our own little corners of life. Like those of our predecessors, our worlds, too, are marked by differences in family background, religion, gender, race–ethnicity, and social class. In these corners, we continue to learn distinctive ways of viewing the world.

One of the beautiful—and fascinating—aspects of sociology is that it enables us to look at both parts of our current reality: being part of a global network *and* our unique experiences in our smaller corners of life. This text reflects both of these worlds, each so vital in understanding who we are.

Origins of Sociology

Tradition versus Science

Just how did sociology begin? Even ancient peoples tried to figure out social life. They, too, asked questions about why war exists, why some people become more powerful than others, and why some are rich, but others are poor. However, they often based their answers on superstition, myth, or even the positions of the stars. They did not *test* their assumptions.

Science, in contrast, requires theories that can be tested by research. Measured by this standard, sociology emerged about the middle of the 1800s when social observers began to use scientific methods to test their ideas.

Sociology was born in social upheaval. The Industrial Revolution had just begun, and masses of people were moving to cities in search of work. This broke their ties to the land—and to a culture that had provided ready answers to the difficult questions of life. The cities greeted them with horrible working conditions: low pay, long hours, and dangerous work. Families lived on the edge of starvation, and children worked alongside the adults. Life no longer looked the same, and tradition, which had provided the answers to social life, no longer could be counted on.

Tradition suffered further blows. With the success of the American and French revolutions, new ideas swept out the old. As the idea that people don't belong to a king and that each person possesses inalienable rights caught fire, many traditional Western monarchies gave way to more democratic forms of government. This stimulated even more new perspectives.

About this time, **the scientific method**—using objective, systematic observations to test theories—was being tried out in chemistry and physics. This approach opened many secrets that had been concealed in nature. With traditional answers failing, the next step was to apply the scientific method to questions about social life. The result was the birth of sociology.

Let's take a quick overview of some of the main figures in this development.

Upsetting the entire social order, the French Revolution removed the past as a sure guide to the present. This stimulated Auguste Comte to analyze how societies change. Shown here is the 1793 Battle of Cholet.

Auguste Comte and Positivism

Auguste Comte (1798–1857) who is credited as the founder of sociology, began to analyze the bases of the social order. Although he stressed that the scientific method should be applied to the study of society, he did not apply it himself.

Auguste Comte (1798–1857) suggested that we apply the scientific method to the social world, a process known as **positivism.** With the bloody upheavals of the French Revolution fresh in his mind—and he knew that the crowds had cheered at the public execution of the king and queen of France—Comte started to wonder what holds society together. Why do we have social order instead of anarchy or chaos? he asked. And when society becomes set on a particular course, what causes it to change?

These were pressing questions, and Comte decided that the scientific method held the key to answering them. Just as the scientific method had revealed the law of gravity, so, too, it would uncover the laws that underlie society. Comte called this new science **sociology**—"the study of society" (from the Greek *logos,* "study of," and the Latin *socius,* "companion," or "being with others"). The purpose of this new science, he said, would be not only to discover social principles but also to apply them to social reform. Comte developed a grandiose view: Sociologists would reform society, making it a better place to live.

Comte did not do what we today call research, and his conclusions have been abandoned. Nevertheless, his insistence that we must observe and classify human activities to uncover society's fundamental laws is well taken. Because he developed and coined the term *sociology,* Comte often is credited with being the founder of sociology.

Herbert Spencer and Social Darwinism

Herbert Spencer (1820–1903), sometimes called the second founder of sociology, coined the term "survival of the fittest." Spencer thought that helping the poor was wrong, that this merely helped the "less fit" survive.

Herbert Spencer (1820–1903), who grew up in England, is sometimes called the second founder of sociology. Spencer disagreed sharply with Comte. He said that sociologists should *not* guide social reform, as this would interfere with a natural process that improves societies. Societies are evolving from a lower form ("barbarian") to higher ("civilized") forms. As generations pass, a society's most capable and intelligent members ("the fittest") survive, while the less capable die out. These fittest members produce a more advanced society—unless misguided do-gooders get in the way and help the less fit (the lower classes) survive.

Spencer called this principle *the survival of the fittest.* Although Spencer coined this phrase, it usually is credited to his contemporary, Charles Darwin. Where Spencer proposed that societies evolve over time as the fittest adapt to their environment, Darwin applied this idea to organisms. Because Darwin is better known, Spencer's idea is called *social Darwinism.* History is fickle, and if fame had gone the other way, we might be speaking of "biological Spencerism."

Like Comte, Spencer did not conduct scientific studies, and his ideas, too, were discarded.

Karl Marx and Class Conflict

Karl Marx (1818–1883) believed that the roots of human misery lay in class conflict, the exploitation of workers by those who own the means of production. Social change, in the form of the workers overthrowing the capitalists, was inevitable from Marx's perspective. Although Marx did not consider himself a sociologist, his ideas have influenced many sociologists, particularly conflict theorists.

Karl Marx (1818–1883) influenced not only sociology, but he also left his mark on world history. Marx's influence has been so great that even the *Wall Street Journal,* that staunch advocate of capitalism, has called him one of the three greatest modern thinkers (the other two being Sigmund Freud and Albert Einstein).

Like Comte, Marx thought that people should try to change society. His proposal for change was radical: revolution. This got him thrown out of Germany, and he settled in England. Marx believed that the engine of human history is **class conflict.** Society is made up of two social classes, he said, and they are natural enemies: the **bourgeoisie** (boo-shwa-ZEE) (the *capitalists,* who own the capital, land, factories, and machines) and the **proletariat** (the exploited workers). Eventually, the workers will unite and break their chains of bondage. The workers' revolution will be bloody, but it will usher in a classless society, one free of exploitation. People will work according to their abilities and receive goods and services according to their needs (Marx and Engels 1848/1967).

Marxism is not the same as communism. Although Marx proposed revolution as the way for workers to gain control of society, he did not develop the political system called *communism*. This is a later application of his ideas. Marx himself was disgusted when he heard debates about his analysis of social life. After listening to some of the positions attributed to him, he shook his head and said, "I am not a Marxist" (Dobriner 1969b:222; Gitlin 1997:89).

Emile Durkheim and Social Integration

Until the time of Emile Durkheim (1858–1917), sociology was viewed as part of history and economics. Durkheim, who grew up in France, wanted to change this, and his major professional goal was to get sociology recognized as a separate academic discipline (Coser 1977). He achieved this goal in 1887 when the University of Bordeaux awarded him the world's first academic appointment in sociology.

Durkheim's second goal was to show how social forces affect people's behavior. To accomplish this, he conducted rigorous research. When he compared the suicide rates of several European countries, Durkheim (1897/1966) found that each country has a different suicide rate—and that these rates remain about the same year after year. He also found that different groups within a country have different suicide rates and that these, too, remain stable from year to year: Males are more likely than females to kill themselves, Protestants more likely than Catholics or Jews, and the unmarried more than the married. From these observations, Durkheim concluded that suicide is not what it appears—individuals here and there deciding to take their lives for personal reasons. Instead, *social factors underlie suicide,* which is why a group's rate remains fairly constant year after year.

In his search for the key social factors in suicide, Durkheim identified **social integration,** the degree to which people are tied to their social group: He found that people who have weaker social ties are more likely to commit suicide. This, he said, explains why Protestants, males, and the unmarried have higher suicide rates. This is how it works: Protestantism encourages greater freedom of thought and action; males are more independent than females; and the unmarried lack the ties that come with marriage. In other words, members of these groups have fewer of the social bonds that keep people from committing suicide. In Durkheim's term, they have less social integration.

Despite the many years that have passed since Durkheim did his research, the principle he uncovered still applies: People who are less socially integrated have higher rates of suicide. Even today, more than a century later, those same groups that Durkheim identified—Protestants, males, and the unmarried—are more likely to kill themselves.

The French sociologist **Emile Durkheim** (1858–1917) contributed many important concepts to sociology. His comparison of the suicide rates of several countries revealed an underlying social factor: People are more likely to commit suicide if their ties to others in their communities are weak. Durkheim's identification of the key role of *social integration* in social life remains central to sociology today.

Durkheim believed that modern societies produce feelings of isolation, much of which comes from the division of labor. In contrast, members of traditional societies, who work alongside family and neighbors and participate in similar activities, experience a high degree of *social integration*. The photo below shows women pounding millet in Mali.

Why is Marx known as a sociologist?

FIGURE 1.1   **How Americans Commit Suicide**

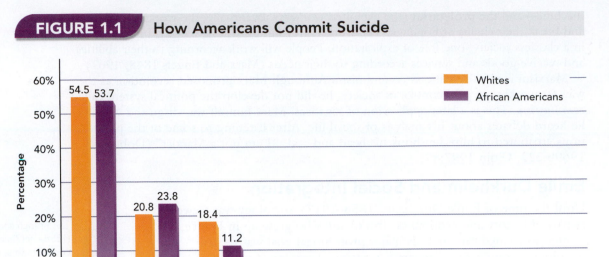

Note: These totals are the mean of years 2001–2008. ("Mean" is explained in Table 1.3 on page 27.)

Source: By the author. Based on CDC, National Center for Injury Prevention and Control Fatal Injury Data, 2011.

Applying Durkheim.   Did you know that 30,000 whites and 2,000 African Americans will commit suicide this year? Of course not. And you probably are wondering if anyone can know something like this before it happens. Sociologists can. How? Sociologists look at **patterns of behavior,** recurring characteristics or events.

The patterns let us be even more specific. Look at Figure 1.1 above. There you can see the methods by which African Americans and whites commit suicide. These patterns are so consistent that we can predict with high certainty that of the 30,000 whites about 16,000 will use guns to kill themselves, and that of the 2,000 African Americans 60 to 70 will jump to their deaths.

These patterns—both the numbers and the way people take their lives—recur year after year. This indicates something far beyond the individuals who kill themselves. They reflect conditions in society, such as the popularity and accessibility of guns. They also reflect conditions that we don't understand. I am hoping that one day this textbook will pique a student's interest enough to investigate these patterns.

Max Weber and the Protestant Ethic

Max Weber (Mahx VAY-ber) (1864–1920), a German sociologist and a contemporary of Durkheim, also became a professor in the new academic discipline of sociology. With Durkheim and Marx, Weber is one of the three most influential of all sociologists, and you will come across his writings and theories in later chapters. For now, let's consider an issue Weber raised that remains controversial today.

Max Weber (1864–1920) was another early sociologist who left a profound impression on sociology. He used cross-cultural and historical materials to trace the causes of social change and to determine how social groups affect people's orientations to life.

Religion and the Origin of Capitalism.   Weber disagreed with Marx's claim that economics is the central force in social change. That role, he said, belongs to religion. Weber (1904/1958) theorized that the Roman Catholic belief system encouraged followers to hold on to traditional ways of life, while the Protestant belief system encouraged its members to embrace change. Roman Catholics were taught that because they were Church members they were on the road to heaven, but Protestants, those of the Calvinist tradition, were told that they wouldn't know if they were saved until Judgment Day. Uncomfortable with this, the Calvinists began to look for "a sign" that they were in God's will. They found this "sign" in financial success, which they took as a blessing that indicated that God was on

How do the patterns of suicide reveal its social nature? (Why is suicide more than a personal or psychological matter?)

their side. To bring about this "sign" and receive spiritual comfort, they began to live frugal lives, saving their money and investing it in order to make even more. This, said Weber, brought about the birth of capitalism.

Weber called this self-denying approach to life the *Protestant ethic*. He termed the desire to invest capital in order to make more money the *spirit of capitalism*. To test his theory, Weber compared the extent of capitalism in Roman Catholic and Protestant countries. He found that capitalism was more likely to flourish in Protestant countries. Weber's conclusion that religion was the key factor in the rise of capitalism was controversial when he made it, and it continues to be debated today (Cantoni 2009).

Sociology in North America

Let's turn to how sociology developed in North America. As we do so, we shall focus on some of the social conditions of this period and the controversy between social reform and social theory.

Sexism at the Time: Women in Early Sociology

As you may have noticed, all the sociologists we have discussed are men. In the 1800s, sex roles were rigid, with women assigned the roles of wife and mother. In the classic German phrase, women were expected to devote themselves to the four K's: *Kirche, Küche, Kinder, und Kleider* (The four C's in English: church, cooking, children, and clothes). To try to break out of this mold meant risking severe disapproval.

Few people, male or female, attained any education beyond basic reading and writing and a little math. Higher education, for the rare few who received it, was reserved primarily for men. Of the handful of women who did pursue higher education, some became prominent in early sociology. Marion Talbot, for example, was an associate editor of the *American Journal of Sociology* for thirty years, from its founding in 1895 to 1925. The influence of some early female sociologists went far beyond sociology. Grace Abbott became the first chief of the U.S. government's Children's Bureau, and Frances Perkins was the first woman to hold a cabinet position, serving twelve years as Secretary of Labor under President Franklin Roosevelt. Jane Addams was awarded the Nobel Prize for Peace, the only sociologist to win this acclaimed honor. The photo wheel on the next page portrays some of these early sociologists.

For the most part, early female sociologists viewed sociology as a path to social reform. They focused on ways to improve society, such as how to stop lynching, integrate immigrants into society, and improve the conditions of workers. As sociology developed in North America, a debate arose about the proper purpose of sociology: Should it be to reform society or to do objective research on society? Those who held the university positions won the debate. They were men who feared that advocacy for social causes would jeopardize the reputation of sociology—and their own university positions. It was these men who wrote the history of sociology. Distancing themselves from the social reformers, they ignored the early female sociologists (Lengermann and Niebrugge 2007). Now that women have regained their voice in sociology—and have begun to rewrite its history—early female sociologists are again, as here, being acknowledged.

Harriet Martineau (1802–1876) provides an excellent example of how the contributions of early female sociologists were ignored. Although Martineau was from England, she is included here because she did extensive analyses of U.S. social customs. Sexism was so pervasive that when Martineau first began to analyze social life, she would hide her writing beneath her sewing when visitors arrived, for writing was "masculine" and sewing "feminine" (Gilman 1911/1971:88). Despite her extensive and acclaimed research on social life in both Great Britain and the United States, until recently Martineau was known primarily for translating Comte's ideas into English.

According to Weber, how did religion bring about capitalism?

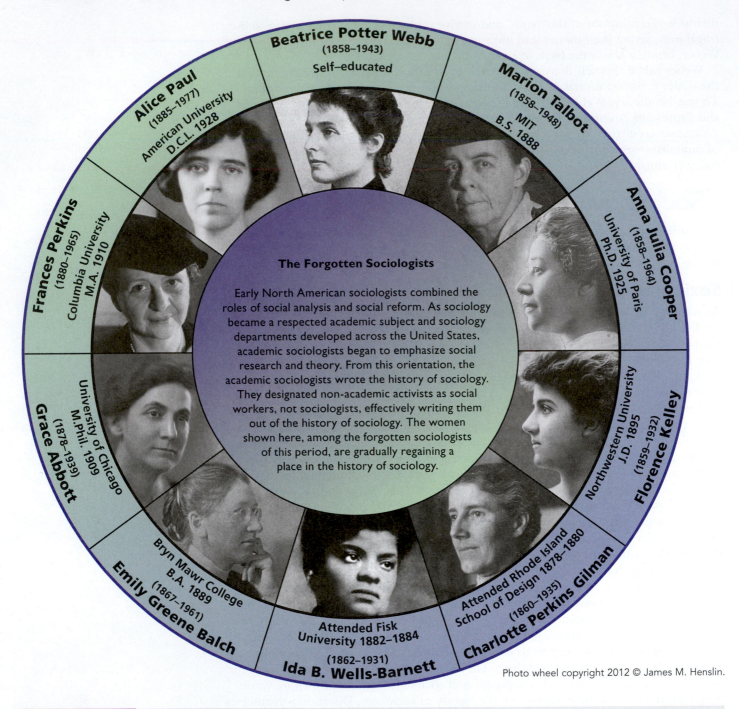

The Forgotten Sociologists

Early North American sociologists combined the roles of social analysis and social reform. As sociology became a respected academic subject and sociology departments developed across the United States, academic sociologists began to emphasize social research and theory. From this orientation, the academic sociologists wrote the history of sociology. They designated non-academic activists as social workers, not sociologists, effectively writing them out of the history of sociology. The women shown here, among the forgotten sociologists of this period, are gradually regaining a place in the history of sociology.

Beatrice Potter Webb
(1858–1943)
Self–educated

Alice Paul
(1885–1977)
American University
D.C.L. 1928

Marion Talbot
(1858–1948)
MIT
B.S. 1888

Frances Perkins
(1880–1965)
Columbia University
M.A. 1910

Anna Julia Cooper
(1858–1964)
University of Paris
Ph.D. 1925

Grace Abbott
(1878–1939)
University of Chicago
M.Phil. 1909

Florence Kelley
(1859–1932)
Northwestern University
J.D. 1895

Emily Greene Balch
(1867–1961)
Bryn Mawr College
B.A. 1889

Charlotte Perkins Gilman
(1860–1935)
Attended Rhode Island
School of Design 1878–1880

Ida B. Wells-Barnett
(1862–1931)
Attended Fisk
University 1882–1884

Photo wheel copyright 2012 © James M. Henslin.

FIGURE 1.2   The Forgotten Sociologists

Racism at the Time: W. E. B. Du Bois

Not only was sexism assumed to be normal during this early period of sociology but so was racism, which made life difficult for African American professionals such as W. E. B. Du Bois (1868–1963). After earning a bachelor's degree from Fisk University, Du Bois became the first African American to earn a doctorate at Harvard. He then studied at the University of Berlin, where he attended lectures by Max Weber. After teaching

What was the role of women in early sociology?

Greek and Latin at Wilberforce University, in 1897 Du Bois moved to Atlanta University to teach sociology and do research. He remained there for most of his career (Du Bois 1935/1992).

The Down-to-Earth Sociology box below features Du Bois' description of race relations when he was in college.

Down-to-Earth Sociology

W. E. B. Du Bois: The Souls of Black Folk

Du Bois wrote more like an accomplished novelist than a sociologist. The following excerpts are from pages 66–68 of *The Souls of Black Folk* (1903). In this book, Du Bois analyzes changes that occurred in the social and economic conditions of African Americans during the thirty years following the Civil War.

For two summers, while he was a student at Fisk, Du Bois taught in a segregated school in a little log cabin "way back in the hills" of rural Tennessee. These excerpts help us understand conditions at that time.

It was a hot morning late in July when the school opened. I trembled when I heard the patter of little feet down the dusty road, and saw the growing row of dark solemn faces and bright eager eyes facing me. . . . There they sat, nearly thirty of them, on the rough benches, their faces shading from a pale cream to deep brown, the little feet bare and swinging, the eyes full of expectation, with here and there a twinkle of mischief, and the hands grasping Webster's blue-black spelling-book. I loved my school, and the fine faith the children had in the wisdom of their teacher was truly marvelous. We read and spelled together, wrote a little, picked flowers, sang, and listened to stories of the world beyond the hill. . . .

On Friday nights I often went home with some of the children,—sometimes to Doc Burke's farm. He was a great, loud, thin Black, ever working, and trying to buy these seventy-five acres of hill and dale where he lived; but people said that he would surely fail and the "white folks would get it all." His wife was a magnificent Amazon, with saffron face and shiny hair, uncorseted and barefooted, and the children were strong and barefooted. They lived in

In the 1800s, most people were poor, and formal education beyond the first several grades was a luxury. This photo depicts the conditions of the people Du Bois worked with.

a one-and-a-half-room cabin in the hollow of the farm near the spring. . . .

Often, to keep the peace, I must go where life was less lovely; for instance, 'Tildy's mother was incorrigibly dirty, Reuben's larder was limited seriously, and herds of untamed insects wandered over the Eddingses' beds. Best of all I loved to go to Josie's, and sit on the porch, eating peaches, while the mother bustled and talked: how Josie had bought the sewing-machine; how Josie worked at service in winter, but that four dollars a month was "mighty little" wages; how Josie longed to go away to school, but that it "looked like" they never could get far enough ahead to let her; how the crops failed and the well was yet unfinished; and, finally, how mean some of the white folks were.

For two summers I lived in this little world. . . . I have called my tiny community a world, and so its isolation made it; and yet there was among us but a half-awakened common consciousness, sprung from common joy and grief, at burial, birth, or wedding; from common hardship in poverty, poor land, and low wages, and, above all, from the sight of the Veil* that hung between us and Opportunity. All this caused us to think some thoughts together; but these, when ripe for speech, were spoken in various languages. Those whose eyes twenty-five and more years had seen "the glory of the coming of the Lord," saw in every present hindrance or help a dark fatalism bound to bring all things right in His own good time. The mass of those to whom slavery was a dim recollection of childhood found the world a puzzling thing: it asked little of them, and they answered with little, and yet it ridiculed their offering. Such a paradox they could not understand, and therefore sank into listless indifference, or shiftlessness, or reckless bravado.

*"The Veil" is shorthand for the Veil of Race, referring to how race colors all human relations. Du Bois' hope, as he put it, was that "sometime, somewhere, men will judge men by their souls and not by their skins" (p. 261).

What was life like for Du Bois' students? What role did race relations play in Du Bois' life?

W(illiam) E(dward) B(urghardt) Du Bois (1868–1963) spent his lifetime studying relations between African Americans and whites. Like many early North American sociologists, Du Bois combined the role of academic sociologist with that of social reformer.

It is difficult to grasp how racist society was at this time. As Du Bois passed a butcher shop in Georgia one day, he saw the fingers of a lynching victim displayed in the window (Aptheker 1990). When Du Bois went to national meetings of the American Sociological Society, restaurants and hotels would not allow him to eat or room with the white sociologists. How times have changed. Today, sociologists not only would boycott such establishments, but they would also refuse to hold meetings in that state. At that time, however, racism, like sexism, prevailed throughout society, rendering it mostly invisible to white sociologists.

Du Bois did extensive research. For about twenty years, he published a book a year on black–white relations. He was also a social activist. Along with Jane Addams and others, Du Bois founded the National Association for the Advancement of Colored People (NAACP). Continuing to battle racism both as a sociologist and as a journalist, Du Bois eventually embraced revolutionary Marxism. He became such an outspoken critic of racism that for years the U.S. State Department, fearing he would criticize the United States, refused to issue him a passport (Du Bois 1968). At age 93, dismayed that so little improvement had been made in race relations, he moved to Ghana, where he died and was buried (Stark 1989).

Jane Addams: Sociologist and Social Reformer

Jane Addams (1860–1935) a recipient of the Nobel Prize for Peace, worked on behalf of poor immigrants. With Ellen G. Starr, she founded Hull-House, a center to help immigrants in Chicago. She was also a leader in women's rights (women's suffrage), as well as the peace movement of World War I.

Although many North American sociologists combined the role of sociologist with that of social reformer, none was as successful as Jane Addams (1860–1935). Like Harriet Martineau, Addams came from a background of wealth and privilege. She attended the Women's Medical College of Philadelphia, but dropped out because of illness (Addams 1910/1981). On one of her trips to Europe, Addams was impressed with work being done to help London's poor. The memory wouldn't leave her, she said, and she decided to work for social justice.

In 1889, Addams co-founded Hull-House, located in Chicago's notorious slums. Hull-House was open to people who needed refuge—to immigrants, the sick, the aged, the poor. Sociologists from the nearby University of Chicago were frequent visitors at Hull-House. With her piercing insights into the social classes, especially the ways in which workers were exploited and rural immigrants adjusted to city life, Addams strived to bridge the gap between the powerful and the powerless. In addition to being one of the founders of the NAACP, she co-founded the American Civil Liberties Union. Two of her major campaigns were for the eight-hour work day and for laws against child labor. Her efforts at social reform were so outstanding that in 1931, she was a co-winner of the Nobel Prize for Peace.

Talcott Parsons and C. Wright Mills: Contrasting Views

C. Wright Mills (1916–1962) was a controversial figure in sociology because of his analysis of the role of the power elite in U.S. society. Today, his analysis is taken for granted by many sociologists and members of the public.

Like Du Bois and Addams, many early North American sociologists worked toward the reform of society. Sociologists such as Robert Park and Ernest Burgess (1921) not only studied crime, drug addiction, juvenile delinquency, and prostitution, but also offered suggestions for how to alleviate these social problems. But by the 1940s, the emphasis had shifted to social theory. A major sociologist of this period, Talcott Parsons (1902–1979), developed abstract models of society that influenced a generation of sociologists. His models of how the parts of society work together harmoniously did nothing to stimulate social activism.

Another sociologist, C. Wright Mills (1916–1962), deplored such theoretical abstractions. Trying to push the pendulum the other way, he urged sociologists to get back to social reform. In his writings, he warned that the nation faced an imminent threat to freedom—the coalescing of interests of a *power elite,* the top leaders of business, politics, and the military. Shortly after Mills' death came the turbulent late 1960s and the 1970s. This precedent-shaking era sparked interest in social activism, making Mills' ideas popular among a new generation of sociologists.

The Continuing Tension: Basic, Applied, and Public Sociology

Basic Sociology.   As we have seen, two contradictory aims—analyzing society versus working toward its reform—have run through North American sociology since its founding. This tension is still with us. Some sociologists see their proper role as **basic sociology,** analyzing some aspect of society, with no goal other than gaining knowledge. Others reply, "Knowledge for what?" They argue that gaining knowledge through research is not enough, that sociologists need to use their expertise to help reform society, especially to help bring justice and better conditions to the poor and oppressed.

Applied Sociology.   As Figure 1.3 shows, one attempt to go beyond basic sociology is **applied sociology,** using sociology to solve problems. Applied sociology goes back to the roots of sociology, for as you will recall, sociologists founded the NAACP. Today's applied sociologists lack the broad vision that the early sociologists had of reforming society, but their application of sociology is wide-ranging. Some work for business firms to solve problems in the workplace, while others investigate social problems such as pornography, rape, pollution, or the spread of AIDS. Sociology is even being applied to find ways to disrupt terrorist groups (Sageman 2008). To see some of the variety of work that applied sociologists do, look at the Down-to-Earth Sociology box on the next page.

Public Sociology.   To get sociologists to apply sociology in a broader way, the American Sociological Association (ASA) is promoting a middle ground between research and reform called **public sociology.** By this term, the ASA refers to harnessing the sociological perspective for the benefit of the public. Of special interest to the ASA is getting politicians and policy makers to apply the sociological understanding of how society works as they develop social policy (American Sociological Association 2004). Public sociology would incorporate both items 3 and 4 of Figure 1.3.

The lines between basic, applied, and public sociology are not always firm (Nickel 2010). In the Cultural Diversity box on page 15, you can see how basic sociology morphed into public sociology.

Social Reform Is Risky.   As some sociologists have found, often to their displeasure, promoting social reform is risky. This is especially the case if they work with oppressed people to demand social change. Always, what someone wants to "reform" is something

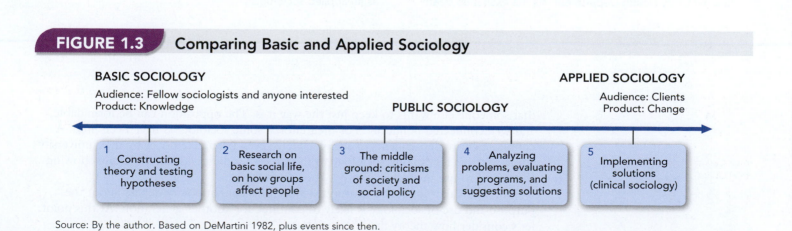

| **FIGURE 1.3** | **Comparing Basic and Applied Sociology** |

BASIC SOCIOLOGY
Audience: Fellow sociologists and anyone interested
Product: Knowledge

PUBLIC SOCIOLOGY

APPLIED SOCIOLOGY
Audience: Clients
Product: Change

| 1 Constructing theory and testing hypotheses | 2 Research on basic social life, on how groups affect people | 3 The middle ground: criticisms of society and social policy | 4 Analyzing problems, evaluating programs, and suggesting solutions | 5 Implementing solutions (clinical sociology) |

Source: By the author. Based on DeMartini 1982, plus events since then.

What is the difference between basic and applied sociology?

Down-to-Earth Sociology

Careers in Sociology: What Applied Sociologists Do

Most sociologists teach in colleges and universities, where they share sociological knowledge with students, as your instructor is doing with you in this course. Applied sociologists, in contrast, work in a wide variety of areas—from counseling children to studying how diseases are transmitted. To give you an idea of this variety, let's look over the shoulders of five applied sociologists.

Leslie Green, who does marketing research at Vanderveer Group in Philadelphia, Pennsylvania, earned her bachelor's degree in sociology at Shippensburg University. She helps to develop strategies to get doctors to prescribe particular drugs. She sets up the meetings, locates moderators for the discussion groups, and arranges payments to the physicians who participate in the research. "My training in sociology," she says, "helps me in 'people skills.' It helps me to understand the needs of different groups, and to interact with them."

Stanley Capela, whose master's degree is from Fordham University, works as an applied sociologist at HeartShare Human Services in New York City. He evaluates how children's programs—such as ones that focus on housing, AIDS, group homes, and preschool education—actually work, compared with how they are supposed to work. He spots problems and suggests solutions. One of his assignments was to find out why it was taking so long to get children adopted, even though there was a long list of eager adoptive parents. Capela pinpointed how the paperwork got bogged down as it was routed through the system and suggested ways to improve the flow of paperwork.

Laurie Banks, who received her master's degree in sociology from Fordham University, analyzes statistics for the New York City Health Department. As she examined death

How can Dora the Explorer be an example of applied sociology? The text explains the reason.

certificates, she noticed that a Polish neighborhood had a high rate of stomach cancer. She alerted the Centers for Disease Control and Prevention, which conducted interviews in the neighborhood. Scientists from the CDC traced the cause to eating large amounts of sausage. In another case, Banks compared birth certificates with school records. She found that lack of prenatal care and problems at birth—low birth weight and birth complications—were linked to low reading skills and behavior problems in school.

Daniel Knapp, who earned a doctorate from the University of Oregon, applied sociology by going to the city dump. Moved by the idea that urban wastes could be recycled and reused, he first tested this idea by scavenging in a small way—at the city dump at Berkeley, California. After starting a company called Urban Ore, Knapp (2005) did research on how to recycle urban wastes and worked to change waste disposal laws. As a founder of the recycling movement in the United States, Knapp's application of sociology continues to influence us all.

Clara Rodriguez, who earned her doctorate at the University of Washington, also illustrates how wide-ranging applied sociology is. Rodriguez is the sociological consultant for *Dora the Explorer*. She advises on the social implications of what the viewers will see on this program. This ranges from advice about Dora as a girl role model to what aspects of Latino culture to present and even to colors, music, and Spanish phrases (Havrilla 2010).

From just these few examples, you can catch a glimpse of the variety of work that applied sociologists do. Some work for corporations, some are employed by government and private agencies, and others run their own businesses. You can also see that you don't need a doctorate in order to work as an applied sociologist.

that someone else wants to keep just the way it is. The opposition can be formidable, and well connected politically. For their efforts, some sociologists have been fired. A couple of entire departments of sociology have even been taken over by their university administrators for "taking sociology to the streets," siding with the poor and showing them how to use the law to improve their lives.

With roots that go back a century or more, this contemporary debate about the purpose and use of sociology is likely to continue for another generation. At this point, let's consider how theory fits into sociology.

When is applied sociology likely to be controversial?

Cultural Diversity in the United States

Unanticipated Public Sociology: Studying Job Discrimination

Basic sociology—research aimed at learning more about some behavior—can turn into public sociology. Here is what happened to Devah Pager (2003) when she was a graduate student at the University of Wisconsin in Madison. She was doing volunteer work in a homeless shelter, and some of the men told her how hard it was to find work if they had been in prison. Were the men exaggerating? she wondered. To find out what difference a prison record makes in getting a job, she sent pairs of college men to apply for 350 entry-level jobs in Milwaukee. One team was African American, and one

U.S.A.

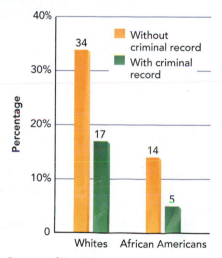

FIGURE 1.4 Call-Back Rates by Race–Ethnicity and Criminal Record

Percentage

- 40%
- 34 — Without criminal record
- 30%
- 17 — With criminal record
- 20%
- 14
- 10%
- 5
- 0

Whites   African Americans

Source: Courtesy of Devah Pager.

was white. Pager prepared identical résumés for the teams, but with one difference: On each team, one of the men said he had served eighteen months in prison for possession of cocaine.

Figure 1.4 shows the difference that the prison record made. Men without a prison record were two or three times more likely to be called back.

But Pager came up with another significant finding. Look at the difference that race–ethnicity made. White men with a prison record were more likely to be offered a job than African American men who had a clean record!

Sociological research often remains in obscure journals, read by only a few specialists. But Pager's findings got around, turning basic research into public sociology. Someone told President George W. Bush about the research, and he announced in his State of the Union speech that he wanted Congress to fund a $300 million program to provide mentoring and other support to help former prisoners get jobs (Kroeger 2004).

Pager repeated her research in New York City and found similar results (Pager et al. 2009).

As you can see, sometimes only a thin line separates basic and public sociology.

For Your Consideration

→ What findings would you expect if women had been included in this study?

Theoretical Perspectives in Sociology

Facts never interpret themselves. To make sense out of life, we place our experiences (our "facts") into a framework of more-or-less related ideas. This gives us a way of interpreting them. Sociologists do this, too, but they place their observations into a conceptual framework called a theory. A **theory** is a general statement about how some parts of the world fit together and how they work. It is an explanation of how two or more "facts" are related to one another.

Sociologists use three major theories: symbolic interactionism, functional analysis, and conflict theory. Each theory is like a lens through which we can view social life. Let's first examine the main elements of each theory, and then apply each to the U.S. divorce rate to see why it is so high. As we do this, you will see how each theory, or perspective, provides a distinct interpretation of social life.

Symbolic Interactionism

The central idea of **symbolic interactionism** is that *symbols*—things to which we attach meaning—are the key to understanding how we view the world and communicate with one another. Two major sociologists who developed this perspective are George Herbert Mead (1863–1931) and Charles Horton Cooley (1864–1929). Let's look at the main elements of this theory.

Symbols in Everyday Life.   Without symbols, our social life would be no more sophisticated than that of animals. For example, without symbols we would have no aunts or uncles, employers or teachers—or even brothers and sisters. I know that this sounds strange, but it is symbols that define our relationships. There would still be reproduction, of course, but no symbols to tell us how we are related to whom. We would not know to whom we owe respect and obligations, or from whom we can expect privileges—two elements that lie at the essence of human relationships.

I know it is vague to say that symbols tell you how you are related to others and how you should act toward them, so let's make this less abstract:

Suppose that you have fallen head over heels in love. Finally, after what seems forever, it is the night before your wedding. As you are contemplating tomorrow's bliss, your mother comes to you in tears. Sobbing, she tells you that she had a child before she married your father, a child that she gave up for adoption. Breaking down, she says that she has just discovered that the person you are going to marry is this child.
   You can see how the symbol will change overnight—and your behavior, too!

George Herbert Mead (1863–1931) is one of the founders of symbolic interactionism, a major theoretical perspective in sociology. He taught at the University of Chicago, where his lectures were popular. Although he wrote little, after his death students compiled his lectures into an influential book, *Mind, Self, and Society.*

The symbols of boyfriend and brother—or girlfriend and sister—are certainly different, and, as you know, each symbol requires rather different behavior.

Not only do relationships depend on symbols, but so does society itself. Without symbols, we could not coordinate our actions with those of others. We could not make plans for a future day, time, and place. Unable to specify times, materials, sizes, or goals, we could not build bridges and highways. Without symbols, we would have no movies or musical instruments, no hospitals, no government, no religion. The class you are taking could not exist—nor could this book. On the positive side, there would be no war.

In Sum: Symbolic interactionists analyze how social life depends on the ways we define ourselves and others. They study face-to-face interaction, examining how people make sense out of life, how they determine their relationships.

Applying Symbolic Interactionism.   Look at Figure 1.5, which shows U.S. marriages and divorces over time. Let's see how symbolic interactionists would use changing symbols to explain this figure. For background, you should understand that marriage used to be a *lifelong commitment*. A hundred years ago (and less) getting divorced was viewed as immoral, a flagrant disregard for public opinion, and the abandonment of adult responsibilities. Let's see what changed.

The meaning of marriage: By the 1930s, young people were coming to view marriage in a different way, a change that was reported by sociologists of the time. In 1933, William Ogburn observed that they were placing more emphasis on the personality of potential mates. Then in 1945, Ernest Burgess and Harvey Locke noted that people were expecting more affection, understanding, and compatibility in marriage. As marriage came to be viewed as an arrangement that was based less on duty and obligation and more on feelings—attraction and intimacy—it became one that could be broken when feelings changed.

How are symbols the basis of human relationships?

FIGURE 1.5   U.S. Marriage, U.S. Divorce

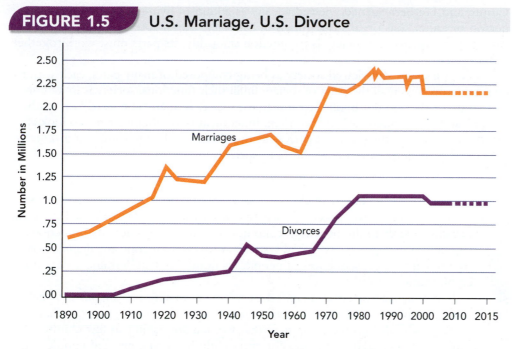

Source: By the author. Based on *Statistical Abstract of the United States* 1998:Table 92 and 2012:Tables 78, 133; earlier editions for earlier years. The broken lines indicate the author's estimates.

The meaning of divorce: As divorce became more common, its meaning changed. Rather than being a symbol of failure, divorce came to indicate freedom and new beginnings. Removing the stigma from divorce shattered a strong barrier that had prevented husbands and wives from breaking up.

The meaning of parenthood: Parents used to have little responsibility for their children beyond providing food, clothing, shelter, and moral guidance. And they needed to do this for only a short time, because children began to contribute to the support of the family early in life. Among many people, parenthood is still like this. In Colombia, for example, children of the poor often are expected to support themselves by the age of 8 or 10. In industrial societies, however, we assume that children are vulnerable beings who must depend on their parents for financial and emotional support for many years—often until they are well into their 20s. The greater responsibilities that we assign to parenthood place heavy burdens on today's couples and, with them, more strain on marriage.

The meaning of love: And we can't overlook the love symbol. As surprising as it may sound, to have love as the main reason for marrying weakens marriage. In some depth of our being, we expect "true love" to deliver constant emotional highs. This expectation sets people up for crushed hopes, as dissatisfactions in marriage are inevitable. When they come, spouses tend to blame one another for failing to deliver the expected satisfaction.

In Sum: Symbolic interactionists look at how changing ideas (or symbols) of marriage, divorce, parenthood, and love put pressure on married couples. No single change is *the* cause of our divorce rate, but, taken together, these changes provide a push toward divorce by making it more acceptable.

Functional Analysis

The central idea of **functional analysis** is that society is a whole unit, made up of interrelated parts that work together. Functional analysis (also known as *functionalism* and *structural functionalism*) is rooted in the origins of sociology. Auguste

How would a symbolic interactionist explain U.S. divorce?

Comte and Herbert Spencer viewed society as a kind of living organism. Just as a person or animal has organs that function together, they wrote, so does society. And like an organism, if society is to function smoothly, its parts must work together in harmony.

Emile Durkheim also viewed society as being composed of many parts, each with its own function. When all the parts of society fulfill their functions, society is in a "normal" state. If they do not fulfill their functions, society is in an "abnormal" or "pathological" state. To understand society, then, functionalists say that we need to look at both *structure* (how the parts of a society fit together to make the whole) and *function* (what each part does, how it contributes to society).

Robert Merton and Functionalism.   Robert Merton (1910–2003) dismissed the organic analogy, but he did maintain the essence of functionalism—the image of society as a whole being composed of parts that work together. Merton used the term *functions* to refer to the beneficial consequences of people's actions: Functions help keep a group (society, social system) in balance. In contrast, *dysfunctions* are the harmful consequences of people's actions. They undermine a system's equilibrium.

Functions can be either manifest or latent. If an action is *intended* to help some part of a system, it is a *manifest function*. For example, suppose that government officials become concerned that women are having so few children. Congress offers a $10,000 bonus for every child born to a married couple. The intention, or manifest function, of the bonus is to increase childbearing within the family unit. Merton pointed out that people's actions can also have *latent functions;* that is, they can have *unintended* consequences that help a system adjust. Let's suppose that the bonus works. As the birth rate jumps, so does the sale of diapers and baby furniture. Because the benefits to these businesses were not the intended consequences, they are latent functions of the bonus.

Robert K. Merton (1910–2003), who spent most of his academic career at Columbia University, was a major proponent of functionalism, one of the main theoretical perspectives in sociology.

Of course, human actions can also hurt a system. Because such consequences usually are unintended, Merton called them *latent dysfunctions*. Let's assume that the government has failed to specify a "stopping point" with regard to its bonus system. To collect more bonuses, some people keep on having children. The more children they have, however, the more they need the next bonus to survive. Large families become common, and poverty increases. Welfare is reinstated, taxes jump, and the nation erupts in protest. Because these results were not intended and because they harmed the social system, they would be latent dysfunctions of the bonus program.

In Sum: From the perspective of functional analysis, society is a functioning unit, with each part related to the whole. Whenever we examine a smaller part, we need to look for its functions and dysfunctions to see how it is related to the larger unit. This basic approach can be applied to any social group, whether an entire society, a college, or even a group as small as a family.

Applying Functional Analysis.   Now let's apply functional analysis to the U.S. divorce rate. Functionalists stress that industrialization and urbanization have undermined the traditional functions of the family. For example, before industrialization, the family formed an economic team. On the farm, where most people lived, each family member had jobs or "chores" to do. The wife was in charge not only of household tasks but also of raising small animals, such as chickens, milking cows, collecting eggs, and churning butter. She also did the cooking, baking, canning, sewing, darning, washing, and cleaning. The daughters helped her. The husband was responsible for caring for large animals, such as horses and cattle, for planting and harvesting, and for maintaining buildings and tools. The sons helped him.

This certainly doesn't sound like life today! But what does it have to do with divorce? Simply put, the husband and wife depended on each other for survival—and there weren't many alternatives.

What are the basic ideas of functional analysis? What are manifest functions? Latent functions?

Other functions also bound family members to one another: educating the children, teaching them religion, providing home-based recreation, and caring for the sick and elderly. To further see how sharply family functions have changed, look at this example from the 1800s:

When Phil became sick, Ann, his wife, cooked for him, fed him, changed the bed linens, bathed him, read to him from the Bible, and gave him his medicine. (She did this in addition to doing the housework and taking care of their six children.) Phil was also surrounded by the children, who shouldered some of his chores while he was sick. When Phil died, the male relatives made the casket while Ann, her sisters, and mother washed and dressed the body. Phil was then "laid out" in the front parlor (the formal living room), where friends, neighbors, and relatives paid their last respects. From there, friends moved his body to the church for the final message and then to the grave they themselves had dug.

In Sum: When the family loses functions, it becomes more fragile, making an increase in divorce inevitable. And these changes in economic production illustrate how the family has lost functions. No longer is making a living a cooperative, home-based effort, where husband and wife depend on one another for their interlocking contributions to a mutual endeavor. Instead, husbands and wives today earn individual paychecks and

Sociologists who use the *functionalist perspective* stress how industrialization and urbanization undermined the traditional *functions* of the family. Before industrialization, members of the family worked together as an economic unit, as in this photo of a farm family in Nebraska in the 1890s. As production moved away from the home, it took with it first the father and, more recently, the mother. One consequence is a major dysfunction, the weakening of family ties.

How do fewer family functions contribute to divorce?

increasingly function as separate components in an impersonal, multinational, and even global system. The fewer functions that family members share, the fewer are their "ties that bind"—and these ties are what help husbands and wives get through the problems they inevitably experience.

Conflict Theory

Conflict theory provides a third perspective on social life. Unlike the functionalists, who view society as a harmonious whole with its parts working together, conflict theorists stress that society is composed of groups that are competing with one another for scarce resources. The surface might show cooperation, but scratch that surface and you will find a struggle for power.

Karl Marx and Conflict Theory.   Karl Marx, the founder of conflict theory, witnessed the Industrial Revolution that transformed Europe. He saw that peasants who had left the land to work in cities earned barely enough to eat. Things were so bad that the average worker died at age 30, the average wealthy person at age 50 (Edgerton 1992:87). Shocked by this suffering and exploitation, Marx began to analyze society and history. As he did so, he developed **conflict theory.** He concluded that the key to human history is *class conflict*. In each society, some small group controls the means of production and exploits those who are not in control. In industrialized societies, the struggle is between the *bourgeoisie,* the small group of capitalists who own the means to produce wealth, and the *proletariat,* the mass of workers who are exploited by the bourgeoisie. The capitalists control the legal and political system: If the workers rebel, the capitalists call on the power of the state to subdue them.

When Marx made his observations, capitalism was in its infancy and workers were at the mercy of their employers. Workers had none of what we take for granted today—minimum wages, eight-hour days, coffee breaks, five-day work weeks, paid vacations and holidays, medical benefits, sick leave, unemployment compensation, Social Security, and, for union workers, the right to strike. Marx's analysis reminds us that these benefits came not from generous hearts, but by workers forcing concessions from their employers.

Conflict Theory Today.   Many sociologists extend conflict theory beyond the relationship of capitalists and workers. They examine how opposing interests run through every layer of society—whether that be a small group, an organization, a community, or the entire society. For example, when police, teachers, and parents try to enforce conformity, this creates resentment and resistance. It is the same when a teenager tries to "change the rules" to gain more independence. Throughout society, then, there is a constant struggle to determine who has authority or influence and how far that dominance goes (Turner 1978; Piven 2008; Manza and McCarthy 2011).

Sociologist Lewis Coser (1913–2003) pointed out that conflict is most likely to develop among people who are in close relationships. These people have worked out ways to distribute power and privilege, responsibilities and rewards. Any change in this arrangement can lead to hurt feelings, resentment, and conflict. Even in intimate relationships, people are in a constant balancing act, with conflict lying uneasily just beneath the surface.

Feminists and Conflict Theory.   Just as Marx examined conflict between capitalists and workers, many feminists analyze conflict between men and women. Their primary focus is the historical, contemporary, and global inequalities of men and women—and how the traditional dominance by men can be overcome to bring about equality of the sexes. Feminists are not united by the conflict perspective, however. They tackle a variety of topics and use whatever theory applies. (Feminism is discussed in Chapter 10.)

Applying Conflict Theory.   To explain why the U.S. divorce rate is high, conflict theorists focus on how men's and women's relationships have changed. For millennia, men dominated women, and women had few alternatives other than to accept their exploitation. As industrialization transformed the world, it brought women the ability to meet

What are basic ideas of conflict theory? What is class conflict?

their basic survival needs without being married. This new ability gave them the power to refuse to bear burdens that earlier generations accepted as inevitable. The result is that today's women are likely to dissolve a marriage that becomes intolerable—or even just unsatisfactory.

In Sum: The dominance of men over women was once considered natural and right. As women gained education and earnings, however, they first questioned and then rejected this assumption. As wives strove for more power and grew less inclined to put up with relationships that they defined as unfair, the divorce rate increased. From the conflict perspective, then, our high divorce rate does not mean that marriage has weakened, but, rather, that women are making headway in their historical struggle with men.

Putting the Theoretical Perspectives Together

Which of these theoretical perspectives is *the* right one? As you have seen, each is a lens that produces a contrasting picture of divorce. The pictures that emerge are quite different from the commonsense understanding that two people are simply "incompatible." Because each theory focuses on different features of social life, each provides a distinct interpretation. Consequently, we need to use all three theoretical lenses to analyze human behavior. By combining the contributions of each, we gain a more comprehensive picture of social life.

Levels of Analysis: Macro and Micro

A major difference among these three theoretical perspectives is their level of analysis. Functionalists and conflict theorists focus on the **macro level;** that is, they examine large-scale patterns of society. In contrast, symbolic interactionists usually focus on the **micro level,** on **social interaction**—what people do when they are in one another's presence. These levels are summarized in Table 1.1.

   To make this distinction between micro and macro levels clearer, let's return to the example of the homeless, with which we opened this chapter. To study homeless people, symbolic interactionists would focus on the micro level. They would analyze

✳ Explore
Living Data
on **mysoclab.com**

TABLE 1.1	Three Theoretical Perspectives in Sociology			
Theoretical Perspective	**Usual Level of Analysis**	**Focus of Analysis**	**Key Terms**	**Applying the Perspective to the U.S. Divorce Rate**
Symbolic Interactionism	Microsociological Examines small-scale patterns of social interaction	Face-to-face interaction, how people use symbols to create social life	Symbols Interaction Meanings Definitions	Industrialization and urbanization changed marital roles and led to a redefinition of love, marriage, children, and divorce.
Functional Analysis (also called functionalism and structural functionalism)	Macrosociological Examines large-scale patterns of society	Relationships among the parts of society; how these parts are functional (have beneficial consequences) or dysfunctional (have negative consequences)	Structure Functions (manifest and latent) Dysfunctions Equilibrium	As social change erodes the traditional functions of the family, family ties weaken, and the divorce rate increases.
Conflict Theory	Macrosociological Examines large-scale patterns of society	The struggle for scarce resources by groups in a society; how the elites use their power to control the weaker groups	Inequality Power Conflict Competition Exploitation	When men control economic life, the divorce rate is low because women find few alternatives to a bad marriage. The high divorce rate reflects a shift in the balance of power between men and women.

Source: By the author.

How would a conflict theorist explain U.S. divorce? Why do we need all three theoretical perspectives?

what homeless people do when they are in shelters and on the streets. They would also analyze their communications, both their talk and their **nonverbal interaction** (gestures, use of space, and so on). The observations I made at the beginning of this chapter about the silence in the homeless shelter, for example, would be of interest to symbolic interactionists.

This micro level, however, would not interest functionalists and conflict theorists. They would focus instead on the macro level; how changes in some parts of society increase homelessness. Functionalists might look at how jobs have dried up—that there is less need for unskilled labor and how millions of jobs have been transferred to workers overseas. Or they might focus on changes in the family—how because of divorce and smaller families many people who can't find work don't have others to fall back on. For their part, conflict theorists would stress the struggle between social classes. They would be interested in how the decisions of international elites affect not only global production and trade but also the local job market, unemployment, and homelessness.

How Theory and Research Work Together

Theory cannot stand alone. As sociologist C. Wright Mills (1959) argued so forcefully, if theory isn't connected to research, it is abstract and empty. It is the same for research. Without theory, research is of little value; it is simply a collection of meaningless "facts."

Theory and research, then, go together like a hand and glove. Every theory must be tested, which requires research. And as sociologists do research, they often come up with surprising findings. Those findings must be explained, and for that, we need theory. As sociologists study social life, they combine research and theory.

Let's turn now to how sociologists do research.

Doing Sociological Research

Around the globe, people make assumptions about the way the world "is." Common sense, the things that "everyone knows are true," may or may not be true. It takes research to find out. To test your own common sense, take the little Down-to-Earth Sociology quiz on the next page.

Because sociologists find all human behavior to be valid research topics, their research ranges from the macro level of the globalization of capitalism to the micro level of social interaction. Shown here is *Tomatina*, a tomato-throwing festival held each year at Buñon, Spain. Sociologists would study the leadership of the organization, relationship of visitors to townspeople, and the activities and interaction of the participants.

How do research and theory work together? What are valid research topics for sociologists?

Down-to-Earth Sociology

Enjoying a Sociology Quiz—Testing Your Common Sense

Some findings of sociology support commonsense understandings of social life, and others contradict them. Can you tell the difference? To enjoy this quiz, complete *all* the questions before turning the page to check your answers.

1. **True/False** More U.S. students are killed in school shootings now than ten or fifteen years ago.
2. **True/False** The earnings of U.S. women have just about caught up with those of U.S. men.
3. **True/False** With life so rushed and more women working for wages, today's parents spend less time with their children than parents of previous generations did.
4. **True/False** It is more dangerous to walk near topless bars than fast-food restaurants.

5. **True/False** Most rapists are mentally ill.
6. **True/False** A large percentage of terrorists are mentally ill.
7. **True/False** Most people on welfare are lazy and looking for a handout. They could work if they wanted to.
8. **True/False** Compared with women, men make more eye contact in face-to-face conversations.
9. **True/False** Couples who lived together before marriage are usually more satisfied with their marriage than couples who did not live together before marriage.
10. **True/False** Because bicyclists are more likely to wear helmets now than a few years ago, their rate of head injuries has dropped.

To understand social life, we need to move beyond "common sense" and learn what is really going on. Let's look at how sociologists do their research.

A Research Model

As shown in Figure 1.6, scientific research follows eight basic steps. This is an ideal model, however, and in the real world of research some of these steps may run together. Some may even be omitted.

1. **Selecting a topic.** First, what do you want to know more about? Let's choose spouse abuse as our topic.
2. **Defining the problem.** The next step is to narrow the topic. Spouse abuse is too broad; we need to focus on a specific area. For example, you may want to know why men are more likely than women to be the abusers. Or perhaps you want to know what can be done to reduce domestic violence.
3. **Reviewing the literature.** You must review the literature to find out what has been published on the problem. You don't want to waste your time rediscovering what is already known.
4. **Formulating a hypothesis.** The fourth step is to formulate a **hypothesis,** a statement of what you expect to find according to predictions that are based on a theory. A hypothesis predicts a relationship between or among **variables,** factors that vary, or change, from one person or situation to another. For example, the statement "Men who are more socially isolated are more likely to abuse their wives than are men who are more socially integrated" is a hypothesis.

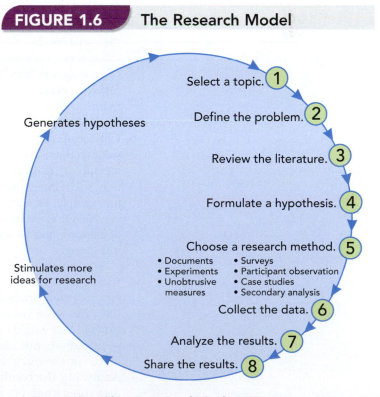

FIGURE 1.6   The Research Model

- Select a topic. 1
- Define the problem. 2
- Review the literature. 3
- Formulate a hypothesis. 4
- Choose a research method. 5
  - Documents • Surveys
  - Experiments • Participant observation
  - Unobtrusive • Case studies
    measures • Secondary analysis
- Collect the data. 6
- Analyze the results. 7
- Share the results. 8

Generates hypotheses

Stimulates more ideas for research

Source: Adapted from Figure 2.2 of Schaefer 1989.

Down-to-Earth Sociology

Testing Your Common Sense—Answers to the Sociology Quiz

1. **False.** More students were shot to death at U.S. schools in the early 1990s than now (National School Safety Center 2012). See page 396.
2. **False.** Over the years, the wage gap has narrowed, but only slightly. On average, full-time working women earn about 70 percent of what full-time working men earn. This low figure is actually an improvement over earlier years. See Figures 10.7 and 10.8 on pages 294–295.
3. **False.** Today's parents actually spend more time with their children (Bianchi et al. 2006). To see how this could be, see Figure 12.2 on page 356.
4. **False.** The crime rate outside fast-food restaurants is considerably higher. The likely reason is that topless bars hire private security and parking lot attendants (Linz et al. 2004).
5. **False.** Sociologists compared the psychological profiles of prisoners convicted of rape and prisoners convicted of other crimes. Their profiles were similar. Like robbery, rape is a learned behavior (Scully and Marolla 1984/2007).

6. **False.** Extensive testing of Islamic terrorists shows that they actually tend to score more "normal" on psychological tests than most "normal" people do. As a group, they are in better mental health than the rest of the population (Sageman 2008b:64).
7. **False.** Most people on welfare are children, young mothers with few skills, or are elderly, sick, mentally challenged, or physically handicapped,. Less than 2 percent fit the stereotype of an able-bodied man. See page 231.
8. **False.** Women make considerably more eye contact (Henley et al. 1985).
9. **False.** The opposite is true. Among other reasons, couples who cohabit before marriage are usually less committed to one another—and a key to marital success is a strong commitment (Dush et al. 2003; Osborne et al. 2007).
10. **False.** Bicyclists today are more likely to wear helmets, but their rate of head injuries is higher. Apparently, they take more risks because the helmets make them feel safer (Barnes 2001).

Your hypothesis will need **operational definitions,** that is, precise ways to measure the variables. In this example, you would need operational definitions for three variables: social isolation, social integration, and spouse abuse.

5. **Choosing a research method.** The means by which you collect your data is called a **research method** (or *research design*). Sociologists use six basic research methods, which are outlined in the next section. You will want to choose the method that will best answer your particular questions.

6. **Collecting the data.** When you gather your data, you have to take care to assure their **validity;** that is, your operational definitions must measure what they are intended to measure. In this case, you must be certain that you really are measuring social isolation, social integration, and spouse abuse—and not something else. Spouse abuse, for example, seems to be obvious. Yet what some people consider to be abuse is not considered abuse by others. Which will you choose? In other words, your operational definitions must be so precise that no one has any question about what you are measuring.

You must also be sure that your data are reliable. **Reliability** means that if other researchers use your operational definitions, their findings will be consistent with yours. If your operational definitions are sloppy, husbands who have committed the same act of violence might be included in some research but excluded in other studies. You would end up with erratic results. You might show a 5 percent rate of spouse abuse, but another researcher may conclude that it is 30 percent. This would make your research unreliable.

7. **Analyzing the results.** You can choose from a variety of techniques to analyze the data you gather. If a hypothesis has been part of your research, you will test it during

Can you summarize the basic research model that sociologists use?

this step. (Some research, especially that done by participant observation, has no hypothesis. You may know so little about the setting you are going to research that you cannot even specify the variables in advance.)

8. **Sharing the results.** To wrap up your research, you will write a report to share your findings with the scientific community. You will review how you did your research, including your operational definitions. You will also show how your findings fit in with the published literature and how they support or refute the theories that apply to your topic. As Table 1.2 on page 26 illustrates, sociologists often summarize their findings in tables.

Let's look in greater detail at the fifth step to see what research methods sociologists use.

Research Methods

As we review the seven research methods (or *research designs*) that sociologists use, we will continue our example of spouse abuse. As you will see, the method you choose will depend on the questions you want to answer.

Surveys

Let's suppose that you want to know how many wives are abused each year. Some husbands also are abused, of course, but let's assume that you are going to focus on wives. An appropriate method for this purpose would be the **survey,** in which you would ask individuals a series of questions. Before you begin your research, however, you must deal with practical matters that face all researchers. Let's look at these issues.

Selecting a Sample.   Ideally, you might want to learn about all wives in the world, but obviously you don't have enough resources to do this. You will have to narrow your **population,** the target group that you are going to study.

Let's assume that your resources (money, assistants, time) allow you to investigate spouse abuse only on your campus. Let's also assume that your college enrollment is large, so you won't be able to survey all the married women who are enrolled. Now you must select a **sample,** individuals from among your target population. How you choose a sample is crucial, for your choice will affect the results of your research. For example, married women enrolled in introductory sociology and engineering courses might have quite different experiences. If so, surveying just one or the other would produce skewed results.

Remember that your goal is to get findings that apply to your entire school. For this, you need a sample that represents the students. How can you get a *representative* sample?

The best way is to use a **random sample.** This does *not* mean that you would stand on some campus corner and ask questions of any woman who happens to walk by. *In a random sample, everyone in your population (the target group) has the same chance of being included in the study.* In this case, because your population is every married woman enrolled in your college, all married women—whether first-year or graduate students, full- or part-time—must have the same chance of being included in your sample.

How can you get a random sample? First, you need a list of all the married women enrolled in your college. Then you assign a number to each name on the list. Using a table of random numbers, you then determine which of these women will become part of your sample. (Tables of random numbers are available in statistics books and online, or they can be generated by a computer.)

A random sample will represent your study's population fairly—in this case, married women enrolled at your college. This means that you will be able to generalize your

To attain their goal of objectivity and accuracy in their research, sociologists must put away their personal opinions or biases.

© Robert Weber/The New Yorker Collection/www.cartoonbank.com

"That's the worst set of opinions I've heard in my entire life."

In doing surveys, why do researchers use samples? What is a random sample?

TABLE 1.2   How to Read a Table

Tables summarize information. Because sociological findings are often presented in tables, it is important to understand how to read them. Tables contain six elements: title, headnote, headings, columns, rows, and source. When you understand how these elements fit together, you know how to read a table.

1. The *title* states the topic. It is located at the top of the table. What is the title of this table? Please determine your answer before looking at the correct answer at the bottom of this page.

2. The *headnote* is not always included in a table. When it is present, it is located just below the title. Its purpose is to give more detailed information about how the data were collected or how data are presented in the table. What are the first eight words of the headnote for this table?

3. The *headings* tell what kind of information is contained in the table. There are three headings in this table. What are they? In the second heading, what does *n* = 25 mean?

4. The *columns* present information arranged vertically. What is the fourth number in the second column and the second number in the third column?

5. The *rows* present information arranged horizontally. In the fourth row, which husbands are more likely to have less education than their wives?

6. The *source* of a table, usually listed at the bottom, provides information on where the data in the table originated. Often, as in this instance, the information is specific enough for you to consult the original source. What is the source for this table?

Comparing Violent and Nonviolent Husbands

Based on interviews with 150 husbands and wives in a Midwestern city who were getting a divorce.

Husband's Achievement and Job Satisfaction	Violent Husbands (*n* = 25)	Nonviolent Husbands (*n* = 125)
He started but failed to complete high school or college.	44%	27%
He is very dissatisfied with his job.	44%	18%
His income is a source of constant conflict.	84%	24%
He has less education than his wife.	56%	14%
His job has less prestige than his father-in-law's.	37%	28%

Source: Modification of Table 1 in O'Brien 1975.

Some tables are much more complicated than this one, but all follow the same basic pattern. To apply these concepts to a table with more information, see page 261.

ANSWERS

1. Comparing Violent and Nonviolent Husbands
2. Based on interviews with 150 husbands and wives
3. Husband's Achievement and Job Satisfaction, Violent Husbands, Nonviolent Husbands. The *n* is an abbreviation for number, and *n* = 25 means that 25 violent husbands were in the sample.
4. 56%, 18%
5. Violent Husbands
6. A 1975 article by O'Brien (listed in the References section of this text).

findings to *all* the married women students on your campus, even if they were not included in your sample.

What if you want to know only about certain subgroups, such as the freshmen and seniors? You could use a **stratified random sample.** You would need a list of the freshmen and senior married women. Then, using random numbers, you would select a sample from each group. This would allow you to generalize to all the freshmen and senior married women at your college, but you would not be able to draw any conclusions about the sophomores or juniors.

No matter what research method you use, you will need a yardstick for comparing your findings. To do this, you will want to know what "average" is in your research. Table 1.3 below discusses ways to measure average.

Asking Neutral Questions.   After you have decided on your population and sample, your next task is to make certain that your questions are neutral. Your questions must allow **respondents,** the people who answer your questions, to express their own opinions. Otherwise, you will end up with biased answers—which are worthless. For example, if you were to ask, "Don't you think that men who beat their wives should go to prison?" you would be tilting the

If sociologists were to study stone throwing, participants and observers, they could use a variety of methods. Based on what you have learned in this chapter, how do you think this activity should be studied? This photo is from Switzerland.

TABLE 1.3	Three Ways to Measure "Average"	
The Mean	**The Median**	**The Mode**
The term *average* seems clear enough. As you learned in grade school, to find the average you add a group of numbers and then divide the total by the number of cases that you added. Assume that the following numbers represent men convicted of battering their wives.	To compute the second average, the *median*, first arrange the cases in order—either from the highest to the lowest or the lowest to the highest. That arrangement will produce the following distribution.	The third measure of average, the *mode,* is simply the cases that occur the most often. In this instance the mode is 57, which is way off the mark.

EXAMPLE

The Mean	The Median		The Mode
321	57	1,795	57
229	57	321	57
57	136	289	136
289	229 or 229		229
136	289	136	289
57	321	57	321
1,795	1,795	57	1,795

The total is 2,884. Divided by 7 (the number of cases), the average is 412. Sociologists call this form of average the *mean.* The mean can be deceptive because it is strongly influenced by extreme scores, either low or high. Note that six of the seven cases are less than the mean. Two other ways to compute averages are the median and the mode.	Then look for the middle case, the one that falls halfway between the top and the bottom. That number is 229, for three numbers are lower and three numbers are higher. When there is an even numbers of cases, the median is the halfway mark between the two middle cases.	Because the mode is often deceptive, and only by chance comes close to either of the other two averages, sociologists seldom use it. In addition, not every distribution of cases has a mode. And if two or more numbers appear with the same frequency, you can have more than one mode.

Do you know the three ways to measure average? What is a stratified random sample?

Improperly worded questions can steer respondents toward answers that are not their own, which produces invalid results.

Doonesbury © G. B. Trudeau. Reprinted with permission of Universal Press Syndicate. All rights reserved.

answer toward agreement with a prison sentence. The *Doonesbury* cartoon illustrates another blatant example of biased questions. For examples of flawed research, see the Down-to-Earth Sociology box on the next page.

Types of Questions   You must also decide whether to use closed-or open-ended questions. **Closed-ended questions** are followed by a list of possible answers. This format would work for questions about someone's age (possible ages would be listed), but not for many other items. For example, how could you list all the opinions that people hold about what should be done to spouse abusers? The answers provided for closed-ended questions can miss the respondent's opinions.

As Table 1.4 illustrates, the alternative is **open-ended questions,** which allow people to answer in their own words. Although open-ended questions allow you to tap the full range of people's opinions, they make it difficult to compare answers. For example, how would you compare these answers to the question "Why do you think men abuse their wives?"

"They're sick."

"I think they must have had problems with their mother."

"We oughta string 'em up!"

Establishing Rapport.   Research on spouse abuse brings up a significant issue. You may have been wondering if women who have been abused will really give honest answers to strangers.

If you were to walk up to women on the street and ask if their husbands have ever beaten them, there would be little reason to take your findings seriously. If, however, you establish **rapport** ("ruh-POUR"), a feeling of trust, with your respondents, victims will talk about personal, sensitive matters. They will share feelings of embarrassment, shame, or other deep emotions. A good example is rape. To go beyond police statistics, each year researchers interview a random sample of 100,000 Americans. They ask them whether they have been victims of burglary, robbery, or other crimes. After establishing rapport, the researchers ask about rape. This National Crime Victimization Survey shows that rape victims will talk about their experiences (Weiss 2009; *Statistical Abstract* 2012:Tables 315, 316).

To gather data on sensitive areas, some researchers use Computer-Assisted Self-Interviewing. In this technique, the interviewer gives the individual a laptop computer, then

TABLE 1.4	Closed- and Open-Ended Questions
A. Closed-Ended Question	**B. Open-Ended Question**
Which of the following best fits your idea of what should be done to someone who has been convicted of spouse abuse? 1. Probation 2. Jail time 3. Community service 4. Counseling 5. Divorce 6. Nothing—It's a family matter	What do you think should be done to someone who has been convicted of spouse abuse?

Can you explain how to establish rapport?

Down-to-Earth Sociology

Loading the Dice: How *Not* to Do Research

The methods of science lend themselves to distortion, misrepresentation, and downright fraud. Consider these findings from surveys:

Americans overwhelmingly prefer Toyotas to Chryslers.
Americans overwhelmingly prefer Chryslers to Toyotas.

Obviously, these opposite conclusions cannot both be true. In fact, both sets of findings are misrepresentations, even though the responses came from surveys conducted by so-called independent researchers. It turns out that some consumer researchers load the dice. Hired by firms that have a vested interest in the outcome of the research, they deliver the results their clients are looking for (Armstrong 2007). Here are six ways to load the dice.

1. **Choose a biased sample.** If you want to "prove" that Americans prefer Chryslers over Toyotas, interview unemployed union workers who trace their job loss to Japanese imports. The answer is predictable. You'll get what you're looking for.
2. **Ask biased questions.** Even if you choose an unbiased sample, you can phrase questions in such a way that you direct people to the answer you're looking for. Suppose that you ask this question:

   We are losing millions of jobs to workers overseas who work for just a few dollars a day. After losing their jobs, some Americans are even homeless and hungry. Do you prefer a car that gives jobs to Americans, or one that forces our workers to lose their homes?

   This question is obviously designed to channel people's thinking toward a predetermined answer—quite contrary to the standards of scientific research. Look again at the *Doonesbury* cartoon.
3. **List biased choices.** Another way to load the dice is to use closed-ended questions that push people into the answers you want. Consider this finding:

   U.S. college students overwhelmingly prefer Levi's 501 to the jeans of any competitor.

   Sound good? Before you rush out to buy Levis, note what these researchers did: In asking students which jeans would be the most popular in the coming year, their list of choices included no other jeans but Levi's 501!

4. **Discard undesirable results.** Researchers can keep silent about results they don't like, or they can continue to survey samples until they find one that matches what they are looking for.
5. **Misunderstand the subjects' world.** This route can lead to errors every bit as great as those just cited. Even researchers who use an adequate sample and word their questions properly can end up with skewed results. They might, for example, fail to anticipate that people may be embarrassed to express an opinion that isn't "politically correct." For example, surveys show that 80 percent of Americans are environmentalists. Is this an accurate figure? Most Americans are probably embarrassed to tell a stranger otherwise. Today, that would be like going against the flag, motherhood, and apple pie.
6. **Analyze the data incorrectly.** Even when researchers strive for objectivity, the sample is good, the wording is neutral, and the respondents answer the questions honestly, the results can still be skewed. The researchers may make a mistake in their calculations, such as entering incorrect data into computer programs. This, too, of course, is inexcusable in science.

Of these six sources of bias, the first four demonstrate fraud. The final two reflect sloppiness, which is also not acceptable in science.

As has been stressed in this chapter, research must be objective if it is to be scientific. The underlying problem with the research cited here—and with so many surveys bandied about in the media as fact—is that survey research has become big business. Simply put, the money offered by corporations has corrupted some researchers.

The beginning of the corruption is subtle. Paul Light, dean at the University of Minnesota, put it this way: "A funder will never come to an academic and say, 'I want you to produce finding X, and here's a million dollars to do it.' Rather, the subtext is that if the researchers produce the right finding, more work—and funding—will come their way."

Sources: Based on Crossen 1991; Goleman 1993; Barnes 1995; Resnik 2000; Augoustinos et al. 2009.

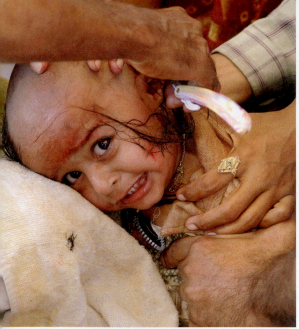

moves aside while he or she answers questions on the computer. In some versions of this method, the individual listens to the questions on headphones and answers on the computer screen. When he or she clicks the "Submit" button, the interviewer has no idea how any question was answered (Guo et al. 2008). Although many people like the privacy that this technique provides, some prefer a live questioner even for sensitive areas of their lives. They say that they want positive feedback from interviewers (Estes et al. 2010).

Participant Observation (Fieldwork)

In **participant observation,** or **fieldwork,** the researcher *participates* in a research setting while *observing* what is happening in that setting. Obviously, this method does not mean that you would sit around and watch someone being abused. But if you wanted to learn how abuse has affected the victims' hopes and goals, their dating patterns, or their marriages, you could use participant observation.

For example, if your campus has a crisis intervention center, you might be able to observe victims of spouse abuse from the time they report the attack through their participation in counseling. With good rapport, you might even be able to spend time with them at their home or with friends. What they say and how they interact with others might help you to understand how the abuse has affected them. This, in turn, could give you insight into how to improve college counseling services.

If you were doing participant observation, you would face this dilemma: How involved should you get in the lives of the people you are observing? Consider this as you read the Down-to-Earth Sociology box on the next page.

Participant observation, participating and observing in a research setting, is usually supplemented by interviewing, asking questions to better understand why people do what they do. In this instance, the sociologist would want to know what this hair removal ceremony in Gujarat, India, means to the child's family and to the community.

Case Studies

To do a **case study,** the researcher focuses on a single event, situation, or individual. The purpose is to understand the dynamics of relationships and power, or even the thinking that motivates people. Sociologist Ken Levi (2009), for example, wanted to study hit men. He would have loved having many hit men to interview, but he had access to only one. He interviewed this man over and over, giving us an understanding of how someone can kill others for money. A case study of spouse abuse would focus on a single wife and husband, exploring the couple's history and relationship.

As you can see, case studies reveal a lot of detail about some particular situation, but the question always remains: How much of this detail applies to other situations? This problem of *generalizability,* which plagues case studies, is the primary reason that few sociologists use this method.

The *research methods* that sociologists choose depend partially on the questions they want to answer. They might want to learn, for example, which forms of publicity are more effective in increasing awareness of spouse abuse as a social problem.

Secondary Analysis

In **secondary analysis,** researchers analyze data that others have collected. For example, if you were to examine the original data from a study of women who had been abused by their husbands, you would be doing secondary analysis.

Analysis of Documents

Documents, or written sources, include books, newspapers, bank records, immigration records, and so on. Sociologists have even used Facebook to study the race-ethnicity of friendships of college students (Wimmer and Lewis 2011). To study spouse abuse, you might examine police reports and court records. These could reveal what percentage of complaints result in arrest and what proportion of the men arrested are

What is participant observation? Case studies? Secondary analysis? Analysis of documents?

Down-to-Earth Sociology

Gang Leader for a Day: Adventures of a Rogue Sociologist

Next to the University of Chicago is an area of poverty so dangerous that the professors warn students to avoid it. One graduate student in sociology, Sudhir Venkatesh, the son of immigrants from India, who was working on a research project with William Julius Wilson, ignored the warning.

With clipboard in hand, Sudhir entered "the projects." Ignoring the glares of the young men standing around, he went into the lobby of a high-rise. Seeing a gaping hole where the elevator was supposed to be, he decided to climb the stairs, where he was almost overpowered by the smell of urine. After climbing five flights, Sudhir came upon some young men shooting craps in a dark hallway. One of them jumped up, grabbed Sudhir's clipboard, and demanded to know what he was doing there.

Sudhir blurted, "I'm a student at the university, doing a survey, and I'm looking for some families to interview."

One man took out a knife and began to twirl it. Another pulled out a gun, pointed it at Sudhir's head, and said, "I'll take him."

Then came a series of rapid-fire questions that Sudhir couldn't answer. He had no idea what they meant: "You flip right or left? Five or six? You run with the Kings, right?"

Grabbing Sudhir's bag, two of the men searched it. They could find only questionnaires, pen and paper, and a few sociology books. The man with the gun then told Sudhir to go ahead and ask him a question.

Sweating despite the cold, Sudhir read the first question on his survey, "How does it feel to be black and poor?" Then he read the multiple-choice answers: "Very bad, somewhat bad, neither bad nor good, somewhat good, very good."

As you might surmise, the man's answer was too obscenity laden to be printed here.

As the men deliberated Sudhir's fate ("If he's here and he don't get back, you know they're going to come looking for him"), a powerfully built man with glittery gold teeth and a sizable diamond earring appeared. The man, known as J. T., who, it turned out, directed the drug trade in the building, asked what was going on. When the younger men mentioned the questionnaire, J. T. said to ask *him* a question.

Amidst an eerie silence, Sudhir asked, "How does it feel to be black and poor?"

"I'm not black," came the reply.

"Well, then, how does it feel to be African American and poor?"

"I'm not African American either. I'm a nigger."

Sudhir was left speechless. Despite his naïveté, he knew better than to ask, "How does it feel to be a nigger and poor?"

As Sudhir stood with his mouth agape, J. T. added, "Niggers are the ones who live in this building. African Americans live in the suburbs. African Americans wear ties to work. Niggers can't find no work."

Not exactly the best start to a research project. But this weird and frightening beginning turned into several years of fascinating research. Over time, J. T. guided Sudhir into a world that few outsiders ever see. Not only did Sudhir get to know drug dealers, crackheads, squatters, prostitutes, and pimps, but he also was present at beatings by drug crews, drive-by shootings done by rival gangs, and armed robberies by the police.

How Sudhir got out of his predicament in the stairwell, his immersion into a threatening underworld—the daily life for many people in "the projects"—and his moral dilemma at witnessing crimes are part of his fascinating experience in doing participant observation of the Black Kings.

Sudhir, who was reared in a middle-class suburb in California, even took over this Chicago gang for a day. This is one reason that he calls himself a rogue sociologist—the decisions he made that day were serious violations of law, felonies that could bring years in prison. There are other reasons, too: During the research, he kicked a man in the stomach, and he was present as the gang planned drive-by shootings.

Sudhir survived, completed his Ph.D., and now teaches at Columbia University.

Source: Based on Venkatesh 2008.

Sudhir Venkatesh, who now teaches at Columbia University, New York City.

For Your Consideration

➔ From this report, what do you see as the advantages of participant observation? Disadvantages? Do you think that doing sociological research justifies being present at beatings? At the planning of drive-by shootings?

How does the Sudhir research illustrate the dilemma of participant observers becoming involved in subjects' lives?

charged, convicted, or put on probation. If these were your questions, police statistics would be valuable.

But for other questions, those records would be useless. If you want to learn about the social and emotional adjustment of the victims, for example police and court records would tell you nothing. Other documents, though, might provide those answers. For example, a crisis intervention center might have records that contain key information—but gaining access to them is almost impossible. Perhaps an unusually cooperative center might ask victims to keep diaries that you could study later.

Experiments

A lot of people say that abusers need therapy. Yet no one knows whether therapy really works. Because **experiments** are useful for determining cause and effect, let's suppose that you propose an experiment to a judge and she gives you access to men who have been arrested for spouse abuse. As in Figure 1.7, you would divide the men randomly into two groups. This helps to ensure that their individual characteristics (attitudes, number of arrests, severity of crimes, education, race–ethnicity, age, and so on) are distributed between the groups. You then would arrange for the men in the **experimental group** to receive some form of therapy. The men in the **control group** would not get therapy.

Your **independent variable,** something that causes a change in another variable, would be therapy. Your **dependent variable,** the variable that might change, would be the men's behavior: whether they abuse women after they get out of jail. Unfortunately, your operational definition of the men's behavior will be sloppy: either reports from the wives or records indicating which men were rearrested for abuse. This is sloppy because some of the women will not report the abuse, and some of the men who abuse their wives will not be arrested. Yet it might be the best you can do.

Let's assume that you choose rearrest as your operational definition. If you find that the men who received therapy are *less* likely to be rearrested for abuse, you can attribute the difference to the therapy. If you find *no difference* in rearrest rates, you can conclude that the therapy was ineffective. If you find that the men who received the therapy have a *higher* rearrest rate, you can conclude that the therapy backfired.

Unobtrusive Measures

Some researchers use **unobtrusive measures,** observing the behavior of people who are not aware that they are being studied. To determine whisky consumption in a town that was legally "dry," sociologists counted the empty bottles in trashcans (Lee 2000).

FIGURE 1.7   **The Experiment**

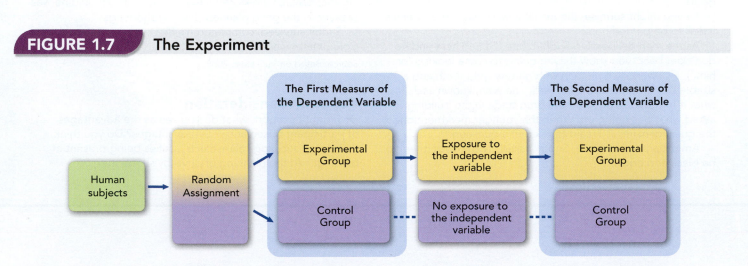

Source: By the author.

Can you explain how experiments work? How do they prove causation?

Researchers have also gone high-tech. When you shop, cameras can follow you from the second you enter a store to the minute you hit the checkout counter, recording each item you touch, as well as every time you pick your nose (Rosenbloom 2010; Singer 2010). Some Web coupons are embedded with bar codes that record your name and Facebook information. The cameras and coupons, which raise ethical issues of invasion of privacy, are part of marketing, not sociological research.

It would be considered unethical to use most unobtrusive measures to research spouse abuse. You could, however, analyze 911 calls. Also, if there were a public forum held by abused or abusing spouses on the Internet, you could record and analyze the online conversations. Ethics in unobtrusive research are still a matter of dispute: To record the behavior of people in public settings, such as a crowd, without announcing that you are doing so is generally considered acceptable. To do this in private settings is not.

To prevent cheating by customers and personnel, casinos use *unobtrusive measures.* Shown here are people examining digitized images from surveillance cameras hidden in the ceiling above the blackjack tables and roulette wheels.

Gender in Sociological Research

You know how significant gender is in your own life, how it affects your orientations and your attitudes. Because gender is also influential in social research, researchers take steps to prevent it from biasing their findings (Davis et al. 2009). In our imagined research on spouse abuse, for example, could a man even do participant observation of women who have been beaten by their husbands? Technically, the answer is yes. But because the women have been victimized by men, they might be less likely to share their experiences and feelings with men. If so, women would be better suited to conduct this research and more likely to achieve valid results. The supposition that these victims will be more open with women than with men, however, is just that—a supposition. Research alone will verify or refute this assumption.

Gender issues can pop up in unexpected ways in sociological research. I vividly recall an incident in San Francisco.

The streets were getting dark, and I was still looking for homeless people. When I saw someone lying down, curled up in a doorway, I approached the individual. As I got close, I began my opening research line, "Hi, I'm Dr. Henslin from. . . ." The individual began to scream and started to thrash wildly. Startled by this sudden, high-pitched scream and by the rapid movements, I quickly backed away. When I later analyzed what had happened, I concluded that I had intruded into a woman's bedroom.

This incident also holds another lesson. Researchers do their best, but they make mistakes. Sometimes these mistakes are minor, and even humorous. The woman sleeping in the doorway wasn't frightened. It was only just getting dark, and there were many people on the street. She was just assertively marking her territory and letting me know in no uncertain terms that I was an intruder. If we make a mistake in research, we pick up and go on. As we do so, we take ethical considerations into account, which is the topic of our next section.

Ethics and Values in Sociological Research

In addition to choosing an appropriate research method, we must also follow the ethics of sociology (American Sociological Association 1999; McKenzie 2009). Research ethics require honesty, truth, and openness (sharing findings with the scientific community). Ethics forbid the falsification of results and condemn

Ethics in social research are of vital concern to sociologists. As discussed in the text, sociologists may disagree on some of the issue's finer points, but none would approve of slipping LSD to unsuspecting subjects like this Marine. This was done to U.S. soldiers in the 1960s under the guise of legitimate testing—just "to see what would happen."

plagiarism—that is, stealing someone else's work. Another ethical guideline states that research subjects should generally be informed that they are being studied and never be harmed by the research. Sometimes people reveal things that are intimate, potentially embarrassing, or otherwise harmful to themselves—and their anonymity must be protected. Finally, although not all sociologists agree, it generally is considered unethical for researchers to misrepresent themselves.

Sociologists take their ethical standards seriously. To illustrate the extent to which they will go to protect their respondents, consider the research conducted by Mario Brajuha.

Ethics: Protecting the Subjects—The Brajuha Research

Mario Brajuha, a graduate student at the State University of New York at Stony Brook, was doing participant observation of restaurant workers. He lost his job as a waiter when the restaurant where he was working burned down—a fire of "suspicious origin," as the police said. When detectives learned that Brajuha had taken field notes, they asked to see them (Brajuha and Hallowell 1986). Because he had promised to keep the information confidential, Brajuha refused to hand them over. When the district attorney subpoenaed the notes, Brajuha still refused. The district attorney then threatened to put Brajuha in jail. By this time, Brajuha's notes had become rather famous, and unsavory characters—perhaps those who had set the fire—also wanted to know what was in them. They, too, demanded to see his notes, and accompanied their demands with threats of a different nature. Brajuha found himself between a rock and a hard place.

For two years, Brajuha refused to hand over his notes, even though he grew anxious and had to appear at several court hearings. Finally, the district attorney dropped the subpoena. When the two men under investigation for setting the fire died, the threats to Brajuha, his wife, and their children ended.

Sociologists applaud the way Brajuha protected his respondents and the professional manner in which he handled himself.

Ethics: Misleading the Subjects—The Humphreys Research

Another ethical problem involves what you tell participants about your research. Although it is considered acceptable for sociologists to do covert participant observation (studying some situation without announcing that they are doing research), to deliberately misrepresent oneself is considered unethical. Let's look at the case of Laud Humphreys, whose research forced sociologists to rethink and refine their ethical stance.

Laud Humphreys, a classmate of mine at Washington University in St. Louis, was an Episcopal priest who decided to become a sociologist. For his Ph.D. dissertation, Humphreys (1970, 1971, 1975) studied social interaction in "tearooms," public restrooms where some men go for quick, anonymous oral sex with other men.

Humphreys found that some restrooms in Forest Park, just across from our campus, were tearooms. He began a participant observation study by hanging around these restrooms. He found that in addition to the two men having sex, a third man—called a "watch queen"—served as a lookout for police and other unwelcome strangers. Humphreys took on the role of watch queen, not only watching for strangers but also observing what the men did. He wrote field notes after the encounters.

Humphreys decided that he wanted to learn about the regular lives of these men. For example, what about the wedding rings that many of the men wore? He came up with an ingenious technique: Many of the men parked their cars near the tearooms, and Humphreys recorded their license plate numbers. A friend in the St. Louis police department gave Humphreys each man's address. About a year later, Humphreys arranged for these men to be included in a medical survey conducted by some of the sociologists on our faculty.

Disguising himself with a different hairstyle and clothing, Humphreys visited the men at home, supposedly to interview them for the medical study. He found that they led conventional lives. They voted, mowed their lawns, and took their kids to Little League games. Many reported that their wives were not aroused sexually or were afraid of getting pregnant because their religion did not allow birth control. Humphreys concluded that heterosexual men were also using the tearooms for a form of quick sex.

This study stirred controversy among sociologists and nonsociologists alike. Many sociologists criticized Humphreys, and a national columnist wrote a scathing denunciation of "sociological snoopers" (Von Hoffman 1970). One of our professors even tried to get Humphreys' Ph.D. revoked. As the controversy heated up and a court case loomed, Humphreys feared that his list of respondents might be subpoenaed. He gave me the list to take from Missouri to Illinois, where I had begun teaching. When he called and asked me to destroy it, I burned the list in my backyard.

Was this research ethical? This question is not decided easily. Although many sociologists sided with Humphreys—and his book reporting the research won a highly acclaimed award—the criticisms continued. At first, Humphreys defended his position vigorously, but five years later, in a second edition of his book (1975), he stated that he should have identified himself as a researcher.

Values: Objectivity and Controversy

Values—beliefs about what is good or desirable in life and the way the world ought to be—are another controversial issue in sociology. Max Weber said that sociology should be **value free.** By this, he meant that a sociologist's values should not affect social research. Instead, **objectivity,** value neutrality, should be the hallmark of social research. If values influence research, he said, sociological findings will be biased.

That bias has no place in research is not a matter of debate. All sociologists agree that no one should distort data to make them fit their values. But it is equally clear that sociologists are infused with arbitrary values of all sorts, for like everyone else, we are members of a particular society at a given point in history. Because values can lead to unintended distortions in how we interpret our research, sociologists stress the need of **replication,** repeating a study in order to compare the new results with the original findings. If an individual's values have distorted the research, replication by others should uncover the bias and correct it.

Despite this consensus, however, values remain a hotly debated topic in sociology (Burawoy 2007; Piven 2007). As summarized in Figure 1.8, this leads us once again to the disagreement about the purposes and uses of sociology. Taking the position that their goal should be to advance the understanding of social life, some sociologists do basic sociology. They gather data on any topic that interests them and use the most appropriate theory to interpret their findings. Convinced that research should have the goal of improving social life, others focus on the social arrangements that harm people—poverty, crime, racism, sexism, war, and other forms of human exploitation.

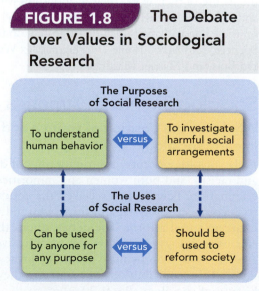

FIGURE 1.8 The Debate over Values in Sociological Research

Source: By the author.

How do ethics influence sociological research? What is the controversy over values in research?

In this book, we'll explore what sociologists do. You will read about research on the macro level, from racism and sexism to the globalization of capitalism. You will also read about research at the micro level of face-to-face interaction—talking, touching, and gestures. This beautiful variety in sociology—and the contrast of going from the larger picture to the smaller picture and back again—is part of the reason that sociology holds such fascination for so many of us. I hope that you also find this variety appealing as you read the rest of this book.

CHAPTER 1 Summary and Review

The Sociological Perspective

What is the sociological perspective?

The **sociological perspective** stresses that people's social experiences—the groups to which they belong and their experiences within these groups—underlie their behavior. C. Wright Mills referred to this as the intersection of biography (the individual) and history (social factors that influence the individual). Pp. 4–5.

Origins of Sociology

When did sociology first appear as a separate discipline?

Sociology emerged in the mid-1800s in western Europe, during the onset of the Industrial Revolution. Industrialization changed all aspects of human existence—where people lived, the nature of their work, their relationships with each other, and how they viewed life. Early sociologists who focused on these social changes include Auguste Comte, Herbert Spencer, Karl Marx, Emile Durkheim, Max Weber, W. E. B. Du Bois, and Harriet Martineau. Pp. 5–9.

Sociology in North America

What was the position of women and minorities in early sociology?

Early sociology occurred during a time of deep sexism and racism, and both women and minorities faced discrimination. Few women received the education required to become sociologists, and those who did tended to focus on social reform. The debate about the proper role of sociology—social reform or objective social analysis—was won by male university professors who ignored the contributions of women as they wrote the history of sociology. Pp. 9–11.

What is the relationship between sociology and social reform?

From its roots, a tension has run between doing **basic sociology** and using sociology to reform society. This tension has never been resolved. Talcott Parsons and C. Wright Mills took opposite positions. Parson's focus was on how the components of society are related to one another. Mills stressed that such a focus does nothing for social reform, which should be the goal of sociologists. This debate about the purpose and use of sociology continues today. **Applied sociology** is the use of sociology to solve problems, usually in specific settings, such as at work or in an organization. The goal of **public sociology** is to benefit the public through the application of sociological data and the sociological perspective. Pp. 11–15.

Theoretical Perspectives in Sociology

What is a theory?

A **theory** is a statement about how facts are related to one another. A theory provides a conceptual framework for interpreting facts. P. 15.

What major theoretical perspectives do sociologists use to interpret social life?

Symbolic interactionists examine how people use symbols (meanings) to develop and share their views of the world. Symbolic interactionists usually focus on the **micro level**—on small-scale, face-to-face interaction. **Functional analysts,** in contrast, focus on the **macro level**—on large-scale patterns of society. Functional theorists stress that a social system is made up of interrelated parts. When working properly, each part contributes to the stability of the whole, fulfilling a function that contributes to the system's equilibrium. **Conflict theorists** also focus on large-scale patterns of society. They stress that society is composed of competing groups that struggle for scarce resources. Pp. 16–21.

With each perspective highlighting different features of social life, and each providing a unique interpretation, no single perspective is adequate. The combined insights of all three yield a more comprehensive picture of social life. Pp. 21–22.

What is the relationship between theory and research?

Theory and research depend on one another. Sociologists use theory to interpret the data they gather. Theory also generates questions that need to be answered by research, while research, in turn, helps to generate theory. Theory without research is not likely to represent real life, while research without theory is merely a collection of unconnected facts. P. 22.

Doing Sociological Research

Why do we need sociological research when we have common sense?

Common sense is unreliable. Research often shows that commonsense ideas are limited or false. Pp. 22–23.

What are the eight basic steps in sociological research?

1. Selecting a topic 2. Defining the problem 3. Reviewing the literature 4. Formulating a **hypothesis** 5. Choosing a **research method** 6. Collecting the data 7. Analyzing the results 8. Sharing the results

These steps are explained on Pp. 23–25.

Research Methods

How do sociologists gather data?

To gather data, sociologists use seven **research methods** (or *research designs*): **surveys, participant observation, case studies, secondary analysis, documents, experiments, and unobtrusive measures.** Pp. 25–33.

Ethics and Values in Sociological Research

How important are ethics in sociological research?

Ethics are of fundamental concern to sociologists, who are committed to openness, honesty, truth, and protecting their subjects from harm. The Brajuha research on restaurant workers and the Humphreys research on "tearooms" illustrate ethical issues of concern to sociologists. Pp. 33–35.

What value dilemmas do sociologists face?

The first dilemma is how to make certain that research is objective and not unintentionally distorted by the researchers' values. To overcome this possible source of bias, sociologists stress **replication.** The second dilemma is whether to do research solely to analyze human behavior or with the goal of reforming harmful social arrangements. Pp. 35–36.

Thinking Critically about Chapter 1

1. Do you think that sociologists should try to reform society or to study it dispassionately?

2. Of the three theoretical perspectives, which one would you prefer to use if you were a sociologist? Why?

3. Considering the macro- and micro-level approaches in sociology, which one do you think better explains social life? Why?

4. Do you think it is right (or ethical) for sociologists to not identify themselves when doing research? To misrepresent themselves? What if identifying themselves as researchers will destroy their access to a research setting or to informants?

Culture

When I first arrived in Morocco, I found the sights that greeted me exotic—not unlike the scenes in *Casablanca* or *Raiders of the Lost Ark*. The men, women, and even the children really did wear those white robes that reached down to their feet. What was especially striking was that the women were almost totally covered. Despite the heat, they wore not only full-length gowns but also head coverings that reached down over their foreheads with veils that covered their faces from the nose down. You could see nothing but their eyes—and every eye seemed the same shade of brown.

And how short everyone was! The Arab women looked to be, on average, 5 feet, and the men only about three or four inches taller. As the only blue-eyed, blond, 6-foot-plus person around, and the only one who was wearing jeans and a pullover shirt, in a world of white-robed short people I stood out like a creature from another planet. Everyone stared. No matter where I went, they stared. Wherever I looked, I saw people watching me intently. Even staring back had no effect. It was so different from home, where, if you caught someone staring at you, that person would look embarrassed and immediately glance away.

> **"Everyone stared. No matter where I went, they stared."**

And lines? The concept apparently didn't even exist. Buying a ticket for a bus or train meant pushing and shoving toward the ticket man (always a man—no women were visible in any public position), who took the money from whichever outstretched hand he decided on.

And germs? That notion didn't seem to exist here either. Flies swarmed over the food in the restaurants and the unwrapped loaves of bread in the stores. Shopkeepers would considerately shoo off the flies before handing me a loaf. They also offered home delivery. I watched a bread vendor deliver a loaf to a woman who was standing on a second-floor balcony. She first threw her money to the bread vendor, and he then threw the unwrapped bread up to her. Unfortunately, his throw was off. The bread bounced off the wrought-iron balcony railing and landed in the street, which was filled with people, wandering dogs, and the ever-present urinating and defecating donkeys. The vendor simply picked up the unwrapped loaf and threw it again. This certainly wasn't his day, for he missed again. But he made it on his third attempt. The woman smiled as she turned back into her apartment, apparently to prepare the noon meal for her family.

Dia de los Muertos (Day of the Dead), California

Watch
The Storytelling Class
on **mysoclab.com**

What Is Culture?

What is culture? The concept is sometimes easier to grasp by description than by definition. For example, suppose you meet a young woman from India who has just arrived in the United States. That her culture is different from yours is immediately evident. You first see it in her clothing, jewelry, makeup, and hairstyle. Next you hear it in her speech. It then becomes apparent by her gestures. Later, you might hear her express unfamiliar beliefs about relationships or what is valuable in life. All of these characteristics are indicative of **culture**—the language, beliefs, values, norms, behaviors, and even material objects that are passed from one generation to the next.

In northern Africa, I was surrounded by a culture quite different from mine. It was evident in everything I saw and heard. The **material culture**—such things as jewelry, art, buildings, weapons, machines, and even eating utensils, hairstyles, and clothing—provided a sharp contrast to what I was used to seeing. There is nothing inherently "natural" about material culture. That is, it is no more natural (or unnatural) to wear gowns on the street than it is to wear jeans.

I also found myself immersed in an unfamiliar **nonmaterial culture,** that is, a group's ways of thinking (its beliefs, values, and other assumptions about the world) and doing (its common patterns of behavior, including language, gestures, and other forms of interaction). North African assumptions that it is acceptable to stare at others in public and to push people aside to buy tickets are examples of nonmaterial culture. So are U.S. assumptions that it is wrong to do either of these things. Like material culture, neither custom is "right." People simply become comfortable with the customs they learn during childhood, and—as when I visited northern Africa—uncomfortable when their basic assumptions about life are challenged.

Culture and Taken-for-Granted Orientations to Life

To develop a sociological imagination, it is essential to understand how culture affects people's lives. If we meet someone from a different culture, the encounter may make us aware of culture's pervasive influence on all aspects of a person's life. Attaining the same level of awareness regarding our own culture, however, is quite another matter. We usually take *our* speech, *our* gestures, *our* beliefs, and *our* customs for granted. We assume that they are "normal" or "natural," and we almost always follow them without question. As anthropologist Ralph Linton (1936) said, "The last thing a fish would ever notice would be water." So also with people: Except in unusual circumstances, most characteristics of our own culture remain imperceptible to us.

Yet culture's significance is profound; it touches almost every aspect of who and what we are. We came into this life without a language; without values and morality; with no ideas about religion, war, money, love, use of space, and so on. We possessed none of these fundamental orientations that are so essential in determining the type of people we become. Yet by this point in our lives, we all have acquired them—and take them for granted. Sociologists call this *culture within us*. These learned and shared ways of believing and of doing (another definition of culture) penetrate our beings at an early age and quickly become part of our taken-for-granted assumptions about what normal behavior is. *Culture becomes the lens through which we perceive and evaluate what is going on around us.* Seldom do we question these assumptions, for, like water to a fish, the lens through which we view life remains largely beyond our perception.

The rare instances in which these assumptions are challenged, however, can be upsetting. Although as a sociologist I try to look at my own culture "from the outside," my trip to Africa quickly revealed how fully I had internalized my own culture. My upbringing in Western culture had given me assumptions about aspects of social life that had become rooted deeply in my being—appropriate eye contact, proper hygiene, and the use of space. But in this part of Africa these assumptions were useless in helping me navigate everyday life. No longer could I count on people to stare only surreptitiously, to take precautions against invisible microbes, or to stand in line in an orderly fashion, one behind the other.

As you can tell from the opening vignette, I found these unfamiliar behaviors unsettling, for they violated my basic expectations of "the way people *ought* to be"—and I did not even realize how firmly I held these expectations until they were challenged so abruptly. When my nonmaterial culture failed me—when it no longer enabled me to make sense out of the world—I experienced a disorientation known as **culture shock.** In the case of buying tickets, the fact that I was several inches taller than most Moroccans and thus able to outreach others helped me to adjust partially to their different ways of doing things. But I never did get used to the idea that pushing ahead of others was "right," and I always felt guilty when I used my size to receive preferential treatment.

An important consequence of culture within us is **ethnocentrism,** a tendency to use our own group's ways of doing things as a yardstick for judging others. All of us learn that the ways of our own group are good, right, and even superior to other ways of life. As sociologist William Sumner (1906), who developed this concept, said, "One's own group is the center of everything, and all others are scaled and rated with reference to it." Ethnocentrism has both positive and negative consequences. On the positive side, it creates in-group loyalties. On the negative side, ethnocentrism can lead to discrimination against people whose ways differ from ours.

The many ways in which culture affects our lives fascinate sociologists. In this chapter, we'll examine how profoundly culture influences everything we are and whatever we do. This will serve as a basis from which you can start to analyze your own assumptions of reality. I should give you a warning at this point: You might develop a changed perspective on social life and your role in it. If so, life will never look the same.

In Sum: To avoid losing track of the ideas under discussion, let's pause for a moment to summarize and, in some instances, clarify the principles we have covered.

1. There is nothing "natural" about material culture. Arabs wear gowns on the street and feel that it is natural to do so. Americans do the same with jeans.
2. There is nothing "natural" about nonmaterial culture. It is just as arbitrary to stand in line as to push and shove.
3. Culture penetrates deeply into our thinking, becoming a taken-for-granted lens through which we see the world and obtain our perception of reality.
4. Culture provides implicit instructions that tell us what we ought to do and how we ought to think. It establishes a fundamental basis for our decision making.
5. Culture also provides a "moral imperative"; that is, the culture that we internalize becomes the "right" way of doing things. (I, for example, believed deeply that it was wrong to push and shove to get ahead of others.)
6. Coming into contact with a radically different culture challenges our basic assumptions of life. (I experienced culture shock when I discovered that my deeply ingrained cultural ideas about hygiene and the use of personal space no longer applied.)
7. Although the particulars of culture differ from one group of people to another, culture itself is universal. That is, all people have culture because society cannot exist without developing shared, learned ways of dealing with the challenges of life.
8. All people are ethnocentric, which has both positive and negative consequences.

What a tremendous photo for sociologists! Seldom are we treated to such cultural contrasts. Can you see how the cultures of these women have given them not only different orientations concerning the presentation of their bodies but also of gender relations, how they expect to relate to men?

What is culture shock? Ethnocentrism? How are they related to our assumptions about life?

For an example of how culture shapes our ideas and behavior, consider dancing with the dead, featured in the Cultural Diversity around the World box below.

Practicing Cultural Relativism

To counter our tendency to use our own culture as the standard by which we judge other cultures, we can practice **cultural relativism;** that is, we can try to understand a culture on its own terms. This means looking at how the elements of a culture fit together, without judging those elements as superior or inferior to our own way of life.

With our own culture embedded so deeply within us, however, practicing cultural relativism can challenge our orientations to life. For example, most U.S. citizens appear to have strong feelings against raising bulls for the purpose of stabbing them to death in front of crowds that shout "Olé!" According to cultural relativism, however, bullfighting must be viewed from the perspective of the culture in which it takes place—*its* history, *its* folklore, *its* ideas of bravery, and *its* ideas of sex roles.

You may still regard bullfighting as wrong, of course, particularly if your culture, which is deeply ingrained in you, has no history of bullfighting. We all possess culturally

Cultural Diversity around the World

Dancing With the Dead

MADAGASCAR

At last the time had come. The family had so looked forward to this day. They would finally be able to take their parents and uncle out of the family crypt and dance with them.

The celebration didn't come cheap, and it had taken several years to save enough money for it. After all, if the dead saw them in old clothing, they would think that they weren't prospering. And the dead needed new silk shrouds, too.

And a band had to be hired—a good one so the dead could enjoy good music.

And, as was customary, friends and relatives had to be invited to the celebration. They would be guests of honor at a feast featuring a roasted zebu, another major expense.

The family members entered the crypt with respect. Carefully removing the dead, they tenderly ran their fingers across the skulls, remembering old times, and sharing the latest family news with the dead. Then, dressing the dead in their new shrouds, with the band playing cheerful tunes, they dance together. The dancing was joyful, as the family members took turns twirling the dead to the musical rhythms.

Everyone was happy, including the dead, who would be put back in their crypt, not to dance again for another four to seven years.

This celebration, which occurs in Madagascar, an island nation off the west coast of Africa, is called *famadihana* (fa-ma-dee-an). Its origin is lost in history, but the dancing is part of what the living owe the dead. "After all," say the Malagasy, "We owe everything to the dead. If they hadn't lived and taken care of us, we wouldn't be here."

Like many people around the world, the traditional Malagasy believe that only a fine line separates the living from the dead. And like many people around the world, they believe that the dead can cross this line and communicate with the living in dreams. The primary distinction is probably the famadihana, a custom that seems to be unique to Madagascar.

As the living know, in a few years, they will join the dead. And a few years after that, these newly dead will join the living in this dance. The celebration of life and death continues.

For Your Consideration

→ How does the famadihana differ from your culture's customs regarding the dead? Why does the famadihana seem strange to Americans and so ordinary to the traditional Malagasy? How has your culture shaped your ideas about death, the dead, and the living?

Based on Bearak 2010; Consulate General of Madagascar in Cape Town 2012.

Use "dancing with the dead" to illustrate how culture shapes our ideas and behavior. What is cultural relativism?

specific ideas about cruelty to animals, ideas that have evolved slowly and match other elements of our culture. In the United States, for example, practices that once were common in some areas—cock fighting, dog fighting, bear–dog fighting, and so on—have been gradually eliminated.

None of us can be entirely successful at practicing cultural relativism. I think you will enjoy the Cultural Diversity box on the next page, but my best guess is that you will evaluate these "strange" foods through the lens of your own culture. Applying cultural relativism, however, is an attempt to refocus that lens so we can appreciate other ways of life rather than simply asserting "Our way is right." Look at the photos on page 46. As you view them, try to appreciate the cultural differences they illustrate about standards of beauty.

Although cultural relativism helps us to avoid cultural smugness, this view has come under attack. In a provocative book, *Sick Societies* (1992), anthropologist Robert Edgerton suggests that we develop a scale for evaluating cultures on their "quality of life," much as we do for U.S. cities. He also asks why we should consider cultures that practice female circumcision, gang rape, or wife beating, or cultures that sell little girls into prostitution, as morally equivalent to those that do not. Cultural values that result in exploitation, he says, are inferior to those that enhance people's lives.

Edgerton's sharp questions and incisive examples bring us to a topic that comes up repeatedly in this text: the disagreements that arise among scholars as they confront contrasting views of reality. It is such questioning of assumptions that keeps sociology interesting.

Many Americans perceive bullfighting as a cruel activity that should be illegal everywhere. To most Spaniards, bullfighting is a sport that pits matador and bull in a unifying image of power, courage, and glory. *Cultural relativism* requires that we suspend our own views in order to grasp the perspectives of others, something easier described than attained.

Components of Symbolic Culture

Sociologists often refer to nonmaterial culture as **symbolic culture,** because it consists of the symbols that people use. A **symbol** is something to which people attach meaning and that they use to communicate with one another. Symbols include gestures, language, values, norms, sanctions, folkways, and mores. Let's look at each of these components of symbolic culture.

Gestures

Gestures, movements of the body to communicate with others, are shorthand ways to convey messages without using words. Although people in every culture of the world use gestures, a gesture's meaning may change completely from one culture to another. North Americans, for example, communicate a succinct message by raising the middle finger in a short, upward stabbing motion. I wish to stress "North Americans," for this gesture does not convey the same message in most parts of the world.

I was surprised to find that this particular gesture was not universal, having internalized it to such an extent that I thought everyone knew what it meant. When I was comparing gestures with friends in Mexico, however, this gesture drew a blank look from them. After I explained its intended meaning, they laughed and showed me their rudest gesture—placing the hand under the armpit and moving the upper arm up and down. To me, they simply looked as if they were imitating monkeys, but to them the gesture meant "Your mother is a whore"—the worst possible insult in that culture.

What does this statement mean? "Cultural relativism helps us to avoid cultural smugness."

Cultural Diversity around the World

You Are What You Eat? An Exploration in Cultural Relativity

Here is a chance to test your ethnocentrism and ability to practice cultural relativity. You probably know that the French like to eat snails and that in some Asian cultures chubby dogs and cats are considered a delicacy ("Ah, lightly browned with a little doggy sauce!"). But did you know that cod sperm is a delicacy in Japan (Halpern 2011)? That flies, scorpions, crickets, and beetles are on the menu of restaurants in parts of Thailand (Gampbell 2006)?

Dusty Friedman, a well-travelled friend, has had some interesting experiences with food. She told me:

When traveling in Sudan, I ate some interesting things that I wouldn't likely eat now that I'm back in our society. Raw baby camel's liver with chopped herbs was a delicacy. So was camel's milk cheese patties that had been cured in dry camel's dung.

We all are ethnocentric when it comes to food preferences. As children, we learn what is and is not food, a view that sticks with us, and we view the world from that perspective. This was driven home to Marston Bates (1967), a zoologist, when he was traveling in Colombia. As he and his hosts were eating roasted ants, they began to talk about the different foods that people like to eat. Bates mentioned that Americans eat frog legs. When he said this, his hosts, who like to munch on crispy ants, looked horrified, as though he had mentioned something vulgar.

You might be able to see yourself eating frog legs and toasted ants, beetles, even flies. (Or maybe not.) Perhaps you could even stomach cod sperm and raw camel liver, maybe even dogs and cats, but here's another test of your ethnocentrism and cultural relativity. Maxine Kingston (1975),

an English professor whose parents grew up in China, wrote:

"Do you know what people in [the Nantou region of] China eat when they have the money?" my mother began. "They buy into a monkey feast. The eaters sit around a thick wood table with a hole in the middle. Boys bring in the monkey at the end of a pole. Its neck is in a collar at the end of the pole, and it is screaming. Its hands are tied behind it. They clamp the monkey into the table; the whole table fits like another collar around its neck. Using a surgeon's saw, the cooks cut a clean line in a circle at the top of its head. To loosen the bone, they tap with a tiny hammer and wedge here and there with a silver pick. Then an old woman reaches out her hand to the monkey's face and up to its scalp, where she tufts some hairs and lifts off the lid of the skull. The eaters spoon out the brains."

What some consider food, even delicacies, can turn the stomachs of others. This ready-to-eat guinea pig was photographed in Lima, Peru.

For Your Consideration

→ What is your opinion about eating toasted ants? Beetles? Flies? Fried frog legs? Cod sperm? About eating puppies and kittens? About eating brains scooped out of a living monkey?

If you were reared in U.S. society, more than likely you think that eating frog legs is okay; eating ants or beetles is disgusting; and eating flies, cod sperm, dogs, cats, and monkey brains is downright repugnant. How would you apply the concepts of ethnocentrism and cultural relativism to your perceptions of these customs?

Gestures not only facilitate communication but also, because they differ around the world, can lead to misunderstanding, embarrassment, or worse. One time in Mexico, for example, I raised my hand to a certain height to indicate how tall a child was. My hosts began to laugh. It turned out that Mexicans use three hand gestures to indicate height: one for people, a second for animals, and yet another for plants. They were amused because I had ignorantly used the plant gesture to indicate the child's height. (See Figure 2.1 on the next page.)

To get along in another culture, then, it is important to learn the gestures of that culture. If you don't, you will fail to achieve the simplicity of communication that gestures allow and you may overlook or misunderstand much of what is

FIGURE 2.1   Gestures to Indicate Height, Southern Mexico

By the author.

happening, run the risk of appearing foolish, and possibly offend people. In some cultures, for example, you would provoke deep offense if you were to offer food or a gift with your left hand, because the left hand is reserved for dirty tasks, such as wiping after going to the toilet. Left-handed Americans visiting Arabs, please note!

Suppose for a moment that you are visiting southern Italy. After eating one of the best meals in your life, you are so pleased that when you catch the waiter's eye, you smile broadly and use the standard U.S. "A-OK" gesture of putting your thumb and forefinger together and making a large "O." The waiter looks horrified, and you are struck speechless when the manager asks you to leave. What have you done? Nothing on purpose, of course, but in that culture this gesture refers to a lower part of the human body that is not mentioned in polite company (Ekman et al. 1984).

Some gestures are so closely associated with emotional messages that the gestures themselves summon up emotions. For example, my introduction to Mexican gestures mentioned on the previous page took place at a dinner table. It was evident that my husband-and-wife hosts were trying to hide their embarrassment at using their culture's obscene gesture at their dinner table. And I felt the same way—not about *their* gesture, of course, which meant nothing to me—but about the one I was teaching them.

Language

The primary way in which people communicate with one another is through **language**—symbols that can be combined in an infinite number of ways for the purpose of communicating abstract thought. Each word is actually a symbol, a sound to which we have attached some particular meaning. Although all human groups have language, there is nothing universal about the meanings given to particular sounds.

Although most *gestures* are learned, and therefore vary from culture to culture, some gestures that represent fundamental emotions such as sadness, anger, and fear appear to be inborn. This crying child whom I photographed in India differs little from a crying child in China—or the United States or anywhere else on the globe. In a few years, however, this child will demonstrate a variety of gestures highly specific to his Hindu culture.

How are gestures an essential part of symbolic culture?

Standards of Beauty

Standards of beauty vary so greatly from one culture to another that what one group finds attractive, another may not. Yet, in its *ethnocentrism*, each group thinks that its standards are the best—that the appearance reflects what beauty "really" is.

As indicated by these photos, around the world men and women aspire to their group's norms of physical attractiveness. To make themselves appealing to others, they try to make their appearance reflect those standards.

Ecuador

United States

Thailand

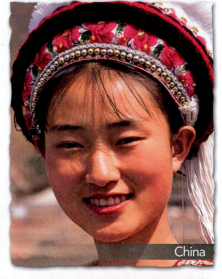
China

Kenya

Cameroon

Tibet

New Guinea

How is beauty an essential part of symbolic culture?

Like gestures, in different cultures the same sound may mean something entirely different—or may have no meaning at all. In German, for example, *gift* means "poison," so if you give a box of chocolates to a non-English-speaking German and say, "Gift, Eat" . . . .

Because *language allows culture to exist,* its significance for human life is difficult to overstate. Consider the following effects of language.

Language Allows Human Experience to Be Cumulative.

By means of language, we pass ideas, knowledge, and even attitudes on to the next generation. This allows others to build on experiences in which they may never directly participate. As a result, humans are able to modify their behavior in light of what earlier generations have learned. This takes us to the central sociological significance of language: *Language allows culture to develop by freeing people to move beyond their immediate experiences.*

Without language, human culture would be little more advanced than that of the lower primates. If we communicated by grunts and gestures, we would be limited to a short time span—to events now taking place, those that have just taken place, or those that will take place immediately—a sort of slightly extended present. You can grunt and gesture, for example, that you want a drink of water, but in the absence of language how could you share ideas concerning past or future events? There would be little or no way to communicate to others what event you had in mind, much less the greater complexities that humans communicate—ideas and feelings about events.

Language Provides a Social or Shared Past.

Without language, we would have few memories, for we associate experiences with words and then use those words to recall the experience. In the absence of language, how would we communicate the few memories we had to others? By attaching words to an event, however, and then using those words to recall it, we are able to discuss the event. This is highly significant, for our talking is far more than "just talk." As we talk about past events, we develop shared understandings about what those events mean. In short, through talk, people develop a shared past.

Language Provides a Social or Shared Future.

Language also extends our time horizons forward. Because language enables us to agree on times, dates, and places, it allows us to plan activities with one another. Think about it for a moment. Without language, how could you ever plan future events? How could you possibly communicate goals, times, and plans? Whatever planning could exist would be limited to rudimentary communications, perhaps to an agreement to meet at a certain place when the sun is in a certain position. But think of the difficulty, perhaps the impossibility, of conveying just a slight change in this simple arrangement, such as "I can't make it tomorrow, but my neighbor can take my place, if that's all right with you."

Language Allows Shared Perspectives.

Our ability to speak, then, provides us with a social (or shared) past and future. This is vital for humanity. It is a watershed that distinguishes us from animals. But speech does much more than this. When we talk with one another, we are exchanging ideas about events; that is, we are sharing perspectives. Our words are the embodiment of our experiences, distilled into a readily exchangeable form, one that is mutually understandable to people who have learned that language. *Talking about events allows us to arrive at the shared understandings that form the basis of social life.*

Not sharing a language while living alongside one another, in contrast, invites miscommunication and suspicion. This risk, which comes with a diverse society, is discussed in the Cultural Diversity box on the next page.

How does *language* provide a shared past, present, and future? How does social life depend on language?

Cultural Diversity in the United States

Miami—Continuing Controversy over Language

Immigration from Cuba and other Spanish-speaking countries has been so vast that most residents of Miami are Latinos. Half of Miami's 400,000 residents have trouble speaking English. Only *one-fourth* of Miamians speak English at home. Controversy erupted when a debate among candidates for mayor of Miami was held only in Spanish. Many English-only speakers are leaving Miami, saying that not being able to speak Spanish is a handicap to getting work. "They should learn Spanish," some reply. As Pedro Falcon, an immigrant from Nicaragua, said, "Miami is the capital of Latin America. The population speaks Spanish."

As the English-speakers see it, this pinpoints the problem: Miami is in the United States, not in Latin America.

Controversy over immigrants and language isn't new. The millions of Germans who moved to the United States in the 1800s brought their language with them. Not only did they hold their religious services in German, but they also opened schools taught in German; published German-language newspapers; and spoke German at home, in the stores, and in the taverns.

Some of their English-speaking neighbors didn't like this a bit. "Why don't those Germans assimilate?" they wondered. "Just whose side would they fight on if we had a war?"

This question was answered, of course, with the participation of German Americans in two world wars. It was even a

Mural on Calle Ocho in Miami

general descended from German immigrants (Eisenhower) who led the armed forces that defeated Hitler.

But what happened to all this German language? The first generation of immigrants spoke German almost exclusively. The second generation assimilated, speaking English at home, but also speaking German when they visited their parents. For the most part, the third generation knew German only as "that language" that their grandparents spoke.

The same thing is happening with the Latino immigrants. Spanish is being kept alive longer, however, because Mexico borders the United States, and there is constant traffic between the countries. The continuing migration from Mexico and other Spanish-speaking countries also feeds the language.

If Germany bordered the United States, there would still be a lot of German spoken here.

Sources: Based on Sharp 1992; Usdansky 1992; Kent and Lalasz 2007; Salomon 2008; Nelson 2011.

Language Allows Shared, Goal-Directed Behavior.   Common understandings enable us to establish a *purpose* for getting together. Let's suppose you want to go on a picnic. You use speech not only to plan the picnic but also to decide on reasons for having the picnic—which may be anything from "because it's a nice day and it shouldn't be wasted studying" to "because it's my birthday." Language permits you to blend individual activities into an integrated sequence. In other words, through discussion you decide where you will go; who will drive; who will bring the hamburgers, the potato chips, the soda; where you will meet; and so on. Only because of language can you participate in such a common yet complex event as a picnic—or build roads and bridges or attend college classes.

In Sum: The sociological significance of language is that it takes us beyond the world of apes and allows culture to develop. Language frees us from the present, actually giving us a social past and a social future. That is, language gives us the capacity to share understandings about the past and to develop shared perceptions about the future. Language also allows us to establish underlying purposes for our activities. In short, *language is the basis of culture.*

How does language both unite and divide people? How is language the basis of culture?

Language and Perception: The Sapir-Whorf Hypothesis

In the 1930s, two anthropologists, Edward Sapir and Benjamin Whorf, became intrigued when they noticed that the Hopi Indians of the southwestern United States had no words to distinguish among the past, the present, and the future. English, in contrast—as well as French, Spanish, Swahili, and other languages—distinguishes carefully among these three time frames. From this observation, Sapir and Whorf began to think that words might be more than labels that people attach to things. *Eventually, they concluded that language has embedded within it ways of looking at the world.* In other words, when we learn a language, we learn not only words but ways of thinking and perceiving (Sapir 1949; Whorf 1956).

The **Sapir-Whorf hypothesis** challenges common sense: It indicates that rather than objects and events forcing themselves onto our consciousness, it is our language that determines our consciousness, and hence our perception of objects and events. Sociologist Eviatar Zerubavel (1991) points out that his native language, Hebrew, does not have separate words for jam and jelly. Both go by the same term, and only when Zerubavel learned English could he "see" this difference, which is "obvious" to native English speakers. Similarly, if you learn to classify students as Jocks, Goths, Stoners, Skaters, Band Geeks, and Preps, you will perceive students in an entirely different way from someone who does not know these classifications.

When I lived in Spain, I was struck by the relevance of the Sapir-Whorf hypothesis. As a native English speaker, I had learned that the term *dried fruits* refers to apricots, apples, and so on. In Spain, I found that *frutos secos* refers not only to such objects but also to things like almonds, walnuts, and pecans. My English makes me see fruits and nuts as quite separate types of objects. This seems "natural" to me, while combining them into one unit seems "natural" to Spanish speakers. If I had learned Spanish first, my perception of these objects would be different.

Although Sapir and Whorf's observation that the Hopi do not have tenses was inaccurate (Edgerton 1992:27), they did stumble onto a major truth about social life. Learning a language means not only learning words but also acquiring the perceptions embedded in that language. In other words, language both reflects and shapes our cultural experiences (Boroditsky 2010). The racial–ethnic terms that our culture provides, for example, influence how we see both ourselves and others, a point that is discussed in the Cultural Diversity box on the next page.

Values, Norms, and Sanctions

To learn a culture is to learn people's **values,** their ideas of what is desirable in life. When we uncover people's values, we learn a great deal about them, for values are the standards by which people define what is good and bad, beautiful and ugly. Values underlie our preferences, guide our choices, and indicate what we hold worthwhile in life.

Every group develops expectations concerning the "right" way to reflect its values. Sociologists use the term **norms** to describe those expectations (or rules of behavior) that develop out of a group's values. The term **sanctions** refers to the reactions people receive for following or breaking norms. A **positive sanction** expresses approval for following a norm, and a **negative sanction** reflects disapproval for breaking a norm. Positive sanctions can be material, such as a prize, a trophy, or money, but in everyday life they usually consist of hugs, smiles, a pat on the back, or even handshakes and "high fives." Negative sanctions can also be material—being fined in court is one example—but negative sanctions, too, are more likely to be symbolic: harsh words, or gestures such as

Many societies relax their *norms* during specified occasions. At these times, known as moral holidays, behavior that is ordinarily not permitted is allowed. Shown here at Mardi Gras in New Orleans is a woman who is about to show her breasts to get beads dropped to her from the balcony. When a moral holiday is over, the usual enforcement of rules follows.

According to the Sapir-Whorf hypothesis, how does language influence our perception?

Cultural Diversity in the United States

Race and Language: Searching for Self-Labels

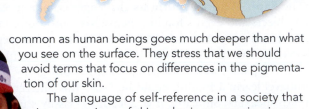

The groups that dominate society often determine the names that are used to refer to racial–ethnic groups. If those names become associated with oppression, they take on negative meanings. For example, the terms *Negro* and *colored people* came to be associated with submissiveness and low status. To overcome these meanings, those referred to by these terms began to identify themselves as *black* or *African American.* They infused these new terms with respect—a basic source of self-esteem that they felt the old terms denied them.

In a twist, African Americans—and to a lesser extent Latinos, Asian Americans, and Native Americans—have changed the rejected term *colored people* to *people of color.* Those who embrace this modified term are imbuing it with meanings that offer an identity of respect. The term also has political meanings. It implies bonds that cross racial–ethnic lines, mutual ties, and a sense of identity rooted in historical oppression.

There is *always* disagreement about racial–ethnic terms, and this one is no exception. Although most rejected the term *colored people,* some found in it a sense of respect and claimed it for themselves. The acronym NAACP, for example, stands for the National Association for the Advancement of Colored People. The new term, *people of color,* arouses similar feelings. Some individuals whom this term would include point out that this new label still makes color the primary identifier of people. They stress that humans transcend race–ethnicity, that what we have in

The ethnic terms we choose—or which are given to us—are major self-identifiers. They indicate both membership in some group and a separation from other groups.

common as human beings goes much deeper than what you see on the surface. They stress that we should avoid terms that focus on differences in the pigmentation of our skin.

The language of self-reference in a society that is so conscious of skin color is an ongoing issue. As long as our society continues to emphasize such superficial differences, the search for adequate terms is not likely to ever be "finished." In this quest for terms that strike the right chord, the term *people of color* may become a historical footnote. If it does, it will be replaced by another term that indicates a changing self-identification within a changing culture.

For Your Consideration

→ What terms do you use to refer to your race–ethnicity? What "bad" terms do you know that others have used to refer to your race–ethnicity? What is the difference in meaning between the terms you use and the "bad" terms? Where does that meaning come from?

---

frowns, stares, clenched jaws, or raised fists. Getting a raise at work is a positive sanction, indicating that you have followed the norms clustering around work values. Getting fired, in contrast, is a negative sanction, indicating that you have violated these norms. The North American finger gesture discussed earlier is, of course, a negative sanction.

Because people can find norms stifling, some cultures relieve the pressure through *moral holidays,* specified times when people are allowed to break norms. Moral holidays such as Mardi Gras often center on getting rowdy. Some activities for which people would otherwise be arrested are permitted—and expected—including public drunkenness and some nudity. The norms are never completely dropped, however—just loosened a bit. Go too far, and the police step in.

Some societies have *moral holiday places,* locations where norms are expected to be broken. Each year, the hometown of the team that wins the Super Bowl becomes a moral holiday place—for one night. One of the more interesting examples is "Party Cove" at Lake of the Ozarks in Missouri, a fairly straightlaced area of the country. During the summer, hundreds of boaters—those operating everything from cabin cruisers to jet skis—moor their vessels together in a highly publicized

Read
Body Ritual Among the Nacirema by Horace Miner
on **mysoclab.com**

cove, where many get drunk, take off their clothes, and dance on the boats. In one of the more humorous incidents, boaters complained that a nude woman was riding a jet ski outside of the cove. The water patrol investigated but refused to arrest the woman because she was within the law—she had sprayed shaving cream on certain parts of her body.

The violation of *mores* is a serious matter. In this case, it is serious enough that the security at a football match in Edmonton, Alberta (Canada) have swung into action to protect the public from seeing a "disgraceful" sight, at least one so designated by this group.

Folkways, Mores, and Taboos

Norms that are not strictly enforced are called **folkways.** We expect people to comply with folkways, but we are likely to shrug our shoulders and not make a big deal about it if they don't. If someone insists on passing you on the right side of the sidewalk, for example, you are unlikely to take corrective action, although if the sidewalk is crowded and you must move out of the way, you might give the person a dirty look.

Other norms, however, are taken much more seriously. We think of them as essential to our core values, and we insist on conformity. These are called **mores** (MORE-rays). A person who steals, rapes, or kills has violated some of society's most important mores. As sociologist Ian Robertson (1987:62) put it,

> A man who walks down a street wearing nothing on the upper half of his body is violating a folkway; a man who walks down the street wearing nothing on the lower half of his body is violating one of our most important mores, the requirement that people cover their genitals and buttocks in public.

It should also be noted that one group's folkways may be another group's mores. Although a man walking down the street with the upper half of his body uncovered is deviating from a folkway, a woman doing the same thing is violating the mores. In addition, the folkways and mores of a subculture (discussed in the next section) may be the opposite of mainstream culture. For example, to walk down the sidewalk in a nudist camp with the entire body uncovered would conform to that subculture's folkways.

A **taboo** refers to a norm so strongly ingrained that even the thought of its violation is greeted with revulsion. Eating human flesh and parents having sex with their children are examples of such behaviors. When someone breaks a taboo, the individual is usually judged unfit to live in the same society as others. The sanctions are severe and may include prison, banishment, or death.

Many Cultural Worlds

Subcultures

Groups of people who occupy some small corner in life, such as an occupation, tend to develop specialized ways to communicate with one another. To outsiders, their talk, even if it is in English, can seem like a foreign language. Here is one of my favorite quotes by a politician:

> There are things we know that we know. There are known unknowns; that is to say, there are things that we now know we don't know. But there are also unknown unknowns; there are things we do not know we don't know. (Donald Rumsfeld, quoted in Dickey and Barry 2006:38)

Whatever Rumsfeld, the former secretary of defense under George W. Bush, meant by his statement probably will remain a known unknown. (Or would it be an unknown known?)

Can you explain the difference between folkways, mores, and taboos?

We have a similar problem in sociology. Try to figure out what this means:

These narratives challenge the "blaming the victim" approach, which has been dominant in the public discourse. The first and oldest is the well-known liberal narrative, here termed the structure/context counter-narrative. The other two counter-narratives—the agency/ resistance counter-narrative and voice/action counter-narrative—are built on the analysis of the structure/context counter-narrative. (Krumer-Nevo and Benjamin 2010:694)

As much as possible, I will spare you from such "insider" talk.

Sociologists and politicians form a **subculture,** *a world within the larger world of the dominant culture.* Subcultures are not limited to occupations, for they include any corner in life in which people's experiences lead them to have distinctive ways of looking at the world. Even if we cannot understand the quotation from Donald Rumsfeld, it makes us aware that politicians don't view life in quite the same way most of us do.

U.S. society contains *thousands* of subcultures. Some are as broad as the way of life we associate with teenagers, others as narrow as those we associate with body builders— or with politicians. Some U.S. ethnic groups also form subcultures: Their values, norms, and foods set them apart. So might their religion, music, language, and clothing. Even sociologists form a subculture. As you are learning, they also use a unique language in their efforts to understand the world.

For a subculture in another society, one that might test the limits of your sense of cultural relativism, read the Down-to-Earth Sociology box on the next page. For a visual depiction of subcultures, see the photo essay on pages 54–55.

Countercultures

Look what a different world this person is living in:

If everyone applying for welfare had to supply a doctor's certificate of sterilization, if everyone who had committed a felony were sterilized, if anyone who had mental illness to any degree were sterilized—then our economy could easily take care of these people for the rest of their lives, giving them a decent living standard—but getting them out of the way. That way there would be no children abused, no surplus population, and, after a while, no pollution. . . .

When the . . . present world system collapses, it'll be good people like you who will be shooting people in the streets to feed their families. (Zellner 1995:58, 65)

Why is salsa dancing a *subculture* and not a counterculture?

Welcome to the world of the Aryan supremacist survivalists, where the message is much clearer than that of politicians—and much more disturbing.

The values and norms of most subcultures blend in with mainstream society. In some cases, however, as with the survivalists quoted above, some of the group's values and norms place it at odds with the dominant culture. Sociologists use the term **counterculture** to refer to such groups. To better see this distinction, consider motorcycle enthusiasts and motorcycle gangs. Motorcycle enthusiasts—who emphasize personal freedom and speed *and* affirm cultural values of success through work or education—are members of a subculture. In contrast, the Hell's Angels, Pagans, and Bandidos not only stress freedom and speed but also value dirtiness and contempt toward women, work, and education. This makes them a counterculture.

An assault on core values is always met with resistance. To affirm their own values, members of the mainstream culture may ridicule, isolate, or even attack members of the counterculture. The Mormons, for example, were driven out of several states before they finally settled in Utah, which was at that time a wilderness. Even there, the federal government would not let them practice *polygyny* (one man having more than one wife), and Utah's statehood was made conditional on its acceptance of monogamy (Anderson 1942/1966; Williams 2007).

Can you explain the difference between subcultures and countercultures?

Down-to-Earth Sociology

2-D: A New Subculture and a Different Kind of Love

"I've experienced so many amazing things because of her. She has really changed my life." —Nisan

Nisan, a 37-year old man who lives in Tokyo, has strong feelings for his girlfriend, Nemu, and loves dating her. Nemu is on the shy side, though, and in restaurants she sits quietly on the chair next to Nisan. When they ride in his Toyota, she sits silently in the passenger's seat. Never once has Nemu uttered even a single word.

The silence hasn't stopped Nisan from spending his vacations with Nemu. They have traveled hundreds of miles to Kyoto and Osaka. This has been a little hard on Nisan's modest budget, but Nemu seems to enjoy the travel. To save money while vacationing, they sleep together in the car. Sometimes they crash on friends' couches (Katayama 2009).

That's Nisan in the photo to the right. And that's Nemu that he is holding.

Nisan isn't joking. He is serious about the feelings that he has for Nemu, a video game character.

And so are the other Japanese men who belong to the 2-D (two-dimensional) subculture. Some of these men have never been able to attract real women. Others have been disappointed in real-life love. For them, cartoon and video characters take on a lifelike reality.

To Westerners raised on Freudian imagery, the 2-D subculture stimulates haunting thoughts. But the Japanese seem to see matters differently. A Japanese author who has written widely on the 2-D subculture—and is himself a member of it—stresses that his subculture exists because romance has

Nisan and Nemu

become a commodity. The mass media glorify good looks and money, he says, which denies romance to many men. Some of these men train their minds to experience romantic love when they look at a cartoon. As one man put it, the pillow covers represent "cute girls who live in my imagination."

Sociologically, we might point out that in Japan the sexes don't mix as easily as they do in the West. About half of Japanese adults, both men and women, have no friends of the opposite sex (Katayama 2009).

The 2-D subculture is growing. Tokyo has shops that feature 2-D products such as body pillows and dolls for men. In some Tokyo restaurants, the waitresses dress up like video-game characters.

There is even an island resort that specializes in honeymoons for men who have fallen in love with their cartoon cuties. The men check into the hotel, pay for a room for two, and immerse themselves in their virtual relationships, controlled through their hand-held devices (Wakabayashi 2010a, 2010b). The local businesses, which sell special meals with heart-shaped dishes and cakes that the lovers give their cartoon characters, are pleased with their new visitors—the flesh-and-blood ones who pay the bills.

For Your Consideration

→ Do you agree with this statement: If a man in the United States were to carry around a body pillow like the one in the photo on this page, he would find less acceptance than do Nisan and the men like him in Japan? If so, why do you think this difference exists? Do you think that 2-D will thrive as a subculture in the United States? Why or why not?

Values in U.S. Society

An Overview of U.S. Values

As you know, the United States is a **pluralistic society,** made up of many different groups. The United States has numerous religious and racial–ethnic groups, as well as countless interest groups that focus on activities as divergent as hunting deer or collecting Barbie dolls. Within this huge diversity, sociologists have tried to identify the country's **core values,** those that are shared by most of the groups that make up U.S. society. Here are ten that sociologist Robin Williams (1965) identified:

1. *Achievement and success.* Americans praise personal achievement, especially outdoing others. This value includes getting ahead at work and school, and attaining wealth, power, and prestige.
2. *Individualism.* Americans cherish the ideal that an individual can rise from the bottom of society to its very top. If someone fails to "get ahead," Americans generally

Looking at Subcultures

Subcultures can form around any interest or activity. Each subculture has its own values and norms that its members share, giving them a common identity. Each also has special terms that pinpoint the group's corner of life and that its members use to communicate with one another. Some of us belong to several subcultures.

As you can see from this photo essay, most subcultures are compatible with the values and norms of the mainstream culture. They represent specialized interests around which its members have chosen to build tiny worlds. Some subcultures, however, conflict with the mainstream culture. Sociologists give the name *countercultures* to subcultures whose values (such as those of outlaw motorcyclists) or activities and goals (such as those of terrorists) are opposed to the mainstream culture. Countercultures, however, are exceptional, and few of us belong to them.

Each subculture provides its members with values and distinctive ways of viewing the world. What values and perceptions do you think are common among body builders? What other subculture do you see in this photo?

Membership in this subculture is not easily awarded. Not only must high-steel ironworkers prove that they are able to work at great heights but also that they fit into the group socially. Newcomers are tested by members of the group, and they must demonstrate that they can take joking without offense.

Specialized values and interests are two of the characteristics that mark subcultures. What values and interests distinguish the modeling subculture?

The subculture that centers around tattooing previously existed on the fringes of society, with seamen and circus folk its main participants. It now has entered mainstream society, but not to this extreme.

The truckdriver subculture, centering on their occupational activities and interests, is also broken into smaller subcultures that reflect their experiences of race–ethnicity.

With their specialized language and activities, surfers are highly recognized as members of a subculture. This surfer is "in the tube."

Why would someone decorate himself like this? Among the many reasons, one is to show solidarity with the football subculture.

Even subcultures can have subcultures. The rodeo subculture is a subculture of "western" subculture. The values that unite its members are reflected in their speech, clothing, and specialized activities, such as the one shown here.

find fault with that individual rather than with the social system for placing road-
blocks in his or her path.

3. *Hard work*. Americans expect people to work hard to achieve financial success and
material comfort.

4. *Efficiency and practicality*. Americans award high marks for getting things done effi-
ciently. Even in everyday life, Americans consider it important to do things fast, and
they seek ways to increase efficiency.

5. *Science and technology*. Americans have a passion for applied science, for using science to control nature—to tame rivers and harness winds—and to develop new
technology, from iPads to pedal-electric hybrid vehicles.

6. *Material comfort*. Americans expect a high level of material comfort. This includes
not only good nutrition, medical care, and housing but also late-model cars and
recreational playthings—from iPhones to motor homes.

7. *Freedom*. This core value pervades U.S. life. It underscored the American Revolution, and Americans pride themselves on their personal freedom.

8. *Democracy*. By this term, Americans refer to majority rule, to the right of everyone
to express an opinion, and to representative government.

9. *Equality*. It is impossible to understand Americans without being aware of the
central role that the value of equality plays in their lives. Equality of opportunity
(part of the ideal culture discussed later) has significantly influenced U.S. history and
continues to mark relations between the groups that make up U.S. society.

10. *Group superiority*. Although it contradicts the values of freedom, democracy, and
equality, Americans regard some groups more highly than others and have done so
throughout their history. The denial of the vote to women, the slaughter of Native
Americans, and the enslavement of Africans are a few examples of how the groups
considered superior have denied equality and freedom to others.

In an earlier publication, I updated Williams' analysis by adding these three values.

1. *Education*. Americans are expected to go as far in school as their abilities and
finances allow. Over the years, the definition of an "adequate" education has
changed, and today a college education is considered an appropriate goal for most
Americans. Those who have an opportunity for higher education and do not take
it are sometimes viewed as doing something "wrong"—not merely as making a bad
choice, but as somehow being involved in an immoral act.

2. *Religiosity*. There is a feeling that "every true American ought to be religious." This
does not mean that everyone is expected to join a church, synagogue, or mosque,
but that everyone ought to acknowledge a belief in a Supreme Being and follow
some set of matching precepts. This value is so pervasive that Americans stamp "In
God We Trust" on their money and declare in their national pledge of allegiance
that they are "one nation under God."

3. *Romantic love*. Americans feel that the only proper basis for marriage is romantic
love. Songs, literature, mass media, and "folk beliefs" all stress this value. Americans
grow misty-eyed at the theme that "love conquers all."

Value Clusters

As you can see, values are not independent units; some cluster together to form a
larger whole. In the **value cluster** that surrounds success, for example, we find hard
work, education, material comfort, and individualism bound up together. Americans
are expected to go far in school, to work hard afterward, and then to attain a high
level of material comfort, which, in turn, demonstrates success. Success is attributed
to the individual's efforts; lack of success is blamed on his or her faults.

Value Contradictions

You probably were surprised to see group superiority on the list of dominant American
values. This is an example of what I mentioned in Chapter 1, how sociology upsets
people and creates resistance. Few people want to bring something like this into the

Explore
Living Data
on **mysoclab.com**

open. It violates today's *ideal* culture, a concept we discuss on the next page. But this is what sociologists do—they look beyond the façade to penetrate what is really going on. And when you look at our history, there is no doubt that group superiority has been a dominant value. It still is, but values change, and this one is diminishing.

Value contradictions, then, are part of culture. Not all values are wrapped in neat packages, and you can see how group superiority contradicts freedom, democracy, and equality. There simply cannot be full expression of freedom, democracy, and equality along with racism and sexism. Something has to give. One way in which Americans in the past sidestepped this contradiction was to say that freedom, democracy, and equality applied only to some groups. The contradiction was bound to surface over time, however, and so it did with the Civil War and the women's liberation movement. *It is precisely at the point of value contradictions, then, that one can see a major force for social change in a society.*

An Emerging Value Cluster

A value cluster of four interrelated core values—leisure, self-fulfillment, physical fitness, and youthfulness—is emerging in the United States. So is a fifth core value—concern for the environment.

1. *Leisure.* The emergence of leisure as a value is reflected in a huge recreation industry—from computer games, boats, vacation homes, and spa retreats to sports arenas, home theaters, adventure vacations, and luxury cruises.
2. *Self-fulfillment.* This value is reflected in the "human potential" movement, which emphasizes becoming "all you can be," and in magazine articles, books, and talk shows that focus on "self-help," "relating," and "personal development."
3. *Physical fitness.* Physical fitness is not a new U.S. value, but the greater emphasis on it is moving it into this emerging cluster. You can see this trend in the publicity given to nutrition, organic foods, weight, and diet; the joggers, cyclists, and backpackers; and the countless health clubs and physical fitness centers.
4. *Youthfulness.* Valuing youth and disparaging old age are also not new, but some analysts note a sense of urgency in today's emphasis on youthfulness. They attribute this to the huge number of aging baby boomers, who, aghast at the physical changes that accompany their advancing years, are attempting to deny or at least postpone their biological fate. One physician even claimed that "aging is not a normal life event, but a disease" (Cowley 1996).
5. *Concern for the environment.* During most of U.S. history, the environment was viewed as something to be exploited—a wilderness to be settled, forests to be cleared for farm land and lumber, rivers and lakes to be fished, and animals to be hunted. One result was the near extinction of the bison and the extinction of the passenger pigeon, a species of bird previously so numerous that its migration would darken the skies for days. Today, Americans have developed a genuine and apparently long-term concern for the environment.

In Sum: Values don't "just happen." They are related to conditions of society. This emerging value cluster is a response to fundamental changes in U.S. culture. Earlier generations of Americans were focused on forging a nation and fighting for economic survival. But today, millions of Americans are freed from long hours of work, and millions retire from work at an age when they anticipate decades of life ahead of them. This value cluster centers on helping people to maintain their health and vigor during their younger years and enabling them to enjoy their years of retirement.

Only when an economy produces adequate surpluses can a society afford these values. To produce both longer lives and retirement, for example, takes a certain stage of economic development. Concern for the environment is another remarkable example. People act on environmental concerns only after they have met their basic needs. The world's poor nations, for example, have a difficult time "affording" this value at this point in their development (Gokhale 2009).

Explain the value cluster that is emerging in U.S. culture. What does "values don't just happen" mean?

When Values Clash

Challenges in core values are met with strong resistance by the people who hold them dear. They see change as a threat to their way of life, an undermining of both their present and their future. Efforts to change gender roles, for example, arouse intense controversy, as do same-sex marriages. Alarmed at such onslaughts against their values, traditionalists fiercely defend historical family relationships and the gender roles they grew up with. Some use the term *culture wars* to refer to the clash in values between traditionalists and those advocating change, but the term is highly exaggerated. Compared with the violence directed against the Mormons, today's culture clashes are mild.

Values as Distorting Lenses

Values and their supporting beliefs are lenses through which we see the world. The views produced through these lenses are often of what life *ought* to be like, not what it is. For example, Americans value individualism so highly that they tend to see almost everyone as free and equal in pursuing the goal of success. This value blinds them to the significance of the circumstances that keep people from achieving success. The dire consequences of family poverty, parents' low education, and dead-end jobs tend to drop from sight. Instead, Americans see the unsuccessful as not putting out enough effort. And they "know" they are right, for the mass media dangle before their eyes enticing stories of individuals who have succeeded despite the greatest of handicaps.

"Ideal" Versus "Real" Culture

Many of the norms that surround cultural values are followed only partially. Differences always exist between a group's ideals and what its members actually do. Consequently, sociologists use the term **ideal culture** to refer to the values, norms, and goals that a group considers ideal, worth aiming for. Success, for example, is part of ideal culture. Americans glorify academic progress, hard work, and the display of material goods as

Values, both those held by individuals and those that represent a nation or people, can undergo deep shifts. It is difficult for many of us to grasp the pride with which earlier Americans destroyed trees that took thousands of years to grow, are located only on one tiny speck of the globe, and that we today consider part of the nation's and world's heritage. But this is a value statement, representing current views. The pride expressed on these woodcutters' faces represents another set of values entirely.

Redwoods, in California
son, Photo Registered

signs of individual achievement. What people actually do, however, usually falls short of the cultural ideal. Compared with their abilities, for example, most people don't work as hard as they could or go as far as they could in school. Sociologists call the norms and values that people actually follow **real culture.**

As you know, our culture is undergoing constant change. A major reason for the barrage of change that we face is that we are adjusting to changing technology. Let's look at this.

Technology in the Global Village

The New Technology

The gestures, language, values, folkways, and mores that we have discussed—all are part of symbolic (nonmaterial) culture. Culture, as you recall, also has a material aspect: *a group's things,* from its houses to its toys. Central to a group's material culture is its technology. In its simplest sense, **technology** can be equated with tools. In a broader sense, technology also includes the skills or procedures necessary to make and use those tools.

We can use the term **new technology** to refer to an emerging technology that has a significant impact on social life. Although people develop minor technologies all the time, most are only slight modifications of existing technologies. Occasionally, however, they develop a technology that makes a major impact on human life. It is primarily to these innovations that the term *new technology* refers. Five hundred years ago, the new technology was the printing press. For us, the new technology consists of computers, satellites, and the Internet.

The sociological significance of technology goes far beyond the tool itself. *Technology sets the framework for a group's nonmaterial culture.* It is obvious that if a group's culture changes, so do the ways people do things. But the effects of technology go far beyond this. Technology also influences how people think and how they relate to

"JUST THINK OF IT AS IF YOU'RE READING A LONG TEXT-MESSAGE."

Technological advances are now so rapid that there can be cultural gaps between generations.

one another. An example is gender relations. Through the centuries and throughout the world, it has been the custom (nonmaterial culture) for men to dominate women. Today's global communications (material culture) make this custom more difficult to maintain. For example, when Arab women watch Western television, they observe an unfamiliar freedom in gender relations. As these women use e-mail and telephones to talk to one another about what they have seen, they both convey and create discontent, as well as feelings of sisterhood. These communications motivate some of them to agitate for social change.

In today's world, the long-accepted idea that it is proper to withhold rights on the basis of someone's sex can no longer be sustained. What usually lies beyond our awareness in this revolutionary change is the role of the new technology, which joins the world's nations into a global communications network.

Cultural Lag and Cultural Change

Three or four generations ago, sociologist William Ogburn (1922/1938) coined the term **cultural lag.** By this, Ogburn meant that not all parts of a culture change at the same pace. When one part of a culture changes, other parts lag behind.

Ogburn pointed out that *a group's material culture usually changes first, with the non-material culture lagging behind*. This leaves the nonmaterial (or symbolic) culture playing a game of catch-up. For example, when we get sick, we can type our symptoms into a computer and get an instant diagnosis and recommended course of treatment. In some tests, computer programs outperform physicians. Yet our customs have not caught up with our technology, and we continue to visit the doctor's office.

Sometimes nonmaterial culture never does catch up. We can rigorously hold onto some outmoded form—one that once was needed, but that long ago was bypassed by technology. Have you ever wondered why our "school year" is nine months long, and why we take summers off? For most of us, this is "just the way it's always been," and we have never questioned it. But there is more to this custom than meets the eye. In the late 1800s, when universal schooling came about, the school year matched the technology of the time. Most parents were farmers, and for survival they needed their children's help at the crucial times of planting and harvesting. Today, generations later, when few people farm and there is no need for the "school year" to be so short, we still live with this cultural lag.

Technology and Cultural Leveling

For most of human history, communication was limited and travel slow. Consequently, in their relative isolation, human groups developed highly distinctive ways of life as they responded to the particular situations they faced. The unique characteristics they developed that distinguished one culture from another tended to change little over time. The Tasmanians, who live on a remote island off the coast of Australia, provide an extreme example. For thousands of years, they had no contact with other people. They were so isolated that they did not even know how to make clothing or fire (Edgerton 1992).

Except in such rare instances as these, humans have always had *some* contact with other groups. During these contacts, people learned from one another, adopting things they found desirable. In this process, called **cultural diffusion,** groups are most open to changes in their technology or material culture. They usually are eager, for example, to adopt superior weapons and tools. In remote jungles in South America one can find metal cooking pots, steel axes, and even bits of clothing spun in mills in South Carolina. Although the direction of cultural diffusion today is primarily from the West to other parts of the world, cultural diffusion is not a one-way street—as bagels, woks, hammocks, and sushi in the United States attest.

With today's travel and communications, cultural diffusion is occurring rapidly. Air travel has made it possible to journey around the globe in a matter of hours. In the not-so-distant past, a trip from the United States to Africa was so unusual that only a few adventurous people made it, and newspapers would herald their feat. Today, hundreds of thousands make the trip each year.

The changes in communication are no less vast. Communication used to be limited to face-to-face speech, written messages that were passed from hand to hand, and visual signals such as smoke or light that was reflected from mirrors. Despite newspapers and even the telegraph, people in some parts of the United States did not hear that the Civil War had ended until weeks and even months after it was over. Today's electronic communications transmit messages across the globe in a matter of seconds, and we learn almost instantaneously what is happening on the other side of the world. During the Iraq War, reporters traveled with U.S. soldiers, and for the first time in history, the public was able to view video reports of battles as they took place. When Navy Seals executed Osama bin Laden under President Obama's orders, Obama and Hillary Clinton watched the helicopter land in bin Laden's compound, listened to reports of the killing, and watched the Seals leave (Schmiddle 2011).

Travel and communication bridge time and space to such an extent that there is almost no "other side of the world" anymore. One result is **cultural leveling,** a process in which cultures become more and more similar to one another. The globalization of capitalism brings with it both technology and Western culture. Japan, for example, has adopted not only capitalism but also Western forms of dress and music, transforming it into a blend of Western and Eastern cultures.

Cultural leveling is apparent to any international traveler. The golden arches of McDonald's welcome visitors to Tokyo, Paris, London, Madrid, Moscow, Hong Kong, and Beijing. When I visited a jungle village in India—no electricity, no running water, and so remote that the only entrance was by a footpath—I saw a young man sporting a cap with the Nike emblem.

Cultural leveling is occurring rapidly, with some strange twists. These men from an Amazon tribe, who have just come back from a week hunting in the jungle, are wearing traditional head-dress and using traditional weapons, but you can easily spot something else that is jarringly out of place.

What is cultural leveling? How does this photo illustrate it?

Although the bridging of geography, time, and culture by electronic signals and the exportation of Western icons do not in and of themselves mark the end of traditional cultures, the inevitable result is some degree of *cultural leveling*. We are producing a blander, less distinctive way of life—U.S. culture with French, Japanese, and Brazilian accents, so to speak. Although the "cultural accent" remains, something vital is lost forever.

CHAPTER 2 Summary and Review

What Is Culture?

How do sociologists understand culture?

All human groups possess **culture**—language, beliefs, values, norms, and material objects that are passed from one generation to the next. **Material culture** consists of objects (art, buildings, clothing, weapons, tools). **Nonmaterial** (or **symbolic**) **culture** is a group's ways of thinking and its patterns of behavior. **Ideal culture** is a group's ideal values, norms, and goals. **Real culture** is people's actual behavior, which often falls short of their cultural ideals. Pp. 40–42.

What are cultural relativism and ethnocentrism?

People are **ethnocentric;** that is, they use their own culture as a yardstick for judging the ways of others. In contrast, those who embrace **cultural relativism** try to understand other cultures on those cultures' own terms. Pp. 42–43.

Components of Symbolic Culture

What are the components of nonmaterial culture?

The central component of nonmaterial culture is **symbols,** anything to which people attach meaning and that they use to communicate with others. Universally, the symbols of nonmaterial culture are gestures, language, values, norms, sanctions, folkways, and mores. Pp. 43–45.

Why is language so significant to culture?

Language allows human experience to be goal-directed, cooperative, and cumulative. It also lets humans move beyond the present and share a past, future, and other common perspectives. According to the **Sapir-Whorf hypothesis,** language even shapes our thoughts and perceptions. Pp. 45–49.

How do values, norms, sanctions, folkways, and mores reflect culture?

All groups have **values,** standards by which they define what is desirable or undesirable, and **norms,** rules or expectations about behavior. Groups use **positive sanctions** to show approval of those who follow their norms and **negative sanctions** to show disapproval of those who do not.

Norms that are not strictly enforced are called **folkways,** while **mores** are norms to which groups demand conformity because they reflect core values. Pp. 49–51.

Many Cultural Worlds

How do subcultures and countercultures differ?

A **subculture** is a group whose values and related behaviors distinguish its members from the general culture. A **counterculture** holds some values that stand in opposition to those of the dominant culture. Pp. 51–53.

Values in U.S. Society

What are some core U.S. values?

Although the United States is a **pluralistic society,** made up of many groups, each with its own set of values, certain values dominate: achievement and success, individualism, hard work, efficiency and practicality, science and technology, material comfort, freedom, democracy, equality, group superiority, education, religiosity, and romantic love. Some values cluster together (**value clusters**) to form a larger whole. **Value contradictions** (such as equality, sexism, and racism) indicate areas of tension which are likely points of social change. Leisure, self-fulfillment, physical fitness, youthfulness, and concern for the environment are emerging core values. Core values do not change without opposition. Pp. 53–59.

Technology in the Global Village

How is technology changing culture?

William Ogburn coined the term **cultural lag** to describe how a group's nonmaterial culture lags behind its changing technology. With today's technological advances in travel and communications, **cultural diffusion** is occurring rapidly. This leads to **cultural leveling,** groups becoming similar as they adopt items from other cultures. Much of the richness of the world's diverse cultures is being lost in the process. Pp. 59–62.

Thinking Critically about Chapter 2

1. Do you favor ethnocentrism or cultural relativism? Explain your position.

2. Do you think that the language change in Miami, Florida (discussed on page 48), indicates the future of the United States? Why or why not?

3. Are you a member of any subcultures? Which one(s)? Why do you think that your group is a subculture and not a counterculture? What is your group's relationship to the mainstream culture?

Socialization

Peru

The old man was horrified when he found out. Life never had been good since his daughter lost her hearing when she was just 2 years old. She couldn't even talk—just fluttered her hands around trying to tell him things.

Over the years, he had gotten used to this. But now . . . he shuddered at the thought of her being pregnant. No one would be willing to marry her; he knew that. And the neighbors, their tongues would never stop wagging. Everywhere he went, he could hear people talking behind his back.

If only his wife were still alive, maybe she could come up with something. What should he do? He couldn't just kick his daughter out into the street.

After the baby was born, the old man tried to shake his feelings, but they wouldn't let loose. Isabelle was a pretty name, but every time he looked at the baby he felt sick to his stomach.

He hated doing it, but there was no way out. His daughter and her baby would have to live in the attic.

Unfortunately, this is a true story. Isabelle was discovered in Ohio in 1938 when she was about 6½ years old, living in a dark room with her deaf-mute mother. Isabelle couldn't talk, but she did use gestures to communicate with her mother. An inadequate diet and lack of sunshine had given Isabelle a disease called rickets.

> "Her behavior toward strangers, especially men, was almost that of a wild animal, manifesting much fear and hostility."

[Her legs] were so bowed that as she stood erect the soles of her shoes came nearly flat together, and she got about with a skittering gait. Her behavior toward strangers, especially men, was almost that of a wild animal, manifesting much fear and hostility. In lieu of speech she made only a strange croaking sound. (Davis 1940/2007:156–157)

When the newspapers reported this case, sociologist Kingsley Davis decided to find out what had happened to Isabelle after her discovery. We'll come back to that later, but first let's use the case of Isabelle to gain insight into human nature.

Society Makes Us Human

"What do you mean, society makes us human?" is probably what you are asking. "That sounds ridiculous. I was born a human." The meaning of this statement will become more apparent as we get into the chapter. Let's start by considering what is human about human nature. How much of a person's characteristics comes from "nature" (heredity) and how much from "nurture" (the **social environment,** contact with others)? Experts are trying to answer the nature–nurture question by studying identical twins who were separated at birth and reared in different environments, such as those discussed in the Down-to-Earth Sociology box.

Down-to-Earth Sociology

Heredity or Environment?
The Case of Jack and Oskar, Identical Twins

Identical twins are almost identical in their genetic makeup. They are the result of one fertilized egg dividing to produce two embryos. (Some differences can appear as genetic codes are copied.) If heredity determines personality—or attitudes, temperament, skills, and intelligence—then identical twins should be identical, or almost so, not only in their looks but also in these characteristics.

The fascinating case of Jack and Oskar helps us unravel this mystery. From their experience, we can see the far-reaching effects of the environment— how social experiences override biology.

Jack Yufe and Oskar Stohr are identical twins. Born in 1932 to a Roman Catholic mother and a Jewish father, they were separated as babies after their parents divorced. Jack was reared in Trinidad by his father. There, he learned loyalty to Jews and hatred of Hitler and the Nazis. After the war, Jack and his father moved to Israel. When he was 17, Jack joined a kibbutz and later served in the Israeli army.

Oskar's upbringing was a mirror image of Jack's. Oskar was reared in Czechoslovakia by his mother's mother, who was a strict Catholic. When Oskar was a toddler, Hitler annexed this area of Czechoslovakia, and Oskar learned to love Hitler and to hate Jews. He joined the Hitler Youth. Like the Boy Scouts, this organization was designed to instill healthy living, love of the outdoors, friendships, and patriotism—but this one added loyalty to Hitler and hatred for Jews.

In 1954, the two brothers met. It was a short meeting, and Jack had been warned not to tell Oskar that they were Jews. Twenty-five years later, in 1979, when they were 47 years old, social scientists at the University of Minnesota brought them together again. These researchers figured that because Jack and Oskar had the same genes, any differences they showed

The relative influence of heredity and the environment in human behavior has fascinated and plagued researchers. Especially intriguing are cases like these twins who, although separated at birth and not knowing one another, each became a firefighter.

would have to be the result of their environment—their different social experiences.

Not only did Jack and Oskar hold different attitudes toward the war, Hitler, and Jews, but their basic orientations to life were also different. In their politics, Jack was liberal, while Oskar was more conservative. Jack was a workaholic, while Oskar enjoyed leisure. And, as you can predict, Jack was proud of being a Jew. Oskar, who by this time knew that he was a Jew, wouldn't even mention it.

This would seem to settle the matter. But there were other things. As children, Jack and Oskar had both excelled at sports but had difficulty with math. They also had the same rate of speech, and both liked sweet liqueur and spicy foods. Strangely, each flushed the toilet both before and after using it, and they each enjoyed startling people by sneezing in crowded elevators.

For Your Consideration

→ Heredity or environment? How much influence does each have? The question is far from settled, but at this point it seems fair to conclude that the *limits* of certain physical and mental abilities are established by heredity (such as ability at sports and aptitude for mathematics), while attitudes are the result of the environment. Basic temperament, though, seems to be inherited. Although the answer is still fuzzy, we can put it this way: For some parts of life, the blueprint is drawn by heredity; but even here the environment can redraw those lines. For other parts, the individual is a blank slate, and it is up to the environment to determine what is written on that slate.

Sources: Based on Begley 1979; Chen 1979; Wright 1995; Segal and Hershberger 2005; Ledger 2009; Johnson et al. 2009; Segal 2011.

Another way is to examine children who have had little human contact. Let's consider such children.

Feral Children

The naked child was found in the forest, walking on all fours, eating grass and lapping water from the river. When he saw a small animal, he pounced on it. Growling, he ripped at it with his teeth. Tearing chunks from the body, he chewed them ravenously.

This is an apt description of reports that have come in over the centuries. Supposedly, these **feral** (wild) **children** could not speak; they bit, scratched, growled, and walked on all fours. They drank by lapping water, ate grass, tore eagerly at raw meat, and showed insensitivity to pain and cold.

Why am I even mentioning stories that sound so exaggerated? Consider what happened in 1798. In that year, such a child was found in the forests of Aveyron, France. "The wild boy of Aveyron," as he became known, would have been written off as another folk myth, except that French scientists took the child to a laboratory and studied him. Like the feral children in the earlier informal reports, this child, too, gave no indication of feeling the cold. Most startling, though, when he saw a small animal, the boy would growl, pounce on it, and devour it uncooked. Even today, the scientists' detailed reports make fascinating reading (Itard 1962).

Ever since I read Itard's account of this boy, I've been fascinated by the seemingly fantastic possibility that animals could rear human children. In 2002, I received a report from a contact in Cambodia that a feral child had been found in the jungles. When I had the opportunity the following year to visit the child and interview his caregivers, I grabbed it. The boy's photo is to the right.

If we were untouched by society, would we be like feral children? By nature, would our behavior be like that of wild animals? This is the sociological question. Unable to study feral children, sociologists have studied isolated children, like Isabelle in our opening vignette. Let's see what we can learn from them.

One of the reasons I went to Cambodia was to interview a feral child—the boy shown here—who supposedly had been raised by monkeys. When I arrived at the remote location where the boy was living, I was disappointed to find that the story was only partially true. When the boy was about two months old, the Khmer Rouge killed his parents and abandoned him. Months later, villagers shot the female monkey who was carrying the baby. Not quite a feral child—but Mathay is the closest I'll ever come to one.

Read

Final Note on a Case of Extreme Isolation
by Kingsley Davis
on **mysoclab.com**

Isolated Children

What can isolated children tell us about human nature? We can first conclude that humans have no natural language, for Isabelle in our opening vignette and others like her are unable to speak.

But maybe Isabelle was mentally impaired. Perhaps she simply was unable to progress through the usual stages of development. It certainly looked that way—she scored practically zero on her first intelligence test. But after a few months of language training, Isabelle was able to speak in short sentences. In just a year, she could write a few words, do simple addition, and retell stories after hearing them. Seven months later, she had a vocabulary of almost 2,000 words. In just two years, Isabelle reached the intellectual level that is normal for her age. She then went on to school, where she was "bright, cheerful, energetic . . . and participated in all school activities as normally as other children" (Davis 1940).

As discussed in the previous chapter, language is the key to human development. Without language, people have no mechanism for developing thought and communicating their experiences. Unlike animals, humans have no instincts that take the place of language. If an individual lacks language, he or she lives in a world of internal silence, without shared ideas, lacking connections to others.

Without language, there can be no culture—no shared way of life—and culture is the key to what people become. Each of us possesses a biological heritage, but this heritage does not determine specific behaviors, attitudes, or values. It is our culture that superimposes the specifics of what we become onto our biological heritage.

An orphanage in Kaliyampoondi, India. The treatment of these children is likely to affect their ability to reason and to function as adults.

Institutionalized Children

Other than language, what else is required for a child to develop into what we consider a healthy, balanced, intelligent human being? We find part of the answer in an intriguing experiment.

The Skeels/Dye Experiment. Back in the 1930s, orphanages were common because parents were more likely than now to die before their children were grown. Children reared in orphanages tended to have low IQs. "Common sense" (which we noted in Chapter 1 is unreliable) made it seem obvious that their low intelligence was because of poor brains ("They're just born that way"). But two psychologists, H. M. Skeels and H. B. Dye (1939), began to suspect a social cause.

Skeels (1966) provides this account of a "good" orphanage in Iowa, one where he and Dye were consultants:

> *Until about six months, they were cared for in the infant nursery. The babies were kept in standard hospital cribs that often had protective sheeting on the sides, thus effectively limiting visual stimulation; no toys or other objects were hung in the infants' line of vision. Human interactions were limited to busy nurses who, with the speed born of practice and necessity, changed diapers or bedding, bathed and medicated the infants, and fed them efficiently with propped bottles.*

Perhaps, thought Skeels and Dye, the problem was the absence of stimulating social interaction, not the children's brains. To test their controversial idea, they selected thirteen infants who were so slow mentally that no one wanted to adopt them. They placed them in an institution for mentally retarded women. They assigned each infant, then about 19 months old, to a separate ward of women ranging in mental age from 5 to 12 and in chronological age from 18 to 50. The women were pleased. They enjoyed taking care of the infants' physical needs—diapering, feeding, and so on. And they also loved to play with the children. They cuddled them and showered them with attention. They even competed to see which ward would have "its baby" walking or talking first. In each ward, one woman became particularly attached to the child and figuratively adopted him or her:

> *As a consequence, an intense one-to-one adult–child relationship developed, which was supplemented by the less intense but frequent interactions with the other adults in the environment. Each child had some one person with whom he [or she] was identified and who was particularly interested in him [or her] and his [or her] achievements. (Skeels 1966)*

The researchers left a control group of twelve infants at the orphanage. These infants received the usual care. They also had low IQs, but they were considered somewhat higher in intelligence than the thirteen in the experimental group. Two and a half years later, Skeels and Dye tested all the children's intelligence. Their findings are startling: Those cared for by the women in the institution gained an average of 28 IQ points while those who remained in the orphanage lost 30 points.

What happened after these children were grown? Did these initial differences matter? Twenty-one years later, Skeels and Dye did a follow-up study. The twelve in the control group, those who had remained in the orphanage, averaged less than a third-grade education. Four still lived in state institutions, and the others held low-level jobs. Only two had married. The thirteen in the experimental group, those cared for by the institutionalized women, had an average education of twelve grades (about normal for that period). Five had completed one or more years of college. One had even gone to graduate school. Eleven had married. All thirteen were self-supporting or were homemakers (Skeels 1966). Apparently, "high intelligence" depends on early, close relations with other humans.

Orphanage Research in India. The Skeels/Dye findings have been confirmed by research in India, where some orphanages are like those that Skeels and Dye studied—dismal places where unattended children lie in bed all day. When researchers added

What does research on institutionalized children tell us about "being human"?

stimulating play and interaction to the children's activities, not only did the children's motor skills improve, but so did their IQs (Taneja et al. 2002).

The longer that children lack stimulating interaction, though, the more difficulty they have intellectually (Meese 2005). From the case of Genie, you can see how important timing is in the development of "human" characteristics.

Timing and Human Development.   Genie was discovered when she was 13 years old. She had been locked in a small room and tied to a chair since she was 20 months old:

Apparently Genie's father (70 years old when Genie was discovered in 1970) hated children. He probably had caused the death of two of Genie's siblings. Her 50-year-old mother was partially blind and frightened of her husband. Genie could not speak, did not know how to chew, was unable to stand upright, and could not straighten her hands and legs. On intelligence tests, she scored at the level of a 1-year-old. After intensive training, Genie learned to walk and to say simple sentences (although they were garbled). Genie's language remained primitive as she grew up. She would take anyone's property if it appealed to her, and she went to the bathroom wherever she wanted. At the age of 21, she was sent to a home for adults who cannot live alone. (Pines 1981)

In Sum: From Genie's pathetic story and from the research on institutionalized children, we can conclude that the basic human traits of intelligence and the ability to establish close bonds with others depend on early interaction with other humans. In addition, there seems to be a period prior to age 13 in which children must learn language and experience human bonding if they are to develop normal intelligence and the ability to be sociable and follow social norms.

Deprived Animals

Finally, let's consider animals that have been deprived of normal interaction. In a series of experiments with rhesus monkeys, psychologists Harry and Margaret Harlow demonstrated the importance of early learning. The Harlows (1962) raised baby monkeys in isolation. They gave each monkey two artificial mothers. One "mother" was only a wire frame with a wooden head, but it did have a nipple from which the baby could nurse. The frame of the other "mother," which had no bottle, was covered with soft terrycloth. To obtain food, the baby monkeys nursed at the wire frame.

When the Harlows (1965) frightened the baby monkeys with a mechanical bear or dog, the babies did not run to the wire-frame "mother." Instead, as shown in the photo to the right, they would cling pathetically to their terrycloth "mother." The Harlows concluded that infant–mother bonding is not the result of feeding but, rather, of what they termed "intimate physical contact." To most of us, this phrase means cuddling.

In one of their many experiments, the Harlows isolated baby monkeys for different lengths of time and then put them in with the other monkeys. Monkeys that had been isolated for shorter periods (about three months) were able to adjust to normal monkey life. They learned to play and engage in pretend fights. Those isolated for six months or more, however, couldn't make the adjustment, and the other monkeys rejected them. In other words, the longer the period of isolation, the more difficult its effects are to overcome. In addition, there seems to be a critical learning stage: If this stage is missed, it may be impossible to compensate for what has been lost. This may have been the case with Genie.

Like humans, monkeys need interaction to thrive. Those raised in isolation are unable to interact with others. In this photograph, we see one of the monkeys described in the text. Purposefully frightened by the experimenter, the monkey has taken refuge in the soft terrycloth draped over an artificial "mother."

What do the case of Genie and research on deprived animals tell us about "being human"?

Because humans are not monkeys, we must be careful about extrapolating from animal studies to human behavior. The Harlow experiments, however, support what we know about children who are reared in isolation.

In Sum: Society Makes Us Human.   Babies do not develop "naturally" into social adults. If children are reared in isolation, their bodies grow, but they become little more than big animals. Without the concepts that language provides, they can't grasp relationships between people (the "connections" we call *brother, sister, parent, friend, teacher,* and so on). And without warm, friendly interactions, they can't bond with others. They don't become "friendly" or cooperate with others. In short, it is through human contact that people learn to be members of the human community. This process by which we learn the ways of society (or of particular groups), called **socialization,** is what sociologists have in mind when they say "Society makes us human."

To add to our understanding of how society makes us human, let's look at how we develop our self-concept, our ability to "take the role of others," and our ability to reason.

Socialization into the Self and Mind

When you were born, you had no ideas. You didn't know that you were a son or daughter. You didn't even know that you were a he or she. How did you develop a **self,** your image of who you are? How did you develop your ability to reason? Let's find out.

Cooley and the Looking-Glass Self

About a hundred years ago, Charles Horton Cooley (1864–1929), a symbolic interactionist who taught at the University of Michigan, concluded that the self is part of how *society* makes us human. He said that *our sense of self develops from interaction with others.* To describe the process by which this unique aspect of "humanness" develops, Cooley (1902) coined the term **looking-glass self.** He summarized this idea in the following couplet:

> *Each to each a looking-glass*
> *Reflects the other that doth pass.*

The looking-glass self contains three elements:

1. *We imagine how we appear to those around us.* For example, we may think that others perceive us as witty or dull.
2. *We interpret others' reactions.* We come to conclusions about how others evaluate us. Do they like us for being witty? Do they dislike us for being dull?
3. *We develop a self-concept.* How we interpret others' reactions to us frames our feelings and ideas about ourselves. A favorable reflection in this *social mirror* leads to a positive self-concept; a negative reflection leads to a negative self-concept.

Note that the development of the self does *not* depend on accurate evaluations. Even if we grossly misinterpret how others think about us, those misjudgments become part of our self-concept. Note also that *although the self-concept begins in childhood, its development is an ongoing, lifelong process.* During our everyday lives, we monitor how others react to us. As we do so, we continually modify the self. The self, then, is never a finished product—it is always in process, even into our old age.

Mead and Role Taking

Another symbolic interactionist, George Herbert Mead (1863–1931), who taught at the University of Chicago, pointed out how important play is in developing a self. As we play with others, we learn to **take the role of the other.** That is, we learn to put ourselves in someone else's shoes—to understand how someone else feels and thinks and to anticipate how that person will act.

Mead analyzed *taking the role of the other* as an essential part of learning to be a full-fledged member of society. At first, we are able to take the role only of *significant others,* as this child is doing. Later we develop the capacity to take the role of the *generalized other,* which is essential not only for cooperation but also for the control of antisocial desires.

What is the looking-glass self? How does it develop?

This doesn't happen overnight. We develop this ability over a period of years (Mead 1934; Denzin 2007). Psychologist John Flavel (1968) asked 8- and 14-year-olds to explain a board game to children who were blindfolded and also to others who were not. The 14-year-olds gave more detailed instructions to those who were blindfolded, but the 8-year-olds gave the same instructions to everyone. The younger children could not yet take the role of the other, while the older children could.

As we develop this ability, at first we can take only the roles of **significant others,** individuals who significantly influence our lives, such as parents or siblings. By assuming their roles during play, such as dressing up in our parents' clothing, we cultivate the ability to put ourselves in the place of significant others.

As our self gradually develops, we internalize the expectations of more and more people. Our ability to take the role of others eventually extends to being able to take the role of "the group as a whole." Mead used the term **generalized other** to refer to our perception of how people in general think of us.

Taking the role of others is essential if we are to become cooperative members of human groups—whether they are family, friends, or co-workers. This ability allows us to modify our behavior by anticipating how others will react—something Genie never learned.

As Figure 3.1 illustrates, we go through three stages as we learn to take the role of the other:

1. *Imitation.* Under the age of 3, we can only mimic others. We do not yet have a sense of self separate from others, and we can only imitate people's gestures and words. (This stage is actually not role taking, but it prepares us for it.)
2. *Play.* During the second stage, from the ages of about 3 to 6, we pretend to take the roles of specific people. We might pretend that we are a firefighter, a wrestler, a nurse, Supergirl, Spider-Man, a princess, and so on. We also like costumes at this stage and enjoy dressing up in our parents' clothing, or tying a towel around our neck to "become" Superman or Wonder Woman.
3. *Team Games.* This third stage, organized play, or team games, begins roughly when we enter school. The significance for the self is that to play these games we must be able to take multiple roles. One of Mead's favorite examples was that of a baseball game, in which each player must be able to take the role of any other player. To play baseball, it isn't enough that we know our own role; we also must be able to anticipate what everyone else on the field will do when the ball is hit or thrown.

Mead also said the self has two parts, the "I" and the "me." The "I" is *the self as subject,* the active, spontaneous, creative part of the self. In contrast, the "me" is *the self as object.* It is made up of attitudes we internalize from our interactions with others. Mead chose these pronouns because in English "I" is the active agent, as in "I shoved him," while "me" is the object of action, as in "He shoved me." Mead stressed that we are not passive in the socialization process. We are not like robots, with pro-grammed software shoved into us. Rather, our "I" actively evaluates the reactions of others and orga-nizes them into a unified whole. Mead added that the "I" even moni-tors the "me," fine-tuning our ideas and attitudes to help us better meet what others expect of us.

In Sum: In studying the details, you don't want to miss the main point, which some find startling: *Both our self and our mind are social products.* Mead stressed that we cannot think without symbols. But where

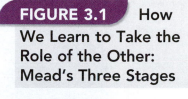

FIGURE 3.1   How We Learn to Take the Role of the Other: Mead's Three Stages

Stage 1: Imitation
(Children under age 3)
No sense of self
Imitate others

↓

Stage 2: Play
(Ages 3 to 6)
Play "pretend" others
(princess, Spider-Man, etc.)

↓

Stage 3: Team Games
(After about age 6 or 7)
Team games
("organized play")
Learn to take multiple roles

Source: By the author.

To help his students understand the term *generalized other*, Mead used baseball as an illustration. Why are team sports and organized games excellent examples to use in explaining this concept?

Why is learning to take the role of the other essential for "becoming human"?

do these symbols come from? Only from society, which gives us our symbols by giving us language. If society did not provide the symbols, we would not be able to think and so would not possess a self-concept or that entity we call the mind. The self and mind, then, like language, are products of society.

Shown here is Jean Piaget with one of the children he studied in his analysis of the development of human reasoning.

Piaget and the Development of Reasoning

The development of the mind—specifically, how we learn to reason—was studied in detail by Jean Piaget (1896–1980). This Swiss psychologist noticed that when young children take intelligence tests, they often give similar wrong answers. This set him to thinking that the children might be using some consistent, but incorrect, reasoning. It might even indicate that children go through some natural process as they learn how to reason.

Stimulated by this intriguing possibility, Piaget set up a laboratory where he could give children of different ages problems to solve (Piaget 1950, 1954; Flavel et al. 2002). After years of testing, Piaget concluded that children go through a natural process as they develop their ability to reason. This process has four stages. (If you mentally substitute "reasoning" or "reasoning skills" for the term *operational* as you review these stages, Piaget's findings will be easier to understand.)

1. **The sensorimotor stage** (from birth to about age 2). During this stage, our understanding is limited to direct contact—sucking, touching, listening, looking. We aren't able to "think." During the first part of this stage, we do not even know that our bodies are separate from the environment. Indeed, we have yet to discover that we have toes. Neither can we recognize cause and effect. That is, we do not know that our actions cause something to happen.
2. **The preoperational stage** (from about age 2 to age 7). During this stage, we *develop the ability to use symbols.* However, we do not yet understand common concepts such as size, speed, or causation. Although we are learning to count, we do not really understand what numbers mean. Nor do we yet have the ability to take the role of the other.
3. **The concrete operational stage** (from the age of about 7 to 12). Although our reasoning abilities are more developed, they remain *concrete.* We can now understand numbers, size, causation, and speed, and we are able to take the role of the other. We can even play team games. Unless we have concrete examples, however, we are unable to talk about concepts such as truth, honesty, or justice. We can explain why Jane's answer was a lie, but we cannot describe what truth itself is.
4. **The formal operational stage** (after the age of about 12). We now are capable of abstract thinking. We can talk about concepts, come to conclusions based on general principles, and use rules to solve abstract problems. During this stage, we are likely to become young philosophers (Kagan 1984). If we were shown a photo of a slave during our concrete operational stage, we might have said, "That's wrong!" Now at the formal operational stage we are likely to add, "If our county was founded on equality, how could anyone own slaves?"

Global Aspects of the Self and Reasoning

Cooley's conclusions about the looking-glass self appear to be true for everyone around the world. So do Mead's conclusions about role taking and the mind and self as social products, although researchers are finding that the self may develop earlier than Mead indicated. The stages of reasoning that Piaget identified probably also occur worldwide, although researchers have found that the stages are not as distinct as Piaget concluded and the ages at which individuals enter the stages differ from one person to another (Flavel et al. 2002). Even during the sensorimotor stage, for example, children show early signs of reasoning, which may indicate an innate ability that is wired into the brain. Although Piaget's theory is being refined, his contribution remains: *A basic structure*

According to Piaget's theory, how do we develop our ability to reason?

underlies the way we develop reasoning, and children all over the world begin with the concrete and move to the abstract.

Interestingly, some people seem to get stuck in the concreteness of the third stage and never reach the fourth stage of abstract thinking (Kohlberg and Gilligan 1971; Suizzo 2000). College, for example, nurtures the fourth stage, and people with this experience apparently have more ability for abstract thought. Social experiences, then, can modify these stages.

Learning Personality, Emotions, and Internal Control

Our personality, emotions, and internal control are also vital aspects of who we are. Let's look at how we learn these essential aspects of our being.

Freud and the Development of Personality

As the mind and the self develop, so does the personality. Sigmund Freud (1856–1939) developed a theory of the origin of personality that has had a major impact on Western thought. Freud, a physician in Vienna in the early 1900s, founded *psychoanalysis,* a technique for treating emotional problems through long-term exploration of the subconscious mind. Let's look at his theory.

Freud believed that personality consists of three elements. Each child is born with the first element, an **id,** Freud's term for inborn drives that cause us to seek self-gratification. The id of the newborn is evident in its cries of hunger or pain. The pleasure-seeking id operates throughout life. It demands the immediate fulfillment of basic needs: food, safety, attention, sex, and so on.

The id's drive for immediate gratification, however, runs into a roadblock: primarily the needs of other people, especially those of the parents. To adapt to these constraints, a second component of the personality emerges, which Freud called the ego. The **ego** is the balancing force between the id and the demands of society that suppress it. The ego also serves to balance the id and the **superego,** the third component of the personality, more commonly called the *conscience.*

The superego represents *culture within us,* the norms and values we have internalized from our social groups. As the *moral* component of the personality, the superego provokes feelings of guilt or shame when we break social rules, or pride and self-satisfaction when we follow them.

According to Freud, when the id gets out of hand, we follow our desires for pleasure and break society's norms. When the superego gets out of hand, we become overly rigid in following those norms and end up wearing a straitjacket of rules that can make our lives miserable. The ego, the balancing force, tries to prevent either the superego or the id from dominating. In the emotionally healthy individual, the ego succeeds in balancing these conflicting demands of the id and the superego. In the maladjusted individual, the ego fails to control the conflict between the id and the superego. Either the id or the superego dominates this person, leading to internal confusion and problem behaviors.

Sociological Evaluation.   Sociologists appreciate Freud's emphasis on socialization—his assertion that the social group into which we are born transmits norms and values that restrain our biological drives. Sociologists, however, object to the view that inborn and subconscious motivations are the primary reasons for human behavior. *This denies the central principle of sociology:* that factors such as social class (income, education, and occupation) and people's roles in groups underlie their behavior (Epstein 1988; Bush and Simmons 1990).

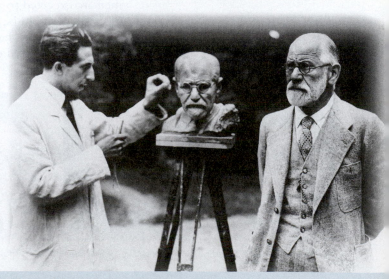

Shown here is Sigmund Freud in 1931 as he poses for a sculptor in Vienna, Austria. Although Freud was one of the most influential theorists of the twentieth century, most of his ideas have been discarded.

How does Freud's theory of the development of personality differ from the sociological perspective?

Feminist sociologists have been especially critical of Freud. Although what I just summarized applies to both females and males, Freud assumed that "male" is "normal." He even referred to females as inferior, castrated males (Chodorow 1990; Gerhard 2000). It is obvious that sociologists need to continue to research how we develop personality.

Socialization into Emotions

As you know so intimately, emotions are also an essential aspect of who you are. Sociologists have found that emotions are not simply the results of our biology. Like the mind, our emotions also depend on socialization (Hochschild 2008). This may sound strange. Don't all people get angry? Doesn't everyone cry? Don't we all feel guilt, shame, sadness, happiness, fear? What has socialization to do with our emotions?

Global Emotions.   At first, it may look as though socialization is not relevant, that we simply express universal feelings. Paul Ekman (1980), a psychologist who studied emotions in several countries, concluded that everyone experiences six basic emotions: anger, disgust, fear, happiness, sadness, and surprise. He also said that we all show the same facial expressions when we feel these emotions. A person from Peru, for example, could tell from just the look on an American's face that she is angry, disgusted, or fearful, and we could tell from the Peruvian's face that he is happy, sad, or surprised. Because we all show the same facial expressions when we experience these six emotions, Ekman concluded that they are hard-wired into our biology.

A study of facial expressions at the Paralympics supports this observation (Matsumoto and Willingham 2009). Upon learning if they had won or lost, those blind from birth had the same facial expressions as those of sighted people, something the blind could not have learned.

Expressing Emotions: Following "Feeling Rules."   If we have universal facial expressions to express basic emotions, then this is biology, something that Darwin noted back in the 1800s (Horwitz and Wakefield 2007:41). What, then, does sociology have to do with them? Facial expressions are only one way by which we show our feelings. We also use our bodies, voices, and gestures.

> *Jane and Sushana have been best friends since high school. They were hardly ever apart until Sushana married and moved to another state a year ago. Jane has been waiting eagerly at the arrival gate for Sushana's flight, which has been delayed. When Sushana exits, she and Jane hug one another, making "squeals of glee" and even jumping a bit.*

If you couldn't tell from their names that these were women, you could tell from their behavior. To express delight, U.S. women are allowed to make "squeals of glee" in public places and to jump as they hug. In contrast, in the exact circumstances, U.S. men are expected to shake hands or to give a brief hug. If they gave out "squeals of glee," they would be violating fundamental "gender rules."

Not only do we have "gender rules" for expressing emotions, but we also have "feeling rules" based on culture, social class, relationships, and settings. Consider *culture.*

What emotions are these people expressing? Are these emotions global? Is their way of expressing them universal?

How do "feeling rules" guide how we express our emotions? How do "feeling rules" operate in your life?

Two close Japanese friends who meet after a long separation don't shake hands or hug—they bow. Two Arab men will kiss. *Social class* is so significant that it, too, cuts across other lines, even gender. Upon seeing a friend after a long absence, upper-class women and men are likely to be more reserved in expressing their delight than are lower-class women and men. *Relationships* also make a big difference. We express our feelings more openly if we are with close friends, more guardedly if we are at a staff meeting with the corporate CEO. The *setting*, then, is also important, with each setting having its own "rules" about emotions. As you know, the emotions you can express at a rock concert differ considerably from those you express in a classroom. If you think about your childhood, you will realize that a good part of your early socialization centered on learning your culture's feeling rules.

What We Feel

Joan, a U.S. woman who had been married for seven years, had no children. When she finally gave birth and the doctor handed her a healthy girl, she was almost overcome with joy. Tafadzwa, in Zimbabwe, had been married for seven years and had no children. When the doctor handed her a healthy girl, she was almost overcome with sadness.

You can easily understand why the U.S. woman felt happy, but why did the woman in Zimbabwe feel sad? The effects of socialization on our emotions go much deeper than guiding how, where, and when we express our feelings. Socialization also affects *what* we feel (Clark 1997; Jasper 2012). In Zimbabwe culture, to not give birth to a male child lowers a woman's social status and is even considered a good reason for her husband to divorce her (Horwitz and Wakefield 2007:43).

Research Needed.   Ekman identified only six emotions as universal in facial expression, but I suspect that there are more. It is likely that people around the world have similar feelings and facial expressions when they experience helplessness, despair, confusion, and shock. We need cross-cultural research to find out whether these emotions are universal. We also need more research into how culture guides us in how we express our feelings and even in what we feel.

Society within Us: The Self and Emotions as Social Control

Much of our socialization is intended to turn us into conforming members of society. Socialization into the self and emotions is essential to this process, for *both the self and our emotions mold our behavior.* Although we like to think that we are "free," consider for a moment just some of the factors that influence how you act: the expectations of your friends and parents, of neighbors and teachers; classroom norms and college rules; city, state, and federal laws. For example, if in a moment of intense frustration, or out of a devilish desire to shock people, you wanted to tear off your clothes and run naked down the street, what would stop you?

The answer is your socialization—*society within you.* Your experiences in society have resulted in a self that thinks along certain lines and feels particular emotions. This helps to keep you in line. Thoughts such as "Would I get kicked out of school?" and "What would my friends (parents) think if they found out?" represent an awareness of the self in relationship to others. So does the desire to avoid feelings of shame and embarrassment. Your *social mirror,* then—the result of your being socialized into a self and emotions—sets up effective internal controls over your behavior. In fact, socialization into self and emotions is so effective that some people feel embarrassed just thinking about running naked in public!

In Sum: Socialization is essential for our development as human beings. From our interaction with others, we learn how to think, reason, and feel. The net result is the shaping of our behavior—including our thinking and emotions—according to cultural standards. This is what sociologists mean when they refer to "*society within us.*"

And remember how we began this chapter—that society makes us human? Socialization into emotions is part of this process.

What does the term "society within us" mean? How is it an essential part of social control?

Socialization into Gender

Socialization into gender is also part of the way that society turns us into certain types of people—and sets up heavy controls over us. Let's get a glimpse of how this happens.

Learning the Gender Map

For a child, society is unexplored territory. A major signpost on society's map is **gender,** the attitudes and behaviors that are expected of us because we are a male or a female. In learning the gender map (called **gender socialization**), we are nudged into different lanes in life—into contrasting attitudes and behaviors. We take direction so well that, as adults, most of us act, think, and even feel according to this gender map, our culture's guidelines to what is appropriate for our sex.

The significance of gender is emphasized throughout this book, and we focus on gender in Chapter 10. For now, though, let's briefly consider some of the *gender messages* that we get from our family and the mass media.

Gender Messages in the Family

Our parents are the first significant others to show us the gender map. Sometimes they do this consciously, perhaps by bringing into play pink and blue, colors that have no meaning in themselves but that are now associated with gender. Our parents' own gender orientations are embedded so firmly that they do most of their gender teaching without being aware of what they are doing.

This is illustrated in a classic study by psychologists Susan Goldberg and Michael Lewis (1969), whose results have been confirmed by other researchers (Connors 1996; Clearfield and Nelson 2006; Best 2010).

Goldberg and Lewis asked mothers to bring their 6-month-old infants into their laboratory, supposedly to observe the infants' development. Covertly, however, they also observed the mothers. They found that the mothers kept their daughters closer to them. They also touched their daughters more and spoke to them more frequently than they did to their sons. By the time the children were 13 months old, the girls stayed closer to their mothers during play, and they returned to their mothers sooner and more often than the boys did.

Then Goldberg and Lewis did a little experiment. They set up a barrier to separate the children from their mothers, who were holding toys. The girls were more likely to cry and motion for help; the boys, to try to climb over the barrier.

The gender roles that we learn during childhood become part of our basic orientations to life. Although we refine these roles as we grow older, they are built on the framework established during childhood.

Goldberg and Lewis concluded that the mothers had subconsciously rewarded their daughters for being passive and dependent, and their sons for being active and independent.

Our family's gender lessons are thorough. On the basis of our sex, our parents give us different kinds of toys. Boys are more likely to get guns and "action figures" that destroy enemies. Girls are more likely to be given dolls and jewelry. Some parents try to choose "gender neutral" toys, but kids know what is popular, and they feel left out if they don't have what the other kids have. The significance of toys in gender socialization can be summarized this way: Most parents would be upset if someone gave their son Barbie dolls.

Play also teaches gender. Parents subtly "signal" to their sons that it is okay for them to participate in more rough-and-tumble play. In general, parents expect their sons to get dirtier and to be more defiant, their daughters to be daintier and more compliant (Gilman 1911/1971; Nordberg 2010). And in large part, parents get what they expect. Such experiences in socialization lie at the heart of the sociological explanation of male–female differences. To see how socialization can trump biology, read the Cultural Diversity box on the next page.

How do gender messages in the family nudge us into behavior considered appropriate for our sex?

Cultural Diversity **around the World**

Women Becoming Men:
The Sworn Virgins

"I will become a man," said Pashe. "I will do it."

The decision was final. Taking a pair of scissors, she soon had her long, black curls lying at her feet. She took off her dress—never to wear one again in her life—and put on her father's baggy trousers. She armed herself with her father's rifle. She would need it.

Going before the village elders, she swore to never marry, to never have children, and to never have sex.

Pashe had become a sworn virgin—and a man.

There was no turning back. The penalty for violating the oath was death. In Albania, where Pashe Keqi lives, and in parts of Bosnia and Serbia, it is the custom for some women to become men. They are neither transsexuals nor lesbians. Nor do they have a sex-change operation, something which is unknown in those parts.

This custom is a practical matter, a way to support the family. In these traditional societies, women must stay home and take care of the children and household. They can go hardly anywhere except to the market and mosque. Women depend on men for survival.

And when there is no man? That is the problem.

Pashe's father was killed in a blood feud. In these traditional groups, when the family patriarch (male head) dies and there are no male heirs, how are the women to survive? In the fifteenth century, people in this area hit upon a solution: One of the women takes an oath of lifelong virginity and takes over the man's role. She then becomes a social he, wears male clothing, carries a gun, owns property, and moves freely throughout the society.

She drinks in the tavern with the men. She sits with the men at weddings. She prays with the men at the mosque.

When a man wants to marry a girl of the family, she is the one who approves or disapproves of the suitor.

In short, the woman really becomes a man. Actually, a *social man*, sociologists would add. Her biology does not change, but her gender does. Pashe had become the man of the house, a status she then occupied her entire life.

Taking this position at the age of 11—she is in her 70s now—also made Pashe responsible for avenging her father's

murder. But when his killer was released from prison, her 15-year-old nephew (she is his uncle) rushed in and did the deed instead.

Sworn virgins walk like men, they talk like men, they hunt with the men, and they take up manly occupations. They become shepherds, security guards, truck drivers, and political leaders. Those around them know that they are biological women, but in all ways they treat them as men. When a sworn virgin talks to women, the women recoil in shyness.

The sworn virgins of Albania are a fascinating cultural contradiction: In the midst of a highly traditional group, one built around male superiority that severely limits women, we find both the belief and practice that a biological woman can do the work of a man and function in all of a man's social roles. The sole exception is marriage.

Under communist rule until 1985, with travel restricted by law and custom, mountainous northern Albania had been cut off from the rest of the world. Now there is a democratic government, and the region is connected to the world by better roads, telephones, and even television. As modern life trickles into these villages, few women want to become men. "Why should we?" they ask. "Now we have freedom. We can go to the city and work and support our families."

Sokol (Zhire) Zmajli, aged 80, changed her name from Zhire to the male name Sokol when she was young. She heads the family household consisting of her nephew, his wife, and their sons and their sons' wives.

For Your Consideration

→ How do the sworn virgins of Albania help to explain what gender is? Apply functionalism: How was the custom and practice of sworn virgins functional for this society? Apply symbolic interactionism: How do symbols underlie and maintain women becoming men in this society? Apply conflict theory: How do power relations between men and women underlie this practice?

Sources: Based on Zumbrun 2007; Bilefsky 2008; Smith 2008.

How do sworn virgins illustrate the social nature of masculinity and femininity?

Gender Messages from Peers

Sociologists stress how this sorting process into gender that begins in the family is reinforced as the child is exposed to other aspects of society. Of those other influences, one of the most powerful is the **peer group,** individuals of roughly the same age who are linked by common interests. Examples of peer groups are friends, classmates, and "the kids in the neighborhood."

As you grew up, you saw girls and boys teach one another what it means to be a female or a male. You might not have recognized what was happening, however, so let's eavesdrop on a conversation between two eighth-grade girls studied by sociologist Donna Eder (2007).

CINDY: The only thing that makes her look anything is all the makeup . . .
PENNY: She had a picture, and she's standing like this. (Poses with one hand on her hip and one by her head)
CINDY: Her face is probably this skinny, but it looks that big 'cause of all the makeup she has on it.
PENNY: She's ugly, ugly, ugly.

Do you see how these girls were giving gender lessons? They were reinforcing images of appearance and behavior that they thought were appropriate for females.

Boys, too, reinforce cultural expectations of gender. Sociologist Melissa Milkie (1994), who studied junior high school boys, found that much of their talk centered on movies and TV programs. Of the many images they saw, the boys would single out those associated with sex and violence. They would amuse one another by repeating lines, acting out parts, and joking and laughing at what they had seen.

If you know boys in their early teens, you've probably seen a lot of behavior like this. You may have been amused, or even have shaken your head in disapproval. But did you peer beneath the surface? Milkie did. What is really going on? The boys, she concluded, were using media images to develop their identity as males. They had gotten the message: "Real" males are obsessed with sex and violence. Not to joke and laugh about murder and promiscuous sex would have marked a boy as a "weenie" or "nerd," labels to be avoided at all costs.

Gender Messages in the Mass Media

As you can see with the boys Milkie studied, a major guide to the gender map is the **mass media,** forms of communication that are directed to large audiences. Let's look further at how media images help teach us *gender,* the behaviors and attitudes considered appropriate for our sex.

Advertising.   From an early age, the media bombard us with stereotypical images. If you are average, you are exposed to a blistering 20,000 commercials a year (Kacen 2011). In commercials geared toward children, boys are more likely to be shown as

The *gender roles* that we learn during childhood become part of our basic orientations to life. Although we refine these roles as we grow older, they remain built around the framework established during childhood.

Frank and Ernest

SOON WE'LL GIVE UP DOLLS AND HOPSCOTCH---BUT THEY'LL BE INTO FOOTBALL FOREVER.

www.cartoonistgroup.com

How do peers teach gender to one another? How have your peers shaped your images of gender?

competing in outdoor settings, while girls are more likely to be portrayed as cooperating in indoor settings. Action figures are pitched to boys, and dolls to girls (Kahlenberg and Hein 2010).

As adults, we are still peppered with ads. Although their purpose is to sell products—from booze and bras to cigarettes and cell phones—these ads continue our gender lessons. I'm sure you have noticed the ads that portray men as dominant and rugged and women as sexy and submissive. The stereotypical images—from cowboys who roam the wide-open spaces to scantily clad women whose physical assets couldn't possibly be real—become part of our own images of the sexes. So do the stereotype-breaking images. Whether overt and exaggerated or subtle and below our awareness, the mass media continue our gender lessons.

Movies and Television.

Television and movies also teach lessons in gender. With male characters outnumbering female characters on prime-time television, one message is that males are more important. But reflecting women's changing position in society, more dominant, aggressive females are also being portrayed. In cartoons, Kim Possible divides her time between cheerleading practice and saving the world from evil. With tongue in cheek, the Powerpuff Girls are touted as "the most elite kindergarten crime-fighting force ever assembled." This changed gender portrayal is especially evident in the violent females who play lead characters in action movies, from the assassin in *Kill Bill* to Angelina Jolie in *Salt* (Gilpatric 2010).

The gender messages, however, are mixed. While girls are presented as more powerful than they used to be, they have to be skinny and gorgeous and wear the latest fashions. Such messages present a dilemma for girls, for continuously thrust before them is a model that is almost impossible to replicate in real life.

But then so are many supermasculine role models held out for boys and men, such as those that Arnold Swarzenegger used to portray.

Video Games.

The movement, color, virtual dangers, unexpected dilemmas, and ability to control the action make video games highly appealing. High school and college students find them a seductive way of escaping from the demands of life. The first members of the "Nintendo Generation," now in their 30s, are still playing video games—with babies on their laps.

Sociologists have begun to study how video games portray the sexes, but we know little about their influence on the players' ideas of gender. The message of male dominance continues, as females are even more underrepresented in video games than on television: 90 percent of the main characters are male (Williams et al. 2009). Some video games, though, do reflect cutting-edge changes in sex roles, the topic of the Mass Media in Social Life box on the next page.

Anime.

Because anime, a Japanese cartoon form, crosses boundaries of video games, television, movies, and books (comic), we shall consider it as a separate category. The depiction of gender roles in anime is far from simple. A pornographic form features passive little girls and women who are exploited sexually by older boys and men, sometimes brutally so. Directed largely to children, another form features big-eyed little girls and fighting little boys. As in the illustration here, young women are also depicted in violent roles. A sociological question yet to be researched is, What gender lessons are children learning from this form of mass media?

In Sum:

"Male" and "female" are such powerful symbols that learning them forces us to interpret the world in terms of gender. As children learn their society's symbols of gender, they learn that

Watch
Play Again
on **mysoclab.com**

The gender messages of *anime*, an increasingly popular art form, are yet to be explored.

How do the mass media teach gender? How have the mass media shaped your images of gender?

Mass Media in Social Life

Lara Croft, Tomb Raider: Changing Images of Women in the Mass Media

With digital advances, video games have crossed the line from games to something that more closely resembles interactive movies. Costing several million dollars to produce and market, some video games introduce new songs by major rock groups (Levine 2008). One game (Grand Theft Auto 4) cost $100 million ("Top 10 . . ." 2010). Sociologically, what is significant is the content of video games. They expose gamers not only to action but also to ideas and images. Just as in other forms of the mass media, the gender images of video games communicate powerful messages.

Lara Croft, an adventure-seeking archeologist and star of Tomb Raider and its many sequels, is the essence of this new gender image. Lara is smart, strong, and able to utterly vanquish foes. With both guns blazing, Lara breaks stereotypical gender roles and dominates what previously was the domain of men. She was the first female protagonist in a field of muscle-rippling, gun-toting macho caricatures (Taylor 1999).

Yet the old remains powerfully encapsulated in the new. As the photos here make evident, Lara is a fantasy girl for young men of the digital generation. No matter her foe, no matter her predicament, Lara oozes sex. Her form-fitting outfits, which flatter her voluptuous figure, reflect the mental images of the men who created this digital character.

Lara has caught young men's fancy to such an extent that they have bombarded corporate headquarters with questions about her personal life. Lara is the star of novels, comic books, and three movies. There are also Lara Croft action figures.

The mass media not only reflect gender stereotypes but also play a role in changing them. Sometimes they do both simultaneously. The images of Lara Croft not only reflect women's changing role in society, but also, by exaggerating the change, they mold new stereotypes.

For Your Consideration

➤ A sociologist who reviewed this text said, "It seems that for women to be defined as equal, we have to become symbolic males—warriors with breasts." Why is gender change mostly one-way—females adopting traditional male characteristics? These two questions should help: Who is moving into the traditional territory of the other? Do people prefer to imitate power or weakness?

➤ Finally, consider just how far stereotypes have actually been left behind. One reward for beating time trials is to be able to see Lara wearing a bikini.

different behaviors and attitudes are expected of boys and girls. First transmitted by the family, these gender messages are reinforced by other social institutions. As these symbols become integrated into our views of the world, we form a picture of "how" males and females "are." As a result, gender serves as a primary basis for **social inequality**—giving privileges and obligations to one group of people while denying them to another.

Agents of Socialization

Individuals and groups that influence our orientations to life—our self-concept, emotions, attitudes, and behavior—are called **agents of socialization.** We have already considered how three of these agents—the family, our peers, and the mass media—influence our ideas of gender. Now we'll look more closely at how agents of socialization prepare us in other ways to take our place in society. We shall consider the family, then the neighborhood, religion, day care, school and peers, and the workplace.

The Family

The first group to have a major impact on us is our family. Our experiences in the family are so intense that their influence is lifelong. These experiences establish our initial motivations, values, and beliefs. In the family, we receive our basic sense of self, ideas about who we are and what we deserve out of life. It is here that we begin to think of ourselves as strong or weak, smart or dumb, good-looking or ugly—or more likely, somewhere in between. And as already noted, the lifelong process of defining ourselves as feminine or masculine also begins in the family.

Let's look at the difference that social class makes in how families socialize their children.

Social Class and Type of Work.   Sociologist Melvin Kohn (1959, 1963, 1977, 2006) found that the main concern of working-class parents is that their children stay out of trouble. They tend to use physical punishment. Middle-class parents, in contrast, focus more on developing their children's curiosity, self-expression, and self-control. They are more likely to reason with their children than to use physical punishment.

These differences puzzled Kohn. As a sociologist, he knew that the answer was life experiences of some sort. He found the answer in the world of work. Blue-collar workers are usually told exactly what to do. Since they expect their children's lives to be like theirs, they stress obedience. The work of middle-class parents, in contrast, requires more initiative, and they socialize their children into the qualities they find valuable.

Kohn was still puzzled. Some working-class parents act more like middle-class parents, and vice versa. As Kohn probed this puzzle, the pieces fell into place. The key turned out to be the parents' type of job. Middle-class office workers, for example, are supervised closely, and Kohn found that they follow the working-class pattern of child rearing, emphasizing conformity. And some blue-collar workers, such as those who do home repairs, have a good deal of freedom. These workers follow the middle-class model in rearing their children (Pearlin and Kohn 1966; Kohn and Schooler 1969).

This photo captures an extreme form of family socialization. The father seems to be more emotionally involved in the goal—and in more pain—than his daughter, as he pushes her toward the finish line in the Teen Tours of America Kid's Triathlon.

The Neighborhood

As all parents know, some neighborhoods are better than others for children. Parents try to move to the better neighborhoods—if they can afford them. Their common-sense evaluations are borne out by sociological research. Children from poor neighborhoods are more likely to get in trouble with the law, to become pregnant, to drop out of school, and even to have worse mental health (Levanthal and Brooks-Gunn 2000; Wheaton and Clarke 2003; Chauhan et al. 2009; DeLuca and Dayton 2009).

Sociologists have also found that the residents of more affluent neighborhoods keep a closer eye on their children than do the residents of poor neighborhoods (Sampson et al. 1999). The basic reason is that the more affluent neighborhoods have fewer families in transition, so the adults are more likely to know the local children and their parents. This better equips them to help keep the children safe and out of trouble.

Religion

How important is religion in your life? Most Americans belong to a local congregation, but what if you are among the 16 percent who do not identify with a religion (Newport 2010)? We would miss the point if we were to assume that religion influences only people who are "religious." Religion plays a powerful role even for people who wouldn't be caught dead near a church, synagogue, or mosque. How? Religious ideas so pervade U.S. society that they provide the foundation of morality for both the religious and the nonreligious.

For many Americans, the influence of religion is more direct. This is especially true for the two of every five Americans who report that during a typical week they attend a religious service (Gallup Poll 2010). On the obvious level, through their participation in religious services they learn doctrines, values, and morality, but the effects of religion on their lives go far beyond this. As they learn beliefs about the hereafter, for example, they also learn what kinds of clothing, speech, and manners are appropriate for formal occasions. Life in congregations also provides them a sense of identity, a feeling of belonging. Religious participation also helps to integrate immigrants into their new society, offers an avenue of social mobility for the poor, provides social contacts for jobs, and for African Americans, has been a powerful influence in social change.

Day Care

It is rare for social science research to make national news, but occasionally it does. This is what happened when researchers published their findings on 1,200 kindergarten children they had studied since they were a month old. They observed the children multiple times both at home and at day care. They also videotaped and made detailed notes on the children's interaction with their mothers (National Institute of Child Health and Human Development 1999; Guensburg 2001). What caught the media's attention? Children who spend more time in day care have weaker bonds with their mothers and are less affectionate to them. They are also less cooperative with others and more likely to fight and to be "mean." By the time they get to kindergarten, they are more likely to talk back to teachers and to disrupt the classroom. This holds true regardless of the quality of the day care, the family's social class, or whether the child is a girl or a boy (Belsky 2006). On the positive side, the children also scored higher on language tests.

Are we producing a generation of "smart but mean" children? This is not an unreasonable question, since the study was well designed and an even larger study of children in England has come up with similar findings (Belsky 2006). Some point out that the differences between children who spend a lot of time in day care and those who spend less time are slight. Others stress that with 5 million children in day care (*Statistical Abstract* 2012:Table 578), slight differences can be significant for society.

Schools are a primary agent of socialization. One of their functions is to teach children the attitudes and skills they are thought to need as adults. As indicated by this photo, in the United States this process starts early.

The researchers continued to test these children as they went through school, and the surprise is how these initial effects of day care have followed the children. At age 15, the children who had lower quality care and those who spent more time in child care did slightly worse academically and had slightly more behavioral problems than the children who had the higher quality care or who spent less time in child care (Vandell et al. 2010).

The School and Peer Groups

As a child's experiences with agents of socialization broaden, the influence of the family decreases. Entry into school marks only one of many steps in this transfer of allegiance. One of the most significant aspects of education is that it exposes children to peer groups that help children resist the efforts of parents and schools to socialize them. The Cultural Diversity box on the next page explores how these new values and ways of looking at the world sometimes even replace those the child learns at home.

When sociologists Patricia and Peter Adler (1998) observed children at two elementary schools in Colorado, they saw how children separate themselves by sex and develop separate gender worlds. The norms that made boys popular were athletic ability, coolness, and toughness. For girls, popularity was based on family background, physical appearance (clothing and use of makeup), and the ability to attract popular boys. In this children's subculture, academic achievement pulled in opposite directions: For boys, high grades lowered their popularity, but for girls, good grades increased their standing among peers.

You know from your own experience how compelling peer groups are. It is almost impossible to go against a peer group, whose cardinal rule seems

Can you explain how religion, day care, school, and peer groups are significant agents of socialization?

Cultural Diversity in the United States

Immigrants and Their Children: Caught between Two Worlds

It is a struggle to adapt to a new culture, for its behaviors and ways of thinking may be at odds with the ones already learned. This can lead to inner turmoil. One way to handle the conflict is to cut ties with your first culture. Doing so, however, can create a sense of loss, one that is perhaps recognized only later in life.

Richard Rodriguez, a literature professor and essayist, was born to working-class Mexican immigrants. Wanting their son to be successful in their adopted land, his parents named him Richard instead of Ricardo. Although this English–Spanish hybrid name indicates his parents' aspirations for their son, it was also an omen of the conflict that Richard would experience.

Like other children of Mexican immigrants, Richard first spoke Spanish—a rich mother tongue that introduced him to the world. Until the age of 5, when he began school, Richard knew only fifty words in English. He describes what happened when he began school:

The change came gradually but early. When I was beginning grade school, I noted to myself the fact that the classroom environment was so different in its styles and assumptions from my own family environment that survival would essentially entail a choice between both worlds. When I became a student, I was literally "remade"; neither I nor my teachers considered anything I had known before as relevant. I had to forget most of what my culture had provided, because to remember it was a disadvantage. The past and its cultural values became detachable, like a piece of clothing grown heavy on a warm day and finally put away.

As happened to millions of immigrants before him, whose parents spoke German, Polish, Italian, and so on, learning English eroded family and class ties and ate away at his ethnic roots. For Rodriguez, language and education were not simply devices that eased the transition to the dominant culture. They also slashed at the roots that had given him life.

To face conflicting cultures is to confront a fork in the road. Some turn one way and withdraw from the new culture—a clue that helps to explain why so many Latinos drop out of U.S. schools. Others go in the opposite direction.

Cutting ties with their family and cultural roots, they wholeheartedly adopt the new culture.

Rodriguez took the second road. He excelled in his new language—so much, in fact, that he graduated from Stanford University and then became a graduate student in English at the University of California at Berkeley. He was even awarded a Fulbright fellowship to study English Renaissance literature at the University of London.

But the past shadowed Rodriguez. Prospective employers were impressed with his knowledge of Renaissance literature. At job interviews, however, they would skip over the Renaissance training and ask him if he would teach the Mexican novel and be an adviser to Latino students. Rodriguez was also haunted by the image of his grandmother, the warmth of the culture he had left behind, and the language and thought to which he had become a stranger.

Richard Rodriguez represents millions of immigrants—not just those of Latino origin but those from other cultures, too—who want to be a part of life in the United States without betraying their past. They fear that to integrate into U.S. culture is to lose their roots. They are caught between two cultures, each beckoning, each offering rich rewards.

For Your Consideration

➔ I saw this conflict firsthand with my father, who did not learn English until after the seventh grade (his last in school). German was left behind, but broken English and awkward expressions remained for a lifetime. Then, too, there were the lingering emotional connections to old ways, as well as the suspicions, haughtiness, and slights of more assimilated Americans. He longed for security by grasping the past, but at the same time, he wanted to succeed in the everyday reality of the new culture. Have you seen similar conflicts?

Sources: Based on Richard Rodriguez 1975, 1982, 1990, 1991, 1995.

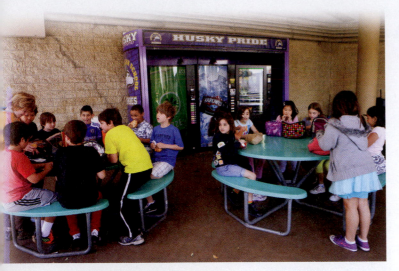

Gradeschool boys and girls often separate themselves by gender, as in this grade school in Beverly Hills, California. The socialization that occurs during self-segregation by gender is a topic of study by sociologists.

to be "conformity or rejection." Anyone who doesn't do what the others want becomes an "outsider," a "nonmember," an "outcast." For preteens and teens just learning their way around in the world, it is not surprising that the peer group rules.

As a result, the standards of our peer groups tend to dominate our lives. If your peers, for example, listen to rap, Nortec, death metal, rock and roll, country, or gospel, it is almost inevitable that you also prefer that kind of music. In high school, if your friends take math courses, you probably do, too (Crosnoe et al. 2008). It is the same for clothing styles and dating standards. Peer influences also extend to behaviors that violate social norms. If your peers are college-bound and upwardly striving, this is most likely what you will be; but if they use drugs, cheat, and steal, you are likely to do so, too.

The Workplace

Another agent of socialization that comes into play somewhat later in life is the workplace. Those initial jobs that we take in high school and college are much more than just a way to earn a few dollars. From the people we rub shoulders with at work, we learn not only a set of skills but also perspectives on the world.

Most of us eventually become committed to some particular line of work, often after trying out many jobs. This may involve **anticipatory socialization,** learning to play a role before entering it. Anticipatory socialization is a sort of mental rehearsal for some future activity. We may talk to people who work in a particular career, read novels about that type of work, or take a summer internship in that field. Such activities allow us to gradually identify with the role, to become aware of what would be expected of us. Sometimes this helps people avoid committing themselves to an empty career, as with some of my students who tried student teaching, found that they couldn't stand it, and then moved on to other fields more to their liking.

An intriguing aspect of work as a socializing agent is that the more you participate in a line of work, the more this work becomes part of your self-concept. Eventually you come to think of yourself so much in terms of the job that if someone asks you to describe yourself, you are likely to include the job in your self-description. You might say, "I'm a teacher," "I'm a nurse," or "I'm a sociologist."

Resocialization

What does a woman who has just become a nun have in common with a man who has just divorced? The answer is that they both are undergoing **resocialization;** that is, they are learning new norms, values, attitudes, and behaviors to match their new situation in life. In its most common form, resocialization occurs each time we learn something contrary to our previous experiences. A new boss who insists on a different way of doing things is resocializing you. Most resocialization is mild—only a slight modification of things we have already learned.

Resocialization can also be intense. People who join Alcoholics Anonymous (AA), for example, are surrounded by reformed drinkers who affirm the destructive effects of excessive drinking. Some students experience an intense period of resocialization when they leave high school and start college—especially during those initially scary days before they find companions, start to fit in, and feel comfortable. The experiences of people who join a cult or begin psychotherapy are even more profound, for they learn views that conflict with their earlier socialization. If these ideas "take," not only does the individual's behavior change but he or she also learns a fundamentally different way of looking at life.

In what ways is the workplace an important agent of socialization? What is resocialization?

Total Institutions

Relatively few of us experience the powerful agent of socialization that sociologist Erving Goffman (1961) called the **total institution.** He coined this term to refer to a place in which people are cut off from the rest of society and where they come under almost total control of the officials who are in charge. Boot camps, prisons, concentration camps, convents, some religious cults, and some military schools, such as West Point, are total institutions.

A person entering a total institution is greeted with a **degradation ceremony** (Garfinkel 1956), an attempt to remake the self by stripping away the individual's current identity and stamping a new one in its place. This unwelcome greeting may involve fingerprinting, photographing, or shaving the head. Newcomers may be ordered to strip, undergo an examination (often in a humiliating, semipublic setting), and then put on a uniform that designates their new status. Officials also take away the individual's *personal identity kit,* items such as jewelry, hairstyle, clothing, and other body decorations used to express individuality.

Total institutions are isolated from the public. The bars, walls, gates, and guards not only keep the inmates in but also keep outsiders out. Staff members supervise the day-to-day lives of the residents. Eating, sleeping, showering, recreation—all are standardized. Inmates learn that their previous statuses—student, worker, spouse, parent—mean nothing. The only thing that counts is their current status.

No one leaves a total institution unscathed, for the experience brands an indelible mark on the individual's self and colors the way he or she sees the world. Boot camp, as described in the Down-to-Earth Sociology box on the next page, is brutal but swift. Prison, in contrast, is brutal and prolonged. Neither recruit nor prisoner, however, has difficulty in knowing that the institution has had profound effects on attitudes and orientations to life.

Socialization Through the Life Course

You are at a particular stage in your life now, and college is a good part of it. You know that you have more stages ahead as you go through life. These stages, from birth to death, are called the **life course** (Elder 1975; 1999). The sociological significance of the life course is twofold. First, as you pass through a stage, it affects your behavior and orientations. You simply don't think about life in the same way when you are 30, are married, and have a baby and a mortgage, as you do when you are 18 or 20, single, and in college. (Actually, you don't even see life the same way as a freshman and as a senior.) Second, your life course differs by social location. Your social class, race–ethnicity, and gender, for example, map out distinctive worlds of experience.

This means that the typical life course differs for males and females, the rich and the poor, and so on. To emphasize this major sociological point, in the sketch that follows I will stress the *historical* setting of people's lives. Because of your particular social location, your own life course may differ from this sketch, which is a composite of stages that others have suggested (Levinson 1978; Carr et al. 1995; Quadagno 2010).

Childhood (from birth to about age 12)

Consider how different your childhood would have been if you had grown up in another historical era. Historian Philippe Ariès (1965) noticed that in European paintings from about A.D. 1000 to 1800 children were always dressed in adult clothing. If they were not depicted stiffly posed, as in a family portrait, they were shown doing adult activities.

From this, Ariès drew a conclusion that sparked a debate among historians. He said that Europeans of this era did not regard childhood as a special time of life. They viewed children as miniature adults and put them to work at an early age. At the age of 7, for example, a boy might leave home for good to learn to be a jeweler or a stonecutter. A girl, in contrast, stayed home until she married, but by the age of 7 she assumed

Down-to-Earth Sociology

Boot Camp as a Total Institution

The bus arrives at Parris Island, South Carolina, at 3 A.M. The early hour is no accident. The recruits are groggy, confused. Up to a few hours ago, the young men were ordinary civilians. Now, as a sergeant sneeringly calls them "maggots," their heads are buzzed (25 seconds per recruit), and they are quickly thrust into the harsh world of Marine boot camp.

Buzzing the boys' hair is just the first step in stripping away their identity so that the Marines can stamp a new one in its place. The uniform serves the same purpose. There is a ban on using the first person "I." Even a simple request must be made in precise Marine style or it will not be acknowledged. ("Sir, Recruit Jones requests permission to make a head call, Sir.")

Every intense moment of the next eleven weeks reminds the recruits, men and women, that they are joining a sub-culture of self-discipline. Here pleasure is suspect and sacrifice is good. As they learn the Marine way of talking, walking, and thinking, they are denied the diversions they once took for granted: television, cigarettes, cars, candy, soft drinks, video games, music, alcohol, drugs, and sex.

A recruit with a drill instructor

Lessons are taught with fierce intensity. When Sgt. Carey checks brass belt buckles, Recruit Robert Shelton nervously blurts, "I don't have one." Sgt. Carey's face grows red as his neck cords bulge. "I?" he says, his face just inches from the recruit. With spittle flying from his mouth, he screams, " 'I' is gone!"

"Nobody's an individual" is the lesson that is driven home again and again. "You are a team, a Marine. Not a civilian. Not black or white, not Hispanic or Indian or some hyphen-ated American—but a Marine. You will live like a Marine, fight like a Marine, and, if necessary, die like a Marine."

Each day begins before dawn with close-order formations. The rest of the day is filled with training in hand-to-hand

combat, marching, running, calisthenics, Marine history, and—always—following orders.

"An M-16 can blow someone's head off at 500 meters," Sgt. Norman says. "That's beautiful, isn't it?"

"Yes, sir!" shout the platoon's fifty-nine voices.

"Pick your nose!" Simultaneously fifty-nine index fingers shoot into nostrils.

The pressure to conform is intense. Those who are sent packing for insubordination or suicidal tendencies are mocked in cadence during drills. ("Hope you like the sights you see/ Parris Island casualty.") As lights go out at 9 P.M., the exhausted recruits perform the day's last task: The entire platoon, in unison, chants the virtues of the Marines.

Recruits are constantly scrutinized. Subpar performance is not accepted, whether it be a dirty rifle or a loose thread on a uniform. The under-performer is shouted at, derided, humiliated. The group suffers for the in-dividual. If one recruit is slow, the entire platoon is punished.

The system works.

One of the new Marines (until graduation, they are recruits, not Marines) says, "I feel like I've joined a new society or religion."

He has.

For Your Consideration

→ Of what significance is the recruits' degradation ceremony? Why are recruits not allowed video games, cigarettes, or calls home? Why are the Marines so unfair as to punish an entire platoon for the failure of an individual? Use concepts in this chapter to explain why the system works.

Sources: Based on Garfinkel 1956; Goffman 1961; Ricks 1995; Dyer 2007.

---

her share of the household tasks. Historians do not deny that these were the customs of that time, but some say that Ariès' conclusion is ridiculous, that other evidence indi-cates that these people viewed childhood as a special time of life (Orme 2002).

Having children work like adults did not disappear with the Middle Ages. This prac-tice was still common around the world in the 1800s. Even today, children in the Least Industrialized Nations work in many occupations—from blacksmiths to waiters. As tourists are shocked to discover, children in these nations also work as street peddlers, hawking everything from shoelaces to chewing gum.

Child rearing, too, used to be remarkably different. Three hundred years ago, parents and teachers considered it their *moral* duty to *terrorize* children. To keep children from "going bad," they would frighten them with bedtime stories of death and hellfire, lock them in dark closets, and force them to witness events like this:

A common moral lesson involved taking children to visit the gibbet [an upraised post on which executed bodies were left hanging], where they were forced to inspect the rotting corpses as an example of what happens to bad children when they grow up. Whole classes were taken out of school to witness hangings, and parents would often whip their children afterwards to make them remember what they had seen. (DeMause 1975)

Industrialization transformed the way we perceive children. When children had the leisure to go to school and postpone taking on adult roles, parents and officials came to think of them as tender and innocent, as needing more care, comfort, and protection. Such attitudes of dependency grew, and today we view children as needing gentle guidance if they are to develop emotionally, intellectually, morally, even physically. We take our view for granted—after all, it is only "common sense." Yet, as you can see, our view is not "natural." It is, instead, rooted in society—in geography, history, and economic development.

In Sum: Childhood is more than biology. Everyone's childhood occurs at some point in history and is embedded in specific social locations, especially social class and gender. *These social factors are as vital as our biology, for they determine what our childhood will be like.* Although a child's *biological* characteristics (such as being small and dependent) are universal, the child's *social* experiences (the kind of life the child lives) are not. Because of this, sociologists say that childhood varies from culture to culture.

Adolescence (ages 13–17)

It might seem strange to you, but adolescence is a *social invention*, not a "natural" age division. In earlier centuries, people simply moved from childhood to young adulthood, with no stopover in between. The Industrial Revolution allowed adolescence to be invented. It brought such an abundance of material surpluses that for the first time in history people in their teens were not needed as workers. At the same time, education became more important for achieving success. As these two forces in industrialized societies converged, they created a gap between childhood and adulthood. The term *adolescence* was coined to indicate this new stage in life (Hall 1904), one that has become renowned for uncertainty, rebellion, and inner turmoil.

From paintings, such as this one of Sir Walter Raleigh from 1602, some historians conclude that Europeans once viewed children as miniature adults who assumed adult roles early in life. From the 1959 photo taken in Harlem, New York, you can see why this conclusion is now being challenged, if not ridiculed.

How does childhood depend on social location: historical, geographical, and gender?

In many societies, manhood is not bestowed upon males simply because they reach a certain age. Manhood, rather, signifies a standing in the community that must be achieved. Shown here is a boy of the Dinka tribe in Sudan being initiated into manhood. To show pain when the six horizontal lines are cut around his head would bring dishonor.

To mark the passage of children into adulthood, tribal societies hold *initiation rites*. This grounds the self-identity, showing these young people how they fit in the society. In the industrialized world, however, adolescents must "find" themselves. They grapple with the dilemma of "I am neither a child nor an adult. Who am I?" As they attempt to carve out an identity that is distinct from both the "younger" world being left behind and the "older" world that still lingers out of reach, adolescents develop their own subcultures, with distinctive clothing, hairstyles, language, gestures, and music. We usually fail to realize that contemporary society, not biology, created this period of inner turmoil that we call *adolescence*.

Transitional Adulthood (ages 18–29)

If society invented adolescence, can it also invent other periods of life? As Figure 3.2 illustrates, this is actually happening now. Postindustrial societies are adding another period of extended youth to the life course, which sociologists call **transitional adulthood** (also known as *adultolescence*).

After high school, millions of young adults postpone adult responsibilities by going to college. They are mostly freed from the control of their parents, yet they don't have to support themselves. After college, many live at home, so they can live cheaply while they establish themselves in a career—and, of course, continue to "find themselves." During this time, people are "neither psychological adolescents nor sociological adults" (Keniston 1971). At some point during this period of extended youth, young adults ease into adult responsibilities. They take a full-time job, become serious about a career, engage in courtship rituals, get married—and go into debt.

The Middle Years (ages 30–65)

The Early Middle Years (ages 30–49).   During their early middle years, most people are more sure of themselves and of their goals in life. As with any point in the life course, however, the self can receive severe jolts. Common upheavals during this period are divorce and losing jobs. It may take years for the self to stabilize after such ruptures.

The early middle years pose a special challenge for many U.S. women, who have been given the message, especially by the media, that they can "have it all." They can be superworkers, superwives, and supermoms—all rolled into one superwoman. Reality, however, hits them in the face: too little time, too many demands, even too little sleep. Something has to give, and attempts to resolve this dilemma are anything but easy.

The Later Middle Years (ages 50–65).   During the later middle years, health issues and mortality begin to loom large as people feel their bodies change, especially if they watch their parents become frail, fall ill, and die. The consequence is a fundamental reorientation in thinking—*from time since birth to time left to live* (Neugarten 1976). With this changed orientation, people attempt to evaluate the past and come to terms with what lies ahead. They compare what they have accomplished with what they had hoped to achieve. Many people also find themselves caring not only for

---

FIGURE 3.2   **Transitional Adulthood: A New Stage in the Life Course**

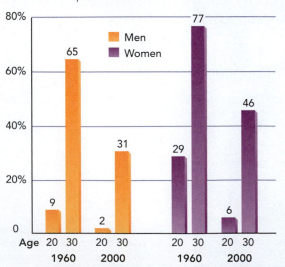

Who has completed the transition?

	Men	Women
Age 20 30	9 65	
1960		
20 30	2 31	
2000		
20 30		29 77
1960		
20 30		6 46
2000		

The bars show the percentage who have completed the transition to adulthood, as measured by leaving home, finishing school, getting married, having a child, and being financially independent.

Source: Furstenberg et al. 2004.

Can you explain why adolescence is not a natural age division, but a social creation?

their own children but also for their aging parents. Because of this double burden, which is often crushing, people in the later middle years sometimes are called the "sandwich generation."

In contrast, many people experience few of these stresses and find late middle age to be the most comfortable period of their lives. They enjoy job security or secure marriages and a standard of living higher than ever before. They have a bigger house (one that may even be paid for), drive newer cars, and take longer and more exotic vacations. The children are grown, the self is firmly planted, and fewer upheavals are likely to occur.

As they anticipate the next stage of life, however, most people do not like what they see.

The Older Years (about age 65 on)

The Transitional Older Years.   In agricultural societies, when most people died early, old age was thought to begin at around age 40. As industrialization brought improved nutrition, medicine, and public health, allowing more people to live longer, the beginning of "old age" gradually stretched out. Today, people who enjoy good health don't think of their 60s as old age, but as an extension of their middle years. This change is so recent that a *new stage of life* seems to be evolving, the period between retirement (averaging about 63) and old age—which people are increasingly coming to see as beginning around age 75 ("Schwab Study" 2008). We can call this stage the *transitional older years*. Increasingly during this stage in the life course, people feel that "time is closing in" on them.

The Later Older Years.   As with the preceding periods of life, except the first one, there is no precise beginning point to this last stage. For some, the 75th birthday may mark entry into this period of life. For others, that marker may be the 80th or even the 85th birthday. For most, this stage is marked by growing frailty and illness; for all who reach this stage, it is ended by death. For some, the physical decline is slow, and a rare few manage to see their 100th birthday mentally alert and in good physical health.

Are We Prisoners of Socialization?

From our discussion of socialization, you might conclude that sociologists think of people as robots: The socialization goes in, and the behavior comes out. People cannot help what they do, think, or feel, for everything is a result of their exposure to socializing agents.

Sociologists do *not* think of people in this way. Although socialization is powerful, and affects all of us profoundly, we have a self. Established in childhood and continually modified by later experience, our self is dynamic. Our self is not a sponge that passively absorbs influences from the environment, but, rather, it is a vigorous, essential part of our being that allows us to act on our environment.

Precisely because people are not robots, individual behavior is hard to predict. The countless reactions of others merge in each of us. As the self develops, we each internalize or "put together" these innumerable reactions, which become the basis for how we reason, react to others, and make choices in life. The result is a unique whole called the *individual*.

Rather than being passive sponges in this process, *each of us is actively involved in the construction of the self*. Our experiences in the family and other groups during childhood lay down our basic orientations to life, but we are not doomed to keep these orientations if we do not like them. We can purposely expose ourselves to other groups and ideas. Those experiences, in turn, have their own effects on our self. In short, we influence our socialization as we make choices. We can change even the self within the limitations of the framework laid down by our social locations. And that self—along with the options available within society—is the key to our behavior.

This January 1937 photo from Sneedville, Tennessee, shows Eunice Johns, age 9, and her husband, Charlie Johns, age 22. The groom gave his wife a doll as a wedding gift. The new husband and wife planned to build a cabin, and, as Charlie Johns phrased it, "go to housekeepin'." This couple illustrates the cultural relativity of life stages, which we sometimes mistake as fixed. It also is interesting from a symbolic interactionist perspective— that of changing definitions.

Students have asked what happened to this couple, so I checked. It turns out that the marriage lasted. The couple had seven children, five boys and two girls. Charlie died in 1997 at age 83, and Eunice in 2006 at age 78. The two were buried in the Johns Family Cemetery.

❋ Explore
Living Data
on **mysoclab.com**

What are transitional adulthood and the transitional older years? How do they illustrate the social basis of the life course?

By the Numbers: Changes Over Time

By the Numbers: Changes Over Time

Percentage of men who complete the transition to adulthood by age 30	
1960	NOW
65%	**31**%

Percentage of women who complete the transition to adulthood by age 30	
1960	NOW
77%	**46**%

About when does old age begin?	
BEFORE INDUSTRI-ALIZATION	NOW (IN TRANSITION)
40	**75**

CHAPTER 3 # Summary and Review

Society Makes Us Human

How much of our human characteristics come from "nature" (heredity) and how much from "nurture" (the social environment)?

Observations of isolated, institutionalized, and **feral children** help to answer the nature–nurture question, as do experiments with monkeys that were raised in isolation. Language and intimate social interaction—aspects of "nurture"—are essential to the development of what we consider to be human characteristics. Pp. 66–70.

Socialization into the Self and Mind

How do we acquire a self?

Humans are born with the *capacity* to develop a **self,** but the self must be socially constructed; that is, its contents depend on social interaction. According to Charles Horton Cooley's concept of the **looking-glass self,** our self develops as we internalize others' reactions to us. George Herbert Mead identified the ability to **take the role of the other** as essential to the development of the self. Mead concluded that even the mind is a social product. Pp. 70–72.

How do children develop reasoning skills?

Jean Piaget identified four stages that children go through as they develop the ability to reason: (1) *sensorimotor,* in which understanding is limited to sensory stimuli such as touch and sight; (2) *preoperational,* in which children develop the ability to use symbols; (3) *concrete operational,* in which reasoning ability is more complex but not yet

capable of complex abstractions; and (4) *formal operational,* or abstract thinking. Pp. 72–73.

Learning Personality, Emotions, and Internal Control

How does Freud's view of personality development differ from the sociological view?

Sigmund Freud viewed personality development as the result of our **id** (inborn, self-centered desires) clashing with the demands of society. The **ego** develops to balance the id and the **super-ego,** the conscience. Sociologists, in contrast, do not examine inborn or subconscious motivations, but, instead, consider how *social* factors such as—social class, gender, race–ethnicity, religion, and education underlie personality. Pp. 73–74.

How does socialization influence emotions?

Socialization influences not only *how we express our emotions* but also *what emotions we feel.* Socialization into emotions is one of the means by which society produces conformity. Pp. 74–76.

Socialization into Gender

How does gender socialization affect our sense of self?

Gender socialization—sorting males and females into different roles—is a primary means of controlling human behavior. Children receive messages about gender even in infancy. A society's ideals of sex-linked behaviors are reinforced by its social institutions. Pp. 76–80.

Agents of Socialization

What are the main agents of socialization?

The **agents of socialization** include the family, neighborhood, religion, day care, school, **peer groups,** the **mass media,** and the workplace. Each has its particular influences in socializing us into becoming full-fledged members of society. Pp. 80–84.

Resocialization

What is resocialization?

Resocialization is the process of learning new norms, values, attitudes, and behavior. Most resocialization is voluntary, but some, as with residents of **total institutions,** is involuntary. Pp. 84–85.

Socialization Through the Life Course

Does socialization end when we enter adulthood?

Socialization occurs throughout the life course. In industrialized societies, the **life course** can be divided into childhood, adolescence, young adulthood, the middle years, and the older years. The West is adding two new stages, **transitional adulthood** and **transitional older years.** Life course patterns vary by geography, history, gender, race–ethnicity, and social class, as well as by individual experiences such as health and age at marriage. Pp. 85–89.

Are We Prisoners of Socialization?

Although socialization is powerful, we are not merely the sum of our socialization experiences. Just as socialization influences our behavior, so we act on our environment and influence even our self-concept. P. 89.

Thinking Critically about Chapter 3

1. What two agents of socialization have influenced you the most? Can you pinpoint their influence on your attitudes, beliefs, values, or other orientations to life?

2. Summarize your views of the "proper" relationships of women and men. What in your socialization has led you to have these views?

3. What is your location in the life course? How does the text's summary of this location compare with your experiences? Explain the similarities and differences.

Social Structure and Social Interaction

Thailand

My curiosity had gotten the better of me. When the sociology convention was over, I climbed aboard the first city bus that came along. I didn't know where the bus was going, and I didn't know where I would spend the night.

This was my first visit to Washington, D.C., so everything was unfamiliar to me. I had no destination, no plans, not even a map. I carried no billfold, just a driver's license shoved into my jeans for emergency identification, some pocket change, and a $10 bill tucked into my sock. My goal was simple: If I saw something interesting, I would get off the bus and check it out.

As we passed row after row of apartment buildings and stores, I could see myself riding buses the entire night. Then something caught my eye. Nothing spectacular—just groups of people clustered around a large circular area where several streets intersected.

I got off the bus and made my way to what turned out to be Dupont Circle. I took a seat on a sidewalk bench. As the scene came into focus, I noticed several streetcorner men drinking and joking with one another. One of the men broke from his companions and sat down next to me. As we talked, I mostly listened.

> "Suddenly one of the men jumped up, smashed the empty bottle against the sidewalk, and . . ."

As night fell, the men said that they wanted to get another bottle of wine. I contributed. They counted their money and asked if I wanted to go with them. As we left the circle, the three men began to cut through an alley. "Oh, no," I thought. "This isn't what I had in mind."

I had but a split second to make a decision. I held back half a step so that none of the three was behind me. As we walked, they passed around the remnants of their bottle. When my turn came, I didn't know what to do. I shuddered to think about the diseases lurking within that bottle. In the semidarkness I faked it, letting only my thumb and forefinger touch my lips and nothing enter my mouth.

When we returned to Dupont Circle, we sat on the benches, and the men passed around their new bottle of Thunderbird. I couldn't fake it in the light, so I passed, pointing at my stomach to indicate that I was having digestive problems.

Suddenly one of the men jumped up, smashed the emptied bottle against the sidewalk, and thrust the jagged neck outward in a menacing gesture. He glared straight ahead at another bench, where he had spotted someone with whom he had some sort of unfinished business. As the other men told him to cool it, I moved slightly to one side of the group—ready to flee, just in case.

Levels of Sociological Analysis

On this sociological adventure, I almost got in over my head. Fortunately, it turned out all right. The man's "enemy" didn't look our way, the man put the broken bottle next to the bench "in case he needed it," and my intriguing introduction to a life that up until then I had only read about continued until dawn.

Sociologists Elliot Liebow (1967/1999), Mitchell Duneier (1999), and Elijah Anderson (1978, 1990, 1990/2006) have written fascinating accounts about men like my companions from that evening. Although streetcorner men may appear to be disorganized—simply coming and going as they please and doing whatever feels good at the moment—sociologists have analyzed how, like us, these men are influenced by the norms and beliefs of our society. This will become more apparent as we examine the two levels of analysis that sociologists use.

Macrosociology and Microsociology

The first level, **macrosociology,** focuses on broad features of society. Conflict theorists and functionalists use this approach to analyze such things as social class and how groups are related to one another. If they were to analyze streetcorner men, for example, they would stress that these men are located at the bottom of the U.S. social class system. Their low status means that many opportunities are closed to them: The men have few job skills, little education, hardly anything to offer an employer. As "able-bodied" men, however, they are not eligible for welfare—even for a two-year limit—so they hustle to survive. As a consequence, they spend their lives on the streets.

In the second level, **microsociology,** the focus is on **social interaction,** what people do when they come together. Sociologists who use this approach are likely to analyze the men's rules, or "codes," for getting along; their survival strategies ("hustles"); how they divide up money, wine, or whatever other resources they have; their relationships with girlfriends, family, and friends; where they spend their time and what they do there; their language; their pecking order; and so on. Microsociology is the primary focus of symbolic interactionists.

Because each approach has a different focus, macrosociology and microsociology yield distinctive perspectives; both are needed to gain a fuller understanding of social life. We cannot adequately understand streetcorner men, for example, without using *macrosociology.* It is essential that we place the men within the broad context of how groups in U.S. society are related to one another—for, as is true for ourselves, the social class of these men helps to shape their attitudes and behavior. Nor can we adequately understand these men without *microsociology,* for their everyday situations also form a significant part of their lives—as they do for all of us.

Let's look in more detail at how these two approaches in sociology work together to help us understand social life.

The Macrosociological Perspective: Social Structure

Why did the street people in our opening vignette act as they did, staying up all night drinking wine, prepared to use a lethal weapon? Why don't *we* act like this? Social structure helps us answer such questions.

The Sociological Significance of Social Structure

To better understand human behavior, we need to understand *social structure,* the framework of society that was already laid out before you were born. **Social structure** refers to the typical patterns of a group, such as the usual relationships

Sociologists use both macro and micro levels of analysis to study social life. Those who use macrosociology to analyze the homeless (or any human behavior) focus on broad aspects of society, such as the economy and social classes. Sociologists who use the microsociological approach analyze how people interact with one another. This photo illustrates social structure (the disparities between power and powerlessness are amply evident). It also illustrates the micro level (the isolation of this man).

between men and women or students and teachers. *The sociological significance of social structure is that it guides our behavior.*

Because this term may seem vague, let's consider how you experience social structure in your own life. As I write this, I do not know your race–ethnicity. I do not know your religion. I do not know whether you are young or old, tall or short, male or female. I do not know whether you were reared on a farm, in the suburbs, or in the inner city. I do not know whether you went to a public high school or to an exclusive prep school. But I do know that you are in college. And this, alone, tells me a great deal about you.

From this one piece of information, I can assume that the social structure of your college is now shaping what you do. For example, let's suppose that today you felt euphoric over some great news. I can be fairly certain (not absolutely, mind you, but relatively confident) that when you entered the classroom, social structure overrode your mood. That is, instead of shouting at the top of your lungs and joyously throwing this book into the air, you entered the classroom in a fairly subdued manner and took your seat.

The same social structure influences your instructor, even if he or she, on the one hand, is facing a divorce or has a child dying of cancer or, on the other, has just been awarded a promotion or a million-dollar grant. Your instructor may feel like either retreating into seclusion or celebrating wildly, but most likely he or she will conduct class in the usual manner. In short, social structure tends to override personal feelings and desires.

Just as social structure influences you and your instructor, so it also establishes limits for street people. They, too, find themselves in a specific location in the U.S. social structure—although it is quite different from yours or your instructor's. Consequently, they are affected in different ways. Nothing about their social location leads them to take notes or to lecture. Their behaviors, however, are as logical an outcome of where they find themselves in the social structure as are your own. In their position in the social structure, it is just as "natural" to drink wine all night as it is for you to stay up studying all night for a crucial examination. It is just as "natural" for you to nod and say, "Excuse me," when you enter a crowded classroom late and have to claim a desk on which someone has already placed books as it is for them to break off the neck of a wine bottle and glare at an enemy. To better understand social structure, read the Down-to-Earth Sociology box on the next page.

In Sum: People learn their behaviors and attitudes because of their location in the social structure (whether they be privileged, deprived, or in between), and they act accordingly. This is as true of street people as it is of us. *The differences in behavior and attitudes are due not to biology (race–ethnicity, sex, or any other supposed genetic factors), but to people's location in the social structure.* Switch places with street people and watch your behaviors and attitudes change!

Because social structure so crucially affects who we are and what we are like, let's look more closely at its major components: culture, social class, social status, roles, groups, and social institutions.

Culture

In Chapter 2, we considered culture's far-reaching effects on our lives. At this point, let's simply summarize its main impact. Sociologists use the term *culture* to refer to a group's language, beliefs, values, behaviors, and even gestures. Culture also includes the material objects that a group uses. Culture is the broadest framework that determines what kind of people we become. If we are reared in Chinese, Arab, or U.S. culture, we will grow up to be like most Chinese, Arabs, or Americans. On the outside, we will look and act like them; and on the inside, we will think and feel like them.

Social Class

To understand people, we must examine the social locations that they hold in life. Especially significant is *social class,* which is based on income, education, and occupational prestige. Large numbers of people who have similar amounts of income and education and who work at jobs that are roughly comparable in prestige make up a

College Football as Social Structure

To gain a better idea of what *social structure* is, think of college football (Dobriner 1969a). You probably know the various positions on the team: center, guards, tackles, ends, quarterback, running backs, and the like. Each is a *status*; that is, each is a social position. For each of the statuses shown in Figure 4.1, there is a *role*; that is, each of these positions has certain expectations attached to it. The center is expected to snap the ball, the quarterback to pass it, the guards to block, the tackles to tackle or block, the ends to receive passes, and so on. Those role expectations guide each player's actions; that is, the players try to do what their particular role requires.

Let's suppose that football is your favorite sport and you never miss a home game at your college. Let's also suppose that you graduate, get a great job, and move across the country. Five years later, you return to your campus for a nostalgic visit. The climax of your visit is the biggest football game of the season. When you get to the game, you might be surprised to see a different coach, but you are not surprised that each playing position is occupied by people you don't know, for all the players you knew have graduated, and their places have been filled by others.

This scenario mirrors *social structure*, the framework around which a group exists. In football, that framework consists of the coaching staff and the eleven playing positions. The game does not depend on any particular individual, but, rather, on *social statuses*, the positions that the individuals occupy. When someone leaves a position, the game can go on because someone else takes over that position or status and plays the role. The game will continue even though not a single individual remains from one period of time to the next. Notre Dame's football team endures today even though Knute Rockne, the Gipper, and his teammates are long dead.

Even though you may not play football, you do live your life within an established social structure. The statuses that you occupy and the roles you play were already in place

FIGURE 4.1   Team Positions (Statuses) in Football

Source: By the author.

before you were born. You take your particular positions in life, others do the same, and society goes about its business. Although the specifics change with time, the game—whether of life or of football—goes on.

For Your Consideration

→ How does social structure influence your life? To answer this question, you can begin by analyzing your social statuses.

---

social class. It is hard to overemphasize this aspect of social structure, for our social class influences not only our behaviors but even our ideas and attitudes. We have this in common, then, with the street people described in the opening vignette: We both are influenced by our location in the social class structure. Theirs may be a considerably less privileged position, but it has no less influence on their lives. Social class is so significant that we shall spend an entire chapter (Chapter 8) on this topic.

Social Status

When you hear the word *status*, you are likely to think of prestige. These two words are wedded together in people's minds. As you saw in the box on football, however, sociologists use **status** in a different way—to refer to the *position* that someone occupies. That position may carry a great deal of prestige, as in the case of a judge or an astronaut, or it may bring little prestige, as in the case of a convenience store clerk or a waitress at the local truck stop. The status may also be looked down on, as in the case of a streetcorner man, an ex-convict, or a thief.

Like other aspects of social structure, statuses are part of our basic framework of living in society. The example I gave of students and teachers who come to class and do what others expect of them despite their particular circumstances and moods illustrates how statuses affect our actions—and those of the people around us. Our statuses—whether daughter or son, teacher or student—serve as guides for our behavior.

Status Sets.   All of us occupy several positions at the same time. You may simultaneously be a son or daughter, a worker, a date, and a student. Sociologists use the term **status set** to refer to all the statuses or positions that you occupy. Obviously your status set changes as your particular statuses change. For example, if you graduate from college, take a full-time job, get married, buy a home, and have children, your status set changes to include the positions of worker, spouse, homeowner, and parent.

Ascribed and Achieved Statuses.   An **ascribed status** is involuntary. You do not ask for it, nor can you choose it. At birth, you inherit ascribed statuses such as your race–ethnicity, sex, and the social class of your parents, as well as your statuses as female or male, daughter or son, niece or nephew. Others, such as teenager and senior citizen, are related to the life course discussed in Chapter 3, and are given to you later in life.

Achieved statuses, in contrast, are voluntary. These you earn or accomplish. As a result of your efforts you become a student, a friend, a spouse, or a lawyer. Or, for lack of effort (or for efforts that others fail to appreciate), you become a school dropout, a former friend, an ex-spouse, or a debarred lawyer. In other words, achieved statuses can be either positive or negative; both college president and bank robber are achieved statuses.

Each status provides guidelines for how we are to act and feel. Like other aspects of social structure, statuses set limits on what we can and cannot do. Because social statuses are an essential part of the social structure, all human groups have them.

Status Symbols.   People who are pleased with their social status often want others to recognize their particular position. To elicit this recognition, they use **status symbols,** signs that identify a status. For example, people wear wedding rings to announce their marital status; uniforms, guns, and badges to proclaim that they are police officers (and not so subtly, to let you know that their status gives them authority over you); and "backward" collars to declare that they are Lutheran ministers or Roman Catholic or Episcopal priests.

Some social statuses are negative and so, therefore, are their status symbols. The scarlet letter in Nathaniel Hawthorne's book by the same title is one example. Another is the CONVICTED DUI (Driving Under the Influence) bumper sticker that some U.S. courts require convicted drunk drivers to display if they wish to avoid a jail sentence.

All of us use status symbols. We use them to announce our statuses to others and to help smooth our interactions in everyday life. Can you identify your own status symbols and what they communicate? For example, how does your clothing announce your statuses of sex, age, and college student?

Master Statuses.   A **master status** cuts across your other statuses. Some master statuses are ascribed. One example is your sex. Whatever you do, people perceive you as a male or as a female. If you are working your way through college by flipping burgers, people see you not only as a burger flipper and a student but also as a *male* or *female* burger flipper and a *male* or *female* college student. Other master statuses are race–ethnicity and age.

Some master statuses are achieved. If you become very, very wealthy (and it doesn't matter whether your wealth comes from a successful invention or from winning the lottery—it is still *achieved* as far as sociologists are concerned), your wealth is likely to become a master status. For example, people might say, "She is a very rich burger flipper"—or, more likely, "She's very rich, and she used to flip burgers!"

Social class and social status are significant factors in social life. Fundamental to what we become, they affect our orientations to life. Can you see how this photo illustrates this point?

Master statuses are those that overshadow our other statuses. Shown here is Stephen Hawking, who is severely disabled by Lou Gehrig's disease. For some, his *master status* is that of a person with disabilities. Because Hawking is one of the greatest physicists who has ever lived, however, his outstanding achievements have given him another *master status*, that of a world-class physicist in the ranking of Einstein.

Similarly, people who become disfigured find, to their dismay, that their condition becomes a master status. For example, a person whose face is scarred from severe burns will be viewed through this unwelcome master status regardless of their occupation or accomplishments. In the same way, people who are confined to wheelchairs can attest to how their wheelchair overrides all their other statuses and influences others' perceptions of everything they do.

Status Inconsistency. Our statuses usually fit together fairly well, but some people have a mismatch among their statuses. This is known as **status inconsistency** (or discrepancy). A 14-year-old college student is an example. So is a 40-year-old married woman who is dating a 19-year-old college sophomore.

These examples reveal an essential aspect of social statuses: Like other components of social structure, our statuses come with built-in *norms* (that is, expectations) that guide our behavior. When statuses mesh well, as they usually do, we know what to expect of people. This helps social interaction to unfold smoothly. Status inconsistency, however, upsets our expectations. In the preceding examples, how are you supposed to act? Are you supposed to treat the 14-year-old as you would a young teenager, or as you would your college classmate? Do you react to the married woman as you would to the mother of your friend, or as you would to a classmate's date?

Roles

All the world's a stage
And all the men and women merely players.
They have their exits and their entrances;
And one man in his time plays many parts . . .

(William Shakespeare, As You Like It, *Act II, Scene 7)*

Like Shakespeare, sociologists see roles as essential to social life. When you were born, **roles**—the behaviors, obligations, and privileges attached to a status—were already set up for you. Society was waiting with outstretched arms to teach you how it expected you to act as a boy or a girl. And whether you were born poor, rich, or somewhere in between, that, too, attached certain behaviors, obligations, and privileges to your statuses.

The difference between role and status is that you *occupy* a status, but you *play* a role (Linton 1936). For example, being a son or daughter is your status, but your expectations of receiving food and shelter from your parents—as well as their expectations that you show respect to them—are part of your role. Or, again, your status is student, but your role is to attend class, take notes, do homework, and take tests.

Roles are like fences. They allow us a certain amount of freedom, but for most of us that freedom doesn't go very far. Suppose that a woman decides that she is not going to wear dresses—or a man that he will not wear suits and ties—regardless of what anyone says. In most situations, they'll stick to their decision. When a formal occasion comes along, however, such as a family wedding or a funeral, they are likely to cave in to norms that they find overwhelming. Almost all of us follow the guidelines for what is "appropriate" for our roles. Few of us are bothered by such constraints, for our **socialization** is thorough, and we usually *want* to do what our roles indicate is appropriate.

What are your master statuses, and how do they influence your life? What is status inconsistency? What are roles?

The sociological significance of roles is that they lay out what is expected of people. As individuals throughout society perform their roles, those many roles mesh together to form this thing called *society*. As Shakespeare put it, people's roles provide "their exits and their entrances" on the stage of life. In short, roles are remarkably effective at keeping people in line—telling them when they should "enter" and when they should "exit," as well as what to do in between.

Groups

A **group** consists of people who interact with one another and who feel that the values, interests, and norms they have in common are important. The groups to which we belong—just like social class, statuses, and roles—are powerful forces in our lives. By belonging to a group, we assume an obligation to affirm the group's values, interests, and norms. To remain a member in good standing, we need to show that we share those characteristics. This means that *when we belong to a group we yield to others the right to judge our behavior*—even though we don't like it!

In the next chapter, we will examine groups in detail. For now, let's look at the next component of social structure, social institutions.

Social Institutions

At first glance, the term *social institution* may seem cold and abstract—with little relevance to your life. In fact, however, **social institutions**—the standard or usual ways that a society meets its basic needs—vitally affect your life. They not only shape your behavior but even color your thoughts. How can this be?

The first step in understanding how this can be is to look at Figure 4.2 on the next page. Look at what social institutions are: the family, religion, education, the economy, medicine, politics, law, science, the military, and the mass media. By weaving the fabric of society, the social institutions set the context for your behavior and orientations to life. Note that each institution satisfies a basic need and has its own groups, statuses, values, and norms. Social institutions are so significant that an entire part of this book, Part IV, focuses on them.

Societies—and Their Transformation

The largest and most complex group that sociologists study is **society,** which consists of people who share a culture and a territory. Society, which surrounds us, sets the stage for our life experiences. *The sociological principle is that the type of society we live in is the fundamental reason for why we become who we are.* Not only does our society lay the broad framework for our behavior, but it also influences the ways we think and feel. Its effects are so significant that if you had grown up in a different society, you would be a different type of person.

Let's try to understand how our society developed. Begin by looking at Figure 4.3 on p. 101. You can see that technology is the key to understanding the sweeping changes that produced our society. Let's review these broad changes. As we do, picture yourself as a member of each society. Consider how your life—even your thoughts and values—would be different as a member of these societies.

Hunting and Gathering Societies

The members of **hunting and gathering societies** have few social divisions and little inequality. As the name implies, in order to survive, these groups depend on hunting animals and gathering plants. In some groups, the men do the hunting, and the women the gathering. In others, both men and women (and children) gather plants, the men hunt large animals, and both men and women hunt small animals. The groups usually have a **shaman,** an individual thought to be able to influence spiritual forces, but shamans, too, must help obtain

⊙ Watch
Ways We Live
on **mysoclab.com**

As society—the largest and most complex type of group—changes, so, too, do the groups, activities, and, ultimately, the type of people who form that society. This photo is of Asa Sandell, Sweden, and Laila Ali, United States, as they fought in Berlin. What social changes can you identify from this photo?

What are the main characteristics of hunting and gathering societies?

FIGURE 4.2   **Social Institutions in Industrial and Postindustrial Societies**

Social Institution	Basic Needs of Society	Some Groups or Organizations	Some Statuses	Some Values	Some Norms
Family	Regulate reproduction, socialize and protect children	Relatives, kinship groups	Daughter, son, father, mother, brother, sister, aunt, uncle, grandparent	Sexual fidelity, providing for your family, keeping a clean house, respect for parents	Have only as many children as you can afford, be faithful to your spouse
Religion	Concerns about life after death, the meaning of suffering and loss; desire to connect with the Creator	Congregation, synagogue, mosque, denomination, charity, clergy associations	Priest, minister, rabbi, imam, worshipper, teacher, disciple, missionary, prophet, convert	God and the holy texts such as the Torah, the Bible, and the Qur'an should be honored	Go to worship services, follow the teachings, contribute money
Education	Transmit knowledge and skills across generations	School, college, student senate, sports team, PTA, teachers' union	Teacher, student, dean, principal, football player, cheerleader	Academic honesty, good grades, being "cool"	Do homework, prepare lectures, don't snitch on classmates
Economy	Produce and distribute goods and services	Credit unions, banks, credit card companies, buying clubs	Worker, boss, buyer, seller, creditor, debtor, advertiser	Making money, paying bills on time, producing efficiently	Maximize profits, "the customer is always right," work hard
Medicine	Heal the sick and injured, care for the dying	AMA, hospitals, pharmacies, HMOs, insurance companies	Doctor, nurse, patient, pharmacist, medical insurer	Hippocratic oath, staying in good health, following doctor's orders	Don't exploit patients, give best medical care available
Politics	Allocate power, determine authority, prevent chaos	Political party, congress, parliament, monarchy	President, senator, lobbyist, voter, candidate, spin doctor	Majority rule, the right to vote as a privilege and a sacred trust	One vote per person, be informed about candidates
Law	Maintain social order, enforce norms	Police, courts, prisons	Judge, police officer, lawyer, defendant, prison guard	Trial by one's peers, innocence until proven guilty	Give true testimony, follow the rules of evidence
Science	Master the environment	Local, state, regional, national, and international associations	Scientist, researcher, technician, administrator, journal editor	Unbiased research, open dissemination of research findings, originality	Follow scientific method, be objective, disclose findings, don't plagiarize
Military	Protection from enemies, enforce national interests	Army, navy, air force, marines, coast guard, national guard	Soldier, recruit, enlisted person, officer, veteran, prisoner, spy	Obedience; to die for one's country is an honor	Follow orders, be ready to go to war, sacrifice for your buddies
Mass Media	Disseminate information, report events, mold public opinion	TV networks, radio stations, publishers, association of bloggers	Journalist, newscaster, author, editor, publisher, blogger	Timeliness, accuracy, freedom of the press	Be accurate, fair, timely, and profitable

Source: By the author.

food. Although these groups give greater prestige to the men hunters, who supply most of the meat, the women gatherers contribute more food to the group, perhaps even four-fifths of their total food supply (Bernard 1992).

Because a region cannot support a large number of people who hunt animals and gather plants (group members do not plant—they only gather what is already there), hunting and gathering societies are small. They usually consist of only twenty-five to

How do social institutions guide your behavior? How do they provide your orientations to life?

forty people. These groups are nomadic. As their food supply dwindles in one area, they move to another location. They place high value on sharing food, which is essential to their survival. Because of disease, drought, and pestilence, children have only about a fifty-fifty chance of surviving to adulthood (Lenski and Lenski 1987).

As in the photo below, all human groups were once hunters and gatherers. Until several hundred years ago, these societies were common, but only about 300 remain today (Stiles 2003). Some were wiped out when different groups took over their lands. Others moved to villages and took up a new way of life. The hunting and gathering groups that remain include the pygmies of central Africa, the aborigines of Australia, and various groups in South America. With today's expanding populations, these groups seem doomed to a similar fate, with their way of life disappearing from the human scene (Lenski and Lenski 1987; Bearak 2010).

Pastoral and Horticultural Societies

About ten thousand years ago, some groups found that they could tame and breed some of the animals they hunted—primarily goats, sheep, cattle, and camels. Others discovered that they could cultivate plants. As a result, hunting and gathering societies branched into two directions, each with different means of acquiring food.

The key to understanding the first branching is the word *pasture;* **pastoral** (or herding) **societies** are based on the *pasturing of animals.* Pastoral societies developed in regions where low rainfall made it impractical to build life around growing crops. Groups that took this turn remained nomadic, for they followed their animals to fresh pasture. The key to understanding the second branching is the word *horticulture,* or plant cultivation. **Horticultural** (or gardening) **societies** are based on the *cultivation of plants by the use of hand tools.* Because they no longer had to abandon an area as the food supply gave out, these groups developed permanent settlements.

As shown in Figure 4.4 on the next page, the *domestication revolution* (the domestication of animals and plants) transformed society. Groups grew larger because the more dependable food supply supported more people. With more food available than was needed for survival, no longer was it necessary for everyone to work at providing food. As a result, a *division of labor* developed. Some people began to make jewelry, others tools, others weapons, and so on. This led to a surplus of objects, which, in turn, stimulated trade. With trading, groups began to accumulate objects they prized, such as gold, jewelry, and utensils.

Figure 4.4 illustrates how these changes led to *social inequality.* Some families (or clans) acquired more goods than others. This led to feuds and war, for groups now possessed animals, pastures, croplands, jewelry, and other material goods to fight about. War, in turn, opened the door to slavery, for people found it convenient to let captives do their drudge work. As individuals passed their possessions on to their descendants, wealth grew more concentrated. So did power, and for the first time, some individuals became chiefs.

FIGURE 4.3   The Social Transformations of Society

Hunting and gathering society

The First Social Revolution: Domestication (of plants and animals)
→ Horticultural society   Pastoral society

The Second Social Revolution: Agricultural (invention of the plow)
→ Agricultural society

The Third Social Revolution: Industrial (invention of the steam engine)
→ Industrial society

The Fourth Social Revolution: Information (invention of the microchip)
→ Postindustrial (information) society

Emerging

The Fifth Social Revolution?: Biotech (decoding of human genome system?)
→ Biotech society?

Note: Not all the world's societies will go through the transformations shown in this figure. Whether any hunting and gathering societies will survive, however, remains to be seen. A few might, perhaps kept on small "reserves" that will be off limits to developers—but open to guided "ethnotours" at a hefty fee.
Source: By the author.

Not many hunting and gathering groups remain on earth. This Hambukushu woman of Botswana is fishing.

How did social inequality emerge? How is it related to changes in society?

FIGURE 4.4 Consequences of Animal Domestication and Plant Cultivation

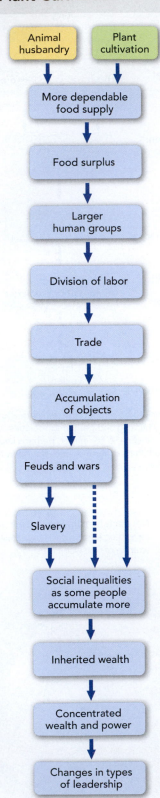

Source: By the author.

Agricultural Societies

The invention of the plow about five or six thousand years ago once again changed social life forever. Compared with hoes and digging sticks, using animals to pull plows is immensely efficient. As the earth was plowed, more nutrients were returned to the soil, making the land more productive. The food surplus of the *agricultural revolution* was unlike anything ever seen in human history. It allowed even more people to engage in activities other than farming. In this new **agricultural society,** people developed cities and what is popularly known as "culture," activities such as philosophy, art, music, literature, and architecture. Accompanied by the inventions of the wheel, writing, and numbers, the changes were so profound that this period is sometimes referred to as "the dawn of civilization."

The social inequality of pastoral and horticultural societies turned out to be only a hint of what was to come. When some people managed to gain control of the growing surplus of resources in agricultural societies, *inequality became a fundamental feature of life in society.* To protect their expanding privileges and power, this elite surrounded itself with armed men. This small group even levied taxes on others, who now had become their "subjects." As conflict theorists point out, this concentration of resources and power—along with the oppression of people not in power—was the forerunner of the state.

Industrial Societies

The *third* social invention also turned society upside down. The **Industrial Revolution** began in Great Britain in 1765 when the steam engine was first used to run machinery. Just as the surplus in the new **industrial society** was greater than anything that preceded it, so also was its social inequality. Thrown off the lands that their ancestors had farmed as tenants for centuries, people flocked to the cities. Homeless, they faced the choice of stealing, starving, or earning the equivalent of a loaf of bread for a day's work. The wealth of some of the men who first harnessed the steam engine and employed these desperate workers outran the imagination of royalty.

The workers' struggle for better conditions was long and brutal. Going on strike was illegal, and during the early 1900s some U.S. strikers were shot by private police and the National Guard. Against these odds, workers gradually won the right to better working conditions. As industrialization continued, bringing an abundance of goods, a surprising change occurred—*the pattern of growing inequality was reversed.* Despite continuing inequality, today's typical worker enjoys a high standard of living in terms of housing, health care, food, material possessions, and access to libraries and education. On an even broader scale of growing equality came the abolition of slavery, the shift from monarchies to more representative political systems, greater rights for women and minorities, and the rights to a jury trial, to cross-examine witnesses, to vote, and to travel. A recent extension of these equalities is the right to set up your own Internet blog where you can bemoan life in your school or criticize the president.

Postindustrial (Information) Societies

If you were to choose one word to characterize our society, what would it be? Of the many candidates, the word *change* would have to rank high. The primary source of the sweeping changes that are transforming our lives is the technology centering on the microchip. The change is so vast that sociologists say that a new type of society has emerged. They call it the **postindustrial** (or **information**) **society.**

Unlike the industrial society, which is marked by turning raw materials into products, the basic components of the posindustrial society are *information and services.* Few people *produce* anything. Rather, they transmit or apply information to provide services that others are willing to pay for.

How did the agricultural revolution contribute to social inequality? How has social inequality decreased? How does it continue?

The changes are so profound that they have led to a *fourth social revolution*. The surface changes of this new technology are obvious. Our purchases are scanned and billed in some remote place. While we ride in cars, trucks, boats, and airplanes, we talk to people in distant cities or even on the other side of the globe. We examine the surface of Mars and probe other remote regions of space. We spend billions of dollars on Internet purchases. Millions of children (and adults) spend countless hours battling virtual video villains.

Beyond such surface changes lie much more fundamental ones: The microchip is transforming relations among people. It is also uprooting our old perspectives and replacing them with new ones. In the Sociology and the New Technology box below, we explore an extreme aspect of virtual reality.

Sociology and the New Technology

Avatar Fantasy Life: The Blurring Lines of Reality

Dissatisfied with your current life? Would you like to become someone else? Maybe someone rich? You can. Join a world populated with virtual people and live out your fantasy.

Second Life and other Internet sites that offer an alternative virtual reality have exploded in popularity. Of the 27 million "residents" of *Second Life*, 450,000 spend twenty to forty hours a week in their alternative life (Alter 2007; "Second Life . . ." 2012).

To start your second life, you select your avatar, a kind of digital hand puppet, to be your persona in this virtual world. Your avatar comes in just a basic form, although you can control its movements just fine. But that bare body certainly won't do. You will want to clothe it. For this, you have your choice of outfits for every occasion. Although you buy them from other avatars in virtual stores, you have to spend real dollars. You might want some hair, too. For that, too, you'll have your choice of designers. And again, you'll spend real dollars. And you might want to have a sex organ. There is even a specialty store for that.

All equipped the way you want to be?

Then it is time to meet other avatars, the virtual personas of real-life people. As you interact with them in this virtual world, you will be able to share stories, talk about your desires in life, and have drinks in virtual bars. You can also buy property and open businesses.

Avatars flirt, too. Some even date and marry.

For most people, this second life is just an interesting game. They come and go, as if playing *Tomb Raider* or *World of Warcraft* now and then. Some people, though, get so caught up in their virtual world that their everyday life shrinks in appeal, and they neglect friends and family. For them, the virtual displaces the real, with the real fading into nonreality.

Ric Hoogestraat in Phoenix, Arizona, operates his avatar, Dutch—a macho motorcycle man, who is also filthy rich—from the time he gets up to the time he goes to bed. Dutch visits his several homes, where he can lounge on specially designed

A scene from Second Life. Each image is an avatar, a real person's fantasy self.

furniture. He pours his favorite drink and from his penthouse watches the sun setting over the ocean (Alter 2007).

Dutch met his wife, Tenaj, on *Second Life*. As courtships go, theirs went well. Their wedding was announced, of course, and about twenty avatar friends attended. They gave the newlyweds real congratulations, in a virtual sort of way.

Dutch and Tenaj have two dogs and pay the mortgage together. They love cuddling and intimate talks. Their love life is quite good, as avatars can have virtual sex.

But Sue is not pleased that Ric spends so much time in his virtual world. Sue feels neglected. She also doesn't appreciate Tenaj. Sue, you see, is also Ric's wife, but in real life.

The whole thing has become more than a little irritating. "I'll try to talk to him or bring him a drink, and he'll be having sex with a cartoon," she says.

The real life counterpart of Tenaj, the avatar, is Janet, who lives in Canada. Ric and Janet have never met—nor do they plan to meet. They haven't even talked on the phone as Ric and Janet—just a lot of sweet talking in their virtual world as Dutch and Tenaj.

For gamers, the virtual always overlaps the real to some extent, but for some the virtual overwhelms the real. A couple from South Korea even let their 3-month-old daughter starve to death while they nurtured a virtual daughter online (Frayer 2010).

For Your Consideration

→ How much time do you spend on computer games? Are you involved in any virtual reality? Do you think that Ric is cheating on Sue? Is this grounds for divorce? (One wife certainly thought so. She divorced her husband when she caught a glimpse of his avatar having sex with an avatar prostitute ["Second Life Affair . . ." 2008]). Other than the sexual aspect, is having a second life really any different from people's involvement in fantasy football? (Keep in mind the term *football widows*.)

How does the microchip affect your life? How does it influence your views of life?

Biotech Societies: Is a New Type of Society Emerging?

- Tobacco that fights cancer. ("Yes, smoke your way to health!")
- Corn that blocks herpes and prevents pregnancy. ("Corn flakes in the morning—and safe sex all day!")
- Goats' milk that contains spider silk to make fishing lines and body armor. ("Got milk? The best bulletproofing.")
- Part-human animals that produce medicines for humans. ("Ah, those liver secretions. Good for what ails you.")
- DNA that you can snap together like Lego blocks. ("Our BioBricks build better life forms.")
- Bacteria that excrete diesel fuel. ("Put our germ droppings in your gas tank.")

I know that such products sound like science fiction, but we *already* have the goats that make spider silk. Human genes have been inserted into animals, and they do produce medicine (Elias 2001; Kristoff 2002; Osborne 2002). The snap-together BioBricks should be available soon (Mooallem 2010). Perhaps one day, you will be able to design your own bacterium—or elephant. We already have the bacteria that produce diesel fuel, but it isn't harvestable yet (Mooallem 2010).

The changes swirling around us are so extensive that we may be stepping into a new type of society. If so, the economy of this new **biotech society** will center on applying and altering genetic structures—both plant and animal—to produce food, medicine, and materials.

If there is a new society—and this is not certain—when did it begin? There are no firm edges to new societies, for each new one overlaps the one it is replacing. The opening to a biotech society could have been 1953, when Francis Crick and James Watson identified the double-helix structure of DNA. Or perhaps historians will trace the date to the decoding of the human genome in 2001.

Whether the changes that are engulfing our lives are part of a new type of society or just a continuation of the one before it is not the main point. Keep your eye on the *sociological significance of these changes: As society is transformed, it sweeps us along with it. The transformation we are experiencing is so fundamental that it will change even the ways we think about the self and life.* We might even see changes in the human species, an implication of the Sociology and the New Technology box on the next page.

In Sum: Each society sets boundaries around its members. By laying a framework of statuses, roles, groups, and social institutions, society establishes the prevailing behaviors and beliefs. It also determines the type and extent of social inequality. These factors, in turn, set the stage for relationships between men and women, racial–ethnic groups, the young and the elderly, the rich and the poor, and so on.

Society is not stagnant, and *you* are affected directly by the sweeping historical changes that transform it. On the obvious level, if you lived in a hunting and gathering society you would not be listening to your favorite music, watching TV, playing video games—or taking this course. On a deeper level, you would not feel the same about life, have the same beliefs, or hold your particular aspirations for the future. Actually, no aspect of your life would be the same. You would be locked into the attitudes and views that come with a hunting and gathering way of life.

What Holds Society Together?

Some of the groups in our society would love to rip others apart. We are also in the midst of social change so extensive that we can barely keep up with it. How does a society manage to hold together? Let's examine two answers that sociologists have proposed.

Mechanical and Organic Solidarity.   Sociologist Emile Durkheim (1893/1933) was interested in how societies manage to create **social integration**—their members united by shared values and other social bonds. He found the answer in what he called **mechanical solidarity.** By this term, Durkheim meant that people who perform

"So, You Want to Be Yourself?" Cloning and the Future of Society

No type of society ends abruptly. The edges are fuzzy, as the old merges into the new. With time speeded up, our information society hasn't even matured, and it looks as though a biotech society is hard on its heels. Let's try to peer over the edge of today's society to glimpse the one that might be pressing on us. If it arrives, what will life be like? We could examine many issues, but since space is limited, let's consider just one: cloning. Since human embryos have been cloned, it seems inevitable that some group somewhere will complete the process. If cloning humans becomes routine—well, consider these two scenarios:

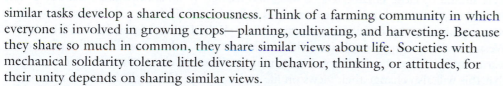

It turns out that you can't have children. You go to your area's cloning clinic, pay the standard fee, and clone either yourself or your spouse. But is that little boy or girl, in effect, either yourself or your spouse—as a child? Or instead of a daughter or son, is this child perhaps your sister or brother?

Or suppose that you love your mother dearly, and she is dying. With her permission, you decide to clone her. Who is the clone? Would you be rearing your own mother?

When we have genetic replicates, we will have to wrestle with new questions of human relationships: What is a clone's relationship to its "parents"? Indeed, what are "parents" and "children"?

Sources: Based on Kaebnick 2000; McGee 2000; Bjerklie et al. 2001; Davis 2001; Weiss 2004; Regalado 2005.

For Your Consideration

→ You might have heard people object that cloning is immoral. But have you heard the opposite, that cloning should be our moral choice? Let's suppose that mass cloning becomes possible. Let's also assume that geneticists trace great creative ability, high intelligence, compassion, and a propensity for peace to specific genes. They also identify a genetic base for the ability to create beautiful poetry, music, and architecture; to excel in mathematics, science, and other intellectual pursuits; even to be successful in love. Why, then, should we leave human reproduction to people who have inferior traits—genetic diseases, low IQs, perhaps even the propensity to be violent? Shouldn't we select people with the finer characteristics to reproduce—and to clone?

---

similar tasks develop a shared consciousness. Think of a farming community in which everyone is involved in growing crops—planting, cultivating, and harvesting. Because they share so much in common, they share similar views about life. Societies with mechanical solidarity tolerate little diversity in behavior, thinking, or attitudes, for their unity depends on sharing similar views.

As societies get larger, they develop different kinds of work, a specialized **division of labor.** Some people mine gold, others sell it, while still others turn it into jewelry. Such a division of labor disperses people into different interest groups where they develop different ideas about life. No longer do they depend on one another to have similar ideas and behaviors. Rather, they depend on one another for the specific work that each person contributes to the whole group.

Durkheim called this new form of solidarity based on interdependence **organic solidarity.** To see why he used this term, think about how you depend on your teacher to guide you through this introductory course in sociology. At the same time, without students your teacher would be without a job. You and your teacher are *like two organs in the same body.* (The "body" in this case is the college or university.) Although each of you performs different tasks, you depend on one another. This creates a form of unity.

Gemeinschaft and Gesellschaft.   Ferdinand Tönnies (1887/1988) also analyzed this fundamental shift in relationships. He used the term *Gemeinschaft* (Guh-MINE-shoft), or "intimate community," to describe village life, the type of society in which everyone knows everyone else. He noted that in the society that was emerging, the personal ties, kinship connections, and lifelong friendships that marked village life were being crowded out by short-term relationships, individual accomplishments, and self-interest. Tönnies called this new type of society *Gesellschaft* (Guh-ZELL-shoft), or "impersonal association." He did not mean that we no longer have intimate ties to family and friends but, rather,

The warm, more intimate relationships of *Gemeinschaft* society are apparent in the photo of Guambian women working together in Colombia. The more impersonal relationships of *Gesellschaft* society are evident in this Internet cafe in Brooklyn, where customers are ignoring one another.

that our lives no longer center on them. Few of us take jobs in a family business, for example, and contracts replace handshakes. Much of our time is spent with strangers and short-term acquaintances.

How Relevant Are These Concepts Today?   I know that *Gemeinschaft, Gesellschaft,* and *mechanical* and *organic solidarity* are strange terms and that Durkheim's and Tönnies' observations must seem like a dead issue. The concern these sociologists expressed, however—that their world was changing from a community in which people were united by close ties and shared ideas and feelings to an anonymous association built around impersonal, short-term contacts—is still very real. In large part, this same concern explains the rise of Islamic fundamentalism (Volti 1995). Islamic leaders fear that Western values will uproot their traditional culture, that cold rationality will replace the warm, informal, personal relationships among families and clans. They fear, rightly so, that this will also change their views on life and morality. Although the terms may sound strange, even obscure, you can see that the ideas remain a vital part of today's world.

In Sum: Whether the terms are *Gemeinschaft* and *Gesellschaft* or *mechanical solidarity* and *organic solidarity,* they indicate that as societies change, so do people's orientations to life. *The sociological point is that social structure sets the context for what we do, feel, and think, and ultimately, then, for the kind of people we become.* As you read the Cultural Diversity box on the next page, which describes one of the few remaining *Gemeinschaft* societies in the United States, think of how fundamentally different your life would be if you had been reared in an Amish family.

The Microsociological Perspective: Social Interaction in Everyday Life

As you have seen, macrosociologists examine the broad features of society. Micro-sociologists, in contrast, examine narrower slices of social life. Their primary focus is *face-to-face interaction*—what people do when they are in one another's presence. Before you study the main features of social interaction, look at the photo essay on pages 108–109. See if you can identify both social structure and social interaction in each of the photos.

continued on page 110

Can you identify the factors that integrate you into society?

Cultural Diversity in the United States

The Amish: *Gemeinschaft* Community in a *Gesellschaft* Society

U.S.A.

One of the best examples of a *Gemeinschaft* community in the United States is the Old Order Amish, followers of a group that broke away from the Swiss-German Mennonite church in the 1600s and settled in Pennsylvania around 1727. Most of today's 225,000 Old Order Amish live in just three states—Pennsylvania, Ohio, and Indiana.

Because Amish farmers use horses instead of tractors, most of their farms are one hundred acres or less. To the ten million tourists who pass through Lancaster County each year, the rolling green pastures, white farmhouses, simple barns, horse-drawn buggies, and clotheslines hung with somber-colored garments convey a sense of peace and innocence reminiscent of another era. Although just sixty-five miles from Philadelphia, "Amish country" is a world away.

The differences are striking—the horses and buggies from so long ago, the language (a dialect of German known as Pennsylvania Dutch), and the plain clothing—often black, no belt, in a style that has remained unchanged for almost 300 years. Beyond these externals is a value system that binds the Amish together, with religion and discipline the glue that maintains their way of life.

Amish life is based on separation from the world—an idea taken from Christ's Sermon on the Mount—and obedience to the church's teachings and leaders. This rejection of worldly concerns, writes sociologist Donald Kraybill (2002), "provides the foundation of such Amish values as humility, faithfulness, thrift, tradition, communal goals, joy of work, a slow-paced life, and trust in divine providence." The Amish believe that violence is bad, even in personal self-defense, and they register as conscientious objectors during times of war. They pay no Social Security, and they receive no government benefits.

To maintain this separation from the world, Amish children attend schools that are run by the Amish, and they attend only until the age of 13. (In 1972, the Supreme Court ruled that Amish parents have the right to take their children out of school after the eighth grade.) To go to school beyond the eighth grade would expose the children to values that would drive a wedge between the children and their community.

The *Gemeinschaft* of village life that has been largely lost to industrialization remains a vibrant part of Amish life. The Amish make their decisions in weekly meetings, where, by consensus, they follow a set of rules, or *Ordnung*, to guide their behavior. Brotherly love and the welfare of the community are paramount values. In times of birth, sickness, and death, neighbors pitch in with the chores. The family is also vital for Amish life. Nearly all Amish marry, and divorce is forbidden. The major events of Amish life take place in the home, including weddings, births, funerals, and church services. In these ways, they maintain the bonds of intimate community.

Because they cannot resist all change, the Amish try to adapt in ways that will least disrupt their core values. Urban sprawl poses a special threat as it has driven up the price of farmland. Unable to afford farms, about half of Amish men now work at jobs other than farming. The men go to great lengths to avoid leaving the home. Most work in farm-related businesses or operate woodcraft shops, but some have taken jobs in factories. With intimate, or *Gemeinschaft*, society essential to the Amish way of life, concerns have grown about how the men who work for non-Amish businesses are being exposed to the outside world. Some are using modern technology such as cell phones and computers at work. During the economic crisis, some who were laid off from their jobs even accepted unemployment checks—violating the fundamental principle of taking no help from the government.

Despite the threats posed by a materialistic and secular culture, the Amish are managing to retain their way of life. Perhaps the most poignant illustration of how greatly the Amish differ from the dominant culture is this: When in 2006 a non-Amish man shot several Amish girls and himself at a one-room school, the Amish community raised funds not only for the families of the dead children but also for the family of the killer.

Sources: Aeppel 1996; Kephart and Zellner 2001; Kraybill 2002; Johnson-Weiner 2007; Scolforo 2008; Buckley 2011.

For Your Consideration

→ Which of your *specific* ideas, attitudes, and behaviors would be different if you had been reared in an Amish family? What do you like and dislike about Amish life? Why?

THROUGH THE AUTHOR'S LENS

Vienna: Social Structure and Social Interaction

We live our lives within social structure. Just as a road is to a car, providing limits to where it can go, so social structure limits our behavior. Social structure—our culture, social class, statuses, roles, group memberships, and social institutions—points us in particular directions in life. Most of this direction-giving is beyond our awareness. But it is highly effective, giving shape to our social interactions, as well as to what we expect from life.

These photos that I took in Vienna, Austria, make visible some of social structure's limiting, shaping, and direction-giving. Most of the social structure that affects our lives is not physical, as with streets and buildings, but social, as with norms, belief systems, obligations, and the goals held out for us because of our ascribed statuses. In these photos, you should be able to see how social interaction takes form within social structure.

Vienna provides a mixture of the old and the new. Stephan's Dom (Cathedral) dates back to 1230, the carousel to now.

And what would Vienna be without its wieners? The word *wiener* actually comes from the name *Vienna*, which is *Wien* in German. *Wiener* means "from Vienna."

The main square in Vienna, Stephan Platz, provides a place to have a cup of coffee, read the newspaper, enjoy the architecture, or just watch the hustle and bustle of the city.

Part of the pull of the city is its offering of rich culture. I took this photo at one of the many operas held in Vienna each night.

In the appealing street cafes of Vienna, social structure and social interaction are especially evident. Can you see both in this photo?

And what would Vienna be without its world-famous beers? With beer stands on the street, the city's entrepreneurs make sure that the beer is within easy reach.

The city offers something for everyone, including unusual places for people to rest and to talk and to flirt with one another.

To be able to hang out with friends, not doing much, but doing it in the midst of stimulating sounds and sights—this is the vibrant city.

© James M Henslin, all photos

How people use space as they interact is studied by sociologists who have a microsociological focus. What do you seen in common in these two photos?

Symbolic Interaction

Symbolic interactionists are especially interested in the symbols people use. They want to know how people look at things and how this, in turn, affects their behavior and orientations to life. Of the many areas of social life that symbolic interactionists study, let's look at stereotypes, personal space, eye contact, smiling, and body language.

Stereotypes in Everyday Life.   You are familiar with how first impressions set the tone for interaction. When you first meet someone, you cannot help but notice certain features, especially the person's sex, race–ethnicity, age, and clothing. Despite your best intentions, your assumptions about these characteristics shape your first impressions. They also influence how you act toward that person—and, in turn, how that person acts toward you. These fascinating aspects of our social interaction are discussed in the Down-to-Earth Sociology box on the next page.

Personal Space.   We all surround ourselves with a "personal bubble" that we go to great lengths to protect. We open the bubble to intimates—to our friends, children, and parents—but we're careful to keep most people out of this space. In a crowded hallway between classes, we might walk with our books clasped in front of us (a strategy often chosen by females). When we stand in line, we make certain there is enough space so that we don't touch the person in front of us and aren't touched by the person behind us.

The amount of space that people prefer varies from one culture to another. South Americans, for example, like to be closer when they speak to others than do people reared in the United States. Anthropologist Edward Hall (1959; Hall and Hall 2012) recounts a conversation with a man from South America who had attended one of his lectures.

He came to the front of the class at the end of the lecture. . . . We started out facing each other, and as he talked I became dimly aware that he was standing a little too close and that I was beginning to back up. Fortunately I was able to suppress my first impulse and remain stationary because there was nothing to communicate aggression in his behavior except the conversational distance. . . .

By experimenting I was able to observe that as I moved away slightly, there was an associated shift in the pattern of interaction. He had more trouble expressing himself. If I shifted to where I felt comfortable (about twenty-one inches), he looked somewhat puzzled and hurt, almost as though he were saying, "Why is he acting that way? Here I am doing everything I can to talk to him in a friendly manner and he suddenly withdraws. Have I done anything wrong? Said something I shouldn't?" Having ascertained that distance had a direct effect on his conversation, I stood my ground, letting him set the distance.

How do you use personal space in your own interactions?

Down-to-Earth Sociology

Beauty May Be Only Skin Deep, But Its Effects Go On Forever

Mark Snyder, a psychologist, wondered whether **stereotypes**—our assumptions of what people are like—might be self-fulfilling. He came up with an ingenious way to test this idea. He (1993) gave college men a Polaroid snapshot of a woman (supposedly taken just moments before) and told them that he would introduce them to her after they talked with her on the telephone. Actually, the photographs—showing either a pretty or a homely woman—had been prepared before the experiment began. The photo was *not* of the woman the men would talk to.

Stereotypes came into play immediately. As Snyder gave each man the photograph, he asked him what he thought the woman would be like. The men who saw the photograph of the attractive woman said that they expected to meet a poised, humorous, outgoing woman. The men who had been given a photo of the unattractive woman described her as awkward, serious, and unsociable.

The men's stereotypes influenced the way they spoke to the women on the telephone, who did *not* know about the photographs. The men who had seen the photograph of a pretty woman were warm, friendly, and humorous. This, in turn, affected the women they spoke to, for they responded in a warm, friendly, outgoing manner. And the men who had seen the photograph of a homely woman? On the phone, they were cold, reserved, and humorless, and the women they spoke to became cool, reserved, and humorless. Keep in mind that the women did not know that their looks had been evaluated—and that the photographs were not even of them. In short, stereotypes tend to produce behaviors that match the stereotype. This principle is illustrated in Figure 4.5.

Beauty might be only skin deep, but it has real consequences. Bosses are more willing to hire individuals whom they perceive as good-looking, others are more willing to interact with them, and they bring in more clients and business. The result is serious money. On average, the more attractive earn between 10 and 15 percent more than plain folks, about $200,000 more over a lifetime (Judge et al. 2009; Hamermesh 2011).

For Your Consideration

➜ Stereotypes have no single, inevitable effect, but they do influence how we react to one another.

➜ Instead of beauty, consider gender and race–ethnicity. How do they influence those who do the stereotyping and those who are stereotyped?

Based on the experiments summarized here, how do you think men would modify their interactions if they were to meet these two women? And if women were to meet these two women, would they modify their interactions in the same way?

FIGURE 4.5   How Self-Fulfilling Stereotypes Work

We see features of the person or hear things about the person.

↓

We fit what we see or hear into stereotypes and then expect the person to act in certain ways.

↓

How we expect the person to act shapes our attitudes and actions.

↓

From how we act, the person gets ideas of how we perceive him or her.

↓

The behaviors of the person change to match our expectations, thus confirming the stereotype.

Source: By the author.

How do stereotypes influence people's behavior? How about yours?

Among the applications of body language is teaching U. S. soldiers to "read" the intent of civilians.

After Hall (1969; Hall and Hall 2012) analyzed situations like this, he observed that North Americans use four different "distance zones."

1. *Intimate distance.* This is the zone that the South American unwittingly invaded. It extends to about 18 inches from our bodies. We reserve this space for comforting, protecting, hugging, intimate touching, and lovemaking.
2. *Personal distance.* This zone extends from 18 inches to 4 feet. We reserve it for friends and acquaintances and ordinary conversations. This is the zone in which Hall would have preferred speaking with the South American.
3. *Social distance.* This zone, extending out from us about 4 to 12 feet, marks impersonal or formal relationships. We use this zone for such things as job interviews.
4. *Public distance.* This zone, extending beyond 12 feet, marks even more formal relationships. It is used to separate dignitaries and public speakers from the general public.

Eye Contact.   One way that we protect our personal bubble is by controlling eye contact. Letting someone gaze into our eyes—unless the person is an eye doctor—can be taken as a sign that we are attracted to that person, even as an invitation to intimacy. Wanting to become "the friendliest store in town," a chain of supermarkets in Illinois ordered its checkout clerks to make direct eye contact with each customer. Female clerks complained that male customers were taking their eye contact the wrong way, as an invitation to intimacy. Management said they were exaggerating. The clerks' reply was, "We know the kind of looks we're getting back from men," and they refused to make direct eye contact with them.

Smiling.   In the United States, we take it for granted that clerks will smile as they wait on us. But it isn't this way in all cultures. Apparently, Germans aren't used to smiling clerks, and when Wal-Mart expanded into Germany, it brought its American ways with it. The company ordered its German clerks to smile at their customers. They did—and the customers complained. The German customers interpreted the smiles as flirting (Samor et al. 2006).

Body Language.   While we are still little children, we learn to interpret **body language,** the ways people use their bodies to give messages to others. This skill in interpreting facial expressions, posture, and gestures is essential for getting through everyday life. Without it—as is the case for people with Asperger's syndrome—we wouldn't know how to react to others. It would even be difficult to know whether someone were serious or joking.

In *dramaturgy*, a specialty within sociology, social life is viewed as similar to the theater. In our everyday lives, we all are actors. Like those in the cast of *South Park*, we, too, perform roles, use props, and deliver lines to fellow actors—who, in turn, do the same.

Applied Body Language.   Our common and essential skill of interpreting body language has become one of the government's tools in its fight against terrorism. Because many of our body messages lie beneath our consciousness, airport personnel and interrogators are being trained to look for telltale facial signs—from a quick downturn of the mouth to rapid blinking—that might indicate nervousness or lying (Davis et al. 2002). The U.S. army is also trying to determine how to apply body language to alert soldiers to danger when interacting with civilians in a military zone (Yager et al. 2009).

This is an interesting twist for an area of sociology that had been entirely theoretical. Let's now turn to dramaturgy, a special area of symbolic interactionism.

Dramaturgy: The Presentation of Self in Everyday Life

It was their big day, two years in the making. Jennifer Mackey wore a white wedding gown adorned with an 11-foot train and 24,000 seed pearls that she and her mother had sewn onto the dress. Next to her at the altar in Lexington, Kentucky, stood her intended, Jeffrey Degler, in black tie. They said their vows, then turned to gaze for a moment at the four hundred guests.

How do you use your body to give messages to others?

That's when groomsman Daniel Mackey collapsed. As the shocked organist struggled to play Mendelssohn's "Wedding March," Mr. Mackey's unconscious body was dragged away, his feet striking—loudly—every step of the altar stairs.

"I couldn't believe he would die at my wedding," the bride said. (Hughes 1990)

Sociologist Erving Goffman (1922–1982) added a new twist to microsociology when he recast the theatrical term **dramaturgy** into a sociological term. Goffman (1959/1999) used the term to mean that social life is like a drama or a stage play: Birth ushers us onto the stage of everyday life, and our socialization consists of learning to perform on that stage. The self that we studied in the previous chapter lies at the center of our performances. We have ideas about how we want others to think of us, and we use our roles in everyday life to communicate these ideas. Goffman called our efforts to manage the impressions that others receive of us **impression management.**

Stages.   Everyday life, said Goffman, involves playing our assigned roles. We have *front stages* on which to perform them, as did Jennifer and Jeffrey. (By the way, Daniel Mackey didn't really die—he had just fainted.) But we don't have to look at weddings to find front stages. Everyday life is filled with them. Where your teacher lectures is a front stage. And if you wait until your parents are in a good mood to tell them some bad news, you are using a front stage. In fact, you spend most of your time on front stages, for a front stage is wherever you deliver your lines. We also have *back stages,* places where we can retreat and let our hair down. When you close the bathroom or bedroom door for privacy, for example, you are entering a back stage.

Role Performance, Conflict, and Strain.   Everyday life brings with it many roles. As discussed earlier, the same person may be a student, a teenager, a shopper, a worker, and a date, as well as a daughter or a son. Although a role lays down the basic outline for a performance, it also allows a great deal of flexibility. The particular emphasis or interpretation that we give a role, our "style," is known as **role performance.** Consider how you play your role as a son or daughter. Perhaps you play the role of ideal daughter or son—being respectful, coming home at the hours your parents set, and so forth. Or this description may not even come close to your particular role performance.

Ordinarily, our statuses are separated sufficiently that we find minimal conflict between them. Occasionally, however, what is expected of us in one status (our role) is incompatible with what is expected of us in another status. This problem, known as **role conflict,** is illustrated in Figure 4.6 on the next page, in which family, friendship, student, and work roles come crashing together. Usually, however, we manage to avoid role conflict by segregating our statuses, although doing so can require an intense juggling act.

Sometimes the *same* status contains incompatible roles, a conflict known as **role strain.** Suppose that you are exceptionally well prepared for a particular class assignment. Although the instructor asks an unusually difficult question, you find yourself knowing the answer when no one else does. If you want to raise your hand, yet don't want to make your fellow students look bad, you will experience role strain. As illustrated in Figure 4.6, the difference between role conflict and role strain is that role conflict is conflict *between* roles, while role strain is conflict *within* a role.

Teamwork.   Being a good role player brings positive recognition from others, something we all covet. To accomplish this, we use **teamwork**—two or more people working together to help a performance come off as planned. If you laugh at your boss's jokes, even though you don't find them funny, you are practicing teamwork to help your boss give a good performance.

If a performance doesn't come off quite right, the team might try to save it by using **face-saving behavior.**

Suppose your teacher is about to make an important point. Suppose also that her lecturing has been outstanding and the class is hanging on every word. Just as she pauses for emphasis, her stomach lets out a loud growl. She might then use a face-saving technique by remarking, "I was so busy preparing for class that I didn't get breakfast this morning."

Read
The Presentation of Self
by Irving Goffman
on **mysoclab.com**

Explore
Living Data
on **mysoclab.com**

FIGURE 4.6   Role Strain and Role Conflict

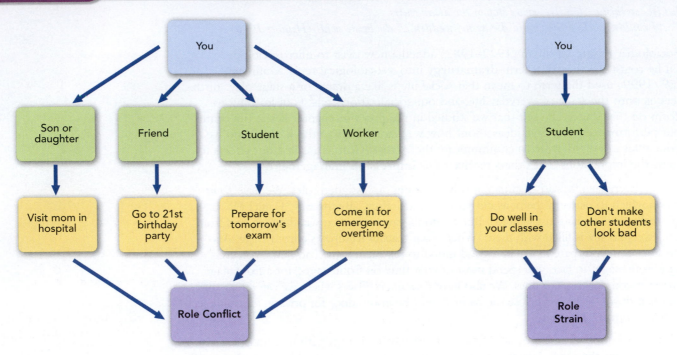

Source: By the author.

It is more likely, however, that both the teacher and class will simply ignore the sound, giving the impression that no one heard a thing—a face-saving technique called *studied nonobservance*. This allows the teacher to make the point or, as Goffman would say, it allows the performance to go on.

Because our own body is identified so closely with the self, a good part of impression management centers on "body messages." The messages that are attached to various body shapes change over time, but, as explored in the Mass Media box on the next page, thinness currently screams "desirability."

Applying Impression Management.   I can just hear someone say, "Impression management is interesting, but is it really important?" It certainly is. Impression management is so significant that it can even make a vital difference in your career. To be promoted, you must be perceived as someone who *should* be promoted. You must appear dominant. Giving this impression is less of a problem for men because stereotypes join masculinity and dominance at the hip. For women, though, stereotypes separate femininity from dominance. To stress dominance, a woman could wear loud clothing and curse. This would get her noticed—but it likely would not put her on the

Both individuals and organizations do *impression management*, trying to communicate messages about the self (or organization) that best meets their goals. At times, these efforts fail.

Can you tell the difference between role strain and role conflict? What is applied impression management?

"Nothing Tastes as Good as Thin Feels": Body Images and the Mass Media

When you stand before a mirror, do you like what you see? To make your body more attractive, do you watch your weight or work out? You have ideas about what you should look like. Where did you get them?

TV and magazine ads keep pounding home the message that our bodies aren't good enough. The way to improve them, of course, is to buy the advertised products: hair extensions, padded bras, diet programs, anti-aging products, and exercise equipment. Muscular hulks show off machines that magically produce "six-pack abs" and incredible biceps—in just a few minutes a day. Female movie stars go through tough workouts without even breaking into a sweat. Women and men get the feeling that attractive members of the opposite sex will flock to them if they purchase that wonder-working workout machine.

Although we try to shrug off such messages, they still penetrate our thinking and feelings, helping to shape ideal images of how we "ought" to look. Those models so attractively clothed and coiffed as they walk down the runway, could they be any thinner? For women, the message is clear: You can't be thin enough. The men's message is also clear: You can't be muscular enough.

With impossibly shaped models at *Victoria's Secret* and skinny models showing off the latest fashions in *Vogue* and *Seventeen*, half of U.S. adolescent girls feel fat and count calories (Grabe et al. 2008). Sixty percent of girls think that the secret to popularity is being thin (Zaslow 2009). Some teens even call the plastic surgeon. Anxious lest their child violate peer ideals and trail behind in her race for popularity, parents foot the bill. Some parents pay $5,000 just to give their daughters a flatter tummy (Gross 1998).

Cruise the Internet, and you will find "thinspiration" videos on YouTube that feature emaciated girls proudly displaying their skeletal frames. You will also find "pro-ana" (pro-anorexic) sites where eating disorders are promoted as a lifestyle choice (Zaslow 2009). The title of this box, "Nothing Tastes as Good as Thin Feels," is taken from one of these sites.

And attractiveness does pay off. U.S. economists studied physical attractiveness and earnings. The result? "Good-looking" men and women earn the most, "average-looking" men and women earn more than "plain" people, and the "ugly" earn the least (Hamermesh 2011). Then there is that interesting cash "bonus" that "attractive" women have: Even if they are bubble-heads, they attract and marry higher-earning men (Kanazawa and Kovar 2004).

More popularity *and* more money? Maybe you can't be thin enough after all. Maybe those exercise machines are a good investment. If only we could catch up with the Japanese who have developed a soap that "sucks the fat right out of your pores" (Marshall 1995). You can practically hear the jingle now.

For Your Consideration

➤ What images do you have of your body? How do cultural expectations of "ideal" bodies underlie your images? Can you recall any advertisements or television programs that have affected your body image?

➤ Most advertising that focuses on weight is directed at women. Women are more likely than men to be dissatisfied with their bodies and to have eating disorders (Honeycutt 1995; Austin et al. 2009). Of all cosmetic surgery, ninety percent is performed on women (American Society of Plastic Surgeons 2011). Do you think that the targeting of women in advertising creates these attitudes and behaviors? Or do you think that these attitudes and behaviors would exist even if there were no such ads? Why?

➤ To counteract the emphasis on being skinny, some clothing companies are featuring "plus-size" models. What do you think of this?

All of us contrast the reality we see when we look in the mirror with our culture's ideal body types. The thinness craze, discussed in this box, encourages some people to extremes, as with Keira Knightley. It also makes it difficult for larger people to have positive self-images. Overcoming this difficulty, Gabourey Sidibe is in the forefront of promoting an alternative image.

path to promotion. Career counselors do advise women to tone down the femininity, but in a different way. They suggest that female executives use makeup that doesn't have to be reapplied during the day, during executive sessions to place their hands on the table, not in their laps—and not to carry a purse, but to stash it inside a briefcase (Needham 2006; Brinkley 2008; Agins 2009).

Male or female, in your own life you will have to find the best way to manage impressions in order to further your career. Much success in the work world depends not on what you know but, instead, on your ability to give the impression that you know what you should know.

Ethnomethodology: Uncovering Background Assumptions

Certainly one of the strangest words in sociology is *ethnomethodology*. To better understand this term, consider the word's three basic components. *Ethno* means "folk" or "people"; *method* means how people do something; *ology* means "the study of." Putting them together, then, *ethno–method–ology* means "the study of how people do things." Specifically, **ethnomethodology** is the study of how people use commonsense understandings to make sense of life.

Let's suppose that during a routine office visit, your doctor remarks that your hair is rather long, then takes out a pair of scissors and starts to give you a haircut. You would feel strange about this, for your doctor would be violating **background assumptions**—your ideas about the way life is and the way things ought to work. These assumptions, which lie at the root of everyday life, are so deeply embedded in our consciousness that we are seldom aware of them, and most of us fulfill them unquestioningly. Thus, your doctor does not offer you a haircut, even if he or she is good at cutting hair and you need one!

The founder of ethnomethodology, sociologist Harold Garfinkel, conducted exercises to reveal our background assumptions. Garfinkel (1967, 2002) asked his students to act as though they did not understand the basic rules of social life. Some tried to bargain with supermarket clerks; others would inch close to people and stare directly at them. They were met with surprise, bewilderment, even anger. In one exercise, Garfinkel asked students to act as though they were boarders in their own homes. They addressed their parents as "Mr." and "Mrs.," asked permission to use the bathroom, sat stiffly, were courteous, and spoke only when spoken to.

All of us have *background assumptions,* deeply ingrained assumptions of how the world operates. What contrasting background assumptions do you think are operating here?

As you can imagine, the other family members didn't know what to make of this (Garfinkel 1967):

> They vigorously sought to make the strange actions intelligible and to restore the situation to normal appearances. Reports (by the students) were filled with accounts of astonishment, bewilderment, shock, anxiety, embarrassment, and anger, and with charges by various family members that the student was mean, inconsiderate, selfish, nasty, or impolite. Family members demanded explanations: What's the matter? What's gotten into you? . . . Are you sick? . . . Are you out of your mind or are you just stupid?

Students can be highly creative when they are asked to break background assumptions. The young children of one of my students were surprised one morning when they came down for breakfast to find a sheet spread on the living room

What background assumptions do you have? How do they help you navigate social life?

floor. On it were dishes, silverware, lit candles—and bowls of ice cream. They, too, wondered what was going on, but they dug eagerly into the ice cream before their mother could change her mind.

This is a risky assignment to give students, however, for breaking some background assumptions can make people suspicious. When a colleague of mine gave this assignment, a couple of his students began to wash dollar bills in a laundromat. By the time they put the bills in the dryer, the police had arrived.

In Sum: Ethnomethodologists explore *background assumptions,* the taken-for-granted ideas about the world that underlie our behavior. Most of these assumptions, or basic rules of social life, are unstated. We learn them as we learn our culture, and we violate them only with risk. Deeply embedded in our minds, they give us basic directions for living everyday life.

The Social Construction of Reality

On a visit to Morocco, in northern Africa, I decided to buy a watermelon. When I indicated to the street vendor that the knife he was going to use to cut the watermelon was dirty (encrusted with filth would be more apt), he was very obliging. He immediately bent down and began to swish the knife in a puddle on the street. I shuddered as I looked at the passing burros that were urinating and defecating as they went by. Quickly, I indicated by gesture that I preferred my melon uncut after all.

"If people define situations as real, they are real in their consequences," said sociologists W. I. and Dorothy S. Thomas in what has become known as *the definition of the situation,* or the **Thomas theorem.** For that vendor of watermelons, germs did not exist. For me, they did. And each of us acted according to our definition of the situation. My perception and behavior did not come from the fact that germs are real but, rather, from *my having grown up in a society that teaches that germs are real.* Microbes, of course, *objectively* exist, and whether or not germs are part of our thought world makes no difference as to whether we are infected by them. Our behavior, however, does not depend on the *objective* existence of something but, rather, on our *subjective interpretation,* on what sociologists call our *definition of reality.* In other words, it is not the reality of microbes that impresses itself on us, but society that impresses the reality of microbes on us.

Sociologists call this the **social construction of reality.** From the social groups to which we belong (the *social* part of this process), we learn ways of looking at life. We learn ways to view Hitler and Osama bin Laden (they're good, they're evil), germs (they exist, they don't exist), and *just about everything else in life.* In short, through our interaction with others, we *construct reality;* that is, we learn ways of interpreting our experiences in life.

Gynecological Examinations.   To better understand the social construction of reality, let's consider what I learned when I interviewed a gynecological nurse who had been present at about 14,000 vaginal examinations, I focused on *how doctors construct social reality in order to define the examination as nonsexual* (Henslin and Biggs 1971/2012). It became apparent that the pelvic examination unfolds much as a stage play does. I will use "he" to refer to the physician because only male physicians were part of this study. Perhaps the results would be different with women gynecologists.

Scene 1 (the patient as person) In this scene, the doctor maintains eye contact with his patient, calls her by name, and discusses her problems in a professional manner. If he decides that a vaginal examination is necessary, he tells a nurse, "Pelvic in room 1." By this statement, he is announcing that a major change will occur in the next scene.

Scene 2 (from person to pelvic) This scene is the depersonalizing stage. In line with the doctor's announcement, the patient begins the transition from a "person" to a "pelvic." The doctor leaves the room, and a female nurse enters to help the patient make the transition. The nurse prepares the "props" for the coming examination and answers any questions the woman might have.

What occurs at this point is essential for the social construction of reality, for *the doctor's absence removes even the suggestion of sexuality*. To undress in front of him could suggest either a striptease or intimacy, thus undermining the reality that the team is so carefully defining: that of nonsexuality.

The patient, too, wants to remove any hint of sexuality, and during this scene she may express concern about what to do with her panties. Some mutter to the nurse, "I don't want him to see these." Most women solve the problem by either slipping their panties under their other clothes or placing them in their purse.

Scene 3 (the person as pelvic) This scene opens when the doctor enters the room. Before him is a woman lying on a table, her feet in stirrups, her knees tightly together, and her body covered by a drape sheet. The doctor seats himself on a low stool before the woman and says, "Let your knees fall apart" (rather than the sexually loaded "Spread your legs"), and begins the examination.

The drape sheet is crucial in this process of desexualization, for it *dissociates the pelvic area from the person*: Leaning forward and with the drape sheet above his head, the physician can see only the vagina, not the patient's face. Thus dissociated from the individual, the vagina is transformed dramaturgically into an object of analysis. If the doctor examines the patient's breasts, he also dissociates them from her person by examining them one at a time, with a towel covering the unexamined breast. Like the vagina, each breast becomes an isolated item dissociated from the person.

In this third scene, the patient cooperates in being an object, becoming, for all practical purposes, a pelvis to be examined. She withdraws eye contact from the doctor, and usually from the nurse, is likely to stare at a wall or at the ceiling, and avoids initiating conversation.

Scene 4 (from pelvic to person) In this scene, the patient becomes "repersonalized." The doctor has left the examining room; the patient dresses and fixes her hair and makeup. Her reemergence as a person is indicated by such statements to the nurse as "My dress isn't too wrinkled, is it?" showing a need for reassurance that the metamorphosis from "pelvic" back to "person" has been completed satisfactorily.

Scene 5 (the patient as person) In this final scene, the patient is once again treated as a person rather than as an object. The doctor makes eye contact with her and addresses her by name. She, too, makes eye contact with the doctor, and the usual middle-class interaction patterns are followed. She has been fully restored.

In Sum: To an outsider to our culture, the custom of women going to a male stranger for a vaginal examination might seem bizarre. But not to us. We learn that pelvic examinations are nonsexual. To sustain this definition requires teamwork— patients, doctors, and nurses, working together to *socially construct reality*.

It is not just pelvic examinations or our views of microbes that make up our definitions of reality. Rather, *our behavior depends on how we define reality*. Our definitions (our constructions) provide the basis for what we do and how we feel. To understand human behavior, then, we must know how people define reality.

The Need for Both Macrosociology and Microsociology

As noted earlier, both microsociology and macrosociology make vital contributions to our understanding of human behavior. Without one or the other, our understanding of social life would be vastly incomplete. The photo essay on the next two pages should help to make clear why we need *both* perspectives.

To illustrate this point, let's consider two groups of high school boys studied by sociologist William Chambliss (1973/2012). Both groups attended Hanibal High School. In one group were eight middle-class boys who came from "good" families and were perceived by the community as "going somewhere." Chambliss calls this group the "Saints." The other group consisted of six lower-class boys who were seen as headed down a dead-end road. Chambliss calls this group the "Roughnecks."

Boys in both groups skipped school, got drunk, got in fights, and vandalized property. The Saints were actually truant more often and involved in more vandalism, but the Saints had a good reputation. It was the Roughnecks who were seen by teachers, the police, and the general community as no good and headed for trouble.

The boys' reputations set them on separate paths. Seven of the eight Saints went on to graduate from college. Three studied for advanced degrees: One finished law school and became active in state politics, one finished medical school, and one went on to earn a Ph.D. The four other college graduates entered managerial or executive training programs with large firms. After his parents divorced, one Saint failed to graduate from high school on time and had to repeat his senior year. Although this boy tried to go to college by attending night school, he never finished. He was unemployed the last time Chambliss saw him.

In contrast, two of the Roughnecks dropped out of high school. They were later convicted of separate murders and sent to prison. Of the four who graduated from high school, two had done exceptionally well in sports and were awarded athletic scholarships to college. They both graduated from college and became high school coaches. Of the two others who completed high school, one became a small-time gambler and the other disappeared "up north," where he was last reported to be driving a truck.

To understand what happened to the Saints and the Roughnecks, we need to grasp *both* social structure and social interaction. Using *macrosociology*, we can place these boys within the larger framework of the U.S. social class system. This reveals how opportunities open or close to people depending on their social class and how people learn different goals as they grow up in different groups. We can then use *microsociology* to follow their everyday lives. We can see how the Saints manipulated their "good" reputations to skip classes and how their access to automobiles allowed them to protect their reputations by spreading their troublemaking around different communities. In contrast, the Roughnecks, who did not have cars, were highly visible. Their lawbreaking, which was limited to a small area, readily came to the attention of the community. Microsociology also reveals how their reputations opened doors of opportunity to the first group of boys while closing them to the other.

It is clear that we need both kinds of sociology, and both are stressed in the following chapters.

Why do we need both macrosociology and microsociology?

When a Tornado Strikes: Social Organization Following a Natural Disaster

As I was watching television on March 20, 2003, I heard a report that a tornado had hit Camilla, Georgia. "Like a big lawn mower," the report said, it had cut a path of destruction through this little town. In its fury, the tornado had left behind six dead and about 200 injured.

From sociological studies of natural disasters, I knew that immediately after the initial shock the survivors of natural disasters work together to try to restore order to their disrupted lives. I wanted to see this restructuring process first-hand. The next morning, I took off for Georgia.

These photos, taken the day after the tornado struck, tell the story of people in the midst of trying to put their lives back together. I was impressed at how little time people spent commiserating about their misfortune and how quickly they took practical steps to restore their lives.

As we look at these photos, try to determine why we need both microsociology and macrosociology to understand what occurs after a natural disaster.

For children, family photos are not as important as toys. This girl has managed to salvage a favorite toy, which will help anchor her to her previous life.

Personal relationships are essential in putting lives together. Consequently, reminders of these relationships are one of the main possessions that people attempt to salvage. This young man, having just recovered the family photo album, is eagerly reviewing the photos.

After making sure that their loved ones are safe, one of the next steps people take is to recover their possessions. The cooperation that emerges among people, as documented in the sociological literature on natural disasters, is illustrated here.

© James M. Henslin, all photos

In addition to the inquiring sociologist, television teams also were interviewing survivors and photographing the damage. This was the second time in just three years that a tornado had hit this neighborhood.

Formal organizations also help the survivors of natural disasters recover. In this neighborhood, I saw representatives of insurance companies, the police, the fire department, and an electrical co-op. The Salvation Army brought meals to the neighborhood.

No building or social institution escapes a tornado as it follows its path of destruction. Just the night before, members of this church had held evening worship service. After the tornado, someone mounted a U.S. flag on top of the cross, symbolic of the church members' patriotism and religiosity—and of their enduring hope.

The owners of this house invited me inside to see what the tornado had done to their home. In what had been her dining room, this woman is trying to salvage whatever she can from the rubble. She and her family survived by taking refuge in the bathroom. They had been there only five seconds, she said, when the tornado struck.

Like electricity and gas, communications need to be restored as soon as possible.

CHAPTER 4 Summary and Review

Levels of Sociological Analysis

What two levels of analysis do sociologists use?

Sociologists use macrosociological and microsociological levels of analysis. In **macrosociology,** the focus is placed on large-scale features of social life, while in **microsociology,** the focus is on **social interaction.** Functionalists and conflict theorists tend to use a macrosociological approach, while symbolic interactionists are more likely to use a micro-sociological approach P. 94.

The Macrosociological Perspective: Social Structure

How does social structure influence our behavior?

The term **social structure** refers to the social envelope that surrounds us and establishes limits on our behavior. Social structure consists of culture, social class, social statuses, roles, groups, and social institutions. Our location in the social structure underlies our perceptions, attitudes, and behaviors. Pp. 94–95.

Culture lays the broadest framework, while **social class** divides people according to income, education, and occupational prestige. Each of us receives **ascribed statuses** at birth; later we add **achieved statuses.** Our behaviors and orientations are further influenced by the **roles** we play, the **groups** to which we belong, and our experiences with social institutions. These components of society work together to help maintain social order. Pp. 95–99.

What are social institutions?

Social institutions are the standard ways that a society develops to meet its basic needs. As summarized in Figure 4.2 (page 100), industrial and postindustrial societies have ten social institutions—the family, religion, education, economy, medicine, politics, law, science, the military, and the mass media. From the functionalist perspective, social institutions meet universal group needs, or *functional requisites.* Conflict theorists stress how society's elites use social institutions to maintain their privileged positions. Pp. 99, 100.

What social revolutions have transformed society?

The discovery that animals and plants could be domesticated marked the *first* social revolution. This transformed **hunting and gathering societies** into **pastoral** and **horticultural societies.** The invention of the plow brought about the *second* social revolution, as societies became **agricultural.**

The invention of the steam engine, which led to **industrial societies,** marked the *third* social revolution. The *fourth* social revolution was ushered in by the invention of the microchip, leading to the **postindustrial** or **information society**. Another new type of society, the **biotech society,** may be emerging. As in the previous social revolutions, little will remain the same. Our attitudes, ideas, expectations, behaviors, relationships—all will be transformed. Pp. 99–104.

What holds society together?

According to Emile Durkheim, in agricultural societies people are united by **mechanical solidarity** (having similar views and feelings). With industrialization comes **organic solidarity** (people depend on one another to do their more specialized jobs). Ferdinand Tönnies pointed out that the informal means of control in *Gemeinschaft* (small, intimate) societies are replaced by formal mechanisms in *Gesellschaft* (larger, more impersonal) societies. Pp. 104–109.

The Microsociological Perspective: Social Interaction in Everyday Life

What is the focus of symbolic interactionism?

In contrast to functionalist and conflict theorists, who as macrosociologists focus on the "big picture," symbolic interactionists tend to be microsociologists who focus on face-to-face social interaction. Symbolic interactionists analyze how people define their worlds, and how their definitions, in turn, influence their behavior. Pp. 106, 110.

Do stereotypes affect social interaction?

Stereotypes are assumptions of what people are like. When we first meet people, we classify them according to our perceptions of their visible characteristics. Our ideas about these characteristics guide our behavior toward them. Our behavior, in turn, may influence them to behave in ways that reinforce our stereotypes. Pp. 110–111.

Do all human groups share a similar sense of personal space?

In examining how people use physical space, symbolic interactionists stress that we surround ourselves with a "personal bubble" that we carefully protect. People from different cultures use "personal bubbles" of varying sizes, so the answer to the question is no. Americans typically use four different "distance zones": intimate, personal, social, and public. Pp. 110, 112.

What is dramaturgy?

Erving Goffman developed **dramaturgy** (or dramaturgical analysis), in which everyday life is analyzed in terms of the stage. At the core of this analysis is **impression management,** our attempts to control the impressions we make on others. Our performances often call for **teamwork** and **face-saving behavior.** Pp. 112–117.

What is the social construction of reality?

The phrase **the social construction of reality** refers to how we construct our views of the world, which, in turn, underlie our actions. **Ethnomethodology** is the study of how people make sense of everyday life. Ethnomethodologists try to uncover **background assumptions,** our basic ideas about the way life is. Pp. 117–119.

The Need for Both Macrosociology and Microsociology

Why are both levels of analysis necessary?

Because each focuses on different aspects of the human experience, both microsociology and macrosociology are necessary for us to understand social life. Pp. 119–121.

Thinking Critically about Chapter 4

1. The major components of social structure are culture, social class, social status, roles, groups, and social institutions. Use social structure to explain why Native Americans have such a low rate of college graduation. (See Table 9.3 on page 261.)

2. Dramaturgy is a form of microsociology. Use dramaturgy to analyze a situation with which you are intimately familiar (such as interaction with your family or friends or in one of your college classes).

3. To illustrate why we need both macrosociology and microsociology to understand social life, analyze the situation of a student getting kicked out of college.

Social Groups and Formal Organizations

When Kody Scott joined the L.A. Crips, his initiation had two parts. Here's the first:

> *"How old is you now anyway?"*
>
> *"Eleven, but I'll be twelve in November."*
>
> *I never saw the blow to my head come from Huck. Bam! And I was on all fours. . . . Kicked in the stomach, I was on my back counting stars in the blackness. A solid blow to my chest exploded pain on the blank screen that had now become my mind. Bam! Blows rained on me from every direction. . . .*
>
> *Then I just started swinging, with no style or finesse, just anger and the instinct to survive. . . . [This] reflected my ability to represent the set [gang] in hand-to-hand combat. The blows stopped abruptly. . . . My ear was bleeding, and my neck and face were deep red. . . .*

Scott's beating was followed immediately by the second part of his initiation. For this, he received the name *Monster,* which he carried proudly:

> *"Give Kody the pump" [12-gauge pump action shotgun] . . . "Tonight we gonna rock they world." . . . Hand slaps were passed around the room. . . . "Kody, you got eight shots, you don't come back to the car unless they all are gone."*

"Bangin'. . . . It's gettin' caught and not tellin'. Killin' and not caring, and dyin' without fear."

> *"Righteous," I said, eager to show my worth. . . .*
>
> *Hanging close to buildings, houses, and bushes, we made our way, one after the other, to within spitting distance of the Bloods. . . . Huck and Fly` stepped from the shadows simultaneously. . . . Boom! Boom! Heavy bodies hitting the ground, confusion, yells of dismay, running. . . . By my sixth shot I had advanced past the first fallen bodies and into the street in pursuit of those who had sought refuge behind cars and trees. . . .*
>
> *Back in the shack we smoked more pot and drank more beer. . . .*
>
> *Tray Ball said, "You got potential, 'cause you eager to learn. Bangin' [being a gang member] ain't no part-time thang, it's full-time, it's a career. . . . It's gettin' caught and not tellin'. Killin' and not caring, and dyin' without fear. It's love for your set and hate for the enemy. You hear what I'm sayin'?"*

Kody adds this insightful remark:

> *. . . The supreme sacrifice was to "take a bullet for a homie" [fellow gang member]. Nothing held a light to the power of the set. If you died on the trigger you surely were smiled upon by the Crip God.*

Excerpts from Scott 1994:8–13, 103.

British Columbia, Canada

Could you be like Kody and shoot strangers in cold blood—just because others tell you to pull the trigger and you want their approval? Although none of us want to think that we could, don't bet on it. You are going to read some surprising things about groups in this chapter.

Groups within Society

Groups, people who think of themselves as belonging together and who interact with one another, are the essence of life in society. Groups are vital for our well-being. They provide intimate relationships and a sense of belonging, something that we all need. This chapter, then, is highly significant for your life.

Before we analyze groups, we should clarify the concept. Two terms sometimes confused with group are *aggregate* and *category*. An **aggregate** consists of people who temporarily share the same physical space but who do not see themselves as belonging together. Shoppers standing in a checkout line or drivers waiting at a red light are an aggregate. A **category** is simply a statistic. It consists of people who share similar characteristics, such as all college women who wear glasses or all men over 6 feet tall. Unlike group members, the individuals who make up a category don't think of themselves as belonging together and they don't interact with one another. These concepts are illustrated in the photos on the next page.

Groups are so influential that they determine who we are. If you think that this is an exaggeration, recall what you read in Chapter 3, that even your mind is a product of society—or, more specifically phrased, of the groups to which you belong. To better understand the influence of groups on your life, let's begin by looking at the types of groups that make up our society.

Primary Groups

How important has your family been to you?

Your first group, the family, has given you your basic orientations to life. Later, among friends, you have found more intimacy and an expanded sense of belonging. These groups are what sociologist Charles Cooley called **primary groups.** By providing intimate, face-to-face interaction, they give us an identity, a feeling of who we are. As Cooley (1909) put it,

> By primary groups I mean those characterized by intimate face-to-face association and cooperation. They are primary in several senses, but chiefly in that they are fundamental in forming the social nature and ideals of the individual.

Producing a Mirror Within.   Cooley called primary groups the "springs of life." By this, he meant that primary groups, such as family and friends, are essential to our emotional well-being. As humans, we have an intense need for face-to-face interaction that generates feelings of self-esteem. By offering a sense of belonging and a feeling of being appreciated—and sometimes even loved—primary groups are uniquely equipped to meet this basic need. From our opening vignette, you can see that gangs are also primary groups.

Primary groups are also significant because their values and attitudes become fused into our identity. We internalize their views, which then become the lenses through which we view life. Even when we are adults—no matter how far we move away from our childhood roots—early primary groups remain "inside" us. There, they continue to form part of the perspective from which we look out onto the world. Ultimately, then, it is difficult, if not impossible, for us to separate the self from our primary groups, for the self and our groups merge into a "we."

Secondary Groups

Compared with primary groups, **secondary groups** are larger, more anonymous, and more formal and impersonal. These groups are based on shared interests or activities, and their members are likely to interact on the basis of specific statuses, such as

Categories, Aggregates, Primary and Secondary Groups

Groups have a deep impact on our actions, views, orientations, even what we feel and think about life. Yet, as illustrated by these photos, not everything that appears to be a group is actually a group in the sociological sense.

The outstanding trait that these three people have in common does not make them a group, but a **category.**

Primary groups such as the family play a key role in the development of the self. As a small group, the family also serves as a buffer from the often-threatening larger group known as society. The family has been of primary significance in forming the basic orientations of this couple, as it will be for their son.

Secondary groups are larger and more anonymous, formal, and impersonal than primary groups. Why are these contestants for Miss Universe an example of a secondary group?

Aggregates are people who happen to be in the same place at the same time.

president, manager, worker, or student. Examples include college classes, the American Sociological Association, and the Democratic Party. Contemporary society could not function without secondary groups. They are part of the way we get our education, make our living, spend our money, and use our leisure time.

As necessary as secondary groups are for contemporary life, they often fail to satisfy our deep needs for intimate association. Consequently, *secondary groups tend to break down into primary groups*. At school and work, we form friendships. Our interaction with our friends is so important that we sometimes feel that if it weren't for them, school or work "would drive us crazy." The primary groups that we form within secondary groups, then, serve as a buffer between ourselves and the demands that secondary groups place on us.

Voluntary Associations.

A special type of secondary group is a **voluntary association**, a group made up of volunteers who organize on the basis of some mutual interest. Some groups are local, consisting of only a few volunteers; others are national, with a paid professional staff.

Americans love voluntary associations and use them to express a wide variety of interests. A visitor entering one of the thousands of small towns that dot the U.S. landscape is often greeted by a highway sign proclaiming the town's voluntary associations: Girl Scouts, Boy Scouts, Kiwanis, Lions, Elks, Eagles, Knights of Columbus, Chamber of Commerce, American Legion, Veterans of Foreign Wars, and perhaps a host of others. One type of voluntary association is so prevalent that a separate sign sometimes indicates which varieties are present in the town: Roman Catholic, Baptist, Lutheran, Methodist, Episcopalian, and so on. Not listed on these signs are many other voluntary associations, such as political parties, unions, health clubs, the National Right to Life, the National Organization for Women, Alcoholics Anonymous, Gamblers Anonymous, Association of Pinto Racers, and Citizens United For or Against This and That.

The Inner Circle and the "Iron Law" of Oligarchy.

A significant aspect of a voluntary association is that its key members, its inner circle, often grow distant from the regular members. They become convinced that only they can be trusted to make the group's important decisions. To see this principle at work, let's look at the Veterans of Foreign Wars (VFW).

Sociologists Elaine Fox and George Arquitt (1985) studied three local posts of the VFW, a national organization of former U.S. soldiers who have served in foreign wars. They found that although the leaders conceal their attitudes from the other members, the inner circle views the rank and file as a bunch of ignorant boozers. Because the leaders can't stand the thought that such people might represent them in the community and at national meetings, a curious situation arises. Although the VFW constitution makes rank-and-file members eligible for top leadership positions, they never become leaders. In fact, the inner circle is so effective in controlling these top positions that even before an election they can tell you who is going to win. "You need to meet Jim," the sociologists were told. "He's the next post commander after Sam does his time."

At first, the researchers found this puzzling. The election hadn't been held yet. As they investigated further, they found that leadership is actually determined behind the scenes. The current leaders appoint their favored people to chair the key committees. This spotlights their names and accomplishments, propelling the members to elect them. By appointing its own members to highly visible positions, then, the inner circle maintains control over the entire organization.

Like the VFW, most organizations are run by only a few of their members. Building on the term *oligarchy*, a system in which many are ruled by a few, sociologist Robert Michels (1876–1936) coined the term *the iron law of oligarchy* to refer to how organizations come to be dominated by a small, self-perpetuating elite (Michels 1911/1949). Most members of voluntary associations are passive, and an elite inner circle keeps itself in power by passing the leadership positions among its members.

What many find disturbing about the iron law of oligarchy is that people are excluded from leadership because they don't represent the inner circle's values—or, in some instances, their background. This is true even of organizations that are committed to democratic principles. For example, U.S. political parties—supposedly the backbone of the nation's representative government—are run by an inner circle that passes leadership positions from one elite member to another. This principle also shows up in the U.S. Congress. With their control of political machinery and access to free mailing, 90 to 95 percent of U.S. senators and representatives who choose to run are reelected (Statistical Abstract 2006:Table 394; Friedman and Holden 2009).

In-Groups and Out-Groups

What groups do you identify with? Which groups in our society do you dislike?

We all have **in-groups,** groups toward which we feel loyalty. And we all have **out-groups,** groups toward which we feel antagonism. For Monster Kody in our opening vignette, the Crips were an in-group, while the Bloods were an out-group. That the Crips—and we—make such a fundamental division of the world has far-reaching consequences for our lives.

Implications for a Socially Diverse Society: Shaping Perception and Morality.
You know the sense of belonging that some groups give you. This can bring positive consequences, such as our tendency to excuse the faults of people we love and to encourage them to do better. Unfortunately, dividing the world into a "we" and "them" also leads to discrimination, hatred, and, as we saw in our opening vignette, even murder.

From this, you can see the sociological significance of in-groups: They shape our perception of the world, our view of right and wrong, and our behavior. Let's look at two examples. The first you see regularly—prejudice and discrimination on the basis of sex.

Here is the fascinating double standard that in-groups produce:

We tend to view the traits of our in-group as virtues, while we perceive those same traits as vices in out-groups. Men may perceive an aggressive man as assertive but an aggressive woman as pushy. They may think that a male employee who doesn't speak up "knows when to keep his mouth shut," while they consider a quiet woman as too timid to make it in the business world (Merton 1949/1968).

The "we" and "they" division of the world can twist perception to such a degree that harming others comes to be viewed as right. The Nazis provide one of the most startling examples. For them, the Jews were an out-group who symbolized an evil that should be eliminated. Many ordinary, "good" Germans shared this view and defended the Holocaust as "dirty work" that someone had to do (Hughes 1962/2005).

An example from way back then, you might say—and the world has moved on. But our inclination to divide the world into in-groups and out-groups has not moved on—nor has the twisting of perception that accompanies it. After the terrorist attacks of September 11, 2001, al-Qaeda became Americans' number one out-group, so much so that top U.S. officials concluded that being "cruel, inhuman, and degrading" to al-Qaeda prisoners was not torture. Officials had one al-Qaeda leader waterboarded 180 times (Shane and Savage 2011). (None of us would want to be waterboarded even once.)

"So long, Bill. This is my club. You can't come in."

How our participation in social groups shapes our self-concept is a focus of symbolic interactionists. In this process, knowing who we are *not* is as significant as knowing who we are.

All of us have *reference groups*—the groups we use as standards to evaluate ourselves. How do you think the reference groups of these members of the KKK who are demonstrating in Jaspar, Texas, differ from those of the police officer who is protecting their right of free speech? Although the KKK and this police officer use different groups to evaluate their attitudes and behaviors, the process is the same.

Caught up in the torture hysteria of the times, Alan Dershowitz, a professor at Harvard Law School who usually takes very liberal views, said that we should make torture legal so judges could issue "torture warrants" (Schulz 2002). Can you see the principle at work—and understand that in-group/out-group thinking can be so severe that even "good people" can support torture? And with a good conscience.

Shades of the Nazis!

Economic downturns are especially perilous in this regard. The Nazis took power during a depression so severe that it was wiping out the middle classes. During our depression, immigrants are being transformed from "nice people who work for low wages at jobs that Americans think are beneath them" to "sneaky people who steal jobs from friends and family." Depressions bring national anti-immigration policies, which can be accompanied by a resurgence of hate groups such as the neo-Nazis, the Ku Klux Klan, and skinheads.

In short, to divide the world into in-groups and out-groups, a natural part of social life, produces both functional and dysfunctional consequences.

Reference Groups

Suppose you have just been offered a good job. It pays double what you hope to make even after you graduate from college. You have only two days to make up your mind. If you accept it, you will have to drop out of college. As you consider the offer, thoughts like this may go through your mind: "My friends will say I'm a fool if I don't take the job . . . but Dad and Mom will practically go crazy. They've made sacrifices for me, and they'll be crushed if I don't finish college. They've always said I've got to get my education first, that good jobs will always be there. . . . But, then, I'd like to see the look on the faces of those neighbors who said I'd never amount to much!"

Evaluating Ourselves.   This is an example of how people use **reference groups,** the groups we refer to when we evaluate ourselves. Your reference groups may include your family, neighbors, teachers, classmates, co-workers, or the members of your church, synagogue, or mosque. If you were like Monster Kody in our opening vignette, the "set" would be your main reference group. Even a group you don't belong to can be a reference group. For example, if you are thinking about going to graduate school, graduate students or members of the profession you want to join may form a reference group.

Reference groups exert tremendous influence on us. For example, if you want to become a corporate executive, you might start to dress more formally, try to improve your vocabulary, read the *Wall Street Journal,* and change your major to business or law. In contrast, if you want to become a rock musician, you might get elaborate tattoos and body piercings, dress in ways your parents and even many of your peers consider extreme, read *Rolling Stone,* drop out of college, and hang around clubs and rock groups.

Exposure to Contradictory Standards in a Socially Diverse Society.   From these examples, you can see how you use reference groups to evaluate your life. When you see yourself as measuring up to a reference group's standards, you feel pleased. But you can experience inner turmoil if your behavior—or aspirations—does not match the group's standards. Although for most of us, wanting to become a corporate executive would create no inner turmoil, it would for someone who had grown up in an Amish home. The Amish strongly disapprove of such aspirations for their children. They ban high school and college education, suits and ties, and corporate employment. Similarly, if you want to join the military and your parents are dedicated pacifists, you

Why are reference groups significant? What are some of yours? How do they influence your life?

We all use *reference groups* to evaluate our accomplishments, failures, values, and attitudes. We compare what we see in ourselves with what we perceive as normative in our reference groups. From these two photos, can you see how the *reference groups* and *social networks* of these youths are not likely to lead them to the same social destination?

likely would feel deep conflict, because your parents would have quite different aspirations for you.

Contradictions that lead to inner turmoil are common because of two chief characteristics of our society—social diversity and social mobility. These expose us to standards and orientations that are inconsistent with those we learned during childhood. The "internal recordings" that play contrasting messages from different reference groups, then, are one price we pay for our social mobility.

Social Networks

Although we live in a huge and diverse society, we don't experience social life as a sea of nameless, strange faces. This is because of the groups we have been discussing. Among these is our **social network**, people who are linked to one another. Your social network includes your family, friends, acquaintances, people at work and school, and even "friends of friends." Think of your social network as a spider's web. You are at the center, with lines extending outward, gradually encompassing more and more people.

If you are a member of a large group, you probably associate regularly with a few people within that group. In a sociology class I was teaching at a commuter campus, six women who didn't know one another ended up working together on a project. They got along well, and they began to sit together. Eventually they planned a Christmas party at one of their homes. This type of social network, the clusters within a group, or its internal factions, is called a **clique** (cleek).

Applied Network Analysis.   Network analysis has moved from theory and laboratory study to the practical world. One of the most striking examples is how U.S. forces located Saddam Hussein. Social scientists analyzed people's relationship to Hussein. They then drew up a "people map," placing names and photos of these people closer and farther from a central photo of Hussein. This let them see who was close enough to Hussein to know where he might be but distant enough to perhaps be willing to cooperate. It worked.

The Small World Phenomenon.   Social scientists have wondered just how extensive the connections are among social networks. If you list everyone you know and each of those individuals lists everyone he or she knows, and you keep doing this, would almost everyone in the United States eventually be included on those lists?

What are social networks? How do your reference groups and social networks affect your behavior?

It would be too cumbersome to test this hypothesis by drawing up such lists, but psychologist Stanley Milgram (1933–1984) came up with an interesting idea. In a classic study known as "the small world phenomenon," Milgram (1967) addressed a letter to "targets": the wife of a divinity student in Cambridge and a stockbroker in Boston. He sent the letter to "starters," who did not know these people. He asked them to send the letter to someone they knew on a first-name basis, someone they thought might know the "target." The recipients, in turn, were asked to mail the letter to a friend or acquaintance who might know the "target," and so on. The question was, Would the letters ever reach the "target"? If so, how long would the chain be?

Think of yourself as part of this study. What would you do if you were a "starter," but the "target" lived in a state in which you knew no one? You would send the letter to someone you know who might know someone in that state. This, Milgram reported, is just what happened. Although none of the senders knew the targets, the letters reached the designated individual in an average of just six jumps.

Milgram's study caught the public's fancy, leading to the phrase "six degrees of separation." This expression means that, on average, everyone in the United States is separated by just six individuals. Milgram's conclusions have become so popular that a game, "Six Degrees of Kevin Bacon," was built around it.

Is the Small World Phenomenon an Academic Myth?

When psychologist Judith Kleinfeld (2002) decided to replicate Milgram's study, she went to the archives at Yale University Library to get more details. Going through Milgram's papers, she found that he had stacked the deck in favor of finding a small world. As mentioned, one of the "targets" was a stockbroker. Kleinfeld found that this person's "starters" were investors in blue-chip stocks. She also found that, on average, only 30 percent of the letters reached their "target."

Since most letters did *not* reach their targets, even with the deck stacked in favor of success, we can draw the *opposite* conclusion: People who don't know one another are dramatically separated by social barriers. As Kleinfeld says, "Rather than living in a small world, we may live in a world that looks like a bowl of lumpy oatmeal, with many small worlds loosely connected and perhaps some small worlds not connected at all." Somehow, I don't think that the phrase "lumpy oatmeal phenomenon" will become standard, but it seems reasonable to conclude that we do *not* live in a small world where everyone is connected by six links.

But not so fast. The plot thickens. Although research with thousands of e-mail chains showed that only about one percent reached their targets (Dodds et al. 2003; Muhamad 2010), other research confirms Milgrm's conclusions. Research on 250 million people who exchanged chat messages showed a link of less than 7, and a study of 700 million people on Facebook showed a connection of less than 5 (Markoff and Sengupta 2011).

The problem seems to be the choice of samples and how researchers measure links. These definitions must be worked out before we can draw solid conclusions. But maybe Milgram did stumble onto the truth.

Building Unntentional Barriers.

Besides geography, the barriers that divide us into separate, small worlds are primarily those of social class, gender, and race–ethnicity. Overcoming these social barriers is difficult because even our own social networks contribute to social inequality, a topic that we explore in the Cultural Diversity box on the next page.

Bureaucracies

About 100 years ago, sociologist Max Weber analyzed the *bureaucracy,* a type of organization that was just emerging and that has since become dominant in social life. To achieve more efficient results, bureaucracies shift the emphasis from traditional relationships based on personal loyalties to the "bottom line." As we look at the characteristics of bureaucracies, we will also consider their implications for our lives.

Cultural Diversity in the United States

How Your Social Networks Perpetuate Social Inequality

Suppose that an outstanding job—great pay, interesting work, opportunity for advancement—has just opened up where you work. Who are you going to tell?

Consider some of the principles we have reviewed. We are part of in-groups, people with whom we identify; we use reference groups to evaluate our attitudes and behavior; and we interact in social networks. Our in-groups, reference groups, and social networks are likely to consist of people whose backgrounds are similar to our own. For most of us, this means that just as social inequality is built into society, so it is built into our relationships. One consequence is that we tend to perpetuate social inequality.

Go back to the extract that opens this box. Who will you tell about the opening for this outstanding job? Most likely it will be someone you know, a friend or someone to whom you owe a favor. And most likely your social network is made up of people who look much like yourself—similar to your age, education, social class, race—ethnicity, and probably also gender. You can see how *our social networks both reflect the inequality in our society and help to perpetuate it.*

When people learn of opportunities, they share this information with their networks. Opportunities then flow to people whose characteristics are similar to theirs.

Consider a network of white men in some corporation. As they learn of opportunities (jobs, investments, real estate, and so on), they share this information with their networks. This causes opportunities and good jobs to flow to people whose characteristics are similar to theirs. This perpetuates the "good old boy"' network, bypassing people who have different characteristics—in this example women and minorities. No intentional discrimination need be involved. It is just a reflection of our contacts, of our everyday interaction.

To overcome this barrier, women and minorities do networking. They try to meet "someone who knows someone" to help advance their careers (Kanter 2009). Like the "good old boys," they go to parties and join clubs, religious organizations, and political parties. They also use Facebook and other online networking sites. The network that African American leaders have cultivated is so tight that one-fifth of the entire national African American leadership knows one another personally. Add some "friends of a friend," and *three-fourths* of the entire leadership belong to the same network (Taylor 1992).

Women also cultivate their own network as they climb the career ladder. The women in this "new girl" network steer business to one another, and like the "good old boys" who preceded them, they have a ready set of reasons to justify their practice of excluding the opposite sex (Jacobs 1997).

For Your Consideration

➔ You can see that the perpetuation of social inequality does not require intentional discrimination. Just as social inequality is built into society, so it is built into our personal relationships. How do you think your social network helps to perpetuate social inequality? How do you think we can break this cycle? How can we create diversity in our social networks?

The Characteristics of Bureaucracies

Do you know what the Russian army and the U.S. postal service have in common? Or the government of Mexico and your college?

The sociological answer to these questions is that all four of these organizations are *bureaucracies.* As Weber (1913/1947) pointed out, **bureaucracies** have

1. *Clear levels, with assignments flowing downward and accountability flowing upward.* Each level assigns responsibilities to the level beneath it, while each lower level is accountable to the level above it for fulfilling those assignments. Figure 5.1 on page 135 shows the bureaucratic structure of a typical university.

When society began to be rationalized, production of items was broken into its components, with individuals assigned only specific tasks. Shown in this wood engraving is the production of glass in Great Britain in the early 1800s.

2. *A division of labor.* Each worker is assigned specific tasks, and the tasks of all the workers are coordinated to accomplish the purpose of the organization. In a college, for example, a teacher does not fix the heating system, the president does not approve class schedules, and a secretary does not evaluate textbooks. These tasks are distributed among people who have been trained to do them.

3. *Written rules.* In their attempt to become efficient, bureaucracies stress written procedures. In general, the longer a bureaucracy exists and the larger it grows, the more written rules it has.

4. *Written communications and records.* Records are kept of much of what occurs in a bureaucracy ("Be sure to CC all immediate supervisors"). In some organizations, workers spend a fair amount of time sending memos and e-mail back and forth.

5. *Impersonality and replaceability.* It is the office that is important, not the individual who holds the office. You work for the organization, not for the replaceable person who heads some post in the organization.

Weber viewed bureaucracies as such a powerful form of social organization that he predicted they would come to dominate social life. He called this process the **rationalization of society,** meaning that bureaucracies, with their rules and emphasis on results, would increasingly dominate our lives. Weber was right. These five characteristics have made bureaucracies

What are the major characteristics of bureaucracies? How do these characteristics help bureaucracies reach their goals?

FIGURE 5.1   The Typical Bureaucratic Structure of a Medium-Sized University

This is a scaled-down version of a university's bureaucratic structure. The actual lines of a university are likely to be much more complicated than those depicted here. A large university may have a chancellor and several presidents under the chancellor, each president being responsible for a particular campus. In this illustration, extensions of authority are shown only for the Vice President for Administration and the College of Social Sciences, but each of the other vice presidents and colleges has similar positions. If the figure were to be extended, departmental secretaries would be shown and, eventually, somewhere, even students.

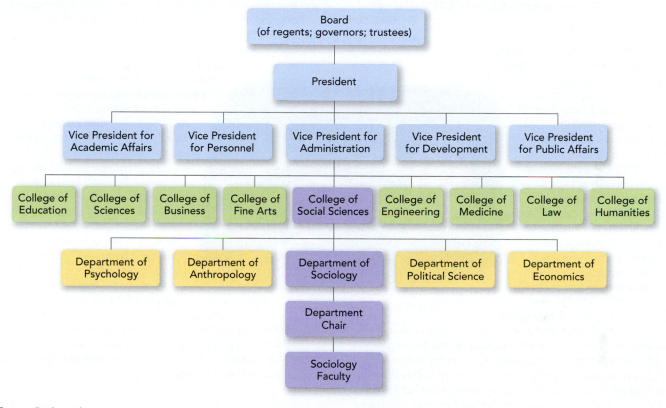

Source: By the author.

so successful that, as illustrated by the Down-to-Earth Sociology box on the next page, they have even begun to take over cooking, one of the most traditional areas of life.

Goal Displacement and the Perpetuation of Bureaucracies

Bureaucracies are so good at harnessing people's energies to reach specific goals that they have become a standard feature of our lives. Once in existence, however, bureaucracies tend to take on a life of their own. In a process called **goal displacement,** even after an organization achieves its goal and no longer has a reason to continue, continue it does.

A classic example is the March of Dimes, organized in the 1930s with the goal of fighting polio (Sills 1957). At that time, the origin of polio was a mystery. The public was alarmed and fearful, for overnight a healthy child could be stricken with this crippling disease. To raise money to find a cure, the March of Dimes placed posters of children on crutches near cash registers in almost every store in the United States. The organization raised money beyond its wildest dreams. When Dr. Jonas Salk developed a vaccine for polio in the 1950s, the threat of polio was wiped out almost overnight.

Did the staff that ran the March of Dimes hold a wild celebration and then quietly fold up their tents and slip away? Of course not. They had jobs to protect, so they

Down-to-Earth Sociology

The McDonaldization of Society

The significance of the McDonald's restaurants that dot the United States—and, increasingly, the world—goes far beyond quick hamburgers, milk shakes, and salads. As sociologist George Ritzer (1993, 1998, 2001) says, our everyday lives are being "McDonaldized." Let's see what he means by this.

The **McDonaldization of society** does not refer just to the robotlike assembly of food. This term refers to the standardization of everyday life, a process that is transforming our lives. Want to do some shopping? Shopping malls offer one-stop shopping in controlled environments. Planning a trip? Travel agencies offer "package" tours. They will transport middle-class Americans to ten European capitals in fourteen days. All visitors experience the same hotels, restaurants, and other scheduled sites— and no one need fear meeting a "real" native. Want to keep up with events? USA Today spews out McNews—short, bland, non-analytical pieces that can be digested between gulps of the McShake or the McBurger.

McDonalds in Xian, China.

Efficiency brings dependability. You can expect your burger and fries to taste the same whether you buy them in Los Angeles or Beijing. Although efficiency also lowers prices, it does come at a cost. Predictability washes away spontaneity. It changes the quality of our lives by producing sameness, a bland version of what used to be unique experiences. In my own travels, for example, had I taken packaged tours I never would have had the eye-opening experiences that

have added so much to my appreciation of human diversity. (Bus trips with chickens in Mexico, hitchhiking in Europe and Africa, and sleeping on a granite table in a nunnery in Italy and in a cornfield in Algeria are just not part of tour agendas.)

For good or bad, our lives are being McDonaldized, and the predictability of packaged settings seems to be our social destiny. When education is rationalized, no longer will our children have to put up with real professors, who insist on discussing ideas endlessly, who never come to decisive answers, and who come saddled with idiosyncrasies. At some point, such an approach to education is going to be a bit of quaint history.

Our programmed education will eliminate the need for discussion of social issues—we will have packaged solutions to social problems, definitive answers that satisfy our need for closure, likely stamped "U.S. government approved." Computerized courses will teach the same answers to everyone—"politically correct" ways to think about social issues. Mass testing will ensure that students regurgitate the programmed responses.

Our looming prepackaged society will be efficient. But we will be trapped in the "iron cage" of bureaucracy—just as Weber warned would happen.

For Your Consideration

→ What do you like and dislike about the standardization of society? What do you think about the author's comments on the future of our educational system?

---

targeted a new enemy—birth defects. But then in 2001 another ominous threat of success reared its ugly head. Researchers finished mapping the human genome system, a breakthrough that held the possibility of eliminating birth defects—and their jobs. Officials of the March of Dimes had to come up with something new—and something that would last. Their new slogan, "Stronger, healthier babies," is so vague that it should ensure the organization's existence forever: We are not likely to ever run out of the need for "stronger, healthier babies."

Then there is NATO (North Atlantic Treaty Organization), formed during the Cold War to prevent Russia from invading Western Europe. The abrupt, unexpected ending of the Cold War removed the organization's purpose. But why waste a perfectly good bureaucracy? As with the March of Dimes, the Western powers found a new goal: to create "rapid response forces" to combat terrorism and "rogue nations" (Tyler 2002). To keep this bureaucracy going, they even allowed Russia to become a junior partner. Russia was pleased—until it felt threatened by NATO's expansion.

What is the McDonaldization of society? Why is it important for your life?

The March of Dimes was founded by President Franklin Roosevelt in the 1930s to fight polio. When a vaccine for polio was discovered in the 1950s, the organization did not declare victory and disband. Instead, its leaders kept the organization intact by creating new goals— first "fighting birth defects," and now "stronger, healthier babies." Sociologists use the term goal displacement to refer to this process of keeping a bureaucracy alive by adopting new goals.

Dysfunctions of Bureaucracies

Although in the long run no other form of social organization is more efficient, as Weber recognized, bureaucracies also have a dark side. Let's look at some of their dysfunctions.

Red Tape: A Rule Is a Rule.   Bureaucracies can be so bound by red tape that when officials apply their rules, the results can defy all logic. I came across an example so ridiculous that it can make your head swim—if you don't burst from laughing first.

In Spain, the Civil Registry of Barcelona recorded the death of a woman named Maria Antonieta Calvo in 1992. Apparently, Maria's evil brother had reported her dead so he could collect the family inheritance.

When Maria learned that she was supposedly dead, she told the Registry that she was very much alive. The bureaucrats at this agency looked at their records, shook their heads, and insisted that she was dead. Maria then asked lawyers to represent her in court. They all refused—because no dead person can bring a case before a judge.

When Maria's boyfriend asked her to marry him, the couple ran into a slight obstacle: No man in Spain (or most other places) can marry a dead woman—so these bureaucrats said, "So sorry, but no license."

After years of continuing to insist that she was alive, Maria finally got a hearing in court. When the judges looked at Maria, they believed that she really was a living person, and they ordered the Civil Registry to declare her alive.

The ending of this story gets even happier, for now that Maria was alive, she was able to marry her boyfriend. I don't know if the two lived happily ever after, but, after overcoming the bureaucrats, they at least had that chance ("Mujer 'resucita'" 2006).

Bureaucratic Alienation.   Perceived in terms of roles, rules, and functions rather than as individuals, many workers begin to feel more like objects than people. Marx termed these reactions **alienation,** a result, he said, of workers being cut off

Technology has changed our lives fundamentally. The connection to each telephone call used to be made by hand. As in this 1940s photo, these connections were made by women. Long-distance calls, with their numerous handmade connections, not only were slower but were also expensive. In 1927, a call from New York to London cost $25 a minute. In today's money this comes to $300 a minute!

What are some functions and dysfunctions of bureaucracies?

Bureaucracies have their dysfunctions and can be slow and even stifling. Most, however, are highly functional in uniting people's efforts toward reaching goals.

from the finished product of their labor. He pointed out that before industrialization workers used their own tools to produce an entire product, such as a chair or table. Now the capitalists own the tools (machinery, desks, computers) and assign each worker only a single step or two in the entire production process. Relegated to performing repetitive tasks that seem remote from the final product, workers no longer identify with what they produce. They come to feel estranged not only from the results of their labor but also from their work environment.

Resisting Alienation.   Because workers want to feel valued and to have a sense of control over their work, they resist alienation. A major form of that resistance is forming primary groups at work. Workers band together in informal settings—at lunch, around desks, or for a drink after work. There, they give one another approval for jobs well done and express sympathy for the shared need to put up with cantankerous bosses, meaningless routines, and endless rules. In these contexts, they relate to one another not just as workers, but also as people who value one another. They flirt, laugh, tell jokes, and talk about their families and goals. Adding this multidimensionality to their work relationships maintains their sense of being individuals rather than mere cogs in a machine.

How is this worker in Houston trying to avoid becoming a depersonalized unit in a bureaucratic-economic machine?

As in the photo to the left, workers often decorate their work areas with personal items. The sociological implication is that of workers who are trying to resist alienation. By staking a claim to individuality, the workers are rejecting an identity as machines that exist to perform functions.

Bureaucratic Incompetence.   In a tongue-in-cheek analysis of bureaucracies, Laurence Peter proposed what has become known as the **Peter principle:** Each employee of a bureaucracy is promoted to his or her *level of incompetence* (Peter and Hull 1969). People who perform well in a bureaucracy come to the attention of those higher up the chain of command and are promoted. If they continue to perform well, they are promoted again. This process continues *until* they are promoted to a level at which they can no longer handle the responsibilities well—their level of incompetence. There they hide behind the work of others, taking credit for the accomplishments of employees under their direction.

In what ways do workers in bureaucracies resist alienation? What is the Peter principle?

Although the Peter principle contains a grain of truth, if it were generally true, bureaucracies would be staffed by incompetents, and these organizations would fail. In reality, bureaucracies are so successful that they have come to dominate our society.

Working for the Corporation

Since you are likely to be working for a bureaucracy after college, let's look at how its characteristics might affect your career.

Self-Fulfilling Stereotypes in the "Hidden" Corporate Culture

As you might recall from Chapter 4, stereotypes can be self-fulfilling. That is, stereotypes can produce the very characteristics that they are built around. The example used there was of stereotypes of appearance and personality. Sociologists have also uncovered **self-fulfilling stereotypes** in corporate life. Let's see how they might affect *your* career.

Self-Fulfilling Stereotypes and Promotions.
Corporate and department heads have ideas of "what it takes" to get ahead. Not surprisingly, since they themselves got ahead, they look for people who have characteristics similar to their own. They feed better information to workers who have these characteristics, bring them into stronger networks, and put them in "fast track" positions. With such advantages, these workers perform better and become more committed to the company. This, of course, confirms the boss's initial expectation or stereotype.

But for workers who don't look or act like the corporate leaders, the opposite happens. Thinking of these people as less capable, the bosses give them fewer opportunities and challenges. When these workers see others get ahead and realize that they are working beneath their own abilities, they lose motivation, become less committed to the company, and don't perform as well. This, of course, confirms the stereotypes the bosses had of them.

In her studies of U.S. corporations, sociologist Rosabeth Moss Kanter (1977, 1983) found such self-fulfilling stereotypes to be part of a "hidden" **corporate culture.** That is, these stereotypes and their powerful effects on workers remain hidden to everyone, even the bosses. What bosses and workers see is the surface: Workers who have superior performance and greater commitment to the company get promoted. To bosses and workers alike, this seems to be just the way it should be. Hidden below this surface, however, are the higher and lower expectations and the open and closed opportunities that produce the attitudes and the accomplishments—or the lack of them.

As corporations grapple with growing diversity, the stereotypes in the hidden corporate culture are likely to give way, although slowly and grudgingly. In the following Thinking Critically section, we'll consider diversity in the workplace.

THINKING CRITICALLY
Managing Diversity in the Workplace

Times have changed. The San Jose, California, electronic phone book lists *ten* times more *Nguyens* than *Joneses* (Albanese 2010). More than half of U.S. workers are minorities, immigrants, and women. Diversity in the workplace is much more than skin color. Diversity includes age, ethnicity, gender, religion, sexual orientation, and social class.

In the past, the idea was for people to join the "melting pot," to give up their distinctive traits and become like the dominant group. With the successes of the civil rights and women's movements, people today are more likely to prize their distinctive traits. Realizing that assimilation (being absorbed into the dominant culture) is probably not

☀️⌐Explore
Living Data
on **mysoclab.com**

The cultural and racial–ethnic diversity of today's work force has led to the need for diversity training.

the wave of the future, most large companies have "diversity training" (Bennett 2010). They hold lectures and workshops so that employees can learn to work with colleagues of diverse cultures.

Diversity training has the potential to build bridges, but it can also backfire. Managers who are chosen to participate can resent it, thinking that it is punishment for some unmentioned insensitivity on their part (Sanchez and Medkik 2004).

Some directors of these programs are so incompetent that they create antagonisms and reinforce stereotypes. For example, the leaders of a diversity training session at the U.S. Department of Transportation had women grope men as the men ran by. They encouraged blacks and whites to insult one another and to call each other names (Reibstein 1996). The intention may have been to increase understanding of others through role reversal and getting hostilities "out in the open," but the approach was moronic. Instead of healing, such behaviors wound and leave scars.

On the positive side is diversity training at Pepsi, where managers are given the assignment of sponsoring a group of employees who are unlike themselves. Men sponsor women, African Americans sponsor whites, and so on. The executives are expected to try to understand the work situation from the perspective of the people they sponsor, to identify key talent, and to personally mentor at least three people in their group. Accountability is built in—the sponsors have to give updates to executives even higher up (Terhune 2005).

As you saw with the examples of groping and name-calling, on the one hand, and making managers accountable, on the other hand—not all diversity programs are equal. It seems logical, then, that different programs will produce different results. And this is what the researchers found. For example, forcing workers to participate in diversity programs or doing the minimum to prevent lawsuits produces resentment. But setting goals for increasing diversity and making managers accountable for reaching these goals increase the diversity of a company's workers.

For Your Consideration

➔ Do you think that corporations and government agencies should offer diversity training? If so, how can we develop diversity training that fosters mutual respect? Can you suggest practical ways to develop workplaces that are not divided by gender and race–ethnicity? ■

Technology and the Control of Workers: Toward a Maximum-Security Society

The microchip is affecting all areas of society. One of the most ominous is the greater potential to create a police state. It is now easier than ever before in history for governments to monitor our behavior, eventually our every move. The Big Brother (as in Orwell's classic novel *1984*) may turn out to be a master computer that makes servants of us all.

We should know shortly. Computers now monitor millions of workers. In some workplaces, cameras even analyze workers' facial expressions (Neil 2008). Other cameras outside the workplace, called "little brothers" (as compared with Orwell's "Big Brother"),

What approaches to managing diversity in the workplace have positive results?

take video images of us as we walk on the street and shop in stores. As some analysts suggest, we seem to be moving toward a *maximum-security society* (Marx 1995; Whitehead 2010). This seems an apt term. As with the workers in the Sociology and the New Technology box below, few of us realize how extensively we are being monitored.

Group Dynamics

Group dynamics is a fascinating area of sociology. This term refers to how groups influence us and how we influence groups. Most of the ways that groups influence us lies below our sense of awareness, however, so let's see if we can bring some of this to the surface. Let's consider how even the size of a group makes a difference and then examine leadership, conformity, and decision making.

Before doing so, we should define **small group,** which is a group small enough so that each member can interact directly with all the others. Small groups can be either primary or secondary. A wife, husband, and children make up a *primary* small group, as do workers who take their breaks together. Students in a small introductory sociology class and bidders at an auction form *secondary* small groups. You might want to look again at the photos on page 127.

Sociology and the New Technology

Cyberloafers and Cybersleuths: Surfing at Work

Few people work constantly at their jobs. Most of us take breaks and, at least once in a while, goof off. We meet fellow workers at the coffee machine, and we talk in the hallway. Much of this interaction is good for the company, for it bonds us to fellow workers and ties us to our jobs.

Our personal lives may even cross over into our workday. Some of us make personal calls from the office. Bosses know that we need to check in with our child's school or make arrangements for a babysitter. They expect such calls. Some even wink as we make a date or nod as we arrange to have our car worked on. And most bosses make personal calls of their own from time to time. It's the abuse that bothers bosses, and it's not surprising that they fire anyone who talks on the phone all day for personal reasons.

Using computers at work for personal purposes is called *cyberslacking*. Many workers download music, gamble, and play games at work. They read books, shop, exchange jokes, send personal e-mail, trade stocks, and post messages in chat rooms. Some visit porno sites. Many monitor their personal social networking sites. Some cyberslackers even operate their own businesses online—when they're not battling virtual enemies during "work."

To take an afternoon off without the boss knowing it, some use remote devices to make their computer switch screens and their printer spew out documents (Spencer 2003). It looks as though they just stepped away from their desk. Some download special audio recordings for their cell phone: Although they may be sitting on the beach when they call the office, their boss hears background sounds of a dentist's drill or of honking horns (Richtel 2004).

Cyberslacking has given birth to *cybersleuths*. Investigators who use software programs can recover every note employees have written, every Web site they have visited, even every keystroke they have made. They can locate offensive words in every e-mail the worker has sent (Tokc-Wilde 2011). They can bring up every file that employees have deleted, every word they've erased. What some workers forget is that "delete" does not mean erase. Hitting the delete button simply pushes the text into the background of our hard drive. As if revealing invisible ink, with a few clicks the cybersleuth can expose our "deleted" information, opening our hidden diary for anyone to read.

For whatever reason, some people get a kick out of posting photos online of themselves drunk, naked, or doing obnoxious things (Barrett and Saul 2011). Photos like this prevent many otherwise qualified applicants from landing a job. Let's suppose that an interviewer has done a little online searching before holding an interview. When he or she looks at the serious new college graduate with the solid academic record sitting on the other side of the desk, can you see why images of bongs, pirate hats, exposed breasts, or drooling, spaced-out looks might come to mind—and how they can torpedo that job interview?

For Your Consideration
→ Do you think that employers have a right to check on what prospective employees have posted online? How about checking what their employees are doing with company computers on company time? How about checking on what their employees are doing on their own time?

Is cybersleuthing fair? How is it related to the potential for a maximum-security society?

Japanese companies encourage their employees to think of themselves not as individuals, but as members of a group. Similarity of appearance and activity help to fuse group identity and company loyalty. Why do you think there are two subgroups in this photo?

Effects of Group Size on Stability and Intimacy

Writing in the early 1900s, sociologist Georg Simmel (1858–1918) analyzed how group size affects people's behavior. He used the term **dyad** for the smallest possible group, which consists of two people. Dyads, which include marriages, love affairs, and close friendships, show two distinct qualities. First, they are the most intense or intimate of human groups. Because only two people are involved, the interaction is focused on them. Second, dyads tend to be unstable. Because dyads require that both members participate, if one member loses interest, the dyad collapses. In larger groups, by contrast, even if one person withdraws, the group can continue, for its existence does not depend on any single member (Simmel 1950).

A **triad** is a group of three people. As Simmel noted, the addition of a third member fundamentally changes the group. With three people, interaction between the first two decreases. This can create strain. For example, with the birth of a child, hardly any aspect of a couple's relationship goes untouched. Attention focuses on the baby, and interaction between the husband and wife diminishes. Despite this, the marriage usually becomes stronger. Although the intensity of interaction is less in triads, they are inherently stronger and give greater stability to a relationship.

Yet, as Simmel noted, triads, too, are unstable. They tend to produce **coalitions**—two group members aligning themselves against one. This common tendency for two people to develop stronger bonds and prefer one another leaves the third person feeling hurt and excluded. Another characteristic of triads is that they often produce an arbitrator or mediator, someone who tries to settle disagreements between the other two. In one-child families, you can often observe both of these characteristics of triads—coalitions and arbitration.

The general principle is this: *As a small group grows larger, it becomes more stable, but its intensity, or intimacy, decreases.* To see why, look at Figure 5.2. As each new person comes into a group, the connections among people multiply. In a dyad, there is only 1 relationship; in a triad, there are 3; in a group of four, 6; in a group of five, 10. If we expand the group to six, we have 15 relationships, while a group of seven yields 21 relationships. If we continue adding members, we soon are unable to follow the connections: A group of eight has 28 possible relationships; a group of nine, 36 relationships; a group of ten, 45; and so on.

It is not only the number of relationships that makes larger groups more stable. As groups grow, they also tend to develop a more formal structure. For example, leaders emerge and more specialized roles come into play. This often results in such familiar offices as president, secretary, and treasurer. This structure provides a framework that helps the group survive over time.

Effects of Group Size on Attitudes and Behavior

You probably have observed the first consequence of group size firsthand. When a group is small, its members act informally, but as the group grows, the members lose their sense of intimacy and become more formal with one another. No longer can the members assume that the others are "insiders" in sympathy with what they say. Now they must take a "larger

---

FIGURE 5.2	The Effects of Group Size on Relationships

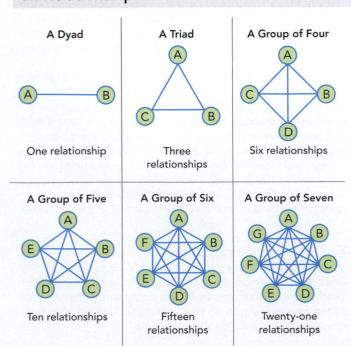

A Dyad — One relationship

A Triad — Three relationships

A Group of Four — Six relationships

A Group of Five — Ten relationships

A Group of Six — Fifteen relationships

A Group of Seven — Twenty-one relationships

audience" into consideration, and instead of merely "talking," they begin to "address" the group. As their speech becomes more formal, their body language stiffens.

You probably have observed a second aspect of group dynamics, too. In the early stages of a party, when only a few people are present, almost everyone talks with everyone else. But as others arrive, the guests break into smaller groups. Some hosts, who want their guests to mix together, make a nuisance of themselves trying to achieve *their* idea of what a group should be like. The division into small groups is inevitable, however, for it follows the basic sociological principles that we have just reviewed. Because the addition of each person rapidly increases connections (in this case, "talk lines"), conversation becomes more difficult. The guests break into smaller groups in which they can look at each other directly and interact comfortably with one another.

Let's turn to a third consequence of group size:

Imagine that you are taking a team-taught course in social psychology and your professors have asked you to join a few students to discuss your adjustment to college life. When you arrive, they tell you that to make the discussion anonymous they want you to sit unseen in a booth. You will participate in the discussion over an intercom, talking when your microphone comes on. The professors say that they will not listen to the conversation, and they leave.

You find the format somewhat strange, to say the least, but you go along with it. You have not seen the other students in their booths, but when they talk about their experiences, you find yourself becoming wrapped up in the problems that they begin to share. One student even mentions how frightening it is to be away from home because of his history of epileptic seizures. Later, you hear this individual breathe heavily into the microphone. Then he stammers and cries for help. A crashing noise follows, and you imagine him lying helpless on the floor. Nothing but an eerie silence follows. What do you do?

Your professors, John Darley and Bibb Latané (1968), staged the whole thing, but you don't know this. No one had a seizure. In fact, no one was even in the other booths. Everything, except your comments, was on tape.

Some participants were told that they would be discussing the topic with just one other student, others with two, and still others with three, four, or five. Darley and Latané found that all students who thought they were part of a dyad rushed out to help. If they thought they were in a triad, only 80 percent went to help—and they were slower in leaving the booth. In six-person groups, only 60 percent went to see what was wrong—and they were even slower.

This experiment demonstrates how deeply group size influences our attitudes and behavior: It even affects our willingness to help one another. Students in the dyad knew that no one else could help the student in trouble. The professor was gone, and it was up to them. In the larger groups, including the triad, students felt a *diffusion of responsibility:* Giving help was no more their responsibility than anyone else's.

Laboratory Findings and the Real World.   Experiments in social psychology can give insight into human behavior—and at the same time, they can woefully miss the mark. Darley and Latane's classic laboratory experiment has serious flaws when it comes to real life. Look at the photos on the next page that I snapped in Vienna, Austria, and you'll see something entirely different. Many people—strangers to one another—were simply passing one another on the sidewalk. But as you can see, no diffusion of responsibility stopped them from immediately helping the man who had tripped and fallen. Other norms and values that people carry within them are also at work, ones that can trump the diffusion of responsibility.

Leadership

All of us are influenced by leaders, so it is important to understand leadership. Let's look at how people become leaders, the types of leaders, and different styles of leadership. Before we do this, though, it is important to clarify that leaders don't

Group size has a significant influence on how people interact. When a group changes from a dyad (two people) to a triad (three people), the relationships among the participants undergo a shift. How do you think the birth of this child affected the relationship between the mother and father?

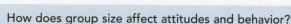

THROUGH THE AUTHOR'S LENS

Helping a Stranger

Serendipity sometimes accompanies sociologists as they do their work, which was certainly the case here. The entire episode took no more than three minutes, and I was fortunate to capture it with my camera. Real life sometimes differs sharply from that portrayed in research laboratories.

As I was walking in Vienna, a city of almost 2 million people, I heard a crashing noise behind me. I turned, and seeing that a man had fallen to the sidewalk, quickly snapped this picture. You can see strangers beginning to help the man. This photo was taken about three seconds after the man fell.

Two strangers are helping the man, with another two ready to pitch in. They have all stopped whatever they were doing to help a man they did not know.

The man is now on his feet, but still a bit shaky. The two who have helped him up are still expressing their concern, especially the young woman.

By this point, the police officer has noticed that I have been taking photos. You can see him coming toward me, his hand on whatever he is carrying at his hip, his shoulders back, glowering and ready for a confrontation. He asked, "What are you doing?" I said, "I am taking pictures" (as though he couldn't see this). He asked, "Do you have to take pictures of this man?" I said, "Yes," and hoping to defuse the situation, added, "I'm a sociologist, and I'm documenting how people help each other in Vienna." He grunted and turned away.

This photo really completes the series, as this individual was acting as the guardian of the community, placing a barrier of protection around the participants in this little drama.

necessarily hold formal positions in a group. **Leaders** are people who influence the behaviors, opinions, or attitudes of others. Even a group of friends has leaders.

Who Becomes a Leader?

Are leaders born with characteristics that propel them to the forefront of a group? No sociologist would agree with such an idea. In general, people who become leaders are perceived by group members as strongly representing their values or as able to lead a group out of a crisis (Trice and Beyer 1991). Leaders tend to be more talkative, outgoing, determined, and self-confident (Ward et al. 2010).

These findings may not be surprising, since such traits are related to what we expect of leaders. Researchers, however, have also discovered traits that seem to have no bearing on the ability to lead. For example, taller people and those judged better looking are more likely to become leaders (Stodgill 1974; Judge and Cable 2004). Some of the factors that go into our choice of leaders are quite subtle, as social psychologists Lloyd Howells and Selwyn Becker (1962) found in a simple experiment. They had groups of five people who did not know one another sit at a rectangular table. Three, of course, sat on one side, and two on the other. After discussing a topic for a set period of time, each group chose a leader. The findings are startling: Although only 40 percent of the people sat on the two-person side, 70 percent of the leaders emerged from there. The explanation is that we tend to interact more with people facing us than with people to our side.

Types of Leaders.

Groups have two types of leaders (Bales 1950, 1953; Cartwright and Zander 1968). The first is easy to recognize. This person, called an **instrumental leader** (or *task-oriented leader*), tries to keep the group moving toward its goals. These leaders try to keep group members from getting sidetracked, reminding them of what they are trying to accomplish. The **expressive leader** (or *socioemotional leader*), in contrast, usually is not recognized as a leader, but he or she certainly is one. This person is likely to crack jokes, to offer sympathy, or to do other things that help to life a group's morale. Both types of leadership are essential: the one to keep the group on track, the other to increase harmony and minimize conflicts.

It is difficult for the same person to be both an instrumental and an expressive leader, for these roles tend to contradict one another. Because instrumental leaders are task oriented, they sometimes create friction as they prod the group to get on with the job. Their actions often cost them popularity. Expressive leaders, in contrast, who stimulate personal bonds and reduce friction, are usually more popular (Olmsted and Hare 1978).

Leadership Styles.

Let's suppose that the president of your college has asked you to head a task force to determine how to improve race relations on campus. You can adopt a number of **leadership styles,** or ways of expressing yourself as a leader. Of the three basic styles, you could be an **authoritarian leader,** one who gives orders; a **democratic leader,** one who tries to gain a consensus; or a **laissez-faire leader,** one who is highly permissive. Which style should you choose?

Social psychologists Ronald Lippitt and Ralph White (1958) carried out a classic study of these leadership styles. They matched boys for IQ, popularity, physical energy, and leadership and assigned them to "craft clubs" made up of five boys each. They trained men in the three leadership styles, and then peered through peepholes, took notes, and made movies as the men rotated among the clubs. To control possible influences of the men's personalities, each man played all three styles.

The *authoritarian* leaders assigned tasks to the boys and told them what to do. They also praised or condemned the boys' work arbitrarily, giving no explanation for why they judged it good or bad. The *democratic* leaders discussed the project with the boys, outlining the steps that would help them reach their goals. When they evaluated the boys' work, they gave "facts" as the bases for their decisions. The *laissez-faire* leaders, who gave the boys almost total freedom to do as they wished, offered help when asked, but made few suggestions. They did not evaluate the boys' projects, either positively or negatively.

The results? The boys under authoritarian leadership grew dependent on their leader. They also became either apathetic or aggressive, with the aggressive boys growing hostile toward their leader. In contrast, the boys in the democratic clubs were friendlier

Explore
Living Data
on **mysoclab.com**

What types of leaders are there? Who becomes a leader? What kinds of leadership styles are there?

Adolf Hitler, shown here in Nuremberg in 1938, was one of the most influential—and evil—persons of the twentieth century. Why did so many people follow Hitler? This question stimulated the research by Stanley Milgram (discussed on pages 147–149).

and looked to one another for approval. When the leader left the room, they continued to work at a steady pace. The boys with laissez-faire management goofed off a lot and were notable for their lack of achievement. The researchers concluded that the democratic style of leadership works best. This conclusion, however, may be biased, as the researchers favored a democratic style of leadership in the first place (Olmsted and Hare 1978). Apparently, this same bias in studies of leadership continues (Cassel 1999).

You may have noticed that only boys and men were involved in this experiment. It is interesting to speculate how the results might differ if we were to repeat the experiment with all-girl groups and with mixed groups of girls and boys and if we used both women and men as leaders. Perhaps you will become the sociologist to study such variations of this classic experiment.

Leadership Styles in Changing Situations. Different situations require different styles of leadership. Suppose that you are leading a dozen backpackers in the mountains, and it is time to make dinner. A laissez-faire style would be appropriate if the backpackers had brought their own food, or perhaps a democratic style if everyone is expected to pitch in. Authoritarian leadership—telling the hikers how to prepare their meals—would create resentment. This, in turn, would likely interfere with meeting the primary goal of the group, which in this case is to have a good time while enjoying nature.

Now assume the same group but a different situation: One of your party is lost, and a blizzard is on its way. This situation calls for you to exercise authority. To simply shrug your shoulders and say "You figure it out" would invite disaster—and probably a lawsuit.

The Power of Peer Pressure: The Asch Experiment

How influential are groups in our lives? To answer this, let's look first at *conformity* in the sense of going along with our peers. Our peers have no authority over us, only the influence that we allow.

Imagine again that you are taking a course in social psychology, this time with Dr. Solomon Asch. You have agreed to participate in an experiment. As you enter his laboratory, you see seven chairs, five of them already filled by other students. You are given the sixth. Soon the seventh person arrives. Dr. Asch stands at the front of the room next to a covered easel. He explains that he will first show a large card with a vertical line on it, then another card with three vertical lines. Each of you is to tell him which of the three lines matches the line on the first card (see Figure 5.3).

Dr. Asch then uncovers the first card with the single line and the comparison card with the three lines. The correct answer is easy, for two of the lines are obviously wrong, and one is exactly right. Each person, in order, states his or her answer aloud. You all answer correctly. The second trial is just as easy, and you begin to wonder why you are there.

Then on the third trial, something unexpected happens. Just as before, it is easy to tell which lines match. The first student, however, gives a wrong answer. The second gives the same incorrect answer. So do the third and the fourth. By now, you are wondering what is wrong. How will the person next to you answer? You can hardly believe it when he, too, gives the same wrong answer. Then it is your turn, and you give what you know is the right answer. The seventh person also gives the same wrong answer.

On the next trial, the same thing happens. You know that the choice of the other six is wrong. They are giving what to you are obviously wrong answers. You don't know what to think. Why aren't they seeing things the same way you are? Sometimes they do, but in twelve trials they don't. Something is seriously wrong, and you are no longer sure what to do.

When the eighteenth trial is finished, you heave a sigh of relief. The experiment is finally over, and you are ready to bolt for the door. Dr. Asch walks over to you with a big smile on his face and thanks you for participating in the experiment. He explains that you were the only real subject in the experiment! "The other six were stooges. I paid them to give those answers," he says. Now you feel real relief. Your eyes weren't playing tricks on you after all.

FIGURE 5.3   Asch's Cards

Card 1   Card 2

The cards used by Solomon Asch in his classic experiment on group conformity

Source: Asch 1952:452–453.

What were the results? Asch (1952) tested fifty people. One-third (33 percent) gave in to the group half the time, providing what they knew to be wrong answers. Another two out of five (40 percent) gave wrong answers, but not as often. One-quarter (25 percent) stuck to their guns and always gave the right answer. I don't know how I would do on this test (if I knew nothing about it in advance), but I like to think that I would be part of the 25 percent. You probably feel the same way about yourself. But why should we feel that we wouldn't be like *most* people?

The results are disturbing, and researchers are still replicating Asch's experiment (Morl and Aral 2011). In our "land of individualism," the group is so powerful that most people are willing to say things that they know are not true. And this was a group of strangers! How much more conformity can we expect when our group consists of friends, people we value highly and depend on for getting along in life? Again, maybe you will become the sociologist to run that variation of Asch's experiment, perhaps using both female and male subjects.

The Power of Authority: The Milgram Experiment

Let's look at the results of another experiment in the following Thinking Critically section.

THINKING CRITICALLY

If Hitler Asked You to Execute a Stranger, Would You? The Milgram Experiment

Imagine that Dr. Stanley Milgram (1963, 1965), a former student of Dr. Asch's, has asked you to participate in a study on punishment and learning. Assume that you do not know about the Asch experiment and have no reason to be wary. When you arrive at the laboratory, you and a second student draw lots for the roles of "teacher" and "learner." You are to be the teacher. When you see that the learner's chair has

Describe the Asch experiment. What are its implications for society?

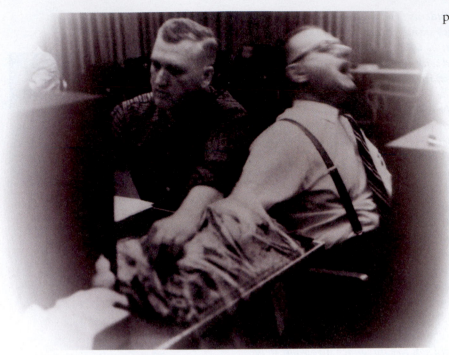

In the 1960s, social psychologists did highly creative but controversial experiments. This photo, taken during Stanley Milgram's experiment, should give you an idea of how convincing the experiment was to the "teacher."

protruding electrodes, you are glad that you are the teacher. Dr. Milgram shows you the machine you will run. You see that one side of the control panel is marked "Mild Shock, 15 volts," while the center says "Intense Shock, 350 Volts," and the far right side reads "DANGER: SEVERE SHOCK."

"As the teacher, you will read aloud a pair of words," explains Dr. Milgram. "Then you will repeat the first word, and the learner will reply with the second word. If the learner can't remember the word, you press this lever on the shock generator. The shock will serve as punishment, and we can then determine if punishment improves memory." You nod, now very relieved that you haven't been designated the learner.

"Every time the learner makes an error, increase the punishment by 15 volts," instructs Dr. Milgram. Then, seeing the look on your face, he adds, "The shocks can be very painful, but they won't cause any permanent tissue damage." He pauses, and then says, "I want you to see." You then follow him to the "electric chair," and Dr. Milgram gives you a shock of 45 volts. "There. That wasn't too bad, was it?" "No," you mumble.

The experiment begins. You hope for the learner's sake that he is bright, but unfortunately he turns out to be rather dull. He gets some answers right, but you have to keep turning up the dial. Each turn makes you more and more uncomfortable. You find yourself hoping that the learner won't miss another answer. But he does. When he received the first shocks, he let out some moans and groans, but now he is screaming in agony. He even protests that he suffers from a heart condition.

How far do you turn that dial?

By now, you probably have guessed that there was no electricity attached to the electrodes and that the "learner" was a stooge who only pretended to feel pain. The purpose of the experiment was to find out at what point people refuse to participate. Does anyone actually turn the lever all the way to "DANGER: SEVERE SHOCK"?

Milgram wanted the answer because millions of ordinary people did nothing to stop the Nazi slaughter of Jews, gypsies, Slavs, homosexuals, people with disabilities, and others whom the Nazis designated as "inferior." The cooperation of so many ordinary people in the face of all this killing seemed bizarre, and Milgram wanted to see how Americans might react to orders from an authority (Russell 2010).

What he found upset Milgram. Some "teachers" broke into a sweat and protested that the experiment was inhuman and should be stopped. But when the experimenter calmly replied that the experiment must go on, this assurance from an "authority" ("scientist, white coat, university laboratory") was enough for most "teachers" to continue, even though the "learner" screamed in agony. Even "teachers" who were "reduced to twitching, stuttering wrecks" continued to follow orders.

Milgram varied the experiments. He used both men and women. In some experiments, he put the "teachers" and "learners" in the same room, so the "teacher" could see the suffering. In others, he put the "learners" in an adjacent room, and had them pound and kick the wall during the first shocks and then go silent. The results varied. When there was no verbal feedback from the "learner," 65 percent of the "teachers" pushed the lever all the way to 450 volts. Of those who could see the "learner,"

Describe the Milgram experiment. What are its implications for society?

40 percent turned the lever all the way. When Milgram added a second "teacher," a stooge who refused to go along with the experiment, only 5 percent of the "teachers" turned the lever all the way.

Milgram's research set off a stormy discussion about research ethics (Nicholson 2011). Researchers agreed that to reduce subjects to "twitching, stuttering wrecks" was unethical, and almost all deception was banned. Universities began to require that subjects be informed of the nature and purpose of social research.

Although researchers were itching to replicate Milgram's experiment, it took almost fifty years before they found a way to satisfy committees that approve research. The findings: People today obey the experimenter at about the same rate that people did in the 1960s (Burger 2009). The results were even higher on *The Game of Death*, a fake game show in France, where the contestants were prodded by the show's host and a shouting audience to administer shocks and win prizes. The contestants kept turning up the dial, with 80 percent of them giving victims what they thought were near-lethal 450-volt shocks (Crumley 2010).

For Your Consideration
➔ Taking into account how significant Milgram's findings are, do you think that the scientific community overreacted to these experiments? Should we allow such research? Consider both the Asch and Milgram experiments, and use symbolic interactionism, functionalism, and conflict theory to explain why groups have such influence over us. ■

Global Consequences of Group Dynamics: Groupthink

Suppose you are a member of the U.S. president's inner circle. It is midnight, and the president has called an emergency meeting. There has just been a terrorist attack, and you must decide how to respond to it. You and the others suggest several options. Eventually, these are narrowed to only a couple of choices, and at some point, everyone seems to agree on what now appears to be "the only possible course of action." To criticize the proposed solution at this point will bring you in conflict with all the other important people in the room, and mark you as "not a team player." So you keep your mouth shut. As a result, each step commits you—and them—more and more to the "only" course of action.

Under some circumstances, as in this example, the influence of authority and peers can lead to **groupthink.** Sociologist Irving Janis (1972, 1982) used this term to refer to the collective tunnel vision that group members sometimes develop. As they begin to think alike, they become convinced that there is only one "right" viewpoint and a single course of action to follow. They take any suggestion of alternatives as a sign of disloyalty. With their perspective narrowed and fully convinced that they are right, they may even put aside moral judgments and disregard risk (Hart 1991; Flippen 1999).

Groupthink can bring catastrophe. Consider the *Columbia* space shuttle disaster of 2003.

Foam broke loose during launch, raising concerns that this might have damaged tiles on the nose cone, making reentry dangerous. Engineers sent e-mails to NASA officials, warning them about the risk. One suggested that the crew do a "space walk" to examine the tiles (Vartabedian and Gold 2003). The team in charge of the Columbia *shuttle, however, disregarded the warnings. Convinced that a piece of foam weighing less than two pounds could not seriously harm the shuttle, they refused to even consider the possibility (Wald and Schwartz 2003). The fiery results of their closed minds were transmitted around the globe.*

Groupthink can lead to consequences even greater than this. In 1941, President Franklin D. Roosevelt and his chiefs of staff had evidence that the Japanese were preparing to attack Pearl Harbor. Refusing to believe it, they decided to continue naval operations as usual. The destruction of the U.S. naval fleet ushered the United States into World War II. During the Vietnam war, U.S. officials had evidence of the strength and determination of the North Vietnamese military. These officials arrogantly threw the evidence aside, refusing to believe that "little, uneducated, bare-foot people in pajamas" could defeat the U.S. military.

In each of these cases, options closed as officials committed themselves to a single course of action. Questioning the decisions would have indicated disloyalty and disregard for "team play." No longer did those in power try to weigh events objectively. Interpreting ongoing events as supporting their one "correct" decision, they plunged ahead, blind to disconfirming evidence and alternative perspectives.

One of the fascinating aspects of groupthink is how it can lead "good" people to do "bad" things. Consider what I mentioned earlier, the aftermath of 9/11. Government officials actually defended torture as moral, "the lesser of two evils." Thought narrowed so greatly that the U.S. Justice Department ruled that the United States was not bound by the Geneva Convention that prohibits torture (Lewis 2005). Even medical professionals, supposedly trained to heal and help people, joined in. They advised the CIA interrogators, telling them when to adjust or stop the water-boarding, slamming prisoners' heads into walls, or shackling a prisoner's arms to the ceiling (Shane 2009).

Do you see the power of groups and groupthink?

Preventing Groupthink.   The leaders of a government tend to surround themselves with an inner circle that closely reflects their own views. In "briefings," written summaries, and "talking points," this inner circle spoon-feeds the leaders information it has selected. As a result, the top leaders, such as the president, are largely cut off from information that does not support their own opinions. You can see how the mental captivity and intellectual paralysis known as groupthink is built into this arrangement.

Perhaps the key to preventing groupthink is the widest possible circulation—especially among a nation's top government officials—of research by social scientists independent of the government and information that media reporters have gathered freely. If this conclusion comes across as an unabashed plug for sociological research and the free exchange of ideas, it is. Giving free rein to diverse opinions can curb groupthink, which—if not prevented—can lead to the destruction of a society and, in today's world of nuclear, chemical, and biological weapons, the obliteration of Earth's inhabitants.

CHAPTER 5 Summary and Review

Groups within Society

How do sociologists classify groups?

Sociologists divide groups into primary groups, secondary groups, in-groups, out-groups, reference groups, and networks. The cooperative, intimate, long-term, face-to-face relationships provided by **primary groups** are fundamental to our sense of self. **Secondary groups** are larger, relatively temporary, and more anonymous, formal, and impersonal than primary groups. **In-groups** provide members with a strong sense of identity and belonging. **Out-groups** also foster identity by showing in-group members what they are *not*. **Reference groups** are groups whose standards we refer to as we evaluate ourselves. **Social networks** consist of social ties that link people together. Pp. 126–131.

What is "the iron law of oligarchy"?

Sociologist Robert Michels noted that formal organizations have a tendency to become controlled by an inner circle that limits leadership to its own members. The dominance of a formal organization by an elite that keeps itself in power is called **the iron law of oligarchy.** Pp. 128–129.

How closely are the members of society related?

We interact within **social networks,** which are vital for our well-being. That we are connected to almost all members of society by just a few degrees, the **small world phenomenon,** has been challenged. Pp. 131-132.

Bureaucracies

What are bureaucracies?

Bureaucracies are social groups characterized by a hierarchy, division of labor, written rules and communications, and impersonality and replaceability of positions. **Goal displacement** is also common. These characteristics make bureaucracies efficient and enduring. Pp. 132–136.

What dysfunctions are associated with bureaucracies?

The dysfunctions of bureaucracies include red tape, alienation, and incompetence (as seen in the **Peter principle**). In Weber's view, the impersonality of bureaucracies tends to produce **alienation** among workers—the feeling that no one cares about them and that they do not really fit in. Marx's view of alienation is somewhat different—workers do not identify with the product of their labor because they participate in only a small part of the production process. Pp. 137–139.

Working for the Corporation

How does the corporate culture affect workers?

Within corporate culture are values and stereotypes that are not readily visible. Often, **self-fulfilling stereotypes** are at work: People who match a corporation's hidden values tend to be put on career tracks that enhance their chance of success, while those who do not match those values are set on a course that minimizes their performance. Pp. 139–140.

Technology and the Control of Workers

What is the maximum-security society?

Computers and surveillance devices are increasingly used to monitor people, especially in the workplace. This technology is being extended to monitoring our everyday lives. Pp. 140–141.

Group Dynamics

How does a group's size affect its dynamics?

The term **group dynamics** refers to how individuals affect groups and how groups influence individuals. In a **small group,** everyone can interact directly with everyone else. As a group grows larger, its intensity decreases but its stability increases. A **dyad,** consisting of two people, is the most unstable of human groups, but it provides the most intimate relationships. The addition of a third person, forming a **triad,** fundamentally alters relationships. Triads are unstable, as **coalitions** (the alignment of some members of a group against others) tend to form. Pp. 141–143.

What characterizes a leader?

A **leader** is someone who influences others. **Instrumental leaders** try to keep a group moving toward its goals, even though this causes friction and they lose popularity. **Expressive leaders** focus on creating harmony and raising group morale. Both types are essential to the functioning of groups. Pp. 143–145.

What are three leadership styles?

Authoritarian leaders give orders, **democratic leaders** try to lead by consensus, and **laissez-faire leaders** are highly permissive. An authoritarian style appears to be more effective in emergency situations, a democratic style works best for most situations, and a laissez-faire style is usually ineffective. Pp. 145–146.

How do groups encourage conformity?

The Asch experiment was cited to illustrate the influence of peer pressure, the Milgram experiment to illustrate the influence of authority. Both experiments demonstrate how easily we can succumb to **groupthink,** a kind of collective tunnel vision. Preventing groupthink requires the free circulation of diverse and opposing ideas. Pp. 146–150.

Thinking Critically about Chapter 5

1. Identify your in-groups and your out-groups. How have your in-groups influenced the way you see the world? And what influence have your out-groups had on you?

2. You are likely to work for a bureaucracy. How do you think that this will affect your orientations to life? How can you make the "hidden culture" work to your advantage?

3. Asch's experiments illustrate the power of peer pressure. How has peer pressure operated in your life? Think about something that you did, despite not wanting to, because of peer pressure.

Arizona

In just a few moments I was to meet my first Yanomamö, my first primitive man. What would it be like? . . . I looked up [from my canoe] and gasped when I saw a dozen burly, naked, filthy, hideous men staring at us down the shafts of their drawn arrows. Immense wads of green tobacco were stuck between their lower teeth and lips, making them look even more hideous, and strands of dark-green slime dripped or hung from their noses. We arrived at the village while the men were blowing a hallucinogenic drug up their noses. One of the side effects of the drug is a runny nose. The mucus is always saturated with the green powder, and the Indians usually let it run freely from their nostrils. . . . I just sat there holding my notebook, helpless and pathetic. . . .

The whole situation was depressing, and I wondered why I ever decided to switch from civil engineering to anthropology in the first place. . . . [Soon] I was covered with red pigment, the result of a dozen or so complete examinations. . . . These examinations capped an otherwise grim day. The Indians would blow their noses into their hands, flick as much of the mucus off that would separate in a snap of the wrist, wipe the residue into their hair, and then carefully examine my face, arms, legs, hair, and the contents of my pockets. I said [in their language], "Your hands are dirty"; my comments were met by the Indians in the following way: they would "clean" their hands by spitting a quantity of slimy tobacco juice into them, rub them together, and then proceed with the examination.

> **"They would "clean" their hands by spitting slimy tobacco juice into them."**

This is how Napoleon Chagnon describes the culture shock he felt when he met the Yanomamö tribe of the rain forests of Brazil. His ensuing months of fieldwork continued to bring surprise after surprise, and often Chagnon (1977) could hardly believe his eyes—or his nose.

If you were to list the deviant behaviors of the Yanomamö, what would you include? The way they appear naked in public? Use hallucinogenic drugs? Let mucus hang from their noses? Or the way they rub hands filled with mucus, spittle, and tobacco juice over a frightened stranger who doesn't dare to protest? Perhaps. But it isn't this simple, for as we shall see, deviance is relative.

What Is Deviance?

Sociologists use the term **deviance** to refer to any violation of norms, whether the infraction is as minor as driving over the speed limit, as serious as murder, or as humorous as Chagnon's encounter with the Yanomamö. This deceptively simple definition takes us to the heart of the sociological perspective on deviance, which sociologist Howard S. Becker (1966) described this way: *It is not the act itself, but the reactions to the act, that make something deviant.* What Chagnon saw disturbed him, but to the Yanomamö those same behaviors represented normal, everyday life. What was deviant to Chagnon was *conformist* to the Yanomamö. From their viewpoint, you *should* check out strangers the way they did—and nakedness is good, as are hallucinogenic drugs. And it is natural to let mucus flow.

I took this photo on the outskirts of Hyderabad, India. Is this man deviant? If this were a U.S. street, he would be. But here? No houses have running water in his neighborhood, and the men, women, and children bathe at the neighborhood water pump. This man, then, would not be deviant in this culture. And yet, he is actually mugging for my camera, making the three bystanders laugh. Does this additional factor make this a scene of deviance?

The Relativity of Deviance.   Chagnon's abrupt introduction to the Yanomamö allows us to see the *relativity of deviance,* a major point made by symbolic interactionists. Because different groups have different norms, *what is deviant to some is not deviant to others.* This principle applies not just to cultures but also to groups within the same society. Look at the photo on this page and the one on page 156. We explore this idea further in the Cultural Diversity box on the next page.

This principle also applies to a specific form of deviance known as **crime,** the violation of rules that have been written into law. In the extreme, an act that is applauded by one group may be so despised by another group that it is punishable by death. Making a huge profit on business deals is one example. Americans who do this are admired. Like Donald Trump and Warren Buffet, they may even write books about their exploits. In China, however, until recently this same act was considered a crime called *profiteering.* Those found guilty were hanged in a public square as a lesson to all.

A Neutral Term.   Unlike the general public, sociologists use the term *deviance* non-judgmentally, to refer to any act to which people respond negatively. When sociologists use this term, it does *not* mean that they agree that an act is bad, just that people judge it negatively. To sociologists, then, *all* of us are deviants of one sort or another, for we all violate norms from time to time.

Stigma.   To be considered deviant, a person does not even have to *do* anything. Sociologist Erving Goffman (1963) used the term **stigma** to refer to characteristics that discredit people. These include violations of norms of appearance (a facial birthmark, a huge nose or ears) and norms of ability (blindness, deafness, mental handicaps). Also included are involuntary memberships, such as being a victim of AIDS or the brother of a rapist. The stigma can become a person's master status, defining him or her as deviant. Recall from Chapter 4 that a master status cuts across all other statuses that a person occupies.

How Norms Make Social Life Possible

No human group can exist without norms, for *norms make social life possible by making behavior predictable.* What would life be like if you could not predict what others would do? Imagine for a moment that you have gone to a store to purchase milk:

Cultural Diversity around the World

Human Sexuality in Cross-Cultural Perspective

Human sexuality illustrates how a group's *definition* of an act, not the act itself, determines whether it will be considered deviant. Let's look at some examples reported by anthropologist Robert Edgerton (1976).

Norms of sexual behavior vary so widely around the world that what is considered normal in one society may be considered deviant in another. In Kenya, a group called the Pokot place high emphasis on sexual pleasure, and they expect that both a husband and wife will reach orgasm. If a husband does not satisfy his wife, he is in trouble—especially if she thinks that his failure is because of adultery. If this is so, the wife and her female friends will sneak up on her husband when he is asleep. The women will tie him up, shout obscenities at him, beat him, and then urinate on him. Before releasing him, as a final gesture of their contempt they will slaughter and eat his favorite ox. The husband's hours of painful humiliation are intended to make him more dutiful concerning his wife's conjugal rights.

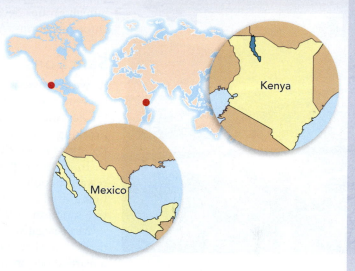

People can also become deviants for following their group's ideal norms instead of its real norms. As with many groups, the Zapotec Indians of Mexico profess that sexual relations should take place exclusively between husband and wife. However, the Zapotec also have a covert norm, an unspoken understanding, that married people will have affairs, but that they will be discreet about them. In one Zapotec community, the *only* person who did not have an extramarital affair was condemned by everyone in the village. The reason was not that she did not have an affair but that she told the other wives the names of the women their husbands were sleeping with. It is an interesting case,

A Pokot married woman, Kenya

for if this virtuous woman had had an affair—and kept her mouth shut—she would not have become a deviant. Clearly, real norms can conflict with ideal norms—another illustration of the gap between ideal and real culture.

For Your Consideration

➤ How do the behaviors of the Pokot wives and husbands mentioned here look from the perspective of U.S. norms? What are those U.S. norms? What norms did the Zapotec woman break? (We discussed this concept in Chapter 2, pages 42–43.)

Suppose the clerk says, "I won't sell you any milk. We're overstocked with soda, and I'm not going to sell anyone milk until our soda inventory is reduced."

You don't like it, but you decide to buy a case of soda. At the checkout, the clerk says, "I hope you don't mind, but there's a $5 service charge on every fifteenth customer." You, of course, are the fifteenth.

Just as you start to leave, another clerk stops you and says, "We're not working anymore. We decided to have a party." Suddenly a CD player begins to blast, and everyone in the store begins to dance. "Oh, good, you've brought the soda," says a different clerk, who takes your package and passes sodas all around.

Life is not like this, of course. You can depend on grocery clerks to sell you milk. You can also depend on paying the same price as everyone else and not being forced to attend a party in the store. Why can you depend on this? Because we are socialized to follow norms, to play the basic roles that society assigns to us.

How do ideal and real norms work together in determining what is deviant?

Violating background assumptions is a common form of deviance. Although we have no explicit rule that says, "Do not put snakes through your nose," we all know that it exists (perhaps as a subcategory of "Don't do strange things in public"). Is this act also deviant for this man in Chennai, India?

Without norms, we would have social chaos. Norms lay out the basic guidelines for how we should play our roles and interact with others. In short, norms bring about **social order,** a group's customary social arrangements. Our lives are based on these arrangements, which is why deviance often is perceived as threatening: *Deviance undermines predictability, the foundation of social life.* Consequently, human groups develop a system of **social control**—formal and informal means of enforcing norms. At the center of social control are sanctions.

Sanctions

As we discussed in Chapter 2, people do not enforce folkways strictly, but they become upset when people break mores (MO-rays). Expressions of disapproval for deviance, called **negative sanctions,** range from frowns and gossip for breaking folkways to imprisonment and death for breaking mores. In general, the more seriously the group takes a norm, the harsher the penalty for violating it. In contrast, **positive sanctions**—from smiles to formal awards—are used to reward people for conforming to norms. Getting a raise is a positive sanction; being fired is a negative sanction. Getting an *A* in intro to sociology is a positive sanction; getting an *F* is a negative one.

Most negative sanctions are informal. You might stare if you observe someone dressed in what you consider to be inappropriate clothing, or you might gossip if a married person you know spends the night with someone other than his or her spouse. Whether you consider the breaking of a norm merely an amusing matter that warrants no sanction or a serious infraction that does, however, depends on your perspective. Let's suppose that a woman appears at your college graduation in a bikini. You might stare, laugh, and nudge the person next to you, but if this is *your* mother, you are likely to feel that different sanctions are appropriate. Similarly, if it is *your* father who spends the night with an 18-year-old college freshman, you are likely to do more than gossip.

In Sum: In sociology, the term *deviance* refers to all violations of social rules, regardless of their seriousness. The term is neutral, not a judgment about the behavior. Deviance is relative, for what is deviant in one group may be conformist in another. Consequently, we must consider deviance from *within* a group's own framework, for it is their meanings that underlie their behavior.

Competing Explanations of Deviance: Sociobiology, Psychology, and Sociology

If social life is to exist, norms are essential. So why do people violate them? To better understand the reasons, it is useful to know how sociological explanations differ from biological and psychological ones.

Biosocial Explanations.   *Sociobiologists* explain deviance by looking for answers within individuals. They assume that **genetic predispositions** lead people to such behaviors as juvenile delinquency and crime (Lombroso 1911; Wilson and Herrnstein 1985; Goozen et al. 2007). An early explanation was that men with an extra Y chromosome (the "XYY" theory) were more likely to become criminals. Another was that people with "squarish, muscular" bodies were more likely to commit **street crime**—acts such as mugging, rape, and burglary. These theories were abandoned when research did not support them.

With advances in the study of genetics, biosocial explanations are being proposed to explain differences in crime by age (juvenile delinquency), sex, race, and social class (Walsh and Beaver 2009). The basic explanation is that over the millennia people with certain characteristics were more likely to survive than were people with different characteristics. As a result, different groups today inherit different propensities (tendencies) for empathy, self-control, and risk-taking.

A universal finding is that in all known societies men commit more violent crimes than women do. There are no exceptions. Here is how sociobiologists explain this. It took only a few pelvic thrusts for men to pass on their genes. After that, they could leave if they wanted to. The women, in contrast, had to carry, birth, and nurture the children. Women who were more empathetic (inclined to nurture their children) engaged in less dangerous behavior. These women passed genes for more empathy, greater self-control, and less risk-taking to their female children. As a result, all over the world, men engage in more violent behavior, which comes from their lesser empathy, lower self-control, and greater tendency for taking risks.

Biosocial theorists stress that deviant behavior does not depend on genes alone. Our inherited propensities (the *bio* part) are modified and stimulated by our environment (the *social* part). Biosocial research is promising and holds the potential of opening a new understanding of deviance.

Psychological Explanations. Psychologists focus on abnormalities *within* the individual. Instead of genes, they examine what are called **personality disorders.** Their supposition is that deviating individuals have deviating personalities (Barnes 2001; Mayer 2007) and that subconscious motives drive people to deviance.

Researchers have never found a specific childhood experience to be invariably linked with deviance. For example, some children who had "bad toilet training," "suffocating mothers," or "emotionally aloof fathers" do become embezzling bookkeepers—but others become good accountants. Just as college students and police officers represent a variety of bad—and good—childhood experiences, so do deviants. Similarly, people with "suppressed anger" can become freeway snipers or military heroes—or anything else. In short, there is no inevitable outcome of any childhood experience. Deviance is not associated with any particular personality.

Sociological Explanations. Sociologists, in contrast with both sociobiologists and psychologists, search for factors *outside* the individual. They look for social influences that "recruit" people to break norms. To account for why people commit crimes, for example, sociologists examine such external influences as socialization, membership in subcultures, and social class. *Social class,* a concept that we will discuss in depth in Chapter 8, refers to people's relative standing in terms of education, occupation, and especially income and wealth.

To explain deviance, sociologists apply the three sociological perspectives—symbolic interactionism, functionalism, and conflict theory. Let's compare these three explanations.

Every society has boundaries that divide what is considered socially acceptable from what is not acceptable. Lady Gaga has made her claim to fame by challenging those boundaries.

The Symbolic Interactionist Perspective

As we examine symbolic interactionism, it will become more evident why sociologists are not satisfied with explanations that are rooted in sociobiology or psychology. A basic principle of symbolic interactionism is that we are thinking beings who act according to how we interpret situations. Let's consider how our membership in groups influences how we view life and, from there, our behavior.

Differential Association Theory

The Theory. Going directly against the idea that biology or personality is the source of deviance, sociologists stress our experiences in groups (Deflem 2006; Chambliss 1973/2012). Consider an extreme: boys and girls who join street gangs and those who join the Scouts. Obviously, each will learn different attitudes and behaviors concerning deviance and conformity. Edwin Sutherland coined the term **differential association** to indicate this: From the *different* groups we *associate* with, we learn to deviate from or conform to society's norms (Sutherland 1924, 1947; McCarthy 2011).

Sutherland's theory is more complicated than this, but he basically said that the different groups with which we associate (our "*different*ial association") give us messages about conformity and deviance. We may receive mixed messages, but we end up with more of one than the other (an "excess of definitions," as Sutherland put it). The end result is an imbalance—attitudes that tilt us in one direction or another. Consequently, we learn to either conform or to deviate.

Watch
Motherhood Manifesto
on **mysoclab.com**

Families.   Since our family is so important for teaching us attitudes, it probably is obvious to you that the family makes a big difference in whether we learn deviance or conformity. Researchers have confirmed this informal observation. Of the many confirming studies, this one stands out: Of all prison inmates across the United States, about *half* have a father, mother, brother, sister, or spouse who has served time in prison (*Sourcebook of Criminal Justice Statistics* 2003:Table 6.0011; Glaze and Maruschak 2008:Table 11). In short, families that are involved in crime tend to set their children on a lawbreaking path.

Friends, Neighborhoods, and Subcultures.   Most people don't know the term *differential association*, but they do know how it works. Most parents want to move out of "bad" neighborhoods because they know that if their kids have delinquent friends, they are likely to become delinquent, too. Sociological research also supports this common observation (Miller 1958; Chung and Steinberg 2006; Church et al. 2009).

In some neighborhoods, violence is so woven into the subculture that even a wrong glance can mean your death ("Why you lookin' at me?") (Gardiner and Fox 2010). If the neighbors feel that a victim deserved to be killed, they refuse to testify because "he got what was coming to him" (Kubrin and Weitzer 2003). Killing can even be viewed as honorable:

Sociologist Ruth Horowitz (1983, 2005), who did participant observation in a lower-class Chicano neighborhood in Chicago, discovered how the concept of "honor" propels young men to deviance. The formula is simple. "A real man has honor. An insult is a threat to one's honor. Therefore, not to stand up to someone is to be less than a real man."

Now suppose you are a young man growing up in this neighborhood. You likely would do a fair amount of fighting, for you would interpret many things as attacks on your honor. You might even carry a knife or a gun, for words and fists wouldn't always be sufficient. Along with members of your group, you would define fighting, knifing, and shooting quite differently from the way most people do.

Members of the Mafia also intertwine ideas of manliness with killing. For them, *to kill is a measure of their manhood*. If a Mafia member were to seduce the *capo*'s wife or girlfriend, for example, the seduction would slash at the *capo*'s manliness and honor. The only course open would be direct retaliation. The offender's body would be found with his penis stuffed in his mouth. However, not all killings are accorded the same respect, for "the more awesome and potent the victim, the more worthy and meritorious the killer" (Arlacchi 1980).

From this example, you can see how relative deviance is. Although killing is deviant to mainstream society, for members of the Mafia, *not* to kill after certain rules are broken is the deviant act.

Prison or Freedom?   As was mentioned in Chapter 3, an issue that comes up over and over again in sociology is whether we are prisoners of socialization. Symbolic interactionists stress that we are not mere pawns in the hands of others. We are not destined to think and act as our groups dictate. Rather, we *help to produce our own orientations to life*. By joining one group rather than another (differential association), for example, we help to shape the self. For instance, one college student may join a feminist group that is trying to change the treatment of women in college, while another associates with women who shoplift on weekends. Their choices point them in different directions. The one who joins the feminist group may develop an even greater interest in producing social change, while the one who associates with shoplifters may become even more oriented toward criminal activities.

To experience a sense of belonging is a basic human need. Membership in groups is a primary way that people meet this need. Regardless of the orientation of the group—whether to conformity, as with the Girl Scouts, or to deviance, as with the Mafia—the process is the same.

Control Theory

Do you ever feel the urge to do something that you know you shouldn't, even something that would get you in trouble? Most of us fight temptations to break society's norms. We find that we have to stifle things inside us—urges, hostilities, raunchy desires of various sorts. And most of the time, we manage to keep ourselves out of trouble.

What is differential association theory? How do family and friends fit into this theory?

The basic question that **control theory** tries to answer is, With the desire to deviate so common, why don't we all just "bust loose"?

The Theory. Sociologist Walter Reckless (1973), who developed control theory, stressed that two control systems work against our motivations to deviate. Our *inner controls* include our internalized morality—conscience, religious principles, ideas of right and wrong. Inner controls also include fears of punishment, feelings of integrity, and the desire to be a "good" person (Hirschi 1969; McShane and Williams 2007). Our *outer controls* consist of people—such as family, friends, and the police—who influence us not to deviate.

The stronger our bonds are with society, the more effective our inner controls are (Hirschi 1969). These bonds are based on *attachments* (our affection and respect for people who conform to mainstream norms), *commitments* (having a stake in society that you don't want to risk, such as your place in your family, being a college student, or having a job), *involvements* (participating in approved activities), and *beliefs* (convictions that certain actions are wrong).

This theory can be summarized as *self*-control, says sociologist Travis Hirschi. The key to learning strong self-control is socialization, especially in childhood. Parents help their children to develop self-control by supervising them and punishing their deviant acts (Gottfredson and Hirschi 1990; Church et al. 2009). They sometimes use shame to keep their children in line. You probably had that forefinger shaken at you. I certainly recall it aimed at me. Do you think that more use of shaming, discussed in the Down-to-Earth Sociology box on the next page, could help increase people's internal controls?

Applying Control Theory.

Suppose that some friends invite you to go to a nightclub with them. When you get there, you notice that everyone seems unusually happy—almost giddy. They seem to be euphoric in their animated conversations and dancing. Your friends tell you that almost everyone here has taken the drug Ecstasy, and they invite you to take some with them.
   What do you do?

Let's not explore the question of whether taking Ecstasy in this setting is a deviant or a conforming act. This is a separate issue. Instead, concentrate on the pushes and pulls you would feel. The pushes toward taking the drug: your friends, the setting, and perhaps your curiosity. Then there are your inner controls—those inner voices of your conscience and your parents, perhaps of your teachers, as well as your fears of arrest and the dangers you've heard about illegal drugs. There are also the outer controls—perhaps the uniformed security guard looking in your direction.

So, what *did* you decide? Which was stronger: your inner and outer controls or the pushes and pulls toward taking the drug? It is you who can best weigh these forces, for they differ with each of us. This little example puts us at the center of what control theory is all about.

Labeling Theory

Suppose for one undesirable moment that people around you thought of you as a "whore," a "pervert," or a "cheat." (Pick one.) What power such a reputation would have—both on how others would see you and on how you would see yourself. How about if you became known as "very intelligent," "gentle and understanding," or "honest to the core"? (Choose one.) You can see that such a reputation would give people different expectations of your character and behavior.

This is what **labeling theory** focuses on, the significance of reputations, how they help set us on paths that propel us into deviance or that divert us away from it.

Rejecting Labels: How People Neutralize Deviance. Not many of us want to be called "whore," "pervert," or "cheat." We resist negative labels, even lesser ones than

The social control of deviance takes many forms, including the actions of the police. Being arrested here is a Florida woman accused of prostitution.

How powerful are labels? Consider Mel Gibson. Previously, he had a sterling reputation (a label) as actor and film maker. After anti-Semitic rants when stopped for drunk driving and, later, threats to a pregnant girlfriend, Gibson's reputation changed abruptly. How do you think his new label will affect his life? Do you think Gibson can rescue his reputation?

Down-to-Earth Sociology

Shaming: Making a Comeback?

Shaming can be effective, especially when members of a primary group use it. In some communities, where the individual's reputation was at stake, shaming was the centerpiece of the enforcement of norms. Violators were marked as deviant and held up for all the world to see. In Nathaniel Hawthorne's *The Scarlet Letter*, town officials forced Hester Prynne to wear a scarlet A sewn on her dress. The A stood for *adulteress*. Wherever she went, Prynne had to wear this badge of shame, and the community expected her to wear it every day for the rest of her life.

As our society grew large and urban, the sense of community diminished, and shaming lost its effectiveness. Now shaming is starting to make a comeback (Appiah 2010). One Arizona sheriff makes the men in his jail wear striped prison uniforms—and pink underwear (Billeaud 2008). They also wear pink while they work in chain gangs. Women prisoners, too, are put in chain gangs and forced to pick up street trash. Online shaming sites have also appeared. Captured on cell phone cameras are bad drivers, older men who leer at teenaged girls, and people who don't pick up their dog's poop (Saranow 2007). Some sites post photos of the offenders, as well as their addresses and phone numbers. In Spain, where one's reputation with neighbors still matters, debt collectors, dressed in tuxedo and top hat, walk slowly to the front door. The sight shames debtors into paying (Catan 2008).

To avoid jail time, this woman in Pennsylvania chose the judge's option of public shaming.

Sociologist Harold Garfinkel (1956) gave the name **degradation ceremony** to an extreme form of shaming. The individual is called to account before the group, witnesses denounce him or her, the offender is pronounced guilty, and steps are taken to strip the individual of his or her identity as a group member. In some courts martial, officers who are found guilty stand at attention before their peers while others rip the insignia of rank from their uniforms. This procedure screams that the individual is no longer a member of the group. Although Hester Prynne was not banished from the group physically, she was banished morally; her degradation ceremony proclaimed her a *moral* outcast from the community. The scarlet A marked her as not "one of them."

Although we don't use scarlet A's today, informal degradation ceremonies still occur. Consider what happened to this New York City police officer (Chivers 2001):

Joseph Gray had been a police officer in New York City for fifteen years. As with some of his fellow officers, alcohol and sex helped relieve the pressures of police work. After spending one afternoon drinking in a topless bar, bleary-eyed, Gray plowed his car into a vehicle carrying a pregnant woman, her son, and her sister. All three died. Gray was accused of manslaughter and drunk driving.

The New York Times and New York television stations kept hammering this story to the public. Three weeks later, Gray resigned from the police force. As he left police headquarters after resigning, an angry crowd surrounded him. Gray hung his head in public disgrace as Victor Manuel Herrera, whose wife and son were killed in the crash, followed him, shouting, "You're a murderer!" (Gray was later convicted of drunk driving and manslaughter.)

For Your Consideration

→ 1. How do you think law enforcement officials might use shaming to reduce law breaking?
2. How do you think school officials could use shaming?
3. Suppose that you were caught shoplifting at a store near where you live. Would you rather spend a week in jail with no one but your family knowing it (and no permanent record) or a week walking in front of the store you stole from wearing a placard that proclaims in bold red capital letters: I AM A THIEF! and in smaller letters says: "I am sorry for stealing from this store and making you pay higher prices"? Why?

What conditions do you think would be necessary for shaming to be effective?

these that others might try to pin on us. Some people are so successful at rejecting labels that even though they beat people up and vandalize property they consider themselves to be conforming members of society. How do they do it?

Sociologists Gresham Sykes and David Matza (1957/1988) studied boys like this. They found that the boys used five **techniques of neutralization** to deflect society's norms.

Denial of responsibility. Some boys said, "I'm not responsible for what happened because . . ." and then they were quite creative about the "becauses." Some said that what happened was an "accident." Other boys saw themselves as "victims" of society. What else could you expect? They were like billiard balls shot around the pool table of life.

Denial of injury. Another favorite explanation was "What I did wasn't wrong because no one got hurt." The boys would define vandalism as "mischief," gang fights as a "private quarrel," and stealing cars as "borrowing." They might acknowledge that what they did was illegal, but claim that they were "just having a little fun."

Denial of a victim. Some boys thought of themselves as avengers. Vandalizing a teacher's car was done to get revenge for an unfair grade, while shoplifting was a way to even the score with "crooked" store owners. In short, even if the boys did accept responsibility and admit that someone had gotten hurt, they protected their self-concept by claiming that the people "deserved what they got."

Condemnation of the condemners. Another technique the boys used was to deny that others had the right to judge them. They might accuse people who pointed their fingers at them of being "a bunch of hypocrites": The police were "on the take," teachers had "pets," and parents cheated on their taxes. In short, they said, "Who are *they* to accuse *me* of something?"

Appeal to higher loyalties. A final technique the boys used to justify their activities was to consider loyalty to the gang more important than the norms of society. They might say, "I had to help my friends. That's why I got in the fight." Not incidentally, the boy may have shot two members of a rival group, as well as a bystander!

In Sum: These techniques of neutralization have implications far beyond this group of boys, for it is not only delinquents who try to neutralize the norms of mainstream society. Look again at these techniques—don't they sound familiar? (1) "I couldn't help myself"; (2) "Who really got hurt?"; (3) "Don't you think she deserved that, after what she did?"; (4) "Who are you to talk?"; and (5) "I had to help my friends—wouldn't you have done the same thing?" All of us attempt to neutralize the moral demands of society, for neutralization helps us to sleep at night.

Embracing Labels: The Example of Outlaw Bikers.   Although most of us resist attempts to label us as deviant, some people revel in a deviant identity. Some teenagers, for example, make certain by their clothing, music, hairstyles, and body art that no one misses their rejection of adult norms. Their status among fellow members of a subculture—within which they are almost obsessive conformists—is vastly more important than any status outside it.

One of the best examples of a group that embraces deviance is a motorcycle gang. Sociologist Mark Watson (1980/2006) did participant observation with outlaw bikers. He rebuilt Harleys with them, hung around their bars and homes, and went on "runs" (trips) with them. He concluded that outlaw bikers see the

While most people resist labels of deviance, some embrace them. In what different ways does this photo illustrate the embracement of deviance?

How do juvenile delinquents neutralize their deviance? How do you?

world as "hostile, weak, and effeminate." Holding this conventional world in contempt, gang members pride themselves on breaking its norms and getting in trouble, laughing at death, and treating women as lesser beings whose primary value is to provide them with services—especially sex. They pride themselves in looking "dirty, mean, and generally undesirable," taking pleasure in shocking people by their appearance and behavior. Outlaw bikers also regard themselves as losers, a view that becomes woven into their unusual embrace of deviance.

📖 **Read**

The Saints and the Roughnecks
by William Chambliss
on **mysoclab.com**

The Power of Labels: The Saints and the Roughnecks.   Labels are powerful. When courts label teenagers as delinquents, it often triggers a process that leads to greater involvement in deviance (DeLisi et al. 2011). We can see how powerful labeling is by referring back to the "Saints" and the "Roughnecks," research that was cited in Chapter 4. (p. 119) As you recall, both groups of high school boys were "constantly occupied with truancy, drinking, wild parties, petty theft, and vandalism." Yet their teachers looked on one group, the Saints, as "headed for success" and the other group, the Roughnecks, as "headed for trouble." By the time they finished high school, not one Saint had been arrested, while the Roughnecks had been in constant trouble with the police.

Why did the members of the community perceive these boys so differently? Chambliss (1973/2012) concluded that this split vision was due to *social class*. As symbolic interactionists emphasize, social class is like a lens that focuses our perceptions. The Saints came from respectable, middle-class families, while the Roughnecks were from less respectable, working-class families. These backgrounds led teachers and the authorities to expect good behavior from the Saints but trouble from the Roughnecks. And, like the rest of us, teachers and police saw what they expected to see.

The boys' social class also affected their visibility. The Saints had automobiles, and they did their drinking and vandalism outside of town. Without cars, the Roughnecks hung around their own street corners, where their drinking and boisterous behavior drew the attention of police, confirming the negative impressions that the community already had of them.

The boys' social class also equipped them with distinct *styles of interaction*. When police or teachers questioned them, the Saints were apologetic. Their show of respect for authority elicited a positive reaction from teachers and police, allowing the Saints to escape school and legal problems. The Roughnecks, said Chambliss, were "almost the polar opposite." When questioned, they were hostile. Even when they tried to assume a respectful attitude, everyone could see through it. Consequently, while teachers and police let the Saints off with warnings, they came down hard on the Roughnecks.

Certainly, what happens in life is not determined by labels alone, but the Saints and the Roughnecks did live up to the labels that the community gave them. As you may recall, all but one of the Saints went on to college. One earned a Ph.D., one became a lawyer, one a doctor, and the others business managers. In contrast, only two of the Roughnecks went to college. They earned athletic scholarships and became coaches. The other Roughnecks did not fare so well. Two of them dropped out of high school, later became involved in separate killings, and were sent to prison. Of the final two, one became a local bookie, and no one knows the whereabouts of the other.

How do labels work? Although the matter is complex, because it involves the self-concept and reactions that vary from one individual to another, we can note that labels open and close doors of opportunity. Unlike its meaning in sociology, the term *deviant* in everyday usage is emotionally charged with a judgment of some sort. This label can lock people out of conforming groups and push them into almost exclusive contact with people who have been similarly labeled.

In Sum: Symbolic interactionists examine how people's definitions of the situation underlie their deviating from or conforming to social norms. They focus on group membership (differential association), how people balance pressures to conform and to deviate (control theory), and the significance of people's reputations (labeling theory).

Can you explain why labels are powerful? How does reputation influence your behavior?

The Functionalist Perspective

When we think of deviance, its dysfunctions are likely to come to mind. Functionalists point out that deviance also has functions.

Can Deviance Really Be Functional for Society?

Most of us are upset by deviance, especially crime, and assume that society would be better off without it. The classic functionalist theorist Emile Durkheim (1893/1933, 1895/1964), however, came to a surprising conclusion. Deviance, he said—including crime—is functional for society, for it contributes to the social order in these three ways:

1. *Deviance clarifies moral boundaries and affirms norms.* By *moral boundaries*, Durkheim referred to a group's ideas about how people should think and act. Deviant acts challenge those boundaries. To call a member into account is to say, in effect, "You broke an important rule, and we cannot tolerate that." Punishing deviants affirms the group's norms and clarifies what it means to be a member of the group.
2. *Deviance encourages social unity.* To affirm the group's moral boundaries by punishing deviants fosters a "we" feeling among the group's members. In saying, "You can't get away with that," the group affirms the rightness of its ways.
3. *Deviance promotes social change.* Not everyone agrees on what to do with people who push beyond their accepted ways of doing things. Some group members may even approve of the rule-breaking behavior. Boundary violations that gain enough support become new, acceptable behaviors. Deviance, then, may force a group to rethink and redefine its moral boundaries, helping groups—and whole societies—to adapt to changing circumstances.

In the Down-to-Earth Sociology box on the next page, you can see these three functions of deviance, as well as the central point of symbolic interactionism, that *deviance* involves a clash of competing definitions.

Strain Theory: How Social Values Produce Deviance

Functionalists argue that crime is a *natural* part of society, not an aberration or some alien element in our midst. Even mainstream values can generate crime. Consider what sociologists Richard Cloward and Lloyd Ohlin (1960) identified as the crucial problem of the industrialized world: the need to locate and train talented people—whether they were born into wealth or into poverty—so that they can take over the key technical jobs of society. When children are born, no one knows which ones will have the ability to become dentists, nuclear physicists, or engineers. To get the most talented people to compete with one another, society tries to motivate *everyone* to strive for success.

We are quite successful in getting almost everyone to want **cultural goals,** usually possessions, wealth, or prestige. But we aren't even close to successful in equalizing access to the **institutionalized means,** the legitimate ways to reach these goals. Many people find their access to success blocked. To explain their reactions, sociologist Robert Merton (1956, 1949/1968) developed **strain theory.** *Strain* refers to the frustrations people feel. It is easy to identify with mainstream norms (such as working hard or pursuing higher education) when those norms help you get ahead, but when they don't seem to be getting you anywhere, you feel frustrated. You might even feel wronged by the system. If mainstream rules seem illegitimate, you experience a gap that Merton called *anomie,* a sense of normlessness.

Table 6.1 on the next page compares the ways that people react to these goals and means. The first reaction, which Merton said is the most common, is *conformity,* using socially acceptable means to try to reach cultural goals. In industrialized societies most people try to get good jobs, a quality education, and so on. If well-paid jobs are unavailable, they take less desirable jobs. If they are denied access to Harvard or Stanford, they go to a state university. Others take night classes and go to vocational schools. In short, most people take the socially acceptable path.

TABLE 6.1	How People Match Their Goals to Their Means		
Do They Feel the Strain That Leads to Anomie?	**Mode of Adaptation**	**Cultural Goals**	**Institutionalized Means**
No	Conformity	Accept	Accept
	Deviant Paths:		
Yes	1. Innovation	Accept	Reject
	2. Ritualism	Reject	Accept
	3. Retreatism	Reject	Reject
	4. Rebellion	Reject/Replace	Reject/Replace

Source: Based on Merton 1968.

Four Deviant Paths. The remaining four responses, which are deviant, represent reactions to the gap that people find between the goals they want and their access to the institutionalized means to reach them. Let's look at each. *Innovators* are people who accept the goals of society but use illegitimate means to try to reach them. Crack dealers, for instance, accept the goal of achieving wealth, but they reject the legitimate avenues for doing so. Other examples are embezzlers, robbers, and con artists.

The second deviant path is taken by people who become discouraged and give up on achieving cultural goals. Yet they still cling to conventional rules of conduct. Merton called this response *ritualism*. Although ritualists have given up on getting ahead at work, they survive by rigorously following the rules of their job. Teachers whose idealism is shattered (who are said to suffer from "burnout"), for example, remain in the classroom, where they teach without enthusiasm. Their response is considered deviant because they cling to the job even though they have abandoned the goal, which may have been to stimulate young minds or to make the world a better place.

People who choose the third deviant path, *retreatism,* reject both the cultural goals and the institutionalized means of achieving them. Some people stop pursuing success and retreat into alcohol or drugs. Although their path to withdrawal is considerably different, women who enter a convent or men a monastery are also retreatists.

The final deviant response is *rebellion*. Convinced that their society is corrupt, rebels, like retreatists, reject both society's goals and its institutionalized means. Unlike retreatists, however, rebels seek to give society new goals, as well as new means for reaching them. Revolutionaries are the most committed type of rebels.

In Sum: Strain theory underscores the sociological principle that deviants are the product of society. Mainstream social values (cultural goals and institutionalized means to reach those goals) can produce strain (frustration, dissatisfaction). People who feel this strain are more likely than others to take the deviant (nonconforming) paths summarized in Table 6.1.

Illegitimate Opportunity Structures: Social Class and Crime

Over and over in this text, you have seen the impact of social class on people's lives—and you will continue to do so in coming chapters. Let's look at how social class produces different types of crime.

Street Crime. In applying strain theory, functionalists point out that industrialized societies have no trouble socializing the poor into wanting to own things. Like others, the poor are bombarded with messages urging them to buy everything from Xboxes and iPods to designer jeans and new cars. Television and movies are filled with

Can you explain the four deviant paths outlined in strain theory?

Down-to-Earth Sociology

The Naked Pumpkin Runners and the Naked Bike Riders: Deviance or Freedom of Self-Expression?

They can hardly sleep the night before Halloween, thinking about how they will carve their pumpkins and all the fun to come. When night falls, they put sneakers on their feet, the pumpkins on their heads, and run into the street. There is nothing between the pumpkins and the sneakers—except whatever nature endowed them with (Simon 2009).

They join one another for their annual chilly, late-night run. Do the gawkers bother them? Maybe a little, but it's all in good fun. The crowd is waiting, hooting and hollering and waving them on.

"Not so fast," reply the police in Boulder, Colorado, where the naked pumpkin run is held on the last day of each October. "You are breaking the law."

If the naked pumpkin run isn't enough, the Boulder police also have to deal with the annual World Naked Bike Ride, which has become so popular that it is held in 70 cities around the world (Vigil 2009). The naked bike rides seem to be a celebration of youth and freedom—and as older people join in, just freedom and maybe the joy of being alive.

Though the Boulder police have prided themselves on tolerance, they don't see the run and ride in quite the same way as the participants do. "The law," they say, "clearly states that no one can show genitalia in public."

The annual Naked Pumpkin Run, Boulder, Colorado

"Are women's breasts genitalia?" they've been asked. "No, those are okay," replied the police. "But watch the rest of it—uh, that is, don't watch . . . uh, that is, don't show anything else. You know what we mean. If you do, we will arrest you, and you'll end up on the sexual offenders list."

"Bad sports," reply the naked pumpkin runners and the naked bike riders, pouting just a bit. "You're trying to ruin our fun."

"We didn't make the laws," the police reply, not pleased about the many who have become angry at their lack of understanding. "We just enforce them."

Trying to recover their tolerance, the police add, "Just wear a thong or a jock strap, and run and ride to your hearts' content."

The American Civil Liberties Union has stepped into the fray, too, saying that nakedness is a form of free speech. Participants should be able to express their, well, whatever it is they are expressing.

For Your Consideration

➔ Here is a basic principle of deviance: As people break rules, sometimes deliberately to test the boundaries of acceptable behavior, the group enforces its norms, or bends them to accommodate the deviants. How do the naked pumpkin runners and the naked bike riders illustrate this principle? What do you think the result will be in Boulder, Colorado?

---

images of middle-class people enjoying luxurious lives. The poor get the message—all full-fledged Americans can afford society's many goods and services.

Yet, for children in poverty, the most common route to success— education—presents a bewildering world. Run by the middle class, schools are at odds with their background. What the poor take for granted is unacceptable in the schools. It is questioned, and mocked. Their speech, for example, is built around nonstandard grammar. It is also often laced with what the middle class considers obscenities. Their ideas of punctuality and their poor preparation in reading and paper-and-pencil skills also make it difficult to fit in. Facing such barriers, the poor are more likely than their more privileged counterparts to drop out of school. Educational failure, of course, slams the door on many legitimate avenues to financial success.

Not all doors slam shut, though. Woven into life in urban slums is what Cloward and Ohlin (1960) called an **illegitimate opportunity structure.** An alternative door to success opens: "hustles" such as robbery, burglary, drug dealing, prostitution, pimping, gambling, and other crimes (Anderson 1978, 1990/2006; Duck and Rawls 2011). Pimps and drug dealers, for example, present an image of a glamorous life— people who are in control and have plenty of "easy money." For many of the poor, the "hustler" becomes a role model.

What do you think the social functions of group public nudity are? What does "illegitimate opportunity structure" mean? Can you give examples?

It should be easy to see, then, why street crime attracts disproportionate numbers of the poor. In the Down-to-Earth Sociology box below, let's look at how gangs are part of the illegitimate opportunity structure that beckons disadvantaged youth.

White-Collar Crime.   Like the poor, the *forms* of crime of the more privileged classes also match their life situation. And how different their illegitimate opportunities are! Physicians don't hold up cabbies, but they do cheat Medicare. Investment managers like Bernie Madoff run fraudulent schemes that cheat people around the world. Mugging, pimping, and burgling are not part of this more privileged world, but evading income tax, bribing public officials, and embezzling are. Sociologist Edwin Sutherland (1949) coined the term **white-collar crime** to refer to crimes that people of respectable and high social status commit in the course of their occupations.

A special form of white-collar crime is **corporate crime,** executives violating the law in order to benefit their corporation. For example, to increase corporate profits, Sears executives defrauded $100 million from victims so poor that they had filed for bankruptcy. To avoid a criminal trial, Sears pleaded guilty. This frightened the parent companies of Macy's and Bloomingdales, which were doing similar things, and they settled out of court (McCormick 1999). Citigroup is notorious for stealing from the poor. In 2004, this firm had to pay $70 million for its crimes (O'Brien 2004). But, like a career criminal, it continued its law-breaking ways. The firm "swept" money from its customers' credit cards, even from the cards of people who had died. Caught red-handed once again—even

Down-to-Earth Sociology

Islands in the Street: Urban Gangs in the United States

For more than ten years, sociologist Martín Sánchez-Jankowski (1991) did participant observation of thirty-seven African American, Chicano, Dominican, Irish, Jamaican, and Puerto Rican gangs in Boston, Los Angeles, and New York City. The gangs earned money through gambling, arson, mugging, armed robbery, and selling moonshine, drugs, guns, stolen car parts, and protection. Sánchez-Jankowski ate, slept, and fought with the gangs, but by mutual agreement he did not participate in drug dealing or other illegal activities. He was seriously injured twice during the study.

Contrary to stereotypes, Sánchez-Jankowski did not find that the motive for joining was to escape a broken home (there were as many members from intact families as from broken homes) or to seek a substitute family (the same number of boys said they were close to their families as those who said they were not). Rather, the boys joined to gain access to money, to have recreation (including girls and drugs), to maintain anonymity in committing crimes, to get protection, and to help the community. This last reason may seem surprising, but in some neighborhoods, gangs protect residents from outsiders and spearhead political change (Kontos et al. 2003). The boys also saw the gang as an alternative to the dead-end—and deadening—jobs held by their parents.

Neighborhood residents are ambivalent about gangs. On the one hand, they fear the violence. On the other hand, many of the adults once belonged to gangs, some gangs provide better protection than the police, and gang members are the children of people who live in the neighborhood.

Particular gangs will come and go, but gangs will likely always remain part of the city. As functionalists point out, gangs fulfill needs of poor youth who live on the margins of society.

For Your Consideration

➤ What functions do gangs fulfill (what needs do they meet)? Suppose that you have been hired as an urban planner for the city of Los Angeles. How could you arrange to meet the needs that gangs fulfill in ways that minimize violence and encourage youth to follow mainstream norms?

What functions do gangs serve? For their members? For society?

stealing from the dead—in 2008 this company was forced to pay another $18 million (Read 2008). *Not one of the corporate thieves at Sears, Macy's, Bloomingdales, or Citigroup spent a day in jail.*

Seldom is corporate crime taken seriously, even when it results in death. In the 1930s, workers were hired to blast a tunnel through a mountain in West Virginia. The company knew the silica dust would kill the miners, and in just three months about 600 died (Dunaway 2008). No owner went to jail. In the 1980s, Firestone executives recalled faulty tires in Saudi Arabia and Venezuela but allowed them to remain on U.S. vehicles. When their tires blew out, about 200 Americans died (White et al. 2001). The photo at the right shows another human cost. Not a single Firestone executive went to jail.

Consider this: Under federal law, causing the death of a worker by *willfully* violating safety rules is a misdemeanor punishable by up to six months in prison. Yet to harass a wild burro on federal lands is punishable by a year in prison (Barstow and Bergman 2003).

At $500 billion a year (Reiman and Leighton 2010), "crime in the suites" actually costs more than "crime in the streets." The physical and emotional costs are another matter. For example, no one has figured out a way to compare the suffering of rape victims with the pain of elderly couples who lost their life savings to Madoff's white-collar fraud.

Fear, however, centers on street crime, especially the violent stranger who can change your life forever. As the Social Map below shows, the chances of such an encounter depend on where you live. You can see that entire regions are safer— or more dangerous–than others. In general, the northern states are safer, and the southern states more dangerous.

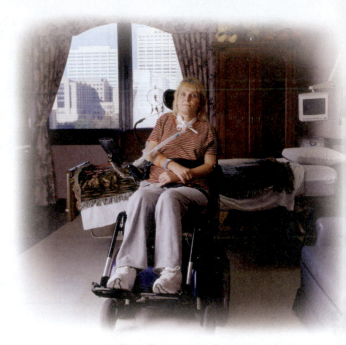

White collar crime usually involves only the loss of property, but not always. To save money, Ford executives kept faulty Firestone tires on their Explorers. The cost? The lives of over 200 people. Shown here in Houston is one of their victims. She survived a needless accident, but was left a quadriplegic. Not one Ford executive spent even a single day in jail.

FIGURE 6.1 How Safe Is Your State? Violent Crime in the United States

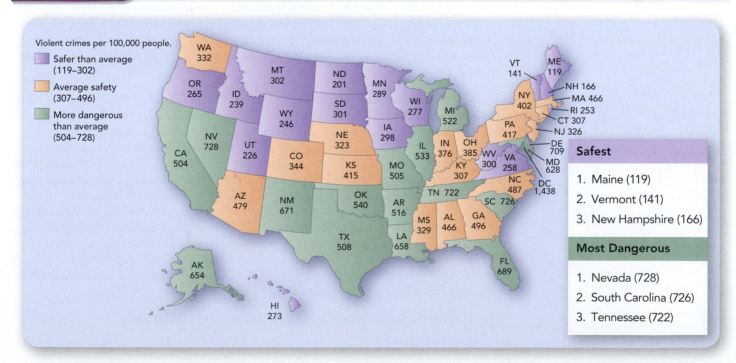

Note: Violent crimes are murder, rape, robbery, and aggravated assault. The chance of becoming a victim of these crimes is six times higher in Nevada, the most dangerous state, than in Maine, the safest state. Washington, D.C., not a state, is in a class by itself. Its rate of 1,438 is *twelve* times higher than Maine's rate.
Source: By the author. Based on *Statistical Abstract of the United States* 2011:Table 304.

How do street crime and white-collar crime reflect opportunity structures?

TABLE 6.2   Women and Crime: What a Difference a Few Years Make

Of all those arrested, what percentage are women?

Crime	1992	2009	Change
Stolen property	12.5%	20.9%	+67%
Car theft	10.8%	17.8%	+65%
Drunken driving	13.8%	22.7%	+64%
Burglary	9.2%	14.9%	+62%
Aggravated assault	14.8%	22.0%	+49%
Robbery	8.5%	11.9%	+40%
Larceny/theft	32.1%	43.6%	+36%
Arson	13.4%	17.3%	+29%
Illegal drugs	16.4%	18.7%	+14%
Forgery and counterfeiting	34.7%	37.7%	+9%
Illegal weapons	7.5%	8.1%	+8%
Fraud	42.1%	44.3%	+5%

Source: By the author. Based on *Statistical Abstract of the United States* 2012:Table 324.

Gender and Crime.   Gender is not just something we are or do. It is a feature of society that surrounds us from birth. Gender pushes us, as male or female, into different corners in life, offering and nurturing some behaviors while it withdraws others. The opportunity to commit crime is one of the many consequences of how society sets up a gender order. The social changes that opened business and the professions to women also brought new opportunities for women to commit crime. From stolen property to illegal weapons, Table 6.2 shows how women have taken advantage of this new opportunity.

In Sum: Functionalists stress that just as the social classes differ in opportunities for income and education, so they differ in opportunities for crime. As a result, street crime is higher among the lower social classes and white-collar crime higher among the higher social classes. The growing crime rates of women illustrate how changing gender roles have given women more access to what sociologists call "illegitimate opportunities."

The Conflict Perspective

Class, Crime, and the Criminal Justice System

TRW sold transistors to the federal government to use in its military satellites. The transistors failed, and the government had to shut down its satellite program. TRW said that the failure was a surprise, that it was due to some unknown defect. U.S. officials then paid TRW millions of dollars to investigate the failure.

Then a whistle blower appeared, informing the government that TRW knew the transistors would fail in satellites even before it sold them. The government sued Northrop Grumman Corporation, which had bought TRW, and the corporation was found guilty (Drew 2009).

What was the punishment for a crime this serious? The failure of these satellites compromised the defense of the United States. When the executives of TRW were put on trial, how long were their prison sentences? Actually, these criminals weren't even put on trial, and not one spent even a night in jail. Grumman was fined $325 million. Then—and this is hard to believe—on the same day, the government settled a lawsuit that Grumman had brought against it for $325 million. Certainly a rare coincidence.

Contrast this backdoor deal between influential people with what happens to the poor who break the law. A poor person who is caught stealing even a $1,000 car can end up serving years in prison. How can a legal system that proudly boasts "justice for all" be so inconsistent? According to conflict theory, this question is central to the analysis of crime and the **criminal justice system**—the police, courts, and prisons that deal with people who are accused of having committed crimes. Let's see what conflict theorists have to say about this.

The Criminal Justice System as an Instrument of Oppression

Conflict theorists regard power and social inequality as the main characteristics of society. The criminal justice system, they stress, is a tool designed by the powerful to maintain their power and privilege. For the poor, in contrast, the law is an instrument of oppression (Spitzer 1975; Reiman 2004; Chambliss 2000, 1973/2012). The idea that the law operates impartially to bring justice, they say, is a cultural myth, promoted by the capitalist class to secure the cooperation of the poor in their own oppression.

The working class and those below them pose a special threat to the power elite. Receiving the least of society's material rewards, they hold the potential to rebel and overthrow the current social order (see Figure 8.5 on page 219). To prevent this, the law comes down hard on its members who get out of line. The working poor and the underclass are a special problem. They are the least rooted in society. They have few skills and only low-paying, part-time, or seasonal work—if they have jobs at all. Because their street crimes threaten the social order that keeps the elite in power, they are punished severely. From this class come *most* of the prison inmates in the United States.

The criminal justice system, then, does not focus on the executives of corporations and the harm they do through manufacturing unsafe products, creating pollution, and manipulating prices. Yet the violations of the capitalist class cannot be ignored totally,

In early capitalism, children worked alongside adults. At that time, just as today, most street criminals came from the *marginal working class,* as did the boys shown in this 1911 yarn mill in Yazoo City, Mississippi.

Why do conflict theorists view the criminal justice system as an instrument of oppression?

for if they become too extreme they might outrage the working class, encouraging them to rise up and revolt. To prevent this, a flagrant violation by a member of the capitalist class is occasionally prosecuted. The publicity given to the case provides evidence of the "fairness" of the criminal justice system, which helps to stabilize the social system—and keeps the powerful in their positions of privilege.

The powerful are usually able to bypass the courts altogether, appearing instead before an agency that has no power to imprison (such as the Federal Trade Commission). These agencies are directed by people from wealthy backgrounds who sympathize with the intricacies of the corporate world. It is they who oversee most cases of price manipulation, insider stock trading, violations of fiduciary duty, and so on. Is it surprising, then, that the typical sanction for corporate crime is a token fine?

In Sum: Conflict theorists stress that the power elite developed the legal system, which is used to stabilize the social order. It helps control the poor, who pose a threat to the powerful, for if they rebel as a group they can dislodge the power elite from their place of privilege. To prevent this, the criminal justice system makes certain that heavy penalties come down on the poor.

Reactions to Deviance

Whether it involves cheating on a sociology quiz or holding up a liquor store, any violation of norms invites reaction. Before we examine reactions in the United States, let's take a little side trip to England. I think you'll enjoy this little excursion in the Cultural Diversity box on page 173.

Street Crime and Prisons

Let's turn back to the United States. Figure 6.2 on page 172 shows the surge in the U.S. prison population. And what a surge! Prisoners have been coming in so fast that the states haven't been able to build prisons fast enough to hold them all. To accommodate their many new guests, the state and federal governments have hired private companies to operate "for-profit" prisons. About 130,000 prisoners are held in these private prisons (*Sourcebook of Criminal Justice Statistics* 2010:Table 6.32.2009).

Actually, the United States has even more prisoners than shown in Figure 6.2, since this total does not include jail inmates. If we add them, the total comes to about 2.3 million people—about one out of every 135 citizens. Not only does the United States have more prisoners than any other nation in the world, but it also has a larger percentage of its population in prison as well (Warren et al. 2008).

Who are these prisoners? Let's compare them with the U.S. population. As you look at Table 6.3 on the next page, several things may strike you. About half (49 percent) of all prisoners are younger than 35, and almost all prisoners are men. Then there is this remarkable statistic: Although African Americans make up just 12.8 percent of the U.S. population, close to two of five prisoners are African Americans. On any given day, *one out of every nine* African American men ages 20 to 34 is in jail or prison. (For Latinos, the rate is one of twenty-six; for whites one of one hundred [Warren et al. 2008].)

Finally, note how marriage and education—two of the major ways that society "anchors" people into mainstream behavior—keeps people out of prison. *Most* prisoners have never married. And look at the power of education, a major component of social class. As I mentioned earlier, social class funnels some people into the criminal justice system and diverts others away from it. You can see how people who drop out of high school have a high chance of ending up in prison—and how unlikely it is for a college graduate to have this unwelcome destination in life.

For about the past twenty years or so, the United States has followed a "get tough" policy. One of the most significant changes was "three-strikes-and-you're-out" laws, which have had unanticipated consequences, as you will see in the following Thinking Critically section.

The cartoonist's hyperbole makes an excellent commentary on the social class disparity of our criminal justice system. Not only are the crimes of the wealthy not as likely to come to the attention of authorities as are the crimes of the poor, but when they do, the wealthy can afford legal expertise that the poor cannot.

"If you want justice, it's two hundred dollars an hour. Obstruction of justice runs a bit more."

Why are any white-collar crimes prosecuted? Why are the punishments for street crimes so severe?

TABLE 6.3	Inmates in U.S. State and Federal Prisons	
Characteristics	Percentage of Prisoners with These Characteristics	Percentage of U.S. Population with These Characteristics
Age		
18–24	15.9%	9.8%
25–34	33.6%	13.5%
35–44	29.1%	14.0%
45–54	14.8%	14.6%
55 and older	6.7%	23.9%
Race–Ethnicity		
African American	38.4%	12.8%
White	34.3%	65.6%
Latino	20.3%	15.4%
Other[a]	6.9%	5.5%
Sex		
Male	93.2%	49.2%
Female	6.8%	50.8%
Marital Status		
Never married	59.8%	26.0%
Divorced	15.5%	10.4%
Married	17.3%	57.3%
Widowed	1.1%	6.4%
Education		
Less than high school	39.7%	13.4%
High school graduate	49.0%	31.2%
Some college[b]	9.0%	26.0%
College graduate	2.4%	29.4%

[a]Asian Americans and Native Americans are included in this category.
[b]Includes associate's degrees.

Source: By the author. Based on *Sourcebook of Criminal Justice Statistics* 2003:Tables 6.000b, 6.28; 2006: Tables 6.34, 6.45; 2009:Table 6.33.2008; *Statistical Abstract of the United States* 2011:Tables 8, 10, 56, 227.

THINKING CRITICALLY

"Three Strikes and You're Out!" Unintended Consequences of Well-Intended Laws

As the violent crime rate soared in the 1980s, Americans grew fearful. They demanded that their lawmakers do something. Politicians heard the message, and many responded by passing "three-strikes" laws in their states. Anyone who is convicted of a third felony receives an automatic mandatory sentence. Although some mandatory sentences carry life imprisonment, judges are not allowed to consider the circumstances. While few of us would feel sympathy if a man convicted of a third brutal rape or a third murder were sent to prison for life, in their haste to appease the public the politicians did not limit the three-strike laws to *violent* crimes. And they did not consider that some minor crimes are considered felonies. As the functionalists would say, this has led to unanticipated consequences.

Here are some actual cases:

- In Los Angeles, a 27-year-old man who stole a pizza was sentenced to 25 years in prison (Cloud 1998).
- In Sacramento, a man passed himself off as Tiger Woods and went on a $17,000 shopping spree. He was sentenced to *200 years* in prison (Reuters 2001).

Why don't the characteristics of prisoners match those of the U.S. population?

- Also in California, Michael James passed a bad check for $94. He was sentenced to 25 years to life (Jones 2008).
- In Utah, a 25-year-old sold small bags of marijuana to a police informant. The judge who sentenced the man to 55 years in prison said the sentence was unjust, but he had no choice (Madigan 2004).
- In New York City, a man who was about to be sentenced for selling crack said to the judge, "I'm only 19. This is terrible." He then hurled himself out of a courtroom window, plunging to his death sixteen stories below (Cloud 1998).

For Your Consideration

➤ Apply the symbolic interactionist, functionalist, and conflict perspectives to the three-strikes laws. For *symbolic interactionism,* what do these laws represent to the public? How does your answer differ depending on what part of "the public" you are referring to? For *functionalism,* who benefits from these laws? What are some of the functions of three-strikes laws? Their dysfunctions? For the *conflict perspective,* which groups are in conflict? Who has the power to enforce their will on others? ■

FIGURE 6.2   How Much Is Enough? The Explosion in the Number of U.S. Prisoners

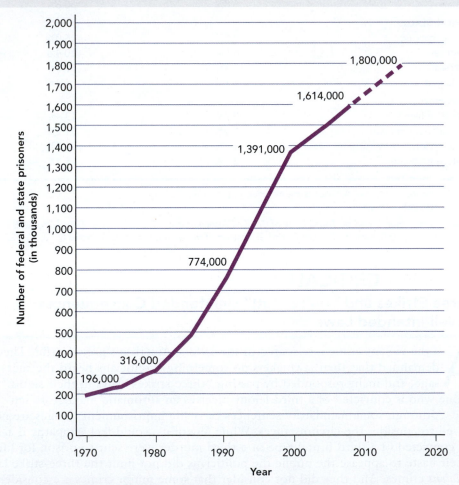

How Much Is Enough? The Explosion in the Number of U.S. Prisoners
Between 1970 and 2009, the U.S. population increased 50 percent, while the number of prisoners increased 823 percent, a rate that is *sixteen times greater* than population growth. If the number of prisoners had grown at the same rate as the U.S. population, we would have about 294,000 prisoners, only one-fifth to one-sixth of today's total. Or if the U.S. population had increased at the same rate as that of U.S. prisoners, the U.S. population would be 1,688,000,000—approximately the population of China and all of Europe combined.

Sources: By the author. Based on *Statistical Abstract of the United States* 1995:Table 349; 2012:Tables 2, 347. The broken line is the author's estimate.

How are the three-strikes laws part of the reason for the explosion in the number of U.S. prisoners?

The Decline in Violent Crime

As you have seen, judges have put more and more people in prison, and legislators have passed the three-strikes laws. As these changes occurred, the crime rate dropped sharply, which has led to a controversy in sociology. Some sociologists conclude that getting tough on criminals is the main reason that violent crime dropped (Conklin 2003; Bhati and Piquero 2008). Others point to higher employment, a drop in drug use, and even abortion (Rosenfeld 2002; Joyce 2009). We can rule out unemployment, for when the unemployment rate shot up with the economic crisis the lower crime rates continued (Oppel 2011). This matter is not yet settled. We'll see what answers future research brings.

Recidivism

If a goal of prisons is to teach their clients to stay away from crime, they are colossal failures. We can measure their failure by the **recidivism rate**—the percentage of former prisoners who are rearrested. For people sent to prison for crimes of violence, within just three years of their release, two out of three

"It's interesting—with each conviction I learn a little more about myself."

Unfortunately, whatever prisoners do learn about themselves in prison—if anything—fails to keep them from coming back.

Cultural Diversity around the World

"Dogging" in England

In some places in England, people like "dogging." This is their term for having sex in public so others can watch. The sex often is between strangers who have arranged to meet through the Internet.

"Dogging" is a strange term, and no one knows its origin. The term might come from voyeurs who doggedly follow people who are having sex. Or it might refer to the similarity to female dogs in heat that have sex with any dog around. Or it might even come from the statement "I'm just going to walk the dog," when they are really going out to do something else entirely.

Regardless of the term's origin, frolicking in the fields is popular. Internet sites even lay out basic rules, such as "Only join in if you are asked."

The Internet sites also rate England's dogging locations. The field in Puttenham, a village an hour's drive from London, is ranked Number 2 in England. The field is mostly used by homosexuals during the day, with heterosexuals taking over at night.

One motorist who stopped his car to use the bushes for a bathroom break was startled when a group of eager men surrounded him. He said that he took the quickest pee in his life.

Dogging isn't legal, but the police mostly ignore it. The police have even warned the public, but in a discreet English way. They have designated the field in Puttenham as a "public sex environment."

Some village residents are upset at the litter left behind, from condoms to tea cups. Others are upset that the dogging field is just 400 yards from the village nursery school. A woman who went to the police to complain showed them a pink vibrator she had found in the field. "What

should we do with it?" asked the officer. Seeing that she was going to get nowhere, she said they could just put it in Lost and Found.

After listening to citizen complaints, the County Council Cabinet wanted to know if anyone had practical solutions. One suggested that the police patrol the site with dogs. Another said they should fill the field with bad-tempered bulls.

Distressed at such inconsiderate reactions, one empathetic cabinet member said, "If you close this site, they wouldn't have anywhere else to go. There might be an increase in suicides."

The citizens and Council members reached a compromise: They would put up a sign. "Don't have sex here" seemed too direct for the English, so the sign, much more polite and circuitous, says, "Do not engage in activities of an unacceptable nature."

Source: Based on Lyall 2010.

For Your Consideration

➤ What do you think the police would do if there were a "dogging" field in your town? What do you think the public's reaction would be? Why do you think the police are so "heavy handed" in the United States while those in England take such a lighter approach?

Compare the reactions to "dogging" in England with the "three-strikes" laws in the United States.

FIGURE 6.3   Recidivism of U.S. Prisoners

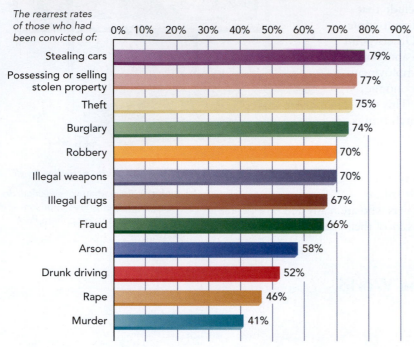

Of 272,000 prisoners released from U.S. prisons, what percentage were rearrested within three years?

The rearrest rates of those who had been convicted of:

Stealing cars	79%
Possessing or selling stolen property	77%
Theft	75%
Burglary	74%
Robbery	70%
Illegal weapons	70%
Illegal drugs	67%
Fraud	66%
Arson	58%
Drunk driving	52%
Rape	46%
Murder	41%

Source: By the author. Based on *Sourcebook of Criminal Justice Statistics* 2003:Table 6.50.
Note: The individuals were not necessarily rearrested for the same crime for which they had originally been imprisoned.

(62 percent) are rearrested, and half (52 percent) are back in prison (*Sourcebook of Criminal Justice Statistics* 2003:Table 6.52). Looking at Figure 6.3, which gives a breakdown of three-year recidivism by type of crime, it is safe to conclude that prisons do not teach people that crime doesn't pay.

The Death Penalty and Bias

As you know, **capital punishment,** the death penalty, is the most extreme measure the state takes. As you also know, the death penalty arouses both impassioned opposition and support. Advances in DNA testing have given opponents of the death penalty a strong argument: Innocent people have been sent to death row, and some have been executed. Others are just as passionate about retaining the death penalty. They point to such crimes as those of the serial killers discussed in the Down-to-Earth Sociology box on the next page.

Geography.   Apart from anyone's personal position on the death penalty, it certainly is clear that the death penalty is not administered evenly. Consider geography: The Social Map on page 176 shows that where people commit murder greatly affects their chances of being put to death.

Social Class.   The death penalty also shows social class bias. As you know from news reports, it is rare for a rich person to be sentenced to death. Although the government does not collect statistics on social class and the death penalty, this common observation is borne out by the education of the prisoners on death row. *Half* of the prisoners on death row (50 percent) have not finished high school (*Sourcebook of Criminal Justice Statistics* 2009:Table 6.81).

Gender.   There is also a gender bias in the death penalty—so strong that it is almost unheard of for a woman to be sentenced to death, much less executed. Although women commit 9.6 percent of the murders, they make up only 1.8 percent of death row inmates (*Sourcebook of Criminal Justice Statistics* 2009: Table 6.81). Even on death row, the gender bias continues: Of those condemned to death, the state is more likely to execute a man than a woman. As Figure 6.5 on page 177 shows, only 0.9 percent of the 5,049 prisoners executed in the United States since 1930 have been women. This gender bias could reflect the women's previous offenses and the relative brutality of their murders, but we need research to determine if this is so.

Race–Ethnicity.   At one point, racial-ethnic bias was so flagrant that it put a stop to the death penalty. Donald Partington (1965), a lawyer in Virginia, was shocked by the bias he saw in the courtroom, and he decided to document it. Going back to 1908, he found that 2,798 men had been convicted for rape and attempted rape in Virginia—56 percent whites and 44 percent blacks. For rape, 41 men had been executed. For attempted rape, 13 had been executed. *All those executed were black.* Not one of the whites was executed.

After listening to evidence like this, in 1972 the Supreme Court ruled in *Furman v. Georgia* that the death penalty, as applied, was unconstitutional. The execution of prisoners

Based on recidivism, how effective are our prisons? Why do you think we have a gender bias in the death penalty?

Down-to-Earth Sociology

The Killer Next Door: Serial Murderers in Our Midst

Here is my experience with serial killers. As I was watching television one night, I was stunned by the images. Television cameras showed the Houston police digging up dozens of bodies from under a boat storage shed. Fascinated, I waited impatiently for spring break. A few days later, I drove from Illinois, where I was teaching, to Houston, where 33-year-old Dean Corll had befriended Elmer Wayne Henley and David Brooks, two teenagers from broken homes. Together, they had killed twenty-seven boys. Elmer and David would pick up young hitchhikers and deliver them to Corll to rape and kill. Sometimes they even brought him their own high school classmates.

I talked to one of Elmer's neighbors, as he was painting his front porch. His 15-year-old son had gone to get a haircut one Saturday morning. That was the last time he saw his son alive. The police refused to investigate. They insisted that his son had run away. On a city map, I plotted the locations of the homes of the local murder victims. Many clustered around the homes of the teenage killers.

I decided to spend my coming sabbatical writing a novel on this case. To get into the minds of the killers, I knew that I would have to "become" them day after day. Corll kept a piece of plywood in his apartment. In each of its corners, he had cut a hole. He and the boys would spread-eagle their handcuffed victims on this board, torturing them for hours. Sometimes, they would even pause to order pizza. As such details emerged, I became uncertain that I could recover psychologically from months-on immersion into torture and human degradation, and I decided not to write the book.

My interviews confirmed what has since become common knowledge about serial killers: They lead double lives so successfully that their friends and family are unaware of their criminal activities. Henley's mother swore to me that her son couldn't possibly be guilty—he was a good boy. Some of Elmer's high school friends told me that that his being involved in homosexual rape and murder was ridiculous—he was interested only in girls. I was interviewing them in Henley's bedroom, and for proof they pointed to a pair of girls' panties that were draped across a lamp shade.

Serial murder is killing three or more victims in separate events. The murders may occur over several days, weeks, or years. The elapsed time between murders distinguishes serial killers from *mass murderers*, those who do their killing all at once. Here are some infamous examples:

- During the 1960s and 1970s, Ted Bundy raped and killed dozens of women in four states.
- Between 1974 and 1991, Dennis Rader killed ten people in Wichita, Kansas. Rader had written to the newspapers, proudly calling himself the BTK (Bind, Torture, and Kill) strangler.

Ted Bundy is shown here with his defense attorney, when he was on trial in Miami for killing two college students. You can get a glimpse of his charm and wit and how, like most serial killers, he blended in with society. Bundy was executed for his murders.

- In the late 1980s and early 1990s, Aileen Wuornos hitchhiked along Florida's freeways. She killed seven men after having had sex with them.
- The serial killer with the most victims appears to be Harold Shipman, a physician in Manchester, England. From 1977 to 2000, during house calls Shipman gave lethal injections to 230 to 275 of his elderly female patients.
- In 2009, Anthony Sowell of Cleveland, Ohio, was discovered living with eleven decomposing bodies of women he had raped and strangled.

Is serial murder more common now than it used to be? Not likely. In the past, police departments had little communication with one another, and seldom did anyone connect killings in different jurisdictions. Today's more efficient communications, investigative techniques, and DNA matching make it easier for the police to know when a serial killer is operating in an area. Part of the perception that there are more serial killers today is also due to ignorance of our history: In our frontier past, for example, serial killers went from ranch to ranch.

For Your Consideration

→ Do you think that serial killers should be given the death penalty? Why or why not? How do your social locations influence your opinion?

stopped—but not for long. The states wrote new laws, and in 1977 they again began to execute prisoners. Since then, 65 percent of those put to death have been white and 35 percent African American (*Statistical Abstract* 2012:Table 352). (Latinos are evidently counted as whites in this statistic.) While living on death row is risky for anyone, the risk is higher for African Americans and Latinos who killed whites. They are more likely to be executed (Jacobs et al. 2007). The most accurate predictor of who will be put to death, though, is somewhat surprising: Those who have the least education

FIGURE 6.4   Executions in the United States

Executions since 1977, when the death penalty was reinstated.

Source: By the author. Based on *Statistical Abstract of the United States* 2012:Table 353.

are the most likely to be executed (Karamouzis and Harper 2007). On Table 6.4 on the next page, you can see the race–ethnicity of the prisoners who are on death row.

Legal Change

Did you know that it is a crime in Saudi Arabia for a woman to drive a car (Usher 2011)? A crime in Florida to sell alcohol before 1 P.M. on Sundays? Or illegal in Wells, Maine, to advertise on tombstones?

As has been stressed in this chapter, deviance, including the form called *crime,* is so relative that it varies from one society to another, and from one group to another within the same society. Crime also varies from one time period to another, as opinions change, as different groups gain access to power, or as we discuss in the following Thinking Critically section as technology changes.

THINKING CRITICALLY
Sexting

Four eighth-grade girls were having a sleepover. As they talked about how they could impress the boys they were interested in, they came up with an idea. They took off their clothes, covered themselves with whipped cream, and sent pictures to boys of themselves licking it off.

It seemed like a good idea at the time, but the girls didn't think so the next day. As they walked to class, the boys stood around leering, laughing, and holding up the girls' images on their cell phones.

The boys who received the images had forwarded them to their friends—who forwarded them to their friends, and so on.

Even some parents received the photos on their cell phones, and, as they say, then all hell broke loose.

How is geography a part of bias in the death penalty?

TABLE 6.4	The Race–Ethnicity of the 3,316 Prisoners on Death Row	
	Percentage	
	on Death Row	in U.S. Population
Whites	44%	65%
African Americans	41%	13%
Latinos	12%	15%
Asian Americans	1%	5%
Native Americans	1%	1%

Source: By the author. Based on *Sourcebook of Criminal Justice Statistics* 2010:Table 6.80 and Figure 9.5 of this text.

Sexting, sending sexually explicit text or images electronically, is a new crime brought about by changing technology. And it is giving lawmakers and enforcers a hard time.

Not to mention teenagers.

If two people over the age of 18 send sexually explicit messages to one another, this is a matter between them. If someone forwards those images, it is still a problem between those individuals. But people under the age of 18 are legally minors, and their sexually explicit photos are classified by law as child pornography.

And what should law enforcers do? If they learn about sexting by minors, can they just ignore it? No, because they are sworn to uphold the law, and sexting comes under the law. And those who are convicted—both those who send the messages and those who pass them on to others—are guilty of producing or disseminating child pornography. So let's prosecute, say some district attorneys. And those who are convicted will have to register as sex offenders for decades!

"Absolutely ridiculous," reply other district attorneys, teachers, and parents. "This is just kids having misguided fun. Let's just teach the kids that they are being foolish and irresponsible."

"You're all getting excited about nothing," says one 17-year-old girl. "You're overlooking the positive side to sexting. You can't get pregnant from it, and you can't transmit STDs. It's a kind of safe sex."

Lawmakers and enforcers are grappling with sexting. Some think that the current laws are good enough, but the general consensus seems to be that the laws passed to prohibit child pornography don't apply to this new behavior. Most proposals for legal change center around educational programs and community service for minors who transmit images of "sexually explicit conduct." Then, of course, there is the more severe penalty—banning the offenders from using cell phones.

For Your Consideration

→ Do you think there should be any sanctions for sexting by minors, or should this be a private matter, much as it is for adults? If you think there should be sanctions, which ones? The same ones for sexters age 13 and age 17? The same sanctions for nudity and for the depiction of activities like penetration, sadism, and masturbation? ■
Source: Based on "What They're Saying…" 2011; Hoffman 2011.

The Medicalization of Deviance: Mental Illness

When the woman drove her car into the river, drowning her two small children strapped to their little car seats, people said that she had "gone nuts," "went bonkers," and just plain "lost it" because of her problems.

Neither Mental Nor Illness? When people cannot find a satisfying explanation for why someone does something weird or is "like that," they often say that a

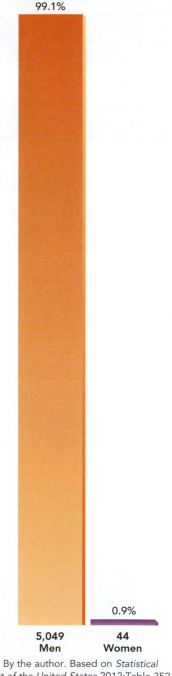

FIGURE 6.5 **Who Gets Executed? Gender Bias in Capital Punishment**

99.1%

0.9%

| 5,049 Men | 44 Women |

Source: By the author. Based on *Statistical Abstract of the United States* 2012:Table 352.

How are the sexting laws an example of an evolving criminal justice system?

People whose behaviors violate norms often are called mentally ill. "Why else would they do such things?" is a common response to deviant behaviors that we don't understand. Mental illness is a label that contains the assumption that there is something wrong "within" people that "causes" their disapproved behavior. The surprise with this man, who changed his legal name to "Scary Guy," is that he speaks at schools across the country, where he promotes acceptance, awareness, love, and understanding.

"sickness in the head" is causing the unacceptable behavior. To *medicalize* something is to make it a medical matter, to classify it as a form of illness that properly belongs in the care of physicians. For the past hundred years or so, especially since the time of Sigmund Freud (1856–1939), the Viennese physician who founded psychoanalysis, there has been a growing tendency toward the **medicalization of deviance.** In this view, deviance, including crime, is a sign of mental sickness. Rape, murder, stealing, cheating, and so on are external symptoms of internal disorders, consequences of a confused or tortured mind, one that should be treated by mental health experts.

Thomas Szasz (1986, 1996, 1998), a renegade in his profession of psychiatry, disagrees. He argues that what are called *mental illnesses are neither mental nor illnesses. They are simply problem behaviors.* Szasz breaks these behaviors for which we don't have a ready explanation into two causes: physical illness and learned deviance.

Some behaviors that are called "mental illnesses" have physical causes. That is, something in an individual's body results in unusual perceptions or behavior. Some depression, for example, is caused by a chemical imbalance in the brain, which can be treated by drugs. The behaviors that are associated with depression—crying, long-term sadness, and lack of interest in family, work, school, or grooming—are only symptoms of a physical problem.

Attention-deficit disorder (ADD) is an example of a new "mental illness" that has come out of nowhere. As Szasz says, "No one explains where this disease came from or why it didn't exist 50 years ago. No one is able to diagnose it with objective tests." ADD is diagnosed because a teacher or parent is complaining about a child misbehaving. Misbehaving children have been a problem throughout history, but now, with doctors looking to expand their territory, this problem behavior has become a sign of "mental illness" that they can treat.

All of us have troubles. Some of us face a constant barrage of problems as we go through life. Most of us continue the struggle, perhaps encouraged by relatives and friends or motivated by job, family responsibilities, religious faith, and life goals. Even when the odds seem hopeless, we carry on, not perfectly, but as best we can.

Some people, however, fail to cope well with life's challenges. Overwhelmed, they become depressed, uncooperative, or hostile. Some strike out at others; and some, in Merton's terms, become retreatists and withdraw into their apartments or homes, refusing to come out. These are *behaviors, not mental illnesses,* stresses Szasz. They may be inappropriate ways of coping, but they are behaviors, not mental illnesses. Szasz concludes that "mental illness" is a myth foisted on a naïve public. Our medical profession uses pseudoscientific jargon that people don't understand so it can expand its area of control and force nonconforming people to accept society's definitions of "normal."

Szasz's controversial claim forces us to look anew at the forms of deviance that we usually refer to as mental illness. To explain behavior that people find bizarre, he directs our attention not to causes hidden deep within the "subconscious," but, instead, to how people learn such behaviors. To ask, "What is the origin of someone's inappropriate or bizarre behavior?" then becomes similar to asking, "Why do some women steal?" "Why do some men rape?" "Why do some teenagers cuss their parents and stalk out of the room, slamming the door?" *The answers depend on those people's particular experiences in life, not on an illness in their minds.* In short, some sociologists find Szasz's renegade analysis refreshing because it indicates that *social experiences,* not some illness of the mind, underlie bizarre behaviors—as well as deviance in general.

The Homeless Mentally Ill

Jamie was sitting on a low wall surrounding the landscaped courtyard of an exclusive restaurant. She appeared unaware of the stares elicited by her layers of mismatched

What is the medicalization of deviance? How can mental illnesses be problem behaviors, not mental illnesses?

clothing, her matted hair and dirty face, and the shopping cart that overflowed with her meager possessions.

After sitting next to Jamie for a few minutes, I saw her point to the street and concentrate, slowly moving her finger horizontally. I asked her what she was doing.

"I'm directing traffic," she replied. "I control where the cars go. Look, that one turned right there," she said, now withdrawing her finger.

"Really?" I said.

After a while she confided that her cart talked to her.

"Really?" I said again.

"Yes," she replied. "You can hear it, too." At that, she pushed the shopping cart a bit.

"Did you hear that?" she asked.

When I shook my head, she demonstrated again. Then it hit me. She was referring to the squeaking wheels!

I nodded.

When I left Jamie, she was pointing to the sky, for, as she told me, she also controlled the flight of airplanes.

To most of us, Jamie's behavior and thinking are bizarre. They simply do not match any reality we know. Could you or I become like Jamie?

Suppose for a bitter moment that you are homeless and have to live on the streets. You have no money, no place to sleep, no bathroom. You do not know *if* you are going to eat, much less where. You have no friends or anyone you can trust. You live in constant fear of rape and other violence. Do you think this might be enough to drive you over the edge?

Consider just the problems involved in not having a place to bathe. (Shelters are often so dangerous that many homeless people prefer to sleep in public settings.) At first, you try to wash in the restrooms of gas stations, bars, the bus station, or a shopping center. But you are dirty, and people stare when you enter and call the management when they see you wash your feet in the sink. You are thrown out and told in no uncertain terms never to come back. So you get dirtier and dirtier. Eventually, you come to think of being dirty as a fact of life. Soon, maybe, you don't even care. The stares no longer bother you—at least not as much.

Mental illness is common among the homeless. This photo was taken in New York City, but it could have been taken in any large city in the United States.

No one will talk to you, and you withdraw more and more into yourself. You begin to build a fantasy life. You talk openly to yourself. People stare, but so what? They stare anyway. Besides, they are no longer important to you.

Jamie might be mentally ill. Some organic problem, such as a chemical imbalance in her brain, might underlie her behavior. But perhaps not. How long would it take you to exhibit bizarre behaviors if you were homeless—and hopeless? The point is that *living on the streets can cause mental illness*—or whatever we want to label socially inappropriate behaviors that we find difficult to classify. *Homelessness and mental illness are reciprocal:* Just as "mental illness" can cause homelessness, so the trials of being homeless, of living on cold, hostile streets, can lead to unusual thinking and behaviors.

The Need for a More Humane Approach

As Durkheim (1895/1964:68) pointed out, deviance is inevitable—even in a group of saints.

Imagine a society of saints, a perfect cloister of exemplary individuals. Crimes, properly so called, will there be unknown; but faults which appear invisible to the layman will create there the same scandal that the ordinary offense does in ordinary society.

With deviance inevitable, one measure of a society is how it treats its deviants. Our prisons certainly don't say much good about U.S. society. Filled with the poor, uneducated, and unskilled, they are warehouses

How are homelessness and mental illness reciprocal (each contributing to the other)?

of the unwanted. White-collar criminals continue to get by with a slap on the wrist while street criminals are punished severely. Some deviants, who fail to meet current standards of admission to either prison or mental hospital, take refuge in shelters, as well as in cardboard boxes tucked away in urban recesses. Although no one has *the* answer, it does not take much reflection to see that there are more humane approaches than these.

Because deviance is inevitable, the larger issues are to find ways to protect people from deviant behaviors that are harmful to themselves or others, to tolerate those behaviors that are not harmful, and to develop systems of fairer treatment for deviants. In the absence of fundamental changes that would bring about an equitable society, most efforts are, unfortunately, like putting a Band-Aid on a gunshot wound. What we need is a more humane social system, one that would prevent the social inequalities that are the focus of the next four chapters.

6 Summary and Review

What Is Deviance?

Deviance (the violation of norms) is relative. What people consider deviant varies from one culture to another and from group to group within the same society. As symbolic interactionists stress, it is not the act, but the reactions to the act, that make something deviant. All groups develop systems of **social control** to punish **deviants**—those who violate their norms. Pp. 154–156.

How do sociological and individualistic explanations of deviance differ?

To explain why people deviate, sociobiologists and psychologists look for reasons *within* the individual, such as **genetic predispositions** or **personality disorders.** Sociologists, in contrast, look for explanations *outside* the individual, in social experiences. Pp. 156–157.

The Symbolic Interactionist Perspective

How do symbolic interactionists explain deviance?

Symbolic interactionists have developed several theories to explain deviance such as **crime,** the violation of norms that are written into law. According to **differential association** theory, people learn to deviate by associating with others. According to **control theory,** each of us is propelled toward deviance, but most of us conform because of an effective system of inner and outer controls. People who have less effective controls deviate. Pp. 157–159.

Labeling theory focuses on how labels (names, reputations) help to funnel people into or divert them away from deviance. People often use **techniques of neutralization** to deflect social norms. Pp. 159–162.

The Functionalist Perspective

How do functionalists explain deviance?

Functionalists point out that deviance, including criminal acts, is functional for society. Functions include affirming norms and promoting social unity and social change. According to **strain theory,** societies socialize their members into desiring **cultural goals.** Many people are unable to achieve these goals in socially acceptable ways—that is, by **institutionalized means.** *Deviants,* then, are people who either give up on the goals or use disapproved means to attain them. Merton identified five types of responses to cultural goals and institutionalized means: conformity, innovation, ritualism, retreatism, and rebellion. **Illegitimate opportunity theory** stresses that some people have easier access to illegal means of achieving goals. Pp. 163–168.

The Conflict Perspective

How do conflict theorists explain deviance?

Conflict theorists take the position that the group in power imposes its definitions of deviance on other groups. From this perspective, the law is an instrument of oppression used by the powerful to maintain their position of privilege. The ruling class, which developed the **criminal** justice system, uses it to punish the crimes of the poor while diverting its own criminal activities away from this punitive system. Pp. 168–170.

Reactions to Deviance

What are common reactions to deviance in the United States?

In following a "get-tough" policy, the United States has imprisoned millions of people. African Americans and Latinos make up a disproportionate percentage of U.S. prisoners. The death penalty shows biases by geography, social class, gender, and race–ethnicity. In line with conflict theory, as groups gain political power, their views are reflected in the criminal code. Sexting legislation was considered in this context. Pp. 170–177.

What is the medicalization of deviance?

The medical profession has attempted to **medicalize** many forms of **deviance,** claiming that they represent mental illnesses. Thomas Szasz disagrees, asserting that they are problem behaviors, not mental illnesses. The situation of homeless people indicates that problems in living can lead to bizarre behavior and thinking. Pp. 177–179.

What is a more humane approach?

Deviance is inevitable, so the larger issues are to find ways to protect people from deviance that harms themselves and others, to tolerate deviance that is not harmful, and to develop systems of fairer treatment for deviants. Pp. 179–180.

Thinking Critically about Chapter 6

1. Select some deviance with which you are personally familiar. (It does not have to be your own—it can be something that someone you know did.) Choose one of the three theoretical perspectives to explain what happened.

2. As explained in the text, deviance can be mild. Recall some instance in which you broke a social rule in dress, etiquette, or speech. What was the reaction? Why do you think people reacted like that? What was your response to their reactions?

3. What do you think should be done about the U.S. crime problem? What sociological theories support your view?

Global Stratification

Chad

Let's contrast two "average" families from around the world:

For Getu Mulleta, 33, and his wife, Zenebu, 28, of rural Ethiopia, life is a constant struggle to avoid starvation. They and their seven children live in a 320-square-foot manure-plastered hut with no electricity, gas, or running water. They have a radio, but the battery is dead. The family farms teff, a grain, and survives on $130 a year.

The Mulletas' poverty is not due to a lack of hard work. Getu works about eighty hours a week, while Zenebu puts in even more hours. "Housework" for Zenebu includes fetching water, cleaning animal stables, and making fuel pellets out of cow dung for the open fire over which she cooks the family's food. Like other Ethiopian women, she eats after the men.

In Ethiopia, the average male can expect to live to age 48, the average female to 50.

The Mulletas' most valuable possession is their oxen. Their wishes for the future: more animals, better seed, and a second set of clothing.

> **They live in a 320-square-foot manure-plastered hut with no electricity, gas, or running water.**

* * * * *

Springfield, Illinois, is home to the Kellys—Rick, 36, Patti, 34, Julie, 10, and Michael, 7. The Kellys live in a three-bedroom, 2½-bath, 2,438-square-foot, ranch-style house with a fireplace, central heating and air conditioning, a basement, and a two-car garage. Their home is equipped with a refrigerator, freezer, washing machine, clothes dryer, dishwasher, garbage disposal, vacuum cleaner, food processor, microwave, and convection stovetop and oven. They also own cell phones, color televisions, a Kindle, digital cameras, an iPod, computers with DVD players, a printer-scanner-fax machine, blow dryers, a juicer, an espresso coffee maker, a pickup truck, and an SUV.

Rick works forty hours a week as a cable splicer for a telephone company. Patti teaches school part-time. Together they make $60,088, plus benefits. The Kellys can choose from among dozens of superstocked supermarkets. They spend $5,187 for food they eat at home, and another $3,543 eating out, a total of 15 percent of their annual income.

In the United States, the average life expectancy is 76 for males, 81 for females.

On the Kellys' wish list are a new hybrid car with satellite radio, a 5,000-gigabyte laptop with Bluetooth wi-fi, a 60-inch LCD TV with surround sound, a boat, a motor home, an ATV, and, oh, yes, farther down the road, an in-ground heated swimming pool. They also have an eye on a cabin at a nearby lake.

Menzel 1994; *Statistical Abstract* 2012:Tables 104, 687, 696, 971.

Systems of Social Stratification

Some of the world's nations are wealthy, others poor, and some in between. This division of nations, as well as the layering of groups of people within a nation, is called *social stratification*. Social stratification is one of the most significant topics we shall discuss in this book, for, as you saw in the opening vignette, it profoundly affects our life chances—from our access to material possessions to the age at which we die.

Social stratification also affects the way we think about life. If you had been born into the Ethiopian family in our opening vignette, you would expect hunger to be a part of life and would not expect all of your children to survive. You would also be illiterate and would assume that your children would be as well. In contrast, if you were one of the U.S. parents, you would expect your children not only to survive, but to go to college as well. You can see that social stratification brings with it not just material things but also ideas of what we can expect out of life.

Social stratification is a system in which groups of people are divided into layers according to their relative property, power, and prestige. It is important to emphasize that social stratification does not refer to individuals. It is a way of ranking large groups of people into a hierarchy according to their relative privileges.

It is also important to note that *every society stratifies its members*. Some societies have greater inequality than others, but social stratification is universal. In addition, in every society of the world, *gender* is a basis for stratifying people. On the basis of their gender, people are either allowed or denied access to the good things offered by their society.

Let's consider three major systems of social stratification: slavery, caste, and class.

Slavery

Slavery, whose essential characteristic is that *some individuals own other people,* has been common throughout world history. The Old Testament even lays out rules for

The Mulleta family of Ethiopia, described in the opening vignette.

What is social stratification? How does it affect people's ideas of what they can expect out of life?

how owners should treat their slaves. So does the Koran. The Romans also had slaves, as did the Africans and Greeks. In classical Greece and Rome, slaves did the work, freeing citizens to engage in politics and the arts. Slavery was most widespread in agricultural societies and least common among nomads, especially hunters and gatherers (Landtman 1938/1968). As we examine the major causes and conditions of slavery, you will see how remarkably slavery has varied around the world.

Causes of Slavery.

Contrary to popular assumption, slavery was usually based not on racism but on one of three other factors. The first was *debt*. In some societies, creditors would enslave people who could not pay their debts. The second was *crime*. Instead of being killed, a murderer or thief might be enslaved by the victim's family as compensation for their loss. The third was *war*. When one group of people conquered another, they often enslaved some of the vanquished. Historian Gerda Lerner (1986) notes that women were the first people enslaved through warfare. When tribal men raided another group, they killed the men, raped the women, and then brought the women back as slaves. The women were valued for sexual purposes, for reproduction, and for their labor.

Roughly twenty-five hundred years ago, when Greece was but a collection of city-states, slavery was common. A city that became powerful and conquered another city would enslave some of the vanquished. Both slaves and slaveholders were Greek. Similarly, when Rome became the supreme power of the Mediterranean area about two thousand years ago, following the custom of the time, the Romans enslaved some of the Greeks they had conquered. More educated than their conquerors, some of these slaves served as tutors in Roman homes. Slavery, then, was a sign of debt, of crime, or of defeat in battle. It was not a sign that the slave was viewed as inherently inferior.

Conditions of Slavery.

The conditions of slavery have varied widely around the world. *In some places, slavery was temporary.* Slaves of the Israelites were set free in the year of jubilee, which occurred every fifty years. Roman slaves ordinarily had the right to buy themselves out of slavery. They knew what their purchase price was, and some were able to meet this price by striking a bargain with their owners and selling their services to others. In most instances, however, slavery was a lifelong condition. Some criminals, for example, became slaves when they were given life sentences as oarsmen on Roman war ships. There they served until death, which often came quickly to those in this exhausting service.

Slavery was not necessarily inheritable. In most places, the children of slaves were slaves themselves. But in some instances, the child of a slave who served a rich family might even be adopted by that family, becoming an heir who bore the family name along with the other sons or daughters of the household. In ancient Mexico, the children of slaves were always free (Landtman 1938/1968:271).

Slaves were not necessarily powerless and poor. In almost all instances, slaves owned no property and had no power. Among some groups, however, slaves could accumulate property and even rise to high positions in the community. Occasionally, a slave might even become wealthy, loan money to the master, and, while still a slave, own slaves himself or herself (Landtman 1938/1968). This, however, was rare.

Slavery in the New World.

To meet the growing need for labor, some colonists tried to enslave Native Americans. This attempt failed miserably, in part because when Indians escaped, they knew how to survive in the wilderness and were able to make their way back to their tribe. The colonists then turned to Africans, who were being brought to North and South America by the Dutch, English, Portuguese, and Spanish.

Because slavery has a broad range of causes, some analysts conclude that racism didn't lead to slavery, but, rather, that slavery led to racism. To defend slavery, U.S. slave owners developed an **ideology,** beliefs that justify social arrangements, making those arrangements seem necessary and fair. They developed the view that their slaves

Under slavery, humans, like horses, could be sold, leased, borrowed, even raffled off.

During my research in India, I interviewed this 8-year-old girl. Mahashury is a *bonded laborer* who was exchanged by her parents for a 2,000 rupee loan (about $14). To repay the loan, Mahashury must do construction work for one year. She will receive one meal a day and one set of clothing for the year. Because this centuries-old practice is now illegal, the master bribes Indian officials, who inform him when they are going to inspect the construction site. He then hides his bonded laborers. I was able to interview and photograph Mahashury because her master was absent the day I visited the construction site.

were inferior. Some even said that they were not fully human. In short, the colonists wove elaborate justifications for slavery, built on the presumed superiority of their own group.

To make slavery even more profitable, slave states passed laws that made slavery *inheritable;* that is, the babies born to slaves became the property of the slave owners (Stampp 1956). These children could be sold, bartered, or traded. To strengthen their control, slave states passed laws making it illegal for slaves to hold meetings or to be away from the master's premises without carrying a pass (Lerner 1972). As sociologist W. E. B. Du Bois (1935/1992:12) noted, "gradually the entire white South became an armed camp to keep Negroes in slavery and to kill the black rebel."

The Civil War did not end legal discrimination. For example, until 1954 many states operated separate school systems for blacks and whites. Until the 1950s, in order to keep the races from "mixing," it was illegal in Mississippi for a white and an African American to sit together on the same seat of a car! There was no outright ban on blacks and whites being in the same car, however, so whites could employ African American chauffeurs.

Slavery Today. Slavery has again reared its ugly head in several parts of the world. The Ivory Coast, Mauritania, Niger, and Sudan have a long history of slavery, and not until the 1980s was slavery made illegal in Mauritania and Sudan (Ayittey 1998). It took until 2003 for slavery to be banned in Niger (Polgreen 2008). Although officially abolished, slavery in this region continues, the topic of the Mass Media box on the next page.

The enslavement of children for work and sex is a problem in Africa, Asia, and South America (*Trafficking in Persons Report* 2011). A unique form of child slavery in some Mideast desert countries is buying little boys around the age of 5 or 6 to race camels. Their screams of terror are thought to make the camels run faster. In Qatar and the United Arab Emirates, which recently banned this practice, robots are supposed to replace the children (de Pastino 2005; Nelson 2009).

Caste

The second system of social stratification is caste. In a **caste system,** birth determines status, which is lifelong. Someone who is born into a low-status group will always have low status, no matter how much that person may accomplish in life. In sociological terms, a caste system is built on ascribed status (discussed on page 97). Achieved status cannot change an individual's place in this system.

Societies with this form of stratification try to make certain that the boundaries between castes remain firm. They practice **endogamy,** marriage within their own group, and prohibit intermarriage. Elaborate rules about *ritual pollution*—touching an inferior caste contaminates the superior caste—keep contact between castes to a minimum.

India's Religious Castes. India provides the best example of a caste system. Based not on race but on religion, the caste system has existed for almost three thousand years (Chandra 1993a; Jaffrelot 2006). India's four main castes are depicted in Table 7.1. These four castes are subdivided into about three thousand subcastes, or *jati*. Each *jati* specializes in a particular occupation. For example, one sub-caste washes clothes, another sharpens knives, and yet another repairs shoes.

The lowest group listed in Table 7.1, the Dalit, make up India's "untouchables." If a Dalit touches someone of a higher caste, that person becomes unclean. Even the shadow of an untouchable can contaminate. Early morning and late afternoons are especially risky, for the long shadows of these periods pose a danger to everyone higher up the caste system. Consequently, Dalits are not allowed

TABLE 7.1	India's Caste System
Caste	**Occupation**
Brahman	Priests and teachers
Kshatriya	Rulers and soldiers
Vaishya	Merchants and traders
Shudra	Peasants and laborers
Dalit (untouchables)	The outcastes; degrading or polluting labor

What Price Freedom? Slavery Today

On the morning of the raid, 10-year-old Adhieu had been watching the cattle. "We were very happy because we would soon leave the cattle camps and return home to our parents. But in the morning, there was shooting. There was yelling and crying everywhere. My uncle grabbed me by the hand, and we ran. We swam across the river. I saw some children drowning. We hid behind a rock."

By morning's end, 500 children were either dead or enslaved. Their attackers were their fellow countrymen—Arabs from northern Sudan. The children who were captured were forced to march hundreds of miles north. Some escaped on the way. Others tried to—and were shot (Akol 1998). This raid occurred in rural Sudan, where children of the Dinka tribe tend the cattle that are essential to the Dinka's way of life.

Public television (PBS) has run film footage of captive children in chains. And escaped slaves have recounted their ordeal in horrifying detail (Salopek 2003; Mende and Lewis 2005).

The United States bombed Serbia into submission for its crimes against humanity, but in the face of this outrage it remained largely silent. A cynic might say that Serbia was located at a politically strategic spot in Europe, but Sudan occupies an area of Africa in which the United States and European powers have had little interest. A cynic might add that these powers fear Arab retaliation, which might take the form of oil embargoes and terrorism. A cynic might also suggest that outrages against black Africans are not as significant to these powers as those against white Europeans. Finally, a cynic might add that this indifference will end as Sudan's oil reserves become more strategic to Western interests.

When the world's most powerful governments didn't act on behalf of the slaves, private groups stepped in. One was Switzerland's Christian Solidarity International (CSI). CSI sent Arab "retrievers" to northern Sudan, where they either bought or abducted slaves. CSI paid the retrievers $100 per slave.

Critics claimed that buying slaves, even to free them, encourages slavery. The money provides motivation to enslave people in order to turn around and sell them. Certainly $100 is a lot of money in Sudan, where the average person makes $92 a month (*Statistical Abstract* 2012:Table 1348).

CSI said that this was a bogus argument. What is intolerable, they said, is to leave women and children in slavery where they are deprived of their freedom and families and are beaten and raped by brutal masters.

For Your Consideration

→ What do you think about buying the freedom of slaves? Can you suggest a workable alternative? Why do you think the U.S. government remained largely silent about this issue, when it invaded other countries such as Serbia and Haiti for human rights abuses? Do you think that, perhaps, political motivations outweigh human rights motivations?

Some U.S. high schools—and even grade schools—raised money to participate in slave buyback programs. If you were a school principal, would you support this? Why or why not?

In this photo, a representative of the Liason Agency Network (on the right) is buying the freedom of the Sudanese slaves (in the background).

in some villages during these times. Anyone who becomes contaminated must follow *ablution,* or washing rituals, to restore purity.

Although the Indian government formally abolished the caste system in 1949, centuries-old practices cannot be eliminated easily, and the caste system remains part of everyday life in India (Beckett 2007). The ceremonies people follow at births, marriages, and deaths, for example, are dictated by caste (Chandra 1993a). The upper castes dread the upward mobility of the untouchables, sometimes even resisting this change with murder and ritual suicide (Crossette 1996; Trofimov 2007). From personal observations in India, I can add that in some villages Dalit children are not allowed in the government schools. If they try to enroll, they are beaten.

In a *caste system*, status is determined by birth and is lifelong. At birth, these women received not only membership in a lower caste but also, because of their gender, a predetermined position in that caste. When I photographed these women, they were carrying sand to the second floor of a house being constructed in Andhra Pradesh, India.

A U.S. Racial Caste System.   Before leaving the subject of caste, we should note that when slavery ended in the United States, it was replaced by a *racial caste system*. From the moment of birth, race marked everyone for life (Berger 1963/2012a). *All* whites, even if they were poor and uneducated, considered themselves to have a higher status than *all* African Americans. As in India and South Africa, the upper caste, fearing pollution from the lower caste, made intermarriage illegal. There were also separate schools, hotels, restaurants, and even toilets and drinking fountains for blacks and whites. In the South, when any white met any African American on a sidewalk, the African American had to move aside. The untouchables of India still must do this when they meet someone of a higher caste (Deliege 2001).

Class

As we have seen, stratification systems based on slavery and caste are rigid. The lines drawn between people are firm, and there is little or no movement from one group to another. A **class system,** in contrast, is much more open, for it is based primarily on money or material possessions, which can be acquired. This system, too, is in place at birth, when children are ascribed the status of their parents. Unlike the other systems, however, individuals can change their social class by what they achieve (or fail to achieve) in life. In addition, no laws specify people's occupations on the basis of birth or prohibit marriage between the classes.

A major characteristic of the class system, then, is its relatively fluid boundaries. A class system allows **social mobility,** movement up or down the class ladder. The potential for improving one's life—or for falling down the class ladder—is a major force that drives people to go far in school and to work hard. In the extreme, the family background that a child inherits at birth may present such obstacles that he or she has little chance of climbing very far—or it may provide such privileges that it makes it almost impossible to fall down the class ladder. Because social class is so significant for our own lives, we will focus on class in the next chapter.

Global Stratification and the Status of Females

In *every* society of the world, gender is a basis for social stratification. In no society is gender the sole basis for stratifying people, but gender cuts across *all* systems of social stratification—whether slavery, caste, or class (Huber 1990). In all these systems, on the basis of their gender, people are sorted into categories and given different access to the good things available in their society.

Did the U.S. ever have a caste system? How does class differ from slavery and caste systems?

Apparently these distinctions always favor males. It is remarkable, for example, that in *every* society of the world men's earnings are higher than women's. Men's dominance is even more evident when we consider female circumcision (see the box on page 285). That most of the world's illiterate are females also drives home women's relative position in society. Of the several hundred million adults who cannot read, about two-thirds are women (UNESCO 2011). Because gender is such a significant factor in what happens to us in life, we shall focus on it more closely in Chapter 10.

The Global Superclass

The growing interconnections among the world's wealthiest people have produced a *global superclass*, one in which wealth and power are more concentrated than ever before. There are only about 6,000 members of this superclass—*the richest 1,000 of them have more wealth than the 2½ billion poorest people on this planet* (Rothkopf 2008:37). Almost all of them are white, and except as wives and daughters, few women are an active part of the superclass. We will have more to say about the superclass in Chapter 11, but for now, let's just stress their incredible wealth. There is nothing in history to compare with what you see in Figure 7.1.

What Determines Social Class?

In the early days of sociology, a disagreement arose about the meaning of social class. Let's compare how Marx and Weber analyzed the issue.

Karl Marx: The Means of Production

As we discussed in Chapter 1, as agricultural society gave way to an industrial one, masses of peasants were displaced from their traditional lands and occupations. Fleeing to cities, they competed for the few available jobs. Paid only a pittance for their labor, they wore rags, went hungry, and slept under bridges and in shacks. In contrast, the factory owners built mansions, hired servants, and lived in the lap of luxury. Seeing this great disparity between owners and workers, Karl Marx (1818–1883) concluded that social class depends on a single factor: people's relationship to the **means of production**—the tools, factories, land, and investment capital used to produce wealth (Marx 1844/1964; Marx and Engels 1848/1967).

Marx argued that the distinctions people often make among themselves—such as clothing, speech, education, paycheck, the neighborhood they live in, even the car they drive—are superficial matters. These things camouflage the only dividing line that counts. There are just two classes of people, said Marx: the **bourgeoisie** (*capitalists*), those who own the means of production, and the **proletariat** (*workers*),

In early industrialization, children worked alongside adults. They worked 12 hours a day Monday to Friday and 15 hours on Saturday, often in dangerous, filthy conditions. In this 1909 protest in New York City, two girls are wearing banners with the slogan "ABOLISH CHILD SLAVERY" in English and Yiddish.

FIGURE 7.1 The Distribution of the Earth's Wealth

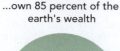

The wealthiest 10 percent of adults worldwide...

10%

90%

...own 85 percent of the earth's wealth

85%

15%

The wealthiest 1 percent of adults worldwide...

1%

99%

...own 40 percent of the earth's wealth

40%

60%

Source: By the author. Based on Rothkopf 2008:37.

Taken at the end of the 1800s, these photos illustrate the contrasting worlds of *social classes* produced by early capitalism. The sleeping boys shown in this classic 1890 photo by Jacob Riis sold newspapers in London. They did not go to school, and they had no home. The children on the right, Cornelius and Gladys Vanderbilt, are shown in front of their parents' estate. They went to school and did not work. You can see how the social locations illustrated in these photos would have produced different orientations to life and, therefore, politics, ideas about marriage, values, and so on—the stuff of which life is made.

those who work for the owners. In short, people's relationship to the means of production determines their social class.

Marx did recognize other groups: farmers and peasants; a *lumpenproletariat* (people living on the margin of society, such as beggars, vagrants, and criminals); and a middle group of self-employed professionals. Marx did not consider these groups social classes, however, for they lack **class consciousness**—a shared identity based on their position in the means of production. In other words, they did not perceive themselves as exploited workers whose plight could be resolved by collective action. Marx thought of these groups as insignificant in the future he foresaw—a workers' revolution that would overthrow capitalism.

The capitalists will grow even wealthier, Marx said, and hostilities will increase. When workers come to realize that capitalists are the source of their oppression, they will unite and throw off the chains of their oppressors. In a bloody revolution, they will seize the means of production and usher in a classless society—and no longer will the few grow rich at the expense of the many. What holds back the workers' unity and their revolution is **false class consciousness,** workers mistakenly thinking of themselves as capitalists. For example, workers with a few dollars in the bank may forget that they are workers and instead see themselves as investors, or as capitalists who are about to launch a successful business.

Max Weber: Property, Power, and Prestige

Max Weber (1864–1920) was an outspoken critic of Marx. Weber argued that property is only part of the picture. *Social class,* he said, has three components: property, power, and prestige (Gerth and Mills 1958; Weber 1922/1978). Some call these the three P's of social class. (Although Weber used the terms *class, power,* and *status,* some sociologists find *property, power,* and *prestige* to be clearer terms. To make them even clearer, you may wish to substitute *wealth* for *property.*)

Property (or wealth), said Weber, is certainly significant in determining a person's standing in society. On this point he agreed with Marx. But, added Weber, ownership is not the only significant aspect of property. For example, some powerful people, such as managers of corporations, *control* the means of production even though they do not *own* them. If managers can control property for their own benefit—awarding themselves huge bonuses and magnificent perks—it makes no practical difference that they do not own the property that they use so generously for their own benefit.

Power, the second element of social class, is the ability to control others, even over their objections. Weber agreed with Marx that property is a major source of power, but he added that it is not the only source. For example, prestige can be turned into power. Two well-known examples are actors Arnold Schwarzenegger, who became governor of California, and Ronald Reagan, who was elected governor of California and president of the United States. Figure 7.2 shows how property, power, and prestige are interrelated.

Prestige, the third element in Weber's analysis, is often derived from property and power, for people tend to admire the wealthy and powerful. Prestige, however, can be based on other factors. Olympic gold medalists, for example, might not own property or be powerful, yet they have high prestige. Some are even able to exchange their prestige for property—such as those who are paid a small fortune for endorsing a certain brand of sportswear or for claiming that they start their day with "the breakfast of champions." In other words, property and prestige are not one-way streets: Although property can bring prestige, prestige can also bring property.

In Sum: For Marx, the only distinction that counted was property, more specifically people's relationship to the means of production. Whether we are owners or workers decides everything else, for this determines our lifestyle and shapes our orientation to life. Weber, in contrast, argued that social class has three components—a combination of property, power, and prestige.

Why Is Social Stratification Universal?

What is it about social life that makes all societies stratified? We shall first consider the explanation proposed by functionalists, which has aroused much controversy in sociology, and then explanations proposed by conflict theorists.

The Functionalist View: Motivating Qualified People

Functionalists take the position that the patterns of behavior that characterize a society exist because they are functional for that society. Because social inequality is universal, inequality must help societies survive. But how?

Davis and Moore's Explanation.   Two functionalists, Kingsley Davis and Wilbert Moore (1945, 1953), wrestled with this question. They concluded that stratification of society is inevitable because

1. Society must make certain that its positions are filled.
2. Some positions are more important than others.
3. The more important positions must be filled by the more qualified people.
4. To motivate the more qualified people to fill these positions, they must offer greater rewards.

To flesh out this functionalist argument, consider college presidents and military generals. The position of college president is more important than that of student because the president's decisions affect a large number of people, including many students. College presidents are also accountable for their performance to boards of trustees. It is the same with generals. Their decisions affect many people and sometimes even determine life and death. Generals are accountable to superior generals and to the country's leader.

Why do people accept demanding, high-pressure positions? Why don't they just take easier jobs? The answer, said Davis and Moore, is that these positions offer greater rewards—more prestige, pay, and benefits. To get highly qualified people to compete with one another, some positions offer a salary of $2 million a year, country club membership, a private jet and pilot, and a chauffeured limousine. For less demanding positions, a $30,000 salary without fringe benefits is enough to get hundreds of people to compete. If a job requires rigorous training, it, too, must offer more salary and benefits. If you can get the same pay with a high school diploma, why suffer through the many tests and term papers that college requires?

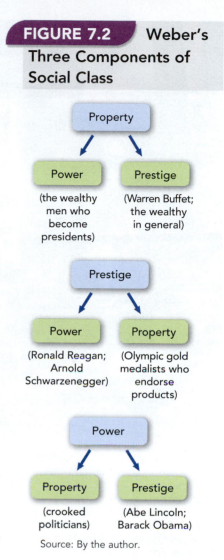

FIGURE 7.2   Weber's Three Components of Social Class

Property

Power
(the wealthy men who become presidents)

Prestige
(Warren Buffet; the wealthy in general)

Prestige

Power
(Ronald Reagan; Arnold Schwarzenegger)

Property
(Olympic gold medalists who endorse products)

Power

Property
(crooked politicians)

Prestige
(Abe Lincoln; Barack Obama)

Source: By the author.

How do functionalists explain why social stratification is universal?

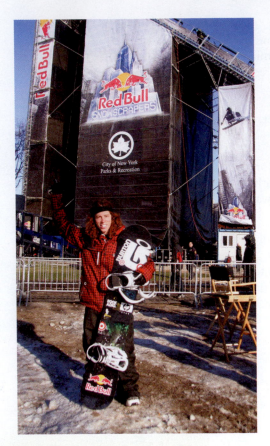

Prestige can sometimes be converted into property or power: Shaun White, the winner of two Olympic gold medals for snowboarding, gained endorsements worth millions. His corporate sponsors include Red Bull, Target, and Hewlett-Packard. He stars in his own video games.

Tumin's Critique of Davis and Moore.   Davis and Moore were not attempting to justify social inequality, just to explain *why* social stratification is universal. Nevertheless, their view makes many sociologists uncomfortable, for they see it as coming close to justifying the inequalities in society. Its bottom line seems to be: The people who contribute more to society are paid more, while those who contribute less are paid less.

Melvin Tumin (1953) was the first sociologist to point out what he saw as major flaws in the functionalist position. Here are three of his arguments.

First, how do we know that the positions that offer the higher rewards are more important? A heart surgeon, for example, saves lives and earns much more than a garbage collector, but this doesn't mean that garbage collectors are less important to society. By helping to prevent contagious diseases, garbage collectors save more lives than heart surgeons do. We need independent methods of measuring importance, and we don't have them.

Second, if stratification worked as Davis and Moore described it, society would be a **meritocracy;** that is, positions would be awarded on the basis of merit. But is this what we have? The best predictor of who goes to college, for example, is not ability but income: The more a family earns, the more likely their children are to go to college (Bailey and Dynarski 2011). Not merit, then, but money—another form of the inequality that is built into society. In short, people's positions in society are based on many factors other than merit.

Third, if social stratification is so functional, it ought to benefit almost everyone. Yet social stratification is *dysfunctional* for many. Think of the people who could have made valuable contributions to society had they not been born in slums, dropped out of school, and taken menial jobs to help support their families. Then there are the many who, born female, are assigned "women's work," thus ensuring that they do not maximize their mental abilities.

In Sum: Functionalists argue that some positions are more important to society than others. Offering higher rewards for these positions motivates more talented people to take them. For example, to get highly capable people to become surgeons—to undergo years of rigorous training and then cope with life-and-death situations, as well as malpractice suits—that position must provide a high payoff.

Next, let's see how conflict theorists explain why social stratification is universal. Before we do, look at Table 7.2 which compares the functionalist and conflict views.

TABLE 7.2	**Functionalist and Conflict Views of Stratification: The Distribution of Resources**		
Why are society's resources (rewards) distributed the way they are?			
	Highest Resources go to those who	**Lowest Resources go to those who**	**Source of Rewards**
The Functionalist View	Perform the most important functions (the most capable and most industrious)	Perform the least important functions (the less capable and less industrious)	Given to motivate people to sacrifice present rewards for future gains
The Conflict View	Occupy the most powerful positions (in society or in an organization)	Occupy the least powerful positions (in society or in an organization)	Seized by those who gain power (and distributed by them to maintain their power)

Source: By the author.

What are the criticisms of functionalism?

The Conflict Perspective: Class Conflict and Scarce Resources

Conflict theorists don't just criticize details of the functionalist argument. Rather, they go for the throat and attack its basic premise. Conflict, not function, they stress, is the reason that we have social stratification. Let's look at the major arguments.

Mosca's Argument.   Italian sociologist Gaetano Mosca argued that every society will be stratified by power. This is inevitable, he said in an 1896 book titled *The Ruling Class,* because:

1. No society can exist unless it is organized. This requires leadership in order to coordinate people's actions.
2. Leadership requires inequalities of power. By definition, some people take leadership positions, while others follow.
3. Because human nature is self-centered, people in power will use their positions to seize greater rewards for themselves.

There is no way around these facts of life, added Mosca. Social stratification is inevitable, and every society will stratify itself along lines of power.

Shown here are sisters Venus and Serena Williams after winning gold medals at the Beijing Olympics. To determine the social class of athletes as highly successful as the Williams sisters presents a sociological puzzle. With their high prestige and growing wealth, what do you think their social class is? Why?

Marx's Argument.   If he were alive to hear the functionalist argument, Karl Marx would be enraged. From his point of view, the people in power are not there because of superior traits, as the functionalists would have us believe. This view is an ideology that members of the elite use to justify their being at the top—and to seduce the oppressed into believing that their welfare depends on keeping quiet and following authorities like sheep. What is human history, Marx asked, except the chronicle of class struggle? All of human history is an account of small groups of people in power using society's resources to benefit themselves and to oppress those beneath them—and of oppressed groups trying to overcome that oppression.

Marx predicted that the workers will revolt. Capitalist ideology now blinds them, but one day class consciousness will throw off that blindfold and expose the truth. When workers realize their common oppression, they will rebel. The struggle to control the means of production may be covert at first, taking such forms as work slowdowns and industrial sabotage. Ultimately, however, resistance will break out into the open. The revolution will not be easy, for the bourgeoisie control the police, the military, and even the educational system, where they implant false class consciousness in the minds of the workers' children.

Current Applications of Conflict Theory.   Just as Marx focused on overarching historic events—the accumulation of capital and power and the struggle between workers and capitalists—so do some of today's conflict sociologists. In analyzing global stratification and global capitalism, they look at power relations among nations, how national elites control workers, and how power shifts as capital is shuffled among nations (Jessop 2010).

Other conflict sociologists, in contrast, examine conflict wherever it is found, not just as it relates to capitalists and workers. They examine how groups *within the same class* compete with one another for a larger slice of the pie (Collins 1999; King et al. 2010). Even within the same industry, for example, union will fight against union for higher salaries, shorter hours, and more power. A special focus is conflict between racial–ethnic groups as they compete for education, housing, and even prestige—whatever rewards society has to offer. Another focus is relations between women and men, which conflict theorists say are best understood as a conflict over power—over who controls society's resources. Unlike functionalists, conflict theorists say that just beneath the surface of what may appear to be a tranquil society lies conflict that is barely held in check.

How do conflict theorists explain why social stratification is universal?

Lenski's Synthesis

As you can see, functionalist and conflict theorists disagree sharply. Is it possible to reconcile their views? Sociologist Gerhard Lenski (1966) thought so. He suggested that surplus is the key. He said that the functionalists are right when it comes to groups that don't accumulate a surplus, such as hunting and gathering societies. These societies give a greater share of their resources to those who take on important tasks, such as warriors who risk their lives in battle. It is a different story, said Lenski, with societies that accumulate surpluses. In them, groups fight over the surplus, and the group that wins becomes an elite. This dominant group rules from the top, controlling the groups below it. In the resulting system of social stratification, where you are born in that society, not personal merit, is important.

In Sum: Conflict theorists stress that in every society groups struggle with one another to gain a larger share of their society's resources. Whenever a group gains power, it uses that power to extract what it can from the groups beneath it. This elite group also uses the social institutions to keep itself in power.

How Do Elites Maintain Stratification?

Suppose that you are part of the ruling elite of your society. You want to make sure that you and your family and friends are going to be able to keep your privileged position for the next generation. How will you accomplish this?

You might think about passing laws and using the police and the military. After all, you are a member of the *ruling elite,* so you have this power. You could use force, but this can lead to resentment and rebellion. It is much more effective to control people's ideas, information, and technology—which is just what the elite try to do. Let's look at some of their techniques.

Soft Control Versus Force

Let's start with Medieval Europe, where we find an excellent example of how ideology is part of "soft" control. At that time, land was the primary source of wealth—and only the nobility and the church could own land. Almost everyone was a peasant (a serf) who worked for these powerful landowners. The peasants farmed the land, took care of the livestock, and built the roads and bridges. Each year, they had to turn over a designated portion of their crops to their feudal lord. Year after year, for centuries, they did so. Why?

The *divine right of kings* was an ideology that made the king God's direct representative on earth—to administer justice and punish evildoers. This theological-political concept was supported by the Roman Catholic Church, whose representatives crowned the king. Shown here is the coronation in 998 of Otto III as king of the Saxony area of Germany.

Controlling People's Ideas.   Why didn't the peasants rebel and take over the land themselves? There were many reasons, not the least of which was that the nobility and church controlled the army. Coercion, however, goes only so far, for it breeds hostility and nourishes rebellion. How much more effective it is to get the masses to *want* to do what the ruling elite desires. This is where *ideology* (beliefs that justify the way things are) comes into play, which the nobility and clergy used to great effect. They developed an ideology known as the **divine right of kings**—the idea that the king's authority comes directly from God. The king delegates authority to nobles, who, as God's representatives, must be obeyed. To disobey is a sin against God; to rebel is to merit physical punishment on earth and eternal suffering in hell.

Controlling people's ideas can be remarkably more effective than using brute force. Although this particular ideology governs few minds today, the elite in *every* society develops ideologies to justify its position at the top. For example, around the world, schools teach that their country's form of government—*no matter what form of government that is*—is good. Religious leaders teach that we owe obedience to authority, that laws are to be obeyed. To the degree that their ideologies are accepted by the masses, the elite remains securely in power.

How did Lenski attempt to reconcile the functionalist and conflict views of social stratification?

Controlling Information.   To maintain their power, elites try to control information. Chinese leaders have put tight controls on Internet cafes and search engines (Blanchard 2010). In North Korea, you can spend six months in a labor camp just for watching a Jackie Chan movie (LaFraniere 2010). Lacking such power, the ruling elites of democracies rely on covert means. A favorite tactic of U.S. presidents is to withhold information "in the interest of national security," a phrase that usually translates as "in the interest of protecting me."

Stifling Criticism.   Like the rest of us, the power elite doesn't like criticism. But unlike the rest of us, they have the power to do something about it. When the U.S. Defense Department found out that an author had criticized its handling of 9/11, it bought and destroyed 9,500 copies of his book (Thompson 2010). Fear is a favorite tactic of the elite. In Thailand, you can be put in prison for criticizing the king or his family (Peck 2009). It was worse in Saddam Hussein's Iraq, where the penalty for telling a joke about Hussein was having your tongue cut out (Nordland 2003).

Big Brother Technology.   The new technology allows the elite to monitor citizens without anyone knowing they are being watched. Computer programs can read the entire contents of a computer in a second—and not leave a trace. Security cameras— "Tiny Brothers"—have sprouted almost everywhere. Face-recognition systems can scan a crowd of thousands, instantly matching the scans with digitized files of individuals. It is likely that the digitized facial image of every citizen will eventually be on file. Dictators have few checks on how they use this technology, but democracies do have some, such as requiring court orders for search and seizure. Such restraints on power always frustrate officials, so they are delighted with our new Homeland Security laws that allow them to spy on citizens without their knowledge.

The new technology, however, is a two-edged sword. Just as it gives the elite powerful tools for monitoring citizens, it also makes it more difficult for them to control information. With international borders meaning nothing to satellite communications, e-mail, and the Internet, information (both true and fabricated) flies around the globe in seconds. Internet users also have free access to some versions of PGP (Pretty Good Privacy) and TrueCrypt, codes that no government has been able to break. Then, too, there is zFone, a voice encryption for telephone calls that prevents wiretappers from understanding what people are saying.

In Sum: To maintain stratification, the elite tries to dominate its society's institutions. In a dictatorship, the elite makes the laws. In a democracy, the elite influences the laws. In both, the elite controls the police and military and can give orders to crush a rebellion—or to run the post office or air traffic control if workers strike. With force having its limits, especially the potential of provoking resistance, most power elites prefer to keep themselves in power by peaceful means, especially by controlling technology and influencing the thinking of their people.

Comparative Social Stratification

Now that we have examined systems of social stratification, considered why stratification is universal, and looked at how elites keep themselves in power, let's compare social stratification in Great Britain and in the former Soviet Union. In the next chapter, we'll look at social stratification in the United States.

Social Stratification in Great Britain

Great Britain is often called England by Americans, but England is only one of the countries that make up the island of Great Britain. The others are Scotland and Wales. In addition, Northern Ireland is part of the United Kingdom of Great Britain and Northern Ireland.

Like other industrialized countries, Great Britain has a class system that can be divided into a lower, a middle, and an upper class. Great Britain's population is about evenly

How do ruling elites maintain their positions (control populations) without using force?

divided between the middle class and the lower (or working) class. A tiny upper class—wealthy, powerful, and highly educated—makes up perhaps 1 percent of the population.

Compared with Americans, the British are very class conscious (Kerswill 2006). Like Americans, they recognize class distinctions on the basis of the type of car a person drives or the stores someone patronizes. But the most striking characteristics of the British class system are language and education. Because these often show up in distinctive speech, accent has a powerful impact on British life. Accent almost always betrays class. As soon as someone speaks, the listener is aware of that person's social class—and treats him or her accordingly (Sullivan 1998).

Education is the primary way by which the British perpetuate their class system from one generation to the next. Almost all children go to neighborhood schools. Great Britain's richest 5 percent, however—who own *half* the nation's wealth—send their children to exclusive private boarding schools. There the children of the elite are trained in subjects that are considered "proper" for members of the ruling class. An astounding 50 percent of the students at Oxford and Cambridge, the country's most elite universities, come from this 5 percent of the population. So do half of the prime minister's cabinet (Neil 2011). To illustrate how powerfully this system of stratified education affects the national life of Great Britain, sociologist Ian Robertson (1987) said,

> Eighteen former pupils of the most exclusive of [England's high schools], Eton, have become prime minister. Imagine the chances of a single American high school producing eighteen presidents!

Social Stratification in the Former Soviet Union

Heeding Karl Marx's call for a classless society, Vladimir Ilyich Lenin (1870–1924) and Leon Trotsky (1879–1940) led a revolution in Russia in 1917. They, and the nations that followed their banner, never claimed to have achieved the ideal of communism, in which all contribute their labor to the common good and receive according to their needs. Instead, they used the term *socialism* to describe the intermediate step between capitalism and communism, in which social classes are abolished but some inequality remains.

To tweak the nose of Uncle Sam, the socialist countries would trumpet their equality and point a finger at glaring inequalities in the United States. These countries, however, also were marked by huge disparities in privilege. Their major basis of stratification was membership in the Communist party. Party members decided who would gain admission to the better schools or obtain the more desirable jobs and housing. The equally qualified son or daughter of a nonmember would be turned down, for such privileges came with demonstrated loyalty to the party.

The Communist party, too, was highly stratified. Most members occupied a low level, where they fulfilled such tasks as spying on fellow workers. For this, they might get easier jobs in the factory or occasional access to special stores to purchase hard-to-find goods. The middle level consisted of bureaucrats who were given better than average access to resources and privileges. At the top level was a small elite: party members who enjoyed not only power but also limousines, imported delicacies, vacation homes, and even servants and hunting lodges. As with other stratification systems around the world, women held lower positions in the party. This was evident at each year's May Day, when the top members of the party reviewed the latest weapons paraded in Moscow's Red Square. Photos of these events showed only men.

The leaders of the USSR became frustrated as they saw the West thrive. They struggled with a bloated bureaucracy, the inefficiencies of central planning, workers who did the minimum because they could not be fired, and a military so costly that it spent one of every eight of the nation's rubles (*Statistical Abstract* 1993:1432, table dropped in later editions). Socialist ideology did not call for their citizens to be deprived, and in an attempt to turn things around, the Soviet leadership initiated reforms. They allowed elections to be held in which more than one candidate ran for an office. (Before this, voters had a choice of only one candidate per office.) They also sold huge chunks of

What are the main characteristics of social stratification in Great Britain? In the former Soviet Union?

state-owned businesses to the public. Overnight, making investments to try to turn a profit changed from a crime into a respectable goal.

Russia's transition to capitalism took a bizarre twist. As authority broke down, a powerful Mafia emerged (Varese 2005; Hignett 2010). These criminal groups are headed by gangsters, corrupt government officials (including members of the secret police, the FSB), and crooked businessmen. In some towns, they buy the entire judicial system—the police force, prosecutors, and judges. They assassinate business leaders, reporters, and politicians who refuse to cooperate. They amass wealth, launder money through banks they control, and buy luxury properties in popular tourist areas in South America, Asia, and Europe. A favorite is Marbella, a watering and wintering spot on Spain's Costa del Sol.

As Moscow reestablishes its authority, Mafia ties have brought wealth to some of the members of this central government. This group of organized criminals is taking its place as part of Russia's new capitalist class.

Global Stratification: Three Worlds

As was noted at the beginning of this chapter, just as the people within a nation are stratified by property, power, and prestige, so are the world's nations. Until recently, a simple model consisting of First, Second, and Third Worlds was used to depict global stratification. *First World* referred to the industrialized capitalist nations, *Second World* to the communist (or socialist) countries, and *Third World* to any nation that did not fit into the first two categories. The breakup of the Soviet Union in 1989 made these terms outdated. In addition, although *first, second,* and *third* did not mean "best," "better," and "worst," they implied it. An alternative classification that some now use—developed, developing, and undeveloped nations—has the same drawback. By calling ourselves "developed," it sounds as though we are mature and the "undeveloped" nations are somehow retarded.

To resolve this problem, I use more neutral, descriptive terms: *Most Industrialized, Industrializing,* and *Least Industrialized* nations. We can measure industrialization with no judgment implied as to whether a nation's industrialization represents "development," ranks it "first," or is even desirable at all. The intention is to depict on a global level the three primary dimensions of social stratification: property, power, and prestige. The Most Industrialized Nations have much greater property (wealth), power (they usually get their way in international relations), and prestige (they are looked up to as world leaders).

As you read this analysis, don't forget the sociological significance of the stratification of nations, its far-reaching effects on people's lives, as illustrated by the two families sketched in our opening vignette.

The contrast between poverty and wealth is a characteristics of all contemporary societies. I took this photo in Riga, the capital of Latvia, one of the countries Russia ruled as a satellite nation.

The Most Industrialized Nations

The Most Industrialized Nations are the United States and Canada in North America; Great Britain, France, Germany, Switzerland, and the other industrialized countries of western Europe; Japan in Asia; and Australia and New Zealand in the area of the world known as Oceania. Although there are variations in their economic systems, these nations are capitalistic. As Table 7.3 shows, although these nations have only 16 percent of the world's people, they possess 31 percent of the earth's land. Their wealth is so enormous that even their poor live better and longer lives than do the average citizens of the Least Industrialized Nations. The Social Map on the next two pages shows the tremendous disparities in income among the world's nations.

TABLE 7.3	Distribution of the World's Land and Population	
	Land	Population
Most Industrialized Nations	31%	16%
Industrializing Nations	20%	16%
Least Industrialized Nations	49%	68%

Sources: By the author. Computed from Kurian 1990, 1991, 1992.

Why does the author propose a model of Most Industrialized, Industrializing, and Least Industrialized Nations?

FIGURE 7.3   Global Stratification: Income[1] of the World's Nations

The Most Industrialized Nations

Nation	Income per Person
1 Luxembourg	$84,700
2 Singapore	$59,900
3 Norway	$53,300
4 Hong Kong	$49,300
5 United States	$48,100
6 Switzerland	$43,400
7 Netherlands	$42,300
8 Austria	$41,700
9 Australia	$40,800
10 Sweden	$40,600
11 Canada	$40,300
12 Denmark	$40,200
13 Finland	$38,300
14 Iceland	$38,000
15 Germany	$37,900
16 Taiwan	$37,900
17 Belgium	$37,600
18 United Kingdom	$35,900
19 France	$35,000
20 Japan	$34,300
21 Korea, South	$31,700
22 Israel	$31,000
23 Italy	$30,100
24 Slovenia	$29,100
25 New Zealand	$27,900
26 Czech Republic	$25,900

The Industrializing Nations

Nation	Income per Person
27 Ireland	$39,500
28 Greenland	$36,500
29 Spain	$30,600
30 Greece	$27,600
31 Slovakia	$23,400
32 Portugal	$23,200
33 Estonia	$20,200
34 Poland	$20,100
35 Hungary	$19,600
36 Lithuania	$18,700
37 Croatia	$18,300
38 Argentina	$17,400
39 Russia	$16,700
40 Chile	$16,100
41 Gabon	$16,000
42 Malaysia	$15,600
43 Latvia	$15,400
44 Mexico	$15,100
45 Mauritius	$15,000
46 Turkey	$14,600
47 Libya	$14,100
48 Bulgaria	$13,500
49 Venezuela	$12,400
50 Romania	$12,300
51 Brazil	$11,600
52 Costa Rica	$11,500
53 South Africa	$11,000
54 Cuba	$9,900
55 China	$8,400

The Least Industrialized Nations

Nation	Income per Person	Nation	Income per Person
56 Botswana[2]	$16,300	72 Ecuador	$8,300
57 Lebanon	$15,600	73 Bosnia	$8,200
58 Uruguay	$15,400	74 Albania	$7,800
59 Belarus	$14,900	75 El Salvador	$7,600
60 Panama	$13,600	76 Guyana	$7,500
61 Kazakhstan	$13,000	77 Turkmenistan	$7,500
62 Macedonia	$10,400	78 Namibia	$7,300
63 Azerbaijan	$10,200	79 Algeria	$7,200
64 Colombia	$10,100	80 Ukraine	$7,200
65 Peru	$10,000	81 Egypt	$6,500
66 Thailand	$9,700	82 Bhutan	$6,000
67 Suriname	$9,500	83 Angola	$5,900
68 Tunisia	$9,500	84 Jordan	$5,900
69 Dominican Republic	$9,300	85 Sri Lanka	$5,600
70 Jamaica	$9,000	86 Paraguay	$5,500
71 Belize	$8,300	87 Armenia	$5,400
		88 Georgia	$5,400

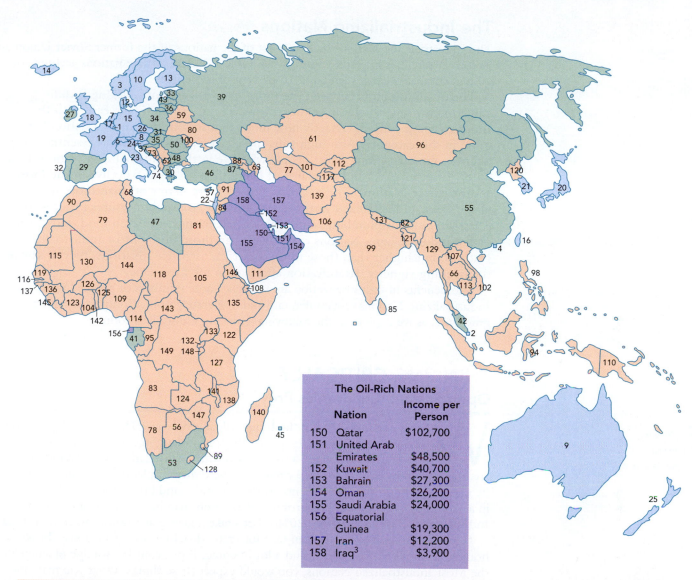

The Oil-Rich Nations

	Nation	Income per Person
150	Qatar	$102,700
151	United Arab Emirates	$48,500
152	Kuwait	$40,700
153	Bahrain	$27,300
154	Oman	$26,200
155	Saudi Arabia	$24,000
156	Equatorial Guinea	$19,300
157	Iran	$12,200
158	Iraq[3]	$3,900

The Least Industrialized Nations

	Nation	Income per Person		Nation	Income per Person		Nation	Income per Person		Nation	Income per Person
89	Swaziland	$5,200	106	Pakistan	$2,800	122	Kenya	$1,700	139	Afghanistan	$1,000
90	Morocco	$5,100	107	Laos	$2,700	123	Cote d'Ivoire	$1,600	140	Madagascar	$1,000
91	Syria	$5,100	108	Djibouti	$2,600	124	Zambia	$1,600	141	Malawi	$900
92	Guatemala	$5,000	109	Nigeria	$2,600	125	Benin	$1,500	142	Togo	$900
93	Bolivia	$4,800	110	Papua-New Guinea	$2,500	126	Burkina Faso	$1,500	143	Central African Republic	$800
94	Indonesia	$4,700				127	Tanzania	$1,500			
95	Congo	$4,600	111	Yemen	$2,500	128	Lesotho	$1,400	144	Niger	$800
96	Mongolia	$4,500	112	Krygyzstan	$2,400	129	Burma	$1,300	145	Sierra Leone	$800
97	Honduras	$4,300	113	Cambodia	$2,300	130	Mali	$1,300	146	Eritrea	$700
98	Philippines	$4,100	114	Cameroon	$2,300	131	Nepal	$1,300	147	Zimbabwe	$500
99	India	$3,700	115	Mauritania	$2,200	132	Rwanda	$1,300	148	Burundi	$400
100	Moldova	$3,400	116	Gambia	$2,100	133	Uganda	$1,300	149	Congo, Dem. Rep.	$300
101	Uzbekistan	$3,300	117	Tajikistan	$2,000	134	Haiti	$1,200			
102	Vietnam	$3,300	118	Chad	$1,900	135	Ethiopia	$1,100			
103	Nicaragua	$3,200	119	Senegal	$1,900	136	Guinea	$1,100			
104	Ghana	$3,100	120	Korea, North	$1,800	137	Guinea-Bissau	$1,100			
105	Sudan	$3,000	121	Bangladesh	$1,700	138	Mozambique	$1,100			

[1]Income is a country's purchasing power parity based on a country's Gross Domestic Product, where the value of a country's goods and services are valued at prices prevailing in the United States. Totals vary from year to year and should be considered as approximations.
[2]Botswana's income is based largely on its diamond mines.
[3]Iraq's oil wealth has been disrupted by war.
Source: By the author. Based on *CIA World Factbook* 2012.

The Industrializing Nations

The Industrializing Nations include most of the nations of the former Soviet Union and its former satellites in eastern Europe. As Table 7.3 shows, these nations account for 20 percent of the earth's land and 16 percent of its people.

The dividing points between the three "worlds" are soft, making it difficult to know how to classify some nations. This is especially the case with the Industrializing Nations. Exactly how much industrialization must a nation have to be in this category? Although soft, these categories do pinpoint essential differences among nations. Most people who live in the Industrializing Nations have much lower incomes and standards of living than do those who live in the Most Industrialized Nations. The majority, however, are better off than those who live in the Least Industrialized Nations. For example, on such measures as access to electricity, indoor plumbing, automobiles, telephones, and even food, most citizens of the Industrializing Nations rank lower than those in the Most Industrialized Nations, but higher than those in the Least Industrialized Nations. As you saw in the opening vignette, stratification affects even life expectancy.

The benefits of industrialization are uneven. Large numbers of people in the Industrializing Nations remain illiterate and desperately poor. Conditions can be gruesome, as we explore in the following Thinking Critically section.

Watch
Slum Features
on **mysoclab.com**

THINKING CRITICALLY

Open Season: Children as Prey

What is childhood like in the Industrializing Nations? The answer depends on who your parents are. If you are the son or daughter of rich parents, childhood can be pleasant—a world filled with luxuries and even servants. If you are born into poverty, but live in a rural area where there is plenty to eat, life can still be good—although there may be no books, television, and little education. If you live in a slum, however, life can be horrible—worse even than in the slums of the Most Industrialized Nations (Barbassa 2010). Let's take a glance at a notorious slum in Brazil.

Not enough food—this you can take for granted—along with wife abuse, broken homes, alcoholism, drug abuse, and a lot of crime. From your knowledge of slums in the Most Industrialized Nations, you would expect these things. What you may not expect, however, are the brutal conditions in which Brazilian slum (*favela*) children live.

Sociologist Martha Huggins (Huggins et al. 2002) reports that poverty is so deep that children and adults swarm through garbage dumps to try to find enough decaying food to keep them alive. You might also be surprised to discover that the owners of some of these dumps hire armed guards to keep the poor out—so that they can sell the garbage for pig food. And you might be shocked to learn that some shop owners hire hit men, auctioning designated victims to the *lowest* bidder!

Life is cheap in the poor nations—but death squads for children? To understand this, we must first note that Brazil has a long history of violence. Brazil also has a high rate of poverty, has only a tiny middle class, and is controlled by a small group of families who, under a veneer of democracy, make the country's major decisions. Hordes of homeless children, with no schools or jobs, roam the streets. To survive, they wash windshields, shine shoes, beg, and steal (Huggins and Rodrigues 2004).

The "respectable" classes see these children as nothing but trouble. They hurt business, for customers feel intimidated when they see begging children—especially teenaged boys—clustered in front of stores. Some shoplift. Others break into the stores. With no effective social institutions to care for these children, one solution is to kill them. As Huggins notes, murder sends a clear message—especially if it is accompanied by ritual torture: gouging out the eyes, ripping open the chest, cutting off the genitals, raping the girls, and burning the victim's body.

Not all life is bad in the Industrializing Nations, but this is about as bad as it gets.

What is life like for the very poor in the Industrializing Nations?

For Your Consideration

Do you think there is anything the Most Industrialized Nations can do about this situation? Or is it, though unfortunate, just an "internal" affair that is up to Brazil to handle as it wishes?

Directed by the police, death squads in the Philippine slums also assassinate rapists and drug dealers ("You Can Die Anytime" 2009). What do you think about this? ■

The Least Industrialized Nations

In the Least Industrialized Nations, most people live on small farms or in villages, have large families, and barely survive. These nations account for 68 percent of the world's people but only 49 percent of the earth's land.

Poverty plagues these nations to such an extent that some families actually *live* in city dumps. This is hard to believe, but look at the photos on the next two pages, which I took in Phnom Penh, the capital of Cambodia. Although wealthy nations have their pockets of poverty, *most* people in the Least Industrialized Nations are poor. *Most* of them have no running water, indoor plumbing, or access to trained teachers or doctors. As we will review in Chapter 14, most of the world's population growth occurs in these nations, placing even greater burdens on their limited resources and causing them to fall farther behind each year.

Homeless people sleeping on the streets is a common sight in India's cities. I took this photo in Chennai (formerly Madras).

How Did the World's Nations Become Stratified?

How did the globe become stratified into such distinct worlds? The commonsense answer is that the poorer nations have fewer resources than the richer nations. As with many commonsense answers, however, this one, too, falls short. Many of the Industrializing and Least Industrialized Nations are rich in natural resources, while one Most Industrialized Nation, Japan, has few. Three theories explain how global stratification came about.

Colonialism

The first theory, **colonialism,** stresses that the countries that industrialized first got the jump on the rest of the world. Beginning in Great Britain about 1750, industrialization spread throughout western Europe. Plowing some of their profits into powerful armaments and fast ships, these countries invaded weaker nations, making colonies out of them (Harrison 1993). After subduing these weaker nations, the more powerful countries left behind a controlling force in order to exploit the nations' labor and natural resources. At one point, there was even a free-for-all among the industrialized European countries as they rushed to divide up an entire continent. As they sliced Africa into pieces, even tiny Belgium got into the act and acquired the Congo, which was *seventy-five* times larger than itself.

The purpose of colonialism was to establish *economic colonies*—to exploit the nation's people and resources for the benefit of the "mother" country. The more powerful European countries would plant their national flags in a colony and send their representatives to run the government, but the United States usually chose to plant corporate flags in a colony and let these corporations dominate the territory's government. Central and South America are prime examples. There were exceptions, such as the U.S. army's conquest of the Philippines, which President McKinley said was motivated by the desire "to educate the Filipinos, and uplift and civilize and Christianize them" (Krugman 2002).

According to colonialism, how did the world's nations become stratified?

The Dump People: Working and Living and Playing in the City Dump of Phnom Penh, Cambodia

I went to Cambodia to inspect orphanages, to see how well the children are being cared for. While in Phnom Penh, Cambodia's capital, I was told about people who live in the city dump. *Live* there? I could hardly believe my ears. I knew that people made their living by picking scraps from the city dump, but I didn't know they actually lived among the garbage. This I had to see for myself.

I did. And there I found a highly developed social organization—an intricate support system. Because words are inadequate to depict the abject poverty of the Least Industrialized Nations, these photos can provide more insight into these people's lives than anything I could say.

After the garbage arrives by truck, people stream around it, struggling to be the first to discover something of value. To sift through the trash, the workers use metal picks, like the one this child is holding. Note that children work alongside the adults.

The children who live in the dump also play there. These children are riding bicycles on a "road," a packed, leveled area of garbage that leads to their huts. The huge stacks in the background are piled trash. Note the ubiquitous Nike.

This is a typical sight—family and friends working together. The trash, which is constantly burning, contains harmful chemicals. Why do people work under such conditions? Because they have few options. It is either this or starve.

© James M. Henslin, all photos

One of my many surprises was to find food stands in the dump. Although this one primarily offers drinks and snacks, others serve more substantial food. One even has chairs for its customers.

The people live at the edge of the dump, in homemade huts (visible in the background). This woman, who was on her way home after a day's work, put down her sack of salvaged items to let me take her picture.

CAMBODIA
★ Phnom Penh

I was surprised to learn that ice is delivered to the dump. This woman is using a hand grinder to crush ice for drinks for her customers. The customers, of course, are other people who also live in the dump.

At the day's end, the workers wash at the community pump. This hand pump serves all their water needs—drinking, washing, and cooking. There is no indoor plumbing. The weeds in the background serve that purpose. Can you imagine drinking water that comes from below this garbage dump?

Not too many visitors to Phnom Penh tell a cab driver to take them to the city dump. The cabbie looked a bit perplexed, but he did as I asked. Two cabs are shown here because my friends insisted on accompanying me.
I know they were curious themselves, but my friends had also discovered that the destinations I want to visit are usually not in the tourist guides, and they wanted to protect me.

Colonialism, then, shaped many of the Least Industrialized Nations. In some instances, the Most Industrialized Nations were so powerful that when dividing their spoils, they drew lines across a map, creating new states without regard for tribal or cultural considerations (Kifner 1999). Britain and France did just this as they divided up North Africa and parts of the Middle East—which is why the national boundaries of Libya, Saudi Arabia, Kuwait, and other countries are so straight. This legacy of European conquests is a background factor in much of today's racial–ethnic and tribal violence: Groups with no history of national identity were incorporated arbitrarily into the same political boundaries.

World System Theory

The second explanation of how global stratification came about was proposed by Immanuel Wallerstein (1974, 1979, 1990). According to **world system theory,** industrialization led to four groups of nations. The first group consists of the *core nations,* the countries that industrialized first (Britain, France, Holland, and later Germany), which grew rich and powerful. The second group is the *semiperiphery.* The economies of these nations, located around the Mediterranean, stagnated because they grew dependent on trade with the core nations. The economies of the third group, the *periphery,* or fringe nations, developed even less. These are the eastern European countries, which sold cash crops to the core nations. The fourth group of nations includes most of Africa and Asia. Called the *external area,* these nations were left out of the development of capitalism altogether. The current expansion of capitalism has changed the relationships among these groups. Most notably, eastern Europe and Asia are no longer left out of capitalism.

The **globalization of capitalism**—the adoption of capitalism around the world—has created extensive ties among the world's nations. Production and trade are now so interconnected that events around the globe affect us all. Sometimes this is immediate, as happens when a civil war disrupts the flow of oil, or—perish the thought—as would be the case if terrorists managed to get their hands on nuclear or biological weapons. At other times, the effects are like a slow ripple, as when a government adopts some policy that gradually impedes its ability to compete in world markets. All of today's societies, then, no matter where they are located, are part of a *world system.*

The interconnections are most evident among nations that do extensive trading with one another. The following Thinking Critically section explores implications of Mexico's *maquiladoras.*

THINKING CRITICALLY

When Globalization Comes Home: *Maquiladoras* South of the Border

Read

The Uses of Global Poverty: How Economic Inequality Benefits the West by Diane Stukulis Eglitis on **mysoclab.com**

Two hundred thousand Mexicans rush to Juarez each year, fleeing the hopelessness of the rural areas in pursuit of a better life. They have no running water or plumbing, but they didn't have any in the country either, and here they have the possibility of a job, a weekly check to buy food for the kids.

The pay is $100 for a 48-hour work week, about $2 an hour (Harris 2008). This may not sound like much, but it is more than twice the minimum daily wage in Mexico.

Assembly-for-export plants, known as *maquiladoras,* dot the Mexican border (Wise and Cypher 2007). The North American Free Trade Agreement (NAFTA) allows U.S. companies to import materials to Mexico without paying tax and to then export the finished products into the United States, again without tax. It's a sweet deal: few taxes and $17 a day for workers starved for jobs.

That these workers live in shacks, with no running water or sewage disposal, is not the employers' concern.

Nor is the pollution. The stinking air doesn't stay on the Mexican side of the border. Neither does the garbage. Heavy rains wash torrents of untreated sewage and industrial wastes into the Rio Grande (M. Lacey 2007).

According to world system theory, how did the world's nations become stratified?

There is also the loss of jobs for U.S. workers. Six of the fifteen poorest cities in the United States are located along the sewage-infested Rio Grande. NAFTA didn't bring poverty to these cities. They were poor before this treaty, but residents resent the transfer of jobs across the border (Thompson 2001).

What if the *maquilas* (*maquiladora* workers) organize and demand better pay? Farther south, even cheaper labor beckons. Workers in Guatemala and Honduras,

A photo taken inside a *maquiladora* in Matamoros, Mexico. The steering wheels are for U.S. automakers.

even more desperate than those in Mexico, will gladly take these jobs (Brown 2008). China, too, is competing for them (Utar and Ruiz 2010).

Many Mexican politicians would say that this presentation is one-sided. "Sure there are problems," they would say, "but this is how it always is when a country industrializes. Don't you realize that the *maqui-ladoras* bring jobs to people who have no work? They also bring roads, telephone lines, and electricity to undeveloped areas." "In fact," said Vicente Fox, when he was the president of Mexico, "workers at the *maquiladoras* make more than the average salary in Mexico—and that's what we call fair wages" (Fraser 2001).

During our economic crisis, the wages of many *maquilas* were cut in half (Muñoz Martinez 2010).

The home of a *maquiladora* worker.

For Your Consideration

Let's apply our three theoretical perspectives.

➤ Some conflict theorists analyze how capitalists try to weaken the bargaining power of workers by exploiting divisions among them. In what is known as the *split labor market*, capitalists pit one group of workers against another to lower the cost of labor. How do you think that *maquiladoras* fit this conflict perspective?

➤ When functionalists analyze a situation, they identify its functions and dysfunctions. What functions and dysfunctions of *maquiladoras* do you see?

➤ Symbolic interactionists analyze how people's experiences shape their views of the world. How would people's experiences in contrasting social locations lead to different answers to "Do *maquiladoras* represent exploitation or opportunity?" What multiple realities do you see here? ■

Culture of Poverty

The third explanation of global stratification is quite unlike the other two. Economist John Kenneth Galbraith (1979) claimed that the cultures of the Least Industrialized Nations hold them back. Building on the ideas of anthropologist Oscar Lewis (1966a,

1966b), Galbraith argued that some nations are crippled by a **culture of poverty,** a way of life that perpetuates poverty from one generation to the next. He explained it this way: Most of the world's poor people are farmers who live on little plots of land. They barely produce enough food to survive. Living on the edge of starvation, they have little room for risk—so they stick closely to tried-and-true, traditional ways. To experiment with new farming techniques is to court disaster, for failure would lead to hunger and death.

Their religion also encourages them to accept their situation, for it teaches fatalism: the belief that an individual's position in life is God's will. For example, in India, the Dalits are taught that they must have done very bad things in a previous life to suffer so. They are supposed to submit to their situation—and in the next life maybe they'll come back in a more desirable state.

Evaluating the Theories

Most sociologists prefer colonialism and world system theory. To them, an explanation based on a culture of poverty places blame on the victim—the poor nations themselves. It points to characteristics of the poor nations, rather than to international political arrangements that benefit the Most Industrialized Nations at the expense of the poor nations. But even taken together, these theories yield only part of the picture. None of these theories, for example, would have led anyone to expect that after World War II, Japan would become an economic powerhouse: Japan had a religion that stressed fatalism, two of its major cities had been destroyed by atomic bombs, and it had been stripped of its colonies.

Each theory, then, yields but a partial explanation, and the grand theorist who will put the many pieces of this puzzle together has yet to appear.

Maintaining Global Stratification

Regardless of how the world's nations became stratified, why do countries remain rich—or poor—year after year? Let's look at two explanations of how global stratification is maintained.

Neocolonialism

Sociologist Michael Harrington (1977) argued that when colonialism fell out of style it was replaced by **neocolonialism.** When World War II changed public sentiment about sending soldiers and colonists to exploit weaker countries, the Most Industrialized Nations turned to the international markets as a way of controlling the Least Industrialized Nations. By selling them goods on credit—weapons that the local elites desire so they can keep themselves in power—the Most Industrialized Nations entrap the poor nations with a circle of debt.

As many of us learn the hard way, owing a large debt and falling behind on payments puts us at the mercy of our creditors. So it is with neocolonialism. The *policy* of selling weapons and other manufactured goods to the Least Industrialized Nations on credit turns those countries into eternal debtors. The capital they need to develop their own industries goes instead as payments toward the debt, which becomes bloated with mounting interest. Keeping these nations in debt forces them to submit to trading terms dictated by the neocolonialists (Carrington 1993; Smith 2001).

Relevance Today. Neocolonialism might seem remote from our own lives, but its heritage affects us directly. Consider the oil-rich Middle Eastern countries, our two wars in the Persian Gulf, and

The maintenance of global stratification has many faces. Here is one, a displaced girl in a United Nations camp in South Darfur, in Sudan.

How does neocolonialism help to maintain global stratification?

the terrorism that emanates from this region (*Strategic Energy Policy* 2001; Mouawad 2007). Although this is an area of ancient civilizations, the countries themselves are recent. Great Britain created Saudi Arabia, drawing its boundaries and even naming the country after the man (Ibn Saud) whom British officials picked to lead it. This created a debt for the Saudi family, which for decades it repaid by providing low-cost oil, which the Most Industrialized Nations need to maintain their way of life. When other nations pumped less oil—no matter the cause, whether revolution or an attempt to raise prices—the Saudis helped keep prices low by making up the shortfall. In return, the United States (and other nations) overlooked the human rights violations of the Saudi royal family, keeping them in power by selling them the latest weapons. This mutually sycophantic arrangement continues.

Multinational Corporations

Multinational corporations, companies that operate across many national boundaries, also help to maintain the global dominance of the Most Industrialized Nations. In some cases, multinational corporations exploit the Least Industrialized Nations directly. A prime example is the United Fruit Company, a U.S. corporation that used to run Central American nations as its own fiefdoms. The CIA would plot and overthrow elected, but uncooperative, governments (CIA 2003), and an occasional invasion by Marines would remind area politicians of the military power that backed U.S. corporations.

Most commonly, however, it is simply by doing business that multinational corporations help to maintain international stratification. A single multinational corporation may manage mining operations in several countries, manufacture goods in others, and market its products around the globe. No matter where the profits are made, or where they are reinvested, the primary beneficiaries are the Most Industrialized Nations, especially the one in which the multinational corporation has its world headquarters.

Buying Political Stability.   In their pursuit of profits, the multinational corporations need cooperative power elites in the Least Industrialized Nations (Wise and Cypher 2007; Jessop 2010). In return for funneling money to the elites and selling them modern weapons, the corporations get a "favorable business climate"—that is, low taxes and cheap labor. The corporations politely call the money they pay to the elites "subsidies" and "offsets"—which are much prettier to the ear than "bribes." Able to siphon money from their country's tax collections and government budgets, these elites live a sophisticated upper-class life in the major cities of their home country. Although most of the citizens of these countries live a hard-scrabble life, the elites are able to send their children to prestigious Western universities, such as Oxford, the Sorbonne, and Harvard.

You can see how this cozy arrangement helps to maintain global stratification. The significance of these payoffs is not so much the genteel lifestyles that they allow the elites to maintain, but the translation of the payoffs into power. They allow the elites to purchase high-tech weapons with which they preserve their positions of privilege, even though they must oppress their people to do so. The result is a political stability that keeps alive this diabolical partnership between the multinational corporations and the national elites.

Unanticipated Consequences.   This, however, is not the full story. An unintentional by-product of the multinationals' global search for cheap resources and labor is to modify global stratification. When corporations move manufacturing from the Most Industrialized Nations to the Least Industrialized Nations, they not only exploit cheap labor but they also bring jobs and money to these nations. Although workers in the Least Industrialized Nations are paid a pittance, it is more than they can earn elsewhere. With new factories come opportunities to develop skills, acquire technology, and accumulate a capital base from which local elites can launch their own factories.

The Pacific Rim nations provide a remarkable example. In return for providing the "favorable business climate" just mentioned, multinational corporations invested billions of dollars in the "Asian tigers" (Hong Kong, Singapore, South Korea, and Taiwan). These nations have developed such a strong capital base that, along with China, they have begun to rival the older capitalist countries. This has also made them subject to

How do multinational corporations help to maintain global stratification?

capitalism's "boom and bust" cycles, and workers and investors in these nations, including those in the *maquiladoras* that you just read about, have their dreams smashed when capitalism suffers a downturn.

Technology and Global Domination

The race between the Most and Least Industrialized Nations to develop and apply the new technologies might seem like a race between a marathon runner and someone with a broken leg. Can the outcome be in doubt? As the multinational corporations amass profits, they are able to invest huge sums in the latest technology while the Least Industrialized Nations are struggling to put scraps on the table.

So it would appear, but the race is not this simple. Although the Most Industrialized Nations have a seemingly insurmountable head start, some of the other nations are shortening the distance between themselves and the front-runners. With cheap labor making their manufactured goods inexpensive, China and India are exporting goods on a massive scale. They are using the capital from these exports to adopt high technology to modernize their infrastructure (transportation, communication, electrical, and banking systems), with the goal of advancing their industry. Although global domination remains in the hands of the West, it could be on the verge of a major shift from West to East.

Strains in the Global System

It is never easy to maintain global stratification. At the very least, a continuous stream of unanticipated events forces the elite to stay on their toes, and at times huge currents of history threaten to sweep them aside. Now matter how secure a stratification system may seem, it always contains unresolved issues. These contradictions can be covered up for a while, but inevitably they rear up. Some are just little dogs nipping at the heels of the world's elites, bringing issues that can be resolved with a few tanks or bombs—or, better, with a scowl and the threat to bomb some opponent. Other issues are of a broader nature, part of huge historical shifts. Baring their teeth, both emerging and old unresolved contradictions snarlingly demand change, even the rearrangement of global power.

Such broad, history changing events are rare, but when they come they bring cataclysmic disruptions. We are now living through such a time. The far-reaching economic–political changes in Russia and China have been accompanied by huge cracks in a creaking global banking system. In desperation, the global powers have pumped trillions of dollars into their economic–political systems. As curious as we are about the outcome and as much as our lives are affected, we don't know the end point of this current strain in the global system and the power elites' desperate attempts to patch up the most glaring inconsistencies in their global domination. As this process of realignment continues, however, it is likely to sweep all of us into its unwelcome net.

CHAPTER 7 Summary and Review

Systems of Social Stratification

What is social stratification?

Social stratification refers to a hierarchy of privilege based on property, power, and prestige. Every society stratifies its members, and in every society men as a group are placed above women as a group. P. 184.

What are three major systems of social stratification?

Three major stratification systems are slavery, caste, and class. The essential characteristic of **slavery** is that some people own other people. Initially, slavery was based not on race but on debt, punishment for crime, or defeat in battle. Slavery could be temporary or permanent and was not necessarily passed on to one's children. North American slavery was gradually buttressed by a racist **ideology.** In a **caste system,** status is determined by birth and is lifelong. A **class system** is much more open than these other systems, for it is based primarily on money or material possessions, which can be acquired. Industrialization encourages the formation of class systems. Gender cuts across all forms of social stratification. Pp. 184–189.

What Determines Social Class?

Karl Marx argued that a single factor determines social class: If you own the means of production, you belong to the **bourgeoisie;** if you do not, you are one of the **proletariat.** Max Weber argued that three elements determine social class: *property, power,* and *prestige.* Pp. 189–191.

Why Is Social Stratification Universal?

To explain why stratification is universal, functionalists Kingsley Davis and Wilbert Moore argued that to attract the most capable people to fill its important positions, society must offer them greater rewards. Melvin Tumin said that if this view were correct, society would be a **meritocracy,** with positions awarded on the basis of merit. Gaetano Mosca argued that stratification is inevitable because every society must have leadership, which by definition means inequality. Conflict theorists argue that stratification is the outcome of an elite emerging as groups struggle for limited resources. Gerhard Lenski suggested a synthesis between the functionalist and conflict perspectives. Pp. 191–194.

How Do Elites Maintain Stratification?

To maintain social stratification within a nation, the ruling class adopts an **ideology** that justifies its current arrangements. It also controls information and uses technology. When all else fails, it turns to brute force. Pp. 194–195.

Comparative Social Stratification

What are key characteristics of stratification systems in other nations?

The most striking features of the British class system are speech and education. In Britain, accent reveals social class,

and almost all of the elite attend private schools. In the former Soviet Union, communism was supposed to abolish class distinctions. Instead, it merely ushered in a different set of classes. Pp. 195–197.

Global Stratification: Three Worlds

How are the world's nations stratified?

The model presented here divides the world's nations into three groups: the Most Industrialized, the Industrializing, and the Least Industrialized. This layering represents relative property, power, and prestige. The oil-rich nations are an exception. Pp. 197–201.

How Did the World's Nations Become Stratified?

The main theories that seek to account for global stratification are **colonialism, world system theory,** and the **culture of poverty.** Pp. 201–206.

Maintaining Global Stratification

How do the Most Industrialized Nations maintain their position?

There are two basic explanations for how the Most Industrialized Nations maintain their dominance. The first, **neocolonialism,** refers to keeping the poorer nations in debt and selling weapons to their elite. The second explanation points to the influence of **multinational corporations.** The new technology gives further advantage to the Most Industrialized Nations. Pp. 206–208.

Strains in the Global System

What strains are showing up in global stratification?

All stratification systems have contradictions that threaten to erupt, forcing the system to change. Currently, capitalism is in crisis, and we seem to be experiencing a global shift in economic (and, ultimately political) power from the West to the East. P. 208.

Thinking Critically about Chapter 7

1. How do slavery, caste, and class systems of social stratification differ?
2. Why is social stratification universal?
3. How do elites maintain stratification (keep themselves in power)?
4. What shifts in global stratification seem to be taking place? Why?

CHAPTER 8

Social Class in the United States

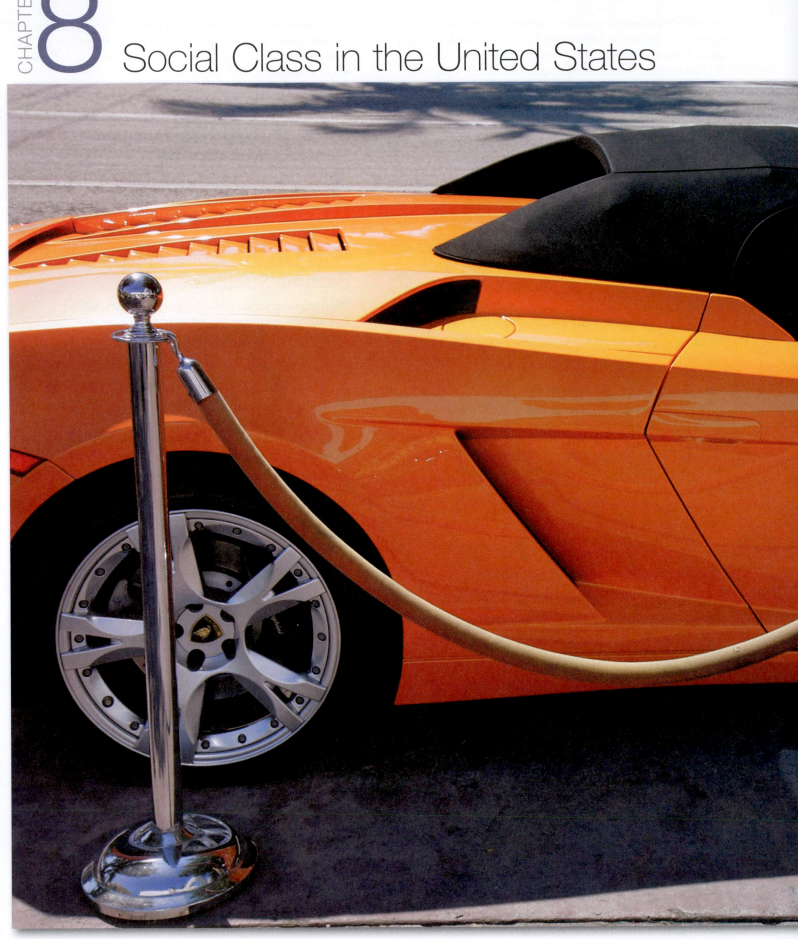

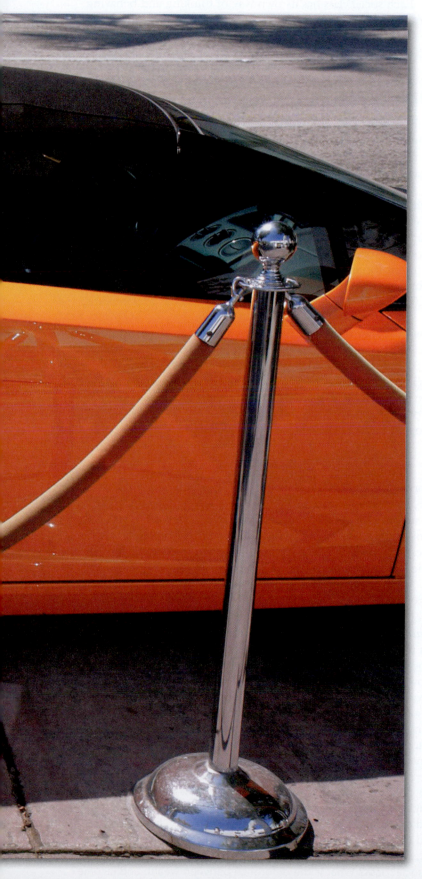

Florida

Ah, New Orleans, that fabled city on the Mississippi Delta. Images from its rich past floated through my head—pirates, treasure, intrigue. Memories from a pleasant vacation stirred my thoughts—the exotic French Quarter with its enticing aroma of Creole food and sounds of earthy jazz drifting through the air.

The shelter for the homeless, however, forced me back to an unwelcome reality. The shelter was like those I had visited in the North, West, and East—only dirtier. The dirt, in fact, was the worst that I had encountered during my research. On top of that, this was the only shelter to insist on payment in exchange for sleeping in one of its filthy beds.

The men here looked the same as the homeless anywhere in the country—disheveled and haggard, wearing that unmistakable expression of sorrow and despair. Except for the accent, you wouldn't know what region you were in. Poverty wears the same tired face wherever you are, I realized. The accent may differ, but the look remains the same.

I had grown used to the sights and smells of abject poverty. Those no longer surprised me. But after my fitful sleep with the homeless that night, I saw something that did. Just a block or so from the shelter, I was startled by a sight so out of step with the misery and despair I had just experienced that I stopped and stared.

> "My mind refused to stop juxtaposing these images of extravagance with the suffering I had just seen."

I felt indignation swelling within me. Confronting me were life-size, full-color photos mounted on the transparent Plexiglas shelter of a bus stop. Staring back at me were images of finely dressed men and women, proudly strutting about as they modeled elegant suits, dresses, diamonds, and furs.

A wave of disgust swept over me. "Something is cockeyed in this society," I thought, as my mind refused to stop juxtaposing these images of extravagance with the suffering I had just seen.

The disjunction that I felt in New Orleans was triggered by the ads, but it was not the first time that I had experienced this sensation. Whenever my research abruptly transported me from the world of the homeless to one of another social class, I experienced a sense of disjointed unreality. Each social class has its own way of thinking and behaving, and because these fundamental orientations to the world contrast so sharply, the classes do not mix well.

What Is Social Class?

If you ask most Americans about their country's social class system, you are likely to get a blank look. If you press the matter, you are likely to get an answer like this: "There are the poor and the rich—and then there are you and I, neither poor nor rich." This is just about as far as most Americans' consciousness of social class goes. Let's try to flesh out this idea.

Our task is made somewhat difficult because sociologists have no clear-cut, agreed-on definition of social class (Crompton 2010). As was noted in the last chapter, conflict sociologists (of the Marxist orientation) see only two social classes: those who own the means of production and those who do not. The problem with this view, say most sociologists, is that it lumps too many people together. Teenage "order takers" at McDonald's who work for $15,000 a year are lumped together with that company's executives who make $500,000 a year—because they both are workers at McDonald's, not owners.

Most sociologists agree with Weber that there is more to social class than just a person's relationship to the means of production. Consequently, most sociologists use the components Weber identified and define **social class** as a large group of people who rank closely to one another in property, power, and prestige. These three elements separate people into different lifestyles, give them different chances in life, and provide them with distinctive ways of looking at the self and the world.

Let's look at how sociologists measure these three components of social class.

Property

Property comes in many forms, such as buildings, land, animals, machinery, cars, stocks, bonds, businesses, furniture, jewelry, and bank accounts. When you add up the value of someone's property and subtract that person's debts, you have what sociologists call **wealth.** This term can be misleading, as some of us have little wealth—especially most college students. Nevertheless, if your net total comes to $10, then that is your wealth. (Obviously, wealth as a sociological term does not mean wealthy.)

A mere one-half percent of Americans owns over a quarter of the entire nation's wealth. Very few minorities are numbered among this 0.5 percent. An exception is Oprah Winfrey, who has had an ultra-successful career in entertainment and investing. Worth $2.7 billion, she is the 215th richest person in the United States. Winfrey has given millions of dollars to help minority children.

Distinguishing Between Wealth and Income. Wealth and income are sometimes confused, but they are not the same. Where *wealth* is a person's net worth, **income** is a flow of money. Income has many sources: The most common is wages or a business, but other sources are rent, interest, and royalties, even alimony, an allowance, or gambling. Some people have much wealth and little income. For example, a farmer may own considerable land (a form of wealth), but bad weather, combined with the high cost of fertilizers and machinery, can cause the income to dry up. Others have much income and little wealth. An executive with a $250,000 annual income may be debt-ridden. Below the surface prosperity—the exotic vacations, country club membership, private schools for the children, sports cars, and an elegant home—the credit cards may be maxed out, the sports cars in danger of being repossessed, and the mortgage payment "past due." Typically, however, wealth and income go together.

How do most sociologists define social class? What is the difference between wealth and income?

Distribution of Property.   Who owns the property in the United States? One answer, of course, is "everyone." Although this statement has some merit, it overlooks how the nation's property is divided among "everyone."

Overall, Americans are worth a hefty sum, about $49 trillion (*Statistical Abstract 2012*:Table 723). This includes all real estate, stocks, bonds, and business assets in the entire country. Figure 8.1 shows how highly concentrated this wealth is. Most wealth, 75 percent, is owned by only *10 percent* of the nation's families. As you can also see from this figure, 1 percent of Americans own more than one-third of all the U.S. assets. As you can also see from this figure, 1 percent of Americans own one-third of all the U.S. assets.

Distribution of Income.   How is income distributed in the United States? Economist Paul Samuelson (Samuelson and Nordhaus 2005) put it this way: "If we made an income pyramid out of a child's blocks, with each layer portraying $500 of income, the peak would be far higher than Mount Everest, but most people would be within a few feet of the ground."

Actually, if each block were 1½-inches tall, the typical American would be just *10 feet off the ground,* for the average per capita income in the United States is about $41,000 per year. (This average income includes every American, even children.) The typical family climbs a little higher, for most families have more than one worker, and together they average about $60,000 a year. Compared with the few families who are on the mountain's peak, the average U.S. family would find itself only 15 feet off the ground. Figure 8.2 portrays these differences.

The fact that some Americans enjoy the peaks of Mount Everest while most—despite their efforts—make it only 10 to 15 feet up the slope presents a striking image of income inequality in the United States. Another picture emerges if we divide the U.S. population into five equal groups and rank them from highest to lowest income. As Figure 8.3 on the next page shows, the top 20 percent of the population receive *half* (50.3 percent) of all income in the United States. In contrast, the bottom 20 percent of Americans receive only 3.4 percent of the nation's income.

Two features of Figure 8.3 are outstanding. First, notice how little change there has been in the distribution of income through the years. Second, look at how income inequality decreased from 1935 to 1970. *Since 1970, the richest 20 percent of U.S. families have grown richer, while the poorest 20 percent have grown poorer.* Despite numerous

FIGURE 8.2

Distribution of the Income of Americans

Some U.S. families have incomes that exceed the height of Mt. Everest, 29,028 feet

Average U.S. family income $60,000 or 15 feet

Average U.S. individual income $41,000 or 10 feet

If a 1½-inch child's block equals $500 of income, the average individual's annual income of $41,000 would represent a height of 10 feet, and the average family's annual income of $60,000 would represent a height of 15 feet. The income of some families, in contrast, would represent a height greater than that of Mt. Everest.

Source: By the author. Based on *Statistical Abstract of the United States* 2012:Tables 681, 696.

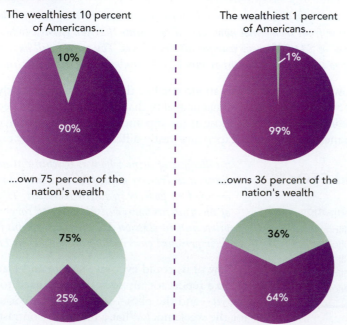

FIGURE 8.1   Distribution of the Property of Americans

The wealthiest 10 percent of Americans...

10%

90%

...own 75 percent of the nation's wealth

75%

25%

The wealthiest 1 percent of Americans...

1%

99%

...owns 36 percent of the nation's wealth

36%

64%

Source: By the author. Based on Allegretto 2011: Table 2.

FIGURE 8.3   The More Things Change, the More They Stay the Same: Dividing the Nation's Income

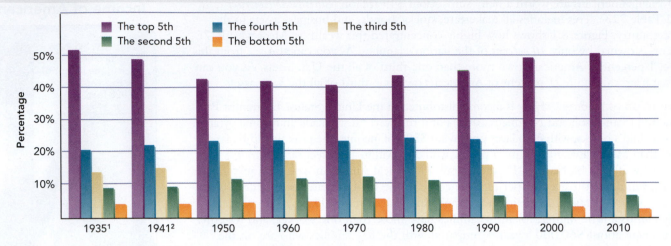

¹Earliest year available. ²No data for 1940.

Source: By the author. Based on *Statistical Abstract of the United States* 1960:Table 417; 1970:Table 489; 2012:Table 694.

government antipoverty programs, the poorest 20 percent of Americans receive *less* of the nation's income today than they did decades ago. The richest 20 percent, in contrast, are receiving more, about as much as they did in 1935.

The chief executive officers (CEOs) of the nation's largest corporations are especially affluent. The *Wall Street Journal* surveyed the 350 largest U.S. companies to find out what they paid their CEOs (Lublin 2011). Their median compensation (including salaries, bonuses, and stock options) came to $9,300,000 a year. (*Median* means that half received more than this amount, and half less.)

The CEOs' income is *225 times* higher than the average pay of U.S. workers (*Statistical Abstract* 2012:Table 681). This does *not* include their income from interest, dividends, or rents. Nor does it include the value of company-paid limousines and chauffeurs, airplanes and pilots, and private boxes at the symphony and sporting events. To really see the disparity, consider this:

Let's suppose that you started working the year Jesus was born and that you worked full time every year from then until now. Let's also assume that you earned today's average per capita income of $41,000 every year for all those years. You would still have to work another 100 years or so to earn the amount received by the highest-paid executive listed in Table 8.1.

Imagine how you could live with an income like this. And this is precisely the point. Beyond these cold numbers lies a dynamic reality that profoundly affects people's lives. The difference in wealth between those at the top and those at the bottom of the U.S. class structure means that people experience vastly different lifestyles. For example,

a colleague of mine who was teaching at an exclusive Eastern university piqued his students' curiosity when he lectured on poverty in Latin America. That weekend, one of the students borrowed his parents' corporate jet and pilot, and in class on Monday, he and his friends related their personal observations on poverty in Latin America.

Few of us could ever say, "Mom and Dad, I've got to do a report for my soc class, so I need to borrow the jet—and the pilot—to run down to South America for the weekend." What a lifestyle! Contrast this with Americans at the low end of the income ladder who lack

TABLE 8.1   The Five Highest-Paid CEOs

Executive	Company	Compensation
Philippe Dauman	Viacom	$84 million
Lawrence Ellison	Oracle	$69 million
Leslie Moonves	CBS	$54 million
Martin Franklin	Jarden	$45 million
Michael White	DIRECTV	$33 million

Note: Compensation includes salary, bonuses, and stock options.
Source: Lublin 2011.

Can you summarize the trends in income distribution in the United States?

the funds to travel even to a neighboring town for the weekend. For parents in poverty, choices may revolve around whether to spend the little they have at the laundromat or on milk for the baby. The elderly might have to choose between purchasing the medicines they need or buying food. In short, divisions of wealth represent not "mere" numbers, but choices that make vital differences in people's lives. Let's explore this topic in the Down-to-Earth Sociology box below.

Down-to-Earth Sociology

How the Super-Rich Live

It's good to see how other people live. It gives us a different perspective on life. Let's take a glimpse at the life of John Castle (his real name). After earning a degree in physics at MIT and an MBA at Harvard, John went into banking and securities, where he made more than $100 million (Lublin 1999).

Wanting to be connected to someone famous, John bought President John F. Kennedy's "Winter White House," an oceanfront estate in Palm Beach, Florida. John spent $11 million to remodel the 13,000-square-foot house so that it would be more to his liking. Among those changes: adding bathrooms numbers fourteen and fifteen. He likes to show off John F. Kennedy's bed and also the dresser that has the drawer labeled "black underwear," carefully hand-lettered by Rose Kennedy.

At his beachfront estate, John gives what he calls "refined feasts" to the glitterati ("On History . . ." 1999). If he gets tired of such activities—or weary of swimming in the Olympic-size pool where JFK swam the weekend before his assassination—John entertains himself by riding one of his thoroughbred horses at his nearby 10-acre ranch. If this fails to ease his boredom, he can relax aboard his custom-built 42-foot Hinckley yacht.

The yacht is a real source of diversion. John once boarded it for an around-the-world trip. He didn't stay on board, though—just joined the cruise from time to time. A captain and crew kept the vessel on course, and whenever John felt like it he would fly in and stay a few days. Then he would fly back to the States to direct his business. He did this about a dozen times, flying perhaps 150,000 miles. An interesting way to go around the world.

How much does a custom-built Hinckley yacht cost? John can't tell you. As he says, "I don't want to know what anything costs. When you've got enough money, price doesn't make a difference. That's part of the freedom of being rich."

Right. And for John, being rich also means paying $1,000,000 to charter a private jet to fly Spot, his Appaloosa horse, back and forth to the vet. John didn't want Spot to

To paraphrase F. Scott Firzgerald, the super-rich are not like you or I. The 414-foot long yacht of Paul Allen, the co-founder of Microsoft, has a swimming pool, two helicopters, and two submarines (one remote controlled for exploring the ocean floor).

have to endure a long trailer ride. Oh, and of course, there was the cost of Spot's medical treatment, another $500,000.

Other wealthy people spend extravagantly, too. Lee Tachman threw a four-day party for three friends. They had massages; ate well; took rides in a helicopter, a fighter jet, Ferraris, and Lamborghinis; and did a little paintballing—all for the bargain price of $50,000. At the 1Oak Lounge in New York City, some customers pay $35,000 for a bottle of champagne (Haughney and Konigsberg 2008). Of course, it is a large bottle.

Parties are fun, but what if you want privacy? You can buy that, too. Wayne Huizenga, the founder of Blockbuster, who sold a half ownership in the Miami Dolphins for $550 million ("Builder Stephen . . ." 2008), bought a 2,000-acre country club, complete with an 18-hole golf course, a 55,000-square-foot-clubhouse, and 68 slips for visiting vessels. The club is so exclusive that its only members are Wayne and his wife (Fabrikant 2005).

Withdrawing into gated estates is fine, but Microsoft co-founder Paul Allen has found another way to gain privacy. He had a 414-foot yacht built. On the *Octopus* are two helicopters, a swimming pool, and a submarine (Freeland 2011).

While the length of Allen's yacht creates an envy among the plutocracy that would make Freud break into a sweat, some might say that Charles Simonyi has even outdone this. He bought a $25 million ticket for a rocket ride to the International Space Station. Simonyi liked the experience so much that he bought a second ticket (Leo 2008). No frequent flyer miles included. But at the rate prices are increasing, $50 million isn't worth what it used to be anyway.

For Your Consideration

→ What effects has social class had on your life? (Go beyond possessions to values, orientations, and outlooks on life.) How do you think you would see the world differently if you were John Castle, Lee Tachman, Paul Allen, Charles Simonyi, or Mrs. Wayne Huizenga?

Power

Let's look at the second component of social class: Power.

The Democratic Facade.   Like many people, you may have said to yourself, "I don't agree with many of the big decisions, like sending soldiers to Afghanistan or Iraq, or launching missiles into Pakistan. *I* don't decide to raise taxes, lower interest rates, or spend $700 billion to bail out Wall Street fools and felons."

And then another part of you may say, "But I do participate in these decisions through my representatives in Congress, and by voting for president." True enough—as far as it goes. The trouble is, it just doesn't go far enough. Such views of being a participant in the nation's "big" decisions are a playback of the ideology we learn at an early age—an ideology promoted by the elites to legitimate and perpetuate their power. Sociologists Daniel Hellinger and Dennis Judd (1991) call this the "democratic facade" that conceals the real source of power in the United States.

Let's try to get a picture of where that power is located.

The Power Elite.   Back in the 1950s sociologist C. Wright Mills (1956) was criticized for insisting that **power**—the ability to get your way despite resistance—was concentrated in the hands of a few, for his analysis contradicted the dominant ideology of equality. As was discussed in earlier chapters, Mills coined the term **power elite** to refer to those who make the big decisions in U.S. society.

Mills and others have stressed how wealth and power coalesce in a group of people who look at the world in the same way—and view themselves as a special elite. They belong to the same private clubs, vacation at the same exclusive resorts, and even hire the same bands for their daughters' debutante balls (Domhoff 2006, 2010). This elite wields extraordinary power in U.S. society, so much so that *most* U.S. presidents have come from this group—millionaire white men from families with "old money" (Baltzell and Schneiderman 1988).

Continuing in the tradition of Mills, sociologist William Domhoff (2006, 2010) argues that this group is so powerful that the U.S. government makes no major decision without its approval. He analyzed how this group works behind the scenes with elected officials to determine both foreign and domestic policy—from setting Social Security taxes to imposing tariffs on imported goods. Although Domhoff's conclusions are controversial—and alarming—they certainly follow logically from the principle that wealth brings power, and extreme wealth brings extreme power.

Prestige

The third component of social class is occupational prestige.

Occupations and Prestige.   What are you thinking about doing after college? Chances are, you don't have the option of lolling under palm trees at the beach. Almost all of us have to choose an occupation and go to work. Look at Table 8.2 to see how the career you are considering stacks up in terms of **prestige** (respect or regard). Because we are moving toward a global society, this table also shows how the rankings given by Americans compare with those of the residents of sixty other countries.

Why do people give more prestige to some jobs than to others? If you look at Table 8.2, you will notice that the jobs at the top share four features:

1. They pay more.
2. They require more education.
3. They involve more abstract thought.
4. They offer greater autonomy (independence, or self-direction).

Now look at the bottom of the list. You can see that people give less prestige to jobs with the opposite characteristics: These jobs pay little, require less education, involve more physical labor, and are closely supervised. In short, the professions and the white-collar jobs are at the top of the list, the blue-collar jobs at the bottom.

One of the more interesting aspects of these rankings is how consistent they are across countries and over time. For example, people in every country rank college professors higher than nurses, nurses higher than social workers, and social workers higher than janitors.

What are Mills' and Domhoff's view on a power elite in the United States?

Similarly, the occupations that were ranked high 25 years ago still rank high today—and likely will rank high in the years to come.

Displaying Prestige. People want others to acknowledge their prestige. In times past, in some countries only the emperor and his family could wear purple—for it was the royal color. In France, only the nobility could wear lace. In England, no one could sit while the king was on his throne. Some kings and queens required that subjects walk backward as they left the room—so that they would not "turn their back" on the "royal presence."

Concern with displaying prestige has not let up. Military manuals specify who must salute whom. The U.S. president enters a room only after everyone else attending the function is present (to show that the president isn't waiting for others). Everyone must also be standing when the president enters. In the courtroom, bailiffs, sometimes armed, make certain that everyone stands when the judge enters.

Status symbols vary with social class. Clearly, only the wealthy can afford certain items, such as yachts and huge estates—or the $35,000 bottle of champagne mentioned in the box on page 215. But beyond affordability lies a class-based preference in status symbols. For example, people who are striving to be upwardly mobile flaunt labels on their clothing or conspicuously carry shopping bags from prestigious stores to show that they have "arrived." The wealthy, who regard the symbols of the "common" classes as cheap and showy, flaunt their own status symbols, such as $75,000 Rolex watches and $50,000 diamond earrings. Like the other classes, they, too, try to outdo one another. They boast about the length of their yacht or casually mention that they have a helicopter fly them to their golf game (Fabrikant 2005)—or that they stayed at the $30,000-a-night room at the Four Seasons in New York City (Feuer 2008).

Do you try to display prestige? Think about your clothing. How much more are you willing to pay for clothing that bears some hot "designer" label? Purses, shoes, jeans, and shirts—many of us pay more if they have some little symbol than if they don't. As we wear them proudly, aren't we actually proclaiming, "See, I had the money to buy this particular item!"? For many of us, prestige is a primary factor in deciding which college to attend. Everyone knows how the prestige of a generic sheepskin from Regional State College compares with a degree from Harvard, Princeton, Yale, or Stanford.

Status Inconsistency

Ordinarily, we have a similar rank on all three dimensions of social class—property, power, and prestige. The homeless men in the opening vignette are an example of these three dimensions lined up. Such people are **status consistent.** Some people, however, have a mixture of high and low ranks. This condition, called **status inconsistency,** leads to some interesting situations.

TABLE 8.2 **Occupational Prestige: How the United States Compares with 60 Countries**

Occupation	United States	Average of 60 Countries
Physician	86	78
Supreme Court judge	85	82
College president	81	86
Astronaut	80	80
Lawyer	75	73
College professor	74	78
Airline pilot	73	66
Architect	73	72
Biologist	73	69
Dentist	72	70
Civil engineer	69	70
Clergy	69	60
Psychologist	69	66
Pharmacist	68	64
High school teacher	66	64
Registered nurse	66	54
Professional athlete	65	48
Electrical engineer	64	65
Author	63	62
Banker	63	67
Veterinarian	62	61
Police officer	61	40
Sociologist	61	67
Journalist	60	55
Classical musician	59	56
Actor or actress	58	52
Chiropractor	57	62
Athletic coach	53	50
Social worker	52	56
Electrician	51	44
Undertaker	49	34
Jazz musician	48	38
Real estate agent	48	49
Mail carrier	47	33
Secretary	46	53
Plumber	45	34
Carpenter	43	37
Farmer	40	47
Barber	36	30
Store sales clerk	36	34
Truck driver	30	33
Cab driver	28	28
Garbage collector	28	13
Waiter or waitress	28	23
Bartender	25	23
Lives on public aid	25	16
Bill collector	24	27
Factory worker	24	29
Janitor	22	21
Shoe shiner	17	12
Street sweeper	11	13

Note. For five occupations not located in the 1994 source, the 1991 ratings were used: Supreme Court judge, astronaut, athletic coach, lives on public aid, and street sweeper.

Sources: Treiman 1977:Appendices A and D; Nakao and Treas 1990, 1994:Appendix D.

How is the display of prestige related to social class?

Sociologist Gerhard Lenski (1954, 1966) analyzed how people try to maximize their **status,** their position in a social group. Individuals who rank high on one dimension of social class but lower on others want people to judge them on the basis of their highest status. Others, however, are also trying to maximize their own positions, so they may respond according to these people's lowest rankings.

A classic study of status inconsistency was done by sociologist Ray Gold (1952). After apartment-house janitors unionized in Chicago, they made more money than some of the tenants whose garbage they carried out. Tenants became upset when they saw their janitors driving more expensive cars than they did. Some attempted to "put the janitor in his place" by making "snotty" remarks to him. For their part, the janitors took delight in finding "dirty" secrets about the tenants in their garbage.

People who are status inconsistent, then, are likely to confront one frustrating situation after another (Dogan 2011). They claim the higher status, but are handed the lower one. This is so frustrating that the resulting tension can affect people's health. Researchers who studied the health of thousands of Europeans over a decade found that men who are status inconsistent are twice as likely to have heart attacks as men who are status consistent. For reasons that no one knows, status inconsistent women do not have a higher risk of heart attacks (Braig et al. 2011).

There are other consequences as well. Lenski (1954) found that people who are status inconsistent tend to be more politically radical. An example is college professors. Their prestige is very high, as we saw in Table 8.2, but their incomes are relatively low. Hardly anyone in U.S. society is more educated, and yet college professors don't even come close to the top of the income pyramid. In line with Lenski's prediction, the politics of most college professors are left of center. This hypothesis may also hold true among academic departments; that is, the higher a department's average pay, the more conservative are the members' politics. Teachers in departments of business and medicine, for example, are among the most highly paid in the university—and they also are the most politically conservative.

Instant wealth, the topic of the Down-to-Earth Sociology box on page 219, provides an interesting case of status inconsistency.

How do you set yourself apart in a country so rich that of its 4.6 million people 79,000 are millionaires? Saeed Khouri (on the right), at an auction in Abu Dhabi paid $14 million for the license plate "1." His cousin was not as fortunate. His $9 million was enough to buy only "5."

Sociological Models of Social Class

The question of how many social classes there are is a matter of debate. Sociologists have proposed several models, but no single one has gained universal support. There are two main models: one that builds on Marx, the other on Weber.

Updating Marx

As Figure 8.4 on page 220 illustrates, Marx argued that there are just two classes—capitalists and workers—with membership based solely on a person's relationship to the means of production. Sociologists have criticized this view, saying that these categories are too broad. For example, because executives, managers, and supervisors don't own the means of production, they would be classified as workers. But what do these people have in common with assembly-line workers? The category of "capitalist" is also too broad. Some people, for example, employ a thousand workers, and their decisions directly affect a thousand families.

Compare these individuals with a man I know in Godfrey, Illinois, who used to fix cars in his

Down-to-Earth Sociology

The Big Win: Life after the Lottery

"If I just win the lottery, life will be good. These problems I've got, they'll be gone. I can just see myself now."

So goes the dream. And many Americans shell out mega-bucks every week, with the glimmering hope that "Maybe this week, I'll hit it big."

Most are lucky to get $20, or maybe just win another scratch-off ticket.

But some do hit it big. What happens to these winners? Are their lives all wine, roses, and chocolate afterward?

We don't have any systematic studies of the big winners, so I can't tell you what life is like for the average winner. But several themes are apparent from reporters' interviews.

The most common consequence of hitting it big is that life becomes topsy-turvy (Bernstein 2007). All of us are rooted somewhere. We have con-nections with others that provide the basis for our orientations to life and how we feel about the world. Sudden wealth can rip these moorings apart, and the resulting *status inconsistency* can lead to a condition sociologists call **anomie.**

First comes the shock. As Mary Sand-erson, a telephone operator in Dover, New Hampshire, who won $66 million, said, "I was afraid to believe it was real, and afraid to believe it wasn't." Mary says that she never slept worse than her first night as a multimillionaire. "I spent the whole time crying—and throwing up" (Tresniowski 1999).

Reporters and TV crews appear on your doorstep. "What are you going to do with all that money?" they demand. You haven't the slightest idea, but in a daze you mumble something.

Then come the calls. Some are welcome. Your Mom and Dad call to congratulate you. But long-forgotten friends and distant relatives suddenly remember how close they really are to you—and strangely enough, they all have emergencies that your money can solve. You even get calls from strangers who have ailing mothers, terminally ill kids, sick dogs . . .

You have to unplug the phone and get an unlisted number.

You might be flooded with marriage proposals. You cer-tainly didn't become more attractive or sexy overnight—or did you? Maybe money makes people sexy.

You can no longer trust people. You don't know what their real motives are. Before, no one could be after your money because you didn't have any. You may even fear kidnappers.

Chris Shaw of Jefferson City, Missouri, shown here, won $256 million. He said he would pay the $1,000 he owes on his truck, take his kids to Disneyworld, and get his teeth fixed. How do you think status inconsistency *will affect his life?*

Before, this wasn't a problem—unless some kidnapper wanted the ransom of a seven-year-old car.

The normal becomes abnormal. Even picking out a wedding gift is a problem. If you give the usual fancy juicer, everyone will think you're stingy. But should you write a check for $25,000? If you do, you'll be invited to every wedding in town—and everyone will expect the same.

Here is what happened to some lottery winners:

When Michael Klinebiel of Rahway, New Jersey, won $2 million, his mother, Phyllis, said that half of it was hers, that she and her son had pooled $20 a month for years to play the lottery. He said they had done this—but he had bought the winning ticket on his own. Phyllis sued her son ("Sticky Ticket" 1998).

Mack Metcalf, a forklift operator in Corbin, Kentucky, hit the jackpot for $34 million. To fulfill a dream, he built and moved into a replica of George Wash-ington's Mount Vernon home. Then his life fell apart—his former wife sued him, his current wife divorced him, and his new girlfriend got $500,000 while he was drunk. Within three years of his "good" fortune, Metcalf had drunk himself to death (Dao 2005).

When Abraham Shakespeare, a dead-broke truck driver's assistant, won $31 million in the Florida lottery, he bought a million-dollar home in a gated community. He lent money to friends to start businesses, even paid for funerals. This evidently wasn't enough. His body was found buried in the yard of a "friend" (Lush 2010; McShane 2010).

Winners who avoid *anomie* seem to be people who don't make sudden changes in their lifestyle or their behavior. They hold onto their old friends and routines—the anchors in life that give them identity and a sense of be-longing. Some even keep their old jobs—not for the money, of course, but because the job anchors them to an identity with which they are familiar and comfortable.

Sudden wealth, in other words, poses a threat that has to be guarded against.

And I can just hear you say, "I'll take the risk!"

For Your Consideration

➤ How do you think your life would change if you won a lottery jackpot of $10 million?

FIGURE 8.4

Marx's Model of the Social Classes

Capitalists
(*Bourgeoisie*, those who own the means of production)

Workers
(*Proletariat*, those who work for the capitalists)

Inconsequential Others
(beggars, etc.)

Source: By the author.

TABLE 8.3

Wright's Modification of Marx's Model of the Social Classes

1. Capitalists
2. Petty bourgeoisie
3. Managers
4. Workers

Source: By the author.

 Read

Media Magic: Making Class Invisible
by Gregory Mantsios
on **mysoclab.com**

backyard. As Frank gained a following, he quit his regular job, and in a few years he put up a building with five bays and an office. Frank is now a capitalist, for he employs five or six mechanics and owns the tools and the building (the "means of production"). But what does he have in common with a factory owner who controls the lives of one thousand workers? Not only is Frank's work different but so are his lifestyle and the way he looks at the world.

To resolve this problem, sociologist Erik Wright (1985) suggests that some people are members of more than one class at the same time. They occupy what he calls **contradictory class locations.** By this, Wright means that a person's position in the class structure can generate contradictory interests. For example, the automobile mechanic-turned-business owner may want his mechanics to have higher wages because he, too, has experienced their working conditions. At the same time, his current interests—making profits and remaining competitive with other repair shops—lead him to resist pressures to raise their wages.

Because of such contradictory class locations, Wright modified Marx's model. As summarized in Table 8.3, Wright identifies four classes: (1) *capitalists,* business owners who employ many workers; (2) *petty bourgeoisie,* small business owners; (3) *managers,* who sell their own labor but also exercise authority over other employees; and (4) *workers,* who simply sell their labor to others. As you can see, this model allows finer divisions than the one Marx proposed, yet it maintains the primary distinction between employer and employee.

Updating Weber

Sociologists Joseph Kahl and Dennis Gilbert (Gilbert and Kahl 1998; Gilbert 2008) developed a six-tier model to portray the class structure of the United States and other capitalist countries. Think of this model, illustrated in Figure 8.5 on the next page, as a ladder. Our discussion starts with the highest rung and moves downward. In line with Weber, on each lower rung you find less property (wealth), less power, and less prestige. Note that in this model education is also a primary measure of class.

The Capitalist Class.   Sitting on the top rung of the class ladder is a powerful elite that consists of just 1 percent of the U.S. population. As you saw in Figure 8.1 on page 213, this capitalist class is so wealthy that it owns one-third of all the nation's wealth. *This tiny 1 percent is worth more than the entire bottom 90 percent of the country* (Beeghley 2008).

Power and influence cling to this small elite. They have direct access to top politicians, and their decisions open or close job opportunities for millions of people. They even help to shape the consciousness of the nation: They own our major media and entertainment outlets—newspapers, magazines, radio and television stations, and sports franchises. They also control the boards of directors of our most influential colleges and universities. The super-rich perpetuate themselves in privilege by passing on their assets and social networks to their children.

The capitalist class can be divided into "old" and "new" money. The longer that wealth has been in a family, the more it adds to the family's prestige. The children of "old" money seldom mingle with "common" folk. Instead, they attend exclusive private schools where they learn views of life that support their privileged position. They don't work for wages; instead, many study business or become lawyers so that they can manage the family fortune. These old-money capitalists (also called "blue-bloods") wield vast power as they use their extensive political connections to protect their economic empires (Sklair 2001; Domhoff 1990, 1999, 2006).

At the lower end of the capitalist class are the *nouveau riche,* those who have "new money." Although they have made fortunes in business, the stock market, inventions, entertainment, or sports, they are outsiders to the upper class. They have not attended the "right" schools, and they don't share the social networks that come with old money.

| FIGURE 8.5 | The U.S. Social Class Ladder |

Social Class	Education	Occupation	Income	Percentage of Population
Capitalist	Prestigious university	Investors and heirs, a few top executives	$1,000,000+	1%
Upper Middle	College or university, often with postgraduate study	Professionals and upper managers	$125,000+	15%
Lower Middle	High school or college; often apprenticeship	Semiprofessionals and lower managers, craftspeople, foremen	About $60,000	34%
Working	High school	Factory workers, clerical workers, low-paid retail sales, and craftspeople	About $36,000	30%
Working Poor	High school and some high school	Laborers, service workers, low-paid salespeople	About $19,000	15%
Underclass	Some high school	Unemployed and part-time, on welfare	Under $12,000	5%

Source: By the author. Based on Gilbert and Kahl 1998 and Gilbert 2008; income estimates are modified from Duff 1995.

Not blue-bloods, they aren't trusted to have the right orientations to life. Even their "taste" in clothing and status symbols is suspect (Fabrikant 2005). Donald Trump, whose money is "new," is not listed in the *Social Register*, the "White Pages" of the blue-bloods that lists the most prestigious and wealthy one-tenth of 1 percent of the U.S. population. Trump says he "doesn't care," but he reveals his true feelings by adding that his heirs will be in it (Kaufman 1996). He is probably right, for the children of the new-moneyed can ascend into the top part of the capitalist class—if they go to the right schools *and* marry old money.

Many in the capitalist class are philanthropic. They establish foundations and give huge sums to "causes." Their motivations vary. Some feel guilty because they have so much while others have so little. Others seek prestige, acclaim, or fame. Still others feel a responsibility—even a sense of fate or purpose—to use their money for doing good. Bill Gates, who has given more money to the poor and to medical research than anyone else in history, seems to fall into this latter category.

The Upper Middle Class.
Of all the classes, the upper middle class is the one most shaped by education. Almost all members of this class have at least a bachelor's degree, and many have postgraduate degrees in business, management, law, or medicine.

With a fortune of $56 billion, Bill Gates, a cofounder of Microsoft Corporation, is the second wealthiest person in the world. His 40,000-square-foot home (sometimes called a "technopalace") in Seattle, Washington, was appraised at $110 million.

Figure 8.5 and the text are an application of Weber's view of social class. Can you compare these six social classes?

These people manage the corporations owned by the capitalist class, operate their own businesses, or pursue professional careers. As Gilbert and Kahl (1998) say,

> [These positions] may not grant prestige equivalent to a title of nobility in the Germany of Max Weber, but they certainly represent the sign of having "made it" in contemporary America. . . . Their income is sufficient to purchase houses and cars and travel that become public symbols for all to see and for advertisers to portray with words and pictures that connote success, glamour, and high style.

Consequently, parents and teachers push children to prepare for upper-middle-class jobs. About 15 percent of the population belong to this class.

The Lower Middle Class.

About 34 percent of the U.S. population are in the lower middle class. Their jobs require that they follow orders given by members of the upper middle class. With their technical and lower-level management positions, they can afford a mainstream lifestyle, although they struggle to maintain it. Many anticipate being able to move up the social class ladder. Feelings of insecurity are common, however, with the threat of inflation, recession, and job insecurity bringing a nagging sense that they might fall down the class ladder (Kefalas 2007).

The distinctions between the lower middle class and the working class on the next rung below are more blurred than those between other classes. In general, however, members of the lower middle class work at jobs that have slightly more prestige, and their incomes are generally higher.

The Working Class.

About 30 percent of the U.S. population belong to this class of relatively unskilled blue-collar and white-collar workers. Compared with the lower middle class, they have less education and lower incomes. Their jobs are also less secure, more routine, and more closely supervised. One of their greatest fears is that of being laid off during a recession. With only a high school diploma, the average member of the working class has little hope of climbing up the class ladder. Job changes usually bring "more of the same," so most concentrate on getting ahead by achieving seniority on the job rather than by changing their type of work. They tend to think of themselves as having "real jobs" and regard the "suits" above them as paper pushers who have no practical experience and don't do "real work" (Morris and Grimes 2005).

The Working Poor.

Members of this class, about 15 percent of the population, work at unskilled, low-paying, temporary and seasonal jobs, such as sharecropping, migrant farm work, housecleaning, and day labor. Most are high school dropouts. Many are functionally illiterate, finding it difficult to read even the want ads. They are not likely to vote (Beeghley 2008), for they believe that no matter what party is elected to office, their situation won't change.

Sociologists use income, education, and occupational prestige to measure social class. For most people, this works well, but not for everyone, especially entertainers. To what social class do DiCaprio, James, Lopez, and Lady Gaga belong? Leonardo DiCaprio makes about $78 million a year, Lebron James $43 million, Jennifer Lopez $25 million, and Lady Gaga $90 million.

Why do highly successful celebrities present a challenge to this sociological model of social class?

Although they work full time, millions of the working poor depend on food stamps and local food banks to survive on their meager incomes (O'Hare 1996b; Bello 2011). It is easy to see how you can work full time and still be poor. Suppose that you are married and have a baby 3 months old and another child 3 years old. Your spouse stays home to care for them, so earning the income is up to you. But as a high-school dropout, all you can get is a minimum wage job. At $7.25 an hour, you earn $290 for 40 hours. In a year, this comes to $15,080—before deductions. Your nagging fear—and recurring nightmare—is of ending up "on the streets."

The Underclass.   On the lowest rung, and with next to no chance of climbing anywhere, is the **underclass.** Concentrated in the inner city, this group has little or no connection with the job market. Those who are employed—and some are—do menial, low-paying, temporary work. Welfare, if it is available, along with food stamps and food pantries, is their main support. Most members of other classes consider these people the "ne'er-do-wells" of society. Life is the toughest in this class, and it is filled with despair. About 5 percent of the population fall into this class.

The homeless men described in the opening vignette of this chapter, and the women and children like them, are part of the underclass. These are the people whom most Americans wish would just go away. Their presence on our city streets bothers passersby from the more privileged social classes—which includes just about everyone. "What are those obnoxious, dirty, foul-smelling people doing here, cluttering up my city?" appears to be a common response. Some people react with sympathy and a desire to do something. But what? Almost all of us just shrug our shoulders and look the other way, despairing of a solution and somewhat intimidated by their presence.

The homeless are the "fallout" of our postindustrial economy. In another era, they would have had plenty of work. They would have tended horses, worked on farms, dug ditches, shoveled coal, and run the factory looms. Some would have explored and settled the West. The prospect of gold would have lured others to California, Alaska, and Australia. Today, however, with no frontiers to settle, factory jobs scarce, and farms that are becoming technological marvels, we have little need for unskilled labor.

© Boris Drucker/The New Yorker Collection/www.cartoonbank.com

"There are plenty of jobs around. People just don't want to work."

A primary sociological principle is that people's views are shaped by their social location. Many people from the middle and upper classes cannot understand how anyone can work and still be poor.

Consequences of Social Class

The man was a C student throughout school. As a businessman, he ran an oil company (Arbusto) into the ground. A self-confessed alcoholic until age forty, he was arrested for drunk driving. With this background, how did he become president of the United States?

Accompanying these personal factors was the power of social class. George W. Bush was born the grandson of a wealthy senator and the son of a businessman who, after serving as a member of the House of Representatives and director of the CIA, became president of the United States. For high school, George W. Bush went to an elite private prep school, Andover; to Yale for his bachelor's degree; and for his MBA to Harvard. He was given $1 million to start his own business. When that business (Arbusto) failed, Bush fell softly, landing on the boards of several corporations. Taken care of even further, he was made the managing director of the Texas Rangers baseball team and allowed to buy a share of the team for $600,000, which he sold for $15 million.

When it was time for him to get into politics, Bush's connections financed his run for governor of Texas and then for the presidency.

Does social class matter? And how! Think of each social class as a broad subculture with distinct approaches to life, so significant that it affects our health, family life,

Again, based on Weber we have a six-class model of stratification. Can you compare these six social classes?

With tough economic times, a lot of people have lost their jobs—and their homes. If this happens, how can you survive? Maybe with a smile and a sense of humor to tap the kindness of strangers. I took this photo outside Boston's Fenway Park.

education, religion, politics, and even our experiences with crime and the criminal justice system. Let's look at how social class affects our lives.

Physical Health

If you want to get a sense of how social class affects health, take a ride on Washington's Metro system. Start in the blighted Southeast section of downtown D.C. For every mile you travel to where the wealthy live in Montgomery County in Maryland, life expectancy rises about a year and a half. By the time you get off, you will find a twenty-year gap between the poor blacks where you started your trip and the rich whites where you ended it. (Cohen 2004)

The principle is simple: As you go up the social-class ladder, health increases. As you go down the ladder, health decreases (Hout 2008). Age makes no difference. Infants born to the poor are more likely to die before their first birthday, and a larger percentage of poor people in their old age—whether 75 or 95—die each year than do the elderly who are wealthy.

How can social class have such dramatic effects? While there are many reasons, here are three. First, social class opens and closes doors to medical care. People with good incomes or with good medical insurance are able to choose their doctors and pay for whatever treatment and medications are prescribed. The poor, in contrast, don't have the money or insurance to afford this type of medical care. How much difference the new health reform will make is yet to be seen.

A second reason is lifestyle, which is shaped by social class. People in the lower classes are more likely to smoke, eat a lot of fats, be overweight, abuse drugs and alcohol, get little exercise, and practice unsafe sex (Chin et al. 2000; Dolnick 2010). This, to understate the matter, does not improve people's health.

There is a third reason, too. Life is hard on the poor. The persistent stresses they face cause their bodies to wear out faster (Geronimus et al. 2010). The rich find life better. They have fewer problems and more resources to deal with the ones they have. This gives them a sense of control over their lives, a source of both physical and mental health.

Mental Health

Sociological research from as far back as the 1930s has found that the mental health of the lower classes is worse than that of the higher classes (Faris and Dunham 1939; Srole et al. 1978; Peltham 2009). Greater mental problems are part of the higher stress that accompanies poverty. Compared with middle- and upper-class Americans, the poor have less job security and lower wages. They are more likely to divorce, to be the victims of crime, and to have more physical illnesses. Couple these conditions with bill collectors and the threat of eviction, and you can see how they can deal severe blows to people's emotional well-being.

People higher up the social class ladder experience stress in daily life, of course, but their stress is generally less, and their coping resources are greater. Not only can they afford vacations, psychiatrists, and counselors, but *their class position also gives them greater control over their lives, a key to good mental health.*

As is starkly evident from the following Thinking Critically section, social class is also important when it comes to the medical care people receive for their mental problems.

How does social class affect people's physical and mental health?

THINKING CRITICALLY
Mental Illness and Inequality in Medical Care

Standing among the police, I watched as the elderly, naked man, looking confused, struggled to put on his clothing. The man had ripped the wires out of the homeless shelter's main electrical box and then led the police on a merry chase as he ran from room to room.

I asked the officers where they were going to take the man, and they replied, "To Malcolm Bliss" (the state hospital). When I commented, "I guess he'll be in there for quite a while," they said, "Probably just a day or two. We picked him up last week—he was crawling under cars at a traffic light—and they let him out in two days."

The police explained that the man must be a danger to himself or to others to be admitted as a long-term patient. Visualizing this old man crawling under cars in traffic and thinking about the possibility of electrocution as he ripped out electrical wires with his bare hands, I marveled at the definition of "danger" that the hospital psychiatrists must be using.

Stripped of its veil, the two-tier system of medical care is readily visible. The poor—such as this confused, naked man—find it difficult to get into mental hospitals. If they are admitted, they are sent to the dreaded state hospitals. In contrast, private hospitals serve the wealthy and those who have good insurance. The rich are likely to be treated with "talk therapy" (forms of psychotherapy), the poor with "drug therapy" (tranquilizers to make them docile, sometimes called "medicinal straitjackets").

For Your Consideration
→ How can we improve the treatment of the mentally ill poor? Take into consideration that the country is in debt and the public does not want higher taxes. What about the more fundamental issue—that of inequality in health care? Should medical care be a commodity that is sold to those who can afford it? Or do all citizens possess a fundamental right to high-quality health care? ■

Family Life

Social class also makes a significant difference in our choice of spouse, our chances of getting divorced, and how we rear our children.

Choice of Husband or Wife.   Members of the capitalist class place strong emphasis on family tradition. They stress the family's history, even a sense of purpose or destiny in life (Baltzell 1979; Aldrich 1989). Children of this class learn that their choice of husband or wife affects not just them, but the entire family, that it will have an impact on the "family line." These background expectations shrink the field of "eligible" marriage partners, making it narrower than it is for the children of any other social class. As a result, parents in this class play a strong role in their children's mate selection.

Divorce.   The more difficult life of the lower social classes, especially the many tensions that come from insecure jobs and inadequate incomes, leads to higher marital friction and a greater likelihood of divorce. Consequently, children of the poor are more likely to grow up in broken homes.

Child Rearing.   As discussed on page 360, lower-class parents focus more on getting their children to follow rules and obey authority, while middle-class parents focus more on developing their children's creative and leadership skills (Lareau and Weininger 2008). Sociologists have traced this difference to the parents' occupations (Kohn 1977). Lower-class parents are closely supervised at work, and they anticipate that their children will have similar jobs. Consequently, they try to teach their children to defer to authority. Middle-class parents, in contrast, enjoy greater independence at work. Anticipating similar jobs for their children, they encourage them to be more creative.

Out of these contrasting orientations arise different ways of disciplining children; lower-class parents are more likely to use physical punishment, while the middle classes rely more on verbal persuasion.

Education

As you saw in Figure 8.5 on page 221, education increases as one goes up the social class ladder. It is not just the amount of education that changes, but also the type of education. Children of the capitalist class bypass public schools. They attend exclusive private schools where they are trained to take a commanding role in society. These schools teach upper-class values and prepare their students for prestigious universities (Beeghley 2008; Stevens 2009).

Keenly aware that private schools can be a key to upward social mobility, some upper-middle-class parents do their best to get their children into the prestigious preschools that feed into these exclusive prep schools. Although some preschools cost $37,000 a year, they have a waiting list (Anderson 2011). Not able to afford this kind of tuition, some parents hire tutors to train their 4-year-olds in test-taking skills so they can get into public kindergartens for gifted students. They even hire experts to teach these preschoolers to look adults in the eye while they are being interviewed for these limited positions (Banjo 2010). You can see how such parental involvement and resources make it more likely that children from the more privileged classes go to college—and graduate.

Religion

One area of social life that we might think would not be affected by social class is religion. ("People are just religious, or they are not. What does social class have to do with it?") As we shall see in Chapter 13, however, the classes tend to cluster in different denominations. Episcopalians, for example, are more likely to attract the middle and upper classes, while Baptists draw heavily from the lower classes. Patterns of worship also follow class lines: The lower classes are attracted to more expressive worship services and louder music, while the middle and upper classes prefer more "subdued" worship.

Politics

As I have stressed throughout this text, people perceive events from their own corner in life. Political views are no exception to this symbolic interactionist principle, and the rich and the poor walk different political paths. The higher that people are on the social class ladder, the more likely they are to vote for Republicans (Hout 2008). In contrast, most members of the working class believe that the government should intervene in the economy to provide jobs and to make citizens financially secure. They are more likely

Donald Trump arriving in Scotland on his private jet. To the right is a middle-aged couple who live in an old motor home parked in Santa Barbara, one of the wealthiest communities in California.

What impact does social class have on education, religion, and politics?

to vote for Democrats. Although the working class is more liberal on *economic* issues (policies that increase government spending), it is more conservative on *social* issues (such as opposing abortion and the Equal Rights Amendment) (Houtman 1995; Hout 2008). People toward the bottom of the class structure are also less likely to be politically active—to campaign for candidates or even to vote (Gilbert 2003; Beeghley 2008).

Crime and Criminal Justice

If justice is supposed to be blind, it certainly is not when it comes to one's chances of being arrested (Henslin 2012). In Chapter 6 (pages 164–167), we discussed how the social classes commit different types of crime. The white-collar crimes of the more privileged classes are more likely to be dealt with outside the criminal justice system, while the police and courts deal with the street crimes of the lower classes. One consequence of this class standard is that members of the lower classes are more likely to be in prison, on probation, or on parole. In addition, since those who commit street crimes tend to do so in or near their own neighborhoods, the lower classes are more likely to be robbed, burglarized, or murdered.

Social Mobility

No aspect of life, then—from work and family life to politics—goes untouched by social class. Because life is so much more satisfying in the more privileged classes, people strive to climb the social class ladder. What affects their chances?

Three Types of Social Mobility

Janice's mom, a single mother, sold used cars at a Toyota dealership. Janice worked summers and part time during the school year, earned her BA, and then her MBA. After college, she worked at IBM, but she missed her home town. When her mom's boss retired, Janice grabbed the opportunity to put a down payment on the Toyota dealership. She has since paid the business off, and has opened another at a second location.

This young woman is being "introduced" to society at a debutante ball in Laredo, Texas. Like you, she has learned from her parents, peers, and education, a view of where she belongs in life. How do you think her view is different from yours?

When grown-up children like Janice end up on a different rung of the social class ladder from the one occupied by their parents, it is called **intergenerational mobility.** You can go up or down, of course. Janice experienced **upward social mobility.** If she had been a child of the dealership's owner, dropped out of college, and ended up selling cars, she would have experienced **downward social mobility.**

We like to think that individual efforts are the reason people move up the class ladder—and their faults the reason they move down. In this example, we can identify intelligence, hard work, and ambition. Although individual factors such as these do underlie social mobility, we must place Janice in the context of **structural mobility.** This second basic type of mobility refers to changes in society that allow large numbers of people to move up or down the class ladder.

Janice grew up during a boom time of easy credit and business expansion. Opportunities were abundant, and colleges were looking for women from working-class backgrounds. It would have been far different for her—and for millions of others—if she had grown up during an economic bust when opportunities were shrinking. As sociologists point out, in analyzing social mobility we must always look at *structural mobility,* how changes in society (its *structure*) make opportunities plentiful or scarce.

The third type of social mobility is **exchange mobility.** This occurs when large numbers of people move up and down the social class ladder, but, on balance, the proportions of the social classes remain about the same. Suppose that a million or so working-class people are trained in some new technology, and they move up the class ladder. Suppose also that

The term *structural mobility* refers to changes in society that push large numbers of people either up or down the social class ladder. A remarkable example was the stock market crash of 1929 when thousands of people suddenly lost their wealth. People who once "had it made" found themselves standing on street corners selling apples or, as depicted here, selling their possessions at fire-sale prices. The crash of 2008 brought similar problems to untold numbers of people.

because of a surge in imports, about a million skilled workers have to take lower-status jobs. Although millions of people change their social class, there is, in effect, an *exchange* among them. The net result more or less balances out, and the class system remains basically untouched.

No matter what type it is, as discussed in the Cultural Diversity box on the next page, social mobility always comes at a cost.

Women in Studies of Social Mobility

About half of sons pass their fathers on the social class ladder, about one-third stay at the same level, and about one-sixth fall down the ladder. (Blau and Duncan 1967; Featherman 1979)

"Only sons!" said feminists in response to these classic studies on social mobility. "Do you think it is good science to ignore daughters? And why do you assign women the class of their husbands? Do you think that wives have no social class position of their own?" (Davis and Robinson 1988). The male sociologists brushed off these objections, replying that there were too few women in the labor force to make a difference.

These sociologists simply hadn't caught up with the times. The gradual but steady increase of women working for pay had caught them unprepared. Although sociologists now include women in their samples, research on the social class of married women is still in its infancy (Beller 2009).

Upwardly mobile women report how important their parents were in their success, how they encouraged them to achieve when they were just children. For upwardly mobile African American women, strong mothers are especially significant (Robinson and Nelson 2010). In their study of women from working-class backgrounds who became managers and professionals, sociologists Elizabeth Higginbotham and Lynn Weber (1992) found this recurring theme: parents encouraging their girls to postpone marriage and get an education. To these understandings from the micro approach, we need to add the macro level. Had there not been a *structural* change in society, the millions of new positions that women occupy would not exist.

Poverty

Many Americans find that the "limitless possibilities" of the American dream are quite elusive. As illustrated in Figure 8.5 on page 221, the working poor and underclass together form about one-fifth of the U.S. population. This translates into a huge number, about 60 million people. Who are these people?

Drawing the Poverty Line

To determine who is poor, the U.S. government draws a **poverty line.** This measure was set in the 1960s, when poor people were thought to spend about one-third of their incomes on food. On the basis of this assumption, each year the government computes a low-cost food budget and multiplies it by 3. Families whose incomes are less than this amount are classified as poor; those whose incomes are higher—even by a dollar—are determined to be "not poor."

This official measure of poverty is grossly inadequate. Poor people actually spend only about 20 percent of their income on food, so to determine a poverty line, we ought to multiply their food budget by 5 instead of 3 (Uchitelle 2001). Another problem is that mothers

How do women fit into studies of social mobility?

Cultural Diversity in the United States

Social Class and the Upward Social Mobility of African Americans

The overview of social class presented in this chapter doesn't apply equally to all the groups that make up U.S. society. Consider geography: What constitutes the upper class of a town of 5,000 people will differ from that of a city of a million. With fewer extremes of wealth and occupation, in small towns family background and local reputation are more significant.

So it is with racial–ethnic groups. All racial–ethnic groups are marked by social class, but what constitutes a particular social class can differ from one group to another—as well as from one historical period to another. Consider social class among African Americans (Landry and Marsh 2011).

The earliest class divisions can be traced to slavery—to slaves who worked in the fields and those who worked in the "big house." Those who worked in the plantation home were exposed more to the customs, manners, and forms of speech of wealthy whites. Their more privileged position—which brought with it better food and clothing, as well as lighter work—was often based on skin color. Mulattos, lighter-skinned slaves, were often chosen for this more desirable work. One result was the development of a "mulatto elite," a segment of the slave population that, proud of its distinctiveness, distanced itself from the other slaves. At this time, there also were free blacks. Not only were they able to own property but some even owned black slaves.

After the War Between the States (as the Civil War is known in the South), these two groups, the mulatto elite and the free blacks, formed an upper class. Proud of their earlier status, they distanced themselves from other blacks. From these groups came most of the black professionals. After World War II, the black middle class expanded as African Americans entered a wider range of occupations. Today, more than half of all African American adults work at white-collar jobs, about 22 percent at the professional or managerial level (Beeghley 2008).

An unwelcome cost greets many African Americans who move up the social class ladder: an uncomfortable distancing from their roots, a separation from significant others—parents, siblings, and childhood friends (hooks 2000; Lacy 2007). The upwardly mobile enter a world unknown to those left behind, one that demands not only different appearance and speech, but also different values, aspirations, and ways of viewing the world. These are severe challenges to the self and often rupture relationships with those left behind.

An additional cost is a subtle racism that lurks beneath the surface of some work settings, poisoning what could be easy, mutually respectful interaction. To be aware that white co-workers perceive you as different—as a stranger, an intruder, or "the other"—engenders frustration, dissatisfaction, and cynicism. To cope, many nourish their racial identity and stress the "high value of black culture and being black" (Lacy and Harris 2008). Some move to neighborhoods of upper-middle-class African Americans, where they can live among like-minded people who have similar experiences (Lacy 2007).

For Your Consideration
→ In the box on upward social mobility on page 83, we discussed how Latinos face a similar situation. Why do you think this is? What connections do you see among upward mobility, frustration, and racial–ethnic identity? How do you think that the upward mobility of whites is different? Why?

who work outside the home and have to pay for child care are treated the same as mothers who don't have this expense. The poverty line is also the same for everyone across the nation, even though the cost of living is much higher in New York than in Alabama. On the other hand, much of the income of the poor is not counted: food stamps, rent assistance, subsidized child care, and the earned income tax credit (DeNavas-Walt et al. 2010). In the face of these criticisms, the Census Bureau has developed alternative ways to measure poverty lines. These show higher poverty, but the official measure has not changed.

That a change in the poverty line can instantly make millions of people poor—or take away their poverty—would be laughable, if it weren't so serious. (The absurdity has not been lost on Parker and Hart, as you can see from their cartoon on the next page).

Watch
American Outrage
on **mysoclab.com**

Why is the poverty line inadequate? Can you review the social mobility of African Americans?

WIZARD OF ID

Although this line is arbitrary, because it is the official measure of poverty, we'll use it to see who in the United States is poor. Before we do this, though, compare your ideas of the poor with the stereotypes explored in the Down-to-Earth Sociology box on page 231.

Who Are the Poor?

The Geography of Poverty.   The Social Map on the next page illustrates how poverty varies by *region*. Note especially the clustering of poverty in the South, a pattern that has prevailed for more than 150 years.

High rates of rural poverty have been a part of the United States from its origin to the present. This 1937 photo shows a 32-year-old woman in California who had seven children and no food.

Down-to-Earth Sociology

Taking Another Fun Quiz: Exploring Stereotypes about the Poor

Do you hold any of these stereotypes? Can you tell which of these statement are true?

Most poor people are lazy. They are poor because they do not want to work. *False.* Half of the poor are too old or too young to work: About 40 percent are under age 18, and another 10 percent are 65 or older. About 30 percent of the working-age poor work at least half the year.

Most of the poor are trapped in a cycle of poverty that few escape. Long-term poverty is the exception. Most poverty lasts less than a year (Lichter and Crowley 2002). Only 12 percent remain in poverty for five or more consecutive years (O'Hare 1996a). Most children who are born in poverty are *not* poor as adults (Ruggles 1989; Corcoran 2001).

There is more poverty in rural than in urban areas. *True.* We'll review this in the following section.

Most African Americans are poor. *False.* This one was easy. We just reviewed some statistics in the box on upward mobility on page 229.

Most of the poor are African Americans. *False.* Look at the second part of Figure 8.7 on page 232. *There are more poor whites than any other group.* The combined total of poor African Americans, Latinos, and Native Americans, however, is larger than the total of poor whites.

Most of the poor are single mothers and their children. *False.* About 38 percent of the poor match this stereotype, but 34 percent of the poor live in married-couple families, 22 percent live alone or with nonrelatives, and 6 percent live in other settings.

Most of the poor live on welfare. *False.* Only about 25 percent of the income of poor adults comes from welfare. About half comes from wages and pensions, and about 22 percent from Social Security.

On a percentage basis, more children than adults are poor. *True.* (Okay, no one holds this stereotype. I just want to make this point. We'll come back to it shortly.)

Sources: O'Hare 1996a, 1996b, with other sources as indicated.

For Your Consideration

➤ What stereotypes of the poor do you (or people you know) hold? How would you test these stereotypes?

FIGURE 8.6 Patterns of Poverty

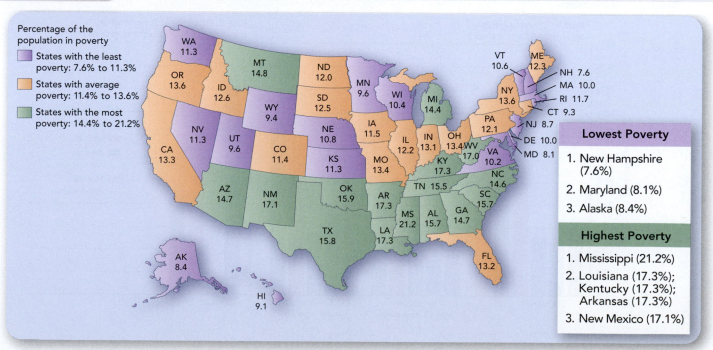

Source: By the author. Based on *Statistical Abstract of the United States* 2011:Table 708.

What does geography have to do with poverty? What are some overarching facts about poverty?

Beyond the awareness of most Americans are the rural poor such as this family in Maine. With low education and few good jobs available, life is hardscrabble. What do you think the future holds for these children?

A second aspect of geography is *rural poverty*. At 16 percent, rural poverty is higher than the national average of 13 percent. Helping to maintain this higher rate are the lower education of the rural poor and the scarcity of rural jobs (Latimer and Woldoff 2010).

A third aspect of geography is the *suburbanization of poverty*. With the extensive migration from the cities to suburbs and the collapse of the housing market, poverty has hit the suburbs—so hard that *most* of the nation's poor now live in the suburbs (Kneebone and Garr 2010). This major change is not likely to be temporary.

Geography, however, is not the main factor in poverty. The greatest predictors of poverty are race–ethnicity, education, and the sex of the person who heads the family. Let's look at these factors.

Race–Ethnicity.   One of the strongest factors in poverty is race–ethnicity. As Figure 8.7 shows, 12 percent of whites are poor, followed closely by Asian Americans at 13 percent. In contrast, 25 percent of Latinos live in poverty, while the total jumps even higher, to 26 percent for African Americans and 27 percent for Native Americans. Because whites are, by far, the largest group in the United States, their lower rate of poverty translates into larger numbers. As a result, there are many more poor whites than poor people of any other racial–ethnic group. As Part 2 of Figure 8.7 shows, close to half (46 percent) of all the poor are whites.

Education.   You are aware that education is a vital factor in poverty, but you may not know just how powerful it is. Look at Figure 8.8. You can see that 1 of every 4 people who drop out of high school is poor but only 3 of 100 people who finish college end up in poverty. As you can see, the chances that someone will be poor become less with each higher level of education. Although this principle applies regardless of race–ethnicity, the figure shows that at every level of education, race–ethnicity makes an impact.

FIGURE 8.7   Race–Ethnicity and U.S. Poverty

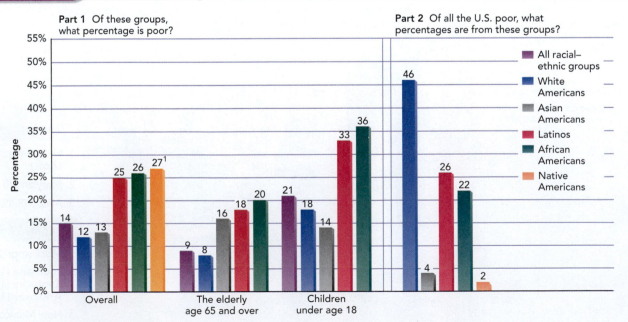

[1] The source does not break this total down by age.

Note: Only these groups are listed in the source. The poverty line is $22,025 for a family of four.

Source: By the author. Based on *Statistical Abstract of the United States* 2011:Tables 709 and 712.

How are race–ethnicity and education related to poverty?

FIGURE 8.8   Who Ends Up Poor? Poverty by Education and Race–Ethnicity

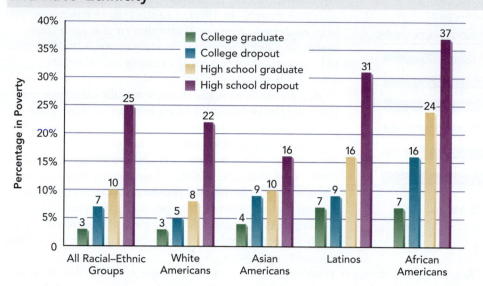

Source: By the author. Based on *Statistical Abstract of the United States* 2007:Table 694. Table dropped in later editions.

The Feminization of Poverty.   One of the best indicators of whether or not a family is poor is family structure. Families headed by both a mother and father are the least likely to be poor, and families headed by only a mother are the most likely to be poor (*Statistical Abstract* 2012:Table 716). The reason for this can be summed up in this one statistic: Women average only 72 percent of what men earn. (If you want to jump ahead, go to Figure 10.7 on page 294.) With our high rate of divorce combined with our high number of births to single women, mother-headed families have become more common. Sociologists call this association of poverty with women the **feminization of poverty.**

Old Age.   As Figure 8.7 on page 232 shows, the elderly are *less* likely than the general population to be poor. This is quite a change. It used to be that growing old increased people's chances of being poor, but government policies to redistribute income—Social Security and subsidized housing, food stamps, and medical care—slashed the rate of poverty among the elderly. Figure 8.7 also shows how the prevailing racial–ethnic patterns carry over into old age. You can see how much more likely elderly African Americans, Latinos, or Native Americans are to be poor than elderly whites. The exception is elderly Asian Americans, who show an unexplained jump in poverty.

Children of Poverty

Children are more likely to live in poverty than are adults or the elderly. This holds true regardless of race–ethnicity, but from Figure 8.7 on page 232, you can see how much greater poverty is among Latino, African American, and Native American children. That millions of U.S. children are reared in poverty is shocking when one considers the wealth of this country and the supposed concern for the well-being of children. This tragic aspect of poverty is the topic of the following Thinking Critically section.

✳️ Explore
Living Data
on **mysoclab.com**

THINKING CRITICALLY
The Nation's Shame: Children in Poverty

One of the most startling statistics in sociology is shown in Figure 8.7. Look at the rate of childhood poverty: For Asian Americans, 1 of 7 children is poor; for whites, 1 of 6; for Latinos and African Americans, an astounding 1 of 3. These percentages translate into incredible numbers—approximately *21 million* children.

What is the feminization of poverty? What causes the poverty of children?

FIGURE 8.9   Births to Single Mothers

Of women with this education who give birth, what percentages are single and married?

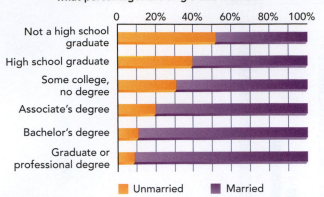

Note: Based on a national sample of all U.S. births in the preceding 12 months.

Source: Dye 2005.

Why do so many U.S. children live in poverty? A major reason is the large number of births to women who are not married, about 1.7 million a year. This number has increased sharply. In 1960, 1 of 20 U.S. children was born to a single woman. Today that total is *eight times higher,* and single women now account for 8 of 20 (41 percent) of all U.S. births (*Statistical Abstract* 2012:Table 86).

But do births to single women actually cause poverty? Consider the obvious: Children born to wealthy single women aren't reared in poverty. Then consider this: In some industrialized countries, the birth rate of single women is higher than ours, *yet our rate of child poverty is higher than theirs* (Garfinkel et al. 2010). Their poverty rate is lower because their governments provide extensive support for rearing these children—from providing day care to health checkups. As the cause of the poverty of children born to single women, then, why can't we point to the lack of government support for children?

Apart from the matter of government policy, births to single women follow patterns that have a negative impact on their children's welfare. The less education a single woman has, the more likely she is to bear children. As you can see from Figure 8.9, births to single women drop with each gain in education. As you know, people with lower education earn less, so this means that the single women who can least afford children are those most likely to give birth. Their children are likely to face the obstacles to building a satisfying life that poverty brings. They are more likely to die in infancy, to go hungry, to be malnourished, to develop more slowly, and to have more health problems. They also are more likely to drop out of school, to become involved in crime, and to have children while still in their teens—thus perpetuating a cycle of poverty.

For Your Consideration

With education so important to obtain jobs that pay well, in light of Figure 8.9, what programs would you suggest for helping women attain more education? What policies would you suggest for reducing child poverty? Be specific and practical. ■

The Dynamics of Poverty

Some have suggested that the poor get trapped in a **culture of poverty** (Lewis 1966; Cohen 2010). They assume that the values and behaviors of the poor "make them fundamentally different from other Americans, and that these factors are largely responsible for their continued long-term poverty" (Ruggles 1989:7).

Lurking behind this concept is the idea that the poor are lazy people who bring poverty on themselves. Certainly, some individuals and families match this stereotype—many of us have known them. But is a self-perpetuating culture—one that poor people transmit across generations and that locks them in poverty—the basic reason for U.S. poverty?

Researchers who began following 5,000 poor U.S. families in 1968 uncovered some surprising findings. Contrary to stereotypes, most poverty is short-lived, lasting only a year or less. Most poverty comes about because of *poverty triggers*, some dramatic life change such as divorce, the loss of a job, or even the birth of a child (O'Hare 1996a). As Figure 8.10 shows, only 12 percent of poverty lasts five years or longer. Contrary to the stereotype of lazy people content to live off the government, few poor people enjoy poverty—and they do what they can to avoid being poor.

Yet from one year to the next, the number of poor people remains about the same. This means that the people who move out of poverty are replaced by people who move into poverty. Most of these newly poor will also move out of poverty within a year.

FIGURE 8.10   How Long Does Poverty Last?

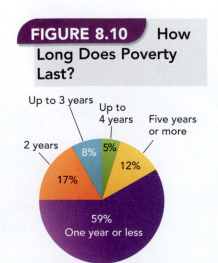

Source: Gottschalk et al. 1994:89.

How is age related to poverty? What is meant by the "dynamics" of poverty?

Some people even bounce back and forth, never quite making it securely out of poverty. Poverty, then, is dynamic, touching a lot more people than the official totals indicate. Although 13 percent of Americans may be poor at any one time, about half of the U.S. population will experience poverty at some point before they turn 65 (Cellini et al. 2008).

Why Are People Poor?

Two explanations for poverty compete for our attention. The first, which sociologists prefer, focuses on *social structure*. Sociologists stress that *features of society* deny some people access to education or training in job skills. They emphasize racial–ethnic, age, and gender discrimination, as well as changes in the job market—fewer unskilled jobs, businesses closing, and manufacturing jobs moving overseas. In short, some people find their escape route from poverty to a better life blocked.

A competing explanation focuses on the *characteristics of individuals*. Sociologists reject explanations such as laziness and lack of intelligence, viewing these as worthless stereotypes. Individualistic explanations that sociologists reluctantly acknowledge include dropping out of school and bearing children in the teen years. Most sociologists are reluctant to speak of such factors in this context, for they appear to blame the victim, something that sociologists bend over backward not to do.

A third explanation is the *poverty triggers* that were just mentioned. People can be living on the edge of poverty, but managing to stay above it, when an unexpected event pushes them over the edge. The main poverty triggers are the loss of a job, pregnancy and the birth of a child, family breakup, and a disabling accident or illness (Cellini et al. 2008).

Welfare Reform

Reforming Welfare. After decades of criticism, the U.S. welfare system was restructured in 1996. A federal law—the Personal Responsibility and Work Opportunity Reconciliation Act—requires states to place a lifetime cap on welfare assistance and compels welfare recipients to look for work and to take available jobs. The maximum length of time that someone can collect welfare is five years. In some states, it is less. Unmarried teen parents who receive assistance must attend school and live at home or in some other adult-supervised setting.

When this law was passed, it set off a storm of criticism. Critics called it an attack on the poor. Defenders replied that the new rules would rescue people from poverty. They would transform welfare recipients into self-supporting and hard-working citizens—and reduce welfare costs. National welfare rolls plummeted, dropping by about 60 percent, but 3 out of 5 who left welfare remained in poverty (Hofferth 2002; Urban Institute 2006). Since the economic crisis that began in 2008, the economy has hemorrhaged millions of jobs. We don't have complete studies yet, but with the lifetime limitations on welfare assistance, one in five low-income single mothers now has no earnings and no cash government assistance (Loprest and Nichols 2011). In both cities and suburbs, you can see people picking through garbage.

Of the former welfare recipients who have kept their jobs, some receive such low pay that they remain in poverty. Consider one of the "success stories":

JoAnne Sims, 37, lives in Erie, New York, with her 7-year-old daughter Jamine. JoAnne left welfare, and now earns $7.25 an hour as a cook for Head Start. Her 37-hour week brings $268 before deductions. With the help of medical benefits and a mother who provides child care, JoAnne "gets by." She says, "From what I hear, a lot of us who went off welfare are still poor . . . let me tell you, it's not easy." (Peterson 2000; earnings updated)

The Conflict View. Conflict theorists have an interesting interpretation of welfare. They say that the purpose of welfare is not to help people, but, rather, to maintain a *reserve labor force*. It is designed to keep the unemployed alive during economic downturns until their labor is needed during the next economic boom. The 1996 law that reduced the welfare rolls fits this model, as it was passed during the longest economic boom in U.S. history. In line with conflict theory, during our current recession some states have softened welfare rules (Eckholm 2009)—as conflict theorists say, in order to keep the reserve labor force ready for the next time it is needed.

Where Is Horatio Alger? The Social Functions of a Myth

In the late 1800s, Horatio Alger was one of the country's most popular authors. The rags-to-riches exploits of his fictional boy heroes and their amazing successes in overcoming severe odds motivated thousands of boys of that period. Although Alger's characters have disappeared from U.S. literature, they remain alive and well in the psyche of Americans. From real-life examples of people of humble origin who climbed the social class ladder, Americans know that anyone who really tries can get ahead. In fact, they believe that most Americans, including minorities and the working poor, have an average or better-than-average chance of getting ahead—obviously a statistical impossibility (Kluegel and Smith 1986).

The accuracy of the **Horatio Alger myth** is less important than the belief that surrounds it—that limitless possibilities exist for everyone. Functionalists would stress that this belief is functional for society. On the one hand, it encourages people to compete for higher positions, or, as the song says, "to reach for the highest star." On the other hand, it places blame for failure squarely on the individual. If you don't make it—in the face of ample opportunities to get ahead—the fault must be your own. The Horatio Alger myth helps to stabilize society: Since the fault is viewed as the individual's, not society's, current social arrangements can be regarded as satisfactory. This reduces pressures to change the system.

As Marx and Weber pointed out, social class penetrates our consciousness, shaping our ideas of life and our "proper" place in society. When the rich look at the world around them, they sense superiority and anticipate control over their own destiny. When the poor look around them, they are more likely to sense defeat and to anticipate that unpredictable forces will batter their lives. Both rich and poor know the dominant ideology, that their particular niche in life is due to their own efforts, that the reasons for success—or failure—lie solely with the self. Like fish that don't notice the water, people tend not to perceive the effects of social class on their own lives.

A society's dominant ideologies are reinforced throughout the society, including its literature. Horatio Alger provided inspirational heroes for thousands of boys. The central theme of these many novels, immensely popular in their time, was rags to riches. Through rugged determination and self-sacrifice, a boy could overcome seemingly insurmountable obstacles to reach the pinnacle of success. (Girls did not strive for financial success, but were dependent on fathers and husbands.)

By the Numbers: Changes Over Time

The richest 20% of Americans receive this percentage of the nation's income		The poorest 20% of Americans receive this percentage of the nation's income		Frequency of births outside of marriage	
1970	NOW	1970	NOW	1960	NOW
41%	50%	6%	3%	1 in 20	8 in 20

How does the Horatio Alger myth shape views of poverty and success? Help does it help stabilize society?

8 Summary and Review

What Is Social Class?

What is meant by the term social class?

Most sociologists have adopted Weber's definition of **social class:** a large group of people who rank closely to one another in terms of property (wealth), power, and prestige. **Wealth**—consisting of the value of property and income—is concentrated in the upper classes. From the 1930s to the 1970s, the trend in the distribution of wealth in the United States was toward greater equality. Since that time, it has been toward greater inequality. Pp. 212–216.

Power is the ability to get one's way even though others resist. C. Wright Mills coined the term **power elite** to refer to the small group that holds the reins of power in business, government, and the military. **Prestige** is linked to occupational status. People's rankings of occupational prestige have changed little over the decades and are similar from country to country. Globally, the occupations that bring greater prestige are those that pay more, require more education and abstract thought, and offer greater independence. Pp. 217–218.

What is meant by the term status inconsistency?

Status is social position. Most people are **status consistent;** that is, they rank high or low on all three dimensions of social class. People who rank higher on some dimensions than on others are status inconsistent. The frustrations of **status inconsistency** tend to produce political radicalism. Pp. 217–218.

Sociological Models of Social Class

What models are used to portray the social classes?

Erik Wright developed a four-class model based on Marx: (1) capitalists (owners of large businesses), (2) petty bourgeoisie (small business owners), (3) managers, and (4) workers. Kahl and Gilbert developed a six-class model based on Weber. At the top is the capitalist class. In descending order are the upper middle class, the lower middle class, the working class, the working poor, and the **underclass.** Pp. 218–223.

Consequences of Social Class

How does social class affect people's lives?

Social class leaves no aspect of life untouched. It affects our chances of benefiting from the new technology, dying early, becoming ill, receiving good health care, and getting divorced. Social class membership also affects child rearing, educational attainment, religious affiliation, political participation, the crimes people commit, and contact with the criminal justice system. Pp. 223–227.

Social Mobility

What are three types of social mobility?

The term **intergenerational mobility** refers to changes in social class from one generation to the next. **Structural mobility** refers to changes in society that lead large numbers of people to change their social class. **Exchange mobility** is the movement of large numbers of people from one social class to another, with the net result that the relative proportions of the population in the classes remain about the same. Pp. 227–230.

Poverty

Who are the poor?

Poverty is unequally distributed in the United States. Racial–ethnic minorities (except Asian Americans), children, households headed by women, and rural Americans are more likely than others to be poor. The poverty rate of the elderly is less than that of the general population. Pp. 230–235.

Why are people poor?

Some social analysts believe that characteristics of *individuals* cause poverty. Sociologists, in contrast, stress the *structural* features of society, such as employment opportunities, to find the causes of poverty. Sociologists generally conclude that life orientations are a consequence, not the cause, of people's position in the social class structure. Pp. 235–236.

How is the Horatio Alger myth functional for society?

The **Horatio Alger myth**—the belief that anyone can get ahead if only he or she tries hard enough—encourages people to strive to get ahead. It also deflects blame for failure from society to the individual. P. 236.

Thinking Critically about Chapter 8

1. The belief that the United States is the land of opportunity draws millions of legal and illegal immigrants to the United States each year. How do the materials in this chapter support or undermine this belief?

2. What three ways is social class having an ongoing impact on your life?

3. What social mobility has your own family experienced? In what ways has this affected your life?

Race and Ethnicity

New Mexico

Imagine that you are an African American man living in Macon County, Alabama, during the Great Depression of the 1930s. Your home is a little country shack with a dirt floor. You have no electricity or running water. You never finished grade school, and you make a living, such as it is, by doing odd jobs. You haven't been feeling too good lately, but you can't afford a doctor.

Then you hear incredible news. You rub your eyes in disbelief. It is just like winning the lottery! If you join *Miss Rivers' Lodge* (and it is free to join), you will get free physical examinations at Tuskegee University *for life*. You will even get free rides to and from the clinic, hot meals on examination days, and a lifetime of free treatment for minor ailments.

You eagerly join *Miss Rivers' Lodge*.

After your first physical examination, the doctor gives you the bad news. "You've got bad blood," he says. "That's why you've been feeling bad. Miss Rivers will give you some medicine and schedule you for your next exam. I've got to warn you, though. If you go to another doctor, there's no more free exams or medicine."

> **"You have just become part of one of the most callous experiments of all time."**

You can't afford another doctor anyway. You are thankful for your treatment, take your medicine, and look forward to the next trip to the university.

What has really happened? You have just become part of what is surely slated to go down in history as one of the most callous experiments of all time, outside of the infamous World War II Nazi and Japanese experiments. With heartless disregard for human life, the U.S. Public Health Service told 399 African American men that they had joined a social club and burial society called *Miss Rivers' Lodge*. What the men were *not* told was that they had syphilis, that there was no real *Miss Rivers' Lodge*, that the doctors were just using this term so they could study what happened when syphilis went untreated. For forty years, the "Public Health Service" allowed these men to go without treatment for their syphilis—and kept testing them each year—to study the progress of the disease. The "public health" officials even had a control group of 201 men who were free of the disease (Jones 1993).

By the way, the men did receive a benefit from "*Miss Rivers' Lodge*," a free autopsy to determine the ravages of syphilis on their bodies.

Laying the Sociological Foundation

As unlikely as it seems, this is a true story. Rarely do race and ethnic relations degenerate to this point, but reports of troubled race relations surprise none of us. Today's newspapers and TV and Internet regularly report on racial problems. Sociology can contribute greatly to our understanding of this aspect of social life—and this chapter may be an eye-opener for you. To begin, let's consider to what extent race itself is a myth.

Race: Myth and Reality

The Reality of Human Variety.   With its 7 billion people, the world offers a fascinating variety of human shapes and colors. Skin colors come in all shades between black and white, heightened by reddish and yellowish hues. Eyes come in shades of blue, brown, and green. Lips are thick and thin. Hair is straight, curly, kinky, black, blonde, and red—and, of course, all shades of brown.

As humans spread throughout the world, their adaptations to diverse climates and other living conditions resulted in this profusion of colors, hair textures, and other physical variations. Genetic mutations added distinct characteristics to the peoples of the globe. In this sense, the concept of **race**—a group of people with inherited physical characteristics that distinguish it from another group—is a reality. Humans do, indeed, come in a variety of colors and shapes.

The Myth of Pure Races.   Humans show such a mixture of physical characteristics—in skin color, hair texture, nose shape, head shape, eye color, and so on—that there are no "pure" races. Instead of falling into distinct types that are clearly separate from one another, human characteristics flow endlessly together. The mapping of the human genome system shows that humans, despite their many visible differences, are strikingly homogenous. The so-called racial groups differ from one another only once in a thousand subunits of the genome (Angler 2000; Frank 2007). As you can see from the example of Tiger Woods, discussed in the Cultural Diversity box on the next page, these minute gradations make any attempt to draw lines of pure race purely arbitrary.

The Myth of a Fixed Number of Races.   Although large groupings of people can be classified by blood type and gene frequencies, even these classifications do not uncover "race." Rather, race is so arbitrary that biologists and anthropologists cannot even agree on how many "races" there are (Smedley and Smedley 2005). Ashley Montagu (1964, 1999), a physical anthropologist, pointed out that some scientists have classified humans into only two "races," while others have found as many as two thousand. Montagu (1960) himself classified humans into forty "racial" groups.

"Race" is so fluid that even a plane ride can change someone's race. If you want to see how, read the Down-to-Earth Sociology box on page 243.

The Myth of Racial Superiority.   Regardless of what anthropologists, biologists, and sociologists say, however, people do divide one another into races, and we are stuck with this term. People also tend to see some races (mostly their own) as superior and others as inferior. As with language, however, no race is better than another. All races have their geniuses—and their idiots. Yet the myth of racial superiority abounds, a myth that is particularly dangerous. Adolf Hitler, for example, believed that the Aryans were a superior race, destined to establish an advanced culture and a new world order. This destiny required them to avoid the "racial contamination" that would come from breeding with inferior races. The Aryans, then, had the "cultural duty" to isolate or destroy races that threatened their racial purity and culture.

Put into practice, Hitler's views left an appalling legacy—the Nazi slaughter of those they deemed inferior: Jews, Slavs, gypsies, homosexuals, and people with mental and physical disabilities. Horrific images of gas ovens and emaciated bodies stacked like cordwood have haunted the world's nations. At Nuremberg, the Allies, flush with victory, put the top Nazis on trial, exposing their heinous deeds to a shocked world. Their public executions, everyone assumed, marked the end of such grisly acts.

Humans show remarkable diversity. Shown here is just one example—He Pingping, from China, who at 2 feet 4 inches, was the world's shortest man, and Svetlana Pankratova, from Russia, who, according to the *Guinness Book of World Records,* is the woman with the longest legs. Race–ethnicity shows similar diversity.

Why is "race" a myth? What are the dangers of the myth of racial superiority?

Cultural Diversity in the United States

Tiger Woods: Mapping the Changing Ethnic Terrain

Tiger Woods, perhaps the top golfer of all time, calls himself *Cablinasian*. Woods invented this term as a boy to try to explain to himself just who he was—a combination of Caucasian, Black, Indian, and Asian (Leland and Beals 1997; Hall 2001). Woods wanted to embrace all sides of his family.

Like many of us, Tiger Woods' heritage is difficult to specify. Analysts who like to quantify ethnic heritage put Woods at one-quarter Thai, one-quarter Chinese, one-quarter white, an eighth Native American, and an eighth African American. From this chapter, you know how ridiculous such computations are, but the sociological question is why many people consider Tiger Woods an African American. The U.S. racial scene is indeed complex, but a good part of the reason is that Woods has dark skin and this is the label the media placed on him. "Everyone has to fit somewhere" seems to be our attitude. If they don't, we grow uncomfortable. And for Tiger Woods, the media chose African American.

The United States once had a firm "color line"—barriers between racial–ethnic groups that you didn't dare cross, especially in dating or marriage. This invisible barrier has broken down, and today such marriages are common (*Statistical Abstract* 2012:Table 60). Several college campuses have interracial student organizations. Harvard has two, one just for students who have one African American parent (Leland and Beals 1997).

As we enter unfamiliar ethnic terrain, our classifications are bursting at the seams. They simply cannot keep pace with our rapid social change. As Kwame Appiah, of Harvard's Philosophy and Afro-American Studies Departments, pointed out, our classifications lead to ridiculous situations. Appiah's sisters are married to men from Norway and Ghana, so his nephews range from light-skinned, blond-haired kids to very black kids. Yet they all are classified as black (Wright 1994).

I marvel at what racial experts the U.S. census takers once were. When they took the census, which is done every ten years, they looked at people and assigned them a race. At various points, the census contained these categories: mulatto, quadroon, octoroon, Negro, black, Mexican, white, Indian, Filipino, Japanese, Chinese, and Hindu. Quadroon (one-fourth black and three-fourths white) and octoroon (one-eighth black and seven-eighths white) proved too difficult to "measure," and these categories were used only in 1890. Mulatto appeared

Tiger Woods as he answers questions at a news conference.

in the 1850 census, and lasted until 1920. The Mexican government complained about Mexicans being treated as a race, and this category was used only in 1930. I don't know whose idea it was to make Hindu a race, but it lasted for three censuses, from 1920 to 1940 (Bean et al. 2004; Tafoya et al. 2005).

Continuing to reflect changing ideas about race–ethnicity, censuses have become flexible, and we now have many choices. In the 2010 census, we were first asked to declare whether we were or were not "Spanish/Hispanic/Latino." After this, we were asked to check "one or more races" that we "consider ourselves to be." We could choose from White; Black, African American, or Negro; American Indian or Alaska Native; Asian Indian, Chinese, Filipino, Japanese, Korean, Vietnamese, Native Hawaiian, Guamanian or Chamorro, and Samoan. There were boxes for Other Asian and Other Pacific Islander, with examples that listed Hmong, Pakistani, and Fijian as races. If these didn't do it, we could check a box called "Some Other Race" and then write whatever we wanted.

Perhaps the census should list Cablinasian, after all. We could also have ANGEL for African-Norwegian-German-English-Latino Americans, DEVIL for those of Danish-English-Vietnamese-Italian-Lebanese descent, and STUDENT for Swedish-Turkish-Uruguayan-Danish-English-Norwegian-Tibetan Americans. As you read farther in this chapter, you will see why these terms make as much sense as the categories we currently use.

For Your Consideration

→ Just why do we count people by "race" anyway? Why not eliminate race from the U.S. census? (Race became a factor in 1790 during the first census. To determine the number of representatives from each state, slaves were counted as three-fifths of whites!) Why is race so important to some people? Perhaps you can use the materials in this chapter to answer these questions.

Based on this box, what is race?

The reason I selected these photos is to illustrate how seriously we must take all preaching of hatred and of racial supremacy, even though it seems to come from harmless or even humorous sources. The strange-looking person with his hands on his hips, who is wearing *lederhosen*, traditional clothing of Bavaria, Germany, is Adolf Hitler. He caused this horrific scene at the Landsberg concentration camp, which, as shown here, the U.S. military forced German civilians to view.

Obviously, they didn't. In the summer of 1994 in Rwanda, Hutus slaughtered about 800,000 Tutsis—mostly with machetes (Gettleman and Kron 2010). In the same decade, Serbs in Bosnia massacred Muslims, giving us a new term, *ethnic cleansing*. As these events sadly attest, **genocide**, the attempt to destroy a group of people because of their presumed race or ethnicity, remains alive and well. Although more recent killings are not accompanied by swastikas and gas ovens, the perpetrators' goal is the same.

The Myth Continues.   The *idea* of race, of course, is far from a myth. Firmly embedded in our culture, it is a powerful force in our everyday lives. That no race is superior and that even biologists cannot decide how people should be classified into races is not what counts. "I know what I see, and you can't tell me any different" seems to be the common attitude. As was noted in Chapter 4, sociologists W. I. and D. S. Thomas (1928) observed, "If people define situations as real, they are real in their consequences." In other words, people act on perceptions and beliefs, not facts. As a result, we will always have people like Hitler and, as illustrated in our opening vignette, officials like those in the U.S. Public Health Service who thought that it was fine to experiment with people whom they deemed inferior. While few people hold such extreme views, most people appear to be ethnocentric enough to believe that their own race is—at least just a little—superior to others.

Ethnic Groups

In contrast to *race,* which people use to refer to supposed biological characteristics that distinguish one group of people from another, **ethnicity** and **ethnic** refer to cultural characteristics. Derived from the word *ethnos* (a Greek word meaning "people" or "nation"), *ethnicity* and *ethnic* refer to people who identify with one another on the basis of common ancestry and cultural heritage. Their sense of belonging may center on their nation or region of origin, distinctive foods, clothing, language, music, religion, or family names and relationships.

People often confuse the terms *race* and *ethnic group*. For example, many people, including many Jews, consider Jews a race. Jews, however, are more properly considered an ethnic group, for it is their cultural characteristics, especially their religion, that bind them together. Wherever Jews have lived in the world, they have intermarried. Consequently, Jews in China may have Chinese features, while some Swedish Jews are blue-eyed blonds. The confusion of race and ethnicity is illustrated in the photo on page 244.

Down-to-Earth Sociology

Can a Plane Ride Change Your Race?

At the beginning of this text (pages 22–24), I mentioned that common sense and sociology often differ. This is especially so when it comes to race. According to common sense, our racial classifications represent biological differences between people. Sociologists, in contrast, stress that what we call races are *social* classifications, not biological categories.

Sociologists point out that *our "race" depends more on the society in which we live than on our biological characteristics.* For example, the racial categories common in the United States are only one of *numerous* ways by which people around the world classify physical appearances. Although various groups use different categories, each group assumes that its categories are natural, merely a response to visible biology.

To better understand this essential sociological point—that race is more social than it is biological—consider this: In the United States, children born to the same parents are all of the same race. "What could be more natural?" Americans assume. But in Brazil, children born to the same parents may be of different races—if their appearances differ. "What could be more natural?" assume Brazilians.

Consider how Americans usually classify a child born to a "black" mother and a "white" father. Why do they usually say that the child is "black"? Wouldn't it be equally as logical to classify the child as "white"? Similarly, if a child has one grandmother who is "black," but all her other ancestors are "white," the child is often considered "black." Yet she has much more "white blood" than "black blood." Why, then, is she considered "black"? Certainly not because of biology.

What "race" are these two Brazilians? Is the child's "race" different from her mother's "race"? The text explains why "race" is such an unreliable concept that it changes even with geography.

Such thinking is a legacy of slavery. In an attempt to preserve the "purity" of their "race" in the face of the many children whose fathers were white slave masters and whose mothers were black slaves, whites classified anyone with even a "drop of black blood" as black. They actually called this the "one-drop" rule.

Even a plane trip can change a person's race. In the city of Salvador in Brazil, people classify one another by color of skin and eyes, breadth of nose and lips, and color and curliness of hair. They use at least seven terms for what we call *white* and *black.* Consider again a U.S. child who has "white" and "black" parents. If she flies to Brazil, she is no longer "black"; she now belongs to one of their several "whiter" categories (Fish 1995).

If the girl makes such a flight, would her "race" actually change? Our common sense revolts at this, I know, but it actually would. We want to argue that because her biological characteristics remain unchanged, her race remains unchanged. This is because we think of race as biological, when *race is actually a label we use to describe perceived biological characteristics.* Simply put, the race we "are" depends on our social location—on who is doing the classifying.

"Racial" classifications are also fluid, not fixed. Even now, you can see change occurring in U.S. classifications. The category "multiracial," for example, indicates changing thought and perception.

For Your Consideration

→ How would you explain to someone that race is more a social classification than a biological one? Can you come up with any arguments to refute this statement? How do you think our racial–ethnic categories will change in the future?

Minority Groups and Dominant Groups

Sociologist Louis Wirth (1945) defined a **minority group** as people who are singled out for unequal treatment and who regard themselves as objects of collective discrimination. Worldwide, minorities share several conditions: Their physical or cultural traits are held in low esteem by the dominant group, which treats them unfairly, and they tend to marry within their own group (Wagley and Harris 1958). These conditions tend to create a sense of identity among minorities (a feeling of "we-ness"). In some instances, even a sense of common destiny emerges (Chandra 1993b).

Surprisingly, a minority group is not necessarily a *numerical* minority. For example, before India's independence in 1947, a handful of British colonial rulers dominated tens of millions of Indians. Similarly, when South Africa practiced apartheid, a smaller group of Afrikaners, primarily Dutch, discriminated against a much larger number of blacks. Accordingly, sociologists refer to those who do the discriminating not as the

Watch
Multiracial Identity
on **mysoclab.com**

How is it possible that a plane ride could change someone's race?

majority, but, rather, as the **dominant group,** for regardless of their numbers, this is the group that has the greater power and privilege.

Possessing political power and unified by shared physical and cultural traits, the dominant group uses its position to discriminate against those with different—and supposedly inferior—traits. The dominant group considers its privileged position to be the result of its own innate superiority.

Emergence of Minority Groups.   A group becomes a minority in one of two ways. The *first* is through the expansion of political boundaries. With the exception of females, tribal societies contain no minority groups. Everyone shares the same culture, including the same language, and belongs to the same group. When a group expands its political boundaries, however, it produces minority groups if it incorporates people with different customs, languages, values, or physical characteristics into the same political entity and discriminates against them. For example, in 1848, after defeating Mexico in war, the United States took over the Southwest. The Mexicans living there, who had been the dominant group prior to the war, were transformed into a minority group, a master status that has influenced their lives ever since. Referring to his ancestors, one Latino said, "We didn't move across the border—the border moved across us."

A *second* way in which a group becomes a minority is by migration. This can be voluntary, as with the millions of people who have chosen to move from Mexico to the United States, or involuntary, as with the millions of Africans who were brought in chains to the United States.

Ethnic Work: Constructing Our Racial-Ethnic Identity

Some of us have a greater sense of ethnicity than others, and we feel firm boundaries between "us" and "them." Others of us have assimilated so extensively into the mainstream culture that we are only vaguely aware of our ethnic origins. With interethnic marriage common, some do not even know the countries from which their families originated—nor do they care. If asked to identify themselves ethnically, they respond with something like "I'm Heinz 57—German and Irish, with a little Italian and French thrown in—and I think someone said something about being one-sixteenth Indian, too."

Why do some people feel an intense sense of ethnic identity, while others feel hardly any? Figure 9.1 portrays four factors, identified by sociologist Ashley Doane, that heighten or reduce our sense of ethnic identity. From this figure, you can see that the keys are relative size, power, appearance, and discrimination. If your group is relatively small, has little power, looks different from most people in society, and is an object of discrimination, you will have a heightened sense of ethnic identity. In contrast, if you belong to the dominant group that holds most of the power, look like most people in the society, and feel no discrimination, you are likely to experience a sense of "belonging"—and to wonder why ethnic identity is such a big deal.

We can use the term **ethnic work** to refer to the way we construct our ethnicity. For people who have a strong ethnic identity, this term refers to how they enhance and maintain their group's distinctions—from clothing, food, and language to religious practices and holidays. For people whose ethnic identity is not as firm, it refers to attempts to recover their ethnic heritage, such as trying to trace family lines or visiting the country or region of their family's origin. As illustrated by the photo essay on page 246 many Americans do ethnic work. This has confounded the experts, who thought that the United States would be a *melting pot,* with most of its groups blending into a sort of

This photo, taken in Ashkelon, Israel, illustrates the difficulty that assumptions about *race* and *ethnicity* posed for Israel. The Ethiopian Jews look so different from other Jews that it took several years for Israeli authorities to acknowledge their "true Jewishness" and allow them to immigrate.

ethnic stew. Because so many Americans have become fascinated with their "roots," some analysts have suggested that
"tossed salad" is a more appropriate term than "melting pot."

Prejudice and Discrimination

With prejudice and discrimination so significant in social life,
let's consider the origin of prejudice and the extent of
discrimination.

Learning Prejudice

Distinguishing Between Prejudice and Discrimination.
Prejudice and discrimination are common throughout the
world. In Mexico, Mexicans of Hispanic descent discriminate against Mexicans of Native American descent; in Israel,
Ashkenazi Jews, primarily of European descent, discriminate against Sephardic Jews, from
the Middle East; in China, the Han and the Uighurs discriminate against each other. In
some places, the elderly discriminate against the young; in others, the young discriminate
against the elderly. And all around the world, men discriminate against women.

   Discrimination is an *action*—unfair treatment directed against someone. Discrimination
can be based on many characteristics: age, sex, height, weight, skin color, clothing, speech,
income, education, marital status, sexual orientation, disease, disability, religion, and
politics. When the basis of discrimination is someone's perception of race, it is known as
racism. Discrimination is often the result of an *attitude* called **prejudice**—a prejudging
of some sort, usually in a negative way. There is also *positive prejudice*, which exaggerates
the virtues of a group, as when people think that some group is superior to others. Most
prejudice, however, is negative and involves prejudging a group as inferior.

Learning from Associating with Others.
As with our other attitudes, we are not
born with prejudice. Rather, we learn prejudice from the people around us. You probably know this, but here is a twist that sociologists have found. Michael Kimmel (2007),
who interviewed neo-Nazi skinheads in Sweden, found that young men were attracted
mostly by the group's tough masculinity, not its hatred of immigrants. Kathleen Blee
(2005, 2011), who interviewed female members of the KKK and Aryan Nations in the

FIGURE 9.1   A Sense of Ethnicity

A Heightened Sense

A Low
Sense

Part of the majority	Smaller numbers
Greater power	Lesser power
Similar to the "national identity"	Different from the "national identity"
No discrimination	Discrimination

Source: By the author. Based on Doane 1997.

This photo, taken in Birmingham, Alabama, provides a glimpse into the intensity and bravery of the civil rights demonstrators of the 1960s.

How does prejudice differ from discrimination? What is the origin of prejudice?

Explorations in Cultural Identity

Ethnic work refers to the ways that people establish, maintain, and transmit their ethnic identity. As shown here, among the techniques people use to forge ties with their roots are dress, dance, and music.

Many African Americans are trying to get in closer contact with their roots. To do this, some use musical performances, as with this group in Philadelphia, Pennsylvania.

Wearing traditional clothing and participating in a parade help to maintain the ethnic identity of these Americans who trace their origin to the Philippines.

Many European Americans are also involved in ethnic work, attempting to maintain an identity more precise than "from Europe." These women of Czech ancestry are performing for a Czech community in a small town in Nebraska.

Many Native Americans have maintained continuous identity with their tribal roots. You can see the blending of cultures in this photo taken at the March Pow Wow in Denver, Colorado.

The *Cinco de Mayo* celebration is used to recall roots and renew ethnic identities. This one was held in Los Angeles, California.

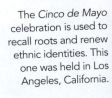

United States, found something similar. They were attracted to the hate group because someone they liked belonged to it. They learned to be racists *after* they joined the group. Both Blee and Kimmel found that the members' racism was not the *cause* of their joining but, rather, joining was the cause of their racism.

The Far-Reaching Nature of Prejudice.   It is amazing how much prejudice people can learn. In a classic article, psychologist Eugene Hartley (1946) asked people how they felt about several racial–ethnic groups. Besides Negroes, Jews, and so on, he included the Wallonians, Pireneans, and Danireans—names he had made up. Most people who expressed dislike for Jews and Negroes showed similar contempt for these three fictitious groups.

Hartley's study shows that prejudice does not depend on negative experiences with others. It also reveals that people who are prejudiced against one racial or ethnic group also tend to be prejudiced against other groups. People can be, and are, prejudiced against people they have never met—and even against groups that do not exist!

The neo-Nazis and the Ku Klux Klan base their existence on prejudice. These groups believe that race is real, that white is best, and that beneath society's surface is a murky river of mingling conspiracies (Ezekiel 1995). What would happen if a Jew attended their meetings? Would he or she survive? In the Down-to-Earth Sociology box on page 249, sociologist Raphael Ezekiel reveals some of the insights he gained during his remarkable study of these groups.

Internalizing Dominant Norms.   People can even learn to be prejudiced against their own group. A national survey found that African Americans think that lighter-skinned African American women are more attractive than those with darker skin (Hill 2002). Participant observation in the ghetto also reveals a preference for lighter skin (Jones 2011). Sociologists call this *internalizing the norms of the dominant group*.

To study the internalization of dominant norms, psychologists Mahzarin Banaji and Anthony Greenwald created the *Implicit Association Test*. In one version of this test, good and bad words are flashed on a screen along with photos of African Americans and whites. Most subjects are quicker to associate positive words (such as "love," "peace," and "baby") with whites and negative words (such as "cancer," "bomb," and "devil") with blacks. Here's the clincher: This is true for *both* whites and blacks (Dasgupta et al. 2000; Greenwald and Krieger 2006). Apparently, we all learn the *ethnic maps* of our culture and, along with them, their route to biased perception.

Individual and Institutional Discrimination

Sociologists stress that we should move beyond thinking in terms of **individual discrimination,** the negative treatment of one person by another. Although such behavior creates problems, it is primarily an issue between individuals. With their focus on the broader picture, sociologists encourage us to examine **institutional discrimination,** that is, to see how discrimination is woven into the fabric of society. Let's look at two examples.

Home Mortgages.   Bank lending provides an excellent illustration of institutional discrimination. Earlier studies using national samples showed that bankers were more likely to reject the loan applications of minorities. When bankers defended themselves by saying that whites had better credit history, researchers retested their data. They found that even when applicants had identical credit, African Americans and Latinos were *60 percent* more likely to be rejected (Thomas 1991, 1992).

The subprime debacle that threw the stock market into a tailspin brought new revelations. Look at Figure 9.2 on the next page. You can see that *minorities are still more likely to be turned down for a loan—whether their incomes are below or above the median income of their community.* Beyond this hard finding lies another just as devastating. In the credit crisis that caused so many to lose their homes, African Americans and Latinos were hit harder than whites. The last set of bars on Figure 9.2 shows a major reason for this: *Banks purposely targeted minorities to charge higher interest rates.* Over the lifetime of a loan, these higher monthly payments can come to an extra $100,000 to $200,000 (Powell and Roberts 2009).

What does "internalizing dominant norms" mean?

FIGURE 9.2   Buying a House: Institutional Discrimination and Predatory Lending

This figure, based on a national sample, illustrates *institutional discrimination*. Rejecting the loan applications of minorities and gouging them with higher interest rates are a nationwide practice, not the acts of a rogue banker here or there. Because the discrimination is part of the banking system, it is also called *systemic discrimination*.

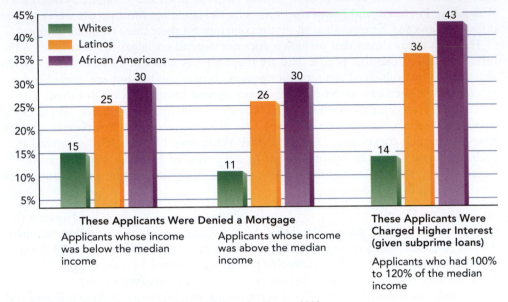

These Applicants Were Denied a Mortgage

Applicants whose income was below the median income

Applicants whose income was above the median income

These Applicants Were Charged Higher Interest (given subprime loans)

Applicants who had 100% to 120% of the median income

Source: By the author. Based on Kochbar and Gonzalez-Barrera 2009.

Would nice bankers really do this? After checking data like these, the Justice Department accused Countrywide Financial, a major mortgage lender, of discriminating against 200,000 Latino and African American borrowers. Countrywide agreed to pay a fine of $335 million, the largest fair-lending settlement in history (Savage 2011).

Health Care.   Losing your home is devastating. Losing your mother or baby is even worse. Look at Table 9.1. You can see that institutional discrimination can be a life-and-death matter. In childbirth, African American mothers are *almost three* times as likely to die as white mothers, while their babies are more than *twice* as likely to die during their first year of life. This is not a matter of biology, as though African American mothers and children are more fragile. It is a matter of *social* conditions, primarily nutrition and medical care.

It is important to understand that discrimination does not have to be deliberate. In some unintentional discrimination, no one is aware of it—neither those being discriminated against nor those doing the discriminating (Harris et al. 2011). Consider knee replacements and coronary bypass surgery. White patients are more likely than either

TABLE 9.1   Race–Ethnicity and Mother/Child Deaths

	Infant Deaths	Maternal Deaths
White Americans	5.6	10.0
African Americans	13.2	26.5

Note: The national database used for this table does not list these totals for other racial–ethnic groups. *White* refers to non-Hispanic whites. *Infant deaths* refers to the number of deaths per year of infants under 1 year old per 1,000 live births. *Maternal deaths* refers to the number of deaths per 100,000 women who give birth in a year.

Source: *Statistical Abstract of the United States* 2012:Table 115.

Can you summarize insititutional discrimination in mortgages and health care?

Latino or African American patients to receive these procedures (Skinner et al. 2003; Popescu 2007). Treatment after a heart attack follows a similar pattern: Whites are more likely than blacks to be given cardiac catheterization, a test to detect blockage of blood vessels. This study of 40,000 patients holds a surprise: Both black *and* white doctors are more likely to give this preventive care to whites (Stolberg 2001).

Researchers do not know why race–ethnicity is a factor in medical decisions. With both white and black doctors involved, we can be certain that physicians *do not intend* to discriminate. Apparently, the implicit bias that comes with the internalization of dominant norms becomes a subconscious motivation for giving or denying access to advanced medical procedures.

Down-to-Earth Sociology

The Racist Mind

Sociologist Raphael Ezekiel wanted to get a close look at the racist mind. The best way to study racism from the inside is to do participant observation (see page 30). But Ezekiel is a Jew. Could he study these groups by participant observation? To find out, Ezekiel told Ku Klux Klan and neo-Nazi leaders that he wanted to interview them and attend their meetings. He also told them that he was a Jew. Surprisingly, they agreed. Ezekiel published his path-breaking research in a book, *The Racist Mind* (1995). Here are some of the insights he gained during his fascinating sociological adventure:

[The leader] builds on mass anxiety about economic insecurity and on popular tendencies to see an Establishment as the cause of economic threat; he hopes to teach people to identify that Establishment as the puppets of a conspiracy of Jews. [He has a] belief in exclusive categories. For the white racist leader, it is profoundly true . . . that the socially defined collections we call races represent fundamental categories. A man is black or a man is white; there are no in-betweens. Every human belongs to a racial category, and all the members of one category are radically different from all the members of other categories. Moreover, race represents the essence of the person. A truck is a truck, a car is a car, a cat is a cat, a dog is a dog, a black is a black, a white is a white. . . . These axioms have a rock-hard quality in the leaders' minds; the world is made up of racial groups. That is what exists for them.

Two further beliefs play a major role in the minds of leaders. First, life is war. The world is made of distinct racial groups; life is about the war between these groups. Second, events have secret causes, are never what they seem superficially. . . . Any myth is plausible, as long as it involves intricate plotting. . . . It does not matter to him what others say. . . . He lives in his ideas and in the little world he has created where they are taken seriously. . . . Gold can be made from the tongues

Raphael Ezekiel

of frogs; Yahweh's call can be heard in the flapping swastika banner. (pp. 66–67)

Who is attracted to the neo-Nazis and Ku Klux Klan? Here is what Ezekiel discovered:

[There is a] ready pool of whites who will respond to the racist signal. . . . This population [is] always hungry for activity—or for the talk of activity—that promises dignity and meaning to lives that are working poorly in a highly competitive world. . . . Much as I don't want to believe it, [this] movement brings a sense of meaning— at least for a while—to some of the discontented. To struggle in a cause that transcends the individual lends meaning to life, no matter how ill-founded or narrowing the cause. For the young men in the neo-Nazi group . . . membership was an alternative to atomization and drift; within the group they worked for a cause and took direct risks in the company of comrades. . . .

When interviewing the young neo-Nazis in Detroit, I often found myself driving with them past the closed factories, the idled plants of our shrinking manufacturing base. The fewer and fewer plants that remain can demand better educated and more highly skilled workers. These fatherless Nazi youths, these high-school dropouts, will find little place in the emerging economy . . . a permanently underemployed white underclass is taking its place alongside the permanent black underclass. The struggle over race merely diverts youth from confronting the real issues of their lives. Not many seats are left on the train, and the train is leaving the station. (pp. 32–33)

For Your Consideration

→ Use functionalism, conflict theory, and symbolic interaction to explain how the leaders and followers of these hate groups view the world. Use these same perspectives to explain why some people are attracted to the message of hate.

How does implicit bias underlie unintentional discrimination? How do hard-core members of hate groups see the world?

Theories of Prejudice

Social scientists have developed several theories to explain prejudice. Let's first look at psychological explanations, then at sociological ones.

Psychological Perspectives

Frustration and Scapegoats.

"Why are we having a depression? The Jews have taken over the banking system, and they want to suck every dollar out of us."

This was a common sentiment in Germany in the 1930s during the depression that helped bring Hitler to power. People often unfairly blame their troubles on a **scapegoat**—often a racial–ethnic or religious minority. Why do they do this? Psychologist John Dollard (1939) suggested that prejudice is the result of frustration. People who are unable to strike out at the real source of their frustration (such as unemployment) look for someone to blame. This person or group becomes a target on which they vent their frustrations. Gender and age are also common targets of scapegoating.

Prejudice and frustration often are related. A team of psychologists led by Emory Cowen (1959) measured the prejudice of a group of students. They then gave the students two puzzles to solve, making sure the students did not have enough time to finish. After the students had worked furiously on the puzzles, the experimenters shook their heads in disgust and expressed disbelief that students couldn't complete such a simple task. They then retested the students. The results? Their scores on prejudice increased. The students had directed their frustrations outward, transferring them to people who had nothing to do with the contempt they had experienced.

The Authoritarian Personality.

"I don't like Swedes. They're too rigid. And I don't like the Italians. They're always talking with their hands. I don't like the Walloneans, either. They're always smiling at something. And I don't like librarians. And my job sucks. Hitler might have had his faults, but he put people to work during the Great Depression."

Have you ever wondered whether some people's personality makes them more inclined to be prejudiced, and others more fair-minded? For psychologist Theodor Adorno, who had fled from the Nazis, this was no idle speculation. With the horrors he had observed still fresh in his mind, Adorno wondered whether there might be a certain type of person who is more likely to fall for the racist spewings of people like Hitler, Mussolini, and those in the Ku Klux Klan.

To find out, Adorno gave three tests to about two thousand people, ranging from college professors to prison inmates (Adorno et al. 1950). He measured their ethnocentrism, anti-Semitism (bias against Jews), and support for strong, authoritarian leaders. People who scored high on one test also scored high on the other two. For example, people who agreed with anti-Semitic statements also said that governments should be authoritarian and that foreign customs pose a threat to the "American" way.

Adorno concluded that highly prejudiced people have deep respect for authority and are submissive to authority figures. He termed this the **authoritarian personality.** These people believe that things are either right or wrong. Ambiguity disturbs them, especially in matters of religion or sex. They become anxious when they confront norms and values that are different from their own. To view people who differ from themselves as inferior assures them that their own positions are right.

Adorno's research stimulated more than a thousand research studies. In general, the researchers found that people who are older, less educated, less intelligent, and from a lower social class are more likely to be authoritarian. Critics say that this doesn't indicate a particular personality, just that the less educated are more prejudiced—which we already knew (Yinger 1965; Ray 1991). Nevertheless, researchers continue to study this concept (McFarland 2010).

Sociological Perspectives

Sociologists find psychological explanations inadequate. They stress that the key to understanding prejudice cannot be found by looking *inside* people, but, rather, by examining conditions *outside* them. For this reason, sociologists focus on how social environments influence prejudice. With this background, let's compare functionalist, conflict, and symbolic interactionist perspectives on prejudice.

Functionalism.

In a television documentary, journalist Bill Moyers interviewed Fritz Hippler, a Nazi who at age 29 was put in charge of the entire German film industry. When Hitler came to power, Hippler said, the Germans were no more anti-Semitic than the French. Hippler was told to increase anti-Semitism in Germany. Obediently, he produced movies that contained vivid scenes comparing Jews to rats—with their breeding threatening to infest the population.

Why was Hippler told to create hatred? Prejudice and discrimination were functional for the Nazis. Defeated in World War I and devastated by fines levied by the victors, Germany was on its knees. Runaway inflation was destroying its middle class. To help unite this fractured Germany, the Nazis created a scapegoat to blame for their troubles. In addition, the Jews owned businesses, bank accounts, fine art, and other property that the Nazis could confiscate. Jews also held key positions (as university professors, reporters, judges, and so on), which the Nazis could give as prizes to their followers. In the end, hatred also showed its dysfunctional face, as the Nazi officials hanged at Nuremberg discovered.

Prejudice becomes practically irresistible when state machinery is used to advance the cause of hatred. To produce prejudice, the Nazis harnessed government agencies, the schools, police, courts, and mass media. The results were devastating. Recall the identical twins featured in the Down-to-Earth Sociology box on page 66. Jack and Oskar had been separated as babies. Jack was brought up as a Jew in Trinidad, while Oskar was reared as a Catholic in Czechoslovakia. Under the Nazi regime, Oskar learned to hate Jews, unaware that he himself was a Jew.

That prejudice is functional and is shaped by the social environment was demonstrated by psychologists Muzafer and Carolyn Sherif (1953). In a boys' summer camp, the Sherifs assigned friends to different cabins and then had the cabin groups compete in sports. In just a few days, strong in-groups had formed. Even lifelong friends began to taunt one another, calling each other "crybaby" and "sissy."

The Sherif study teaches us several important lessons about social life. Note how it is possible to arrange the social environment to generate either positive or negative feelings about people, and how prejudice arises if we pit groups against one another in an "I win, you lose" situation. You can also see that prejudice is functional, how it creates in-group solidarity. And, of course, it is obvious how dysfunctional prejudice is, when you observe the way it destroys human relationships.

Conflict Theory.

"The Japanese have gone on strike? They're demanding a raise? And they even want a rest period? We'll show them who's boss. Hire those Koreans who've been trying to get work."

This did happen. When Japanese workers in Hawaii struck, owners of plantations hired Koreans (Jeong and You 2008). The division of workers along racial–ethnic and gender lines is known as a **split labor market** (Du Bois 1935/1992; Roediger 2002). Although today's exploitation of these divisions is more subtle, whites are aware that other racial–ethnic groups are ready to take their jobs, African Americans often perceive Latinos as competitors (Cose 2006), and men know that women are eager to get promoted. All of this helps to keep workers in line.

Conflict theorists, as you will recall, focus on how groups compete for scarce resources. Owners want to increase profits by holding costs down, while workers want better food, health care, housing, education, and leisure. Divided, workers are weak, but united, they gain strength. The *split labor market* is one way that owners divide workers so they can't take united action to demand higher wages and better working conditions.

Another tactic that owners use is the **reserve labor force.** This is simply another term for the unemployed. To expand production during economic booms, companies hire those who don't have jobs. When the economy contracts and they no longer need these workers, they lay them off. That there are people without jobs who are desperately looking for work is a lesson not lost on workers who have jobs. They fear eviction and worry about having their cars and furniture repossessed. Many know they are just one or two paychecks away from ending up "on the streets."

Just like the boys in the Sherif experiment, African Americans, Latinos, whites, and others see themselves as able to make gains only at the expense of other groups. Sometimes this rivalry shows up along very fine racial–ethnic lines, such as that in Miami between Haitians and African Americans, who distrust each other as competitors. Divisions among workers deflect anger and hostility away from the power elite and direct these powerful emotions toward other racial and ethnic groups. Instead of recognizing their common class interests and working for their mutual welfare, workers learn to fear and distrust one another.

Symbolic Interactionism.

"I know her qualifications are good, but yikes! She's ugly. I don't want to have to see her every day. Let's hire the one with the nice curves."

While conflict theorists focus on the role of the owner (or capitalist) class in exploiting racial and ethnic divisions, symbolic interactionists examine how labels affect perception and create prejudice.

How Labels Create Prejudice.

Symbolic interactionists stress that *the labels we learn affect the ways we perceive people*. Labels cause **selective perception;** that is, they lead us to see certain things while they blind us to others. If we apply a label to a group, we tend to perceive its members as all alike. We shake off evidence that doesn't fit (Simpson and Yinger 1972). Shorthand for emotionally charged stereotypes, some racial and ethnic labels are especially powerful. As you know, the term *nigger* is not neutral. Nor are *honky, cracker, spic, mick, kike, limey, kraut, dago, guinea,* or any of the other scornful words people use to belittle ethnic groups. As in the little vignette above, *ugly* can work in a similar way. Such words overpower us with emotions, blocking out rational thought about the people to whom they refer (Allport 1954).

Labels and Self-Fulfilling Stereotypes.

Some stereotypes not only justify prejudice and discrimination but also produce the behavior depicted in the stereotype. We examined this principle in Chapter 4 in the box on beauty (p. 111). Let's consider Group X. According to stereotypes, the members of this group are lazy, so they don't deserve good jobs. ("They are lazy and wouldn't do the job well.") Denied the better jobs, most members of Group X do "dirty work," the jobs few people want. ("That's the right kind of work for that kind of people.") Since much "dirty work" is sporadic, members of Group X are often seen "on the streets." The sight of their idleness reinforces the original stereotype of laziness. The discrimination that created the "laziness" in the first place passes unnoticed.

To apply these three theoretical perspectives and catch a glimpse of how amazingly different things were in the past, read the Down-to-Earth Sociology box on the next page.

Down-to-Earth Sociology

The Man in the Zoo

The Bronx Zoo in New York City used to keep a 22-year-old pygmy in the Monkey House. The man—and the orangutan he lived with—became the most popular exhibit at the zoo. Thousands of visitors would arrive daily and head straight for the Monkey House. Eyewitnesses to what they thought was a lower form of human in the long chain of evolution, the visitors were fascinated by the pygmy, especially by his sharpened teeth.

To make the exhibit even more alluring, the zoo director had animal bones scattered in front of the man.

I know it sounds as though I must have made this up, but this is a true story. The World's Fair was going to be held in St. Louis in 1904, and the Department of Anthropology wanted to show villages from different cultures. They asked Samuel Verner, an explorer, if he could bring some pygmies to St. Louis to serve as live exhibits. Verner agreed, and on his next trip to Africa, in the Belgian Congo he came across Ota Benga (or Otabenga), a pygmy who had been enslaved by another tribe. Benga, then about age 20, said he was willing to go to St. Louis. After Verner bought Benga's freedom for some cloth and salt, Benga recruited another half dozen pygmies to go with them.

After the World's Fair, Verner took the pygmies back to Africa. When Benga found out that a hostile tribe had wiped out his village and killed his family, he asked Verner if he could return with him to the United States. Verner agreed.

When they returned to New York, Verner ran into financial trouble and wrote some bad checks. No longer able to care for Benga, Verner left him with friends at the American Museum of Natural History. After a few weeks, they grew tired of Benga's antics and turned him over to the Bronx Zoo. The zoo officials put Benga on display in the Monkey House, with this sign:

The African Pygmy, 'Ota Benga.' Age 23 years. Height 4 feet 11 inches. Weight 103 pounds. Brought from the Kasai River, Congo Free State, South Central Africa by Dr. Samuel P. Verner. Exhibited each afternoon during September

Ota Benga, 1906, on exhibit in the Bronx Zoo.

Exhibited with an orangutan, Benga became a sensation. An article in the *New York Times* said it was fortunate that Benga couldn't think very deeply, or else living with monkeys might bother him.

When the Colored Baptist Ministers' Conference protested that exhibiting Benga was degrading, zoo officials replied that they were "taking excellent care of the little fellow." They added that "he has one of the best rooms at the primate house." (I wonder what animal had the best room.)

Not surprisingly, this reply didn't satisfy the ministers. When they continued to protest, zoo officials decided to let Benga out of his cage. They put a white shirt on him and let him walk around the zoo. At night, Benga slept in the monkey house.

Benga's life became even more miserable. Zoo visitors would follow him, howling, jeering, laughing, and poking at him. One day, Benga found a knife in the feeding room of the Monkey House and flourished it at the visitors. Unhappy zoo officials took the knife away.

Benga then made a little bow and some arrows and began shooting at the obnoxious visitors. This ended the fun for the zoo officials. They decided that Benga had to leave.

After living in several orphanages for African American children, Benga ended up working as a laborer in a tobacco factory in Lynchburg, Virginia.

Always treated as a freak, Benga was desperately lonely. In 1916, at about the age of 32, in despair that he had no home or family to return to in Africa, Benga ended his misery by shooting himself in the heart.

Source: Based on Bradford and Blume 1992; Crossen 2006; Richman 2006.

For Your Consideration

1. See what different views emerge as you apply the three theoretical perspectives (functionalism, symbolic interactionism, and conflict theory) to exhibiting Benga at the Bronx Zoo.
2. How does the concept of ethnocentrism apply to this event?
3. Explain how the concepts of prejudice and discrimination apply to what happened to Benga.

Global Patterns of Intergroup Relations

In their studies of racial–ethnic relations around the world, sociologists have found six basic ways that dominant groups treat minority groups. These patterns are shown in Figure 9.3 on the next page. Let's look at each.

Can you explain how a human could have ever been a zoo exhibit?

FIGURE 9.3   Global Patterns of Intergroup Relations: A Continuum

INHUMANITY →   HUMANITY →

REJECTION   ACCEPTANCE

Genocide	Population Transfer	Internal Colonialism	Segregation	Assimilation	Multiculturalism (Pluralism)
The dominant group tries to destroy the minority group (e.g., Germany and Rwanda)	The dominant group expels the minority group (e.g., Native Americans forced onto reservations)	The dominant group exploits the minority group (e.g., low-paid, menial work)	The dominant group structures the social institutions to maintain minimal contact with the minority group (e.g., the U.S. South before the 1960s)	The dominant group absorbs the minority group (e.g., American Czechoslovakians)	The dominant group encourages racial and ethnic variation; when successful, there is no longer a dominant group (e.g., Switzerland)

Source: By the author.

Genocide

When gold was discovered in northern California in 1849, the fabled "Forty-Niners" rushed in. In this region lived 150,000 Native Americans. To get rid of them, the white government put a bounty on their heads. It even reimbursed the whites for their bullets. The result was the slaughter of 120,000 Native American men, women, and children. (Schaefer 2004)

Could you ever participate in genocide? Don't be too quick in answering. Gaining an understanding of how ordinary people take part in genocide will be our primary goal in this section. In the events depicted in the little vignette above, those who did the killing were regular people—people like you and I. The killing was promoted by calling the Native Americans "savages," making them appear inferior, as somehow less than human. Killing them, then, didn't seem the same as killing whites in order to take their property.

It is true that most Native Americans died not from bullets, but from the diseases the whites brought with them. Measles, smallpox, and the flu came from another continent, and the Native Americans had no immunity against them (Dobyns 1983; Schaefer 2012). But to accomplish the takeover of their resources, the settlers and soldiers destroyed the Native Americans' food supply (crops and buffalos). From all causes, about *95 percent* of Native Americans died (Thornton 1987; Churchill 1997). Ordinary, "good" people were intent on destroying the "savages."

Now consider last century's two most notorious examples of genocide. In Germany during the 1930s and 1940s, Hitler and the Nazis attempted to destroy all Jews. In the 1990s, in Rwanda, the Hutus tried to destroy all Tutsis. One of the horrifying aspects of these two slaughters is that the killers did not crawl out from under a rock someplace. In some cases, it was even the victims' neighbors and friends who did the killing. *Their killing was facilitated by labels that marked the victims as enemies who deserved to die* (Huttenbach 1991; Browning 1993; Gross 2001).

In Sum: Labels are powerful; dehumanizing ones even more so. They help people to **compartmentalize**—to separate their acts of cruelty from their sense of being good and decent people. To regard members of some group as inferior opens the door to treating them inhumanely. In some cases, these labels help people to kill—and to still retain a good self-concept (Bernard et al. 1971). In short, *labeling the targeted group as inferior or even less than fully human facilitates genocide.*

Population Transfer

There are two types of **population transfer:** indirect and direct. *Indirect transfer* is achieved by making life so miserable for members of a minority that they leave "voluntarily." Under the bitter conditions of czarist Russia, for example, millions of Jews made this "choice." *Direct transfer* occurs when a dominant group expels a minority. Examples include the

U.S. government relocating Native Americans to reservations and transferring Americans of Japanese descent to internment camps during World War II.

Internal Colonialism

In Chapter 7, the term *colonialism* was used to refer to one way that the Most Industrialized Nations exploit the Least Industrialized Nations (p. 199). Conflict theorists use the term **internal colonialism** to describe how a country's dominant group exploits minority groups for its economic advantage. The dominant group manipulates the social institutions to suppress minorities and deny them full access to their society's benefits. Slavery, reviewed in Chapter 7, is an extreme example of internal colonialism, as was the South African system of *apartheid*. Although the dominant Afrikaners despised the minority, they found its presence necessary. As Simpson and Yinger (1972) put it, who else would do the hard work?

Segregation

Internal colonialism is often accompanied by **segregation**—the separation of racial or ethnic groups. Segregation allows the dominant group to maintain social distance from the minority and yet to exploit their labor as cooks, cleaners, chauffeurs, nannies, factory workers, and so on. In the U.S. South until the 1960s, by law African Americans and whites had to use separate public facilities—hotels, schools, swimming pools, bathrooms, and even drinking fountains. In thirty-eight states, laws prohibited marriage between blacks and whites. Violators could be sent to prison (Mahoney and Kooistra 1995). The last law of this type was repealed in 1967 (Spickard 1989). In the villages of India, an ethnic group, the Dalits (untouchables), is forbidden to use the village pump. Dalit women must walk long distances to streams or pumps outside of the village to fetch their water (author's notes).

Assimilation

Assimilation is the process by which a minority group is absorbed into the mainstream culture. There are two types. In *forced assimilation,* the dominant group refuses to allow the minority to practice its religion, to speak its language, or to follow its customs. Before the fall of the Soviet Union, for example, the dominant group, the Russians, required that Armenian children attend schools where they were taught in Russian. Armenians could celebrate only Russian holidays, not Armenian ones. *Permissible assimilation,* in contrast, allows the minority to adopt the dominant group's patterns in its own way and at its own speed.

Multiculturalism (Pluralism)

A policy of **multiculturalism,** also called **pluralism,** permits or even encourages racial–ethnic variation. The minority groups are able to maintain their separate identities, yet participate freely in the country's social institutions, from education to politics. Switzerland provides an outstanding example of multiculturalism. The Swiss population includes four ethnic groups: French, Italians, Germans, and Romansh. These groups have kept their own languages, and they live peacefully in political and economic unity. Multiculturalism has been so successful that none of these groups can properly be called a minority.

Racial–Ethnic Relations in the United States

Writing about race–ethnicity is like stepping onto a minefield: One never knows where to expect the next explosion. Serbian students have written to me, saying that I have been unfair to their group. So have American whites. Even basic terms are controversial. Some people classified as *African Americans* reject this term because they identify

Amid fears that Japanese Americans were "enemies within" who would sabotage industrial and military installations on the West Coast, in the early days of World War II Japanese Americans were transferred to "relocation camps." To make sure they didn't get lost, the children were tagged like luggage.

Can you give examples of internal colonization, segregation, assimilation, and multiculturalism in the United States?

FIGURE 9.4   Race–Ethnicity of the U.S. Population

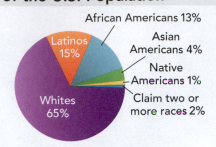

- African Americans 13%
- Latinos 15%
- Asian Americans 4%
- Native Americans 1%
- Claim two or more races 2%
- Whites 65%

Source: By the author. See Figure 9.5.

themselves as blacks. Similarly, some Latinos prefer the term *Hispanic American,* but others reject it, saying that it ignores the Native American side of their heritage. Some would limit the term *Chicanos*—commonly used to refer to Americans from Mexico—to those who have a sense of ethnic oppression and unity; they say that it does not apply to those who have assimilated.

No term that I use here, then, will satisfy everyone. Racial–ethnic identity is fluid, constantly changing, and all terms carry a risk as they take on politically charged meanings. Nevertheless, as part of everyday life, we classify ourselves and one another as belonging to distinct racial–ethnic groups. As Figures 9.4 and 9.5 show, on the basis of these self-identities, whites make up 65 percent of the U.S. population, minorities (African Americans, Asian Americans, Latinos, and Native Americans) 33 percent. Between 1 and 2 percent claim membership in two or more racial–ethnic groups.

FIGURE 9.5   U.S. Racial–Ethnic Groups

[a]This figure, which follows convention and lists Latinos as a separate category, brings into focus the problem of counting "racial–ethnic" groups. Because Latinos can be of any racial–ethnic group, I have reduced the total of the groups with which they self-identify by the number of Latinos who identify with those groups.
[b]Interestingly, this total is six times higher than all the Irish who live in Ireland.
[c]Includes French Canadian.
[d]Includes "Scottish-Irish."
[e]Most Latinos trace at least part of their ancestry to Europe.
[f]In descending order, the largest groups of Asian Americans are from China, the Philippines, India, Korea, Vietnam, and Japan. See Figure 9.9 on page 265. Also includes those who identify themselves as Native Hawaiian or Pacific Islander.
[g]Includes Native Alaskans.

Americans of European Descent[a]
199,491,000
65%

Group	Number	Percentage of Americans
German	50,272,000	16.5%
Irish[b]	36,278,000	11.9%
English/British	28,630,000	9.4%
Italian	17,749,000	5.8%
French[c]	11,526,000	3.8%
Polish	9,887,000	3.25%
Scottish[d]	9,365,000	3.1%
Dutch	4,929,000	1.6%
Norwegian	4,643,000	1.5%
Swedish	4,390,000	1.4%
Russian	3,130,000	1.0%
Welsh	1,980,000	0.6%
Czech	1,914,000	0.5%
Hungarian	1,539,000	0.5%
Danish	1,459,000	0.5%
Portuguese	1,419,000	0.5%
Greek	1,351,000	0.4%
Swiss	997,000	0.3%
Others	839,300	0.2%

Americans of African, Asian, North, Central, and South American, and Pacific Island Descent
104,743,000
33%

Group	Number	Percentage of Americans
Latino[e]	46,944,000	15.4%
African American	39,059,000	12.8%
Asian American[f]	13,549,000	4.5%
Native American[g]	3,083,000	1.0%
Arab	1,546,000	0.5%

Claim Two or More Race–Ethnicities 2%   5,167,000   1.7%

Overall Total:
309,401,000

Percentage of Americans

Source: By the author. Based on *Statistical Abstract of the United States* 2010:Table 10; 2011:Table 52.

USA—the land of diversity.

Why are racial–ethnic terms problematic? What are the major racial–ethnic groups in the United States?

FIGURE 9.6   The Distribution of Dominant and Minority Groups

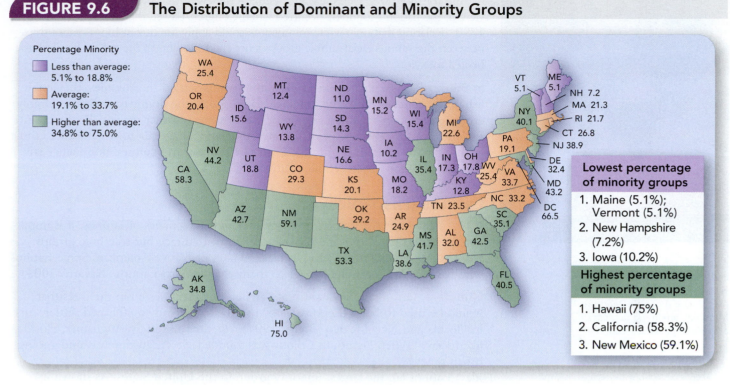

Source: By the author. Based on *Statistical Abstract of the United States* 2011:Table 19.

As you can see from the Social Map, the distribution of dominant and minority groups among the states seldom comes close to the national average. This is because minority groups tend to be clustered in regions. The extreme distributions are represented by Maine and Vermont, each of which has only 5 percent minority, and by Hawaii, where minorities outnumber whites 75 percent to 25 percent. With this as background, let's review the major groups in the United States, going from the largest to the smallest.

European Americans

Benjamin Franklin said, "Why should the Palatine boors (Germans) be suffered to swarm into our settlements and by herding together establish their language and manners to the exclusion of ours? Why should Pennsylvania, founded by the English, become a colony of aliens, who will shortly be so numerous as to germanize us instead of our anglifying them?" (in Alba and Nee 2003:17)

At the founding of this nation, White Anglo Saxon Protestants (**WASPs**) held deep prejudices against other whites. There was practically no end to their disdainful stereotypes of **white ethnics**—immigrants from Europe whose language and other customs differed from theirs. The English despised the Irish, viewing them as dirty, lazy drunkards, but they also painted Poles, Jews, Italians, and others with similar disparaging brushstrokes. From the little vignette, you can see that they didn't like Germans either.

The political and cultural dominance of the WASPs placed intense pressure on immigrants to assimilate into the mainstream culture. The children of most immigrants embraced the new way of life and quickly came to think of themselves as Americans rather than as Germans, French, Hungarians, and so on. They dropped their distinctive customs, especially their language, often viewing them as symbols of shame. This second generation of immigrants was sandwiched between two worlds: "the old country" of their parents and their new home. Their children, the third generation, had an easier adjustment, for they had fewer customs to discard. As white ethnics assimilated into this Anglo-American culture, the meaning of WASP expanded to include them.

At the founding of the United States, what was the relationship of WASPs and white ethnics?

As immigrants assimilate into a new culture, they learn and adapt new customs. These Muslim girls at an elementary school in Dearborn, Michigan, are in the process of assimilating into U.S. culture.

And for those who weren't white? Perhaps the event that best illustrates the racial view of the nation's founders occurred when Congress passed the Naturalization Act of 1790, declaring that only white immigrants could apply for citizenship. Relationships between the various racial–ethnic groups since the founding of the nation has, at best, been a rocky one.

In Sum: Because Protestant English immigrants settled the colonies, they established the culture—from the dominant language to the dominant religion. Highly ethnocentric, they regarded as inferior the customs of other groups. Because white Europeans took power, they determined the national agenda to which other ethnic groups had to react and conform. Their institutional and cultural dominance still sets the stage for current ethnic relations.

Latinos (Hispanics)

A Note on Terms. Before reviewing major characteristics of Latinos, it is important to stress that *Latino* and *Hispanic* refer not to a race but to ethnic groups. Latinos may identify themselves as black, white, or Native American. Some Latinos who have an African heritage refer to themselves as Afro-Latinos (Navarro 2003).

Numbers, Origins, and Locations. When birds still nested in the trees that would be used to build the *Mayflower*, Latinos had already established settlements in Florida and New Mexico (Bretos 1994). (As the folks in St. Augustine, Florida, like to say, "When Plymouth Colony was founded, St. Augustine was undergoing urban renewal.")

Today, Latinos are the largest minority group in the United States. As shown in Figure 9.7, about 32 million people trace their origin to Mexico, 4 million to Puerto Rico, almost 2 million to Cuba, and about 8 million to Central and South America.

Although Latinos are officially tallied at 47 million, another 9 million Latinos are living here illegally. About 7 million are from Mexico, and the rest from Central and South America (*Statistical Abstract* 2012:Table 45). Most Latinos are citizens or legal residents, but before our economic crisis each year about 700,000 Latinos were arrested, most as they crossed the border (*Statistical Abstract* 2012:Table 531). With this vast migration, about 20 million more Latinos live in the United States than Canadians (34 million) live in Canada. As Figure 9.8 shows, two-thirds live in just four states: California, Texas, Florida, and New York.

Our economic crisis, accompanied by sanctions against employers for hiring undocumented workers, has turned the river of migration into a trickle. Now about the same number of people are returning home to Mexico as are coming here to find work (Jordan 2012). The unauthorized entry into the United States aroused pubic concern. One response was the plan to construct a wall along the 2,000-mile border between Mexico and the United States. After building just 53 miles of the wall at the horrendous cost of $1 billion, the wall was cancelled (Preston 2011). Civilian groups such as the Minutemen also patrol the border, but unofficially. To avoid conflict with the U.S. Border Patrol, the Minutemen do not carry guns. A second unofficial group, the Techno Patriots, patrols the border as well, using computers and thermal imaging cameras. When they confirm illegal crossings, they call the Border Patrol, whose agents make the arrests (Archibold and Preston 2008; Marino 2008).

FIGURE 9.7 — Geographical Origins of U.S. Latinos

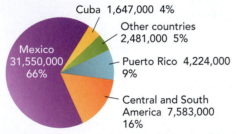

Cuba 1,647,000 4%
Other countries 2,481,000 5%
Mexico 31,550,000 66%
Puerto Rico 4,224,000 9%
Central and South America 7,583,000 16%

Source: By the author. Based on *Statistical Abstract of the United States* 2011:Table 37.

FIGURE 9.8 — Where U.S. Latinos Live

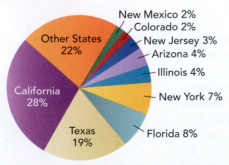

New Mexico 2%
Colorado 2%
New Jersey 3%
Arizona 4%
Illinois 4%
Other States 22%
New York 7%
California 28%
Florida 8%
Texas 19%

Source: By the author. Based on *Statistical Abstract of the United States* 2011:Table 19.

How extensive is illegal immigration? What are some reactions to it?

Cultural Diversity in the United States

The Illegal Travel Guide

Manuel was a drinking buddy of Jose, a man I had met in Colima, Mexico. At 45, Manuel was friendly, outgoing, and enterprising.

Manuel, who had lived in the United States for seven years, spoke fluent English. Preferring to live in his hometown in Colima, where he palled around with his childhood friends, Manuel always seemed to have money and free time.

When Manuel invited me to go on a business trip with him, I accepted. I never could figure out what he did for a living or how he could afford a car, a luxury that none of his friends had. As we traveled from one remote village to another, Manuel would sell used clothing that he had heaped in the back of his older-model Ford station wagon.

At one stop, Manuel took me into a dirt-floored, thatched-roof hut. While chickens ran in and out, Manuel whispered to a slender man who was about 23 years old. The poverty was overwhelming. Juan, as his name turned out to be, had a partial grade school education. He also had a wife, four hungry children under the age of 5, and two pigs—his main food supply. Although eager to work, Juan had no job, for there was simply no work available in this remote village.

As we were drinking a Coke, which seems to be the national beverage of Mexico's poor, Manuel explained to me that he was not only selling clothing—he was also lining up migrants to the United States. For a fee, he would take a man to the border and introduce him to a "wolf," who would help him cross into the promised land.

When I saw the hope in Juan's face, I knew nothing would stop him. He was borrowing every cent he could from every friend and relative to scrape the money together. Although he risked losing everything if apprehended and he would be facing unknown risks, Juan would make the trip, for wealth beckoned on the other side. He knew people who had been to the United States and spoke glowingly of its opportunities. Manuel, of course, the salesman he was, stoked the fires of hope.

Looking up from the children playing on the dirt floor with chickens pecking about them, I saw a man who loved his family. In order to make the desperate bid for a better life, he would suffer an enforced absence, as well as the uncertainties of a foreign culture whose language he did not know.

Juan opened his billfold, took something out, and slowly handed it to me. I looked at it curiously. I felt tears as I saw the tenderness with which he handled this piece of paper. It was his passport to the land of opportunity: a Social Security card made out in his name, sent by a friend who had already made the trip and who was waiting for Juan on the other side of the border.

It was then that I realized that the thousands of Manuels scurrying about Mexico and the millions of Juans they are transporting can never be stopped, for only the United States can fulfill their dreams of a better life.

A "coyote" leads two people across the Rio Grande into Texas.

For Your Consideration

➤ The vast stream of immigrants illegally crossing the Mexican–U.S. border has become a national issue. What do you think is the best way to deal with this issue? Why?

How does your social location affect your view?

Despite walls and patrols, as long as there is a need for unskilled labor and millions of Mexicans live in poverty, undocumented workers will continue to come to the United States. To gain insight into why, see the Cultural Diversity box on the next page.

Spanish Language.   The Spanish language distinguishes most Latinos from other U.S. ethnic groups. With 35 million people speaking Spanish at home, the United States has become one of the largest Spanish-speaking nations in the world (*Statistical Abstract* 2012:Table 53).

Because about half of Latinos are unable to speak English, or can do so only with difficulty, many millions face a major obstacle to getting good jobs.

The growing use of Spanish has stoked controversy (Fund 2007). Perceiving the prevalence of Spanish as a threat, Senator S. I. Hayakawa of California initiated an "English-only" movement in 1981. The constitutional amendment that he sponsored never got off the ground, but thirty states have passed laws that declare English their official language.

Diversity.   For Latinos, country of origin is highly significant. Those from Puerto Rico, for example, feel that they have little in common with people from Mexico, Venezuela, or El Salvador—just as earlier immigrants from Germany, Sweden, and England felt they had little in common with one another. A sign of these divisions is that many refer to themselves in terms of their country of origin, such as *puertorrique-ños* or *cubanos,* rather than as Latino or Hispanic.

As with other ethnic groups, Latinos are separated by social class. The half-million Cubans who fled Castro's rise to power in 1959, for example, were mostly well-educated, well-to-do professionals or businesspeople. In contrast, the "boat people" who fled later were mostly lower-class refugees, people with whom the earlier arrivals would not have associated in Cuba. The earlier arrivals, who are firmly established in Florida and who control many businesses and financial institutions, distance themselves from the more recent immigrants.

With 15.4 percent of the U.S. population, the potential political power of Latinos is remarkable. Several Latinos have been elected governors, and in 2010 Susana Martinez became the first Latina to govern a state (New Mexico). In the Senate, we might expect fifteen U.S. senators to be Latino. But there are only *four*. In addition, Latinos hold only 5 percent of the seats in the U.S. House of Representatives (*Statistical Abstract* 2012:Table 413).

As Latinos have become more visible in U.S. society and more vocal in their demands for equality, they have come face to face with African Americans who fear that Latino gains in employment and at the ballot box come at their expense (Hutchinson 2008). This rivalry even shows up in prison, where hostility between Latino and African American gangs sometimes escalates into violence (Thompson 2009). (To better understand why, review the experiment with boys at a summer camp on page 251.) If Latinos and African Americans were to work together—since combined they make up more than one-fourth of the U.S. population—their unity would produce an unstoppable political force.

Comparative Conditions.   To see how Latinos are doing on major indicators of well-being, look at Table 9.2 on the next page. As you can see, compared with white Americans and Asian Americans, Latinos have less income, higher unemployment, and more poverty. They are also less likely to own their homes. We get another view if we focus on education. In Table 9.3 on the next page, you can see that Latinos are the most likely to drop out of high school and the least likely to graduate from college. In a postindustrial society that increasingly requires advanced skills, these totals indicate that huge numbers of Latinos will be left behind.

The umbrella term of *Latino* (or *Hispanic*) conceals as much as it reveals. To understand comparative conditions, we need to also look at people's country of origin, which remains highly significant not only for self-identity but also for determining life chances. As you can see from Table 9.2, Latinos who trace their roots to Cuba have less poverty and are more likely to own their homes. In contrast, those who trace their origin to Puerto Rico score lower on these indicators of well-being.

For millions of people, the United States represents a land of opportunity and freedom from oppression. Shown here are Cubans who reached the United States by transforming their 1950s truck into a boat.

How do Latinos rank on major indicators of well-being?

| TABLE 9.2 | Race–Ethnicity and Comparative Well-Being | | | | | | | |

Racial–Ethnic Group	Income		Unemployment		Poverty		Home Ownership	
	Median Family Income	Compared to Whites	Percentage Unemployed	Compared to Whites	Percentage Below Poverty Line	Compared to Whites	Percentage Who Own Their Homes	Compared to Whites
Whites	$70,835	—	7.3%	—	9.3%	—	73%	—
Latinos	$43,437	39% lower	10.5%	31% higher	21.3%	129% higher	49%	33% lower
Cuba	NA[1]	NA	5.0%	32% higher	16.8%	81% higher	58%	21% lower
Central/South America	NA	NA	NA	NA	18.9%	103% higher	40%	45% lower
Mexico	NA	NA	8.4%	14% higher	24.8%	166% higher	49%	33% lower
Puerto Rico	NA	NA	8.6%	16% higher	25.2%	171% higher	38%	48% lower
African Americans	$41,874	41% lower	12.3%	41% higher	24.1%	159% higher	46%	37% lower
Asian Americans[2]	$80,101	13% higher	6.6%	10% lower	10.5%	13% higher	60%	14% lower
Native Americans	$43,190	39% lower	NA	NA	24.2%	160% higher	55%	25% lower

[1]Not Available
[2]Includes Pacific Islanders

Source: By the author. Based on *Statistical Abstract of the United States* 2011:Tables 36, 37, 626.

| TABLE 9.3 | Race–Ethnicity and Education | | | | | | |

Racial–Ethnic Group	Education Completed				Doctorates		
	Less Than High School	High School	Some College	College (BA or Higher)	Number Awarded	Percentage of all U.S. Doctorates[1]	Percentage of U.S. Population
Whites	9.9%	29.3%	30.0%	19.3%	26,908	57.1	65.6
Latinos	39.2%	25.9%	21.8%	8.9%	2,267	3.6	15.4
African Americans	19.3%	31.4%	31.7%	11.5%	2,604	6.1	12.8
Asian Americans	14.9%	16.0%	19.5%	29.8%	2,734	5.7	4.5
Native Americans	24.3%	30.3%	32.5%	8.7%	127	0.4	1.0

[1]Percentage after the doctorates awarded to nonresidents are deducted from the total.

Source: By the author. Based on *Statistical Abstract of the United States* 2011:Tables 36, 37, 296, and Figure 9.5 of this text.

African Americans

It was 1955, in Montgomery, Alabama. As specified by law, whites took the front seats of the bus, and blacks went to the back. As the bus filled up, blacks had to give up their seats to whites.

When Rosa Parks, a 42-year-old African American woman and secretary of the Montgomery NAACP, was told that she would have to stand so that white folks could sit, she refused (Bray 1995). She stubbornly sat there while the bus driver raged and whites felt insulted. Her arrest touched off mass demonstrations, led 50,000 blacks to boycott the city's buses for a year, and thrust an otherwise unknown preacher into a historic role.

Reverend Martin Luther King, Jr., who had majored in sociology at Morehouse College in Atlanta, Georgia, took control. He organized car pools and preached nonviolence. Incensed at this radical organizer and at the stirrings in the normally compliant black community, segregationists also put their beliefs into practice—by bombing the homes of blacks and dynamiting their churches.

How do the racial-ethnic groups compare on indicators of well-being, including education?

Explore
Living Data
on **mysoclab.com**

After slavery was abolished, the Southern states passed legislation (*Jim Crow* laws) to segregate blacks and whites. In 1896, the U.S. Supreme Court ruled in *Plessy v. Ferguson* that it was a reasonable use of state power to require "separate but equal" accommodations for blacks. Whites used this ruling to strip blacks of the political power they had gained after the Civil War. Declaring political primaries to be "white," they prohibited blacks from voting in them. Not until 1944 did the Supreme Court rule that political primaries weren't "white" and were open to all voters. White politicians then passed laws that only people who could read could vote—and they determined that most African Americans were illiterate. Not until 1954 did African Americans gain the legal right to attend the same public schools as whites, and, as recounted in the vignette on page 261, even later to sit where they wanted on a bus.

Rising Expectations and Civil Strife.   The barriers came down, but they came down slowly. In 1964, Congress passed the Civil Rights Act, making it illegal to discriminate on the basis of race. African Americans were finally allowed in "white" restaurants, hotels, theaters, and other public places. Then in 1965, Congress passed the Voting Rights Act, banning the fraudulent literacy tests that the Southern states had used to keep African Americans from voting.

African Americans then experienced what sociologists call **rising expectations.** They expected that these sweeping legal changes would usher in better conditions in life. In contrast, the lives of the poor among them changed little, if at all. Frustrations built up, exploding in Watts in 1965, when people living in that ghetto of central Los Angeles

Until the 1960s, the South's public facilities were segregated. Some were reserved for whites, others for blacks. This *apartheid* was broken by blacks and whites who worked together and risked their lives to bring about a fairer society. Shown here is a 1963 sit-in at a Woolworth's lunch counter in Jackson, Mississippi. Sugar, ketchup, and mustard are being poured over the heads of the demonstrators.

What is the relationship of rising expectations and civil strife?

took to the streets in the first of what were termed the *urban revolts*. When a white supremacist assassinated King on April 4, 1968, inner cities across the nation erupted in fiery violence. Under threat of the destruction of U.S. cities, Congress passed the sweeping Civil Rights Act of 1968.

Continued Gains.   Since then, African Americans have made remarkable gains in politics, education, and jobs. At 9 percent, the number of African Americans in the U.S. House of Representatives is *two to three times* what it was a generation ago (*Statistical Abstract* 1989:Table 423; 2012:Table 413). As college enrollments increased, the middle class expanded, and today 40 percent of all African American families make more than $50,000 a year. One in four earns more than $75,000, and one in eight over $100,000 (*Statistical Abstract* 2012:Table 696).

African Americans have become prominent in politics. Jesse Jackson (another sociology major) competed for the Democratic presidential nomination in 1984 and 1988. In 1989, L. Douglas Wilder was elected governor of Virginia, and in 2006 Deval Patrick became governor of Massachusetts. These accomplishments, of course, pale in comparison to the election of Barack Obama as president of the United States in 2008.

In 2009, Barack Obama was sworn in as the 44th president of the United States. He is the first minority to achieve this political office.

Current Losses.   Despite these remarkable gains, African Americans continue to lag behind in politics, economics, and education. Only *one* U.S. senator is African American, many fewer than the twelve or thirteen we would expect based on the percentage of African Americans in the U.S. population. As Tables 9.2 and 9.3 on page 261 show, African Americans average only 59 percent of white income, experience much more unemployment and poverty, and are less likely to own their homes or to have college educations. That two of five of African American families have incomes over $50,000 is only part of the story. Table 9.4 shows the other part—that one of every five or six African American families makes less than $15,000 a year.

The upward mobility of millions of African Americans into the middle class has created two worlds of African American experience—one educated and affluent, the other uneducated and poor. Concentrated among the poor are those with the least hope, the most despair, and the violence that so often dominates the evening news. Although homicide rates have dropped to their lowest point in thirty-five years, African Americans are *six* times more likely to be murdered than whites (*Statistical Abstract* 2012:Table 312).

Race or Social Class? A Sociological Debate.   This division of African Americans into "haves" and "have-nots" has fueled a sociological controversy (Landry and Marsh 2011). Sociologist William Julius Wilson (1978, 2000, 2007) argues that social class has become more important than race in determining the life chances of African Americans. Before civil rights legislation, he says, the African American experience was dominated by race. Throughout the United States, African Americans were excluded from avenues of

TABLE 9.4	Race–Ethnicity and Income Extremes	
	Less than $15,000	Over $100,000
Asian Americans	6.9%	37.7%
Whites	7.2%	27.0%
African Americans	17.9%	12.1%
Latinos	15.3%	12.4%

Note: These are family incomes. Only these groups are listed in the source.

Source: By the author: Based on *Statistical Abstract of the United States* 2012:Table 695.

What are current gains and losses of African Americans? What is the debate on race or social class?

Sociologists disagree about the relative significance of race and social class in determining social and economic conditions of African Americans. William Julius Wilson, shown here, is an avid proponent of the social class side of this debate.

economic advancement: good schools and good jobs. When civil rights laws opened new opportunities, African Americans seized them. Just as legislation began to open doors to African Americans, however, manufacturing jobs dried up, and many blue-collar jobs were moved to the suburbs. As better-educated African Americans obtained white-collar jobs, they moved out of the inner city. Left behind were those with poor education and few skills.

Wilson stresses how significant these two worlds of African American experience are. The group that is stuck in the inner city lives in poverty, attends poor schools, and faces dead-end jobs or welfare. This group is filled with hopelessness and despair, combined with apathy or hostility. In contrast, those who have moved up the social class ladder live in comfortable homes in secure neighborhoods. Their jobs provide decent incomes, and they send their children to good schools. With middle-class experiences shaping their views on life, their aspirations and values have little in common with those of African Americans who remain poor. According to Wilson, then, social class—not race—is the more significant factor in the lives of African Americans.

Some sociologists reply that this analysis overlooks the discrimination that continues to underlie the African American experience. They note that African Americans who do the same work as whites average less pay (Willie 1991; Herring 2002) and even receive fewer tips (Lynn et al. 2008). This, they argue, points to racial discrimination, not to social class.

What is the answer to this debate? Wilson would reply that it is not an either-or question. My book is titled *The **Declining** Significance of Race,* he would say, not *The **Absence** of Race.* Certainly racism is still alive, he would add, but today social class is more central to the African American experience than is racial discrimination. He stresses that we need to provide jobs for the poor in the inner city—for work provides an anchor to a responsible life (Wilson 1996, 2007).

Racism as an Everyday Burden.

Researchers sent out 5,000 résumés in response to help wanted ads in the Boston and Chicago Sunday papers. The résumés were identical, except some applicants had white-sounding names, such as Emily and Brandon, while others had black-sounding names, such as Lakisha and Jamal. Although the qualifications of these supposed job applicants were identical, the white-sounding names elicited 50 percent more callbacks than the black-sounding names (Bertrand and Mullainathan 2002).

Certainly racism continues as a regular feature of society, often something that whites, not subjected to it, are only vaguely aware of. But for those on the receiving end, racism can be an everyday burden. Here is how an African American professor describes his experiences:

[One problem with] being black in America is that you have to spend so much time thinking about stuff that most white people just don't even have to think about. I worry when I get pulled over by a cop. . . . I worry what some white cop is going to think when he walks over to our car, because he's holding on to a gun. And I'm very aware of how many black folks accidentally get shot by cops. I worry when I walk into a store, that someone's going to think I'm in there shoplifting. . . . And I get resentful that I have to think about things that a lot of people, even my very close white friends whose politics are similar to mine, simply don't have to worry about. (Feagin 1999:398)

Asian Americans

I have stressed in this chapter that our racial–ethnic categories are based more on social factors than on biological ones. This point is again obvious when we examine the category *Asian American.* As Figure 9.9 shows, those who are called Asian Americans came to the United States from many nations. *With no unifying culture or "race," why should people from so many backgrounds be clustered together and assigned a single label?* Think about it. What culture or race–ethnicity do Samoans and Vietnamese have in common? Or Laotians and Pakistanis? Or people from Guam and those from China? Those from Japan and those from India? Yet all these groups—and more—are lumped together and called Asian Americans. Apparently, the U.S. government is not satisfied until it is able to pigeonhole everyone into some racial–ethnic category.

Since *Asian American* is a standard term, however, let's look at the characteristics of the 14 million people who are lumped together and assigned this label.

A Background of Discrimination.

> *Lured by gold strikes in the West and an urgent need for unskilled workers to build the railroads, 200,000 Chinese immigrated between 1850 and 1880. When the famous golden spike was driven at Promontory, Utah, in 1869 to mark the completion of the railroad to the West Coast, white workers prevented Chinese workers from being in the photo—even though Chinese made up 90 percent of Central Pacific Railroad's labor force (Hsu 1971).*

After the railroad was complete, the Chinese competed with whites for other jobs. Anglos then formed vigilante groups to intimidate them. They also used the law. California's 1850 Foreign Miners Act required Chinese (and Latinos) to pay $20 a month in order to work—when wages were a dollar a day. The California Supreme Court ruled that Chinese could not testify against whites (Carlson and Colburn 1972). In 1882, Congress passed the Chinese Exclusion Act, suspending all Chinese immigration for ten years. Four years later, the Statue of Liberty was dedicated. The tired, the poor, and the huddled masses it was intended to welcome were obviously not Chinese.

When immigrants from Japan arrived, they encountered *spillover bigotry,* a stereotype that lumped Asians together, depicting them as sneaky, lazy, and untrustworthy. After Japan attacked Pearl Harbor in 1941, conditions grew worse for the 110,000 Japanese Americans who called the United States their home. U.S. authorities feared that Japan would invade the United States and that the Japanese Americans would fight on Japan's side. They also feared that Japanese Americans would sabotage military installations on the West Coast. Although no Japanese American had been involved in even a single act of sabotage, on February 19, 1942, President Franklin D. Roosevelt ordered that everyone who was *one-eighth Japanese or more* be confined in detention centers (called "internment camps"). These people were charged with no crime, and they had no trials. Japanese ancestry was sufficient cause for being imprisoned.

Diversity.

As you can see from Tables 9.2 and 9.4 on pages 261 and 263, the income of Asian Americans has outstripped that of all groups, including whites. This has led to the stereotype that all Asian Americans are successful. Are they? Their poverty rate is actually higher than that of whites, as you can also see from Table 9.2. As with Latinos, country of origin is significant: Poverty is unusual among Chinese and Japanese Americans, but it clusters among Americans from Southeast Asia. Altogether, between 1 and 2 million Asian Americans live in poverty.

Reasons for Success.

The high average incomes of Asian Americans can be traced to three major factors: family life, educational achievement, and assimilation into mainstream culture. Of all ethnic groups,

---

FIGURE 9.9   Countries of Origin of Asian Americans

Source: By the author. Based on U.S. Census Bureau 2010.

Of the racial–ethnic groups in the United States, Asian Americans have the highest rate of intermarriage.

including whites, Asian American children are the most likely to grow up with two parents and the least likely to be born to either a teenaged or single mother (*Statistical Abstract* 2012:Tables 69, 86). Common in these families is a stress on self-discipline, thrift, and hard work (Suzuki 1985; Bell 1991). This early socialization provides strong impetus for the other two factors.

The second factor is their unprecedented rate of college graduation. As Table 9.3 on page 261 shows, 50 percent of Asian Americans complete college. To realize how stunning this is, compare their rate with those of the other groups shown on this table. Educational achievement, in turn, opens doors to economic success.

The most striking indication of the third factor, assimilation, is a high rate of intermarriage. Of Asian Americans who graduate from college, about 40 percent of the men and 60 percent of the women marry a non–Asian American (Qian and Lichter 2007). The intermarriage of Japanese Americans is so extensive that two of every three of their children have one parent who is not of Japanese descent (Schaefer 2012). The Chinese are close behind (Alba and Nee 2003).

Asian Americans are becoming more prominent in politics. With more than half of its citizens being Asian American, Hawaii has elected Asian American governors and sent several Asian American senators to Washington, including the two now serving there (Lee 1998; *Statistical Abstract* 2012:Table 413). The first Asian American governor outside of Hawaii was Gary Locke, who served from 1997 to 2005 as governor of Washington, a state in which Asian Americans make up less than 6 percent of the population. In 2008 in Louisiana, Piyush Jindal became the first Indian American governor.

Native Americans

"I don't go so far as to think that the only good Indians are dead Indians, but I believe nine out of ten are—and I shouldn't inquire too closely in the case of the tenth. The most vicious cowboy has more moral principle than the average Indian."

—Teddy Roosevelt, 1886
(President of the United States 1901–1909)

Diversity of Groups.   This quote from Teddy Roosevelt provides insight into the rampant racism of earlier generations. Yet, even today, thanks to countless grade B Westerns, some Americans view the original inhabitants of what became the United States as uncivilized savages, a single group of people subdivided into separate tribes.

The European immigrants to the colonies, however, encountered diverse groups of people who spoke over 700 languages. Their variety of cultures ranged from nomadic hunters and gatherers to farmers who lived in wooden houses (Schaefer 2004). Each group had its own norms and values—and the usual ethnocentric pride in its own culture.

Native Americans, who numbered about 10 million, had no immunity to the diseases the Europeans brought with them. With deaths due to disease—and warfare, a much lesser cause—their population plummeted. The low point came in 1890, when the census reported only 250,000 Native Americans. If the census and the estimate of the original population are accurate, Native Americans had been reduced to about *one-fortieth* their original size. The population has never recovered, but Native Americans now number

This depiction breaks stereotypes, but is historically accurate. Shown here is an Iroquois fort. Can you guess who the attackers are?

about 3 million (see Figure 9.5 on p. 256). Native Americans, who today speak 150 different languages, do not think of themselves as a single people who fit neatly within a single label (McLemore 1994).

From Treaties to Genocide and Population Transfer.

At first, the Native Americans tried to accommodate the strangers, since there was plenty of land for both the few newcomers and themselves. Soon, however, the settlers began to raid Indian villages and pillage their food supplies (Horn 2006). As wave after wave of settlers arrived, Pontiac, an Ottawa chief, saw the future—and didn't like it. He convinced several tribes to unite in an effort to push the Europeans into the sea. He almost succeeded, but failed when the English were reinforced by fresh troops (McLemore 1994).

A pattern of deception evolved. The U.S. government would make treaties to buy some of a tribe's land, with the promise to honor forever the tribe's right to what it had not sold. European immigrants, who continued to pour into the United States, would then disregard these boundaries. The tribes would resist, with death tolls on both sides. The U.S. government would then intervene—not to enforce the treaty it had made, but to force the tribe off its lands. In its relentless drive westward, the U.S. government embarked on a policy of genocide. It assigned the U.S. cavalry the task of "pacification," which translated into slaughtering Native Americans who "stood in the way" of this territorial expansion.

The acts of cruelty perpetrated by the Europeans against Native Americans appear endless, but two are especially notable. The first is the Trail of Tears. The U.S. government adopted a policy of population transfer (see Figure 9.3 on p. 254), which it called *Indian Removal*. The goal was to confine Native Americans to specified areas called *reservations*. In the winter of 1838–1839, the U.S. Army rounded up 15,000 Cherokees and forced them to walk a thousand miles from the Carolinas and Georgia to Oklahoma. Conditions were so brutal that about 4,000 of those who were forced to make this midwinter march died along the way. The second, the symbolic end of Native American resistance to the European expansion, took place in 1890 at Wounded Knee, South Dakota. There, the U.S. cavalry gunned down 300 men, women, and children of the Dakota Sioux tribe. After the massacre, the soldiers threw the bodies into a mass grave (Thornton 1987; Lind 1995; DiSilvestro 2006).

The Invisible Minority and Self-Determination.

Native Americans can truly be called the invisible minority. Because about half live in rural areas and one-third in just three states—Oklahoma, California, and Arizona—most other Americans are hardly aware of a Native American presence in the United States. The isolation of about half of Native Americans on reservations further reduces their visibility (Schaefer 2012).

The systematic attempts of European Americans to destroy the Native Americans' way of life and their forced resettlement onto reservations continue to have deleterious effects. The rate of suicide among Native Americans is high, and their life expectancy is lower than that of the nation as a whole (Murray et al. 2006; Crosby et al. 2011). Table 9.3 on page 261 shows that their educational attainment also lags behind most groups: Only 13 percent graduate from college.

Native Americans are experiencing major changes. In the 1800s, U.S. courts ruled that Native Americans did not own the land on which they had been settled and had no right to develop its resources. They made Native Americans wards of the state, and the Bureau of Indian Affairs treated them like children (Mohawk 1991; Schaefer 2012). Then, in the 1960s, Native Americans won a series of legal victories that gave them control over reservation lands. With this legal change, many Native American tribes have opened businesses—ranging from fish canneries to industrial parks that serve metropolitan areas. The Skywalk, opened by the Hualapai, which offers breathtaking views of the Grand Canyon, gives an idea of the varieties of businesses to come (Lacey 2011).

Read
Race Specific Policies and the Truly Disadvantaged by William Julius Wilson on **mysoclab.com**

What major issues do Native Americans face?

It is the casinos, though, that have attracted the most attention. In 1988, the federal government passed a law that allowed Native Americans to operate gambling establishments on reservations. Now over 200 tribes have casinos. *They bring in $26 billion a year, more than all the casinos in Las Vegas* (Pratt 2011; *Statistical Abstract* 2012:Table 1258). The Oneida tribe of New York, which has only 1,000 members, runs a casino that nets $232,000 a year for each man, woman, and child (Peterson 2003). This huge amount, however, pales in comparison with that of the Mashantucket Pequot tribe of Connecticut. With only 700 members, the tribe brings in more than $2 million a day just from slot machines (Rivlin 2007). Incredibly, one tribe has only *one* member: She has her own casino (Bartlett and Steele 2002).

One of the most significant changes for Native Americans is **pan-Indianism.** This emphasis on common elements that run through their cultures is an attempt to develop an identity that goes beyond the tribe. Pan-Indianism ("We are all Indians") is a remarkable example of the plasticity of ethnicity. It embraces and substitutes for individual tribal identities the label "Indian"—originally imposed by Spanish and Italian sailors who thought they had reached the shores of India. As sociologist Irwin Deutscher (2002:61) put it, "The peoples who have accepted the larger definition of who they are, have, in fact, little else in common with each other than the stereotypes of the dominant group which labels them."

Looking Toward the Future

Back in 1903, sociologist W. E. B. Du Bois said, "The problem of the twentieth century is the problem of the color line—the relation of the darker to the lighter races." Incredibly, over a hundred years later, the color line remains one of the most volatile topics facing the United States. From time to time, the color line takes on a different complexion, as with the war on terrorism and the corresponding discrimination directed against people of Middle Eastern descent.

In another hundred years, will yet another sociologist lament that the color of people's skin still affects human relationships? Given our past, it seems that although racial–ethnic walls will diminish, some even crumbling, the color line is not likely to disappear. Let's close this chapter by looking at two issues we are currently grappling with, immigration and affirmative action.

The Immigration Debate

Throughout its history, the United States has both welcomed immigration and feared its consequences. The gates opened wide (numerically, if not in attitude) for waves of immigrants in the 1800s and early 1900s. During the past twenty years, a new wave of immigration has brought close to a million new residents to the United States each year. Today, more immigrants (38 million) live in the United States than at any other time in the country's history (*Statistical Abstract* 2007:Table 5; 2012:Table 40).

In contrast to earlier waves, in which immigrants came almost exclusively from western Europe, the current wave of immigrants is so diverse that it is changing the U.S. racial–ethnic mix. If current trends in immigration (and birth) persist, in about fifty years the "average" American will trace his or her ancestry to Africa, Asia, South America, the Pacific Islands, the Middle East—almost anywhere but white Europe. This change is discussed in the Cultural Diversity box on the next page.

Cultural Diversity in the United States

Glimpsing the Future: The Shifting U.S. Racial–Ethnic Mix

During the next twenty-five years, the population of the United States is expected to grow by about 22 percent. To see what the U.S. population will look like at that time, can we simply add 22 percent to our current racial–ethnic mix? The answer is a resounding no. As you can see from Figure 9.10, some groups will grow much more than others, giving us a different-looking United States. Some of the changes in the U.S. racial–ethnic mix will be dramatic. In twenty-five years, one of every nineteen Americans is expected to have an Asian background, and in the most dramatic change, almost one of four is expected to be of Latino ancestry.

The basic causes of this fundamental shift are the racial–ethnic groups' different rates of immigration and birth. Both will change the groups' proportions of the U.S. population, but immigration is by far the more important. From Figure 9.10, you can see that the proportion of non-Hispanic whites is expected to shrink, that of Native Americans and African Americans to remain about the same, and that of Latinos to increase sharply.

For Your Consideration

→ This shifting racial–ethnic mix is one of the most significant events occurring in the United States. To better understand its implications, apply the three theoretical perspectives.

Use the *conflict perspective* to identify the groups that are likely to be threatened by this change. Over what resources are struggles likely to develop? What impact do you think this changing mix might have on European Americans? On Latinos? On African Americans? On Asian Americans? On Native Americans? What changes in immigration laws (or their enforcement) can you anticipate?

To apply the *symbolic interactionist perspective*, consider how groups might perceive one another differently as their proportions of the population change. How do you think that these changed perceptions will affect people's behavior?

To apply the *functionalist perspective*, try to determine how each racial–ethnic group will benefit from this changing mix. How will other parts of society (such as businesses) benefit? What functions and dysfunctions can you anticipate for politics, economics, education, or religion?

FIGURE 9.10   Projections of the Racial–Ethnic Makeup of the U.S. Population

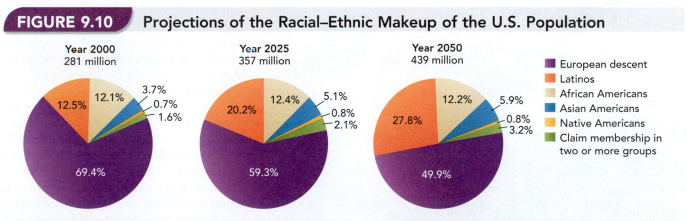

Source: By the author. Based on U.S. Census Bureau 2009; *Statistical Abstract of the United States* 2012:Table 12. I modified the projections based on the new census category of membership in two or more groups and trends in interethnic marriage.

In some states, the future is arriving much sooner than this. In California, racial–ethnic minorities have become the majority. California has 21 million minorities and 15 million whites (*Statistical Abstract* 2012:Table 18). Californians who request new telephone service from Pacific Bell can speak to customer service representatives in Spanish, Korean, Vietnamese, Mandarin, Cantonese—or English.

As in the past, there is concern that "too many" immigrants will change the character of the United States. "Throughout the history of U.S. immigration," write sociologists Alejandro Portés and Rubén Rumbaut (1990), "a consistent thread has been the fear that the 'alien element' would somehow undermine the institutions of the country and would lead it down the path of disintegration and decay." A hundred years ago, the widespread fear was that the immigrants from southern Europe would bring communism with them. Today, some fear that Spanish-speaking immigrants threaten the primacy of the English language. In addition, the age-old fear that immigrants will take jobs away from native-born Americans remains strong. Finally, minority groups that struggled for political representation fear that newer groups will gain political power at their expense.

Affirmative Action

Affirmative action in our multicultural society lies at the center of a national debate about racial–ethnic relations. In this policy, initiated by President Kennedy in 1961, goals based on race (and sex) are used in hiring, promotion, and college admission. Sociologist Barbara Reskin (1998) examined the results of affirmative action. She concluded that although it is difficult to separate the results of affirmative action from economic booms and busts and the greater numbers of women in the workforce, affirmative action has had a modest impact.

The results may have been modest, but the reactions to this program have been anything but modest. Affirmative action has been at the center of controversy for two generations. Liberals, both white and minority, say that this program is the most direct way to level the playing field of economic opportunity. If whites are passed over, this is an unfortunate cost that we must pay if we are to make up for past discrimination. In contrast, conservatives, both white and minority, agree that opportunity should be open to all, but claim that putting race (or sex) ahead of an individual's training and ability to perform a job is reverse discrimination. Because of their race (or sex), qualified people who had nothing to do with past inequality are discriminated against. They add that affirmative action stigmatizes the people who benefit from it, because it suggests that they hold their jobs because of race (or sex), rather than merit.

This national debate crystallized with a series of controversial rulings. One of the most significant was *Proposition 209,* a 1996 amendment to the California state constitution. This amendment made it illegal to give preference to minorities and women in hiring, promotion, and college admissions. Despite appeals by a coalition of civil rights groups, the U.S. Supreme Court upheld this California law.

A second significant ruling was made by the U.S. Supreme Court in 2003. White students who had been denied admission to the University of Michigan claimed that they had been discriminated against because less qualified applicants had been admitted on the basis of their race. The Court ruled that universities can give minorities an edge in admissions, but there must be a meaningful review

The United States is the most racially–ethnically diverse society in the world. This can be our central strength, with our many groups working together to build a harmonious society, a stellar example for the world. Or it can be our Achilles heel, with us breaking into feuding groups, a Balkanized society that marks an ill-fitting end to a grand social experiment. Our reality will probably fall somewhere between these extremes.

What is affirmative action? Why is it controversial?

of individual applicants. Mechanical systems, such as giving extra points because of race, are unconstitutional. This murky message, which satisfied no one, as no one knew what it really meant, is being challenged (Liptak 2010).

To remove ambiguity, opponents of affirmative action put amendments to several state constitutions on the ballot. The amendments, which make it illegal for public institutions to even consider race or sex in hiring, in awarding contracts, or in college admissions, failed in some states, such as Colorado, but became law in Michigan and Nebraska (Lewin 2007; Kaufman and Fields 2008).

With constitutional battles continuing and people feeling that they are being discriminated against (Norton and Sommers 2011), the issue of affirmative action in a multicultural society is likely to remain center stage for quite some time.

Toward a True Multicultural Society

The United States has the potential to become a society in which racial–ethnic groups not only coexist, but also respect one another—and thrive—as they work together for mutually beneficial goals. In a true multicultural society, the minority groups that make up the United States would participate fully in the nation's social institutions while maintaining their cultural integrity. Reaching this goal will require that we understand that "the biological differences that divide one race from another add up to a drop in the genetic ocean." For a long time, we have given racial categories an importance they never merited. Now we need to figure out how to reduce them to the irrelevance they deserve. In short, we need to make real the abstraction called equality that we profess to believe (Cose 2000).

By the Numbers: Changes Over Time

Percentage of Americans who claim membership in these groups:

European descent		
2000	NOW	2050
69%	65%	50%

Latino descent		
2000	NOW	2050
13%	15%	28%

African descent		
2000	NOW	2050
12%	13%	12%

Asian descent		
2000	NOW	2050
3.7%	4.5%	5.9%

Native American descent		
2000	NOW	2050
0.7%	1.0%	0.8%

What is needed to have a true multicultural society?

CHAPTER 9 Summary and Review

Laying the Sociological Foundation

How is race both a reality and a myth?

In the sense that different groups inherit distinctive physical traits, race is a reality. There is no agreement regarding what constitutes a particular race, however, or even how many races there are. In the sense of one race being superior to another and of there being pure races, race is a myth. The *idea* of race is powerful, shaping basic relationships among people. Pp. 240–242.

How do race and ethnicity differ?

Race refers to inherited biological characteristics; **ethnicity,** to cultural ones. Members of ethnic groups identify with one another on the basis of common ancestry and cultural heritage. Pp. 242–243.

What are minority and dominant groups?

Minority groups are people who are singled out for unequal treatment by members of the **dominant group,** the group with more power and privilege. Minorities originate with migration or the expansion of political boundaries. Pp. 243–244.

What heightens ethnic identity, and what is "ethnic work"?

A group's relative size, power, physical characteristics, and amount of discrimination heighten or reduce ethnic identity. **Ethnic work** is the process of constructing and maintaining an ethnic identity. For people without a firm ethnic identity, ethnic work is an attempt to recover one's ethnic heritage. For those with strong ties to their culture of origin, ethnic work involves enhancing group distinctions. Pp. 244–245.

Prejudice and Discrimination

Why are people prejudiced?

Prejudice is an attitude, and **discrimination** is an action. Like other attitudes, prejudice is learned in association with others. Prejudice is so extensive that people can show prejudice against groups that don't even exist. Minorities also internalize the dominant norms, and some show prejudice against their own group. Pp. 245–247.

How do individual and institutional discrimination differ?

Individual discrimination is the negative treatment of one person by another, while **institutional discrimination** is negative treatment that is built into social institutions. Institutional discrimination can occur without the awareness of either the perpetrator or the object of discrimination. Discrimination in health care is one example. Pp. 247–249.

Theories of Prejudice

How do psychologists explain prejudice?

Psychological theories of prejudice stress the **authoritarian personality** and frustration displaced toward **scapegoats.** Pp. 250–251.

How do sociologists explain prejudice?

Sociological theories focus on how different social environments increase or decrease prejudice. *Functionalists* stress the benefits and costs that come from discrimination. *Conflict theorists* look at how the groups in power exploit racial–ethnic divisions in order to control workers and maintain power. *Symbolic interactionists* stress how labels create **selective perception** and self-fulfilling prophecies. Pp. 251–253.

Global Patterns of Intergroup Relations

What are the major patterns of minority and dominant group relations?

Beginning with the least humane, they are **genocide, population transfer, internal colonialism, segregation, assimilation,** and **multiculturalism (pluralism).** Pp. 253–255.

Racial–Ethnic Relations in the United States

What are the major racial–ethnic groups in the United States?

From largest to smallest, the major groups are European Americans, Latinos, African Americans, Asian Americans, and Native Americans. Pp. 255–257.

What are some issues in racial–ethnic relations and characteristics of minority groups?

Latinos are divided by social class and country of origin. African Americans are increasingly divided into middle and lower classes, with two sharply contrasting worlds of experience. On many measures, Asian Americans are better off than white Americans, but their well-being varies with their country of origin. For Native Americans, the primary issues are poverty, nationhood, and settling treaty obligations. The overarching issue for minorities is overcoming discrimination. Pp. 257–268.

Looking Toward the Future

What main issues dominate U.S. racial–ethnic relations?

The main issues are immigration, affirmative action, and how to develop a true multicultural society. The answers affect our future. Pp. 268–271.

Thinking Critically about Chapter 9

1. How many races do your friends or family think there are? Do they think that one race is superior to the others? What do you think their reaction would be to the sociological position that racial categories are primarily social?

2. A hundred years ago, sociologist W. E. B. Du Bois said, "The problem of the twentieth century is the problem of the color line—the relation of the darker to the lighter races." Why do you think that the color line remains one of the most volatile topics facing the nation?

3. If you were appointed head of the U.S. Civil Service Commission, what policies would you propose to reduce racial–ethnic strife in the United States? Be ready to explain the sociological principles that might give your proposals a higher chance of success.

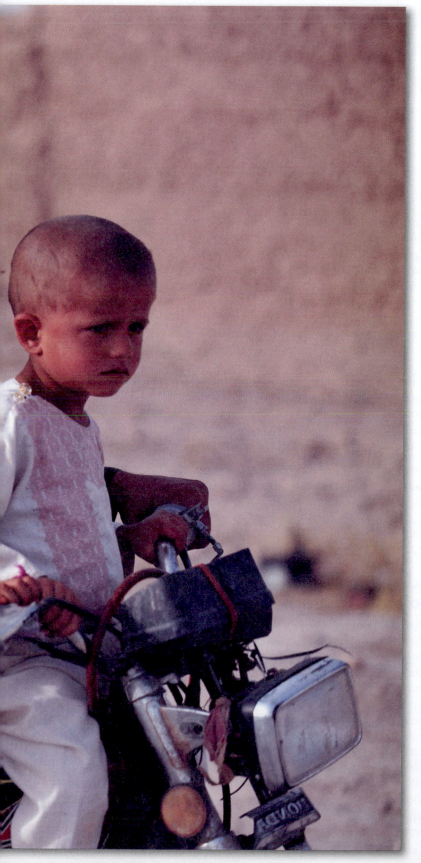

Afghanistan

In Tunis, the capital of Tunisia, on Africa's northern coast, I met some U.S. college students and spent a couple of days with them. They wanted to see the city's red light district, but I wondered whether it would be worth the trip. I already had seen other red light districts, including the unusual one in Amsterdam where a bronze statue of a female prostitute lets you know you've entered the area; the state licenses the women and men, requiring that they have medical checkups (certificates must be posted); and the prostitutes add sales tax to the receipts they give customers. The prostitutes sit behind lighted picture windows while customers stroll along the narrow canal side streets and do "window shopping" from the outside. Tucked among the brothels are day care centers, bakeries, and clothing stores. Amsterdam itself is an unusual place—in cafes, you can smoke marijuana but not tobacco.

I decided to go with them. We ended up on a wharf that extended into the Mediterranean. Each side was lined with a row of one-room wooden shacks, crowded one against the next. In front of each open door stood a young woman. Peering from outside into the dark interiors, I could see that each door led to a tiny room with an old, well-worn bed.

> The prostitutes sit behind lighted picture windows while customers stroll along the narrow canal side streets and do "window shopping" from the outside.

The wharf was crowded with men who were eyeing the women. Many of the men wore sailor uniforms from countries that I couldn't identify.

As I looked more closely, I could see that some of the women had runny sores on their legs. Incredibly, with such visible evidence of their disease, customers still sought them out.

With a sick feeling in my stomach and the desire to vomit, I kept a good distance between the beckoning women and myself. One tour of the two-block area was more than sufficient.

Somewhere nearby, out of sight, I knew that there were men whose wealth derived from exploiting these women who were condemned to live short lives punctuated by fear and misery.

In the previous chapter, we considered how race–ethnicity affects people's well-being and their position in society. In this chapter, we examine **gender stratification**—males' and females' unequal access to property, power, and prestige.

We also explore the prejudice and discrimination directed to people because of their age. Gender and age are especially significant because, like race–ethnicity, they are *master statuses;* that is, they cut across *all* aspects of social life. We all are labeled male or female and are assigned an age category. These labels are powerful, because they convey images and expectations about how we should act and serve as a basis of power and privilege.

Inequalities of Gender

Let's begin by considering the distinctions between sex and gender.

Issues of Sex and Gender

Read

Night to His Day: The Social Construction of Gender by Judith Lorber on **mysoclab.com**

When we consider how females and males differ, the first thing that usually comes to mind is **sex,** the *biological characteristics* that distinguish males and females. *Primary sex characteristics* consist of a vagina or a penis and other organs related to reproduction. *Secondary sex characteristics* are the physical distinctions between males and females that are not directly connected with reproduction. These characteristics become clearly evident at puberty when males develop larger muscles, lower voices, more body hair, and greater height, while females develop breasts and form more fatty tissue and broader hips.

Gender, in contrast, is a *social,* not a biological, characteristic. **Gender** consists of whatever behaviors and attitudes a group considers proper for its males and females. *Sex* refers to male or female, and *gender* refers to masculinity or femininity. In short, you inherit your sex, but you learn your gender as you learn the behaviors and attitudes your culture asserts are appropriate for your sex.

As the photo montage on the next page illustrates, the expectations associated with gender differ around the world. They vary so greatly that some sociologists suggest that we replace the terms *masculinity* and *femininity* with *masculinities* and *femininities.*

The Sociological Significance of Gender.   *The sociological significance of gender is that it is a device by which society controls its members.* Gender sorts us, on the basis of sex, into different life experiences. It opens and closes doors to property, power, and prestige. Like social class, gender is a structural feature of society.

Before examining inequalities of gender, let's consider why the behaviors of men and women differ.

Gender Differences in Behavior: Biology or Culture?

Why are most males more aggressive than most females? Why do women enter "nurturing" occupations, such as teaching young children and nursing, in far greater numbers than men? To answer such questions, many people respond with some variation of "They're just born that way."

Is this the correct answer? Certainly biology plays a significant role in our lives. Each of us begins as a fertilized egg. The egg, or ovum, is contributed by our mother, the sperm that fertilizes the egg by our father. At the very instant the egg is fertilized, our sex is determined. Each of us receives twenty-three chromosomes from the ovum and twenty-three from the sperm. The egg has an X chromosome. If the sperm that fertilizes the egg also has an X chromosome, the result is a girl (XX). If the sperm has a Y chromosome, the result is a boy (XY).

Differences in how we display gender often lie below our awareness. How males and females use social space is an example. In this unposed photo from Grand Central Station in New York City, you can see how males tend to sprawl out, females to enclose themselves. Why do you think this difference exists? Biology? Socialization? Both?

Standards of Gender

Each human group determines its ideas of "maleness" and "femaleness." As you can see from these photos of four women and four men, standards of gender are arbitrary and vary from one culture to another. Yet, in its ethnocentrism, each group thinks that its preferences reflect what gender "really" is. As indicated here, around the world men and women try to make themselves appealing by aspiring to their group's standards of gender.

Mexico

Jordan

Kenya

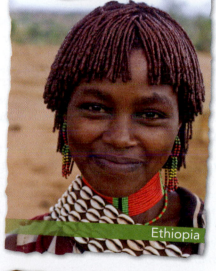
Ethiopia

Brazil

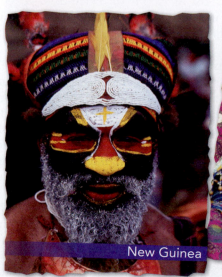
New Guinea

India

Tibet

How does gender depend on culture?

The Dominant Position in Sociology.   That's the biology. Now, the sociological question is, Does this biological difference control our behavior? Does it, for example, make females more nurturing and submissive and males more aggressive and domineering? Here is the quick sociological answer: The dominant sociological position is that *social* factors, not biology, are the reasons people do what they do.

Let's apply this position to gender. If biology were the principal factor in human behavior, all around the world we would find women behaving in one way and men in another. Men and women would be just like male spiders and female spiders, whose genes tell them what to do. In fact, however, ideas of gender vary greatly from one culture to another—and, as a result, so do male–female behaviors.

Despite this, to see why the door to biology is opening just slightly in sociology, let's consider a medical accident and a study of Vietnam veterans.

Opening the Door to Biology
A Medical Accident.

In 1963, 7-month-old identical twin boys were taken to a doctor for a routine circumcision. The physician, not the most capable person in the world, was using a heated needle. He turned the electric current too high and accidentally burned off the penis of one of the boys.

You can imagine the parents' disbelief—and then their horror—as the truth sank in. What could they do? After months of soul-searching and tearful consultations with experts, the parents decided that their son should have a sex-change operation (Money and Ehrhardt 1972). When he was 22 months old, surgeons castrated the boy, using the skin to construct a vagina. The parents then gave the child a new name, Brenda, dressed him in frilly clothing, let his hair grow long, and began to treat him as a girl. Later, physicians gave Brenda female steroids to promote female puberty (Colapinto 2001).

At first, the results were promising. When the twins were 4 years old, the mother said (remember that the children are biologically identical):

One thing that really amazes me is that she is so feminine. I've never seen a little girl so neat and tidy. . . . She likes for me to wipe her face. She doesn't like to be dirty, and yet my son is quite different. I can't wash his face for anything. . . . She is very proud of herself, when she puts on a new dress, or I set her hair. . . . She seems to be daintier. (Money and Ehrhardt 1972)

If the matter were this clear-cut, we could use this case to conclude that gender is determined entirely by nurture. Seldom are things in life so simple, however, and a twist occurs in this story.

Despite this promising start and her parents' coaching, Brenda did not adapt well to femininity. She preferred to mimic her father shaving, rather than her mother putting on makeup. She rejected dolls, favoring guns and her brother's toys. She liked rough-and-tumble games and insisted on urinating standing up. Classmates teased her and called her a "cavewoman" because she walked like a boy. At age 14, she was expelled from school for beating up a girl who teased her. Despite estrogen treatment, she was not attracted to boys. At age 14, when despair over her inner turmoil brought her to the brink of suicide, her father, in tears, told Brenda about the accident and her sex change.

"All of a sudden everything clicked. For the first time, things made sense, and I understood who and what I was," the twin said of this revelation. David (his new name) was given testosterone shots and, later, had surgery to partially reconstruct a penis. At age 25, David married a woman and adopted her children (Diamond and Sigmundson 1997; Colapinto 2001). There is an unfortunate end to this story, however. In 2004, David committed suicide.

David Reimer, whose story is recounted here.

Why is the door to biology slowly opening in sociology?

The Vietnam Veterans Study. Time after time, researchers have found that boys and men who have higher levels of testosterone tend to be more aggressive. In one study, researchers compared the testosterone levels of college men in a "rowdy" fraternity with those of men in a fraternity that had a reputation for academic achievement. Men in the "rowdy" fraternity had higher levels of testosterone (Dabbs et al. 1996). In another study, researchers found that prisoners who had committed sex crimes and other crimes of violence had higher levels of testosterone than those who had committed property crimes (Dabbs et al. 1995). The samples were small, however, leaving the nagging uncertainty that these findings might be due to chance.

Then in 1985, the U.S. government began a health study of Vietnam veterans. To be certain that the study was representative, the researchers chose a random sample of 4,462 men. Among the data they collected was a measurement of testosterone. This sample supported the earlier studies. When the veterans with higher testosterone levels were boys, they were more likely to get in trouble with parents and teachers and to become delinquents. As adults, they were more likely to use hard drugs, to get into fights, to end up in lower-status jobs, and to have more sexual partners. Those who married were more likely to have affairs, to hit their wives, and, it follows, to get divorced (Dabbs and Morris 1990; Booth and Dabbs 1993).

This makes it sound like biology is the basis for behavior. Fortunately for us sociologists, there is another side to this research, and here is where *social class,* the topic of Chapter 8, comes into play. The researchers compared high-testosterone men from higher and lower social classes. The men from lower social classes were more likely to get in trouble with the law, do poorly in school, and mistreat their wives (Dabbs and Morris 1990). You can see, then, that *social* factors such as socialization, subcultures, life goals, and self-definitions were significant in these men's behavior.

In Sum: Sociologists acknowledge that biological factors are involved in some human behavior other than reproduction and childbearing (Udry 2000). Alice Rossi, a feminist sociologist and former president of the American Sociological Association, suggested that women are better prepared biologically for "mothering" than are men. Rossi (1977, 1984) said that women are more sensitive to the infant's soft skin and to their nonverbal communications.

Perhaps Rossi expressed it best when she said that the issue is not either biology or society. Instead, whatever biological predispositions nature provides are overlaid with culture. A task of sociologists is to discover how social factors modify biology, especially as sociologist Janet Chafetz (1990:30) said, to determine how "different" becomes translated into "unequal."

Sociologists study the social factors that underlie human behavior, the experiences that mold us, funneling us into different directions in life. The research on Vietnam veterans discussed in the text indicates how the sociological door is opening slowly to also consider biological factors in human behavior. This March 31, 1967, photo shows soldiers of the 1st Cavalry Division carrying a buddy who had just been shot.

Gender Inequality in Global Perspective

Around the world, gender is *the* primary division between people. To catch a glimpse of how remarkably gender expectations differ with culture, look at the photo essay on the next two pages. Every society sorts men and women into separate groups and gives them different access to property, power, and prestige. These divisions *always* favor men-as-a-group. After reviewing the historical record, historian and feminist Gerda Lerner (1986) concluded that "there is not a single society known where women-as-a-group have decision-making power over men (as a group)." Consequently, sociologists classify females as a *minority group.* Because females outnumber males, you may find this strange. The term *minority group* applies, however, because it refers to people who are discriminated against on the basis

From research on Vietnam veterans: How do social factors of human behavior override biological ones?

Work and Gender: Women at Work in India

Traveling through India was both a pleasant and an eye-opening experience. The country is incredibly diverse, the people friendly, and the land culturally rich. For this photo essay, wherever I went—whether city, village, or country-side—I took photos of women at work.

From these photos, you can see that Indian women work in a wide variety of occupations. Some of their jobs match traditional Western expectations, and some diverge sharply from our gender stereotypes. Although women in India remain subservient to men—with the women's movement hardly able to break the cultural surface—women's occupations are hardly limited to the home. I was surprised at some of the hard, heavy labor that Indian women do.

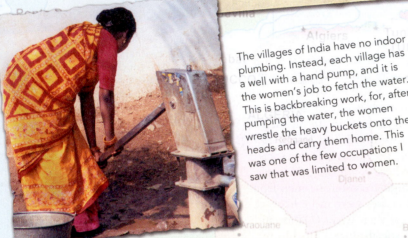

The villages of India have no indoor plumbing. Instead, each village has a well with a hand pump, and it is the women's job to fetch the water. This is backbreaking work, for, after pumping the water, the women wrestle the heavy buckets onto their heads and carry them home. This was one of the few occupations I saw that was limited to women.

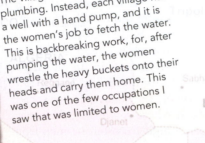

I visited quarries in different parts of India, where I found men, women, and children hard at work in the tropical sun. This woman works 8½ hours a day, six days a week. She earns 40 rupees a day (about 90 cents). Men make 60 rupees a day (about $1.35). Like many quarry workers, this woman is a bonded laborer. She must give half of her wages to her master.

Indian women are highly visible in public places. A storekeeper is as likely to be a woman as a man. This woman is selling glasses of water at a beach on the Bay of Bengal. The structure on which her glasses rest is built of sand.

Women also take care of livestock. It looks as though this woman dressed up and posed for her photo, but this is what she was wearing and doing when I saw her in the field and stopped to talk to her. While the sheep are feeding, her job is primarily to "be" there, to make certain the sheep don't wander off or that no one steals them.

© Jim Henslin, all photos

Sweeping the house is traditional work for Western women. So it is in India, but the sweeping has been extended to areas outside the home. These women are sweeping a major intersection in Chennai. When the traffic light changes here, the women will continue sweeping, with the drivers swerving around them. This was one of the few occupations that seems to be limited to women.

As in the West, food preparation in India is traditional women's work. Here, however, food preparation takes an unexpected twist. Having poured rice from the 60-pound sack onto the floor, these women in Chittoor search for pebbles or other foreign objects that might be in the rice.

When I saw this unusual sight, I had to stop and talk to the workers. From historical pictures, I knew that belt-driven machines were common on U.S. farms 100 years ago. This one in Tamil Nadu processes sugar cane. The woman feeds sugar cane into the machine, which disgorges the stalks on one side and sugar cane juice on the other.

This woman belongs to the Dhobi subcaste, whose occupation is washing clothes. She stands waist deep at this same spot doing the same thing day after day. The banks of this canal in Hyderabad are lined with men and women of her caste, who are washing linens for hotels and clothing for more well-to-do families.

A common sight in India is women working on construction crews. As they work on buildings and on highways, they mix cement, unload trucks, carry rubble, and, following Indian culture, carry loads of bricks atop their heads. This photo was taken in Raipur, Chhattisgarh.

of physical or cultural characteristics, regardless of their numbers (Hacker 1951). Women around the world struggle against gender discrimination. For an extreme case, see the Mass Media in Social Life box on the next page.

How Did Females Become a Minority Group?

Have females always been a minority group? Some analysts speculate that in hunting and gathering societies, women and men were social equals (Leacock 1981; Hendrix 1994) and that horticultural societies also had less gender discrimination than is common today (Collins et al. 1993). In these societies, women may have contributed about 60 percent of the group's total food. Yet, around the world, gender is the basis for discrimination.

How, then, did it happen that women became a minority group? The main theory that has been proposed to explain the origin of **patriarchy**—men dominating society— centers on human reproduction (Lerner 1986; Friedl 1990). In early human history, life was short. Because people died young, if the group were to survive, women had to give birth to many children. This brought severe consequences for women. To survive, an infant needed a nursing mother. If there were no woman to nurse the child, it died. With a child at her breast or in her uterus, or one carried on her hip or on her back, women were not able to stay away from camp for as long as the men could. They also had to move slower. Around the world, then, women assumed the tasks that were associated with the home and child care, while men hunted the large animals and did other tasks that required both greater speed and longer absences from the base camp (Huber 1990).

This led to men becoming dominant. When the men left the camp to hunt animals, they made contact with other tribes. They traded with them, gaining new possessions—and they also quarreled and waged war with them. It was also the men who

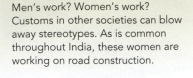

Men's work? Women's work? Customs in other societies can blow away stereotypes. As is common throughout India, these women are working on road construction.

Why do sociologists call women a minority group? What theory, based on reproduction, explains how women became a minority group?

Mass Media in Social Life

Women in Iran: The Times Are Changing, Ever So Slowly

A woman's testimony in court is worth half that of a man's testimony.

A woman may inherit from her parents only half what her brother inherits.

A woman who has sex with a man who is not her husband can be stoned to death.

A woman who refuses to cover her hair in public can receive 80 lashes with a whip.

Not exactly equality.

As you would expect, Iranian women don't like it. Until now, though, there was little that they could do. Controlled by their fathers until they marry and afterward by their husbands, women for the most part didn't know that life could be different.

Now the mass media along with a new literacy are spearheading change in gender relations. Iranian women are logging onto the Internet, and they are reading books. Those who watch satellite television, which is illegal, are seeing pictures of other ways of life, an unfamiliar equality and mutual respect between women and men.

Thanks to the mass media, their eyes are being opened to the fact that not all the women in the world live under the thumbs of men. From this awareness is coming the realization that they don't have to live like this either, that there is a potential for new relationships.

This awareness and the glimmer of hope that another way of life can be theirs have stimulated a women's movement. The movement is small—and protest remains dangerous. Some women have been fined, and for others it is worse. Women are being arrested for being "feminists." Punishment is fines and prison. Security forces sometimes rape these offenders. Other protestors find brutality at home, from their husbands, fathers, or brothers.

Despite the danger, women are continuing to protest. They are even pressing for new rights in the Iranian courts. They are demanding divorce from abusive husbands—and some are getting it.

Not much has changed yet. A man can still divorce his wife whenever he wants, while a woman who wants to divorce a husband must go through a lengthy procedure and never can be sure she will be granted the divorce. A husband also gets automatic custody of any children over the age of 7.

But as women continue their struggle, change will come. One sign of hope: Iraninan politicians, embarrassed by the international outcry, are allowing fewer women to be stoned to death. But women continue to be buried up to their necks in the ground and then stoned.

That there are fewer stonings, though, is at least a beginning.

Sources: Based on Fathi 2009; Semple 2009; U.S. Department of State 2011.

A sign of fundamental change is Iranian women protesting in public. Can the genie be put back in the bottle? Unlikely.

For Your Consideration

➤ What do you think gender relations will be like in Iran ten years from now? Why?

➤ If the women's movement in Iran becomes popular and effective, do you think that relationships between men and women will be about the same as in the United States? Why or why not?

---

made and controlled the instruments of power and death, the weapons that were used for hunting and warfare. The men heaped prestige upon themselves as they returned to the camp triumphantly, leading captured prisoners and displaying their new possessions or the large animals they had killed to feed the women and children.

Contrast this with the women. Their activities were routine, dull, and taken-for-granted. The women kept the fire going, took care of the children, and did the cooking. There was nothing triumphant about what they did—and they were not perceived as risking their lives for the group. The women were "simply there," awaiting the return of their men, ready to acclaim their accomplishments.

Men, then, took control of society. Their sources of power were their weapons, items of trade, and the knowledge they gained from their contacts with other groups. Women did not have access to these sources of power, which the men enshrouded in secrecy. The women became second-class citizens, subject to whatever the men decided.

A theory of how *patriarchy* originated centers on childbirth. Because only women give birth, they assumed tasks associated with home and child care, while men hunted and performed other survival tasks that required greater strength, speed, and absence from home. Following in the steps of her female ancestors, this woman in Yangshou, China, while she works, takes care of her grandchild.

What background factors underlie the women's movement in the Arab world?

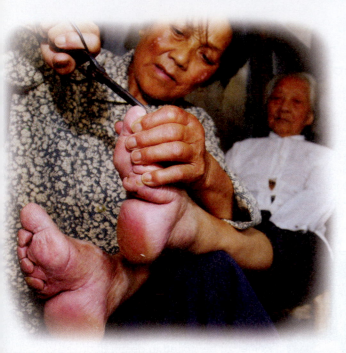

Foot binding was practiced in China until about 1900. Tiny feet were a status symbol. Making it difficult for a woman to walk, small feet indicated that a woman's husband did not need his wife's labor. To make the feet even smaller, sometimes the baby's feet were broken and wrapped tightly. Some baby's toes were cut off. This photo was taken in Hubel Province, China. The woman getting the pedicure is reportedly 105 years old.

Global Violence Against Women

A global human rights issue is violence against women. Historical examples include foot binding in China, witch burning in Europe, and *suttee* (burning the living widow with the body of her dead husband) in India. Today we have rape, wife beating, female infanticide, and the kidnapping of women to be brides. There is also forced prostitution, which was probably the case in our opening vignette. Another notorious example is female circumcision, the topic of the Cultural Diversity box on the next page.

"Honor killings" are another form of violence against women (Yardley 2010a). In some societies, such as India, Jordan, Kurdistan, and Pakistan, a woman who is thought to have brought disgrace on her family is killed by a male relative—usually a brother or her husband, but sometimes her father or uncles. What threat to a family's honor can be so severe that men kill their own daughters, wives, or sisters? The usual reason is sex outside of marriage. Virginity at marriage is so prized in these societies that even a woman who has been raped is in danger of becoming the victim of an honor killing (Zoepf 2007; Falkenberg 2008). Killing the girl or woman—even one's own sister or mother—removes the "stain" she has brought to the family and restores its honor in the community. Sharing this view, the police in these countries generally ignore honor killings, viewing them as private family matters.

In Sum: Inequality is not some accidental, hit-or-miss affair. Rather, each society's institutions work together to maintain the group's particular forms of inequality. Customs, often venerated throughout history, both justify and maintain these arrangements. In some cases, the prejudice and discrimination directed at females are so extreme they result in their enslavement and death.

Gender Inequality in the United States

As we review gender inequality in the United States, let's begin by taking a brief look at how change in this vital area of social life came about. Before we do so, though, you might enjoy the historical snapshot presented in the Down-to-Earth Sociology box on page 286.

Fighting Back: The Rise of Feminism

In the nation's early history, the second-class status of women was taken for granted. A husband and wife were legally one person—him (Chafetz and Dworkin 1986). Women could not vote, buy property in their own names, make legal contracts, or serve on juries. How could things have changed so much in the last hundred years that these examples sound like fiction?

A central lesson of conflict theory is that power yields privilege. Like a magnet, power draws society's best resources to the elite. Because men tenaciously held onto their privileges and used social institutions to maintain their dominance, basic rights for women came only through prolonged and bitter struggle.

Feminism—the view that biology is not destiny and that stratification by gender is wrong and should be resisted—met with strong opposition, both by men who had privilege to lose and by women who accepted their status as morally correct. In 1894, for example, Jeannette Gilder said that women should not have the right to vote: "Politics is too public, too wearing, and too unfitted to the nature of women" (Crossen 2003).

Feminists, then known as suffragists, struggled against such views. In 1916, they founded the National Woman's Party, and in 1917 they began to picket the White House. After picketing for six months, the women were arrested. Hundreds were sent to prison,

How is gender inequality related to violence? Who were the suffragists?

Cultural Diversity **around the World**

Female Circumcision

"Lie down there," the excisor suddenly said to me [when I was 12], pointing to a mat on the ground. No sooner had I laid down than I felt my frail, thin legs grasped by heavy hands and pulled wide apart. . . . Two women on each side of me pinned me to the ground . . . I underwent the ablation of the labia minor and then of the clitoris. The operation seemed to go on forever. I was in the throes of agony, torn apart both physically and psychologically. It was the rule that girls of my age did not weep in this situation. I broke the rule. I cried and screamed with pain . . . !

Afterwards they forced me, not only to walk back to join the other girls who had already been excised, but to dance with them. I was doing my best, but then I fainted. . . . It was a month before I was completely healed. When I was better, everyone mocked me, as I hadn't been brave, they said. (Walker and Parmar 1993:107–108)

Worldwide, about 140 million females have been circumcised, mostly in Muslim Africa and in some parts of Malaysia and Indonesia (Lazaro 2011). In Egypt and Indonesia, between 90 and 97 percent of the women have been circumcised (Slackman 2007; Leopold 2012). In some cultures, the surgery occurs seven to ten days after birth, but in others it is not performed until girls reach adolescence. Among most groups, it takes place between the ages of 4 and 8. Because the surgery is usually done without anesthesia, the pain is so excruciating that adults hold the girl down. In urban areas, physicians sometimes perform the operation; in rural areas, a neighborhood woman usually does it.

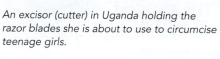

An excisor (cutter) in Uganda holding the razor blades she is about to use to circumcise teenage girls.

In some cultures, only the girl's clitoris is cut off; in others, more is removed. In Sudan, the Nubia cut away most of the girl's genitalia, then sew together the remaining outer edges. They bind the girl's legs from her ankles to her waist for several weeks while scar tissue closes up the vagina. They leave a small opening the diameter of a pencil for the passage of urine and menstrual fluids. When a woman marries, the opening is enlarged further. After birth, the vagina is again sutured shut; this cycle of surgically closing and opening begins anew with each birth.

What are the reasons for circumcising girls? Some groups believe that it reduces female sexual desire, making it more likely that a woman will be a virgin at marriage and, afterward, remain faithful to her husband. Others think that women can't bear children if they aren't circumcised.

The surgery has strong support among many women. Some mothers and grandmothers even insist that the custom continue. Their concern is that their daughters marry well, and in some of these societies uncircumcised women are considered impure and are not allowed to marry.

Feminists respond that female circumcision is a form of ritual torture to control female sexuality. They point out that men dominate the societies that practice it.

Change is on its way: A social movement to ban female circumcision has developed, and the World Health Organization has declared that female circumcision is a human rights issue. Fifteen African countries have now banned the circumcision of females. Without sanctions, though, these laws accomplish little. In Egypt, which prohibited female circumcision in 1996, almost all girls continue to be circumcised (Leopold 2012).

Health workers have hit upon a strategy that is meeting some success. To overcome resistance to change, they begin teaching village women about germs and hygiene. They then trace current health problems such as incontinence to female circumcision. When enough support has been gained, an entire village will publicly abandon the practice. As other villages do the same, the lack of circumcision no longer remains an obstacle to marriage.

Sources: As cited, and Lightfoot-Klein 1989; Merwine 1993; Chalkley 1997; Collymore 2000; Tuhus-Dubrow 2007; UNIFEM 2008; Lazaro 2011.

For Your Consideration

➤ Do you think the members of one culture have the right to interfere with the customs of another culture? If so, under what circumstances? What makes us right and them wrong? What if some African nation said that the U.S. custom of circumcising males is wrong—and wanted the United Nations to take action?

Finally, how would you respond to this Somali woman who said, "The Somali woman doesn't need an alien woman telling her how to treat her private parts"?

Down-to-Earth Sociology

Women and Smoking: Let's Count the Reasons

(A humorous, but serious, look at historical changes in gender)

Why Women Shouldn't Smoke

1. *Smoking turns a woman into a tramp.*

   "A man may take out a woman who smokes for a good time, but he won't marry her, and if he does, he won't stay married."

   Editorial in *The Washington Post*, 1914

2. *Women who smoke drive men wild. They break up families and even make men kill.*

   "Young fellows go into our restaurants to find women folks sucking cigarettes. The . . . next thing you know the young fellows, vampired by these smoking women, desert their homes, their wives and children, rob their employers and even commit murder so that they can get money to lavish on these smoking women."

   A New York City alderman

3. *Smoking ruins women's sleep—and it is bad for their skin.*

   "The cigarette habit indulged by women tends to cause nervousness and insomnia and ruins the complexion. This is one of the most evil influences in American life today."

   Hugh S. Cumming, surgeon general of the U.S., 1920

4. *Women just aren't as good as men at smoking.*

   "Women really don't know how to smoke. One woman smoking one cigarette at a dinner table will stir up more smoke than a whole tableful of men smoking cigars. Neither do they know how to hold their cigarettes properly."

   The manager of a Manhattan hotel, 1920s

An ad from 1929

(And with cancer, you'll lose even more weight!)

Why Women Should Smoke

1. *Smoking prevents fat ankles.*

   "You can't hide fat, clumsy ankles. When tempted to overindulge, reach for a Lucky."

   The American Tobacco Company, 1930s

Challenging Gender

Opposition to women smoking was so strong that the police in New York City warned women not to light up—even in their own cars. Women's colleges also got into the act. Smith College students who were seen smoking, even off campus, were given a demerit. This was serious—three demerits and a woman would be kicked out of college.

Why do you think there was such strong opposition to women smoking in the early 1900s? Men were free to smoke wherever they wanted—in hotels and restaurants, in the street and at work, and in bars, which at that time were off limits to women.

Smoking was part of how women were breaking out of their traditional roles, a gender change that threatened the privileged position of men. Despite the strong opposition, more and more women began to smoke. As they continued to challenge the privileges of men in this and other areas of social life, they ushered in the gender relations that we have today.

For Your Consideration

→ Today if a woman in Saudi Arabia drives a car, she is arrested. How is this a parallel to men's reaction to U.S. women smoking in the early 1930s?

---

including Lucy Burns, a leader of the National Woman's Party. The extent to which these women had threatened male privilege is demonstrated by how they were treated in prison.

Two men brought in Dorothy Day [the editor of a periodical that promoted women's rights], twisting her arms above her head. Suddenly they lifted her and brought her body down twice over the back of an iron bench. . . . They had been there a few minutes when Mrs. Lewis, all doubled over like a sack of flour, was thrown in. Her head struck the iron bed and she fell to the floor senseless. As for Lucy Burns, they handcuffed her wrists and fastened the handcuffs over [her] head to the cell door. (Cowley 1969)

In the early 1900s, men were offended by women smoking. Why?

This *first wave* of the women's movement had a radical branch that wanted to reform all the institutions of society and a conservative branch whose concern was to win the vote for women (Freedman 2001). The conservative branch dominated, and after winning the right to vote in 1920, the movement basically dissolved.

The *second wave* began in the 1960s. Sociologist Janet Chafetz (1990) points out that up to this time most women thought of work as a temporary activity intended to fill the time between completing school and getting married. For an example of how children's books reinforced such thinking, see Figure 10.1 on the next page. As more women took jobs and began to regard them as careers, however, they compared their working conditions with those of men. This shift in their reference group changed the way women viewed their conditions at work. The result was a second wave of protest against gender inequalities. The goals of this second wave (which continues today) are broad, ranging from raising women's pay to changing policies on violence against women.

A *third wave* of feminism has emerged. It has many divisions, but three main aspects are apparent. The first is a greater focus on the problems of women in the Least Industrialized Nations (Spivak 2000; Hamid 2006). Some are fighting battles against conditions long since overcome by women in the Most Industrialized Nations. The second is a criticism of the values that dominate work and society. Some feminists argue that competition, toughness, calloused emotions, and independence represent "male" qualities and need to be replaced with cooperation, connection, openness, and interdependence (England 2000). A third aspect is an emphasis on women's sexual pleasure (Swigonski and Reheim 2011).

Sharp disagreements among feminists have emerged regarding male–female relationships. Some, for example, defend their use of "erotic capital," women's sexual

The "first wave" of the U.S. women's movement met enormous opposition. The women in this 1920 photo had just been released after serving two months in jail for picketing the White House. Lucy Burns, mentioned on page 286, is the second woman on the left. Alice Paul, who was placed in solitary confinement and is a subject of this 1920 protest, is featured in the photo circle of early female sociologists in Chapter 1, page 10.

Can you contrast the three waves of feminism?

FIGURE 10.1   Teaching Gender

Mother and Sally

Mother can sew.
Jane can sew.

"I will help," said Dick.
"I will help you with the pigs."

Father

The "Dick and Jane" readers were the top selling readers in the United States in the 1940s and 1950s. In addition to reading, they taught "gender messages." What gender message do you see here?

Housework is "women's work," a lesson girls should learn early in life.

Besides learning words like "pigs" (relevant at that historical period), boys and girls also learned that rough outside work was for men.

What does this page teach children other than how to read the word "Father"? (Look to the left to see what Sally and Jane and Mother are doing.)

Source: From *Dick and Jane: Fun with Our Family*, Illustrations © copyright 1951, 1979, and *Dick and Jane: We Play Outside*, copyright © 1965, Pearson Education, Inc., published by Scott, Foresman and Company. Used with permission.

As women accomplish more in areas traditionally dominated by men, do you think that the definition of femininity will change? If so, how?

attractiveness and seductiveness, to get ahead at work. Others deplore this as a denial of ability and betrayal of equality (Hakim 2010).

Although U.S. women enjoy fundamental rights today, gender inequality continues to play a central role in social life. Let's first consider gender inequality in health care.

Gender Inequality in Health Care

Medical researchers were perplexed. Reports were coming in from all over the country: Women were twice as likely as men to die after coronary bypass surgery. Researchers at Cedars-Sinai Medical Center in Los Angeles checked their own records. They found that of 2,300 coronary bypass patients, 4.6 percent of the women died as a result of the surgery, compared with 2.6 percent of the men.

These findings presented a sociological puzzle. To solve it, researchers first turned to biology (Bishop 1990). In coronary bypass surgery, a blood vessel is taken from one part of the body and stitched to an artery on the surface of the heart. Perhaps the surgery was more difficult to do on women because of their smaller arteries. To find out, researchers measured the amount of time that surgeons kept patients on the heart-lung machine while they operated. They were surprised to learn that women spent *less* time on the machine than men. This indicated that the surgery was not more difficult to perform on women.

As the researchers probed, a surprising answer unfolded: unintended sexual discrimination. When women complained of chest pains, their doctors took them only *one-tenth as seriously* as when men made the same complaints. How do we know this? Doctors were *ten* times more likely to give men exercise stress tests and radioactive heart scans. They also sent men to surgery on the basis of abnormal stress tests, but they waited until women showed clear-cut symptoms of heart disease before sending them to surgery. Patients with more advanced heart disease are more likely to die during and after heart surgery.

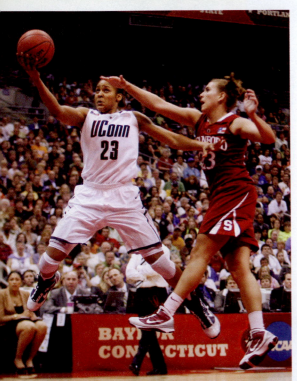

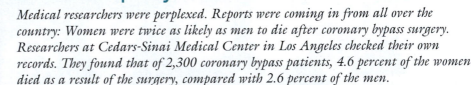

How is gender inequality in health care a life-or-death matter?

Although these findings have been publicized among physicians, the problem continues (Jackson et al. 2011). Perhaps as more women become physicians, the situation will change, since female doctors are more sensitive to women's health problems. For example, they are more likely to order Pap smears and mammograms (Lurie et al. 1993). In addition, as more women join the faculties of medical schools, we can expect women's health problems to receive more attention in the training of physicians. Even this might not do it, however, as no one knows how stereotyping of the sexes produces this deadly discrimination, and women, too, hold our cultural stereotypes.

In contrast to unintentional sexism in heart surgery, there is a type of surgery that is a blatant form of discrimination against women. This is the focus of the Down-to-Earth Sociology box below.

Down-to-Earth Sociology

Cold-Hearted Surgeons and Their Women Victims

While doing participant observation in a hospital, sociologist Sue Fisher (1986) was surprised to hear surgeons recommend total hysterectomy (removal of both the uterus and the ovaries) *when no cancer was present*. When she asked why, the male doctors explained that the uterus and ovaries are "potentially disease producing." They also said that these organs are unnecessary after the childbearing years, so why not remove them? Doctors who reviewed hysterectomies confirmed this gender-biased practice. *Ninety percent* of hysterectomies are avoidable. Only ten percent involve cancer (Costa 2011).

Greed is a powerful motivator in many areas of social life, and it rears its ugly head in surgical sexism (Domingo and Pellicer 2009). Surgeons make money when they do hysterectomies, and the more of them that they do, the more money they make. Since women, to understate the matter, are reluctant to part with these organs, surgeons find that they have to "sell" this operation. As you read how one resident explained the "hard sell" to sociologist Diana Scully (1994), you might think of a used car salesperson:

> You have to look for your surgical procedures; you have to go after patients. Because no one is crazy enough to come and say, "Hey, here I am. I want you to operate on me." You have to sometimes convince the patient that she is really sick—if she is, of course [laughs], and that she is better off with a surgical procedure.

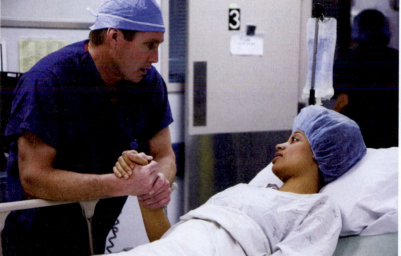

Used-car salespeople would love to have the powerful sales weapon that these surgeons have at their disposal: To "convince" a woman to have this surgery, the doctor puts on a serious face and tells her that the examination has turned up *fibroids* in her uterus—and they *might* turn into *cancer*. This statement is often sufficient to get the woman to buy the surgery. She starts to picture herself lying at death's door, her sorrowful family gathered at her death bed. Then the used car salesperson—I mean, the surgeon—moves in to clinch the sale. Keeping a serious face and emitting an "I-know-how-you-feel" look, the surgeon starts to make arrangements for the surgery. What the surgeon withholds is the rest of the truth—that a lot of women have fibroids, that fibroids usually do *not* turn into cancer, and that the patient has several alternatives to surgery.

In case it is difficult for someone to see how this is sexist, let's change the context just a little. Let's suppose that the income of some female surgeons depends on selling a specialized operation. To sell it, they systematically suggest to older men the benefits of castration—since "those organs are no longer necessary, and might cause disease."

For Your Consideration

→ Hysterectomies are now so common that one of three U.S. women eventually has her uterus surgically removed (Whiteman et al. 2008). Why do you think that surgeons are so quick to operate? How can women find alternatives to surgery?

Gender Inequality in Education

What a contrast with today. Until 1832, women were not allowed to attend college with men. When women did start to attend college with men, they had to wash the men's clothing, clean their rooms, and serve them their meals (Flexner 1971/1999).

How the times have changed. So much so that this quote sounds like a joke. Gradually, like out-of-fashion clothing, such ideas were discarded. As Figure 10.2 shows, by 1900 one-third of college students were women, and today more women than men attend college. The overall average differs with racial–ethnic groups, as you can see from Figure 10.3 on page 291. African Americans have the most women relative to men, and Asian Americans the least. Another indication of how extensive the change is: Women now earn 57 percent of all bachelor's degrees and 60 percent of all master's degrees (*Statistical Abstract* 2012:Table 299).

Figure 10.4 on the next page illustrates another major change—how women have increased their share of professional degrees. The greatest change is in dentistry: In 1970, across the entire United States, only 34 women earned degrees in dentistry. Today, that total has jumped to 2,300 a year. As you can also see, almost as many women as men now become dentists, lawyers, and physicians. It is likely that women will soon outnumber men in earning these professional degrees.

Gender Tracking.   With such extensive changes, it would seem that gender equality has been achieved, or at least almost so, and in some instances—as with the changed sex ratio in college—we have a new form of gender inequality. If we look closer, however, we find something beneath the surface. Underlying these degrees is *gender tracking;* that is, college degrees tend to follow gender, which reinforces male–female

✳ ⌐Explore
Living Data
on **mysoclab.com**

FIGURE 10.2   **Changes in College Enrollment, by Sex**

What percentages of U.S. college students are female and male?

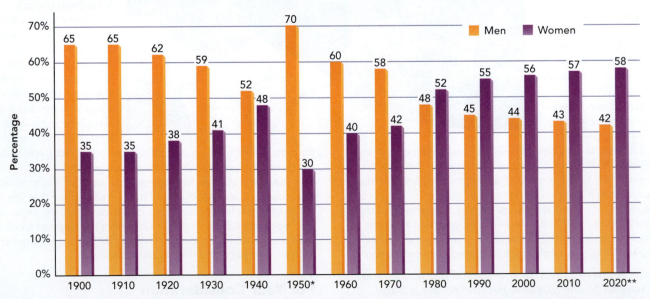

* This sharp drop in female enrollment occurred when large numbers of male soldiers returned from World War II and attended college under the new GI Bill of Rights.

** Author's estimate.

Source: By the author. Based on *Statistical Abstract of the United States* 1938:Table 114; 1959:Table 158; 1991:Table 261; 2012:Table 277.

FIGURE 10.3   **College Students, by Sex and Race–Ethnicity**

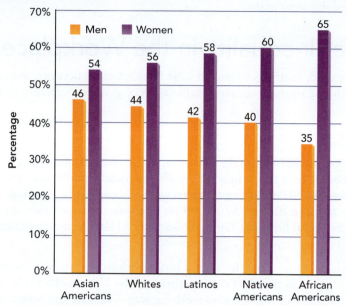

Note: This figure can be confusing. To read it, ask: What percentage of a particular group in college are men or women? (For example, what percentage of Asian American college students are men or women?)

Source: By the author. Based on *Statistical Abstract of the United States* 2012:Table 279.

distinctions. Here are two extremes: Men earn 95 percent of the associate degrees in the "masculine" field of construction trades, while women are awarded 96 percent of the associate degrees in the "feminine" field of "family and consumer sciences" (*Statistical Abstract* 2012:Table 301). Because gender socialization gives men and

FIGURE 10.4   **Gender Changes in Professional Degrees**

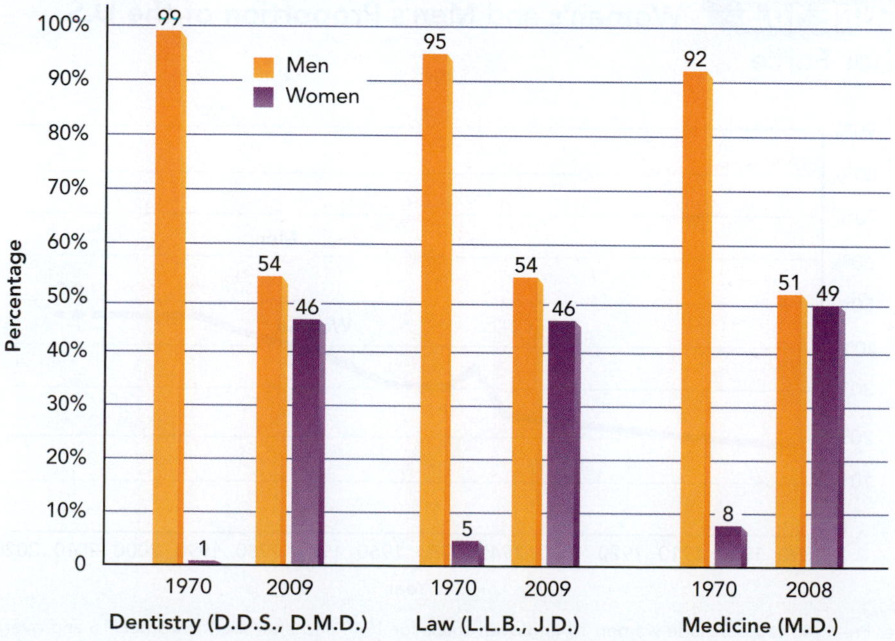

Percentage

	Dentistry (D.D.S., D.M.D.)	Law (L.L.B., J.D.)	Medicine (M.D.)
Men	99 / 54	95 / 54	92 / 51
Women	1 / 46	5 / 46	8 / 49

1970   2009   1970   2009   1970   2008

Source: By the author. Based on *Digest of Education Statistics* 2007:Table 269; *Statistical Abstract of the United States* 2012:Table 303.

women different orientations to life, they enter college with gender-linked aspirations. Socialization—not some presumed innate characteristic—channels men and women into different educational paths.

Gender Inequality in the Workplace

To examine the work setting is to make visible basic relations between men and women. Let's begin with one of the most remarkable areas of gender inequality at work, the pay gap.

The Pay Gap

After college, you might like to take a few years off, travel around Europe, sail the oceans, or maybe sit on a beach in some South American paradise and drink piña coladas. But chances are, you are going to go to work instead. Since you have to work, how would you like to make an extra $700,000 on your job? If this sounds appealing, read on. I'm going to reveal how you can make an extra $1,465 a month between the ages of 25 and 65.

Historical Background.   First, let's get a broad background to help us understand today's situation. One of the chief characteristics of the U.S. workforce is the steady growth in the numbers of women who work for wages outside the home. Figure 10.5 shows that in 1890 about one of every five paid workers was a woman. By 1940, this ratio had grown to one of four; by 1960 to one of three; and today it is almost one of two. As shown in this figure, during the next few years we can expect that the ratio will remain 53 percent men and 47 percent women.

Geographical Factors.   Women who work for wages are not distributed evenly throughout the United States. From the Social Map on the next page, you can see that where a woman lives makes a difference in how likely she is to work outside the home. Why is there such a clustering among the states? The geographical patterns that you

---

FIGURE 10.5   Women's and Men's Proportion of the U.S. Labor Force

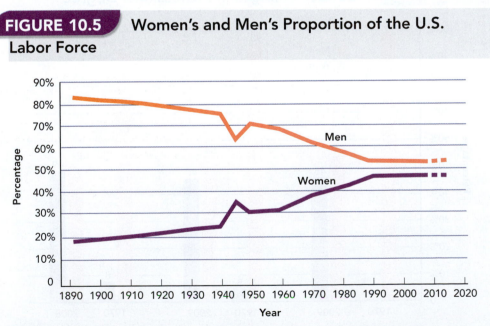

Note: Pre-1940 totals include women 14 and over: totals for 1940 and after are for women 16 and over. Broken lines are the author's projections.

Sources: By the author. Based on Women's Bureau of the United States 1969:10; *Manpower Report to the President*, 1971:203, 205; Mills and Palumbo 1980:6, 45; *Statistical Abstract of the United States* 2012: Table 587.

How has the proportion of women and men in the U.S. workforce changed over time?

FIGURE 10.6   Women in the Workforce

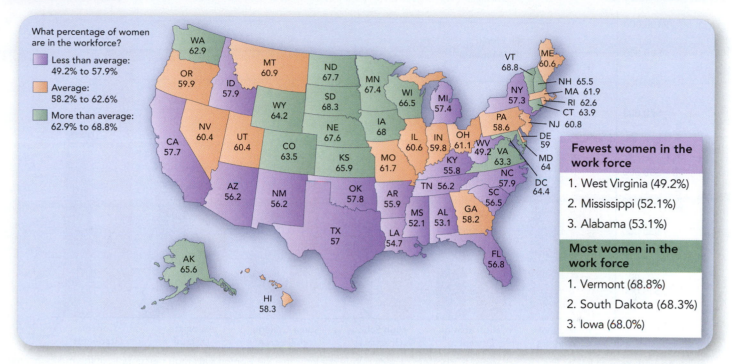

What percentage of women are in the workforce?

Less than average: 49.2% to 57.9%

Average: 58.2% to 62.6%

More than average: 62.9% to 68.8%

WA 62.9
OR 59.9
ID 57.9
MT 60.9
ND 67.7
MN 67.4
WI 66.5
MI 57.4
VT 68.8
ME 60.6
NH 65.5
NY 57.3
MA 61.9
RI 62.6
CT 63.9
NJ 60.8
WY 64.2
SD 68.3
IA 68
PA 58.6
DE 59
NV 60.4
UT 60.4
CO 63.5
NE 67.6
IL 60.6
IN 59.8
OH 61.1
WV 49.2
VA 63.3
MD 64
DC 64.4
CA 57.7
KS 65.9
MO 61.7
KY 55.8
NC 57.9
TN 56.2
SC 56.5
AZ 56.2
NM 56.2
OK 57.8
AR 55.9
MS 52.1
AL 53.1
GA 58.2
TX 57
LA 54.7
FL 56.8
AK 65.6
HI 58.3

Fewest women in the work force

1. West Virginia (49.2%)
2. Mississippi (52.1%)
3. Alabama (53.1%)

Most women in the work force

1. Vermont (68.8%)
2. South Dakota (68.3%)
3. Iowa (68.0%)

Source: By the author. Based on *Statistical Abstract of the United States* 2011:Table 593.

see on this map reflect regional subcultural differences about which we currently have little understanding.

The "Testosterone Bonus".   Now, back to how you can make an extra $700,000 at work—and maybe even more. You might be wondering if this is hard to do. Actually, it is simple for some and impossible for others. As Figure 10.7 on the next page shows, all you have to do is be born a male. If we compare full-time workers, based on current differences in earnings, this is how much more money the *average male* can expect to earn over the course of his career. Now if you want to boost that annual difference to $30,600 for a whopping career total of $1,225,000, be both a male and a college graduate. Hardly any single factor pinpoints gender discrimination better than these totals. As you can see from Figure 10.7, the pay gap shows up at *all* levels of education.

For college students, the gender gap in pay begins with the first job after graduation. You might know of a particular woman who was offered a higher salary than most men in her class, but she would be an exception. On average, employers start men out at higher salaries than women, and although women advance in salary at roughly the same rate as men, they never catch up from the men's starting "testosterone bonus" (Carter 2010; Weinberger 2011; Smith 2012). Depending on your sex, then, you will either benefit from the pay gap or be victimized by it.

The pay gap is so great that U.S. women who work full time average *only 72 percent* of what men are paid. As you can see from Figure 10.8 on page 295, the pay gap used to be even worse. A gender gap in pay occurs not only in the United States but also in *all* industrialized nations.

Reasons for the Gender Pay Gap.   What logic can underlie the gender pay gap? As we just saw, college degrees are gender linked, so perhaps this gap is due to career choices. Maybe women are more likely to choose lower-paying jobs, such as teaching grade school, while men are more likely to go into better-paying fields, such as business and engineering. Actually, this is true, and researchers have found that about *half* of the gender pay gap is due to such factors. And the balance? It consists of a

FIGURE 10.7   The Gender Pay Gap, by Education[1]

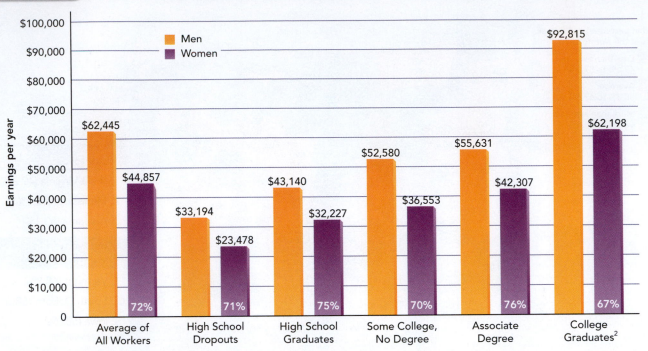

[1]Full-time workers in all fields. The percentage at the bottom of each purple bar indicates the women's average percentage of the men's income.
[2]Bachelor's and all higher degrees, including professional degrees.

Source: By the author. Based on *Statistical Abstract of the United States* 2012:Table 703.

combination of gender discrimination (Jacobs 2003; Roth 2003) and what is called the "child penalty"—women missing out on work experience and opportunities while they care for children (Hundley 2001; Wilde et al. 2010).

The CEO Gap.   As a final indication of the extent of the U.S. gender pay gap, consider this. Of the nation's top 500 corporations (the so-called Fortune 500), only twelve are headed by women (VenderMey 2011).

I examined the names of the CEOs of the 350 largest U.S. corporations, and I found that your best chance to reach the top is to be named (in this order) John, Robert, James, William, or Charles. Edward, Lawrence, and Richard are also advantageous names. Amber, Katherine, Leticia, and Maria apparently draw a severe penalty. Naming your baby girl John or Robert might seem a little severe, but it could help her reach the top. (I say this only slightly tongue-in-cheek. One of the few women to head a Fortune 500 company—before she was fired and given $21 million severance pay—had a man's first name: Carleton Fiorina of Hewlett-Packard. Carleton's first name is actually Cara, but knowing what she was facing in the highly competitive business world, she dropped this feminine name to go by her masculine middle name.)

Is the Glass Ceiling Cracking?

"First comes love, then comes marriage, then comes flex time and a baby carriage."
—Said by a supervisor at Novartis who refused to hire women (Carter 2010)

This supervisor's statement reflects blatant discrimination. Most gender discrimination in the workplace, however, seems to be unintentional, with much of it based on gender stereotypes.

Apart from cases of overt discrimination, then, what keeps women from breaking through the **glass ceiling,** the mostly invisible barrier that prevents women from reaching the executive suite? The "pipelines" that lead to the top of a company are its marketing,

FIGURE 10.8   **The Gender Gap over Time: What Percentage of Men's Income Do Women Earn?**

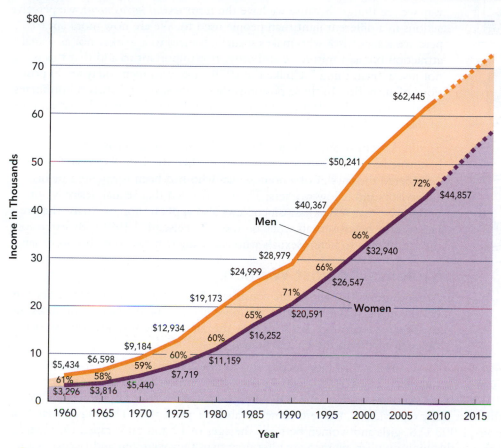

Source: By the author. Based on *Statistical Abstract of the United States* 1995:Table 739; 2002:Table 666; 2012:Table 703, and earlier years. Broken lines indicate the author's estimate.

sales, and production positions, those that directly affect the corporate bottom line (Hymowitz 2004; DeCrow 2005). Men, who dominate the executive suite, stereotype women as being good at "support" but less capable than men of leadership (Belkin 2007). They steer women into human resources or public relations. In these positions, successful projects are not appreciated in the same way as those that bring corporate profits—and bonuses for their managers.

Another reason for the strength of the glass ceiling is that women lack mentors—successful executives who take an interest in them and teach them the ropes. Lack of a mentor is no trivial matter, for mentors can provide opportunities to develop leadership skills that open the door to the executive suite (Hymowitz 2007; Yakaboski and Reinert 2011).

Sexual Harassment—and Worse

Sexual harassment—unwelcome sexual attention at work or at school, which may affect job or school performance or create a hostile environment—was not recognized as a problem until the 1970s. Before this, women considered unwanted sexual comments, touches, looks, and pressure to have sex as a personal matter, something between her and some "turned on" man—or an obnoxious one.

With the prodding of feminists, women began to perceive unwanted sexual advances at work and school as part of a *structural* problem. That is, they began to realize that the issue was more than a man here or there doing obnoxious things

As the glass ceiling slowly cracks, women are gradually gaining entry into the top positions in society. Shown here is Virginia Rometty, the first woman to head IBM.

Is the glass ceiling cracking? What keeps women from breaking through it?

"Of course it isn't a case of sexual discrimination. We just don't think you're the right man for the job."

Although crassly put by the cartoonist, behind the glass ceiling lies this background assumption.

because he was attracted to a woman; rather, men were using their positions of authority to pressure women for sex.

Effects on Perception.   As symbolic interactionists stress, labels affect the way we see things. Because we have the term *sexual harassment,* we perceive actions in a different light than people used to. We are now more apt to perceive a supervisor who makes sexual advances to a worker not as sexual attraction but as a misuse of authority. It is important to add that this is not just a "man thing." Unlike the 1970s, many women today are in positions of authority. In those positions they, too, sexually harass subordinates (Settles et al. 2011). With most authority still vested in men, however, most of the sexual harassers are men.

Sexual Orientation.   Originally, sexual desire was an element of sexual harassment, but no longer. This changed when the U.S. Supreme Court considered the lawsuit of a homosexual who had been tormented by his supervisors and fellow workers. The Court ruled that sexual desire is not necessary—that sexual harassment laws also apply to homosexuals who are harassed by heterosexuals while on the job (Felsenthal 1998). By extension, the law applies to heterosexuals who are sexually harassed by homosexuals.

Violence Against Women

Around the world, one of the consistent characteristics of violence is its gender inequality. That is, females are more likely to be the victims of males, not the other way around. Let's see how this almost-one-way street in gender violence applies to the United States.

Forcible Rape.   The fear of rape is common among U.S. women, a fear that is far from groundless. The U.S. rate is 0.52 per 1,000 females (*Statistical Abstract* 2012:Table 314). If we exclude the very young and women over 50, those who are the least likely rape victims, the rate comes to about 1 per 1,000. This means that 1 of every 1,000 U.S. girls and women between the ages of 12 and 50 is raped *each year.* Despite this high number, women are safer now than they were ten and twenty years ago. The rape rate then was much higher than today.

Although any woman can be a victim of sexual assault—and victims include babies and elderly women—the typical victim is 16 to 19 years old. As you can see from Table 10.1, sexual assault peaks at those ages and then declines.

Women's most common fear seems to be an attack by a stranger—a sudden, violent abduction and rape. However, contrary to the stereotypes that underlie these fears, most victims know their attackers. As you can see from Table 10.2, about one of three rapes is committed by strangers.

Males are also victims of rape, which is every bit as devastating for them as it is for female victims (Choudhary et al. 2010). Rape in prison is a special problem, sometimes tolerated by prison guards, at times even encouraged as punishment for prisoners who have given them problems (Donaldson 1993; Buchanan 2010).

Date (Acquaintance) Rape.   What has shocked so many about date rape (also known as *acquaintance rape*) are studies showing how common it is (Littleton et al. 2008). Researchers who used a nationally representative sample of women enrolled in U.S. colleges and universities with 1,000 students or more found that 1.7 percent had been raped during the preceding six months. Another 1.1 percent had been victims of attempted rape (Fisher et al. 2000).

With 11 million women enrolled in college, 2.8 percent (1.7 plus 1.1) means that over a quarter of a million college women were victims of rape or of attempted rape *in just the past six months.* (This

TABLE 10.1	Age of Rape Victims
Age	Rate per 1,000 Females
12–15	1.9
16–19	3.3
20–24	2.3
25–34	1.3
35–49	0.8
50–64	0.3
65 and Older	0.09

Sources: By the author. A ten-year average, based on *Statistical Abstract of the United States*; 2002:Table 303; 2003:Table 295; 2004:Table 322; 2005:Table 306; 2006:Table 308; 2007:Table 312; 2008:Table 316; 2009:Table 305; 2010:Table 305; 2012:Table 316.

Why is sexual harassment a structural problem, not just a personal problem? What are the typical ages of rape victims?

TABLE 10.2	Relationship of Victims and Rapists
Relationship	**Percentage**
Relative	7%
Known Well	33%
Casual Acquaintance	23%
Stranger	34%
Not Reported	2%

Sources: By the author. A ten-year average, based on *Statistical Abstract of the United States*; 2002:Table 296; 2003:Table 323; 2004–2005:Table 307; 2006:Table 311; 2007: Table 315; 2008:Table 316; 2009:Table 306; 2010:Table 306; 2011:Table 313.

The most common drug used to facilitate date rape is alcohol, not GHB.

conclusion assumes that the rate is the same in colleges with fewer than 1,000 students, which has not been verified.) Most of the women told a friend what happened, but only *5 percent* reported the crime to the police (Fisher et al. 2003).

Murder.   All over the world, men are more likely than women to be killers. Figure 10.9 illustrates this gender pattern in U.S. murders. Note that although females make up about 51 percent of the U.S. population, they don't even come close to making up 51 percent of the nation's killers. As you can see from this figure, when women are murdered, about 9 times out of 10 the killer is a man.

Violence in the Home.   In the family, too, women are the typical victims. Spouse battering, marital rape, and incest are discussed in Chapter 12, pages 375–376. Two forms of violence against women—honor killings and genital circumcision—are discussed on pages 284 and 285.

Feminism and Gendered Violence.   Feminist sociologists have been especially effective in bringing violence against women to the public's attention. Some use symbolic interactionism, pointing out that to associate strength and virility with violence—as is done in many cultures—is to promote violence. Others use conflict theory. They argue that men are losing power, and that some men turn violently against women as a way to reassert their declining power and status (Reiser 1999; Meltzer 2002; Xie et al. 2011).

Solutions.   There is no magic bullet for this problem of gendered violence, but to be effective, any solution must break the connection between violence and masculinity. This would require an educational program that encompasses schools, churches, homes, and the media. Given the gunslinging heroes of the Wild West and other American icons, as well as the violent messages that are so prevalent in the mass media, including video games, it is difficult to be optimistic that a change will come any time soon.

Our next topic, women in politics, however, gives us much more reason for optimism.

The Changing Face of Politics

Women could take over the United States! Think about it. There are eight million more women than men of voting age. But look at Table 10.3 on the next page. Although women voters greatly outnumber men voters, men greatly outnumber women in political office. The remarkable gains women have made in recent elections can take our eye off the broader picture. Since 1789 almost 2,000 men have served in the U.S. Senate. And how many women? Only 38, including 17 current senators. Not

FIGURE 10.9	Killers and Their Victims

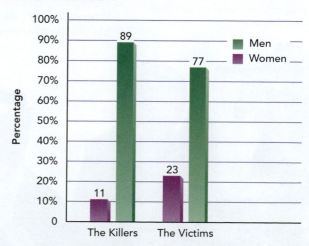

Source: By the author. Based on *Statistical Abstract of the United States* 2012:Tables 311, 324.

What is the relationship of victims and rapists? What is the pattern of gender and murder?

TABLE 10.3	U.S. Women in Political Office	
	Percentage of Offices Held by Women	Number of Offices Held by Women
National Office		
U.S. Senate	17%	17
U.S. House of Representatives	17%	73
State Office		
Governors	12%	6
Lt. Governors	18%	9
Attorneys General	8%	4
Secretaries of State	24%	12
Treasurers	20%	10
State Auditors	16%	8
State Legislators	24%	1,800

Source: Center for American Women and Politics 2010.

until 1992 was the first African American woman (Carol Moseley-Braun) elected to the U.S. Senate. No Latina or Asian American woman has yet been elected to the Senate (National Women's Political Caucus 1998, 2011; *Statistical Abstract* 2012:Table 413).

We are in the midst of fundamental change. In 2002, Nancy Pelosi was the first woman to be elected by her colleagues as minority leader of the House of Representatives. Five years later, in 2007, they chose her as the first female Speaker of the House. These posts made her the most powerful woman ever in Congress. Another significant event occurred in 2008 when Hillary Clinton came within a hair's breadth of becoming the presidential nominee of the Democratic party. That same year, Sarah Palin was chosen as the Republican vice-presidential candidate. We can also note that more women are becoming corporate executives, and, as indicated in Figure 10.4 (on page 291), more women are also becoming lawyers. In these positions, women are traveling more and making statewide and national contacts. Along with other societal changes allowing women more freedom, such as the increasing view of child care as a responsibility of both mother and father, it is only a matter of time until a woman occupies the Oval Office.

Glimpsing the Future—with Hope

Women's fuller participation in the decision-making processes of our social institutions has shattered stereotypes that tended to limit females to "feminine" activities and push males into "masculine" ones. As structural barriers continue to fall and more activities are degendered, both males and females will have greater freedom to pursue activities that are more compatible with their abilities and desires as individuals.

As females and males develop a new consciousness both of their capacities and of their potential, relationships will change. Distinctions between the sexes will not disappear, but there is no reason for biological differences to be translated into social inequalities. Our potential, as sociologist Alison Jaggar (1990) observed, is for gender equality to become less a goal than a background condition for living in society.

Hillary Clinton broke through the glass ceiling in politics when she was elected senator from New York: She also came close to being the Democratic nominee for president. She is shown here in her position as Secretary of State, meeting with Arab leaders in Morocco.

How are gender and politics changing? Are we close to gender equality in politics? What support do you have for your answer?

Inequalities of Aging

In 1928, Charles Hart, who was working on his Ph.D. in anthropology, did fieldwork with the Tiwi people, who live on an island off the northern coast of Australia. Because every Tiwi belongs to a clan, they assigned Hart to the bird (Jabijabui) clan and told him that a particular woman was his mother. Hart described the woman as "toothless, almost blind, withered." He added that she was "physically quite revolting and mentally rather senile." He then recounted this remarkable event:

Toward the end of my time on the islands an incident occurred that surprised me because it suggested that some of them had been taking my presence in the kinship system much more seriously than I had thought. I was approached by a group of about eight or nine senior men. . . . They were the senior members of the Jabijabui clan and they had decided among themselves that the time had come to get rid of the decrepit old woman who had first called me son and whom I now called mother. . . . As I knew, they said, it was Tiwi custom, when an old woman became too feeble to look after herself, to "cover her up." This could only be done by her sons and brothers and all of them had to agree beforehand, since once it was done, they did not want any dissension among the brothers or clansmen, as that might lead to a feud. My "mother" was now completely blind, she was constantly falling over logs or into fires, and they, her senior clansmen, were in agreement that she would be better out of the way. Did I agree?

I already knew about "covering up." The Tiwi, like many other hunting and gathering peoples, sometimes got rid of their ancient and decrepit females. The method was to dig a hole in the ground in some lonely place, put the old woman in the hole and fill it in with earth until only her head was showing. Everybody went away for a day or two and then went back to the hole to discover to their great surprise, that the old woman was dead, having been too feeble to raise her arms from the earth. Nobody had "killed" her; her death in Tiwi eyes was a natural one. She had been alive when her relatives last saw her. I had never seen it done, though I knew it was the custom, so I asked my brothers if it was necessary for me to attend the "covering up."

They said no and that they would do it, but only after they had my agreement. Of course I agreed, and a week or two later we heard in our camp that my "mother" was dead, and we all wailed and put on the trimmings of mourning. (C. W. M. Hart in Hart and Pilling 1979:125–126)

Aging in Global Perspective

We won't deal with the question of whether it was moral or ethical for Hart to agree that the old woman should be "covered up." What is of interest for our purposes is how the Tiwi treated their frail elderly—or, more specifically, their frail *female* elderly. You probably noticed that the Tiwi "covered up" only old women. As was noted earlier, females are discriminated against throughout the world. As this incident makes evident, in some places that discrimination extends even to death.

Every society must deal with the problem of people growing old, and of some becoming frail. Although few societies choose to bury old people alive, all societies must decide how to allocate limited resources among their citizens. With the percentage of the population that is old increasing in many nations, these decisions are generating tensions between the generations.

The Social Construction of Aging

The way the Tiwi treated frail elderly women reflects one extreme of how societies cope with aging. Another extreme, one that reflects an entirely different attitude, is illustrated by the Abkhasians, an agricultural people who live in Georgia, a republic of the former Soviet Union. The Abkhasians pay their elderly high respect and look to them

Watch
Ways We Live
on **mysoclab.com**

for guidance. They would no more dispense with their elderly by "covering them up" than we would "cover up" a sick child in our culture.

The Abkhasians may be among the longest-lived people on earth. Many claim to live past 100—some beyond 120 and even 130 (Benet 1971; Robbins 2006). Although researchers have concluded that the extreme claims are bogus (Young et al. 2010), government records do indicate that many Abkhasians do live to a very old age.

Three main factors appear to account for their long lives. The first is their diet, which consists of little meat, much fresh fruit, vegetables, garlic, goat cheese, cornmeal, buttermilk, and wine. The second is their lifelong physical activity. They do slow down after age 80, but even after the age of 100 they still work about four hours a day. The third factor—a highly developed sense of community—lies at the very heart of the Abkhasian culture. From childhood, each individual is integrated into a primary group and remains so throughout life. There is no such thing as a nursing home, nor do the elderly live alone. Because they continue to work and contribute to the group's welfare, the elderly aren't a burden to anyone. They don't vegetate, nor do they feel the need to "fill time" with bingo and shuffleboard. In short, the elderly feel no sudden rupture between what they "were" and what they "are."

The examples of the Tiwi and the Abkhasians reveal an important sociological principle: Like gender, aging is *socially constructed*. That is, nothing in the nature of aging summons forth any particular viewpoint. Rather, attitudes toward the aged are rooted in society and, therefore, differ from one social group to another. As we shall see, even the age at which people are considered old depends not on biology, but on culture.

This 104-year old woman in Bama Yao, China, has slowed down but has not retired. As in her earlier years, she still does spinning and remains an active member of her community.

Except for interaction within families, age groups in Western culture are usually kept fairly separate. The idea of having a day care center in the same building as a nursing home breaks this tradition. This photo was taken in Seattle, Washington.

Industrialization and the Graying of the Globe

As was noted in previous chapters, industrialization is occurring worldwide. With industrialization comes a higher standard of living, including more food, a purer water supply, and more effective ways of fighting the diseases that kill children. As a result, when a country industrializes, more of its people reach older ages. The Social Map on the next page illustrates this principle.

From this global map, you can see that the industrialized countries have the highest percentage of elderly. The range among nations is broad, from just 1 of 45 citizens in nonindustrialized Uganda to *nine* times more—1 of 5—in postindustrial Japan (*Statistical Abstract* 2012:Table 1334). In just two decades, *half* the population of Italy and Japan will be older than 50 (Kinsella and Phillips 2005). The graying of the globe is so new that *two-thirds of all people who have ever passed age 50 in the history of the world are alive today* (Zaslow 2003).

As the numbers of elderly continue to grow, analysts have become alarmed about future liabilities for their care. This issue is especially troubling in western Europe and Japan, which have the largest percentage of citizens over age 60. The basic issue is, How can nations provide high-quality care for their growing numbers of elderly without burdening future generations with impossible taxes? Although more and more nations around the world are confronting this issue, no one has found a solution yet.

The Graying of America

As Figure 10.11 on the next page illustrates, the United States is part of this global trend. This figure shows how U.S. **life expectancy,** the number of years people can expect to live, has increased since 1900. To me, and perhaps to you, it is startling to realize that a hundred years ago the average U.S. man didn't make it to his 50th birthday, while the average U.S. woman died

What does "the social construction of aging" mean? Can you give an example?

FIGURE 10.10 The Graying of the Globe

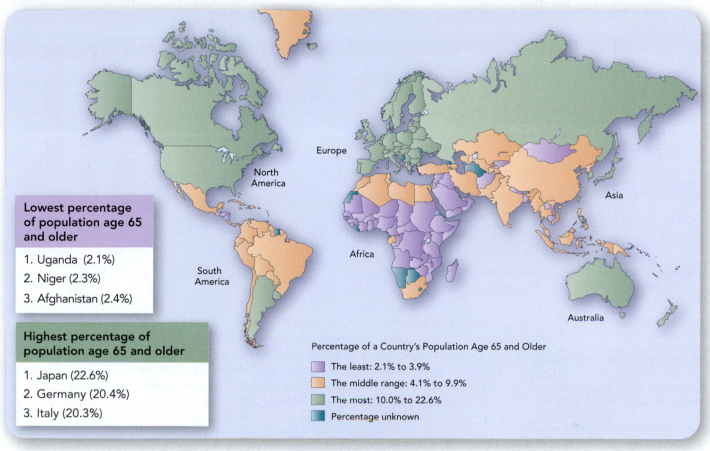

Lowest percentage of population age 65 and older

1. Uganda (2.1%)
2. Niger (2.3%)
3. Afghanistan (2.4%)

Highest percentage of population age 65 and older

1. Japan (22.6%)
2. Germany (20.4%)
3. Italy (20.3%)

Europe

North America

Asia

Africa

South America

Australia

Percentage of a Country's Population Age 65 and Older

- The least: 2.1% to 3.9%
- The middle range: 4.1% to 9.9%
- The most: 10.0% to 22.6%
- Percentage unknown

Source: By the author. Based on *Statistical Abstract of the United States* 2011:Table 1333.

FIGURE 10.11 U.S. Life Expectancy by Year of Birth

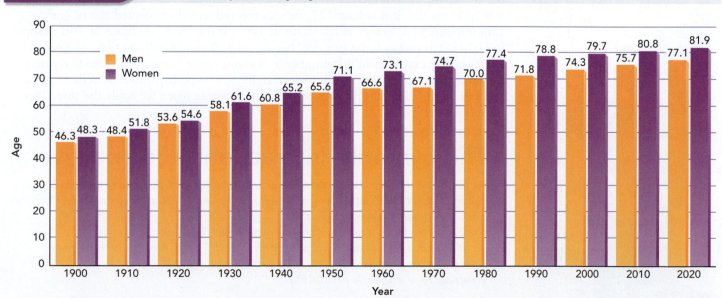

Men
Women

Year	Men	Women
1900	46.3	48.3
1910	48.4	51.8
1920	53.6	54.6
1930	58.1	61.6
1940	60.8	65.2
1950	65.6	71.1
1960	66.6	73.1
1970	67.1	74.7
1980	70.0	77.4
1990	71.8	78.8
2000	74.3	79.7
2010	75.7	80.8
2020	77.1	81.9

Age

Year

Sources: By the author. Based on *Historical Statistics of the United States, Colonial Times to 1970*, Bicentennial Edition, Part I, Series B, 107–115; *Statistical Abstract of the United States* 2012:Table 104.

What indicators are there that the globe is "graying"?

FIGURE 10.12   The Graying of America: Americans Age 65 and Older

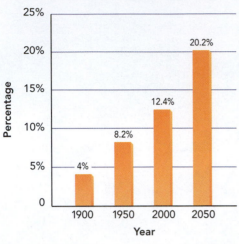

Source: By the author. Based on *Statistical Abstract of the United States* 2012:Table 9, and earlier years.

FIGURE 10.13   The Median Age of the U.S. Population

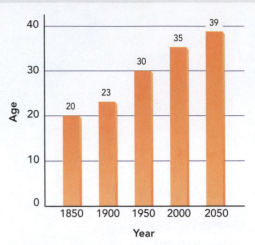

Source: By the author. Based on *Statistical Abstract of the United States* 2000:Table 14; 2012:Table 9, and earlier years.

When does old age begin? And what activities are appropriate for the elderly? From this photo that I took of Munimah, a 65-year-old bonded laborer in Chennai, India, you can see how culturally relative these questions are. No one in Chennai thinks it is extraordinary that this woman makes her living by carrying heavy rocks all day in the burning, tropical sun. Working next to her in the quarry is her 18-year-old son, who breaks the rocks into the size that his mother carries.

shortly after her 50th birthday. Since then, we've added about *30* years to our life expectancy, and Americans born today can expect to live into their 70s or 80s.

The term **graying of America** refers to this growing percentage of older people in the U.S. population. Look at Figure 10.12 above. In 1900 only 4 percent of Americans were age 65 and older. Today 13 percent are. The average 65-year-old can expect to live another 19 years (*Statistical Abstract* 2012:Table 107). U.S. society has become so "gray" that, as Figure 10.13 shows, the median age has almost *doubled* since 1850. Today, there are 8 million *more* elderly Americans than there are teenagers.

As anyone who has ever visited Florida knows, the elderly population is not distributed evenly around the country. (As Jerry Seinfeld sardonically noted, "There's a law that when you get old, you've got to move to Florida.") The Social Map on the next page shows how uneven this distribution is.

Although more people are living to old age, the maximum length of life possible, the **life span,** has not increased. No one knows, however, just what that maximum is. We do know that it is at least 122, for this was the well-documented age of Jeanne Louise Calment of France at her death in 1997. If the birth certificate of Tuti Yusupova in Uzbekistan proves to be genuine, her age of 130 would indicate that the human life span may exceed even this number by a comfortable margin. It is also likely that advances in genetics will extend the human life span—perhaps to hundreds of years.

Let's see the different pictures of aging that emerge when we apply the three theoretical perspectives.

The Symbolic Interactionist Perspective

At first, the audience sat quietly as the developers explained their plans to build a high-rise apartment building. After a while, people began to shift uncomfortably in their seats. Then they began to show open hostility.

"That's too much money to spend on those people," said one.

"You even want them to have a swimming pool?" asked another incredulously.

Finally, one young woman put their attitudes in a nutshell when she asked, "Who wants all those old people around?"

When physician Robert Butler (1975, 1980) heard these complaints about plans to build apartments for senior citizens, he began to realize how deeply antagonistic feelings toward

What does "graying of America" mean? Why is this term accurate?

FIGURE 10.14   As Florida Goes, So Goes the Nation

Source: By the author. Based on *Statistical Abstract of the United States* 2011:Table 18. Projections to 2015.

the elderly can run. He coined the term **ageism** to refer to prejudice and discrimination directed against people because of their age. Let's see how ageism developed in U.S. society.

Shifting Meanings of Growing Old

As we have seen, there is nothing inherent in old age to produce any particular attitude, negative or not. Some historians point out that in early U.S. society old age was regarded positively (Cottin 1979; Fleming et al. 2003). In colonial times, growing old was seen as an accomplishment because so few people made it to old age. With no pensions, the elderly continued to work at jobs that changed little over time. They were viewed as storehouses of knowledge about work skills and sources of wisdom about how to live a long life.

The coming of industrialization eroded these bases of respect. The better sanitation and medical care allowed more people to reach old age, and no longer was being elderly an honorable distinction. Industrialization's new forms of mass production also made young workers as productive as the elderly. Coupled with mass education, this stripped away the elderly's superior knowledge (Cowgill 1974; Hunt 2005).

A basic principle of symbolic interactionism is that we perceive both ourselves and others according to the symbols of our culture. When the meaning of old age changed from an asset to a liability, not only did younger people come to view the elderly differently but the elderly also began to perceive themselves in a new light. This shift in meaning is demonstrated in the way people lie about their age: They used to say that they were older than they were, but now claim to be younger than their true ages (Clair et al. 1993).

However, once again, the meaning of old age is shifting—and this time in a positive direction. This is largely because most of today's U.S. elderly can take care of themselves financially, and many are well-off. As the vast numbers of the baby boom generation enter their elderly years, their better health and financial strength will contribute to still more positive images of the elderly. If this symbolic shift continues, the next step—now in process—is to celebrate old age as a time of renewal.

How have Americans' ideas about the elderly changed over time?

Old age will be viewed not as a period that precedes death, but, rather, as a new stage of growth.

Even theories of old age have taken a more positive tone. A theory that goes by the mouthful *gerotranscendence* was developed by Swedish sociologist Lars Tornstam. The thrust of this theory is that as people grow old they transcend their limited views of life. They become less self-centered and begin to feel more at one with the universe. Coming to see things as less black and white, they develop subtler ways of viewing right and wrong and tolerate more ambiguity (Manheimer 2005; Hyse and Tornstam 2009). However, this theory seems to miss the mark. I have seen some elderly people grow softer and more spiritual, but I have also seen others turn bitter, close up, and become even more judgmental of others. The theory's limitations should become apparent shortly.

The Influence of the Mass Media

Read
Growing Old in an Arab American Family by Hani Fakhouri
on **mysoclab.com**

In Chapter 3 (pp. 77, 79–80), we noted that the mass media help to shape our ideas about both gender and relationships between men and women. As a powerful source of symbols, the media also influence our ideas of the elderly, the topic of the Mass Media box on the next page.

In Sum: Symbolic interactionists stress that old age has no inherent meaning. There is nothing about old age to automatically summon forth responses of honor and respect, as with the Abkhasians, or any other response. Culture shapes how we perceive the elderly, including the ways we view our own aging. In short, the social modifies the biological.

Stereotypes, which play such a profound role in social life, are a basic area of sociological investigation. In contemporary society, the mass media are a major source of stereotypes.

The Functionalist Perspective

Functionalists analyze how the parts of society work together. Among the components of society are **age cohorts**—people who were born at roughly the same time and who pass through the life course together. *Age cohorts* might seem to be merely an abstract term, but they have a huge impact on your life. When you finish college, for example, if the age cohort nearing retirement is large (a "baby boom" generation), more jobs will be available to you and your peers. In contrast, if it is small (a "baby bust" generation), fewer jobs will be open.

Let's consider people who are about to retire or who have retired recently. We will review theories that focus on how people adjust to retirement.

Disengagement Theory

Think about how disruptive it would be if the elderly left their jobs only when they died or became incompetent. How does society get the elderly to leave their positions so younger people can take them? According to **disengagement theory,** developed by Elaine Cumming and William Henry (1961), this is the function of pensions.

How is the meaning of "old age" changing today?

The Cultural Lens: Shaping Our Perceptions of the Elderly

The mass media profoundly influence our perception of people. What we hear and see on television and in the movies, the songs we listen to, the books and magazines we read—all become part of the cultural lens through which we view the world. The media shape our images of minorities and dominant groups; men, women, and children; people with disabilities; those from other cultures—and the elderly.

The shaping of our images and perception of the elderly is subtle, so much so that it usually occurs without our awareness. The elderly, for example, are underrepresented on television and in most popular magazines. This leaves a covert message—that the elderly are of little consequence and can be safely ignored.

The media also reflect and reinforce stereotypes of *gender age*. Older male news anchors are likely to be retained, while female anchors who turn the same age are more likely to be transferred to less visible positions. Similarly, in movies older men are more likely to play romantic leads—and to play them opposite much younger rising stars.

The message might be subtle, but it is not lost. The more television that people watch, the more they perceive the elderly in negative terms. The elderly, too,

Aging is more than biology. In some cultures, Mariah Carey, 43, would be considered elderly. Carey is shown here with her husband, Nick Cannon, 31.

internalize these negative images, which, in turn, influences the ways they view themselves. These images are so powerful that they affect the elderly's health, even the way they walk (Donlon et al. 2005).

We become fearful of growing old, and we go to great lengths to deny that we are losing our youth. Fear and denial play into the hands of advertisers, of course, who exploit our concerns. They help us deny this biological reality by selling us hair dyes, skin creams, and other products that are designed to conceal even the appearance of old age. For these same reasons, plastic surgeons do a thriving business as they remove telltale signs of aging.

The elderly's growing numbers and affluence translate into economic clout and political power. It is inevitable, then, that the media's images of the elderly will change. An indication of that change is shown in the photo at left.

For Your Consideration

➤ What other examples of fear and denial of growing old are you familiar with? What examples of older men playing romantic leads with younger women can you give? Of older women and younger men? Why do you think we have gender age?

Pensions get the elderly to *disengage* from their positions and hand them over to younger people. Retirement, then, is a mutually beneficial arrangement between two parts of society.

Evaluation of the Theory.   Certainly pensions do entice the elderly to leave their jobs so a younger generation can step in. I think we all know this, so it isn't much of a theory. Critics have also pointed out that the elderly don't really "disengage." People who quit their jobs don't sit in rocking chairs and watch the world go by. Instead of disengaging, the retired *exchange* one set of roles for another (Jerrome 1992). They find these new ways of conducting their lives, which often center on friendship, no less satisfying than their earlier roles. In addition, the meaning of retirement has changed since this "theory" was developed. Less and less does retirement mean an end to work. Millions slow down, staying at their jobs, but putting in fewer hours. Others work as consultants part-time. Some switch careers, even in their 60s, some even in their 70s. If disengagement theory is ever resurrected, it must come to grips with our new patterns of retirement.

Activity Theory

Are retired people more satisfied with life? (All that extra free time and not having to kowtow to a boss must be nice.) Are intimate activities more satisfying than formal ones? Such questions are the focus of **activity theory.** Although we could consider this theory from other perspectives, we are examining it from the functionalist perspective because its focus is how disengagement is functional or dysfunctional.

Researchers are exploring factors that can make old age an enjoyable period of life, those conditions that increase people's mental, social, emotional, and physical well-being. As research progresses, do you think we will reach the point where the average old person will be in this woman's physical condition?

Evaluation of the Theory.   A study of retired people in France found that some people are happier when they are more active, but others prefer less involvement (Keith 1982). Similarly, most people find informal, intimate activities, such as spending time with friends, to be more satisfying than formal activities. But not everyone does. In one study, 2,000 retired U.S. men reported formal activities to be as important as informal ones. Even solitary tasks, such as doing home repairs, had about the same impact as intimate activities on these men's life satisfaction (Beck and Page 1988). It is the same for spending time with adult children. "Often enough" for some parents is "not enough" or even "too much" for others. In short, researchers have discovered the obvious: What makes life satisfying for one person doesn't work for another. (This, of course, can be a source of intense frustration for retired couples.)

Continuity Theory

Another theory of aging called **continuity theory** focuses, as its name implies, on how the elderly continue ties with their past (Wang and Shultz 2010). When they retire, many people take on new roles that are similar to the ones they gave up. For example, a former CEO might serve as a consultant, a retired electrician might do small electrical repairs, or a pensioned banker might take over the finances of her church. Researchers have found that people who are active in multiple roles (wife, author, mother, intimate friend, church member, etc.) are better equipped to handle the changes that come with growing old. Social class is also significant: With their greater resources, people from higher social classes adjust better to the challenges of aging.

Evaluation of the Theory.   The basic criticism of continuity theory is that it is too broad (Hatch 2000). We all have anchor points based on our particular experiences in life, and we all rely on them to make adjustments to the changes we encounter. This applies to people of all ages beyond infancy. This theory is really a collection of loosely connected ideas, with no specific application to the elderly.

In Sum: The *broader* perspective of the functionalists is how society's parts work together to keep society running smoothly. If the younger workers had to fight to take over the jobs of the elderly, it would be disruptive to society. To make this process work smoothly, the elderly are offered pensions, which entice them to leave their positions. Functionalists also use a *narrower* perspective, focusing on how individuals adjust to their retirement. The findings of this narrower perspective are too mixed to be of much value—except that people who have better resources and are active in multiple roles adjust better to old age (Crosnoe and Elder 2002).

Because U.S. workers do not have to retire by any certain age, it is also important to study how people decide to keep working or to retire in the first place. After they retire, how do they reconstruct their identities and come to terms with their changed lives? As the United States grows even grayer, these should prove productive areas of sociological theory and research.

For a unique view of continuity into old age, one I think you will enjoy, read the Down-to-Earth Sociology box on the next page.

The Conflict Perspective

As you know, the conflict perspective's guiding principle is how social groups struggle to control power and resources. How does this apply to society's age groups? Regardless of whether the young and old recognize it, say conflict theorists, they are opponents in a struggle that threatens to throw society into turmoil. Let's look at how the passage of Social Security legislation fits the conflict view.

Down-to-Earth Sociology

Feisty to the End: Gender Roles among the Elderly

This image of my father makes me smile—not because he was arrested as an old man, but, rather, because of the events that led to his arrest. My dad had always been a colorful character, ready with endless ribald jokes and a hearty laugh. He carried these characteristics into his old age.

In his late 70s, my dad was living in a small apartment in a complex for the elderly in Minnesota. The adjacent building was a nursing home, the next destination for the residents of these apartments. None of them liked to think about this "home," because no one survived it—yet they all knew that this would be their destination. Under the watchful eye of these elderly neighbors, care in the nursing home was fairly good. Until they were transferred to this unwelcome last stopping-place, life for them went on "as usual" in the complex for the elderly.

According to the police report and my dad's account, here is what happened:

Dad was sitting in the downstairs lounge with other residents, waiting for the mail to arrive, a daily ritual that the residents looked forward to. For some reason known only to him, my dad hooked his cane under the dress of an elderly woman, lifted up her skirt, and laughed. Understandably, this upset her, as well as her husband, who was standing next to her. Angry, the man moved toward my father, threatening him.

I say "moved," rather than "lunged," because this man was using a walker. My dad started to run away from this threat. Actually, "run" isn't quite the right word. "Hobbled" would be a better term.

My dad fled as fast as he could using his cane, while the other man pursued him as fast as he could using his walker.

During their elderly years, men and women continue to exhibit aspects of the gender roles that they learned and played in their younger years.

Wheezing and puffing, the two went from the lounge into the long adjoining hall, pausing now and then to catch their breath. Tiring the most, the other man gave up the pursuit. He then called the police.

When the police officer arrived, he said, "Uncle Marv, I'm sorry, but I'm going to have to arrest you." (This event occurred in a small town, and the officer assigned this case turned out to be Dad's nephew.)

Dad went before a judge, who could hardly keep a straight face. He gave Dad a small fine and warned him to behave himself. The apartment manager also gave Dad a warning: One more incident, and he would have to move out of the complex.

Dad's wife wasn't too happy about the situation, either.

This event was brought to mind by a newspaper account of a fight that broke out at the food bar of a retirement home ("Melee Breaks . . ." 2004). It seems that one elderly man criticized the way another man was picking through the salad. When a fight broke out between the two, several elderly people were hurt as they tried either to intervene or to flee.

For Your Consideration

→ People carry their personalities, values, and other traits into old age. Among these characteristics are gender roles. What examples of gender roles do you see in the events related here? Are you familiar with how old people continue to show their femininity or masculinity?

Fighting for Resources: Social Security Legislation

In the 1920s, before Social Security provided an income for the aged, two-thirds of all citizens over 65 had no savings and could not support themselves (Holtzman 1963; Crossen 2004). Destitution in old age loomed even larger for workers during the Great Depression, and in 1930 Francis Townsend, a physician, started a movement to rally older citizens. He soon had one-third of all Americans over age 65 enrolled in his Townsend Clubs. They demanded that the federal government impose a national sales tax of 2 percent to provide $200 a month for every person over 65 ($2,100 a month in today's money). In 1934, the Townsend Plan went before Congress. Because it called for such high payments and many were afraid that it would destroy people's incentive to save for the future, members of Congress looked for a way to reject the plan without appearing to oppose the elderly. When President Roosevelt announced his own, more modest Social Security plan in 1934, Congress embraced it (Schottland 1963; Amenta 2006).

FIGURE 10.15 Social Security Payments to Beneficiaries

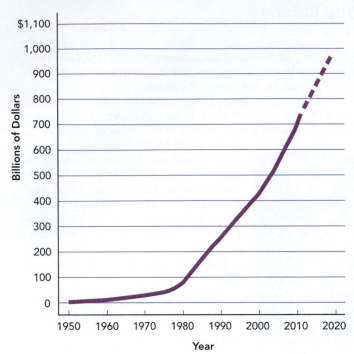

Source: By the author. Based on *Statistical Abstract of the United States* 1997: Table 518; 2012:Table 474. Broken line indicates the author's projections.

To provide jobs for younger people, the new Social Security law required that workers retire at age 65. It did not matter how well people did their work, or how much they needed the pay. For decades, the elderly protested. Finally, in 1986, Congress eliminated mandatory retirement. Today, almost 90 percent of Americans retire by age 65, but most do so voluntarily. No longer can they be forced out of their jobs simply because of age.

Let's look at what has happened to this groundbreaking legislation since it was passed.

Intergenerational Competition and Conflict

Social Security came about not because the members of Congress had generous hearts, but out of a struggle between competing interest groups. As conflict theorists stress, equilibrium between competing groups is only a temporary balancing of oppositional forces, one that can be upset at any time. Following this principle, could conflict between the elderly and the young be in our future? Let's consider this possibility.

If you listen closely, you can hear ripples of grumbling—complaints that the elderly are getting more than their fair share of society's resources. The huge costs of Social Security and Medicare are a special concern. As incredible as it may seem, *three of every five* tax dollars (60 percent) is spent on these two programs (*Statistical Abstract* 2012:Tables 474, 475). (Total U.S. government receipts are $2,173,000,000, and the total outlay for Medicare and Social Security is $1,307,000,000.) As Figure 10.15 shows, Social Security payments were $781 million in 1950; now they run *950 times* higher. Now look at Figure 10.16 on the next page, which shows the nation's huge—and growing—medical bill to care for the elderly. Like gasoline poured on a bonfire, these soaring costs may well fuel an intergenerational showdown.

Figure 10.17 on the next page shows another area of concern that can fuel an intergenerational conflict. You can see how greatly the condition of the elderly improved as the government transferred resources to them. But look also at the matching path of children's poverty. You can see that it is higher now than it was in 1967—and in all the years in between. Our economic crisis is having a severe toll on the nation's children.

Did the decline in the elderly's rate of poverty come at the expense of the nation's children? Of course not. Congress could have decided to finance the welfare of children just as it did that of the elderly. It chose not to. Why? Following conflict theorists, the reason is that the elderly, not the children, launched a broad assault on Congress. The lobbyists for the elderly put a lot of grease in the political reelection machine.

Figure 10.17 could indicate another reason for coming intergenerational conflict. If we take a 9 percent poverty rate as a goal for the nation's children—to match what the government has accomplished for the elderly—where would the money come from? If the issue gets pitched as a case of taking money from the elderly to give it to children, it can divide the generations. To get people to think that they must choose between pathetic children and suffering old folks can splinter voters into opposing groups. Would improving the welfare of children ever be presented in such a crass way? Ask yourself this: Do politicians ever try to manipulate the emotions of voters to get elected?

In Sum: Age groups are one of society's many groups that are competing for scarce resources. At some point, this competition may break into conflict.

Why might Social Security lead to conflict between the generations?

FIGURE 10.16   **Health Care Costs for the Elderly and Disabled**

✳ Explore
Living Data
on **mysoclab.com**

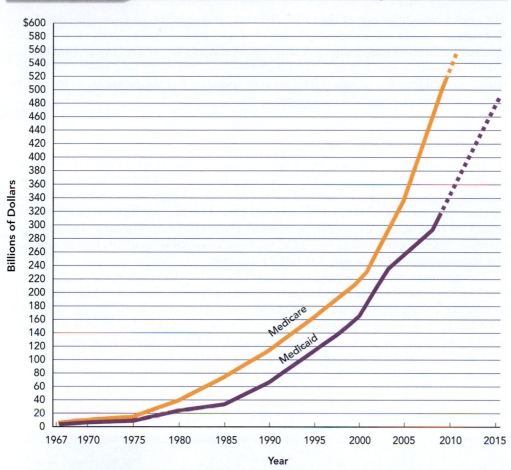

Note: Medicare is intended for the elderly and disabled, Medicaid for the poor. About 72 percent of Medicare ($373 billion) and 20 percent of Medicaid payments ($63 billion) go for medical care for the elderly (*Statistical Abstract* 2012:Tables 144, 151).

Source: By the author. Based on *Statistical Abstract of the United States* various years, and 2012:Tables 144, 151. Broken lines indicate the author's projections.

FIGURE 10.17   **Age and Trends in Poverty**

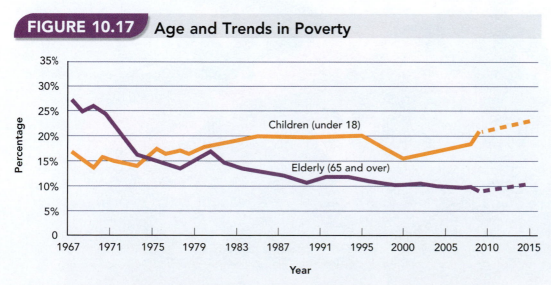

Source: By the author. Based on *Statistical Abstract of the United States*, various years, and 2012:Table 713. Broken lines indicate the author's projections.

Why might Medicare and Medicaid lead to conflict between the generations?

Looking toward the Future

Let's not lose sight of one of the major changes stressed in this chapter—that for the first time in human history huge numbers of people are becoming elderly. It is inevitable that such a fundamental change will have a powerful impact on societies around the world, so much so that it might even transform them. We don't have space to explore such potential transformations, which are only speculative at the moment, so let's try to catch a glimpse of a new approach to aging.

New Views of Aging

As huge numbers of Americans move into old age, the elderly have begun not only to challenge the demeaning stereotypes of the aged but also to develop new perspectives of aging. These new approaches build on the idea that old age should not be viewed as "a-time-close-to-death," but, rather, as a new period of life, one with its specific challenges, to be sure, but also one to be enjoyed, even celebrated. This new time of life provides unique opportunities to pursue interests, to develop creativity, and to enhance the appreciation of life's beauty and one's place in it.

This approach to aging is new, so we don't know the directions it will take. But if this emphasis continues, it will change how younger people view the elderly—as well as how the elderly view themselves. Negative stereotypes of weak old people living out their last years while they get ready to die might even be replaced with stereotypes of robust, engaged, thriving older adults (Manheimer 2005). No stereotype will encompass the reality of the elderly, of course, as the aged differ among themselves as much as younger people differ.

More and more, the goal of the elderly is to enjoy themselves—and with more resources at their disposal, more and more are able to do so. The goal of the Red Hat Society, with chapters around the nation, is simply for women to have fun.

What new views of aging are developing?

By the Numbers: Changes Over Time

Percentage of college students who are women	
1970	**NOW**
42%	**57**%

Percentage of dental school graduates who are women	
1970	**NOW**
1%	**46**%

Percentage of medical school graduates who are women	
1970	**NOW**
8%	**49**%

Women make up this percentage of the U.S. labor force		
1890	**1970**	**NOW**
18%	**38**%	**47**%

Percentage of men's salary earned by women	
1970	**NOW**
59%	**72**%

OTHER NUMBERS Number of U.S. senators since 1789	
MEN	**WOMEN**
2,000	**38**

Number of workers paying into Social Security for each beneficiary	
1950	**NOW**
16	**4**

Annual Social Security payments to beneficiaries	
1950	**NOW**
$781	**$720**
MILLION	**BILLION**

Life expectancy of the average American	
1900	**NOW**
47	**78**
YEARS	**YEARS**

Median age in the United States		
1900	**NOW**	**2050**
23	**37**	**39**

Americans age 65 and older		
1900	**NOW**	**2050**
4%	**13**%	**20**%

Percent in poverty			
Elderly		Children	
1970	**NOW**	**1970**	**NOW**
25%	**9**%	**16**%	**20**%

CHAPTER 10 Summary and Review

Issues of Sex and Gender

What is gender stratification?

The term **gender stratification** refers to unequal access to property, power, and prestige on the basis of sex. Each society establishes a structure that, on the basis of sex and gender, opens and closes doors to its privileges. P. 276.

How do sex and gender differ?

Sex refers to biological distinctions between males and females. It consists of both primary and secondary sex characteristics. **Gender,** in contrast, is what a society considers proper behaviors and attitudes for its male and female members. *Sex* physically distinguishes males from females; *gender* refers to what people call "masculine" and "feminine." P. 276.

Why do the behaviors of males and females differ?

The "nature versus nurture" debate refers to whether differences in the behaviors of males and females are caused by inherited (biological) or learned (cultural) characteristics. Almost all sociologists take the side of nurture. In recent years, however, sociologists have begun to cautiously open the door to biology. Pp. 276–279.

Gender Inequality in Global Perspective

How did females become a minority group?

Patriarchy, or male dominance, appears to be universal. The origin of discrimination against females is lost in history, but the primary theory of how females became a minority group in their own societies focuses on the physical limitations imposed by childbirth. Pp. 279–283.

What are some forms of global violence against females?

The major forms discussed are honor killings and female circumcision. Pp. 284.

Gender Inequality in the United States

Is the feminist movement new?

In what is called the "first wave," feminists made political demands for change in the early 1900s—and were met with hostility, and even violence. The "second wave" began in the 1960s and continues today. A "third wave" has emerged. Pp. 284–288.

What forms do gender inequality in health care and education take?

Physicians don't take women's health complaints as seriously as those of men, and they exploit women's fears, performing unnecessary hysterectomies. More women than men attend college, and each tends to select fields that are categorized as "feminine." Pp. 288–292.

How does gender inequality show up in the workplace?

All occupations show a gender gap in pay. For college graduates, the lifetime pay gap runs over a million dollars in favor of men. **Sexual harassment** also continues to be a reality of the workplace. Pp. 292–296.

What is the relationship between gender and violence?

Overwhelmingly, the victims of rape and murder are females. Conflict theorists point out that men use violence to maintain their power and privilege. Pp. 296–297.

What is the trend in gender inequality in politics?

Women continue to be underrepresented in politics, but the trend toward greater political equality is firmly in place. Pp. 297–298.

Aging in Global Perspective

How are the elderly treated around the world?

There is no single set of attitudes, beliefs, or policies regarding the aged. Rather, they vary around the world, from exclusion and killing to integration and honor. The global trend is for more people to live longer. Pp. 299–302.

The Symbolic Interactionist Perspective

What does the social construction of aging mean?

Nothing in the nature of aging produces any particular set of attitudes. Rather, attitudes toward the elderly are rooted in society and differ from one social group to another. Pp. 302–304.

The Functionalist Perspective

How is retirement functional for society?

Functionalists focus on how the withdrawal of the elderly from positions of responsibility benefits society. **Disengagement theory** examines retirement as a device for ensuring that a society's positions of responsibility are passed smoothly from one generation to the next. **Activity theory** examines how people adjust when they retire. **Continuity theory** focuses on how people adjust to growing old by continuing their roles and coping techniques. Pp. 304–306.

The Conflict Perspective

Is there conflict among different age groups?

Social Security legislation is an example of one generation making demands on another generation for limited resources. As the number of retired people grows, there are relatively fewer workers to support them. The mushrooming costs of social security, Medicare, and Medicaid are growing concerns. Pp. 306–310.

Looking toward the Future

What trends indicate the future for gender and aging?

The trends are positive: Increasing equality and political participation for women and, for the elderly, longer lives, less poverty, and the development of creative aging. P. 310.

Thinking Critically about Chapter 10

1. What is your position on the "nature versus nurture" (biology or culture) debate? What materials in this chapter support your position?

2. Why do you think that the gender gap in pay exists all over the world?

3. How does culture influence our ideas about the elderly?

South Africa

In 1949, George Orwell wrote *1984,* a book about a time in the future when a government known as "Big Brother" dominates society, dictating almost every aspect of each individual's life. Even loving someone is considered sinister—a betrayal of the supreme love and total allegiance that all citizens owe Big Brother.

Despite the danger, Winston and Julia fall in love. They delight in each other, but they must meet furtively, always with the threat of discovery hanging over their heads. When informers turn them in, interrogators separate Julia and Winston and try to destroy their affection and restore their loyalty to Big Brother.

Winston's tormentor is O'Brien, who straps Winston into a chair so tightly that he can't even move his head. O'Brien explains that inflicting pain is not always enough to break a person's will, but everyone has a breaking point. There is some worst fear that will push anyone over the edge.

O'Brien tells Winston that he has discovered his worst fear. Then he sets a cage with two starving giant sewer rats on the table next to Winston. O'Brien picks up a hood connected to the door of the cage and places it over Winston's head. He then explains that when he presses the lever, the door of the cage will slide up, and the rats will shoot out like bullets and bore straight into Winston's face. Winston's eyes, the only part of his body that he can move, dart back and forth, revealing his terror. Speaking so quietly that Winston has to strain to hear him, O'Brien adds that the rats sometimes attack the eyes first, but sometimes they burrow through the cheeks and devour the tongue. When O'Brien places his hand on the lever, Winston realizes that the only way out is for someone else to take his place. But who? Then he hears his own voice screaming, "Do it to Julia! . . . Tear her face off. Strip her to the bones. Not me! Julia! Not me!"

> Even loving someone is considered sinister—a betrayal of the supreme love and total allegiance that all citizens owe Big Brother.

Orwell does not describe Julia's interrogation, but when Julia and Winston see each other later, they realize that each has betrayed the other. Their love is gone. Big Brother has won.

Winston's and Julia's misplaced loyalty had made them political heretics, a danger to the state, for every citizen had the duty to place the state above all else in life. To preserve the state's dominance over the individual, their allegiance to one another had to be stripped from them. As you see, it was.

Politics: Establishing Leadership

Although seldom as dramatic as the interrogations of Winston and Julia, politics is always about power and authority. Let's explore this topic that is so significant for our lives.

Power, Authority, and Violence

To exist, every society must have a system of leadership. Some people must have power over others. As Max Weber (1913/1947) pointed out, we perceive power as either legitimate or illegitimate. *Legitimate* power is called **authority.** This is power that people accept as right. In contrast, *illegitimate* power—called **coercion**—is power that people do not accept as just.

> *Imagine that you are on your way to buy the hot new cell phone that is on sale for $250. As you approach the store, a man jumps out of an alley and shoves a gun in your face. He demands your money. Frightened for your life, you hand over your $250. After filing a police report, you head back to college to take a sociology exam. You are running late, so you step on the gas. As you hit 85, you see flashing blue and red lights in your rearview mirror. Your explanation about the robbery doesn't faze the officer—or the judge who hears your case a few weeks later. She first lectures you on safety and then orders you to pay $50 in court costs plus $10 for every mile over 65. You pay the $250.*

The mugger, the police officer, and the judge—all have power, and in each case you part with $250. What, then, is the difference? The difference is that the mugger has no authority. His power is *illegitimate*—he has no *right* to do what he did. In contrast, you acknowledge that the officer has the right to stop you and that the judge has the right to fine you. They have authority, or *legitimate* power.

Authority and Legitimate Violence

As sociologist Peter Berger observed, it makes little difference whether you willingly pay the fine that the judge levies against you or refuse to pay it. The court will get its money one way or another.

> *There may be innumerable steps before its application [of violence], in the way of warnings and reprimands. But if all the warnings are disregarded, even in so slight a matter as paying a traffic ticket, the last thing that will happen is that a couple of cops show up at the door with handcuffs and a Black Maria [paddy wagon]. Even the moderately courteous cop who hands out the initial traffic ticket is likely to wear a gun—just in case. (Berger 1963)*

The ultimate foundation of any political order is violence, never more starkly demonstrated than when a government takes a human life. This iconic photo from the war in Vietnam shows the chief of the national police shooting a suspected Viet Cong officer.

What is the difference between authority and coercion?

The *government*, then, also called the **state,** claims a monopoly on legitimate force or violence. This point, made by Max Weber (1946, 1922/1978)—that the state claims both the exclusive right to use violence and the right to punish everyone else who uses violence—is crucial to our understanding of politics. If someone owes you $100, you cannot take the money by force, much less imprison that person. The state, in contrast, can. The ultimate proof of the state's authority is that you cannot kill someone because he or she has done something that you consider absolutely horrible—but the state can. As Berger (1963) summarized this matter, "*Violence is the ultimate foundation of any political order.*"

But just why do people accept power as legitimate? Max Weber (1922/1978) identified three sources of authority: traditional, rational–legal, and charismatic. Let's examine each.

Traditional Authority

Throughout history, the most common basis for authority has been tradition. **Traditional authority,** which is based on custom, is the hallmark of tribal groups. In these societies, custom dictates basic relationships. For example, birth into a particular family makes an individual the chief, king, or queen. As far as members of that society are concerned, this is the right way to determine who shall rule because "We've always done it this way."

Although traditional authority declines with industrialization, it never dies out. Even though we live in a postindustrial society, parents continue to exercise authority over their children *because* parents always have had such authority. From generations past, we inherit the idea that parents should discipline their children, choose their doctors and schools, and teach them religion and morality.

Rational–Legal Authority

The second type of authority, **rational–legal authority,** is based not on custom but on written rules. *Rational* means reasonable, and *legal* means part of law. Thus *rational–legal* refers to matters that have been agreed to by reasonable people and written into law (or regulations of some sort). The matters that are agreed to may be as broad as a constitution that specifies the rights of all members of a society or as narrow as a contract between two individuals. Because bureaucracies are based on written rules, rational–legal authority is also called *bureaucratic authority*.

Rational–legal authority comes from the *position* that someone holds, not from the person who holds that position. In the United States, for example, the president's authority comes from the legal power assigned to that office, as specified in a written constitution, not from custom or the individual's personal characteristics. In rational–legal authority, everyone—no matter how high the office held—is subject to the organization's written rules. In governments based on traditional authority, the ruler's word may be law; but in those based on rational–legal authority, the ruler's word is subject to the law.

Charismatic Authority

Joan of Arc is an example of **charismatic authority,** the third type of authority Weber identified. (*Charisma* is a Greek word that means a gift freely and graciously given [Arndt and Gingrich 1957].) People are drawn to a charismatic individual because they believe that individual has been touched by God or has been endowed by nature with exceptional qualities (Lipset 1993). The armies did not follow Joan of Arc because it was the custom to do so, as in traditional authority. Nor did they risk their lives fighting alongside her because she held a position defined by written rules, as in rational–legal authority. Instead, people followed her because they were attracted by her outstanding traits. They saw her as a messenger of God, fighting on the side of justice, and they accepted her leadership because of these appealing qualities.

One of the best examples of charismatic authority is Joan of Arc, shown here mounted and armored.

How is the state based on violence? Can you contrast traditional, rational–legal, and charismatic authority?

Charismatic authorities can be of any morality, from the saintly to the most bitterly evil. Like Joan of Arc, Adolf Hitler attracted throngs of people, providing the stuff of dreams and arousing them from disillusionment to hope. This poster from the 1930s, titled *Es Lebe Deutschland* ("Long Live Germany"), illustrates the qualities of leadership that Germans of that period saw in Hitler.

The Threat Posed by Charismatic Leaders.   Kings and queens owe allegiance to tradition, and presidents to written laws. To what, however, do charismatic leaders owe allegiance? Their authority resides in their ability to attract followers, which is often based on their sense of a special mission or calling. Not tied to tradition or the regulation of law, charismatic leaders pose a threat to the established political order. Following their personal inclination, charismatic leaders can inspire followers to disregard—or even to overthrow—traditional and rational–legal authorities.

This threat does not go unnoticed, and traditional and rational–legal authorities often oppose charismatic leaders. If they are not careful, however, their opposition can arouse even more positive sentiment in favor of the charismatic leader, who might be viewed as an underdog persecuted by the powerful. Occasionally the Roman Catholic Church faces such a threat, as when a priest claims miraculous powers that appear to be accompanied by amazing healings. As people flock to this individual, they bypass parish priests and the formal ecclesiastical structure. This transfer of allegiance from the organization to an individual threatens the church hierarchy. Consequently, church officials may encourage the priest to withdraw from the public eye, perhaps to a monastery, to rethink matters. This defuses the threat, reasserts rational–legal authority, and maintains the stability of the organization.

The Transfer of Authority

The orderly transfer of authority from one leader to another is crucial for social stability. Under traditional authority, people know who is next in line. Under rational–legal authority, people might not know who the next leader will be, but they do know how that person will be selected. South Africa provides a remarkable example of the orderly transfer of authority under a rational–legal organization. This country had been ripped apart by decades of racial–ethnic strife, including horrible killings committed by each side. Yet, by maintaining its rational–legal authority, the country was able to transfer power peacefully from the dominant group led by President de Klerk to the minority group led by Nelson Mandela.

Charismatic authority has no rules of succession, making it less stable than either traditional or rational–legal authority. Because charismatic authority is built around a single individual, the death or incapacitation of a charismatic leader can mean a bitter struggle for succession. To avoid this, some charismatic leaders make arrangements for an orderly transition of power by appointing a successor. This step does not guarantee orderly succession, for the followers may not have the same confidence in the designated heir as did the charismatic leader. A second strategy is for the charismatic leader to build an organization. As the organization develops rules or regulations, it transforms itself into a rational–legal organization. Weber used the term **routinization of charisma** to refer to the transition of authority from a charismatic leader to either traditional or rational–legal authority.

The transfer of authority in Cuba after Fidel Castro became ill is a remarkable example of the routinization of charisma. Castro was charismatic, attracting enough followers to overthrow Cuba's government. He ruled through a combination of personal charisma and bureaucratic machinery. Castro set up an organized system to transfer authority to his non-charismatic brother, Raul, who, in turn, made certain that authority was transferred in an orderly manner to the state bureaucracies (Hoffman 2011).

Types of Government

How do the various types of government—monarchies, democracies, dictatorships, and oligarchies—differ? As we compare them, let's also look at how the state arose and why the concept of citizenship was revolutionary.

Monarchies: The Rise of the State

Early societies were small and needed no extensive political system. They operated more like an extended family. As surpluses developed and societies grew larger, cities evolved—perhaps around 3500 B.C. (Fischer 1976). **City-states** then came into being, with power radiating outward from the city like a spider's web. Although the ruler of each city controlled the immediate surrounding area, the land between cities remained in dispute. Each city-state had its own **monarchy,** a king or queen whose right to rule was passed on to the monarch's children. If you drive through Spain, France, or Germany, you can still see evidence of former city-states. In the countryside, you will see only scattered villages. Farther on, your eye will be drawn to the outline of a castle on a faraway hill. As you get closer, you will see that the castle is surrounded by a city. Several miles farther, you will see another city, also dominated by a castle. Each city, with its castle, was once a center of power.

City-states often quarreled, and wars were common. The victors extended their rule, and eventually a single city-state was able to wield power over an entire region. As the size of these regions grew, the people slowly began to identify with the larger region. That is, they began to see distant inhabitants as "we" instead of "they." What we call the *state*—the political entity that claims a monopoly on the use of violence within a territory—came into being.

Democracies: Citizenship as a Revolutionary Idea

The United States had no city-states. Each colony, however, was small and independent like a city-state. After the American Revolution, the colonies united. With the greater strength and resources that came from political unity, they conquered almost all of North America, bringing it under the power of a central government.

This classic painting, "Siege at Yorktown" by Louis Coulder, depicts George Washington and Jean de Rochambeau giving the final orders for the attack on Yorktown in 1781. This turned out to be the decisive battle of the American Revolution, allowing the fledgling U.S. democracy to proceed.

What are city-states? How are they related to "the rise of the state"?

Democracy (or "democratization") is a global social movement. People all over the world yearn for the freedoms that are taken for granted in the Western democracies. Shown here is a man in a remote village in Indonesia, where democracy has gained a foothold.

The government formed in this new country was called a **democracy.** (Derived from two Greek words—*demos* [common people] and *kratos* [power]—democracy literally means "power to the people.") Because of the bitter antagonisms associated with the revolution against the British king, the founders of the new country were distrustful of monarchies. They wanted to put political decisions into the hands of the people.

This was not the first democracy the world had seen, but such a system had been tried before only with smaller groups. Athens, a city-state of Greece, practiced democracy 2,500 years ago, with each free male above a certain age having the right to be heard and to vote. Members of some Native American tribes, such as the Iroquois, also elected their chiefs, and in some, women were able to vote and to hold the office of chief. (The Incas and Aztecs of Mexico and Central America had monarchies.)

Because of their small size, tribes and cities were able to practice **direct democracy.** That is, they were small enough for the eligible voters to meet together, express their opinions, and then vote publicly—much like a town hall meeting today. As populous and spread out as the United States was, however, direct democracy was impossible, and the founders invented **representative democracy.** Certain citizens (at first only white male landowners) voted for men to represent them in Washington. Later, the vote was extended to men who didn't own property, to African American men, and, finally, to women.

Today we take the concept of citizenship for granted. What is not evident to us is that this idea had to be envisioned in the first place. There is nothing natural about citizenship; it is simply one way in which people choose to define themselves. Throughout most of human history, people were thought to *belong* to a clan, to a tribe, or even to a ruler. The idea of **citizenship**—that by virtue of birth and residence people have basic rights—is quite new to the human scene.

The concept of representative democracy based on citizenship—perhaps the greatest gift the United States has given to the world—was revolutionary. Power was to be vested in the people themselves, and government was to flow from the people. That this concept was revolutionary is generally forgotten, but its implementation meant *the reversal of traditional ideas. It made the government responsive to the people's will, rather than the people being responsive to the government's will.* To keep the government responsive to the needs of its citizens, people were expected to express dissent. In a widely quoted statement, Thomas Jefferson observed:

> *A little rebellion now and then is a good thing. . . . It is a medicine necessary for the sound health of government. . . . God forbid that we should ever be twenty years without such a rebellion. . . . The tree of liberty must be refreshed from time to time with the blood of patriots and tyrants. (In Hellinger and Judd 1991)*

The idea of **universal citizenship**—of *everyone* having the same basic rights by virtue of being born in a country (or by immigrating and becoming a naturalized citizen)—flowered slowly, and came into practice only through fierce struggle. When the United States was founded, for example, this idea was still in its infancy. Today, it seems inconceivable to Americans that sex or race–ethnicity should be the basis for denying anyone the right to vote, hold office, make a contract, testify in court, or own property. For earlier generations of property-owning white American men, however, it seemed just as inconceivable that women, racial–ethnic minorities, and the poor should be *allowed* such rights.

Dictatorships and Oligarchies: The Seizure of Power

If an individual seizes power and then dictates his will to the people, the government is known as a **dictatorship.** If a small group seizes power, the government is called an **oligarchy.** The occasional coups in Central and South America and Africa, in which military leaders seize control of a country, are often oligarchies. Although one individual may be named president, often it is military officers, working behind the scenes, who make the decisions. If their designated president becomes uncooperative, they remove him from office and appoint another.

Monarchies, dictatorships, and oligarchies vary in the amount of control they wield over their citizens. **Totalitarianism** is almost *total* control of a people by the government. In Nazi Germany, Hitler organized a ruthless secret police force, the Gestapo, which searched for any sign of dissent. Spies even watched how moviegoers reacted to newsreels, reporting those who did not respond "appropriately" (Hippler 1987). Saddam Hussein acted just as ruthlessly toward Iraqis. The lucky ones who opposed Hussein were shot; the unlucky ones had their eyes gouged out, were bled to death, or were buried alive (Amnesty International 2005). The punishment for telling a joke about Hussein was to have your tongue cut out.

People around the world find great appeal in the freedom that is inherent in citizenship and representative democracy. Those who have no say in their government's decisions, or who face prison or even death for expressing dissent, find in these ideas the hope for a brighter future. With today's electronic communications, people no longer remain ignorant of whether they are more or less politically privileged than others. This knowledge produces pressure for greater citizen participation in government—and for governments to respond to their citizens' concerns. As electronic communications develop further, this pressure will increase.

The U.S. Political System

With this global background, let's examine the U.S. political system. We shall consider the two major political parties and examine voting patterns and the role of lobbyists and PACs.

Political Parties and Elections

After the founding of the United States, numerous political parties emerged. By the time of the Civil War, however, two parties dominated U.S. politics: the Democrats, who in the public mind are associated with the working class, and the Republicans, who are associated with wealthier people (Burnham 1983). In pre-elections, called *primaries,* the voters decide who will represent their party. The candidates chosen by each party then campaign, trying to appeal to the most voters. The Social Map on the next page shows how Americans align themselves with political parties.

Slices from the Center.   Although the Democrats and Republicans have somewhat contrasting philosophical principles, each party represents *slightly different slices of the center.* Each party may ridicule the other and promote different legislation—and they do fight hard battles—but they both firmly support such fundamentals of U.S. political philosophy as free public education; a strong military; freedom of religion, speech, and assembly; and, of course, capitalism—especially the private ownership of property. This makes it difficult to distinguish a conservative Democrat from a liberal Republican.

The extremes are easy to see, however. Deeply committed Democrats support legislation that transfers income from those who are richer to those who are poorer or that controls wages, working conditions, and competition. Deeply committed Republicans, in contrast, oppose such legislation.

Those who are elected to Congress may cross party lines. That is, some Democrats vote for legislation proposed by Republicans, and vice versa. This happens because officeholders support their party's philosophy, but not necessarily its specific proposals. When it comes to a particular bill, such as raising the minimum wage, some conservative Democrats may view the measure as unfair to small employers and vote with the Republicans against the bill. At the same time, liberal Republicans—feeling that the proposal is just, or sensing a dominant sentiment in voters back home—may side with its Democratic backers.

Although the Democrats and the Republicans represent slightly different slices of the center, those differences arouse extreme emotions, pandered to by both parties. Occasionally, voters get tired of the constant posing.

FIGURE 11.1   Which Political Party Dominates?

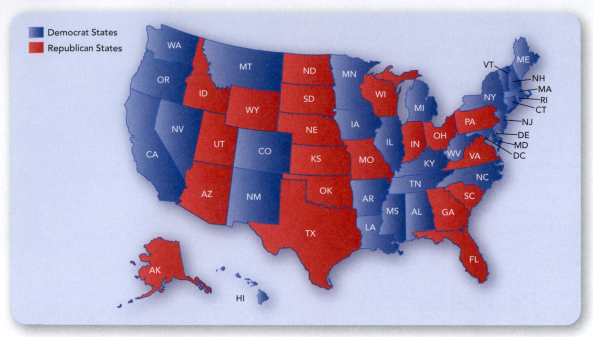

Note: Domination by a political party does not refer to votes for president or Congress. This social map is based on the composition of the states' upper and lower houses. When different parties dominate a state's houses, the total number of legislators was used. In Nebraska, where no parties are designated, the percentage vote for president was the determining factor.

Source: By the author. Based on *Statistical Abstract of the United States* 2011:Table 411.

✳ Explore
Living Data
on **mysoclab.com**

Third Parties.   Third parties sometimes play a role in U.S. politics, but to gain power, they must also support these centrist themes. Any party that advocates radical change is doomed to a short life. Because most Americans consider votes for them as wasted, third parties do not do well at the polls. Two exceptions are the Bull Moose party, whose candidate, Theodore Roosevelt, won more votes in 1912 than William Howard Taft, the Republican presidential candidate, and the United We Stand (Reform) party, founded by billionaire Ross Perot, which won 19 percent of the vote in 1992. Amidst internal bickering, the Reform Party declined rapidly and fell off the political map (Bridgwater 1953; *Statistical Abstract* 1995:Table 437; 2012:Table 403).

Voting Patterns

Year after year, Americans show consistent voting patterns. From Table 11.1 on the next page, you can see that the percentage of people who vote increases with age. This table also shows how significant race–ethnicity is. Non-Hispanic whites are more likely to vote than are African Americans, although when Barack Obama ran for president in 2008, their totals were almost identical. You can also see that both whites and African Americans are much more likely to vote than are Latinos and Asian Americans.

Look at education on Table 11.1. Notice how voting increases with each level of education. Education is so significant that college graduates are twice as likely to vote as are high school dropouts. You can also see how much more

From *The Wall Street Journal*, permission Cartoon Features Syndicate

Why do third parties have little chance of success in the United States?

TABLE 11.1	Who Votes for President?					
	1988	**1992**	**1996**	**2000**	**2004**	**2008**
Overall						
Americans Who Voted	57%	61%	54%	55%	58%	58%
Age						
18–20	33%	39%	31%	28%	41%	41%
21–24	46%	46%	33%	35%	43%	47%
25–34	48%	53%	43%	44%	47%	49%
35–44	61%	64%	55%	55%	57%	55%
45–64	68%	70%	64%	64%	67%	65%
65 and older	69%	70%	67%	68%	69%	68%
Sex						
Male	56%	60%	53%	53%	56%	56%
Female	58%	62%	56%	56%	60%	60%
Race–Ethnicity						
Whites	64%	70%	56%	56%	60%	60%
African Americans	55%	59%	51%	54%	56%	61%
Asian Americans	NA	54%	NA	25%	30%	32%
Latinos	48%	52%	27%	28%	28%	32%
Education						
High school dropouts	41%	41%	34%	34%	35%	34%
High school graduates	55%	58%	49%	49%	52%	51%
Some college	65%	69%	61%	60%	66%	65%
College graduates	78%	81%	73%	72%	74%	73%
Marital Status						
Married	NA	NA	66%	67%	71%	70%
Divorced	NA	NA	50%	53%	58%	59%
Labor Force						
Employed	58%	64%	55%	56%	60%	60%
Unemployed	39%	46%	37%	35%	46%	49%
Income[1]						
Under $20,000	NA	NA	NA	NA	48%	52%
$20,000 to $30,000	NA	NA	NA	NA	58%	56%
$30,000 to $40,000	NA	NA	NA	NA	62%	62%
$40,000 to $50,000	NA	NA	NA	NA	69%	65%
$50,000 to $75,000	NA	NA	NA	NA	72%	71%
$75,000 to $100,000	NA	NA	NA	NA	78%	76%
Over $100,000	NA	NA	NA	NA	81%	92%

[1]The primary source changed the income categories in 2004, making the data from earlier presidential election years incompatible.

Sources: By the author. Based on Casper and Bass 1996; Jamieson et al. 2002; Holder 2006; File and Crissey 2010:Table 1; *Statistical Abstract of the United States* 1991:Table 450; 1997:Table 462; 2012:Table 399.

likely the employed are to vote. And look at how powerful income is in determining voting. At each higher income level, people are more likely to vote. Finally, note that women are more likely than men to vote.

Social Integration.   How can we explain these voting patterns? It is useful to look at the extremes. You can see from this table that those who are most likely to vote are the older, more educated, affluent, and employed. Those who are least likely to vote are the younger, less educated, poor, and unemployed. From these extremes, we can draw this principle: The more that people feel they have a stake in the political system, the more likely they are to vote. They have more to protect, and they feel that voting can make a

What are some major voting patterns? How is social integration related to voting patterns in U.S. presidential elections?

difference. In effect, people who have been rewarded more by the political and economic system feel more socially integrated. They vote because they perceive that elections make a difference in their lives, including the type of society in which they and their children live.

Alienation. In contrast, those who gain less from the system—in terms of education, income, and jobs—are more likely to feel alienated from politics. Perceiving themselves as outsiders, many feel hostile toward the government. Some feel betrayed, believing that politicians have sold out to special-interest groups. They ask, "How can you tell if politicians are lying?" and reply, "Whenever you see their lips moving."

Apathy. But we must go beyond this. From Table 11.1, you can see that many highly educated people with good incomes stay away from the polls. They are not alienated, but many do not vote because of **voter apathy,** or indifference. Their view is that "next year will just bring more of the same, regardless of who is in office." A common attitude of those who are apathetic is "What difference will my one vote make when there are millions of voters?" Many also see little difference between the two major political parties. Only about *half* of the nation's eligible voters cast ballots in presidential elections (*Statistical Abstract* 2012:Table 398).

The Gender and Racial–Ethnic Gaps in Voting. Historically, men and women voted the same way, but now we have a *political gender gap*. That is, men and women are somewhat more likely to vote for different presidential candidates. As you can see from Table 11.2, men are more likely to favor the Republican candidate, while women are more likely to vote Democratic. This table also illustrates the much larger racial–ethnic gap in politics. Note how few African Americans vote for a Republican presidential candidate.

As we saw in Table 11.1, voting patterns reflect life experiences, especially people's economic conditions. On average, women earn less than men, and African Americans earn less than whites. As a result, at this point in history, women and African Americans tend to look more favorably on government programs that redistribute income, and they are more likely to vote for Democrats. As you can see in this table, Asian American voters, with their higher average incomes, are an exception to this pattern. Attempted

◉ Watch
Street Fight
on **mysoclab.com**

TABLE 11.2	How the Two-Party Presidential Vote Is Split					
	1988	**1992**	**1996**	**2000**	**2004**	**2008**
Women						
Democrat	50%	61%	65%	56%	53%	57%
Republican	50%	39%	35%	44%	47%	43%
Men						
Democrat	44%	55%	51%	47%	46%	52%
Republican	56%	45%	49%	53%	54%	48%
African Americans						
Democrat	92%	94%	99%	92%	90%	99%
Republican	8%	6%	1%	8%	10%	1%
Whites						
Democrat	41%	53%	54%	46%	42%	44%
Republican	59%	47%	46%	54%	58%	56%
Latinos						
Democrat	NA	NA	NA	61%	58%	66%
Republican	NA	NA	NA	39%	42%	34%
Asian Americans						
Democrat	NA	NA	NA	62%	77%	62%
Republican	NA	NA	NA	38%	23%	38%

Sources: By the author. Based on Gallup Poll 2008; *Statistical Abstract of the United States* 1999:Table 464; 2002:Table 372; 2012:Table 404.

What are alienation and apathy? What gender and racial–ethnic gaps show up in voting for U.S. presidents?

explanations are far from satisfactory (Wong et al. 2011), but the reason could be a lesser emphasis on individualism in the Asian American subculture.

Lobbyists and Special-Interest Groups

Suppose that you are president of the United States, and you want to make milk more affordable for the poor. As you check into the matter, you find that part of the reason prices are high is because the government is paying farmers billions of dollars a year in price supports. You propose to eliminate these subsidies.

Immediately, large numbers of people leap into action. They contact their senators and representatives and hold news conferences. Your office is flooded with calls, faxes, and e-messages.

Reuters and the Associated Press distribute pictures of farm families—their Holsteins grazing contentedly in the background—and inform readers that your harsh proposal will destroy these hard-working, healthy, happy, good Americans who are struggling to make a living. President or not, you have little chance of getting your legislation passed.

Lobbying by Special-Interest Groups.   What happened? The dairy industry went to work to protect its special interests. A **special-interest group** consists of people who think alike on a particular issue and can be mobilized for political action. The dairy industry is just one of thousands of such groups that employ **lobbyists,** people who are paid to influence legislation on behalf of their clients. Members of Congress who want to be reelected must pay attention to them, for they represent blocs of voters who share an interest in some proposed legislation. Well financed and able to contribute huge sums, lobbyists can deliver votes to you—or to your opponent.

Lobbying has led to a *revolving door*. People who served as assistants to the president or to powerful senators are sought after as lobbyists (Vidal et al. 2010). With their contacts swinging open the doors of the powerful, some even go to work for the same companies they regulated when they worked for the president (Delaney 2010).

To try to reign in some of this influence peddling, Congress made it illegal for former senators to lobby for two years after they leave office. Yet senators do lobby immediately after leaving office. How do you suppose they get around this law? It's all in the name. They hire themselves out to lobbying firms as *strategic advisors*. They then lobby—excuse me—"strategically advise" their former colleagues ("It's So Much Nicer . . ." 2008).

The Money.   Buying votes is what especially bothers people. In response to publicity, Congress passed laws that limit the amount that corporations and individuals can give to candidates. To get around this law, special-interest groups form **political action committees (PACs)** to solicit contributions from many, and then hand over huge sums to politicians. The amounts are mind-boggling. Each year, about 4,500 PACs shell out almost a half billion dollars to politicians (*Statistical Abstract* 2012:Tables 422, 423). A few PACs represent broad social interests such as environmental protection. Most, however, represent the financial interests of specific groups, such as the banking, dairy, defense, and oil industries.

In a surprise decision in 2010, the Supreme Court opened the floodgates to bank-rolling politicians. In *Citizens United v. Federal Election Commission*, the Court ruled that laws that limit the amount corporations can contribute to politicians violate the First Amendment, which guarantees the right to political speech (Liptak 2010). By extension, individuals should have the same right, but until a case comes before the Court regarding the limits on giving by individuals, corporations have more constitutional rights to fund candidates than individuals do.

What are lobbyists? Special-interest groups? PACs? What role do they play in U.S. elections?

Who Rules the United States?

With lobbyists and PACs wielding such influence, just whom do U.S. senators and representatives really represent? This question has led to a lively debate among sociologists.

The Functionalist Perspective: Pluralism

Functionalists view the state as having arisen out of the basic needs of the social group. To protect themselves from oppressors, people formed a government and gave it the monopoly on violence. The risk is that the state can turn that force against its own citizens. To return to the example used earlier, states have a tendency to become muggers. Thus, people must find a balance between having no government—which would lead to **anarchy,** a condition of disorder and violence—and having a government that protects them from violence, but that also may turn against them. When functioning well, then, the state is a balanced system that protects its citizens both from one another *and* from government.

What keeps the U.S. government from turning against its citizens? Functionalists say that **pluralism,** a diffusion of power among many special-interest groups, prevents any one group from gaining control of the government and using it to oppress the people (Bentley 1908; Dahl 1961, 1982; Lemann 2008). To keep the government from coming under the control of any one group, the founders of the United States set up three branches of government: the executive branch (the president), the judiciary branch (the courts), and the legislative branch (the Senate and House of Representatives). Each is sworn to uphold the Constitution, which guarantees rights to citizens, and each can nullify the actions of the other two. This system, known as **checks and balances,** was designed to ensure that no one branch of government dominates the others.

In Sum: Our pluralist society has many parts—women, men, racial–ethnic groups, farmers, factory and office workers, religious organizations, bankers, bosses, the unemployed, the retired—as well as such broad categories as the rich, middle class, and poor. No group dominates. Rather, as each group pursues its own interests, it is balanced by other groups that are pursuing theirs. To attain their goals, groups must make compromises and work together. Because these groups have political muscle to flex at the polls, politicians try to design policies that please as many groups as they can. This, say functionalists, makes the political system responsive to the people, and no one group rules.

The Conflict Perspective: The Power Elite

If you focus on the lobbyists scurrying around Washington, stress conflict theorists, you get a blurred image of superficial activities. What really counts is the big picture, not its fragments. The important question is, Who holds the power that determines the country's overarching policies? For example, who determines interest rates—and their impact on the price of our homes? Who sets policies that encourage the transfer of jobs from the United States to countries where labor costs less? And the ultimate question of power: Who is behind the decision to go to war?

Sociologist C. Wright Mills (1956) took the position that the country's most important matters are not decided by lobbyists or even by Congress. Rather, the decisions that have the greatest impact on the lives of Americans—and people across the globe—are made by a **power elite.** As depicted in Figure 11.2, the power elite consists of the top leaders of the largest corporations, the most powerful generals and admirals of the armed forces, and certain elite

Read

The Power Elite by C. Wright Mills on on **mysoclab.com**

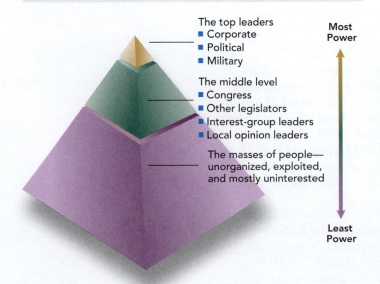

FIGURE 11.2   **Power in the United States: The Model Proposed by C. Wright Mills**

The top leaders
- Corporate
- Political
- Military

The middle level
- Congress
- Other legislators
- Interest-group leaders
- Local opinion leaders

The masses of people— unorganized, exploited, and mostly uninterested

Most Power

Least Power

Source: Based on Mills 1956.

politicians—the president, the president's cabinet, and senior members of Congress who chair the major committees. It is they who wield power, who make the decisions that direct the country and shake the world.

Are the three groups that make up the power elite—the top business, political, and military leaders—equal in power? Mills said that they were not, but he didn't point to the president and his staff or even to the generals and admirals as the most powerful. Instead, he said that the corporate leaders are the most dominant. Because all three segments of the power elite view capitalism as essential to the welfare of the country, Mills said that business interests take center stage in setting national policy.

Sociologist William Domhoff (1990, 2006) uses the term **ruling class** to refer to the power elite. He focuses on the 1 percent of Americans who belong to the super-rich, the powerful capitalist class analyzed in Chapter 8 (pp. 220–221). Members of this class control our top corporations and foundations, even the boards that oversee our major universities. It is no accident, says Domhoff, that from this group come most members of the president's cabinet and the ambassadors to the most powerful countries of the world.

In Sum: Conflict theorists take the position that a *power elite* dominates the United States. With connections that extend to the highest centers of power, this ruling class determines the economic and political conditions under which the rest of the country operates (Domhoff 1990, 1998, 2007). They say that we should not think of the power elite (or ruling class) as some secret group that meets to agree on specific matters. Rather, the group's unity springs from the members having similar backgrounds and orientations to life. All have attended prestigious private schools, belong to exclusive clubs, and are millionaires many times over. Their behavior stems not from some grand conspiracy to control the country but from a mutual interest in solving the problems that face big business.

Which View Is Right?

The functionalist and conflict views of power in U.S. society cannot be reconciled. Either competing interests block any single group from being dominant, as functionalists assert, or a power elite oversees the major decisions of the United States, as conflict theorists maintain. The answer may have to do with the level you look at. Perhaps at the middle level of power depicted in Figure 11.2, the competing groups do keep each other at bay, and none can dominate. If so, the functionalist view would apply to this level. But which level holds the key to U.S. power? Perhaps the functionalists have not looked high enough, and activities at the peak remain invisible to them. On that level, does an elite dominate? To protect its mutual interests, does a small group make the major decisions of the United States?

Sociologists passionately argue this issue, but with mixed data, we don't yet know the answer. We await further research.

War and Terrorism: Implementing Political Objectives

Some students wonder why I include war and terrorism as topics of politics. The reason is that war and terrorism are tools used to try to accomplish political goals. The Prussian military analyst Carl von Clausewitz, who entered the military at the age of twelve and rose to the rank of major-general, put it best when he said "War is merely a continuation of politics by other means."

Let's look at this aspect of politics.

Why Countries Go to War

War, armed conflict between nations (or politically distinct groups), is simply *one option* that politicians choose for dealing with disagreements. Why do they choose this option? As usual, sociologists answer this question not by focusing on factors *within* humans, such as aggressive impulses, but by looking for *social* causes—conditions in society that encourage or discourage combat between nations.

Few want to say that we honor war, but we do. Its centrality in the teaching of history and the honoring of the patriots who founded a country are two indications. A third is the display of past weapons in parks and museums. Shown here are children playing in a park in Poland, where an instrument of war has become a toy for children.

The hatred and vengeance of adults become the children's heritage. The headband of this 4-year-old Palestinian boy reads: "Friends of Martyrs."

Sociologist Nicholas Timasheff (1965) identified three essential conditions of war. The *first* is an antagonistic situation in which two or more states confront incompatible objectives. For example, each may want the same land or resources. The *second* is a cultural tradition of war. Because their nation has fought wars in the past, the leaders of a group see war as an option for dealing with serious disputes with other nations. The *third* is a "fuel" that heats the antagonistic situation to a boiling point, so that politicians cross the line from thinking about war to actually waging it.

Timasheff identified seven such "fuels." He found that war is likely if a country's leaders see the antagonistic situation as an opportunity to achieve one or more of these objectives:

1. *Revenge:* settling "old scores" from earlier conflicts
2. *Power:* dominating a weaker nation
3. *Prestige:* defending the nation's "honor"
4. *Unity:* uniting rival groups within their country
5. *Position:* protecting or exalting the leaders' positions
6. *Ethnicity:* bringing under their rule "our people" who are living in another country
7. *Beliefs:* forcibly converting others to religious or political beliefs

You can use these three essential conditions and seven fuels to analyze any war. They will help you understand why politicians choose this political action called war.

The Flesh and Blood of War.   Sociological analysis can be cold and dispassionate. These "fuels" of war are like this: accurate and insightful, but cold. Throughout this book, I've tried to bring you the flesh and blood of topics, to help you see the ways that people experience life. So let's do this again.

Behind these "fuels" are politicians who make the bloody choice to go to war. They do not fight the war themselves, of course. They sit back and watch it from the comfort of their homes and offices. Some even profit from the war by making investments in companies that produce weapons. For most politicians, the deaths are bloodless affairs. It is young men, and increasingly young women, who do the killing—and dying—for them. Some soldiers are killed on the battlefield; others survive but are mutilated for the rest of their lives. Many who survive with their bodies intact suffer emotionally. Some of my students have shared their suffering with me, but let me close this section with one of the most powerful statements I have come across. A soldier from California wrote this just before he put a bullet through his brain (Smith 1980):

I can't sleep anymore. When I was in Vietnam, we came across a North Vietnamese soldier with a man, a woman, and a three- or four-year-old girl. We had to shoot them all. I can't get the little girl's face out of my mind. I hope that God will forgive me . . . I can't.

Terrorism

Mustafa Jabbar, in Najaf, Iraq, is proud of his first born, a baby boy. Yet he said, "I will put mines in the baby and blow him up." (Sengupta 2004)

Can feelings really run so deep that a father would sacrifice his only son? Some groups nourish hatred, endlessly chronicling the injustices and atrocities of their archenemy. Stirred in a cauldron of bitter hatred, antagonism can span generations, its embers sometimes burning for centuries. The combination of perceived injustice and righteous hatred fuels the desire to strike out— but what can a group do if it is weaker than its enemy? Unable to meet its more powerful opponent on the battlefield, one option is **terrorism,** violence intended to create fear in order to bring about political objectives. And, yes, if the hatred is strong enough, that can mean blowing up your only child.

Suicide terrorism, a weapon sometimes chosen by the weaker group, captures headlines around the world. Among the groups that have used suicide terrorism are the Palestinians against the Israelis and the Iraqis and

Why do countries go to war? Why do some groups choose terrorism as an instrument of war?

Afghanistanis against U.S. troops. The suicide terrorism that has had the most profound effects on our lives is the attack on the World Trade Center and the Pentagon under the direction of Osama bin Laden. What kind of sick people become suicide terrorists? This is the topic of the Down-to-Earth Sociology box below.

The suicide attacks on New York and Washington are tiny in comparison with the threat of weapons of mass destruction. If terrorists unleash biological, nuclear, or chemical weapons, the death toll could run in the millions. We've had a couple of scares. A shipment of

Down-to-Earth Sociology

Who Are the Suicide Terrorists? Testing Your Stereotypes

Some events in life leave us perplexed, not knowing what to make of things. For most of us, suicide terrorism is like this. We don't know any suicide bombers, so it is hard to imagine someone becoming one.

Let's see if we can flesh out our mental files a bit. Sociologist Marc Sageman (2008a,b) wondered about terrorists, too. Finding that his mental files were inadequate to understand them, he decided that research might provide the answer. Sageman had an unusual advantage for gaining access to data—he had been in the CIA. Through his contacts, he studied 400 al-Qaeda terrorists who had targeted the United States. He was able to examine thousands of pages of their trial records.

So let's use Sageman's research to test some common ideas. I think you'll find that the data blow away stereotypes of terrorists.

- Here's a common stereotype. Terrorists come from backgrounds of poverty. Cunning leaders take advantage of their frustration and direct it toward striking out at an enemy.

  Not true. Three-quarters of the terrorists came from the middle and upper classes.

- How about this image, then—the deranged loner? We carry around images like this concerning serial and mass murderers. It is a sort of catch-all stereotype that we have. These people can't get along with anyone; they stew in their loneliness and misery; and all this bubbles up in misapplied violence. You know, the workplace killer sort of image, loners "going postal."

  Not this one, either. Sageman found that 90 percent of the terrorists came from caring, intact families. On top of this, 73 percent were married, and most of them had children.

- Let's try another one. Terrorists are uneducated, ignorant people, so those cunning leaders can manipulate them easily.

What does a suicide bomber look like? This young married mother of two little children blew herself up at the Erez crossing in the Gaza Strip, killing four Israelis. She had this photo taken at home before her death.

We have to drop this one, too. Sageman found that 63 percent of the terrorists had gone to college. Three-quarters worked in professional and semi-professional occupations. Many were scientists, engineers, and architects.

What? Most terrorists are intelligent, educated, family-oriented, professional people? How can this be? Sageman found that these people had gone through a process of radicalization. Here was their trajectory:

1. *Moral outrage.* They became angry, even enraged, about something that they felt was terribly wrong.
2. *Ideology.* They interpreted their moral outrage within a radical, militant interpretation of Islamic teachings.
3. *Shared outrage and ideology.* They found like-minded people, often on the Internet, especially in chat rooms.
4. *Group decision*: They decided that an act of terrorism was called for.

In one sense, however, the image of the loner does come close. Seventy percent of these terrorists committed themselves to extreme acts while they were living away from the country where they grew up. They became homesick, sought out people like themselves, and ended up at radical mosques where they learned a militant script. Constantly, then, sociologists seek to understand the relationship between the individual and the group. This fascinating endeavor sometimes blows away stereotypes.

For Your Consideration

→ 1. How do you think we can reduce the process of radicalization that turns people into terrorists?
2. Sageman concludes that this process of radicalization has produced networks of homegrown, leaderless terrorists, ones that don't need al-Qaeda to direct them. He also concludes that this process will eventually wear itself out. Do you agree? Why or why not?

How do research findings on suicide terrorists contradict stereotypes of who they are?

enriched uranium that was being smuggled out of Europe was intercepted just before it landed in terrorist hands (Sheets and Broad 2007a,b). This chilling possibility was brought home to Americans in 2001 when anthrax powder was mailed to a few select victims.

It is sometimes difficult to tell the difference between war and terrorism. This is especially so in civil wars when the opposing sides don't wear uniforms and attack civilians. Africa is embroiled in such wars. In the Down-to-Earth Sociology box below, we look at one aspect of these wars, that of child soldiers.

Down-to-Earth Sociology

Child Soldiers

When rebels entered 12-year-old Ishmael Beah's village in Sierra Leone, they lined up the boys (Beah 2007). One of the rebels said, "We are going to initiate you by killing these people. We will show you blood and make you strong."

Before the rebels could do the killing, shots rang out and the rebels took cover. In the confusion, Ishmael escaped into the jungle. When he returned, he found his family dead and his village burned.

With no place to go and rebels attacking the villages, killing, looting, and raping, Ishmael continued to hide in the jungle. As he peered out at a village one day, he saw a rebel carrying the head of a man, which he held by the hair. With blood dripping from where the neck had been, Ishmael said that the head looked as though it were still feeling its hair being pulled.

Months later, government soldiers found Ishmael. The "rescue" meant that he had to become a soldier—on their side, of course. Ishmael's indoctrination was short but to the point. Hatred is a strong motivator.

> "You can revenge the death of your family, and make sure that more children do not lose their parents," the lieutenant said. "The rebels cut people's heads off. They cut open pregnant women's stomachs and take the babies out and kill them. They force sons to have sex with their mothers. Such people do not deserve to live. This is why we must kill every single one of them. Think of it as destroying a great evil. It is the highest service you can perform for your country."

Along with thirty other boys, most of whom were ages 13 to 16, with two just 7 and 11, Ishmael was trained to shoot and clean an AK-47.

Banana trees served for bayonet practice. With thoughts of disemboweling evil rebels, the boys would slash at the leaves. The things that Ishmael had seen, he did.

Killing was difficult at first, but after a while, as Ishmael says, "killing became as easy as drinking water."

The corporal thought that the boys were sloppy with their bayonets. To improve their performance, he held a contest.

A boy soldier in Somalia.

He chose five boys and placed them opposite five prisoners with their hands tied. He told the boys to slice the men's throats on his command. The boy whose prisoner died the quickest would win the contest.

> "I stared at my prisoner," said Ishmael. "He was just another rebel who was responsible for the death of my family. The corporal gave the signal with a pistol shot, and I grabbed the man's head and sliced his throat in one fluid motion. His eyes rolled up, and he looked me straight in the eyes before they suddenly stopped in a frightful glance. I dropped him on the ground and wiped my bayonet on him. The corporal, who was holding a timer, proclaimed me the winner. The other boys clapped at my achievement."

> "No longer was I running away from the war," adds Ishmael. "I was in it. I would scout for villages that had food, drugs, ammunition, and the gasoline we needed. I would report my findings to the corporal, and the entire squad would attack the village. We would kill everyone."

Ishmael was one of the lucky ones. Of the approximately 300,000 child soldiers worldwide, Ishmael is one of the few who has been rescued and given counseling at a UNICEF rehabilitation center. Ishmael has also had the remarkable turn of fate of graduating from college in the United States and becoming a permanent U.S. resident.

Source: Based on Beah 2007; quotations are summaries.

For Your Consideration

→ 1. Why are there child soldiers?
  2. What can be done to prevent the recruitment of child soldiers? Why don't we just pass a law that requires a minimum age to serve in the military?
  3. How can child soldiers be helped? Which agencies should be involved, taking what actions?

Why are there child soldiers? How can this problem be solved?

The Economy: Work in the Global Village

If you are like most students, you are wondering how changes in the economy are going to affect your chances of getting a good job. Let's see if we can shed some light on this question. We'll begin with this story:

The sound of her alarm rang in Kim's ears. "Not Monday already," she groaned. "There must be a better way of starting the week." She pressed the snooze button on the clock (from Germany) to sneak another ten minutes' sleep. In what seemed like just thirty seconds, the alarm once again shrilly insisted that she get up and face the week.

Still bleary-eyed after her shower, Kim peered into her closet and picked out a silk blouse (from China), a plaid wool skirt (from Scotland), and leather shoes (from Italy). She nodded, satisfied, as she added a pair of simulated pearls (from Taiwan). Running late, she hurriedly ran a brush (from Mexico) through her hair. As Kim wolfed down a bowl of cereal (from the United States) topped with milk (from the United States), bananas (from Costa Rica), and sugar (from the Dominican Republic), she turned on her kitchen television (from Korea) to listen to the weather forecast.

Gulping the last of her coffee (from Brazil), Kim grabbed her briefcase (from India), purse (from Spain), and jacket (from Malaysia), left her house, and quickly climbed into her car (from Japan). As she glanced at her watch (from Switzerland), she hoped that the traffic would be in her favor. She muttered to herself as she pulled up at a stoplight (from Great Britain) and eyed her gas gauge. She muttered again when she pulled into a station and paid for gas (from Saudi Arabia), for the price had risen over the weekend. "My paycheck never keeps up with prices," she moaned.

When Kim arrived at work, she found the office abuzz. Six months ago, New York headquarters had put the company up for sale, but there had been no takers. The big news was that both a German company and a Canadian company had put in bids over the weekend. No one got much work done that day, as the whole office speculated about how things might change.

The Transformation of Economic Systems

Although this vignette may be slightly exaggerated, many of us are like Kim: We use a multitude of products from around the world, and yet we're concerned about our country's ability to compete in global markets. Today's **economy**—our system of producing and distributing goods and services—differs radically from past economies. The products that Kim uses make it apparent that today's economy knows no national boundaries. To better understand how global forces affect the U.S. economy—and your life—let's begin by summarizing the sweeping historical changes we reviewed in Chapter 4.

Preindustrial Societies: The Birth of Inequality

The earliest human groups, *hunting and gathering societies*, had a **subsistence economy.** In small groups of about twenty-five to forty, people lived off the land. They gathered plants and hunted animals in one location and then moved to another place as these sources of food ran low. Because these people had few possessions, they did little trading with one another. With no excess to accumulate, as was mentioned in Chapter 4, everybody owned as much (or, really, as little) as everyone else.

Then people discovered how to breed animals and cultivate plants. The more dependable food supply in what became *pastoral and horticultural societies* allowed humans to settle down in a single place. Human groups grew larger, and for the first time in history, it was no longer necessary for everyone to work at producing food.

What does "we live in a global market" mean? What in your life reflects a global market?

Some people became leather workers, others weapon makers, and so on. This new division of labor produced a surplus, and groups traded items with one another. The primary sociological significance of surplus and trade is this: They fostered *social inequality*, for some people accumulated more possessions than others. The effects of that change remain with us today.

The plow brought the next major change, ushering in *agricultural societies*. Plowing the land made it more productive, allowing even more people to specialize in activities other than producing food. More specialized divisions of labor followed, and trade expanded. Trading centers then developed, which turned into cities. As power passed from the heads of families and clans to a ruling elite, social, political, and economic inequalities grew.

Industrial Societies: The Birth of the Machine

The steam engine, invented in 1765, ushered in *industrial societies*. Based on machines powered by fuels, these societies created a surplus unlike anything the world had seen. This, too, stimulated trade among nations and brought even greater social inequality. A handful of individuals opened factories and exploited the labor of many.

Then came more efficient machines. As the surpluses grew even greater, the emphasis gradually changed—from producing goods to consuming them. In 1912, sociologist Thorstein Veblen coined the term **conspicuous consumption** to describe this fundamental change in people's orientations. By this term, Veblen meant that the Protestant ethic identified by Weber—an emphasis on hard work, savings, and a concern for salvation (discussed on pages 8–9)—was being replaced with an eagerness to show off wealth by the "elaborate consumption of goods."

Postindustrial Societies: The Birth of the Information Age

In 1973, sociologist Daniel Bell noted that *a new type of society was emerging*. This new society, which he called the *postindustrial society*, has six characteristics: (1) a service sector so large that *most* people work in it, (2) a vast surplus of goods, (3) even more extensive trade among nations, (4) a wider variety and quantity of goods available to the average person, (5) an information explosion, and (6) a *global village*—that is, the world's nations are linked by fast communications, transportation, and trade.

To see why analysts use the term *postindustrial society* to describe the United States, look at Figure 11.3. The change in work shown in this figure is without parallel in human history. In the 1800s, most U.S. workers were farmers. Today, farmers make up about 1 percent of the workforce. With the technology of the 1800s, a typical farmer produced enough food to feed five people. With today's powerful machinery and hybrid seeds, a farmer now feeds about eighty. In 1940, about half of U.S. workers wore a blue collar; then changing technology shrank the market for blue-collar jobs. White-collar work continued its ascent, reaching the dominant position it holds today.

Biotech Societies: The Merger of Biology and Economics

As we discussed in Chapter 4, we may be on the verge of yet another new type of society. This one is being ushered in by advances in biology, especially the deciphering of the human genome system. Although the specifics of this new society have yet to unfold, the marriage of biology and economics should yield even greater surpluses and more extensive trade. The technological advances that will emerge in this new society may allow us to lead longer and healthier lives. Its effects on inequality between the nations are likely to be spotty. Some poorer nations may be able to import the new technology and develop their economies, while others remain in poverty.

Implications for Your Life

The broad changes in societies that I have just sketched may seem to be abstract matters, but they are far from irrelevant to your life. Whenever society changes, so do our lives. Consider the information explosion. When you graduate from college, you will most likely

The commonsense meaning of *market* is a place where people exchange or buy and sell goods. Such old-fashioned markets remain common in the Least Industrialized Nations, such as this floating one in Bangkok, Thailand. Here people find the social interaction every bit as rewarding as the goods and money that they exchange.

As societies changed from preindustrial to industrial, how did economies change?

do some form of "knowledge work." Instead of working in a factory, you will manage information or design, sell, or service products. The type of work you do has profound implications for your life. It produces social networks, nurtures attitudes, and even affects how you view yourself and the world. To better understand this, consider how vastly different your outlook on life would be if you were one of the children discussed in the Cultural Diversity box on the next page.

It is the same with the global village. Think of the globe as being divided into three neighborhoods—the three worlds of industrialization and postindustrialization that we reviewed in Chapter 7. Some nations are located in the poor part of the village. Their citizens do menial work and barely eke out a living. Life is so precarious that some even starve to death, while their fellow villagers in the rich neighborhood feast on steak and lobster, washed down with vintage Chateau Lafite Rothschild. It's the same village, but what a difference the neighborhood makes.

Now visualize any one of the three neighborhoods. Again you will see gross inequalities. Not everyone who lives in the poor neighborhood is poor, and some areas of the rich neighborhood are packed with poor people. The United States is the global economic leader, occupying the most luxurious mansion in the best neighborhood, and is spearheading the new biotech society.

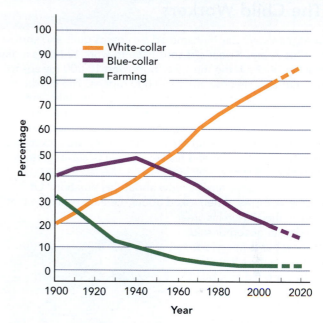

FIGURE 11.3 The Revolutionary Change in the U.S. Workforce

Source: By the author. Based on *Statistical Abstract of the United States*, various years, and 2012:Tables 616, 620.

World Economic Systems

Now that we have sketched the main historical changes in world economic systems, let's compare capitalism and socialism, the two main economic systems in force today. This will help us to understand where the United States stands in the world economic order.

Capitalism

People who live in a capitalist society may not understand its basic tenets, even though they see them reflected in their local shopping malls and fast-food chains. Table 11.3 distills the many businesses of the United States down to their basic components. As you can see, **capitalism** has three essential features: (1) *private ownership of the means of production* (individuals own the land, machines, and factories); (2) *market competition* (competing with one another, the owners decide what to produce and set the prices for their products); and (3) *the pursuit of profit* (the owners try to sell their products for more than they cost).

What State Capitalism Is. No country has pure capitalism. Pure capitalism, known as **laissez-faire capitalism** (literally "hands off" capitalism), means that the government doesn't interfere in the market. The current form of U.S. capitalism is *state* (or *welfare*)

TABLE 11.3	Comparing Capitalism and Socialism
Capitalism	**Socialism**
1. Individuals own the means of production.	1. The public owns the means of production.
2. Based on competition, the owners determine production and set prices.	2. Central committees plan production and set prices; no competition.
3. The pursuit of profit is the reason for distributing goods and services.	3. No profit motive in the distribution of goods and services.

Source: By the author.

What are the three main characteristics of capitalism?

Cultural Diversity **around the World**

The Child Workers

In Afghanistan, Zar Muhammad expresses guilt and sorrow that his 7- and 8-year-old sons have to work 12 hours a day making bricks in the mud. Zar borrowed 10,000 rupees to get married. He now owes 150,000 rupees. The children have to work alongside him to try to pay the debt. But the debt continues to grow: rent to the kiln owner for their mud house, electricity, and food, and sometimes emergency medicine for the children. They are locked in a cycle that makes Zar and his sons servants/slaves forever (Kamber 2011).

Does the government know about this situation? Of course, it knows. When asked about the 5,000 children that work in the kilns in his area, the district governor said, "I know this is not good for kids, but we have to build our buildings, build our country. The work provides income for the children's families" (Kamber 2011).

In Zambia, nine-year-old Alone Banda works in an abandoned quarry. Using a bolt, he breaks rocks into powder. In a week, he makes enough powder to fill half a cement bag. Alone gets $3 for the half bag.

It is still a slow death for Alone. Robbed of his childhood and breathing rock dust continuously, Alone is likely to come down with what the quarry workers call a "heavy chest," an early sign of silicosis.

The amount Alone makes is pitiful, but without it he and his grandmother would starve to death. As one mother said, "If I feel pity for them, what are they going to eat?" (Wines 2006).

As with the photo I took of an 8-year-old girl in India (page 186), some children work in construction, others in factories.

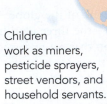

Children work as miners, pesticide sprayers, street vendors, and household servants. They weave carpet in India, race camels in the Middle East, and, all over the world, work as prostitutes. In the poverty-stricken areas of some of these countries, people live on less than $1 a day. The few dollars the children earn make the difference between life and death.

Besides poverty, there is also a cultural factor. In many parts of the world, people view children differently than we do in the West. The idea that children have the right to be educated and to be spared from adult burdens is fairly new in history. A major factor shaping our views of life is economics, and when prosperity comes to these other countries, so will this new perspective.

The answer to "What is the proper role of children in an economy?" varies by social class, culture, economic development, and historical period. On the left is a boy working in a Pennsylvania coal mine about 1880. On the right is a four-year-old boy pounding stones in a quarry in Benin.

For Your Consideration

→ How do you think the wealthier nations can help alleviate the suffering of child workers? Before industrialization, and for a period afterwards, having children work was also common in the West. Just because our economic system has changed, bringing with it different ideas of childhood and of the rights of children, do we have the right to impose our changed ideas on other nations?

---

capitalism. Private citizens own the means of production and pursue profits, but they do so within a vast system of laws designed to protect the welfare of the population and—not incidentally—ensure that the government can collect taxes.

Consider this example:

Suppose that you discover what you think is a miracle tonic: It will grow hair, erase wrinkles, and dissolve excess fat. If your product works, you will become an overnight sensation—not only a multimillionaire, but also the toast of television talk shows and the darling of Hollywood.

But don't count on your money or fame yet. You still have to reckon with market restraints, the laws and regulations of welfare capitalism that limit your capacity to produce and sell. First, you must comply with local and state laws. You must obtain a business license and a state tax number that allows you to buy your ingredients without paying sales taxes. Then come the federal regulations. You cannot simply take your product to local stores and ask them to sell it; you first must seek approval from federal agencies that monitor compliance with the Pure Food and Drug Act. This means that you must prove that your product will not cause harm to the public. Your manufacturing process is also subject to federal, state, and local laws concerning fraud, hygiene, and the disposal of hazardous wastes.

Suppose that you overcome these obstacles, and your business prospers. Other federal agencies will monitor your compliance with laws concerning minimum wages, Social Security taxes, and discrimination on the basis of race, gender, religion, or disability. State agencies will examine your records to see whether you have paid unemployment and sales taxes. Finally, as your shadowy but ever-present business partner, the Internal Revenue Service will look over your shoulder and demand about 35 percent of your profits.

In short, the U.S. economic system is highly regulated and is far from an example of laissez-faire capitalism.

Socialism

What Socialism Is.   As Table 11.3 on page 333 shows, **socialism** also has three essential components: (1) public ownership of the means of production, (2) central planning, and (3) the distribution of goods without a profit motive.

In socialist economies, the government owns the means of production—not only the factories but also the land, railroads, oil wells, and gold mines. Unlike capitalism, in which **market forces**—supply and demand—determine both what will be produced and the prices that will be charged, a central committee decides that the country needs X number of toothbrushes, Y toilets, and Z shoes. The committee decides how many of each will be produced, which factories will produce them, what price will be charged for the items, and where they will be distributed.

Socialism is designed to eliminate competition, for goods are sold at predetermined prices regardless of the demand for an item or the cost of producing it. The goal is not to make a profit, nor is it to encourage the consumption of goods that are in low demand (by lowering the price) or to limit the consumption of hard-to-get goods (by raising the price). Rather, the goal is to produce goods for the general welfare and to distribute them according to people's needs, not their ability to pay.

In a socialist economy *everyone* in the economic chain works for the government. The members of the central committee who set production goals are government employees, as are the supervisors who implement their plans, the factory workers who produce the merchandise, the truck drivers who move it, and the clerks who sell it. Those who buy the items may work at different jobs—in offices, on farms, or in day care centers—but they, too, are government employees.

Socialism in Practice.   Just as capitalism does not exist in a pure form, neither does socialism. Although the ideology of socialism calls for resources to be distributed according to need and not the ability to pay, socialist countries found it necessary to pay higher salaries for some jobs in order to entice people to take on greater responsibilities. Factory managers, for example, always earned more than factory workers. These differences in pay follow the functionalist argument of social stratification presented in Chapter 7 (pp. 191–192). By narrowing the huge pay gaps that characterize capitalist nations, however, socialist nations established considerably greater equality of income.

The wealthy, whether capitalist or socialist, can buy most anything, including trophy spouses. It is usually successful men who marry women much younger than themselves, such as Nicolas Cage, age 48, shown here with his wife, Alice, age 25. This pattern will continue, but with changing norms we can expect more financially successful women to marry younger men.

What are the three main characteristics of socialism?

Democratic Socialism.   Dissatisfied with the greed and exploitation of capitalism and the lack of freedom and individuality of socialism, Sweden and Denmark developed **democratic socialism** (also called *welfare socialism*). In this form of socialism, both the state and individuals produce and distribute goods and services. The government owns and runs the steel, mining, forestry, and energy concerns, as well as the country's telephones, television stations, and airlines. Remaining in private hands are the retail stores, farms, factories, and most service industries.

Ideologies of Capitalism and Socialism

Not only do capitalism and socialism have different approaches to producing and distributing goods but they also represent opposing belief systems. *Capitalists* believe that market forces should determine both products and prices. They also believe that profits are good for humanity. The potential to make money stimulates people to produce and distribute goods, as well as to develop new products. Society benefits, as the result is a more abundant supply of goods at cheaper prices.

Socialists take an opposite view of profits. They consider profits to be immoral. An item's value is based on the work that goes into it, said Karl Marx. The only way there can be profit, he stressed, is by paying workers less than the value of their labor. Profit, he said, is the *excess value* that has been withheld from workers. Socialists believe that the government should protect workers from this exploitation. To do so, the government should own the means of production, using them not to generate profit but to produce items that match people's needs, not their ability to pay.

Capitalists and socialists paint each other in such stark colors that *each perceives the other system as one of exploitation*. Capitalists believe that socialists violate people's basic right to make their own decisions and to pursue opportunity. Socialists believe that capitalists violate people's basic right to be free from poverty. With each side claiming moral superiority while viewing the other as a threat to its very existence, the last century witnessed the world split into two main blocs. In what was known as the *Cold War*, the West armed itself to defend and promote capitalism, the East to defend and promote socialism.

Criticisms of Capitalism and Socialism

In India, an up-and-coming capitalist giant, the construction of a 27-story building is almost complete (Yardley 2010). It comes with a grand ballroom, nine elevators, a fifty-seat theater, a six-story garage, and three helipads on the roof.

The occupants are ready to move in—all five of them—a husband, wife, and their three children. From their perch, they will be able to view the teeming mass of destitute people below.

The primary criticism leveled against capitalism is that it leads to social inequality. Capitalism, say its critics, produces a tiny top layer of wealthy people who exploit an immense bottom layer of poorly paid workers. Another criticism is that the tiny top layer wields vast political power. Those few who own the means of production reap huge profits, accrue power, and get legislation passed that goes against the public good.

The first criticism leveled against socialism is that it does not respect individual rights. Others (in the form of some government agency) control people's lives. They decide where people will live, work, and go to school. In China, they even determine how many children women may bear (Mosher 1983, 2006). Critics make a second point—that central planning is grossly inefficient and that socialism is not capable of producing much wealth. They say that its greater equality really amounts to giving almost everyone an equal chance to be poor.

The Convergence of Capitalism and Socialism

Regardless of the validity of these mutual criticisms, as nations industrialize they come to resemble one another. They urbanize, encourage higher education, and produce similar divisions of labor (such as professionals and skilled technicians; factory workers and factory managers). Similar values also emerge (Kerr 1983). By itself, this tendency would make capitalist and socialist nations grow more alike, but another factor also brings them

Can you contrast the ideologies of capitalism and socialism? Can you summarize the criticisms of each?

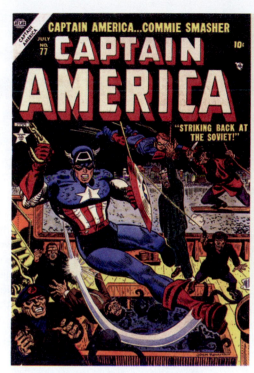

Тов. Ленин ОЧИЩАЕТ землю от нечисти.

For about 60 years, the capitalist and socialist (communist) countries were locked in a life-death struggle called the *Cold War*. Each used propaganda to promote its economic-political system. The 1920 anticapitalist poster from Russia depicts Lenin cleansing the world of the rich and privileged (called "filth" in the Russian caption). Even private enterprise got involved, as you can see from this anticommunist U.S. comic book from the 1950s.

closer to one another: Despite their incompatible ideologies, both capitalist and socialist systems have adopted features from the other (Form 1979).

That capitalism and socialism are growing similar is known as **convergence theory.** Fundamental changes in socialist countries give evidence for this coming hybrid, or mixed, economy. For example, Russians suffered from shoddy goods and shortages, and their standard of living lagged severely behind that of the West. To try to catch up, in the 1980s and 1990s the rulers of Russia made the private ownership of property legal and abandoned communism. Making a profit—which had been a crime—was encouraged. China joined the change, but kept a communist government. In its converged form of "capunism," capitalists joined the Communist Party. The convergence is so great that when the Western governments instituted stimulus plans to counter the economic crisis, China joined in with a huge stimulus plan of its own (Batson 2009). Even Western banks are now welcome in China. Among other things, they provide specialized services to China's 960,000 new millionaires (Yenfang 2011)—and, of course, to China's 115 new billionaires (Flannery 2011). The change is so remarkable that some textbooks in China now give more space to Bill Gates than to Mao (Guthrie 2008). The Cultural Diversity box on the next page provides a glimpse of the new capitalism in China.

Changes in capitalism also support this theory. The United States has adopted many socialist practices. One of the most obvious is that the government collects money from some individuals to pay for benefits given to others. It had none of these when the country was founded: unemployment compensation (taxes paid by workers are distributed to those who no longer produce a profit); subsidized housing, food, and medical care (paid for by the many and given to the poor and elderly with no motive of profit); welfare (taxes from the many are distributed to the needy); a minimum wage (the government, not the employer, determines the minimum that workers receive); and Social Security (the retired do not receive what they paid into the system, but, rather, money that the government collects from current workers).

Convergence is continuing. In 2008, when Wall Street and auto firms started to buckle, the U.S. government stepped in to shore up these businesses. In some cases, the government even bought the companies, fired CEOs, and set salary limits. Such an extended embrace of socialist principles indicates that the United States has produced its own version of a mixed economy.

What events indicate that convergence theory is right?

Cultural Diversity around the World

The New Competitor: The Chinese Capitalists

Socialism has the virtue of making people more equal. Socialism's equality, however, translates into distributing poverty throughout a society. Under socialism, almost everyone becomes equally poor.

Capitalism, in contrast, has the virtue of producing wealth. A lot of people remain poor, however, leaving deep gaps between wealth and poverty, one that produces envy and sometimes creates social unrest.

Chinese leaders realized the wealth-producing capacity of capitalism and wanted that for their people (Karon 2011). In the Chinese version they produced—capitalism directed by communists—wealth has increased at an astonishing rate. In all the world's history, this new capitalism has lifted the largest number—*a half billion*—of people out of poverty in the shortest time. The poor who are left behind, however, aren't happy when their land is taken from them to help make others wealthy. The anger and resentment have kept the Party busy sending out the army to squelch riots.

In Beijing, the capital of China, stands a mansion built by Zhang Yuchen. This is no ordinary mansion, like those built by China's other newly rich. This imposing building is a twin of the Chateau de Maisons-Laffitte, an architectural landmark on the Seine River outside Paris. At a cost of $50 million, the Beijing replica matches the original edifice detail for detail. The architects even used the original blueprints of the French chateau, and the building features the same Chantilly stone (Kahn 2004, 2007).

Building the chateau and its housing development of luxury homes made eight hundred farmers landless. But if they get angry, the spiked fence, the moat, and the armed guards—looking sharp in their French-style uniforms complete with capes and kepis—will keep the peasants out of the chateau.

In most places, you need connections to become wealthy. In China, this means connections with the

Like a debutante being introduced to society, the Chinese capunists presented themselves on the world stage at the Beijing Olympics. This photo is from the games' closing ceremonies.

Communist Party, for this group still holds the power. Yuchen has those connections. As a member of the Party, it was his job to direct Beijing's construction projects. With his deep connections, Yuchen was able to get the wheat fields farmed by the peasants rezoned from farmland to a "conservation area." He was even able to divert a river so he could build the moat around the chateau, one of the finishing touches on his architectural wonder.

Beneath such ostentatious examples of capitalistic excess lies this irony: China is doing capitalism better than the capitalist countries. Using the state machinery, their leaders have proven themselves more nimble in reacting to competition, in seizing opportunities for profit, and for accumulating vast amounts of capital. The capitalist nations have become envious, especially as the Chinese model of capitalism—at least at this historical point—is proving competitively superior (Bremmer 2011; Karon 2011).

For Your Consideration

➔ When China has completed its transition to capitalism, what do you think the final version will look like (that is, what characteristics do you think it will have)? Where will the top Party leaders fit in the class system that is emerging? Why? (To answer this, consider the connections and resources of the elite.)

The Globalization of Capitalism

Capitalism has made the world's countries part of the same broad economic unit. When the economic crisis hit the United States, it spread quickly around the world. To decide what they should do, the leaders of the top 20 producers of consumer goods met in Washington. The Chinese leaders said that no one should worry about them not being a team player; they knew that their actions would affect other nations. (Yardley and Brasher 2008)

Can you make an argument that there is or is not capitalism in communist China?

The globalization of capitalism is so significant that its impact on our lives may rival that of the Industrial Revolution. As Louis Galambos, a historian of business, says, "This new global business system will change the way everyone lives and works" (Zachary 1995).

Let's look, then, at how capitalism is changing the face of the globe.

A New Global Structure and the Displacement of Workers

The globalization of capitalism has forged a new world structure. Three primary trading blocs (groups of countries) have emerged: North and South America, dominated by the United States; Europe, dominated by Germany; and Asia, dominated by China and Japan. Functionalists stress that this new global division benefits not only the multinational giants but also the citizens of the world.

Consider free trade. Free trade increases competition, which, in turn, drives the search for greater productivity. This lowers prices and brings a higher standard of living. Free trade also has dysfunctions. As production moves to countries where labor costs are lower, millions of U.S., U.K., French, and Spanish workers have lost their jobs. Functionalists point out that this is a temporary dislocation, that as the Most Industrialized Nations lose factory jobs, their workers shift into service and high-tech jobs. Perhaps. But the millions of workers searching in vain for jobs that no longer exist would disagree.

Certainly the adjustment has been anything but easy. As the U.S. steel industry lost out to global competition, for example, the plant closings created "rust belts" in the northern states. The globalization of capitalism has also brought special challenges to small towns across the country, which already were suffering long-term losses because of urbanization. Their struggle to survive is the topic of the photo essay on the next two pages.

Stagnant Paychecks

With extensive automation, the productivity of U.S. workers has increased year after year, making them some of the most productive in the world (*Statistical Abstract* 2012:Tables 1353, 1355). One might think, therefore, that their pay would be increasing. This brings us to a disturbing trend, one that bothers Americans and is an underlying reason that so many workers have lost their homes to foreclosure.

Look at Figure 11.4. The gold bars show current dollars. These are the dollars the average worker finds in his or her paycheck. You can see that since 1970 the average pay of U.S. workers has soared from just over $3 an hour to over $19 an hour. Workers today are bringing home about *six* times as many dollars as workers used to.

But let's strip away the illusion. Look at the purple bars, which show the dollars adjusted for inflation, the *buying power* of those paychecks. You can see how inflation has surpressed the value of the dollars that workers earn. Today's workers, with their $19 an hour, can buy little more than workers in 1970 could with their "measly" $3 an hour. The question is not "How could workers live on just $3 an hour back then?" but, rather, "*How can workers get by on a 62-cent-an-hour raise that*

FIGURE 11.4   Average Hourly Earnings of U.S. Workers in Current and Constant Dollars

Note: Constant dollars are dollars adjusted for inflation with 1982–1984 as the base.

Source: By the author. Based on *Statistical Abstract of the United States* 1992:Table 650; 1999:Table 698; 2012:Table 644.

What are the world's main trading blocs? What is meant by "stagnant paychecks"?

THROUGH THE AUTHOR'S LENS

Small Town USA: Struggling to Survive

All across the nation, small towns are struggling to survive. Parents and town officials are concerned because so few young adults remain in their home town. There is little to keep them there, and when they graduate from high school, most move to the city. With young people leaving and old ones dying, the small towns are shriveling.

How can small towns contend with cutthroat global competition when workers in some countries are paid a couple of dollars a day? Even if you open a store, down the road Wal-Mart sells the same products for about what you pay for them—and offers much greater variety.

There are exceptions: Some small towns are located close to a city, and they receive the city's spillover. A few possess a rare treasure—some unique historical event or a natural attraction—that draws visitors with money to spend. Most of the others, though, are drying up, left in a time warp as history shifts around them. This photo essay tells the story.

People do whatever they can to survive. This enterprising proprietor uses the building for an unusual combination of purposes: a "plant world," along with the sale of milk, eggs, bread, and, in a quaint southern touch, cracking pecans.

I was struck by the grandiosity of people's dreams, at least as reflected in the names that some small-towners give their businesses. Donut Palace has a nice ring to it—inspiring thoughts of wealth and royalty (note the crowns). Unfortunately, like so many others, this business didn't make it.

In striking contrast to the grandiosity of some small-town business names is the utter simplicity of others. *Cafe* tells everyone that some type of food and drinks are served here. Everyone in this small town knows the details.

The small towns are filled with places like this— small businesses, locally owned, that have enough clientele for the owner and family to eke out a living. They have to offer low prices because there is a fast-food chain down the road. Fixing the sign? That's one of those "I'll get-to-its."

© James M. Henslin, all photos

One of the few buildings consistently in good repair in the small towns is the U.S. Post Office. Although its importance has declined in the face of telecommunications, for "small towners" the post office still provides a vital link with the outside world.

With little work available, it is difficult to afford adequate housing. This house, although cobbled together and in disrepair, is a family's residence.

There is no global competition for this home-grown business. Shirley has located her sign on a main highway just outside Niceville, Florida. By the looks of the building, business could be better.

This general store used to be the main business in the area: It even has a walk-in safe. It has been owned by the same family since the 1920s, but is no longer successful. To get into the building, I had to find out where the owner (shown here) lived, knock on her door, and then wait while she called around to find out who had the keys.

This is a successful business. The store goes back to the early 1900s, and the proprietors have capitalized on the "old timey" atmosphere.

took 40 years to get?" That's less than two cents an hour per year! Incredibly, despite workers having more college and more technical training, despite the use of computers, and much higher productivity, their purchasing power increased just 62 cents an hour between 1970 and 2010. What can you buy with those 62 cents?

Actually, after taxes and Social Security, we should ask, What can you do with the 40 cents.

The New Economic System and the Old Divisions of Wealth

Suppose that you own a business that manufactures widgets. You are paying your workers an average $152 a day ($19 an hour including vacation pay, sick pay, unemployment benefits, Social Security, and so on). Widgets similar to yours are being manufactured in Thailand, where workers are paid $8 a day. Those imported widgets are being sold in the same stores that feature your widgets.

We are in the midst of the globalization of capitalism. The explosion that is sending products around the world brings new ways of thinking to people in the Least Industrialized Nations. Many ideas are subtle, such as what refreshing drinks are.

How does the globalization of capitalism increase competition and lower prices?

How long do you think you could stay in business? Even if your workers were willing to drop their pay in half—which they aren't willing to do—you still couldn't compete.

What do you do? Your choices are simple. You can continue as you are and go broke, try to find some other product to manufacture (which, if successful, will soon be made in Thailand or India or China)—or you can close up your plant here and manufacture your widgets in Thailand.

What happens when oil tankers wear out? They go to Bangladesh, where they are turned into scrap. These workers, an expendable part of the global economic system that we are all a part of, are exposed to PCBs, asbestos, and other toxins. For this, they earn $1–$2 a day.

These are not easy times for workers. One disruption after another. High insecurity with layoffs, plant closings, and the prospect of more of the same. The insecurity is especially hard-hitting on the most desperate of workers, the less-skilled and those who live from paycheck to paycheck. How can they compete with people overseas who work for peanuts? They suffer the wrenching adjustments that come from having their jobs pulled out from under them, looking for work and finding only jobs that pay lower wages—if that, watching their savings go down the drain, postponing their retirement, and seeing their children disillusioned about the future. The photo above indicates some of the consequences for workers in the Least Industrialized Nations.

What about the wealthy? In these tough economic times, aren't they being hurt, too? Some rich individuals do get on the wrong side of investments and lose their collective shirts. In general, though, the wealthy do just fine in these challenging economic times. How can I be so sure, you might be wondering. Take a look at Figure 11.5 on the next page.

Each rectangle on the left of this figure represents a fifth of the U.S. population, about 62 million people. The rectangles of the inverted pyramid on the right show the percentage of the nation's income that goes to each fifth of the population. You can see that half of the entire country's income goes to the richest fifth of Americans. Only 3 percent goes to the poorest fifth.

This gap has been growing over the years, and it now is *greater* than it has been in generations. The transition to a postindustrial economy and the globalization of capitalism has increased our income inequalities. The common folk saying that the rich are getting richer and the poor are getting poorer is certainly an apt observation,

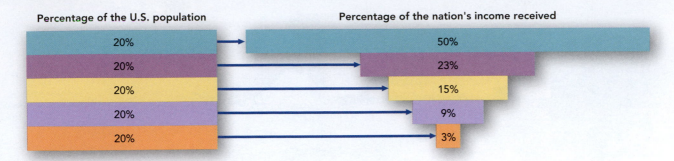

FIGURE 11.5   The Inverted Income Pyramid: The Proportion of Income Received by Each Fifth of the U.S. Population

Source: By the author. Based on *Statistical Abstract of the United States* 2012:Table 694.

well supported by social research. What implications of this division of the nation's wealth do you see for our future?

The Global Superclass

At the top of the multinational corporations is an overlapping membership; that is, people serve on the boards of several corporations. The leaders of the globe's top multinational companies overlap to such a degree that they form a small circle, one that we can call the **global superclass** (Rothkopf 2008). The superclass is not only extremely wealthy, as we reviewed in Chapter 7 (see Figure 7.1, p. 189), but it is also extremely powerful. These people have access to the top circles of political power around the globe. With their multiple layers of security to ensure their privacy and safety, it is difficult to do research on the super class. But how would you like to listen to a member of this superclass describe their tight connections? Here is your chance.

Every country has its large financial institutions that are central to the development of that country, and everyone else in finance knows somebody who will know the head of one of those companies. That person knows a senior person in their government that could be useful in a situation. . . . the key is the network. . . . it is twenty, thirty, fifty people worldwide who ultimately drive the decisions. (Rothkopf 2008:129–130)

Twenty to fifty individuals who make the world's major decisions! Could this possibly be true? The individual who said this, Stephen Schwarzman, is an insider who is worth about $9 billion (Freeland 2011). Pay attention to this real-life example of how this interconnected global power works out in practice:

When Schwarzman, a co-founder of Blackstone, an investment company, had a problem with some policy of the German government, he called a German friend. The friend arranged for Schwarzman to meet with the Chancellor of Germany. After listening to Schwarzman, the Chancellor agreed to support a change in Germany's policy.

Do you see the power that is concentrated in this small group? The U.S. members can call the U.S. president, the English members can ring up the British prime minister, and so on. They know how to get and give favors, to move vast amounts of capital from country to country, and to open and close doors to investments around the world.

This concentration of power is new to the world scene. Working behind the scenes, the global superclass affects our present and our future. To close this chapter, let's look at this aspect of our changing political and economic order.

A New World Order?

So far, the use of war and terrorism to try to dominate the globe has failed. A New World Order, however, might be on its way, ushered in not by violence, but by changing economic-political conditions.

Trends toward Unity

Perhaps the key *political* event in our era is the globalization of capitalism. Why the term political? Because politics and economics are twins, with each setting the stage for the other. Look at the economic-political units being developed. The United States, Canada, and Mexico have formed a North American Free-Trade Agreement (NAFTA). Ten Asian countries with a combined population of a half billion people have formed a regional trading partnership called ASEAN (Association of South East Asian Nations). Struggling for dominance is an even more encompassing group called the *World* Trade Organization. These coalitions of trading partners are making national borders increasingly insignificant.

The European Union (EU) may indicate the future. Transcending their national boundaries, twenty-seven European countries (with a combined population of 450 million) formed this economic and political unit. These nations adopted a single, cross-national currency, the euro, which replaced their marks, francs, liras, pesetas, and lats. The EU also established a military staff in Brussels, Belgium.

Could this process continue until there is just one state (or empire) that envelops the earth? It is possible. The United Nations is striving to become the legislative

OUR CARELESSNESS
Their Secret Weapon

PREVENT FOREST FIRES

U. S. DEPT. OF AGRICULTURE
FOREST SERVICE

Hinter den
Feindmächten:

der Jude

All governments—all the time—use propaganda to influence public opinion. During times of war, the propaganda becomes more obvious. Note how ugly Hitler and Tojo are depicted on the World War II poster from the United States—and this is just an ad to prevent forest fires! The second poster was produced by the Nazis, letting the Germans know that the United States and the Soviet Union were run by Jews. It reads "Behind the enemy, the Jew."

What trends or events indicate that a new global order may be on its way?

body of the world, wanting its decisions to supersede those of any individual nation. The UN operates a World Court (formally titled the International Court of Justice). It also has a small multinational army and has sent "peacekeeping" troops to several nations. And there is also now a *World Bank*.

Strains in the Global System

Although the globalization of capitalism and its encompassing trade organizations could lead to a single world government, the developing global system is experiencing strains that threaten to rip the system apart. Unresolved items constantly rear up, demanding realignments of the current arrangements of power. Although these pressures are resolved on a short-term basis, over time their cumulative weight leads to a gradual shift in global stratification.

The economic crisis that exposed a debt-ridden global financial system teetering on the edge of global disaster also laid bare some of the interconnections that unite its elements. In 2012, when the crisis threatened to tear the European Union apart, sending its individual members sulking back into their solitary units, the United States stepped in. By pouring billions of dollars into the European Central Bank and the International Monetary Fund, the United States helped European banks to keep credit flowing and hold the economic-political union together. No longer are economic-political problems limited to local areas, to regions, or even to continents. Larger and larger Band-Aids are needed to prop the tattered union together.

If we take a broad historical view, we see that a particular group or culture can dominate only so long. Its dominance always comes to an end, to be replaced by another group or culture. The process of decline is usually slow and can last hundreds of years (Toynbee 1946). Life today, though, is so speeded-up that the future looms into the present at a furious pace. The decline of U.S. dominance—like that of Great Britain—could come fairly quickly, although certainly not without resistance and bloodshed. The shape of the new political arrangements of world power is anyone's guess, but it certainly will include an ascendant China (Kissinger 2011).

As the economic and political arrangements of the present give way, future generations will face a new world. Whatever the particular shape of future stratification, it is likely that a super-dominant group of more-or-less integrated economic-political elites will be directing it. This super class will not belong to any single nation, and the alliances that forge its dominance in the new global scheme of things will pay little attention to international borders. This process may well lead to a one-world government, perhaps to a dictatorship or an oligarchy that controls the world's resources and people. If so, we could end up with living under a government like that of Winston and Julia in our opening vignette.

Only time will tell.

What strains are showing up in the global financial system?

By the Numbers: Changes Over Time

Purchasing power of the U.S. dollar	
1941	NOW
$1.00	$0.05

Average hourly earnings of workers, in current U.S. dollars	
1970	NOW
$3.23	$19.07

Average hourly earnings of workers, in constant (1984) U.S. dollars	
1970	NOW
$8.29	$8.91

Percentage of U.S. workforce made up of white-collar workers	
1900	NOW
20%	80%

Percentage of U.S. workforce made up of blue-collar workers	
1900	NOW
40%	19%

Percentage of U.S. workforce made up by farmers	
1900	NOW
30%	1%

The average U.S. farmer produces enough food to feed this many people	
1800	NOW
5	80

Men who voted in the presidential election	
1988	2008
56%	56%

Women who voted in the presidential election	
1988	2008
58%	60%

High school drop-outs who voted in the presidential election	
1988	2008
41%	34%

College graduates who voted in the presidential election	
1988	2008
78%	73%

Latinos who voted in the presidential election	
1988	2008
48%	32%

African Americans who voted in the presidential election	
1988	2008
55%	61%

CHAPTER 11 Summary and Review

Power, Authority, and Violence

How are authority and coercion related to power?

Authority is power that people view as legitimately exercised over them, while **coercion** is power they consider unjust. The **state** is a political entity that claims a monopoly on violence over some territory. Pp. 316–317.

What kinds of authority are there?

Max Weber identified three types of authority. In **traditional authority**, power is derived from custom—patterns set down in the past serve as rules for the present. In **rational–legal authority** (also called *bureaucratic authority*), power is based on law and written rules. In **charismatic authority**, power is derived from loyalty to an individual to whom people are attracted. Charismatic authority, which undermines traditional and rational–legal authority, has built-in problems in transferring authority to a new leader. Pp. 317–318.

Types of Government

How are the types of government related to power?

In a **monarchy**, power is based on hereditary rule; in a **democracy**, power is given to the ruler by citizens; in a **dictatorship**, power is seized by an individual; and in an **oligarchy**, power is seized by a small group. Pp. 318–321.

The U.S. Political System

What are the main characteristics of the U.S. political system?

The U.S. political system is dominated by the Democratic and Republican parties, which represent slightly different centrist positions. The differences are most obvious in those who take extreme positions. Pp. 321–322.

Voter turnout is higher among people who are more socially integrated—those who sense a greater stake in the outcome of elections, such as the more educated and well-to-do. **Lobbyists** and **special-interest groups**, such as **political action committees (PACs)**, play a significant role in U.S. politics. Pp. 322–325.

Who Rules the United States?

Is the United States controlled by a ruling class?

In a view known as **pluralism**, functionalists say that no one group holds power, that the country's many competing interest groups balance one another. Conflict theorists, who focus on the top level of power, say that the United States is governed by a **power elite**, a **ruling class** made up of the top corporate, political, and military leaders. At this point, the matter is not settled. Pp. 326–327.

War and Terrorism: Implementing Political Objectives

How are war and terrorism related to politics?

War and **terrorism** are both means of attempting to accomplish political objectives. Timasheff identified three essential conditions of war and seven fuels that bring about war. His analysis can be applied to terrorism. Nuclear, biological, and chemical terrorism are major threats. Pp. 327–331.

The Transformation of Economic Systems

How are economic systems linked to types of societies?

In early societies (hunting and gathering), small groups lived off the land and produced little or no surplus. Economic systems grew more complex as people discovered how to domesticate animals and grow plants (pastoral and horticultural societies), farm (agricultural societies), and manufacture (industrial societies). As people produced a *surplus*, trade developed. Trade, in turn, brought social inequality as some people accumulated more than others. Service industries dominate the postindustrial societies. If a biotech society is emerging, its consequences, too, will be far reaching. Pp. 331–333.

World Economic Systems

How do the major economic systems differ?

The world's two major economic systems are capitalism and socialism. In **capitalism**, private citizens own the means of production and pursue profits. In **socialism**, the state owns the means of production and has no goal of profit. Adherents of each have developed ideologies that defend their own systems and paint the other as harmful or even evil. As expected from **convergence theory,** each system has adopted features of the other. Pp. 333–338.

The Globalization of Capitalism

What is the new global structure?

The world's nations are forming major trading blocs. As multinational corporations seek the lowest costs of production, millions of jobs are transferred to nations where workers are paid little. This is causing great suffering to workers who are losing their jobs and to those whose pay is stagnant. At the same time, an ultrawealthy and powerful **global superclass** has risen. Pp. 338–345.

A New World Order?

Is humanity headed toward a world political system?

The globalization of capitalism and the trend toward regional economic and political unions may indicate that a world economic-political system is developing. Competing interests and internal contradictions might prevent a New World Order from developing, but if one does emerge, the consequences for human welfare could be calamitous. Pp. 345–346.

Thinking Critically about Chapter 11

1. What are the three sources of authority, and how do they differ from one another?

2. Apply the three essential conditions of war and its seven fuels to a recent (or current) war that the United States has been (or is) a part of.

3. What global forces are affecting the U.S. economy? What consequences are they having? How might they affect your own life?

Marriage and Family

I was living in a remote village in the state of Colima, Mexico. I had chosen this nondescript town a few kilometers from the ocean because it had no other Americans, and I wanted to immerse myself in the local culture.

The venture was successful. I became friends with my neighbors, who were curious about why a gringo was living in their midst. After all, there was nothing about their drab and dusty town to attract tourists. So why was this gringo there, this guy who looked so different from them and who had the unusual custom of jogging shirtless around the outskirts of town and among the coconut and banana trees? This was their burning question, while mine was "What is your life like?"

We satisfied one another. I explained to them what a sociologist is. Although they never grasped why I would want to know about *their* way of life, they accepted my explanation. And I was able to get my questions answered. I was invited into their homes—by the men. The women didn't talk to men outside the presence of their husbands, brothers, or other women. The women didn't even go out in public unless they were accompanied by someone. Another woman would do, just so they weren't alone. The women did the cooking, cleaning, and child care. The men worked in the fields.

I was culturally startled one day at my neighbor's house. The man had retired from the fields, and he and his wife, as the custom was, were being supported by their sons who worked in the fields. When I saw the bathroom, with a homemade commode made of clay—these were poor people—I asked him about the used toilet paper thrown into a pile on the floor. He explained

> It was his wife's job to pick up the used toilet paper.

that the sewer system couldn't handle toilet paper. He said that I should just throw mine onto the pile, adding that it was his wife's job to pick up the used toilet paper and throw it out.

I became used to the macho behavior of the men. This wasn't too unlike high-school behavior—a lot of boisterous man-to-man stuff—drinking, joking, and bragging about sexual conquests. The sex was vital for proving manhood. When the men took me to a whorehouse (to help explain their culture, they said), they couldn't understand why I wouldn't have sex with a prostitute. Didn't I find the women attractive? Yes, they were good looking. Weren't they sexy? Yes, very much so. Was I a real man? Yes. Then why not? My explanation about being married didn't faze them one bit. They were married, too—and a real man had to have sex with more women than just his wife.

Explanations of friendship with a wife and respect for her fell on deaf cultural ears.

Florida

Marriage and Family in Global Perspective

These men and I were inhabiting the same physical space, but our cultural space—which we carry in our heads and show in our behavior—was worlds apart. My experiences with working-class men in this remote part of Mexico helped me understand how marriage and family can vastly differ from one culture to another. To broaden our perspective for understanding this vital social institution, let's look at how marriage and family customs differ around the world.

What Is a Family?

Every human group in the world organizes its members in families. The world's cultures, though, display so much variety that the term *family* is difficult to define. Although the Western world regards a family as a husband, wife, and children, other groups have family forms in which men have more than one wife (**polygyny**) or women more than one husband (**polyandry**). How about the obvious? Can we define the family as the approved group into which children are born? That would be overlooking the Banaro of New Guinea. In this group, a young woman must give birth *before* she can marry—and she *cannot* marry the father of her child (Murdock 1949).

Such remarkable variety means that we have to settle for a broad definition. A **family** consists of people who consider themselves related by blood, marriage, or adoption. A **household,** in contrast, consists of people who occupy the same housing unit—a house, apartment, or other living quarters.

We can classify families as **nuclear** (husband, wife, and children) and **extended** (including people such as grandparents, aunts, uncles, and cousins in addition to the nuclear unit). Sociologists also refer to the **family of orientation** (the family in which an individual grows up) and the **family of procreation** (the family that is formed when a couple has its first child).

What Is Marriage?

We have the same problem here. For just about every element you might regard as essential to marriage, some group has a different custom.

Consider the sex of the bride and groom. Until recently, opposite sex was taken for granted. Then in the 1980s and 1990s, several European countries legalized same-sex marriages. Canada and several U.S. states soon followed.

At least one thing has to be universal in marriage: We can at least be sure that the bride and groom are alive. So you would think. But even for this there is an exception. On the Loess Plateau in China, if a son dies without a wife, his parents look for a dead woman to be his bride. After buying one—from the parents of a dead unmarried daughter—the dead man and woman are married and then buried together. Happy that their son will have intimacy in the after-life, the parents throw a party to celebrate the marriage (Fremson 2006).

With such encompassing cultural variety, we can define **marriage** this way—a group's approved mating arrangements, usually marked by a ritual of some sort (the wedding) to indicate the couple's new public status.

Common Cultural Themes

Despite this diversity, several common themes run through marriage and family. As Table 12.1 illustrates, all societies use marriage and family to establish patterns of mate selection, descent, inheritance, and authority. Let's look at these patterns.

Mate Selection.   Each human group establishes norms to govern who marries whom. If a group has norms of **endogamy,** it specifies that its members must marry *within* their group. For example, some groups prohibit interracial marriage. In contrast, norms of **exogamy** specify that people must marry *outside*

Often one of the strongest family bonds is that of mother–daughter. The young artist, an eleventh grader, wrote: "This painting expresses the way I feel about my future with my child. I want my child to be happy and I want her to love me the same way I love her. In that way we will have a good relationship so that nobody will be able to take us apart. I wanted this picture to be alive; that is why I used a lot of bright colors."

What is a family? What is marriage? Why are they so difficult to define?

TABLE 12.1	Common Cultural Themes: Marriage in Traditional and Industrialized Societies	
Characteristic	**Traditional Societies**	**Industrial (and Postindustrial) Societies**
What is the structure of marriage?	*Extended* (marriage embeds spouses in a large kinship network of explicit obligations)	*Nuclear* (marriage brings fewer obligations toward the spouse's relatives)
What are the functions of marriage?	Encompassing (see the six functions listed on page 355)	More limited (many functions are fulfilled by other social institutions)
Who holds authority?	*Patriarchal* (authority is held by males)	Although some patriarchal features remain, authority is divided more equally
How many spouses at one time?	Most have one spouse (*monogamy*), while some have several (*polygamy*)	One spouse
Who selects the spouse?	Parents, usually the father, select the spouse	Individuals choose their own spouses
Where does the couple live?	Couples usually reside with the groom's family (*patrilocal residence*), less commonly with the bride's family (*matrilocal residence*)	Couples establish a new home (*neolocal residence*)
How is descent figured?	Usually figured from male ancestors (*patrilineal kinship*), less commonly from female ancestors (*matrilineal kinship*)	Figured from male and female ancestors equally (*bilineal kinship*)
How is inheritance figured?	Rigid system of rules; usually patrilineal, but can be matrilineal	Highly individualistic; usually bilineal

Source: By the author.

their group. The best example of exogamy is the **incest taboo,** which prohibits sex and marriage among designated relatives.

As you can see from Table 12.1, how people find mates varies around the world, from fathers selecting them, with no input from those who are to marry, to the highly individualistic, personal choices common in Western cultures. Changes in mate selection are the focus of the Sociology and the New Technology box on the next page.

Descent.   How are you related to your father's father or to your mother's mother? You would think that the answer to this question would be the same all over the world—but it isn't. Each society has a **system of descent,** the way people trace kinship over generations. We use a **bilineal system,** for we think of ourselves as related to *both* our mother's and our father's sides of the family. "Doesn't everyone?" you might ask. Ours, however, is only one logical way to reckon descent. Some groups use a **patrilineal system,** tracing descent only on the father's side; they don't think of children as being related to their mother's relatives. Others follow a **matrilineal system,** tracing descent only on the mother's side, and not considering children to be related to their father's relatives. The Naxi of China don't even have a word for *father* (Hong 1999).

Inheritance.   Marriage and family are also used to determine rights of inheritance. In a bilineal system, property is passed to both males and females, in a patrilineal system only to males, and in a matrilineal system (the rarest form), only to females. No system is natural. Rather, each matches a group's ideas of justice and logic.

Authority.   Some form of **patriarchy,** a social system in which men-as-a-group dominate women-as-a-group, runs through all societies. Contrary to what some think, there are no historical records of a true **matriarchy,** a society in which women-as-a-group dominate men-as-a-group. Although U.S. family patterns are becoming more **egalitarian,** or equal, some of today's customs still reflect their patriarchal origin. One of the most obvious is the U.S. naming pattern: Despite some changes, the typical bride still takes the groom's last name, and children usually receive the father's last name.

What common cultural themes run through marriage? How does marriage differ in traditional and industrialized societies?

Finding a Mate: Not the Same as It Used to Be

Things haven't changed entirely. Boys and girls still get interested in each other at their neighborhood schools, and men and women still meet at college. Friends still serve as matchmakers and introduce friends, hoping they might click. People still meet at churches and bars, at the mall and at work.

But the Internet has intruded on these traditional arrangements. Dating sites offer thousands of potential companions, lovers, or spouses. For a low monthly fee, you can meet the person of your dreams—or so they promise.

The photos on these sites are fascinating. Some seem to be lovely people, warm, attractive, and vivacious. Others seem okay, although perhaps a bit needy. Then there are the pitiful, and one wonders whether they will ever find a mate, or even a hookup, for that matter. Some are desperate, begging for someone—anyone—to contact them: women trying to look sexy, their exposed flesh suggesting the promise of a good time, and men trying to look like hulks, their muscular presence promising the same.

With Internet postings having lost much of their stigma, electronic matchmaking is changing the way we find mates. A fifth of heterosexual couples now meet online. For homosexuals, the total swells to three-fifths of couples (Rosenbloom 2011).

If you want to meet a mate online, though, you can expect to be fed a few lies. Researchers have found that to "put their best foot forward" women say that they weigh less than they do. And men? They say they are taller than they are (Rosenbloom 2011). But this seems to be in line with what you could expect in meeting someone at a bar, or wherever you would meet someone for the first time. To make a good impression, most people stretch the truth. (Do they really scuba dive, or is that something they would just like to do?)

Are there dangers? The Craigslist rapists and all that. Certainly there are, and you have to watch out for shady characters lurking on the Net. How do you know that the engaging person you are corresponding with is not already married, does not have a dozen kids, or is not a child molester or a rapist? But what makes

such concerns unique to Internet dating? Aren't those the same kind of issues you need to be concerned about when meeting someone at school, a party, or even in the supermarket?

Even though the form is changing, the substance appears to be about the same. Maybe Internet dating is just tradition dressed up in different clothing.

For Your Consideration

➤ Have you used an electronic dating site? Would you consider using one? Why or why not?

Snapshots

© Jason Love/www.CartoonStock.com

Tall, Dark, and Handsome chats with Buxom Blonde.

Marriage and Family in Theoretical Perspective

As we have seen, human groups around the world have many forms of mate selection, ways to trace descent, and ways to assign authority. Although these patterns are arbitrary, each group perceives its own forms of marriage and family as natural. Now let's see what pictures emerge when we view marriage and family theoretically.

The Functionalist Perspective: Functions and Dysfunctions

Functionalists stress that to survive, a society must fulfill basic functions (that is, meet its basic needs). When functionalists look at marriage and family, they examine how they are related to other parts of society, especially the ways that marriage and family contribute to the well-being of society.

How is the Internet changing dating for some?

Why the Family Is Universal.   Although the form of marriage and family varies from one group to another, the family is universal. The reason for this, say functionalists, is that the family fulfills six needs that are basic to the survival of every society. These needs, or functions, are (1) economic production, (2) socialization of children, (3) care of the sick and aged, (4) recreation, (5) sexual control, and (6) reproduction. To make certain that these functions are performed, every human group has adopted some form of the family.

Functions of the Incest Taboo.   Functionalists note that the incest taboo helps families to avoid *role confusion*. This, in turn, helps parent socialize children. For example, if father–daughter incest were allowed, how should a wife treat her daughter—as a daughter or as a second wife? Should the daughter consider her mother as a mother or as the first wife? Would her father be a father or a lover? And would the wife be the husband's main wife or the "mother of the other wife"? And if the daughter had a child by her father, what relationships would everyone have? Maternal incest would also lead to complications every bit as confusing as these.

The incest taboo also forces people to look outside the family for marriage partners. Anthropologists theorize that *exogamy* was especially functional in tribal societies, for it forged alliances between tribes that otherwise might have killed each other off. Today, exogamy still extends both the bride's and the groom's social networks by adding and building relationships with their spouse's family and friends.

The Conflict Perspective: Struggles between Husbands and Wives

Anyone who has been married or who has seen a marriage from the inside knows that—despite a couple's best intentions—conflict is a part of marriage. Conflict inevitably arises between two people who live intimately and who share most everything in life—from their goals and checkbooks to their bedroom and children. At some point, their desires and approaches to life clash, sometimes mildly, at other times quite harshly. Conflict among married people is so common that it is the grist of soap operas, movies, songs, and novels.

Power is the source of such conflict in marriage. Who has it? And who resents not having it? Throughout history, husbands have had more power, and wives have resented it. In the United States, as I'm sure you know, wives have gained more and more power in marriage. Do you think that one day wives will have more power than their husbands?

You probably are saying that such a day will never come. But maybe wives have *already* reached this point. From time to time, you've seen some surprising things in this book. Now look at Figure 12.1. Based on a national sample, this figure shows who makes decisions concerning the family's finances and purchases, what to do on the weekends, and even what to watch on television. As you can see, wives now have more control over the family purse and make more of these decisions than do their husbands. These findings are such a surprise that we await confirmation by future studies.

The Symbolic Interactionist Perspective: Gender, Housework, and Child Care

Changes in Traditional Gender Orientations.   The chapter's opening vignette gave you a glimpse into extreme traditional gender roles. Apart from the specifics mentioned there, throughout the generations housework and child care have been regarded as "women's work." As women put in more hours at paid work, men gradually did more housework and took more responsibility for the care of their children. Ever so slowly, cultural ideas shifted, with housework, care of children, and paid labor coming to be regarded as the responsibilities of both men and women. Let's examine this shift.

FIGURE 12.1   **Who Makes the Decisions at Home?**

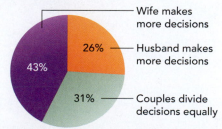

- Wife makes more decisions — 43%
- Husband makes more decisions — 26%
- Couples divide decisions equally — 31%

Note: Based on a nationally representative sample, with questions on who chooses weekend activities, buys things for the home, decides what to watch on television, and manages household finances.

Source: Morin and Cohn 2008.

What six functions do marriage and family perform? What is the conflict perspective on marriage?

In Hindu marriages, the roles of husband and wife are firmly established. Neither this woman, whom I photographed in Chittoor, India, nor her husband question whether she should carry the family wash to the village pump. Women here have done this task for millennia. As India industrializes, as happened in the West, who does the wash will be questioned—and may eventually become a source of strain in marriage.

Who Does What?   Figure 12.2 illustrates several significant changes that have taken place in U.S. families. The first is likely to surprise you. If you look closely at this figure, you will see that not only are husbands spending more time taking care of the children but so are wives. This is fascinating: How can children be getting *more* attention from their parents than they used to? *Both* husbands and wives are spending more time in child care?

This flies in the face of our mythical past, the *Leave-It-to-Beaver* images that color our perception of the present. We know that families are not leisurely lolling through their days as huge paychecks flow in, so if parents are spending more time with their children, just where is the time coming from?

Today's parents are squeezing out more hours for their children by spending less time on social activities and by participating less in organizations. But this accounts for only some of the time. To get the rest of the answer, look again at Figure 12.2. This time focus on the hours that husbands and wives spend doing housework. You can see that men are doing more housework than they used to, but women are spending so much less time on housework that the total hours that husbands and wives spend on housework have dropped from 38.9 to 29.1 hours a week. This leaves a lot more time to spend with the children.

Finally, from Figure 12.2, you can see that husbands and wives spend their time differently. In what sociologists call a *gendered division of labor*, husbands still take the primary responsibility for earning the income and wives the primary responsibility for taking care of the house and children. You can also see that a shift is taking place in this traditional gender orientation: Wives now spend more time than they used to earning the family income, while husbands are spending more time on housework and child care. In light of these trends and with changing ideas of gender—of what is considered appropriate for husbands and wives—we can anticipate greater marital equality in the future.

| FIGURE 12.2 | In Two-Paycheck Marriages, How Do Husbands and Wives Divide Up Their Responsibilities? |

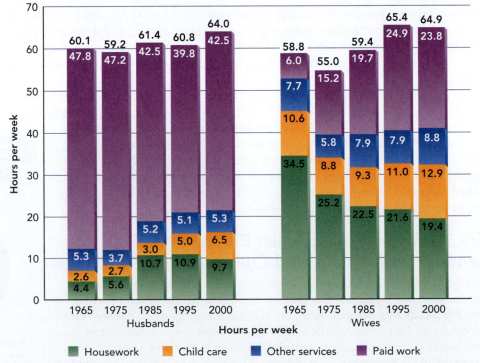

Source: By the author. Based on Bianchi et al. 2006. Housework hours are from Table 5.1, child care from Table 4.1, and work hours and total hours from Table 3.4. Other services is derived by subtracting the hours for housework, child care, and paid work from the total hours.

What is a symbolic interactionist perspective on marriage and family? What are some implications of Figure 12.2?

The Family Life Cycle

We have seen how the forms of marriage and family vary widely, looked at marriage and family theoretically, and examined major changes in family relationships. Now let's discuss love, courtship, and the family life cycle.

Love and Courtship in Global Perspective

Have you ever been sick over love? Some people can't eat, and they are obsessed with thoughts of the one they love. When neuroscientists decided to study "love sickness," they found that it is real: Love feelings light up the same area of the brain that lights up when cocaine addicts are craving coke (Fisher et al. 2010).

Evidently, then, love can be an addiction. From your own experience, you probably know the power of **romantic love**—mutual sexual attraction and idealized feelings about one another. Because romantic love plays such a significant role in Western life—and often is regarded as the *only* proper basis for marriage—social scientists have probed this concept with the tools of the trade: experiments, questionnaires, interviews, and observations. In a fascinating experiment, psychologists Donald Dutton and Arthur Aron discovered that fear can produce romantic love (Rubin 1985). Here's what they did.

Why does romantic love so captivate us? One reason may be because it is addictive.

> About 230 feet above the Capilano River in North Vancouver, British Columbia, a rickety footbridge sways in the wind. It makes you feel like you might fall into the rocky gorge below. A more solid footbridge crosses only ten feet above the shallow stream.
>
> The experimenters had an *attractive* woman approach men who were crossing these bridges. She told them she was studying "the effects of exposure to scenic attractions on creative expression." She showed them a picture, and they wrote down their associations. The sexual imagery in their stories showed that the men on the unsteady, frightening bridge were more sexually aroused than were the men on the solid bridge. More of these men also called the young woman afterward—supposedly to get information about the study.

You may have noticed that this research was really about sexual attraction, not love. The point, however, is that romantic love usually begins with sexual attraction. Finding ourselves sexually attracted to someone, we spend time with that person. If we discover mutual interests, we may label our feelings "love." Apparently, then, *romantic love has two components*. The first is emotional, a feeling of sexual attraction. The second is cognitive, a label that we attach to our feelings. If we attach this label, we describe ourselves as being "in love."

Marriage

Ask Americans why they married, and they will say that they were "in love." Contrary to folklore, whatever love is, it certainly is not blind. That is, love does not hit us willy-nilly, as if Cupid had shot darts blindly into a crowd. If it did, marital patterns would be unpredictable. When we look at who marries whom, however, we can see the social channels that love follows.

The Social Channels of Love and Marriage.   The most highly predictable social channels are age, education, social class, and race–ethnicity. For example, a Latina with a college degree whose parents are both physicians is likely to fall in love with and marry a Latino slightly older than herself who has graduated from college. Similarly, a girl who drops out of high school and whose parents are on welfare is likely to fall in love with and marry a man who comes from a background similar to hers.

Sociologists use the term **homogamy** to refer to the tendency of people who have similar characteristics to marry one another. Homogamy occurs largely as a result of *propinquity,* or spatial nearness. This is a sociological way of saying that we tend to "fall in love" with and

FIGURE 12.3 Marriages between Whites and African Americans: The Race–Ethnicity of the Husbands and Wives

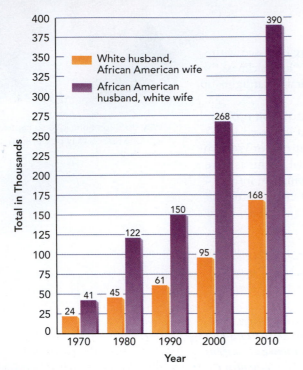

Source: By the author. *Based on Statistical Abstract of the United States* 1990:Table 53; 2012:Table 60.

marry someone who lives near us or someone we meet at school, church, work, or a neighborhood bar. The people with whom we associate are far from a random sample of the population, for social filters produce neighborhoods, schools, and places of worship that follow racial–ethnic and social class lines.

As with all social patterns, there are exceptions. Although 93 percent of married Americans choose someone of their same racial–ethnic background, 7 percent do not. Seven percent doesn't sound like much, but with 60 million married couples in the United States, this comes to over 4 million couples (*Statistical Abstract* 2012:Table 60).

One of the more dramatic changes in U.S. marriage is the increase in marriages between African Americans and whites. Today it is difficult to realize how norm-shattering such marriages used to be, but they were once illegal in 40 states (Staples 2008). In Mississippi, the penalty for interracial marriage was *life in prison* (Crossen 2004b). Despite the risks, a few couples crossed the "color line," but it took the social upheaval of the 1960s to break this barrier permanently. In 1967, the U.S. Supreme Court struck down the state laws that prohibited such marriages.

Figure 12.3 shows this change. Look at the race–ethnicity of the husbands and wives in these marriages, and you will see that here, too, Cupid's arrows don't hit random targets. Why do you think this particular pattern exists? Why do you think it is changing?

Childbirth

Ideal Family Size.   The number of children that Americans consider ideal has changed over the years. As you can see from Figure 12.4, preferences have moved to having fewer children. The research shows an interesting religious divide, not between

✳Explore
Living Data
on **mysoclab.com**

FIGURE 12.4 The Number of Children Americans Think Are Ideal

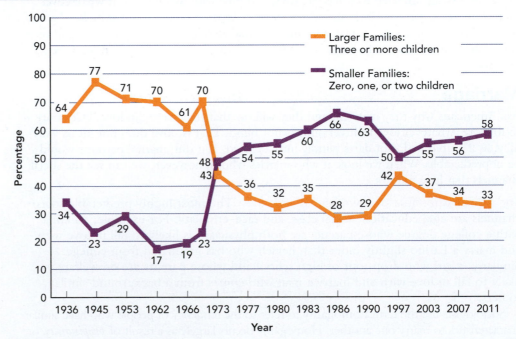

Source: By the author, based on Gallup Poll 2011.

How has the ideal U.S. family size changed over time?

Protestants and Roman Catholics, who give the same answers, but by church attendance. Those who attend services more often prefer larger families than those who attend less often. The last couple of polls reveal an unexpected change: Younger Americans (ages 18 to 34) prefer larger families than do those who are older than 34 (Gallup Poll 2011).

If they had their way, some couples would specify not just the number of children but also their characteristics, the topic of the Sociology and the New Technology box below.

Child Rearing

With mothers and fathers spending so many hours away from home at work, we must ask: Who's minding the kids while the parents are at work?

Married Couples and Single Mothers.   Figure 12.6 on page 360 compares the child care arrangements of single and married mothers. As you can see, their overall arrangements are similar. A main difference, though, is that when married women are at work the child is more likely to be under the father's care or in day care. For single mothers,

---

Sociology and the New Technology

What Color Eyes? How Tall? Designer Babies on the Way

You can't carry a tune, but you want your daughter to be musical? You're short, but you want to make sure that your son is tall? You want your child to be a basketball star or a scientist?

Welcome to the world of Designer Baby Clinics, where you can put in your order. Not like fast food, of course, for it will still take the usual nine months. But you will get what you ordered.

Or at least this is the promise. A few technical details must still be worked out, but these hurdles are falling rapidly.

The allure of designer babies is apparent. To pick superior qualities for your child—this is sort of like being able to pick a superior college. To be able to do so much good for your child!

But with this allure come moral dilemmas. Let's suppose that a couple wants a green-eyed blond girl. As Figure 12.5 shows, the technicians will fertilize several eggs, test the embryos, and plant the one(s) with the desired characteristics in a uterus. And the ones that are not used? They will be flushed down the drain. Some people find this objectionable.

Others are concerned that selecting certain characteristics represents a bias against people who have different characteristics. To order a tall designer baby, for example, is this a bias against short people?

If this isn't quite clear, perhaps this will help. If there is a preference for boys, a lot of female embryos will be discarded.

There is also the issue of a super race. If we can produce people who are superior physically and intellectually, should we?

Or here is another issue. Two deaf parents want their child to share their subculture, not to be a part of the hearing world, which they fear will drive a wedge between them and their child (Naik 2009). Would it be moral or immoral to produce a deaf child?

Oh, the moral dilemmas our technologies bring!

For Your Consideration
→ What are your answers to the questions raised in this box? On what do you base your answers?

FIGURE 12.5   On the Way to Designer Babies

A woman's eggs are fertilized with sperm in a lab, creating several embryos.

A single cell is removed from each embryo, and then tested for biomarkers associated with females, green eyes, and blond hair.

Only embryos with the biomarkers for the required traits are placed in the woman's womb.

The procedure virtually guarantees that the child will be female and increases the probability it will have green eyes and blond hair.

Source: Adapted from Naik 2009. Reproduced with permission.

What pattern of child preference (breaking at age 34) has emerged? What moral or social issues do "designer babies" raise?

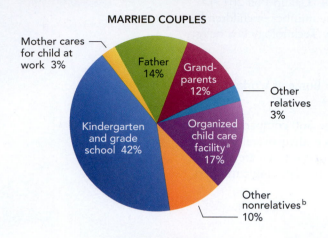

FIGURE 12.6 Who Takes Care of Preschoolers while Their Mothers Are at Work?

MARRIED COUPLES

Mother cares for child at work 3%
Father 14%
Grand-parents 12%
Other relatives 3%
Organized child care facility[a] 17%
Other nonrelatives[b] 10%
Kindergarten and grade school 42%

SINGLE MOTHERS

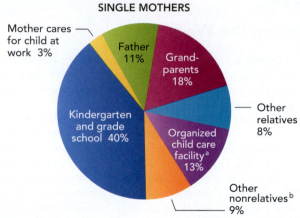

Mother cares for child at work 3%
Father 11%
Grand-parents 18%
Other relatives 8%
Organized child care facility[a] 13%
Other nonrelatives[b] 9%
Kindergarten and grade school 40%

[a]Includes day care centers, nursery schools, preschools, and Head Start programs. [b]Includes in-home babysitters and other nonrelatives providing care in either the child's or the provider's home.

Source: *America's Children in Brief 2010*:Table FAM3A.

One of the most demanding, exasperating—and also fulfilling—roles in life is that of parent. To really appreciate this cartoon, perhaps one has to have experienced this part of the life course.

"Your attitude is sucking all the fulfillment out of motherhood."

Barbara Smaller/The New Yorker Collection/www.cartoonbank.com

grandparents and other relatives are more likely to fill in for the absent father.

Day Care.   From Figure 12.6, you can see that about one of six or seven children is in day care. The broad conclusions of research on day care were reported in Chapter 3 (p. 82). Apparently only a minority of U.S. day care centers offer high-quality care as measured by whether they provide stimulating learning activities, emotional warmth, and attentiveness to children's needs (Bergmann 1995; Blau 2000; Belsky 2009). A primary reason for this dismal situation is the low salaries paid to day care workers, who average only about $17,000 a year ("Career Guide. . ." 2011).

It is difficult for parents to judge the quality of day care, since they don't know what takes place when they are not there. If you ever look for day care, two factors best predict that children will receive quality care: staff who have taken courses in early childhood development and a low ratio of children per staff member (Blau 2000; Belsky et al. 2007). If you have nagging fears that your children might be neglected or even abused, choose a center that streams live webcam images on the Internet. While at work, you can "visit" each room of the day care center via cyberspace and monitor your toddler's activities and care.

Social Class.   Do you think that social class makes a difference in how people rear their children? If you answered "yes," you are right. But what difference? And why? Sociologists have found that working-class parents tend to think of children as wild flowers that develop naturally, while in the middle-class mind children are like wild flowers that need a lot of nurturing if they are to bloom (Lareau 2002). These contrasting views make a world of difference in how people rear their children. Working-class parents are more likely to set limits for their children and then let them choose their own activities, while middle-class parents are more likely to try to push their children into activities that they think will develop their thinking and social skills.

Sociologist Melvin Kohn (1963, 1977; Kohn and Schooler 1969) also found that the type of work that parents do has an impact on how they rear their children. Because members of the working class are closely supervised on their jobs, where they are expected to follow explicit rules, their concern is less with their children's motivation and more with their outward conformity. These parents are more apt to use physical punishment—which brings about outward conformity without regard for internal attitude. Middle-class workers, in contrast, are expected to take more initiative on the job. Consequently, middle-class parents have more concern that their children develop curiosity and self-expression. They are also more likely to withdraw privileges or affection than to use physical punishment.

Family Transitions

The later stages of family life bring their own pleasures to be savored and problems to be solved. Let's look at two transitions—children staying home longer and adults adjusting to widowhood.

"Adultolescents" and the Not-So-Empty Nest.   Adolescents, especially the young men, used to leave home after finishing high school. (My high school graduation present was a suitcase.) When the last child left home at about age 17 to 19, the husband and wife were left with what was called an *empty nest.* Today's nest is not as empty as it used to be. With prolonged education and the higher cost of establishing a household, U.S. children are leaving home later. Many stay home during college, while others who strike out on their own find the cost or responsibility too great and return home. Much to their own disappointment, some even leave and return to the parents' home several times. As a result, 18 percent of all U.S. 25- to 29-year-olds are living with their parents. About 15 percent of this still-at-home group have children (U.S. Census Bureau 2010:Table A2).

This major historical change in how people become adults is playing out before our eyes. With the path to adulthood changing abruptly, its contours—its roadmap—are still being worked out. Although "adultolescents" enjoy the protection of home, they have to work out issues about turf, authority, and responsibilities—items that both the children and parents thought were long ago resolved.

Widowhood.   As you know, women are more likely than men to become widowed. There are two reasons for this: On average, women live longer than men, and they usually marry men older than they are. For either women or men, the death of a spouse tears at the self, clawing at identities that had merged through the years. With the one who had become an essential part of the self gone, the survivor, as in adolescence, once again confronts the perplexing question "Who am I?"

The death of a spouse produces what is called the *widowhood effect:* The impact of the death is so strong that surviving spouses tend to die earlier than expected. The "widowhood effect" is not even across the board, however, and those who have gone through anticipatory grief suffer fewer health consequences (Elwert and Christakis 2008). Apparently learning that their spouse was going to die gave them time to make preparations that smoothed the transition—from arranging finances to preparing themselves psychologically for being alone. You can see how saying goodbye and cultivating treasured last memories would help people adjust to the impending death of an intimate companion. Sudden death, in contrast, rips the loved one away, offering no chance for this predeath healing.

Diversity in U.S. Families

It is important to note that there is no such thing as *the* American family. Rather, family life varies widely throughout the United States. In several contexts, we have seen how significant social class is in our lives. Its significance will continue to be evident as we examine diversity in U.S. families.

African American Families

Note that the heading reads African American *families,* not *the* African American family. There is no such thing as *the* African American family any more than there is *the* white family or *the* Latino family. The primary distinction is not between African Americans and other groups, but between social classes (Willie and Reddick 2003). Because African Americans who are members of the upper class follow the class interests reviewed in Chapter 8—preservation of privilege and family fortune—they are especially concerned about the family background of those whom their children marry (Gatewood 1990). To them, marriage is viewed as a merger of family lines. Children of this class marry later than children of other classes.

Read

Women and Men in the Caregiving Role by Rhonda J. V. Montgomery and Mary McGlinn Datwyler on **mysoclab.com**

What are "adultolescents"? What problems do they and their parents face? What identity crisis does widowhood bring?

There is no such thing as *the* African American family, any more than there is *the* Native American, Asian American, Latino, or Irish American family. Rather, each racial–ethnic group has different types of families, with the primary determinant being social class.

Middle-class African American families focus on achievement and respectability. Both husband and wife are likely to work outside the home. A central concern is that their children go to college, get good jobs, and marry well—that is, marry people like themselves, respectable and hardworking, who want to get ahead in school and pursue a successful career.

African American families in poverty face all the problems that cluster around poverty (Wilson 2007; Bryant et al. 2010). Because the men are likely to be unemployed with few marketable skills, it is difficult for them to fulfill the cultural roles of husband and father. Consequently, these families are likely to be headed by a woman and to have a high rate of births to single women. Divorce and desertion are also more common than among other classes. Sharing scarce resources and "stretching kinship" are primary survival mechanisms. People who have helped out in hard times are considered brothers, sisters, or cousins to whom one owes obligations as though they were blood relatives; and men who are not the biological fathers of their children are given fatherhood status (Stack 1974; Hall 2008). Sociologists use the term *fictive kin* to refer to this stretching of kinship.

From Figure 12.7 you can see that, compared with other groups, African American families are the least likely to be headed by married couples and the most likely to be headed by women. Because African American women tend to go farther in school than African American men, they are more likely than women in other racial–ethnic groups to marry men who are less educated than themselves (Eshleman 2000; Harford 2008).

Latino Families

As Figure 12.7 shows, the proportion of Latino families headed by married couples and women falls in between that of whites and Native Americans. The effects of social

FIGURE 12.7   Family Structure: U.S. Families with Children under Age 18 Headed by Mothers, Fathers, and Both Parents

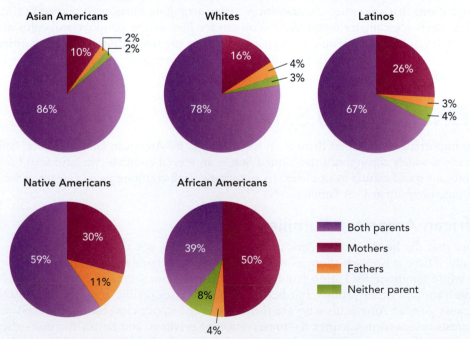

Note: Because of rounding, the individual percentages sometimes total 101%.

Sources: By the author. For Native Americans, Kreider and Elliott 2009:Table 1. For other groups, *Statistical Abstract of the United States* 2012:Table 69.

How do middle-class African American families and those in poverty differ?

class on families, which I just sketched, also apply to Latinos. In addition, families differ by country of origin. Families from Mexico, for example, are more likely to be headed by a married couple than are families from Puerto Rico (*Statistical Abstract* 2012:Table 37). The longer that Latinos have lived in the United States, the more their families resemble those of middle-class Americans (Falicov 2010).

With such wide variety, experts disagree on what is distinctive about Latino families (Falicov 2010). Some researchers have found that Latino husbands–fathers play a stronger role than husbands–fathers in white and African American families (Vega 1990; Torres et al. 2002). Others point to the Spanish language, the Roman Catholic religion, and a strong family orientation coupled with a disapproval of divorce. But such characteristics are limited, as there are Latino families who are Protestants, don't speak Spanish, and so on. Still others emphasize loyalty to the extended family, with an obligation to support the extended family in times of need (Cauce and Domenech-Rodriguez 2002), but this, too, is hardly unique to Latino families.

With such diversity among Latino families, you can see how difficult it is to draw generalizations. The sociological point that runs through all studies of Latino families, however, is this: Social class is more important in determining family life than is either being Latino or a family's country of origin.

Asian American Families

As you can see from Figure 12.7 on the previous page, Asian American children are more likely than children in other racial–ethnic groups to grow up with both parents. As with the other groups, family life also reflects social class. In addition, because Asian Americans emigrated from many different countries, their family life reflects those many cultures (Jeong and You 2008). As with Latino families, the more recent their immigration, the more closely their family life reflects the patterns in their country of origin (Glenn 1994; Jeong and You 2008).

Despite such differences, sociologist Bob Suzuki (1985) identified several distinctive characteristics of Asian American families. They tend to retain Confucian values that provide a framework for family life: humanism, collectivity, self-discipline, hierarchy, respect for the elderly, moderation, and obligation. Obligation means that each member of a family owes respect to other family members and has a responsibility never to bring shame on the family. Conversely, a child's success brings honor to the family (Zamiska 2004). To control their children, Asian American parents are more likely to use shame and guilt than physical punishment.

Seldom does the ideal translate into the real, and so it is here. The children born to Asian immigrants confront a bewildering world of incompatible expectations—those of the new culture and those of their parents. As a result, they experience more family conflict and mental problems than do children of Asian Americans who are not immigrants (Meyers 2006; Ying and Han 2008).

Native American Families

Perhaps the most significant issue that Native American families face is whether to follow traditional values or to assimilate into the dominant culture (Frosch 2008). This primary distinction creates vast differences among families. The traditionals speak native languages and emphasize distinctive Native American values and beliefs. Those who have assimilated into the broader culture do not.

As with other groups, there is no such thing as *the* Latino family. Some Latino families speak little or no English, while others have assimilated into U.S. culture to such an extent that they no longer speak Spanish.

What is distinctive about Latino families? About African American families?

To search for *the* Native American family would be fruitless. There are rural, urban, single-parent, extended, nuclear, rich, poor, traditional, and assimilated Native American families, to name just a few. Shown here is a family from the Comanche tribe in New Mexico.

Figure 12.7 on page 362 depicts the structure of Native American families. You can see that it is closer to Latinos than to any other group. In general, Native American parents are permissive with their children and avoid physical punishment. Elders play a much more active role in their children's families than they do in most U.S. families: Elders, especially grandparents, not only provide child care but also teach and discipline children. Like others, Native American families differ by social class.

In Sum: From this brief review, you can see that race–ethnicity signifies little for understanding family life. Rather, social class and culture hold the keys. The more resources a family has, the more it assumes the characteristics of a middle-class nuclear family. Compared with the poor, middle-class families have fewer children and fewer unmarried mothers. They also place greater emphasis on educational achievement and deferred gratification.

One-Parent Families

An indication of how extensively U.S. families are changing is the increase in one-parent families. From Figure 12.8 on the next page, you can see that the percentage of U.S. children who live with two parents (not necessarily their biological parents) has dropped sharply. Divorce is not the only reason. Another is that single women who give birth are taking longer to get married (Gibon-Davis 2011). The concerns—even alarm—that are expressed about one-parent families may have more to do with their poverty than with children being reared by one parent. Because women head most one-parent families, these families tend to be poor. Although most divorced women earn less than their former husbands, four of five (81 percent) children of divorce live with their mothers (U.S. Census Bureau 2010:Table C3).

To understand the typical one-parent family, then, we need to view it through the lens of poverty, for this is its primary source of strain. The results are serious, not just for these parents and their children but also for society. Children from one-parent families are more likely to have behavioral problems in school, to drop out of school, to get arrested, to have physical and emotional health problems, and to get divorced (McLanahan and Sandefur 1994; McLanahan and Schwartz 2002; Amato and Cheadle 2005; Wen 2008; Waldfogel et al. 2010). If female, they are more likely to have sex at a younger age and to bear children while still unmarried teenagers.

As you know, whether a child has one or two parents makes a vital difference in that child's life, but recent research has brought a surprise. For the child's adjustment, it does not matter if those parents are a man and a woman, a man and a man or a woman and a woman. Two women or two men who rear children together apparently do as well as a husband and wife (Farr et al. 2010).

Couples without Children

While most married women give birth, about one of five does not (Livingston and Cohn 2010). This is *double* what it was thirty years ago. As you can see from Figure 12.9, childlessness varies by racial–ethnic group, with whites and Asian Americans representing the extremes. From this figure, you can also see that except for women with Ph.D.s, the more education women have, the less likely they are to have children.

Some couples are infertile, but most childless couples have made a *choice* to not have children—and they prefer the term *childfree* rather than *childless*. Some decide before marriage that they will never have children, often to attain a sense of freedom—to pursue a career, to travel, and to have less stress (Letherby 2002; Koropeckyj-Cox 2007). In many cases, the couple simply postponed the date they were going to have their first child until either it was too late to have children or it seemed too uncomfortable to add a child to their lifestyle.

With trends firmly in place—more education and careers for women, advances in contraception, legal abortion, the high cost of rearing children, and an emphasis on possessing more material things—the proportion of women who never bear children is likely to increase. Consider this statement in a newsletter:

We are DINKS (Dual Incomes, No Kids). We are happily married. I am 43; my wife is 42. We have been married for almost twenty years. . . . Our investment strategy has a lot to do with our personal philosophy: "You can have kids—or you can have everything else!"

Blended Families

The **blended family,** one whose members were once part of other families, is an increasingly significant type of family in the United States. Two

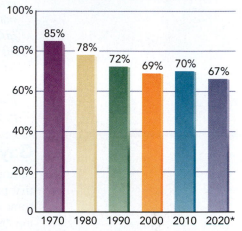

FIGURE 12.8   The Decline of Two-Parent Families

The percentage of children under 18 who live with both parents

Year	Percentage
1970	85%
1980	78%
1990	72%
2000	69%
2010	70%
2020*	67%

*Author's estimate. 2010 is based on slight increases since 2000.

Source: By the author. Based on *Statistical Abstract of the United States* 1995:Table 79; 2012:Table 69.

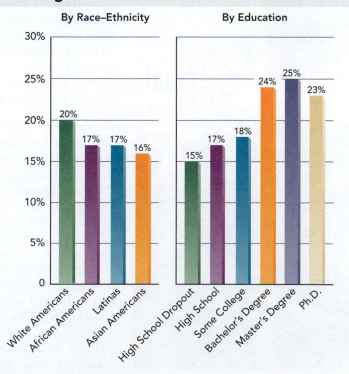

FIGURE 12.9   What Percentage of U.S. Married Women Ages 40–44 Have Never Given Birth?

By Race–Ethnicity

Group	Percentage
White Americans	20%
African Americans	17%
Latinas	17%
Asian Americans	16%

By Education

Group	Percentage
High School Dropout	15%
High School	17%
Some College	18%
Bachelor's Degree	24%
Master's Degree	25%
Ph.D.	23%

Source: By the author. Based on Livingston and Cohn 2010.

Why can we expect the percentage of U.S. women who never give birth to increase? What are blended families?

divorced people who marry and each bring their children into a new family unit form a blended family. With divorce common, millions of children spend some of their childhood in blended families. I've never seen a better explanation of how blended families can complicate family relationships than what one of my freshman students wrote:

> I live with my dad. I should say that I live with my dad, my brother (whose mother and father are also my mother and father), my half sister (whose father is my dad, but whose mother is my father's last wife), and two stepbrothers and stepsisters (children of my father's current wife). My father's wife (my current stepmother, not to be confused with his second wife who, I guess, is no longer my stepmother) is pregnant, and soon we all will have a new brother or sister. Or will it be a half brother or half sister?
>
> If you can't figure this out, I don't blame you. I have trouble myself. It gets very complicated around Christmas. Should we all stay together? Split up and go to several other homes? Who do we buy gifts for, anyway?

Gay and Lesbian Families

Although a handful of U.S. states allow people of the same sex to marry, 41 states have laws that prohibit same-sex marriages (Dematteis 2011). Walking a fine conceptual tightrope, some states avoid the term *marriage* but give legal status to same-sex unions by recognizing "registered domestic partnerships." Most gay and lesbian couples lack the legal rights—either marriage or civil unions—that support their relationship.

What are same-sex relationships like? Like everything else in life, these couples cannot be painted with a single brush stroke. Sociologists Philip Blumstein and Pepper Schwartz (1985), who interviewed same-sex couples, found their main struggles to be housework, money, careers, problems with relatives, and sexual adjustment. If these sound familiar, they should be, as they are the same problems that heterosexual couples face. A major difference is that many of these couples face a stigma, sometimes accompanied by discrimination, because they are of the same sex. As you can imagine, this complicates the relationship.

Being fought in U.S. courts is whether or not marriage should be limited to heterosexual couples. Passions on both sides are deep, as illustrated by the two sides of the issue shown here.

As with heterosexual couples, same-sex relationships also sour, and for all the same reasons—disagreements about sex, how to spend money, how to rear children, romantic triangles, and so on. Since about thirty percent of lesbian couples and seventeen percent of gay couples are rearing children, break-ups bring the usual problems of custody and visitation (Gartrell et al. 2011.)

If this sounds like "more of the same," it is. Except for the sex of the individuals, same-sex and heterosexual relationships are quite similar. A major difference is that only in the few states that allow same-sex marriages or civil unions do same-sex couples have to confront a legal system when they break up.

Adoption by Gay and Lesbian Couples.   Adoption by gay and lesbian couples has been a hot-button issue across the United States. A primary fear of heterosexuals is that children reared by homosexuals will somehow be pressured into becoming homosexuals (Lewin 2009). With this concern in mind and following their professional curiosity, sociologists and psychologists have compared the children adopted by heterosexual and gay and lesbian couples. The results are consistent: The children reared by homosexual parents have about the same adjustment as children reared by heterosexual parents (Gelderen et al. 2012). Their children are not more likely to have a gay or lesbian sexual orientation (Farr et al. 2010; Tasker 2010).

Why do gay and lesbian couples want to adopt children? To explore this question, anthropologist Ellen Lewin (2009) interviewed homosexual couples in San Francisco and Chicago who had adopted children. The reasons they gave are about the same as you would expect of heterosexual couples: to establish a family, love of children, wanting to give parentless children a home, to feel more adult, and to give meaning to one's life.

How are the problems that same-sex couples face similar to those heterosexual couples face? How do they differ?

Trends in U.S. Families

As is apparent from this discussion, marriage and family life in the United States is undergoing fundamental change. Let's look at some of the major trends.

The Changing Timetable of Family Life: Marriage and Childbirth

Figure 12.10 illustrates one of the most significant changes in U.S. marriages. As you can see, the average age of first-time brides and grooms declined from 1890 to about 1950. In 1890, the typical first-time bride was 22, but by 1950, she had just left her teens. For about twenty years, there was little change. Then in 1970, the average age started to increase sharply. *Today's average first-time bride and groom are older than at any other time in U.S. history.*

Since postponing marriage is today's norm, it may surprise you to learn that *most* U.S. women used to be married before they turned 24. To see this remarkable change, look at Figure 12.11 on the next page. This change is so engrained in our culture that the percentage of women between 20 and 24 who are married is now *less than a fourth* of what it was in 1970. For men, it is *less than a third.* Just as couples are postponing marriage, so they are putting off having children. Today's average U.S. woman now has her first child at age 25, the highest age in U.S. history (Mathews and Hamilton 2009).

Why have these changes occurred? The primary reason is cohabitation. Although Americans have postponed the age at which they first marry, they have *not* postponed the age at which they first set up housekeeping with someone of the opposite sex. Let's look at this trend.

Watch
Motherhood Manifesto
on **mysoclab.com**

FIGURE 12.10   **When Do Americans Marry? The Changing Age at First Marriage**

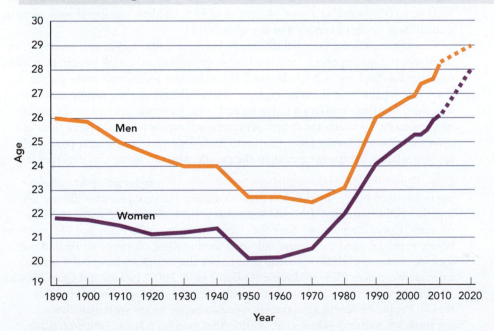

Note: This is the median age at first marriage. The broken lines indicate the author's estimate.

Source: By the author. Based on U.S. Census Bureau 2010.

What are the historical trends in age at first marriage? In being single for Americans ages 20–24? For age at first child?

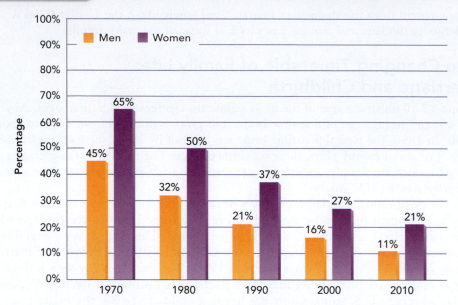

FIGURE 12.11   Americans Ages 20–24 Who Are Married

Source: By the author. Based on *Statistical Abstract of the United States* 1993:Table 60; 2002:Table 48; 2012:Table 57.

FIGURE 12.12   Cohabitation in the United States

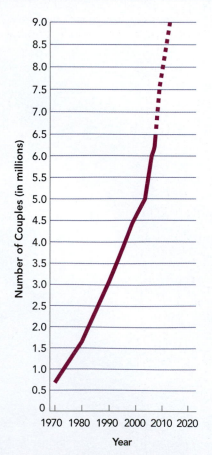

Note: Broken line indicates author's estimate.

Source: By the author. Based on U.S. Census Bureau 2007 and *Statistical Abstract of the United States* 1995:Table 60; 2012:Table 63.

Cohabitation

Figure 12.12 shows the increase in **cohabitation,** adults living together in a sexual relationship without being married. This figure is one of the most remarkable in sociology. I know of no other social trend that increases this steeply and consistently. Cohabitation is *twelve times* more common than it was in the 1970s. From a furtive activity, cohabitation has moved into the mainstream, and today about two-thirds of couples who marry have cohabited (Huang et al. 2011). Cohabitation has become so common that about 44 percent of U.S. children will spend some time in a cohabiting family (Kennedy and Bumpass 2011).

Commitment is the essential difference between cohabitation and marriage. In marriage, the assumption is permanence; in cohabitation, couples agree to remain together for "as long as it works out." For marriage, individuals make public vows that legally bind them as a couple; for cohabitation, they simply move in together. Marriage requires a judge to authorize its termination, but if a cohabiting relationship sours, the couple separates, telling friends and family that "it didn't work out." In the Down-to-Earth Sociology box on the next page, let's explore what cohabitation means to the people who are living this experience.

Does Cohabitation Make Marriage Stronger?   If couples set up housekeeping before they marry, are they less likely to divorce than couples who did not live together before marriage? It would seem that cohabitation would make marriage stronger. Cohabiting couples have the chance to work out so many real-life problems before marriage—and they marry only after sharing these experiences. To find out, sociologists compared divorce rates. It turns out that couples who cohabit before marriage were *more* likely to divorce (Osborne et al. 2007; Lichter and Qian 2008).

This went directly against what we would expect. Sociologists suggested this reason: People are less picky about choosing someone to live with than choosing someone to marry (Dush et al. 2003). After couples cohabit, however, many experience a "push" toward marriage—from having common possessions, pets, and children to the subtle and not-so-subtle hints of family and friends. As a result, many end up marrying someone they would not otherwise have chosen as a spouse.

Why was the divorce rate higher among those who cohabited before marriage?

Down-to-Earth Sociology

"You Want Us to Live Together? What Do You Mean by That?"

What has led to the surge of cohabitation in the United States? Let's consider two fundamental changes in U.S. culture.

The first is changed ideas of sexual morality. It is difficult for today's college students to grasp the sexual morals that prevailed before the 1960's sexual revolution. Almost everyone used to consider sex before marriage to be immoral. Premarital sex existed, to be sure, but it took place furtively and often with guilt. To live together before marriage was called "shacking up," and the couple was said to be "living in sin." A double standard prevailed: It was the woman's responsibility to say no to sex before marriage, so she was considered to be the especially sinful one in cohabitation.

And today—with premarital sex socially acceptable, and loads of sexual partners around—why rush into marriage? For those inclined to "settle down" somewhat, cohabitation offers a fairly safe alternative. It provides both sexual and emotional satisfactions within an ongoing relationship that does not require the long-term commitment of marriage.

Cohabitation also provides protection from divorce. Marriage sometimes seems so fragile and risky, as if it isn't going to last no matter how hard you try to make it work. Cohabitation removes this threat by offering an intimate relationship in which divorce is impossible. You can break up, but you can't get divorced.

And cohabitation is cheaper. You can set up housekeeping without the cost of a wedding—those expensive announcements, booking the church or hall, the reception, the honeymoon. You don't even have to fork over for a license.

From the outside, all cohabitation may look the same, but not to the people who are living together. As you can see from Table 12.2, for about 10 percent of couples, cohabitation is a substitute for marriage. These couples consider themselves married but for some reason don't want a marriage certificate. Some object to marriage on philosophical grounds ("What difference does a piece of paper make?"); others do not yet have a legal divorce from a spouse. Almost half of cohabitants (46 percent) view cohabitation as a step on the path to marriage. For them, cohabitation is more than "going steady" but less than engagement. Another 15 percent of couples are simply "giving it a try." They want to see what marriage to one another might be like. For the least committed, about 29 percent, cohabitation is a form of dating. It provides a dependable source of sex and emotional support.

If you look at these couples a half dozen years after they began to live together, you can see how important these different levels of commitment are. As you can see from Table 12.2, couples who view cohabitation as a substitute for marriage are the least likely to marry and the most likely to continue to cohabit. For couples who see cohabitation as a step toward marriage, the outcome is just the opposite: They are the most likely to marry and the least likely to still be cohabiting. Couples who are the most likely to break up are those who "tried" cohabitation and those for whom cohabitation was a form of dating.

For Your Consideration

➤ Can you explain why the meaning of cohabitation makes a difference in whether couples marry? Can you classify cohabiting couples you know into these four types? Do you think there are other types? If so, what?

TABLE 12.2	The Meaning of Cohabitation: What a Difference It Makes				
				After 5 to 7 Years	
				Of Those Still Together	
What Cohabitation Means	Percent of Couples	Split Up	Still Together	Married	Cohabitating
Substitute for Marriage	10%	35%	65%	37%	63%
Step Toward Marriage	46%	31%	69%	73%	27%
Trial Marriage	15%	51%	49%	66%	34%
Coresidential Dating	29%	46%	54%	61%	39%

Source: Recomputed by the author from Bianchi and Casper 2000.

What different meanings does cohabitation have? What differences do those meanings make for getting married?

As cohabitation has developed into a more essential part of the courtship/mating process, the initial findings of higher divorce are washing out. The latest research shows that of the recently married the divorce rate of those who did and did not cohabit before marriage is about the same (Manning and Cohen 2011). If this finding holds, we can conclude that cohabitation neither weakens nor strengthens marriage.

Children of Cohabiting Parents: A Surprising Finding.   Kammi Schmeer (2011), a sociologist who compared the health of children of married and cohabiting parents, found something that surprised her. It likely will surprise you, too. On average, the children of cohabiting parents aren't as healthy as the children of married parents. Schmeer suggests that one possibility for this finding is that there is more conflict in cohabiting relationships. But this is just a guess, and no one yet knows the reason. As this is just a single study, we must be cautious about drawing conclusions. We'll see what further research shows.

Divorce and Remarriage

The topic of family life would not be complete without considering divorce. Let's first try to determine how much divorce there is.

Ways of Measuring Divorce

You probably have heard that the U.S. divorce rate is 50 percent, a figure that is popular with reporters. The statistic is true in the sense that each year about half as many divorces are granted as there are marriages performed. The totals are roughly 2 million marriages and 1 million divorces (*Statistical Abstract* 2012:Table 133).

© Sidney Harris, ScienceCartoonPlus.com

" I NOW PRONOUNCE YOU SECOND HUSBAND AND FOURTH WIFE."

This fanciful depiction of marital trends may not be too far off the mark.

What is wrong, then, with saying that the divorce rate is about 50 percent? Think about it for a moment. Why should we compare the number of divorces and marriages that take place during the same year? The couples who divorced do not—with rare exceptions—come from the group that married that year. The one number has *nothing* to do with the other, so in no way do these two statistics reveal the divorce rate.

What figures should we compare, then? Couples who divorce come from the entire group of married people in the country. Since the United States has 60 million married couples, and about 1 million of them get divorced in a year, the divorce rate for any given year is less than 2 percent. A couple's chances of still being married at the end of a year are over 98 percent—not bad odds—and certainly much better odds than the mass media would have us believe. As the Social Map on the next page shows, the "odds"—if we want to call them that—depend on where you live.

Over time, of course, each year's small percentage adds up. A third way of measuring divorce, then, is to ask, "Of all U.S. adults, what percentage are divorced?" Figure 12.14 on answers this question. You can see how divorce has increased over the years and how race–ethnicity makes a difference for the likelihood that couples will divorce.

Figure 12.14 shows us the percentage of Americans who are currently divorced, but we get yet another answer if we ask the question, "What percentage of Americans has ever been divorced?" This percentage increases with each age group, peaking when people reach their 50s ("Marital History . . ." 2004). Overall, about 43 to 46 percent of marriages end in divorce (Amato 2010), so a divorce rate of 50 percent is actually fairly accurate.

National statistics are fine, but you probably want to know if sociologists have found anything that will tell you about *your* chances of divorce. This is the topic of the Down-to-Earth Sociology box on page 372.

What is the surprising finding about the children of cohabiting parents? What are different ways to measure divorce?

FIGURE 12.13   The "Where" of U.S. Divorce

Annual divorces per 1,000 people

- Lower than average: 2.2 to 3.1
- Average: 3.3 to 4.1
- Higher than average: 4.3 to 6.5

Lowest divorce rate

1. Massachusetts (2.2)
2. North Dakota (2.4)
3. Illinois (2.6)

Highest divorce rate

1. Nevada (6.5)
2. Arkansas (5.9)
3. Wyoming (5.5)

Note: Data for California, Georgia, Hawaii, Indiana, Louisiana, and Minnesota, based on the earlier editions in the source, have been decreased by the average decrease in U.S. divorce.

Source: By the author. Based on *Statistical Abstract of the United States* 1995:Table 149; 2002:Table 111; 2010:Table 126.

FIGURE 12.14   What Percentage of Americans Are Divorced?

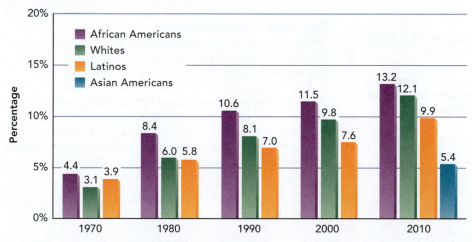

Legend:
- African Americans
- Whites
- Latinos
- Asian Americans

Year	African Americans	Whites	Latinos	Asian Americans
1970	4.4	3.1	3.9	
1980	8.4	6.0	5.8	
1990	10.6	8.1	7.0	
2000	11.5	9.8	7.6	
2010	13.2	12.1	9.9	5.4

Note: This figure shows the percentage who are divorced and have not remarried, not the percentage who have ever divorced. Only these racial–ethnic groups are listed in the source. The source only recently added data on Asian Americans.

Source: By the author. Based on *Statistical Abstract of the United States* 1995:Table 58; 2012:Table 56.

Children of Divorce

Emotional Problems.   Children whose parents divorce are more likely than children reared by both parents to experience emotional problems and to become juvenile delinquents (Amato and Sobolewski 2001; Wallerstein et al. 2001). They are less likely

What patterns of divorce do you see in Figure 12.13? In Figure 12.14?

Down-to-Earth Sociology

"What Are *Your* Chances of Getting Divorced?"

As you have seen, over a lifetime about half of all marriages fail. If you have that 50 percent figure dancing in your head while you are getting married, you might as well make sure that you have an escape door open even while you're saying "I do."

Not every group carries the same risk of divorce. For some, the risk is much higher; for others, much lower. Let's look at some factors that reduce people's risk. As Table 12.3 shows, sociologists have worked out percentages that you might find useful. As you can see, people who go to college, participate in a religion, wait to get married before having children, and earn higher incomes have a much better chance that their marriages will last. You can also see that having parents who did not divorce is significant. If you reverse these factors, you will see how the likelihood of divorce increases for people who have a baby before they marry, who marry in their teens, and so on. It is important to note, however, that these

Divorces are often messy. To settle the question of who gets the house, a couple in Cambodia sawed their house in half.

factors reduce the risk of divorce for *groups* of people, not for any particular individual.

Three other factors increase the risk for divorce, but for these, sociologists have not computed percentages: The first will probably strike you as strange—if a couple's firstborn child is a girl (Ananat and Michaels 2007; Dahl and Moretti 2008). Apparently, men prefer sons, and if the firstborn is a boy, the father is more likely to stick around. The second factor is more obvious: The more co-workers you have who are of the opposite sex, the more likely you are to get divorced (McKinnish 2007). (I'm sure you can figure out why.) No one knows the reason for the third factor: working with people who are recently divorced (Aberg 2003). It could be that divorced people are more likely to "hit" on their fellow workers—and human nature being what it is. . . .

For Your Consideration

→ Why do you think that people who go to college have a lower risk of divorce? How would you explain the other factors shown in Table 12.3 or discussed in this box?

Why can't you figure your own chances of divorce by starting with some percentage (say 14 percent less likelihood of divorce if your parents are not divorced, another 13 percent for going to college, and so on)? To better understand this, you might want to read the section on the misuse of statistics on page 377.

TABLE 12.3 What Reduces the Risk of Divorce?	
Factors That Reduce People's Chances of Divorce	**How Much Does This Decrease the Risk of Divorce?**
Some college (vs. high-school dropout)	−13%
Affiliated with a religion (vs. none)	−14%
Parents not divorced	−14%
Age 25 or over at marriage (vs. under 18)	−24%
Having a baby 7 months or longer after marriage (vs. before marriage)	−24%
Annual income over $25,000 (vs. under $25,000)	−30%

Note: These percentages apply to the first ten years of marriage.

Source: Whitehead and Popenoe 2004.

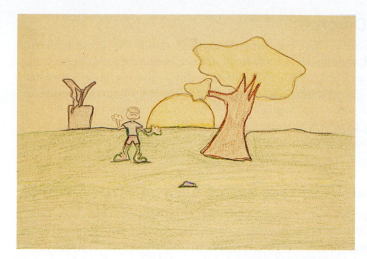

It is difficult to capture the anguish of the children of divorce, but when I read these lines by the fourth-grader who drew these two pictures, my heart was touched:

Me alone in the park . . .

All alone in the park.

My Dad and Mom are divorced

that's why I'm all alone.

This is me in the picture with my son.

We are taking a walk in the park.

I will never be like my father.

I will never divorce my wife and kid.

to complete high school and to graduate from college (McLanahan and Schwartz 2002). Finally, their children are more likely to divorce, perpetuating a marriage–divorce cycle (Cui and Fincham 2010).

Is the greater maladjustment of the children of divorce a serious problem? This question initiated a lively debate between two psychologists. Judith Wallerstein claims that divorce scars children, making them depressed and leaving them with insecurities that follow them into adulthood (Wallerstein et al. 2001). Mavis Hetherington replies that 75 to 80 percent of children of divorce function as well as children who are reared by both of their parents (Hetherington and Kelly 2003).

Without meaning to weigh in on either side of this debate, it doesn't seem to be a simple case of the glass being half empty or half full. If 75 to 80 percent of children of divorce don't suffer long-term harm, this leaves one-fourth to one-fifth who do. Any way you look at it, one-fourth or one-fifth of a million children each year is a lot of kids who are having a lot of problems.

What helps children adjust to divorce?   Children of divorce who feel close to both parents make the best adjustment, and those who don't feel close to either parent make the worst adjustment (Richardson and McCabe 2001). Other studies show that children adjust well if they experience little conflict, feel loved, live with a parent who is making a good adjustment, and have consistent routines. It also helps if their family has adequate money to meet its needs. Children also adjust better if a second adult can be counted on for support (Hayashi and Strickland 1998). Sociologist Urie Bronfenbrenner (1992) said this person is like the third leg of a stool, giving stability to the smaller family unit. Any adult can be the third leg, he says—a relative, friend, or even a former mother-in-law—but the most powerful stabilizing third leg is the father, the ex-husband.

Perpetuating Divorce.   When the children of divorce grow up and marry, they are more likely to divorce than are adults who grew up in intact families. Have researchers found any factors that increase the chances that the children of divorce will have successful marriages? Actually, they have. They are more likely to have a lasting marriage if they marry someone whose parents did not divorce. These marriages have more trust and less conflict. If both husband and wife come from broken families, however, it is not good news. Those marriages tend to have less trust and more conflict, leading to a higher chance of divorce (Wolfinger 2011).

What helps children adjust to divorce? Why are children of divorce more likely to divorce?

Grandchildren of Divorce

Paul Amato and Jacob Cheadle (2005), the first sociologists to study the grandchildren of people who had divorced, found that the effects of divorce continue across generations. Using a national sample, they compared grandchildren—those whose grandparents had divorced with those whose grandparents had not divorced. Their findings are astounding. The grandchildren of divorce have weaker ties to their parents, don't go as far in school, and don't get along as well with their spouses. As these researchers put it, when parents divorce, the consequences ripple through the lives of children who are not yet born.

Fathers' Contact with Children after Divorce

With most children living with their mothers after divorce, how often do fathers see their children? As you can see from Table 12.4, researchers have found four main patterns. The most common pattern is for fathers to see their children frequently after the divorce, and to keep doing so. But as you can see, a similar number of fathers have little contact with their children both right after the divorce and during the following years.

Which fathers are more likely to see and talk often to their children? It is men who were married to the mothers of the children, especially those who are older, more educated, and have higher incomes. In contrast, men who were cohabiting with the mothers, as well as younger, less educated men with lower incomes, tend to have less contact with their children. If their former wife marries, the fathers tend to see their children less (Berger et al. 2012).

TABLE 12.4 Fathers' Contact with Their Children after Divorce			
Frequent[1]	Minimal[2]	Decreased[3]	Increased[4]
38%	32%	23%	8%

[1]Maintains contact once a week or more through the years
[2]Little contact after the divorce, maybe 2 to 6 times a year
[3]Frequent contact after the divorce but less through the years
[4]Has little contact after the divorce but increases it through the years. Sometimes called the "divorce activated" father.

Source: By the author: Based on Cheadle et al. 2010.

The Ex-Spouses

Women are more likely than men to feel that divorce is giving them a "new chance" in life. A few couples manage to remain friends through it all—but they are the exception. The spouse who initiates the divorce usually gets over it sooner (Kelly 1992; Wang and Amato 2000) and remarries sooner (Sweeney 2002).

Divorce does not necessarily mean the end of a couple's relationship. Many divorced couples maintain contact because of their children. For others, the *continuities*, as sociologists call them, represent lingering attachments (Vaughan 1985; Masheter 1991; author's file 2005). The former husband may help his former wife paint a room or move furniture; she may invite him over for a meal or to watch television. They might even go to dinner or to see a movie together. Some couples even continue to make love after their divorce.

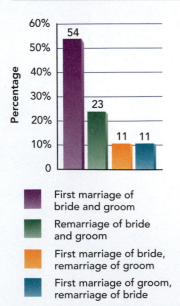

FIGURE 12.15　The Marital History of U.S. Brides and Grooms

- First marriage of bride and groom
- Remarriage of bride and groom
- First marriage of bride, remarriage of groom
- First marriage of groom, remarriage of bride

Source: By the author. Based on *Statistical Abstract of the United States* 2000:Table 145. Table dropped in later editions.

Remarriage

As Figure 12.15 shows, most divorced people marry other divorced people. You may be surprised that the women who are most likely to remarry are young mothers and those with less education (Glick and Lin 1986; Schmiege et al. 2001). Apparently women who are more educated and more independent (no children) can afford to be more selective. Men are more likely than women to remarry, perhaps because they have a larger pool of potential mates.

How do remarriages work out? The divorce rate of remarried people *without* children is the same as that of first marriages. Those who bring children into a new marriage, however, are more likely to divorce again (MacDonald and DeMaris 1995). Certainly remarriages with children are more complicated and stressful. A lack of clear norms to follow may also play a role (Coleman et al. 2000). As sociologist Andrew Cherlin (1989) noted, we lack satisfactory names for stepmothers, stepfathers,

What patterns show up: Of divorced fathers' with their children? Of ex-spouses? In how remarriages work out?

stepbrothers, stepsisters, stepaunts, stepuncles, stepcousins, and stepgrandparents. At the very least, these awkward terms to use, but they also represent ill-defined relationships.

Two Sides of Family Life

Let's first look at situations in which marriage and family have gone seriously wrong and then try to answer the question of what makes marriage work.

The Dark Side of Family Life: Battering, Child Abuse, Marital Rape, and Incest

The dark side of family life involves events that people would rather keep in the dark. We shall look at spouse battering, child abuse, rape, and incest.

Spouse Battering.   From his own research and his review of the research of others, sociologist Murray Straus concludes that wives attack their husbands as often as husbands attack their wives (Straus and Gelles 1988; Straus 1992; Straus 2011). Gender equality may exist in *initiating* marital violence, but it certainly vanishes when it comes to the *effects* of violence. As you know, women are much more likely to be injured. You also know that the primary reason is that most husbands are bigger and stronger than their wives, putting women at a physical disadvantage in this literal battle of the sexes.

Gender equality in initiating violence goes against the dominant idea of our society, which generally lays the blame at the feet of men. This is another of the surprising findings in sociology. And it has serious implications: If we want to curb violence, we should *not* concentrate on men, but, instead, on both men and women.

The basic sociological question, then, is how to socialize *both* males and females to handle frustration and disagreements without resorting to violence. We do not yet have this answer.

Child Abuse.

> I answered an ad about a lakeside house in a middle-class neighborhood that was for sale by owner. As the woman showed me through her immaculate house, I was surprised to see a plywood box in the youngest child's bedroom. About 3 feet high, 3 feet wide, and 6 feet long, the box was perforated with holes and had a little door with a padlock. Curious, I asked what it was. The woman replied matter-of-factly that her son had a behavior problem, and this was where they locked him for "time out." She added that other times they would tie him to a float, attach a line to the dock, and put him in the lake.
>
> I left as soon as I could. With thoughts of a terrorized child filling my head, I called the state child abuse hotline.

As you can tell, what I saw upset me. Most of us are bothered by child abuse— helpless children being victimized by their parents and other adults who are supposed to love, protect, and nurture them. The most gruesome of these cases make the evening news: The 4-year-old girl who was beaten and raped by her mother's boyfriend, passed into a coma, and three days later passed out of this life; the 6- to 10-year-old children whose stepfather videotaped them engaging in sex acts. Unlike these cases, which made headlines in my area, most child abuse is never brought to our attention: the children who live in filth, who are neglected—left alone for hours or even days at a time—or who are beaten with extension cords—cases like the little boy I learned about when I went house hunting.

Child abuse is extensive. Each year, U.S. authorities receive about 2 million reports of children being abused or neglected. About 800,000 of these cases are substantiated (*Statistical Abstract* 2012:Table 343). The excuses that parents make are incredible.

To reduce marital violence, why should the focus be on *both* husbands and wives? Why don't abused wives "just leave"?

Of those I have read, the most fantastic is what a mother said to a Manhattan judge: "I slipped in a moment of anger, and my hands accidentally wrapped around my daughter's windpipe" (LeDuff 2003).

Incest.   Sexual relations between certain relatives (for example, between brothers and sisters or between parents and children) constitute **incest.** Incest is most likely to occur in families that are socially isolated (Smith 1992). Sociologist Diana Russell (n.d.) found that incest victims who experience the greatest trauma are those who were victimized the most often, whose assaults occurred over longer periods of time, and whose incest was "more intrusive"—for example, sexual intercourse as opposed to sexual touching.

Incest can occur between any family members, but apparently the most common form is sex between children. An analysis of 13,000 cases of sibling incest showed that in three-fourths of the cases the sex is initiated by a brother who is five years older than his sister (Krienert and Walsh 2011). In one-fourth of the cases, the victim is a younger brother, and in 13 percent of the cases it is the sister who is the offender. Most offenders are between the ages of 13 and 15, and most victims are age 12 or younger. In most cases, the parents treat the incest as a family matter to be dealt with privately.

The Bright Side of Family Life: Successful Marriages

Successful Marriages.   After examining divorce and family abuse, one could easily conclude that marriages seldom work out. This would be far from the truth, however, for about three of every five married Americans report that they are "very happy" with their marriages (Whitehead and Popenoe 2004). (Keep in mind that each year divorce eliminates about a million unhappy marriages.) To find out what makes marriage successful, sociologists Jeanette and Robert Lauer (1992) interviewed 351 couples who had been married fifteen years or longer. Fifty-one of these marriages were unhappy, but the couples stayed together for religious reasons, because of family tradition, or "for the sake of the children."

Of the others, the 300 happy couples, all

1. Think of their spouses as best friends
2. Like their spouse as a person
3. Think of marriage as a long-term commitment
4. Believe that marriage is sacred
5. Agree with their spouses on aims and goals
6. Believe that their spouses have grown more interesting over the years
7. Strongly want the relationship to succeed
8. Laugh together

Sociologist Nicholas Stinnett (1992) used interviews and questionnaires to study 660 families from all regions of the United States and parts of South America. He found that happy families

1. Spend a lot of time together
2. Are quick to express appreciation
3. Are committed to promoting one another's welfare
4. Do a lot of talking and listening to one another
5. Are religious
6. Deal with crises in a positive manner

Here are three more important factors: Marriages are happier when the partners get along with their in-laws (Bryant et al. 2001), find leisure activities that they both enjoy (Crawford et al. 2002), and agree on how to spend money (Bernard 2008).

Symbolic Interactionism and the Misuse of Statistics

Many students are concerned that divorce statistics mean they won't have a successful marriage. Because sociology is not just about abstract ideas, but is really about our lives, it is important to stress that you are an individual, not a statistic. That is, if the divorce rate were 33 percent or 50 percent, this would *not* mean that if you marry, your chances of getting divorced are 33 percent or 50 percent. This is a misuse of statistics—and a common one at that. Divorce statistics represent all marriages and have absolutely *nothing* to do with any individual marriage. Our own chances depend on our own situations—especially the way we approach marriage.

To make this point clearer, let's apply symbolic interactionism. From a symbolic interactionist perspective, we create our own worlds. That is, because our experiences don't come with built-in meanings, we interpret our experiences and act accordingly. As we do so, we can create a self-fulfilling prophecy. For example, if we think that our marriage might fail, we are more likely to run when things become difficult. If we think that our marriage is going to work out, we are more likely to stick around and to do things to make the marriage successful. The folk saying "There are no guarantees in life" is certainly true, but it does help to have a vision that a good marriage is possible and that it is worth the effort to achieve.

The Future of Marriage and Family

What can we expect of marriage and family in the future? Despite its many problems, then, marriage is in no danger of becoming a relic of the past. Marriage is so functional that it exists in every society. Consequently, the vast majority of Americans will continue to find marriage vital to their welfare.

Certain trends are firmly in place: cohabitation, births to single women, and age at first marriage. As more married women join the workforce, wives will continue to gain marital power. In the midst of changing marriage and family, our culture will continue to be haunted by distorted images of marriage and family: the bleak ones portrayed in the mass media and the rosy ones perpetuated by cultural myths. Sociological research can help to correct these distortions and allow us to see how our own family experiences fit into the patterns of our culture. Sociological research can also help to answer the big question: How do we formulate social policies that will support and enhance family life?

By the Numbers: Changes Over Time

Americans who want 3 or more children	
1936	**NOW**
64%	**33**%

Americans who want 0, 1, or 2 children	
1936	**NOW**
34%	**58**%

Number of marriages with a white wife and an African American husband	
1970	**NOW**
41,000	**390,000**

Number of marriages with an African American wife and a white husband	
1970	**NOW**
24,000	**168,000**

Number of hours per week wives do housework	
1965	**NOW**
34.5	**19.4**

Number of hours per week husbands do housework	
1965	**NOW**
4.4	**9.7**

Number of cohabitating couples	
1970	**NOW**
523,000	**6,500,000**

White Americans divorced	
1970	**NOW**
3.1%	**10.3**

African Americans divorced	
1970	**NOW**
4.4%	**11.4**%

Average age of first-time bride	
1970	**NOW**
20	**26**

Average age of first-time groom	
1970	**NOW**
23	**28**

Women ages 20–24 who are married	
1970	**NOW**
65%	**21**%

Men ages 20–24 who are married	
1970	**NOW**
45%	**11**%

Children who live with both parents	
1970	**NOW**
85%	**70**%

CHAPTER 12 Summary and Review

Marriage and Family in Global Perspective

What is a family—and what themes are universal?

Family is difficult to define. There are exceptions to every element that one might consider essential. Consequently, **family** is defined broadly—as people who consider themselves related by blood, marriage, or adoption. Universally, **marriage** and family are mechanisms for governing mate selection, reckoning descent, and establishing inheritance and authority. Pp. 352–354.

Marriage and Family in Theoretical Perspective

What is a functionalist perspective on marriage and family?

Functionalists examine the functions and dysfunctions of family life. Examples include the **incest taboo** and how weakened family functions increase divorce. Pp. 354–355.

What is a conflict perspective on marriage and family?

Conflict theorists focus on inequality in marriage, especially unequal power between husbands and wives. P. 355.

What is a symbolic interactionist perspective on marriage and family?

Symbolic interactionists examine the contrasting experiences and perspectives of men and women in marriage. They stress that only by grasping the perspectives of wives and husbands can we understand their behavior. Pp. 355–356.

The Family Life Cycle

What are the major elements of the family life cycle?

The major elements are love and courtship, marriage, childbirth, child rearing, and the family in later life. Most mate selection follows predictable patterns of age, social class, race–ethnicity, and religion. Child-rearing patterns vary by social class. Pp. 357–361.

Diversity in U.S. Families

How significant is race–ethnicity in family life?

The primary distinction is social class, not race–ethnicity. Families of the same social class are likely to be similar, regardless of their race–ethnicity. Pp. 361–364.

What other diversity do we see in U.S. families?

Also discussed are one-parent, childless (childfree), **blended,** and gay and lesbian families. Each has its unique characteristics, but social class is important in determining their primary characteristics. Poverty is especially significant for single-parent families, most of which are headed by women. Pp. 364–367.

Trends in U.S. Families

What major changes characterize U.S. families?

Two changes are postponement of first marriage and childbirth and an increase in **cohabitation.** Pp. 367–370.

Divorce and Remarriage

What is the current divorce rate?

Depending on what numbers you choose to compare, you can produce almost any rate you wish, from 50 percent to less than 2 percent. Pp. 370–371.

How do children and their parents adjust to divorce?

Divorce is difficult for children, who as adults are also more likely to divorce. Divorce even affects the grandchildren of divorced parents. Most divorced fathers do not maintain ongoing relationships with their children. Pp. 371–374.

Two Sides of Family Life

What are the two sides of family life?

The dark side is abuse—spouse battering, child abuse, and **incest,** all of which revolve around the misuse of family power. The bright side is that most people find marriage and family to be rewarding. Pp. 375–377.

The Future of Marriage and Family

What is the likely future of marriage and family?

We can expect cohabitation, births to unmarried women, and age at first marriage to increase. The growing numbers of women in the workforce are likely to continue to shift the balance of marital power. P. 377.

Thinking Critically about Chapter 12

1. Functionalists stress that the family is universal because it provides basic functions for individuals and society. What functions does *your* family provide? *Hint:* In addition to the section "The Functionalist Perspective," also consider the section "Common Cultural Themes."

2. Explain why social class is more important than race–ethnicity in determining a family's characteristics.

3. Apply this chapter's contents to your own experience with marriage and family. What social factors affect your family life? In what ways is your family life different from that of your grandparents when they were your age?

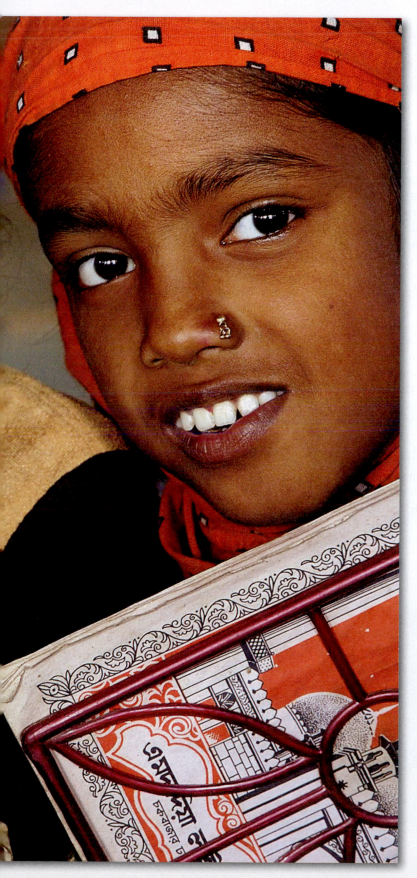

Bangladesh

Kathy Spiegel was upset. Horace Mann, the school principal in her hometown in Oregon, had asked her to come to his office. He explained that Kathy's 11-year-old twins had been acting up in class. They were disturbing other children and the teacher—and what was Kathy going to do about this?

Kathy didn't want to tell Mr. Mann what he could do with the situation. *That* would have gotten her kicked out of the office. Instead, she bit her tongue and said she would talk to her daughters.

* * * * *

On the other side of the country, Jim and Julia Attaway were pondering their own problem. When they visited their son's school in the Bronx, they didn't like what they saw. The boys looked like they were little gangsta wannabes, and the girls dressed and acted as though they were sexually active. Their own 13-year-old son had started using street language at home, and it was becoming increasingly difficult to talk to him.

> "The boys looked like they were junior gang members, and the girls . . ."

* * * * *

In Minneapolis, Denzil and Tamika Jefferson were facing a much quieter crisis. They found life frantic as they hurried from one school activity to another. Their 13-year-old son attended a private school, and the demands were so intense that it felt like the junior year in high school. They no longer seemed to have any relaxed family time together.

* * * * *

In Atlanta, Jaime and Maria Morelos were upset at the ideas that their 8-year-old daughter had begun to express at home. As devout first-generation Protestants, Jaime and Maria felt moral issues were a top priority, and they didn't like what they were hearing.

* * * * *

Kathy talked the matter over with her husband, Bob. Jim and Julia discussed their problem, as did Denzil and Tamika and Jaime and Maria. They all came to the same conclusion: The problem was not their children. The problem was the school their children attended. All four sets of parents also came to the same solution: home schooling for their children.

Home schooling might seem to be a radical solution to today's education problems, but it is one that the parents of 1½ million U.S. children have chosen. We'll come back to problems in education, and possible solutions, but, first, let's take a broad look at education.

Education: Transferring Knowledge and Skills

Education in Global Perspective

Have you ever wondered why people need a high school diploma to sell cars or to join the U.S. Marines? You will learn what you know on the job. Why do employers insist on diplomas and degrees? Why don't they simply use on-the-job training?

In some cases, job skills must be mastered before you are allowed to do the work. On-the-job training was once adequate to become an engineer or an airline pilot, but with changes in information and technology it is no longer sufficient. This is precisely why doctors display their credentials so prominently. Their framed degrees declare that an institution of higher learning has certified them to work on your body.

But testing in algebra or paragraph construction to sell gizmos at Radio Shack? Sociologist Randall Collins (1979) observed that industrialized nations have become **credential societies.** By this, he means that employers use diplomas and degrees as *sorting devices* to determine who is eligible for a job. Because employers don't know potential workers, they depend on schools to weed out the incapable. For example, when you graduate from college, potential employers will presume that you are a responsible person—that you have shown up for numerous classes, have turned in scores of assignments, and have demonstrated basic writing and thinking skills. They will then graft their particular job skills onto this foundation, which has been certified by your college.

Education and Industrialization

In the early years of the United States, there was no free public education. Parents with an average income could not afford to send their children even to grade school. As the country industrialized during the 1800s, political and civic leaders recognized the need for an educated workforce. They also feared the influx of "foreign" values, for this was a period of high immigration. They looked on public education as a way to reach two major goals: producing more educated workers and "Americanizing" immigrants (Hellinger and Judd 1991).

As industrialization progressed and fewer people made their living from farming, formal education came to be regarded as essential to the well-being of society. With the distance to the nearest college too far and the cost of tuition and lodging too great, few high school graduates were able to attend college. As is discussed in the Down-to-Earth Sociology box on page 384, this predicament gave birth to community colleges. As you can see from Figure 13.1 on the next page, receiving a bachelor's degree in the United States is now *twice* as common as completing high school used to be.

To place our own educational system in perspective, let's look at education in three countries at different levels of industrialization. This will help us see how education is related to a nation's culture and its economy.

In this photo from the 1890s in Washington, D.C., you can catch a glimpse of public schools in their infancy. As with the present, students then were also taught skills useful for their adult lives. The specific skills taught in schools have certainly changed.

FIGURE 13.1 Educational Achievement in the United States

Explore
Living Data
on mysoclab.com

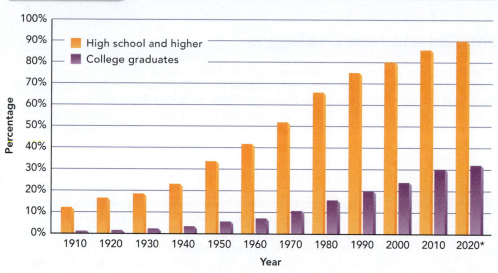

- High school and higher
- College graduates

Year: 1910, 1920, 1930, 1940, 1950, 1960, 1970, 1980, 1990, 2000, 2010, 2020*

Note: Americans 25 years and over. Asterisk indicates author's estimate. College graduates are included in both categories (High school and higher, and College graduates).

Sources: By the author. Based on National Center for Education Statistics 1991:Table 8; *Statistical Abstract of the United States* 2012:Table 229.

Education in the Most Industrialized Nations: Japan

The yells of children pierce the night, belting out the elements—"Lithium! Magnesium!"—as an instructor displays abbreviations from the periodic table. Next, two dozen flags stream by as the ten-year-olds shout out the names of the corresponding countries. Later they identify 20 constellations they have committed to memory. Timers on desks push older students as they practice racing through different tests. The scene at this juku *(cram school) on the edge of Tokyo, repeats itself nightly at 50,000 cram schools across Japan. ("Testing Times" 2011)*

What an emphasis on education. Japanese parents pay over $3,000 a year to enroll a child in a cram school. Even one in five first-graders is enrolled in these schools, which opearate after the regular school day. In grade school, children work as a group, all mastering the same skills and materials. On any one day, children all over Japan even study the same page from the same textbook ("Less Rote . . ." 2000). This uniformity is accompanied by a personal touch: Teachers are required to visit each student's home once a year (Yamamoto and Brinton 2010).

A central sociological principle of education is that a nation's education reflects its culture. Working as a group reflects the core Japanese value of solidarity with the group. In the workforce, people who are hired together are not expected to compete with one another for promotions; instead, they work as a team and are promoted as a group (Ouchi 1993). Japanese education reflects this group-centered approach to life.

In a fascinating cultural contradiction, college admission in Japan is highly competitive (Yamamoto and Brinton 2010). The Scholastic Assessment Test (SAT), taken by college-bound high school students in the United States, is voluntary, but Japanese seniors who want to attend college must take a national test. U.S. students who perform poorly on their tests can usually find some college to attend—as long as their parents can pay the tuition. Until recently, in Japan only the top scorers—rich and poor alike—were admitted to college. Because of Japan's low birth rate, this is changing. The pool of students has shrunk, and Japan's colleges have begun to compete for students (McNeill 2008).

School is over—but not for these students. After the regular school day, hundreds of thousands of students in Japan attend 50,000 cram (juku) schools.

Can you give a brief history of U.S. educational achievement?

Down-to-Earth Sociology

Community Colleges: Facing Old and New Challenges

I attended a junior college in Oakland, California. From there, with fresh diploma in hand, I transferred to a senior college—a college in Fort Wayne, Indiana, that had no freshmen or sophomores.

I didn't realize that my experimental college matched the vision of some of the founders of the community college movement. In the early 1900s, they foresaw a system of local colleges that would be accessible to the average high school graduate—a system so extensive that it would be unnecessary for universities to offer courses at the freshman and sophomore levels (Manzo 2001).

A group with an equally strong opinion questioned whether preparing high school graduates for entry to four-year colleges and universities should be the goal of junior colleges. They insisted that the purpose of junior colleges should be vocational preparation, to equip people for the job market as electricians and other technicians. In some regions, where the proponents of transfer dominated, the admissions requirements for junior colleges were higher than those of Yale (Pedersen 2001). This debate was never won by either side, and you can still hear its echoes today (Hanson 2010).

The name *junior* college also became a problem. Some felt that the word *junior* made their institution sound as though it weren't quite a real college. A struggle to change the name followed, and several decades ago *community* college won out.

The name change didn't settle the debate about whether the purpose was preparing students to transfer to universities or training them for jobs, however. Community colleges continue to serve this dual purpose.

Community colleges have become such an essential part of the U.S. educational system that 37 percent of all undergraduates in the United States are enrolled in them (*Statistical Abstract* 2012:Table 279). They have become the major source of the nation's emergency medical technicians, firefighters, nurses, and police officers. Most students are

nontraditional students: Many are age 25 or older, come from the working class, have jobs and children, and attend college part-time (Panzarella 2008; Osterman 2010).

To help students who are not seeking occupational certificates transfer to four-year colleges and universities, many community colleges work closely with four-year public and private universities (College Board 2011b). Some provide admissions guidance on how to enter flagship state schools. Others coordinate courses, making sure that they match the university's title and numbering system, as well as its rigor of instruction and grading. More than a third offer honors programs that prepare talented students to transfer with ease into these schools (Padgett 2005).

As with this college in Maine, community colleges have opened higher education to millions of students who would not otherwise have access to college because of cost or distance.

An emerging trend is for community colleges to become four-year colleges without changing their names. Some are now granting work-related baccalaureate degrees in such areas as teaching, nursing, and public safety (Hanson 2010). This raises the question: Will these community colleges eventually develop into full four-year colleges. If so, will this create the need to establish community colleges to replace them?

Community colleges face the challenges of securing adequate budgets in the face of declining resources, adjusting to changing job markets, and maintaining quality instruction. Other challenges include offering effective remedial courses; meeting the shifting needs of students, such as teaching students for whom English is a second language; and providing on-campus day care for parents. To help students succeed, community colleges need to improve their orientation programs and find better ways to monitor their students' progress (Panzarella 2008; Osterman 2010).

For Your Consideration

→ Do you think the primary goal of community colleges should be to prepare students for jobs or to prepare them to transfer to four-year colleges and universities? Why?

As in the United States, children from the richer families score higher on college admission tests and are more likely to go to college (Yamamoto and Brinton 2010). In each country, to be born into a richer family means to inherit privileges that help you in life. Among these privileges, which sociologists call **social capital,** are having more highly educated parents, encouragement and pressure to bring home top grades, and cultural experiences that translate into higher test scores.

Education in the Industrializing Nations: Russia

After the Russian Revolution of 1917, the Soviet Communist Party changed the nation's educational system. At that time, as in most countries, education was limited to children of the elite. The communists expanded the educational system until eventually it encompassed all children. Following the sociological principle that education reflects culture, the new government made certain that socialist values dominated its schools, for it saw education as a means to undergird the new political system. As a result, schoolchildren were taught that capitalism was evil and that communism was the salvation of the world. Every classroom was required to prominently display photographs of Lenin and Stalin.

Education, including college, was free. Just as the economy was directed from central headquarters in Moscow, so was education. Schools stressed mathematics and the natural sciences. Each school followed the same state-prescribed curriculum, and all students in the same grade used the same textbooks. To prevent critical thinking, which might lead to criticisms of communism, there were few courses in the social sciences. Students memorized course materials, repeating lectures on oral exams (Deaver 2001).

Russia's switch from communism to capitalism brought a change in culture—especially new ideas about profit, private property, and personal freedom. This, in turn, meant that the educational system had to adjust to the country's changing values and views of the world. Not only did the photos of Lenin and Stalin come down, but also, for the first time, private, religious, and even foreign-run schools were allowed. For the first time as well, teachers were able to encourage students to think for themselves.

The problems that Russia confronted in "reinventing" its educational system are mind-boggling. Tens of thousands of teachers who had been teaching students to memorize Party-dictated political answers had to learn new methods of instruction. As the economy faltered during Russia's early transition to capitalism, school budgets dwindled. Some teachers went unpaid for months; instead of money, at one school teachers were given toilet paper and vodka (Deaver 2001). Teachers are now paid regularly (and in money), but the salaries are low. University professors average only about $500 a month (Nemtsova 2008). Abysmal salaries have encouraged corruption, and some students pay for good grades and for admission to the better schools ("Russia Sets Out to . . ." 2007).

During this transition to the new education, the president of Russia, Vladimir Putin, declared that the new history books did not do justice to Russia's glorious past. Educational bureaucrats immediately jumped into action, and now officials inspect the content of history books to make certain they are sufficiently patriotic (Rapoport 2009). We can confidently predict that Russia's educational system will continue to glorify Russia's historical exploits and reinforce its values and world views—no matter how they might change.

Education in the Least Industrialized Nations: Egypt

Education in the Least Industrialized Nations stands in sharp contrast to that in the industrialized world. Because most of the citizens of these nations work the land or take care of families, there is little emphasis on formal schooling. Mandatory attendance laws are not enforced. As we saw in Figure 7.3 (pp. 198–199), many people

Can you summarize education in Japan and Russia?

The poverty of the Least Industrialized Nations carries over to their educational systems. This primary school in Khatta Village, Pakistan, is better off than some, which have no books, paper, or even buildings, just a blackboard on the street.

The cartoonist captures a primary reason that we have become a credential society.

"Hey, how come no diplomas?" "Oh, I'm self-taught."

© Robert Mankoff/The New Yorker Collection/www.cartoonbank.com

in the Least Industrialized Nations live on less than $1,000 a year. Consequently, in some of these nations few children go to school beyond the first couple of grades. As was once common around the globe, it is primarily the wealthy in the Least Industrialized Nations who have the means and the leisure for formal education—especially anything beyond the basics. As an example, let's look at education in Egypt.

Although the Egyptian constitution guarantees six years of free school for all children, many poor children receive no education at all. For those who do attend school, qualified teachers are few, and classrooms are crowded. As a result, one-third to one-half of Egyptians are illiterate, with more men than women able to read and write (UNESCO 2011). After the six years of grade school, students are tracked. Most study technical subjects for three years, and are then done with school, while others follow these three years with two years of academic subjects: arts, science, or mathematics ("Egyptian Overview" 2010).

The emphasis is on memorizing facts to pass national tests. With concerns that this approach leaves minds less capable of evaluating life and opens the door to religious extremism, Egyptian educators have pressed for critical thinking to be added to the curriculum (Gauch 2006). To become more competitive in the global economy, the government has requested independent evaluation of its educational system ("Reviews of National Policies . . ." 2010). So far little has changed. But as Egypt industrializes as part of the globalization of capitalism, this will likely forge educational reforms.

The Functionalist Perspective: Providing Social Benefits

A central position of functionalism is that when the parts of society are working properly, each contributes to the well-being or stability of that society. The positive things that people intend their actions to accomplish are known as **manifest functions.** The positive consequences they did not intend are called **latent functions.** Let's look at the functions of education.

Teaching Knowledge and Skills

Education's most obvious manifest function is to teach knowledge and skills—whether the traditional three R's or their more contemporary counterparts, such as computer literacy. Each generation must train the next to fill the group's significant positions. Because our postindustrial society needs highly educated people, the schools supply them.

Cultural Transmission of Values

Another manifest function of education is the **cultural transmission of values,** a process by which schools pass on a society's core values from one generation to the next. Consequently, schools in a socialist society stress values that support socialism, while schools in a capitalist society teach values that support capitalism. U.S. schools, for example, stress the significance of private property, individualism, and competition.

Can you summarize education in Egypt? What is the "cultural transmission of values?"

Regardless of a country's economic system, loyalty to the state is a cultural value, and schools around the world teach patriotism. U.S. schools—as well as those of Russia, France, China, and other countries around the world—extol the society's founders, their struggle for freedom from oppression, and the goodness of the country's social institutions. Seldom is this function as explicit as it is in Japan, where the law requires that schools "cultivate a respect for tradition and culture, and love for the nation and homeland" (Nakamura 2006).

To visualize what the functionalists mean, consider how differently a course in U.S. history would be taught in Cuba; Iran; and Muncie, Indiana.

Social Integration

Schools also bring about *social integration*. They promote a sense of national identity by having students salute the flag and sing the national anthem. One of the best examples of how U.S. schools promote political integration is the teaching of mainstream ideas and values to tens of millions of immigrants. Coming to regard themselves as Americans, the immigrants give up their earlier national and cultural identities (Carper 2000; G. Thompson 2009).

This integrative function of education goes far beyond making people similar in their appearance, speech, or even ways of thinking. *To forge a national identity is to stabilize the political system.* If people identify with a society's institutions and *perceive them as the basis of their own welfare,* they have no reason to rebel. This function is especially significant when it comes to the lower social classes, from which most social revolutionaries emerge. The wealthy already have a vested interest in maintaining the status quo, but getting the lower classes to identify with a social system *as it is* goes a long way toward preserving the system in its current state.

People with disabilities often have found themselves left out of the mainstream of society. To overcome this, U.S. schools have added a manifest function, **mainstreaming,** or inclusion. As in the photo at the right, this means that educators try to incorporate students with disabilities into regular school activities. Wheelchair ramps are provided for people who cannot walk; interpreters who use sign language may attend classes with students who cannot hear. Exceptions include most blind students, who attend special schools, as well as people with severe learning disabilities. Most inclusion goes fairly smoothly, but mainstreaming students with emotional and behavioral problems disrupts classrooms, frustrates teachers, and increases teacher turnover (Tomsho and Golden 2007). The disruption is so serious that the other children learn less, as measured by their scores in math and reading (Fletcher 2010).

Gatekeeping (Social Placement)

Sociologists Talcott Parsons (1940), Kingsley Davis, and Wilbert Moore (Davis and Moore 1945) pioneered a view called **social placement,** more commonly known as **gatekeeping.** They pointed out that some jobs require few skills and can be performed by people of lesser intelligence. Other jobs, such as that of physician, require high intelligence and advanced education. It is up to the schools to sort the capable from the incapable. They do this, say the functionalists, on the basis of merit, the students' abilities and ambitions.

To open the doors of opportunity for some is to close them to others. The question is what opens and closes those doors. Is it merit, as the functionalists argue? To accomplish gatekeeping, schools use some form of **tracking,** sorting students into different educational "tracks" or programs on the basis of their perceived abilities. Some U.S. high schools funnel students into one of three tracks: general, college prep, or honors. Students on the lowest track are likely to go to work after high school, or to take vocational courses. Those on the highest track usually attend prestigious colleges. Those in between usually attend a local college or regional state university.

You can also see that the impact of gatekeeping is lifelong. Tracking affects people's opportunities for jobs, income, and lifestyle. When tracking was challenged—that it is based more on social class than merit, which perpetuates social inequality—schools

Children with disabilities used to be sent to special schools. In a process called *mainstreaming* or inclusion, they now attend regular schools. Shown here is a 10-year-old girl with a rare genetic defect attending classes in Boiling Springs, Pennsylvania.

What is gatekeeping? How do schools perform this function?

retreated from formal tracking. Placing students in "ability groups" and "advanced" classes, however, serves the same purpose (Catsambis et al. 2012).

Replacing Family Functions

Over the years, the functions of U.S. schools have expanded, and they now rival some family functions. Child care is an example. Grade schools do double duty as babysitters for families in which both parents work, or for single working mothers. Child care has always been a latent function of formal education, for it was an unintended consequence. Now, however, with two wage earners in most families, child care has become a manifest function, and some schools offer child care both before and after the school day. Some high schools even provide nurseries for the children of their teenaged students (Bosman 2007).

Another function is providing sex education, and, as in 500 school-based health centers, birth control (Elliott 2007). This has stirred controversy, for some families resent schools taking this function away from them. Disagreement over values has fueled the social movement for home schooling, featured in the chapter's opening vignette.

In Sum: Functionalists analyze the functions, the benefits, that schools provide society. Not only do the schools teach the knowledge and skills needed by the next generation, but they also stabilize society by forging a national identity. A controversial function is gatekeeping, sorting students for various levels of jobs. Schools have expanded their domain, taking over some functions formerly performed by families.

The Conflict Perspective: Perpetuating Social Inequality

Unlike functionalists, who look at the benefits of education, conflict theorists examine how *the educational system reproduces the social class structure*. By this, they mean that schools perpetuate the social divisions of society and help members of the elite maintain their dominance.

Let's look, then, at how education is related to social classes, how it helps people inherit *social capital*, the life opportunities that were laid down before they were born.

The Hidden Curriculum: Reproducing the Social Class Structure

The term **hidden curriculum** refers to the attitudes and the unwritten rules of behavior that schools teach in addition to the formal curriculum. Examples are obedience to authority and conformity to mainstream norms. Conflict theorists stress that the hidden curriculum helps to perpetuate social inequalities.

Conflict theorists stress that education reproduces a country's social class system. In the United States, the social classes attend separate schools—private capitalist class, middle class, and inner city. In each of these types of schoools, children learn perspectives of the world that match their place in it. Shown here is a student at The Andrews School in Willoughby, Ohio. What do you think the *hidden curriculum is* at this school?

To understand this central point, consider the way English is taught. Schools for the middle class—whose teachers know where their students are headed—stress "proper" English and "good" manners. In contrast, the teachers in inner-city schools—who also know where *their* students are headed—allow ethnic and street language in the classroom. *Each type of school is helping to reproduce the social class structure.* That is, each is preparing students to work in positions similar to those of their parents. The social class of some children destines them for higher positions. For these jobs, they need "refined" speech and manners. The social destiny of others is low-status jobs. For this type of work, they need only to obey rules (Bowles and Gintis 1976, 2002). Teaching these students "refined" speech and manners would be wasted effort. In other words, even the teaching of English and manners helps keep the social classes intact across generations.

How are schools replacing family functions? What does "reproducing the social class structure" mean? What is the "hidden curriculum"?

For a humorous but serious account of how teachers perpetuate social classes even though they do not intend to do so, read the Down-to-Earth Sociology box below.

Tilting the Tests: Discrimination by IQ

Even intelligence tests help to keep the social class system intact. Let's look at an example. How would you answer this question?

> **A symphony is to a composer as a book is to a(n) ___**
> ___ *paper* ___ *sculptor* ___ *musician* ___ *author* ___ *man*

You probably had no difficulty coming up with "author" as your choice. Wouldn't any intelligent person have done so?

Down-to-Earth Sociology

How I Became a Fairy: Education and the Perpetuation of Social Inequality

I was excited about going to school. With its recess, scissors, and coloring, kindergarten turned out to be fun. Like the other boys, recess and rough-and-tumble games on the playground were my favorite activities.

First grade whizzed by, and I looked forward to second grade. Those big second graders had told me about how they were learning to read. How magical to be able to make out words from those strange marks on paper.

My second-grade teacher took her job seriously. She taught us how to sound out each letter. I couldn't figure out how s-a-i-d could be pronounced sed. It didn't seem to fit with what I was being taught, but I accepted it.

I liked learning. Each lesson seemed to unfold a different part of the world.

I tried my very best. And I learned and did well.

Then my teacher divided our class into two groups. She called the slower readers Elves, and the better readers Fairies. (These were simpler times.)

I was an elf.

Disappointment flooded over me! I knew that I should be a fairy. In the fairy group were my friends, the boys I played with during recess and after school—the lawyers' son, Jerry, the doctor's son, Jon, and the principal's son, Jacky. Roseau was a small town on the Canadian border in Minnesota, and we all lived just a few blocks from one another.

The teacher took turns teaching each group. She would go around the circle, having each student read aloud. As I heard the fairies read, I knew that my reading was just as good as theirs, actually better than some. I had to get this across to the teacher. But how?

From your experiences in grade school, can you tell if or how your teachers unintentionally helped perpetuate social class divisions?

When my turn came, I decided to read loudly and deliberately. She had no or few corrections for me, and would then move on to other elves, explaining to them over and over how to attach the right sounds to the letters, and from there how to form words.

After several reading lessons, with me continuing the loud reading, she looked at me and said, "I think you belong in the other group." She then allowed me to move my chair into their little circle.

And I went home, triumphantly announcing to my mother, "I'm a fairy!"

For Your Consideration

➔ Please don't get lost in the humor of this homely story. My parents were ill-educated and poor, farmers' children who had moved into town. Everyone in this little town knew precisely how everyone else ranked. Hidden within the teacher's awareness was this perception of social class. She thought that the students from advantaged homes—the children of professionals and those who had more money (there were no really wealthy people in town) could read better—and for the most part, she was right. She pegged the poorer students as poor readers, and for the most part, she was right.

But not entirely. What had happened was a misclassification of ability based on social class. This same process—occurring in a myriad of ways from well-meaning teachers throughout the U.S. school system—continues today. It is an essential part of, as we sociologists are fond of saying, how the educational system perpetuates the social class structure.

Did you see anything like this in your grade school?

In point of fact, this question raises a central issue in intelligence testing. Not all intelligent people would know the answer. This question contains *cultural biases*. Children from some backgrounds are more familiar with the concepts of symphonies, composers, and sculptors than are other children. This tilts the test in their favor.

To make the bias clearer, try to answer this question:

If you throw two dice and "7" is showing on the top, what is facing down?

___ *seven* ___ *snake eyes* ___ *box cars* ___ *little Joes* ___ *eleven*

Adrian Dove (n.d.), a social worker in Watts, a poor area of Los Angeles, suggested this question. Its cultural bias should be obvious—that it allows children from some social backgrounds to perform better than others. Unlike the first question, this one is not tilted to the middle-class experience. In other words, IQ (intelligence quotient) tests measure not only intelligence but also acquired knowledge.

You should now be able to perceive the bias of IQ tests that use such words as *composer* and *symphony*. A lower-class child may have heard about rap, rock, gangsta, or jazz, but not about symphonies. One consequence of this bias to the middle-class experience is that the children of the poor score lower on IQ tests. Then, to match their supposedly inferior intelligence, these children are assigned to less demanding courses. Their inferior education helps them reach their social destiny, their lower-paying jobs in adult life. As conflict theorists view them, then, IQ tests are another weapon in an arsenal designed to maintain the social class structure across the generations.

Stacking the Deck: Unequal Funding

Read

How Corporations Are Buying Their Way into America's Classrooms by Steven Manning

on **mysoclab.com**

Conflict theorists stress that the way schools are funded stacks the deck against the poor. Because public schools are supported largely by local property taxes, the richer communities (where property values and incomes are higher) have more to spend on their children, and the poorer communities have less to spend on theirs. Consequently, the richer communities can offer higher salaries and take their pick of the most highly qualified and motivated teachers. They can also afford to buy the latest textbooks, computers, and software, as well as offer courses in foreign languages, music, and the arts. This, stress conflict theorists, means that in *all* states the deck is stacked against the poor.

The Bottom Line: Family Background

Reproducing the Social Class Structure. The end result of unequal funding, IQ tests, and the other factors we have discussed is this: Family background is more important than test scores in predicting who attends college. In a classic study, sociologist Samuel Bowles (1977) compared the college attendance of high school students who were the most and least intellectually prepared for college. Figure 13.2 shows the results. Of the students who scored the highest on tests, 90 percent of those from affluent homes went to college, but only half of the high-scorers from low-income homes went to college. Of the least prepared, those who scored the lowest, 26 percent from affluent homes went to college, while only 6 percent from poorer homes did so.

Other sociologists have confirmed this classic research (Carnevale and Rose 2003; Bailey and Dynarski 2011). Regardless of personal abilities, children from more well-to-do families are more likely not only to go to college but also to attend the nation's most elite schools. This, in turn, piles advantage upon advantage, because they get higher-paying and more prestigious jobs when they graduate. The elite colleges are the icing on the cake of these students' more privileged birth.

Reproducing the Racial–Ethnic Structure. Conflict theorists point out that the educational system reproduces not only the U.S. social class structure but also its racial–ethnic divisions. From Figure 13.3 on the next page,

FIGURE 13.2 **Who Goes to College? Comparing Social Class and Ability in Determining College Attendance**

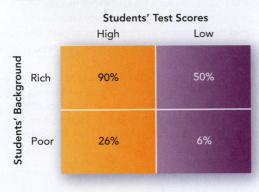

Students' Test Scores

	High	Low
Rich	90%	50%
Poor	26%	6%

Students' Background

Source: Bowles 1977.

you can see that, compared with whites, African Americans and Latinos are much less likely to complete high school and, of those who do, much less likely to go to college. Because adults with only high school diplomas usually end up with low-paying, dead-end jobs, you can see how this supports the conflict view—that education is helping to reproduce the racial–ethnic structure for the next generation.

In Sum: U.S. schools closely reflect the U.S. social class system. They equip the children of the elite with the tools they need to maintain their dominance, while they prepare the children of the poor for lower-status positions. Because education's doors of opportunity swing wide open for some but have to be pried open by others, conflict theorists say that the educational system perpetuates social inequality across generations (or, as they often phrase it, helps to reproduce the social class structure). In fact, they add, this is one of its primary purposes.

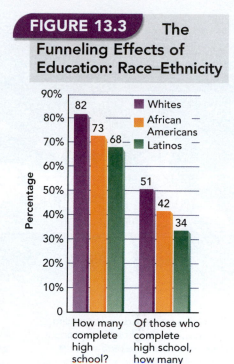

FIGURE 13.3   The Funneling Effects of Education: Race–Ethnicity

Note: The source gives totals only for these three groups.

Source: By the author. Based on *Statistical Abstract of the United States* 2012:Table 273.

The Symbolic Interactionist Perspective: Teacher Expectations

As you have seen, functionalists look at how education benefits society, and conflict theorists examine how education perpetuates social inequality. Symbolic interactionists, in contrast, study face-to-face interaction in the classroom. They have found that what teachers expect of their students has profound consequences for how students do in school.

The Rist Research

Why do some people get tracked into college prep courses and others into vocational ones? There is no single answer, but in what has become a classic study, sociologist Ray Rist came up with some intriguing findings. Rist (1970, 2007) did participant observation in an African American grade school with an African American faculty. He found that after only eight days in the classroom, the kindergarten teacher felt that she knew the children's abilities well enough to assign them to three separate worktables. To Table 1, Mrs. Caplow assigned those she considered to be "fast learners." They sat at the front of the room, closest to her. Those whom she saw as "slow learners," she assigned to Table 3, located at the back of the classroom. She placed "average" students at Table 2, in between the other tables.

This seemed strange to Rist. He knew that the children had not been tested for ability, yet their teacher was certain that she could identify the bright and slow children. Investigating further, Rist found that social class was the underlying basis for assigning the children to the different tables. Middle-class students were separated out for Table 1, and children from poorer homes were assigned to Tables 2 and 3. The teacher paid the most attention to the children at Table 1, who were closest to her, less to Table 2, and the least to Table 3. As the year went on, children from Table 1 perceived that they were treated better and came to see themselves as smarter. They became the leaders in class activities and even called children at the other tables "dumb." Eventually, the children at Table 3 disengaged themselves from many classroom activities. At the end of the year, only the children at Table 1 had completed the lessons that prepared them for reading.

This early tracking stuck. Their first-grade teacher looked at the work these students had done, and she placed students from Table 1 at her Table 1. She treated her tables much as the kindergarten teacher had, and the children at Table 1 again led the class.

The children's reputations continued to follow them. The second-grade teacher reviewed their scores and also divided her class into three groups. The first she named the "Tigers" and, befitting their name, gave them challenging readers. Not surprisingly, the Tigers came from the original Table 1 in kindergarten. The second group she called the "Cardinals." They came from the original Tables 2 and 3. Her third group consisted of children she had failed the previous year, whom she called the "Clowns." The Cardinals and Clowns were given less advanced readers.

How does the Rist research illustrate the effects of social class in education?

Education can be a dangerous thing. Socrates, who taught in Greece about 400 years before the birth of Christ, was forced to take poison because his views challenged those of the establishment. Usually, however, educators reinforce the perspectives of the elite, teaching students to take their place within the social structure. This 1787 painting, "The Death of Socrates," is by J. L. David (1748–1825).

Rist concluded that *each child's journey through school was determined by the eighth day of kindergarten!* As we saw with the Saints and Roughnecks, in Chapter 4, labels can be so powerful that they can set people on courses of action that affect the rest of their lives.

What occurred was a **self-fulfilling prophecy.** This term, coined by sociologist Robert Merton (1949/1968), refers to a false assumption of something that is going to happen but which then comes true simply because it was predicted. For example, if people believe an unfounded rumor that a credit union is going to fail because its officers have embezzled their money, they all rush to the credit union to demand their money. The prediction—although originally false—is now likely to come true.

How Do Teacher Expectations Work?

Sociologist George Farkas (Farkas et al. 1990a; Farkas et al. 1990b; Farkas 1996) became interested in how teacher expectations affect grades. Using a stratified sample of students in a large school district in Texas, he found that teacher expectations produced gender and racial–ethnic biases. *On the gender level:* Even though boys and girls had the same test scores, girls on average were given higher course grades. *On the racial–ethnic level:* Asian Americans who had the same test scores as the other groups averaged higher grades.

At first, this may sound like more of the same old news—another case of discrimination. But this explanation doesn't fit, which is what makes the finding fascinating. Look at who the victims are. It is most unlikely that the teachers would be prejudiced against boys and whites. To interpret these unexpected results, Farkas used symbolic interactionism. He observed that some students "signal" to their teachers that they are "good students." They show an eagerness to cooperate, and they quickly agree with what the teacher says. They also show that they are "trying hard." The teachers pick up these signals and reward these "good students" with better grades. Girls and Asian Americans, the researcher concluded, are better at giving these signals so coveted by teachers.

We do not have enough information on how teachers communicate their expectations to students. Nor do we know much about how students "signal" messages to teachers. Perhaps you will become the educational sociologist who will shed more light on this significant area of human behavior.

Problems in U.S. Education—and Their Solutions

Now that we've looked at some of the dynamics within the classroom, let's turn to three problems facing U.S. education—mediocrity, cheating, and violence—and consider potential solutions.

Mediocrity

The Rising Tide of Mediocrity.   Since I know you love taking tests, let's see how you do on these three questions:

1. *How many goals are on a basketball court? a. 1   b. 2   c. 3   d. 4*
2. *How many halves are in a college basketball game? a. 1   b. 2   c. 3   d. 4*
3. *How many points does a three-point field goal account for in a basketball game?*
   a. 1   b. 2   c. 3   d. 4

I know this sounds like a joke, but it isn't. Sociologist Robert Benford (2007) got his hands on a copy of a twenty-question final examination given to basketball players who took a credit course on coaching principles at the University of Georgia. It is usually difficult to refer to athletes, sports, and academics in the same breath, but this is about as mediocre as mediocrity can get.

Let's move to a broader view of the mediocrity that plagues our educational system like pollution plagues gasoline engines:

- Arizona officials gave their high school sophomores a math test that covered the math that sophomores should know. One of ten passed.
- New York City officials, in contrast, were so pleased at their test results that they called a press conference. They boasted that 80 percent of their students were proficient at math—and they had the test results to prove it. When the students took a federal test, the results dropped just a bit—to 34 percent (Medina 2009).
- Pennsylvania officials figured out a solution to their students' miserable test results: Students who can't pass their exit exam can do "projects" instead.
- Not to be outdone in this race to the bottom, Arkansas dropped its passing score in math to 24 out of 100 (Urbina 2010).

The SAT Tests.   How are we doing on our SAT tests? The news is mixed. First the good news. Look at Figure 13.4. You can see how the scores dropped from the 1960s to 1980. At that point, educators sounded an alarm—and even Congress expressed concern. School officials decided that they had better do something if they didn't want to lose their jobs. They raised their standards, and the SAT scores started to climb. The recovery in math is encouraging. Today's high school seniors score the same in math as seniors did in the 1960s. Administrators are requiring more of math teachers, and teachers are requiring more of students. Each is performing according to these higher expectations.

But then there is the bad news. Look at the verbal scores on Figure 13.4. Their drop from the 1960s is even larger than the drop in math, and they are continuing to go down. No one knows why these scores remain so low, but the usual suspects have been rounded up: "dummied down" textbooks, less rigorous teaching, and less reading because of television, videos, and computer games.

The news is actually worse than what you see on this figure. To accomodate today's less prepared students, those who develop the SAT made it easier. They shortened the test, dropped the section on analogies and antonyms, and gave students more time to take the test. The test makers then "rescored" the totals of previous years to match the easier test. This "dummying down" of the SAT is a form of grade inflation, the topic to which we shall now turn.

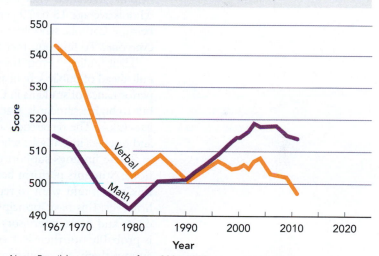

FIGURE 13.4   **National Results of the Scholastic Assessment Test (SAT)**

Note: Possible scores range from 200 to 800.

Sources: By the author. Based on College Board 2011a; *Statistical Abstract of the United States* 2012:Table 267.

Grade Inflation, Social Promotion, and Functional Illiteracy.   The letter grade C used to indicate average, and since more students are average than superior, high school teachers used to give about twice as many *C*'s as *A*'s. Now they give more *A*'s than *C*'s. Students aren't smarter—grading is just easier. Grades have become so inflated that some of today's *A*'s are the *C*'s of years past. **Grade inflation** is so pervasive that *47 percent* of all college freshmen have an overall high school grade point average of *A*. This is more than *twice* what it was in 1970 (*Statistical Abstract* 2012:Table 286). Grade inflation has also hit the Ivy League. At Harvard University, *half* of the course grades are *A*'s and *A–*'s. *Ninety* percent of Harvard students graduate with honors. To rein in "honor inflation," the Harvard faculty voted to limit the number of students who graduate with honors to 60 percent of a class (Hartocollis 2002; Douthat 2005).

Why does the word *mediocre* apply to the average U.S. high school? What is grade inflation?

On average, students in Roman Catholic schools score higher on national tests than students in public schools. Is it because Roman Catholic schools have better students, or because they do better teaching? The text reports the sociological findings.

Easy grades and declining standards have been accompanied by **social promotion,** passing students from one grade to the next even though they have not learned the basic materials. One result is **functional illiteracy,** high school graduates who never mastered even things they should have learned in grade school. Some have difficulty with reading and writing. Others can't fill out job applications. Some can't even figure out whether they get the right change at the grocery store.

Raising Standards for Teachers.   It is one thing to identify problems, quite another to find solutions for them. How can we solve mediocrity? To offer a quality education, we need quality teachers. Don't we already have them? Most teachers are qualified and, if motivated, can do an excellent job. But a large number of teachers are not qualified. Consider what happened in California, where teachers must pass an educational skills test. The teachers did so poorly that to fill the classrooms officials had to drop the passing grade to the tenth-grade level. These teachers are college graduates—and they are expected to perform at the tenth-grade level (Schemo 2002). I don't know about you, but I think this situation is a national disgrace. If we want to improve teaching, we need to insist that teachers meet high standards.

Raising Standards for Students.   What else can we do to improve the quality of education? An older study by sociologists James Coleman and Thomas Hoffer (1987) provides helpful guidelines. They wanted to see why the test scores of students in Roman Catholic schools average 15 to 20 percent higher than those of students in public schools. Is it because Catholic schools attract better students, while public schools have to put up with everyone? To find out, they tested 15,000 students in public and Catholic high schools.

Their findings? From the sophomore through the senior years, students at Catholic schools pull ahead of public school students by a full grade in verbal and math skills. The superior test performance of students in Catholic schools, they concluded, is not due to better students, but to higher standards. Catholic schools have not watered down their curricula as have public schools. The researchers also underscored the importance of parental involvement. Parents and teachers in Catholic schools reinforce each other's commitment to learning.

These findings support the basic principle reviewed earlier about teacher expectations: Students perform better when they are expected to meet higher standards. To this, you might want to reply, "Of course. I knew that. Who wouldn't?" Somehow, however, this basic principle is lost on many teachers, who expect little of their students and have supervisors who accept low student performance. The reason, actually, is probably not their lack of awareness of such basics, but, rather, the organization that entraps them, a bureaucracy in which ritual replaces performance. To understand this point better, you may want to review Chapter 5.

A Warning about Higher Standards.   If we raise standards, we can expect to upset students and their parents. It is soothing to use low standards and to pat students on the head and tell them they are doing well. But it upsets people if you do rigorous teaching and use high standards to measure performance. When Florida decided that its high school seniors needed to pass an assessment test in order to receive a diploma, 13,000 students failed the test. Parents of failed students protested. Did they demand better teaching? Or that bad teachers be fired? No. They wanted the state to drop the new test. In their anger, they asked people to boycott Disney World and to not buy Florida orange juice (Canedy 2003). What positive steps to improve their children's learning!

Let's look at a second problem in education.

Cheating

The cheating I'm referring to is not what you saw in your social studies or mathematics class in high school. I'm referring to cheating by *teachers and school administrators.* Listen to this:

The state school board of Georgia ordered an investigation after computer scanners showed that teachers in 191 schools had erased students' answers on reading and math tests and penciled in correct ones (Gabriel 2010). The cheating was apparently led by the superintendant of Atlanta's school system (Severson 2011).

The school district was facing pressure to show that their teaching had improved, and this was a quick way to do it. It is not far-fetched to think that these same teachers cheated on tests when they were students.

Now look at how states fake their high school graduation rates:

Mississippi keeps two sets of books: The one sent to Washington reports the state's graduation rate at 87 percent. The other, which the state keeps, reports that 63 percent of its students graduate. Other states do the same. California reports its totals at 83 percent and 67 percent (Dillon 2008).

Why do high school administrators across the nation fake their graduation rates? The reason is that federal agencies publish these reports, and states don't want to look bad. Also, Washington might reduce the money it gives them. It's like a girl telling her parents that she received a B in English when she really received a D. She didn't want to look bad, and her allowance might be cut.

School administrators can be quite creative in producing fake numbers. Some count the number of students who begin their senior year, and report the percentage of these seniors who graduate. This conveniently overlooks all those who drop out in the freshman, sophomore, and junior years. Some even encourage high school students who are doing poorly to drop out before they reach their senior year. This way, they won't be counted as dropouts (Dillon 2008).

The Solution to Cheating.   The solution to this problem is fairly simple. Zero tolerance. Develop a straightforward measurement of high school graduation and require all states to follow it. A simple measure is to compare the number of those who graduate from high school with the number who entered high school in the ninth grade four years earlier, minus those who died and those who transferred out plus those who transferred in. Federal officials can spot-check records across the nation. With loss of job the punishment, we could expect honesty in reporting to jump immediately. Real graduation rates would help pinpoint where the problems are, helping us to know where to focus solutions. If you don't know where it's broken, you don't know where to fix it.

Let's turn to the third problem.

Violence

Some U.S. schools have deteriorated to the point that safety is an issue. In these schools, uniformed guards and metal detectors have become permanent fixtures. Everywhere, school officials fear that "it could happen here." In an era of bomb threats and armed sociopaths, some states now require lockdown, or "Code Blue," drills: The classrooms—each equipped with a phone—are locked, the windows are locked, and the shades are drawn. The students are told to remain absolutely silent, while a school official wanders the halls, like an armed intruder, listening for the slightest sound that would indicate that someone is in a classroom (Kelley 2008).

School shootings are a national concern. For a surprising analysis of deaths at school, read the Mass Media box on the next page.

The Need for Educational Reform

Most of the changes in education are merely minor adjustments to a flawed system: giving this test instead of that test, requiring more memorizing or less memorizing, measuring progress this way instead of that way, tinkering with the curriculum, or motivating teachers and students by this carrot or that carrot. Each might be important in its own way, but each is but a minute adjustment to the details of a system that needs to be overhauled from top to bottom.

We are unlikely to do this.

How do some school administrators cheat? How can we stop it?

School Shootings: Exploding a Myth

This frame from a home video shows Eric Harris (on the left) and Dylan Klebold (on the right) as they pretend that they are searching for victims. They put their desires into practice in the infamous Columbine High School shootings.

The media sprinkle their reports of school shootings with such dramatic phrases as "alarming proportions," "outbreak of violence," and "out of control." They give us the impression that wackos walk our hallways, ready to spray our schools with gunfire. Parents used to consider schools safe havens, but no longer. Those naïve thoughts have been shattered by the bullets that have ripped through schools—or at least by the media's portrayal of growing danger and violence in our schools.

Have our schools really become war zones, as the mass media would have us believe? Certainly events such as those at Columbine High School and Virginia Tech are disturbing, but we need to probe deeper than newspaper headlines and televised images.

When we do, we find that the media's sensationalist reporting has created a myth. Contrary to "what everyone knows," *there is no trend toward greater school violence.* In fact, the situation is just the opposite—*the trend is toward greater safety at school.* Despite the dramatic school shootings that make screaming headlines, as you can see from Table 13.1, shooting deaths at schools are *decreasing.* The average number of annual shooting deaths for 1992 to 2000 is twenty-eight, which is *more than twice* as high as the annual average of thirteen for 2000 to 2010.

This is not to say that school shootings are not a serious problem. Even one student being wounded or killed is too many. But, contrary to the impression fostered by the media, school shooting deaths have dropped sharply.

A headline like "Schools Safer Than Ever!" simply doesn't get much attention—nor bring in much advertising revenue.

This is one reason that we need sociology: to quietly, dispassionately search for facts so we can better understand the events that shape our lives. The first requirement for solving any problem is accurate data, for how can we create rational solutions that are based on hysteria? The information presented in this box may not make for sensational headlines, but it does serve to explode one of the myths that the media have created.

For Your Consideration

→ How do you think we can reduce school shootings? How about school violence of any sort?

TABLE 13.1	Exploding a Myth: Deaths at U.S. Schools[1]				
	Victims				
School Year	**Shooting Deaths**	**Other Deaths[2]**	**Boys**	**Girls**	**Total**
1992–1993	45	11	49	7	56
1993–1994	41	12	41	12	53
1994–1995	16	5	18	3	21
1995–1996	29	7	26	10	36
1996–1997	15	11	18	8	26
1997–1998	36	8	27	17	44
1998–1999	25	6	24	7	31
1999–2000	16	16	26	6	32
2000–2001	19	5	20	4	24
2001–2002	4	2	6	0	6
2002–2003	14	8	16	6	22
2003–2004	29	13	37	5	42
2004–2005	20	8	20	8	28
2005–2006	5	0	4	1	5
2006–2007	16	4	13	7	20
2007-2008	3	0	3	0	3
2008-2009	10	3	11	2	13
2009-2010	5	2	4	3	7
Total 1992–2010	348	121	363	106	469
Mean 1992–2009	19.3	6.7	20.2	5.9	26.1

[1]Includes all school-related homicides, even those that occurred on the way to or from school. Includes suicides, school personnel killed at school by other adults, and even adults who had nothing to do with the school but who were found dead on school property. Source does not report on deaths at colleges, only K–12 (kindergarten through high school).
[2]Beating, hanging, jumping, stabbing, slashing, strangling, or heart attack.
Source: By the author. Based on National School Safety Center 2012.

Religion: Establishing Meaning

Let's look at the main characteristics of a second significant social institution.

What Is Religion?

Sociologists who do research on religion analyze the relationship between society and religion and study the role that religion plays in people's lives. They do not try to prove that one religion is better than another. Nor is it their goal to verify or disprove anyone's faith. As was mentioned in Chapter 1, sociologists have no tools for deciding that one course of action is more moral than another, much less for determining that one religion is the "correct" one. Religion is a matter of faith—and sociologists deal with empirical matters, things they can observe or measure. When it comes to religion, then, sociologists study the effects of religious beliefs and practices on people's lives. They also analyze how religion is related to stratification systems. Unlike theologians, however, sociologists do not try to evaluate the truth of a religion's teachings.

Emile Durkheim was highly interested in religion, probably because he was reared in a mixed-religion family, by a Protestant mother and a Jewish father. Durkheim decided to find out what all religions have in common. After surveying religions around the world, in 1912 he published his findings in *The Elementary Forms of the Religious Life.* Here are Durkheim's three main findings. The first is that the world's religions are so varied that they have no specific belief or practice in common. The second is that all religions develop a community centering on their beliefs and practices. The third is that all religions separate the sacred from the profane. By **sacred,** Durkheim referred to aspects of life having to do with the supernatural that inspire awe, reverence, deep respect, even fear. By **profane,** he meant aspects of life that are not concerned with religion but, instead, are part of ordinary, everyday life.

Durkheim (1912/1965) summarized his conclusions by saying:

A religion is a unified system of beliefs and practices relative to sacred things, that is to say, things set apart and forbidden—beliefs and practices which unite into one single moral community called a Church, all those who adhere to them.

Religion, then, has three elements:

1. *Beliefs* that some things are sacred (forbidden, set apart from the profane)
2. *Practices* (rituals) centering on the things considered sacred
3. *A moral community* (a church) resulting from a group's beliefs and practices

Durkheim used the word **church** in an unusual sense, to refer to any "moral community" centered on beliefs and practices regarding the sacred. In Durkheim's sense, *church* refers to Buddhists bowing before a shrine, Hindus dipping in the Ganges River, and Confucians offering food to their ancestors. Similarly, the term *moral community* does not imply morality in the sense familiar to most of us—of ethical conduct. Rather, a moral community is simply a group of people who are united by their religious practices—and that would include sixteenth-century Aztec priests who each day gathered around an altar to pluck out the beating heart of a virgin.

To better understand the sociological approach to religion, let's see what pictures emerge when we apply the three theoretical perspectives.

When I visited a Hindu temple in Chattisgargh, India, I was impressed by the colorful and expressive statues on its roof. Here is a close-up of some of those figures, which represent some of the millions of gods that Hindus worship.

What three elements of religion did Durkheim identify? What are "sacred" and "profane"?

One of the many functions of religion is providing emotional comfort. This photo was taken in a Wesleyan church in Williamsville, New York.

Religion can promote social change, as was evident in the U.S. civil rights movement. Dr. Martin Luther King, Jr., a Baptist minister, shown here in his famous "I have a dream" speech, was the foremost leader of this movement.

The Functionalist Perspective

Functionalists stress that religion is universal because it meets universal human needs. Let's look at some of the functions—and dysfunctions—of religion.

Functions of Religion

Questions about Ultimate Meaning. Around the world, religions provide answers to perplexing questions about ultimate meaning—such as the purpose of life, why people suffer, and the existence of an afterlife. Those answers give followers a sense of purpose, a framework in which to live. Instead of seeing themselves buffeted by random events in an aimless existence, believers see their lives as fitting into a divine plan.

Emotional Comfort. The answers that religion provides about ultimate meaning bring comfort by assuring people that there is a purpose to life, even to suffering. The religious rituals that enshroud crucial events such as illness and death assure the individual that others care.

Social Solidarity. Religious teachings and practices unite believers into a community that shares values and perspectives ("we Jews," "we Christians," "we Muslims"). The religious rituals that surround marriage, for example, link the bride and groom with a broader community that wishes them well. So do other religious rituals, such as those that celebrate birth and mourn death.

Guidelines for Everyday. The teachings of religion are not all abstractions. They also provide practical guidelines for everyday life. For example, four of the ten commandments delivered by Moses to the Israelites concern God, but the other six contain instructions for getting along with others, from how to avoid problems with parents and neighbors to warnings about lying, stealing, and having affairs.

What are some of the functions of religion? Can you give examples?

The consequences for people who follow these guidelines can be measured. For example, people who attend church are more likely to exercise and less likely to abuse alcohol, nicotine, and illegal drugs than are people who don't go to church (Gillum 2005; Wallace et al. 2007; Newport et al. 2012). In general, churchgoers follow a healthier lifestyle than people who don't go to church—and they live longer.

Social Control.   Although a religion's guidelines for everyday life usually apply only to its members, nonmembers feel a spillover. Religious teachings, for example, are incorporated into criminal law. In an earlier United States, people could be arrested for blasphemy and adultery. Some states still have laws that prohibit the sale of alcohol before noon on Sunday, laws whose purpose was to get people out of the saloons and into the churches.

Social Change.   Although religion is often so bound up with the prevailing social order that it resists social change, religion occasionally spearheads change. In the 1960s, for example, the civil rights movement, whose goals were to desegregate public facilities and abolish racial discrimination at Southern polls, was led by religious leaders, especially leaders of African American churches such as Martin Luther King, Jr. Churches also served as centers at which demonstrators were trained and rallies were organized. Other churches were centers for resisting this change.

Dysfunctions of Religion

Functionalists also examine ways in which religion is *dysfunctional*, that is, how it can bring harmful results. Two dysfunctions are persecution and war and terrorism.

Religion as Justification for Persecution.   Beginning in the 1100s and continuing into the 1800s, in what has become known as the Inquisition, special commissions of the Roman Catholic Church tortured accused heretics. In 1692, Protestant leaders in Salem, Massachusetts, executed twenty-one women and men who were accused of being witches. In 2001, in the Democratic Republic of the Congo, about 1,000 alleged witches were hacked to death (Jenkins 2002). In Angola, children who are accused of being witches are beaten and then killed or expelled (LaFraniere 2007). Similarly, it seems fair to say that the Aztec religion had its dysfunctions—at least for the virgins who were offered to appease angry gods. In short, religion has been used to justify oppression and any number of brutal acts.

War and Terrorism.   History is filled with wars based on religion—commingled with politics. Between the eleventh and fourteenth centuries, for example, Christian monarchs conducted nine bloody Crusades in an attempt to wrest control of the region they called the Holy Land from the Muslims. The suicide terrorists we focused on in Chapter 11 are a current example.

The Symbolic Interactionist Perspective

Symbolic interactionists focus on the meanings that people give their experiences, especially how they use symbols. Let's apply this perspective to religious symbols, rituals, and beliefs to see how they help to forge a community of like-minded people.

Religious Symbols

Suppose that it is about two thousand years ago and you have just joined a new religion. You have come to believe that a recently crucified Jew named Jesus is the Messiah, the Lamb of God offered for your sins. The Roman leaders are persecuting the followers of Jesus. They hate your religion because you and your fellow believers will not acknowledge Caesar as God.

Christians are few in number, and you are eager to have fellowship with other believers. But how can you tell who is a believer? Spies are everywhere. The government has sworn to destroy this new religion, and you do not relish the thought of being fed to lions in the Colosseum.

What are some dysfunctions of religion?

Symbolic interactionists stress that a basic characteristic of humans is that they attach meaning to objects and events and then use representations of those objects or events to communicate with one another. Michaelangelo's *Pietà*, depicting Mary tenderly holding her son, Jesus, after his crucifixion, is one of the most acclaimed symbols in the Western world. It is admired for its beauty by believers and nonbelievers alike.

You use a simple technique. While talking with a stranger, as though doodling absentmindedly in the sand or dust, you casually trace the outline of a fish. Only fellow believers know the meaning—that, taken together, the first letter of each word in the Greek sentence "Jesus (is) Christ the Son of God" spell the Greek word for fish. If the other person gives no response, you rub out the outline and continue the interaction as usual. If there is a response, you eagerly talk about your new faith.

All religions use symbols to provide identity and create social solidarity for their members. For Muslims, the primary symbol is the crescent moon and star; for Jews, the Star of David; for Christians, the cross. For members, these are not ordinary symbols, but sacred emblems that evoke feelings of awe and reverence. In Durkheim's terms, religions use symbols to represent what the group considers sacred and to separate the sacred from the profane.

A symbol is a condensed way of communicating. Worn by a fundamentalist Christian, for example, the cross says, "I am a follower of Jesus Christ. I believe that He is the Messiah, the promised Son of God, that He loves me, that He died to take away my sins, that He rose from the dead and is going to return to earth, and that through Him I will receive eternal life."

That is a lot to pack into one symbol—and it is only part of what the symbol means to a fundamentalist believer. To people in other traditions of Christianity, the cross conveys somewhat different meanings—but to all Christians, the cross is a shorthand way of expressing many meanings. So it is with the Star of David, the crescent moon and star, the cow (expressing to Hindus the unity of all living things), and the various symbols of the world's many other religions.

Rituals

Rituals, ceremonies or repetitive practices, are also symbols that help to unite people into a moral community. Some rituals, such as the bar mitzvah of Jewish boys and the holy communion of Christians, are designed to create in devout believers a feeling of closeness with God and unity with one another. Rituals include kneeling and praying at set times; bowing; crossing oneself; singing; lighting candles and incense; reading scripture; and following prescribed traditions at processions, baptisms, weddings, and funerals. The photo essay on pages 402–403 features annual rituals held in Spain during Holy Week (the week that leads into the Christian holiday of Easter).

Beliefs

Symbols, including rituals, develop from beliefs. The belief may be vague ("God is") or highly specific ("God wants us to prostrate ourselves and face Mecca five times each day"). Religious beliefs include not only *values* (what is considered good and desirable in life—how we ought to live) but also a **cosmology,** a unified picture of the world. For example, the Jewish, Christian, and Muslim belief that there is only one God, the creator of the universe, who is concerned about the actions of humans and who will hold us accountable for what we do, is a cosmology. It presents a unifying picture of the universe.

Religions use rituals to create community—a sense of being connected with one another and, in this case, also a sense of being connected with God. Shown here is a Sikh temple in Penjab, India.

Religious Experience

The term **religious experience** refers to a sudden awareness of the supernatural or a feeling of coming into contact with God. Some people undergo a mild version, such as feeling closer to God when they look at a mountain, watch a sunset, or listen to a certain piece of music. Others report a life-transforming experience. St. Francis of Assisi, for example, said that he became aware of God's presence in every living thing.

Some Protestants use the term **born again** to describe people who have undergone such a life-transforming religious experience. These people say that they came to the realization that they had sinned, that Jesus had died for their sins, and that God wants them to live a new life. Their worlds become transformed. They look forward to the Resurrection and to a new life in heaven and they see relationships with spouses, parents, children, and even bosses in a new light. They also report a need to make changes in how they interact with others so that their lives reflect their new, personal commitment to Jesus as their "Savior and Lord." They describe a feeling of beginning life anew; hence the term *born again*.

The Conflict Perspective

In general, conflict theorists are highly critical of religion. They stress that religion supports the status quo and helps to maintain social inequalities. Let's look at some of their analyses.

Opium of the People

Karl Marx, an avowed atheist who believed that the existence of God was impossible, set the tone for conflict theorists with this statement: "Religion is the sigh of the oppressed creature, the sentiment of a heartless world. . . . It is the opium of the people" (Marx 1844/1964). Marx meant that for oppressed workers religion is like a drug that helps addicts forget their misery. By diverting thoughts toward future happiness in an afterlife, religion takes the workers' eyes off their suffering in this world, reducing the possibility that they will overthrow their chains by rebelling against their oppressors.

Legitimating Social Inequalities

Conflict theorists stress that religion legitimates social inequalities. By this, they mean that religion teaches that the existing social arrangements represent what God desires. For example, during the Middle Ages, Christian theologians decreed the *divine right of kings*. This doctrine meant that God determined who would become king and set him on the throne. The king ruled in God's place, and it was the duty of a king's subjects to be loyal to him (and to pay their taxes). To disobey the king was to disobey God.

In what was perhaps the supreme technique of legitimating the social order (and one that went even a step farther than the divine right of kings), the religion of ancient Egypt held that the pharaoh himself was a god. The emperor of Japan was similarly declared divine. If this were so, who could ever question his decisions? Today's politicians would give their right arms for such a religious teaching.

Conflict theorists point to many other examples of how religion legitimates the social order. In India, Hinduism supports the caste system by teaching that anyone who tries to change caste will come back in the next life as a member of a lower caste—or even as an animal. In the decades before the American Civil War, Southern ministers used scripture to defend slavery, saying that it was God's will—while Northern ministers legitimated *their* region's social structure by using scripture to denounce slavery as evil (Ernst 1988; Nauta 1993; White 1995).

In the 1700s, men and women sat in separate sections during their meetings. This one is a bit different, with the division by floors. Do you think sex-segregated seating supports the conflict perspective that religion reflects and legitimates social inequalities? Why or why not?

What is the conflict perspective on religion? What does "legitimating social inequalities" mean?

Holy Week in Spain

Religious groups develop rituals designed to evoke memories, create awe, inspire reverence, and stimulate social solidarity. One of the primary means by which groups, religious and secular, accomplish these goals is through the display of symbols.

I took these photos during Holy Week in Spain—in Malaga and Almuñecar. Throughout Spain, elaborate processions feature *tronos* that depict the biblical account of Jesus' suffering, death, and resurrection. During the processions in Malaga, the participants walk slowly for about two minutes; then because of the weight of the *tronos*, they rest for about two minutes. They repeat this process for about six hours a day.

Bands, sometimes several of them, are part of the processions.

The procession in the village was more informal. This Roman soldier has an interesting way of participating—and keeping tabs—on his little daughter. The girl is distributing candy.

A group of participants exiting the Church of the Incarnation for Malaga's Easter procession.

Parents gave a lot of attention to their children both during the preparations and during the processions. This photo was taken during one of the repetitive two-minute breaks.

Beneath the costumes are townspeople and church members who know one another well. They enjoy themselves prior to the procession. This man is preparing to put on his hood.

During the short breaks at the night processions, children from the audience would rush to collect dripping wax to make wax balls. This was one way that the audience made themselves participants in the drama.

SPAIN

Some *tronos* are so heavy that they require many men to carry them. (Some were carried by over 100 men.) This photo was taken in Malaga, on Monday of Holy Week.

For the Good Friday procession, I was fortunate to be able to photograph the behind-the-scenes preparations, which are seldom seen by visitors. Shown here are finishing touches being given to the Mary figure.

The village's town square was packed with people awaiting the procession. From one corner of the square, the *trono* of Jesus was brought in. Then from another, that of Mary ("reuniting" them, as I was told). During this climactic scene, the priest on the balcony on the left read a message.

© **James M. Henslin**, all photos

"We're thinking maybe it's time you started getting some religious instruction. There's Catholic, Protestant, and Jewish—any of those sound good to you?"

For some Americans, religion is an "easy-going, makes-little-difference" matter, as expressed in this cartoon. For others, religious matters are firmly held, and followers find even slight differences of faith to be significant.

Religion and the Spirit of Capitalism

Max Weber disagreed with the conflict perspective. Religion, he said, does not merely reflect and legitimate the social order and impede social change. Rather, religion's focus on the afterlife is a source of profound social change.

To explain his conclusions, Weber wrote *The Protestant Ethic and the Spirit of Capitalism* (1904–1905/1958). He said that:

1. Capitalism represents a fundamentally different way of thinking about work and money. *Traditionally, people worked just enough to meet their basic needs, not so that they could have a surplus to invest.* To accumulate money (capital) as an end in itself, not just to spend it, was a radical departure from traditional thinking. People even came to consider it a duty to invest money so they could make profits. They reinvested these profits to make even more profits. Weber called this new approach to work and money the **spirit of capitalism.**

2. Why did the spirit of capitalism develop in Europe and not, for example, in China or India, where people had similar material resources and education? According to Weber, *religion was the key*. The religions of China and India, and indeed Roman Catholicism in Europe, encouraged a traditional approach to life, not thrift and investment. Capitalism appeared when Protestantism came on the scene.

3. What was different about Protestantism, especially Calvinism? John Calvin taught that God had predestined some people to go to heaven, and others to hell. Neither church membership nor feelings about your relationship with God could assure you that you were saved. You wouldn't know your fate until after you died.

4. "Am I predestined to hell or to heaven?" Calvin's followers wondered. As they wrestled with this question, they concluded that church members have a duty to live as though they are predestined to heaven—for good works are a demonstration of salvation.

5. This conclusion motivated Calvinists to lead moral lives *and* to work hard, to use their time productively, and to be frugal—for idleness and needless spending were signs of worldliness. Weber called this self-denying approach to life the **Protestant ethic.**

6. As people worked hard and spent money only on necessities (a pair of earrings or a second pair of dress shoes would have been defined as sinful luxuries), they had money left over. Because it couldn't be spent, this capital was invested, which led to a surge in production.

7. Weber's analysis can be summed up this way: The change in religion (from Catholicism to Protestantism, especially Calvinism) led to a fundamental change in thought and behavior (the *Protestant ethic*). The result was the *spirit of capitalism*. For this reason, capitalism originated in Europe and not in places where religion did not encourage capitalism's essential elements: the accumulation of capital and its investment and reinvestment.

Although Weber's analysis has been influential, it has not lacked critics. Hundreds of scholars have attacked it, some for overlooking the lack of capitalism in Scotland (a Calvinist country), others for failing to explain why the Industrial Revolution was born in England (not a Calvinist country). Hundreds of other scholars have defended Weber's argument, and sociologists continue to test Weber's theory (Becker 2009; Basten and Betz 2008). Currently, sociologists are not in agreement on this matter.

At this point in history, the Protestant ethic and the spirit of capitalism are not confined to any specific religion or even to any part of the world. Rather, they

According to Weber's analysis, how did religion produce capitalism?

have become cultural traits that have spread to societies around the globe (Greeley 1964; Yinger 1970). U.S. Catholics have about the same approach to life as do U.S. Protestants. In addition, Hong Kong, Japan, Malaysia, Singapore, South Korea, and Taiwan—not exactly Protestant countries—have embraced capitalism. China, Russia, and Vietnam are in the midst of doing so.

Types of Religious Groups

Sociologists have identified four types of religious groups: cult, sect, church, and ecclesia. Why do some of these groups meet with hostility, while others tend to be accepted? For an explanation, look at Figure 13.5.

Let's explore what sociologists have found about these four types of religious groups. The summary that follows is a modification of analyses by sociologists Ernst Troeltsch (1931), Liston Pope (1942), and Benton Johnson (1963).

Cult

The word *cult* conjures up bizarre images—shaven heads, weird music, brainwashing— and even ritual suicide may come to mind. Cults, however, are not necessarily weird, and few practice "brainwashing" or bizarre rituals. In fact, *all religions began as cults* (Stark 1989). A **cult** is simply a new or different religion whose teachings and practices put it at odds with the dominant culture and religion. Because the term *cult* arouses such negative meanings in the public mind, however, some scholars prefer to use the term *new religion* instead. As is evident from the Cultural Diversity box on the next page, "new" can mean that an old religion is making its appearance in a culture that is not familiar with it.

Cults often originate with a **charismatic leader,** an individual who inspires people because he or she seems to have extraordinary gifts, qualities, or abilities. **Charisma** refers to an outstanding gift or to some exceptional quality. People feel drawn to both the person and the message because they find something highly appealing about the individual—in some instances, almost a magnetic charm.

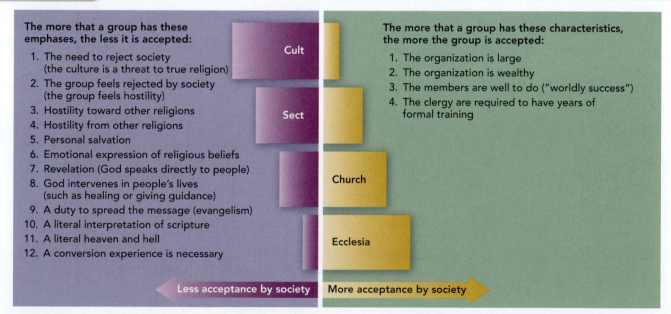

FIGURE 13.5   **Religious Groups: From Hostility to Acceptance**

The more that a group has these emphases, the less it is accepted:

1. The need to reject society (the culture is a threat to true religion)
2. The group feels rejected by society (the group feels hostility)
3. Hostility toward other religions
4. Hostility from other religions
5. Personal salvation
6. Emotional expression of religious beliefs
7. Revelation (God speaks directly to people)
8. God intervenes in people's lives (such as healing or giving guidance)
9. A duty to spread the message (evangelism)
10. A literal interpretation of scripture
11. A literal heaven and hell
12. A conversion experience is necessary

The more that a group has these characteristics, the more the group is accepted:

1. The organization is large
2. The organization is wealthy
3. The members are well to do ("worldly success")
4. The clergy are required to have years of formal training

Cult

Sect

Church

Ecclesia

← Less acceptance by society

More acceptance by society →

Note: Any religious organization can be placed somewhere on this continuum, based on its having "more" or "less" of these characteristics and emphases. The varying proportions of the rectangles are intended to represent the group's relative characteristics and emphases.

Sources: By the author. Based on Troeltsch 1931; Pope 1942; and Johnson 1963.

What is a cult? What is a charismatic leader?

Cultural Diversity in the United States

Human Heads and Animal Blood: The Toleration of Religion

As the customs officials looked over the line of people who had just gotten off the plane from Haiti, there was nothing to make this particular woman stand out. She would have passed through without a problem, except for one thing: A routine search turned up something that struck the custom agents as somewhat unusual—a human head.

The head had teeth, hair, pieces of skin, and some dirt. It had evidently been dug up from some grave, probably in Haiti.

The 30-year-old woman, who lives in Florida, practiced voodoo. The head was for her religious rituals.

The woman was arrested. Her crime was not filing a report that she was carrying "organic material" ("Mujer con Cabeza . . ." 2006).

* * * * *

The Santeros from Cuba who live in Florida sacrifice animals. They meet in apartments, where, following a Yoruba religion, they kill goats and chickens. Calling on their gods, they first ask permission to sacrifice the animals. After sacrificing them, they pour out the animals' blood, which opens and closes the doors of their destiny. They also cut off the animals' heads and place them at locations in the city that represent the four directions of the compass. This is done to terrorize their enemies and give them safety. The heads also protect the city from hurricanes and other destructive forces.

When city officials in Hialeah, Florida, learned that the Santeros were planning to build a church in their city, they

A follower of Voodoo holding a chicken before it is sacrificed in a ceremony in Saut d'Eau, Haiti.

passed a law against the sacrifice of animals within the city limits. The Santeros appealed to the U.S. Supreme Court, claiming discrimination, because the law was directed against them. The Court ruled in their favor.

City officials of Euless, Texas, were shocked when they learned that Jose Merced was sacrificing goats in his home. They sent in the police (Associated Press 2009). Merced appealed to the federal circuit court, saying that the officials were violating his rights as a Santeria priest. He can now sacrifice goats at home.

For Your Consideration

→ What do you think the limitations on religious freedom should be? Should people be allowed to sacrifice animals as part of their religious practices?

→ If the Santeros can sacrifice animals, why shouldn't people who practice voodoo be able to use human heads if they want to? (Assume that the relatives of the dead person have given their permission.)

The most popular religion in the world began as a cult. Its handful of followers believed that an unschooled carpenter who preached in remote villages in a backwater country was the Son of God, that he was killed and came back to life. Those beliefs made the early Christians a cult, setting them apart from the rest of their society. Persecuted by both religious and political authorities, these early believers clung to one another for support. Many cut off associations with friends who didn't accept the new message. To others, the early Christians must have seemed deluded and brainwashed.

So it was with Islam. When Muhammad revealed his visions and said that God's name was really Allah, only a few people believed him. To others, he must have seemed crazy, deranged.

Most cults fail. Not many people believe the new message, and the cult fades into obscurity. Some, however, succeed and make history. Over time, large numbers of people may come to accept the message and become followers of the religion. If this happens, the new religion changes from a cult to a sect.

How do the customs of voodoo and the Santeros test the limits of religious tolerance?

Sect

A **sect** is larger than a cult, but its members still feel tension between their views and the prevailing beliefs and values of the broader society. A sect may even be hostile to the society in which it is located. At the very least, its members remain uncomfortable with many of the emphases of the dominant culture; in turn, nonmembers tend to be uncomfortable with members of the sect.

If a sect grows, its members tend to gradually make peace with the rest of society. To appeal to a broader base, the sect shifts some of its doctrines, redefining matters to remove some of the rough edges that create tension between it and the rest of society. As the members become more respectable in the eyes of the society, they feel less hostility and little, if any, isolation. If a sect follows this course, as it grows and becomes more integrated into society, it changes into a church.

Like other aspects of culture, religion is filled with background assumptions that usually go unquestioned. In this photo, which I took in Amsterdam, what background assumption of religion is this woman violating?

Church

At this point, the religious group is highly bureaucratized—probably with national and international headquarters that give direction to the local congregations, enforce rules about who can be ordained, and control finances. The relationship with God has grown less intense. The group is likely to have less emphasis on personal salvation and emotional expression. Worship services are likely to be more sedate, with formal sermons and written prayers read before the congregation. Rather than being recruited from the outside by personal evangelism, most new members now come from within, from children born to existing members. Rather than joining through conversion—seeing the new truth—children may be baptized, circumcised, or dedicated in some other way. At some designated age, children may be asked to affirm the group's beliefs in a ceremony, such as a confirmation or bar mitzvah.

Ecclesia

Finally, some groups become so well integrated into a culture, and so strongly allied with their government, that it is difficult to tell where one leaves off and the other takes over. In these *state religions,* also called **ecclesia,** the government and religion work together to try to shape society. There is no recruitment of members, for citizenship makes everyone a member. For most people in the society, the religion is part of a cultural identity, not an eye-opening experience. Sweden provides a good example of how extensively religion and government intertwine in an ecclesia. In the 1860s, all citizens had to memorize Luther's *Small Catechism* and be tested on it annually (Anderson 1995). Today, Lutheranism is still associated with the state, but most Swedes come to church only for baptisms, marriages, and funerals.

Unlike cults and sects, which perceive God as personally involved with and concerned about people, ecclesias envision God as more impersonal and remote. Reflecting this view of the supernatural, church services tend to be highly formal, directed by ministers or priests who, after undergoing training in approved schools or seminaries, follow prescribed rituals.

Variations in Patterns

Obviously, not all religious groups go through all these stages—from cult to sect to church to ecclesia. Some die out because they fail to attract enough members. Others, such as the Amish, remain sects. And, as is evident from the few countries that have state religions, very few religions ever become ecclesias.

In addition, these classifications are not perfectly matched in the real world. For example, although the Amish are a sect, they place little or no emphasis on recruiting others. The early Quakers, another sect, shied away from emotional expressions of their beliefs. They would quietly meditate in church, with no one speaking, until God gave someone a message to share with others. Finally, some groups that become churches may retain a few characteristics of sects, such as an emphasis on evangelism or a personal relationship with God.

Although all religions began as cults, not all varieties of a particular religion begin that way. For example, some **denominations**—"brand names" within a major religion, such as Baptists or Reform Judaism—begin as splinter groups. Some members of a church disagree with *particular* aspects of the church's teachings (not its main message), and they break away to form their own organization.

Religion in the United States

To better understand religion in U.S. society, let's first find out who belongs to religious groups and then look at the groups themselves.

Characteristics of Members

About 65 percent of Americans belong to a church, synagogue, or mosque. What are the characteristics of people who hold formal membership in a religion?

Explore
Living Data
on **mysoclab.com**

Social Class.   Religion in the United States is stratified by social class. As you can see from Figure 13.6 below, some religious groups are "top-heavy," and others are "bottom-heavy." The most top-heavy are Jews; the most bottom-heavy are Jehovah's Witnesses. This figure provides further confirmation that churchlike groups tend to appeal to people who have more "worldly" success, while the more sectlike groups attract people who have less "worldly" success.

From this figure, you can see how *status consistency* (a concept we reviewed in Chapter 8) applies to religious groups. If a group ranks high (or low) on education, it is also likely to rank high (or low) on income and occupational prestige. Jews, for example, rank the highest on education, income, and occupational prestige, while Jehovah's Witnesses rank the lowest on these three measures of social class. As you can see, the Mormons are status inconsistent. They rank second in income, fourth in education, and tie for sixth in occupational prestige. Even more status inconsistent is the Assembly of God. Their members tie for third in occupational prestige but rank only eighth in income and ninth in education. This inconsistency is so jarring that there could be a problem with the sample.

| FIGURE 13.6 | **Social Class and Religious Affiliation** |

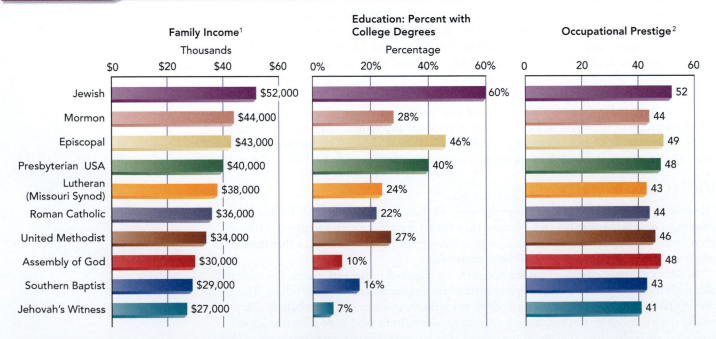

[1] Since the income data were reported, inflation has run approximately 20 percent or so.
[2] Higher numbers mean that more of the group's members work at occupations that have higher prestige, generally those that require more education and pay more. For more information on occupational prestige, see Table 8.2 on page 217.

Source: By the author. Based on Smith and Faris 2005.

How is church membership related to social class?

Race–Ethnicity. All major religious groups draw from the nation's many racial–ethnic groups. Like social class, however, race–ethnicity tends to cluster. People of Irish descent are likely to be Roman Catholics; those with Greek ancestors are likely to belong to the Greek Orthodox Church. African Americans are likely to be Protestants—more specifically, Baptists—or to belong to fundamentalist sects.

Although many churches are integrated, it is with good reason that Sunday morning between 10 and 11 A.M. has been called "the most segregated hour in the United States." African Americans tend to belong to African American churches, while most whites see only whites in theirs. The segregation of churches is based on custom, not on law.

Characteristics of Religious Groups

Let's examine features of the religious groups in the United States.

Diversity. With its 300,000 congregations and hundreds of denominations, no religious group even comes close to being a dominant religion in the United States (*Statistical Abstract* 2012:Tables 75, 76). Table 13.2 illustrates some of this remarkable diversity.

Pluralism and Freedom. It is the U.S. government's policy not to interfere with religions. The government's position is that its obligation is to ensure an environment in which people can worship as they see fit. Religious freedom is so extensive that anyone can start a church and proclaim himself or herself a minister, revelator, or any other desired term. The exceptions to this hands-off policy are startling. The most notorious exception in recent times occurred in Waco, Texas. When armed agents of the Bureau of Alcohol, Tobacco, and Firearms attacked the compound of the Branch Davidians, an obscure religious group, eighty-two men, women, and children were

TABLE 13.2	How U.S. Adults Identify with Religion	
Religious Group	**Number of Members**	**Percentage of U.S. Adults**
Christian	**176,000,000**	**78.4%**
Protestant	115,000,000	51.3%
Evangelical churches	59,000,000	26.3%
Mainline churches	41,000,000	18.1%
Historical black churches	16,000,000	6.9%
Roman Catholic	54,000,000	23.9%
Mormon	3,800,000	1.7%
Jehovah's Witness	1,600,000	0.7%
Orthodox, Greek, Russian	1,400,000	0.6%
Other Christian	700,000	0.3%
Other Religions	**11,000,000**	**4.7%**
Jewish	3,800,000	1.7%
Buddhist	1,600,000	0.7%
Muslim	1,400,000	0.6%
Hindu	900,000	0.4%
Other faiths	2,700,000	1.2%
(Unitarians, New Age, Native American religions, Liberal)		
No Identity with a Religion	**36,000,000**	**16.1%**
Nothing in particular	27,000,000	12.1%
Agnostic	5,400,000	2.4%
Atheist	3,600,000	1.6%
Don't Know or Refused	**1,800,000**	**0.8%**

Note: Due to rounding, totals may not add to 100. Based on a sample of 35,000 of the 225 million Americans age 18 and over.

Source: U.S. Religious Landscape Survey 2008:5.

How is church membership related to race–ethnicity?

burned to death. A second is the government's infiltration of mosques to monitor the activities of Arab immigrants (Elinson 2004; ACLU 2010). Other limitations to this policy are discussed in the Cultural Diversity box on page 406.

Toleration. The general religious toleration of Americans can be illustrated by three prevailing attitudes: (1) "All religions have a right to exist—as long as they don't try to brainwash or hurt anyone." (2) "With all the religions to choose from, how can anyone tell which one—if any—is true?" (3) "Each of us may be convinced about the truth of our religion—and that is good—but don't be obnoxious by trying to convince others that you have the exclusive truth." (See the photo on page 405.)

The Electronic Church. What began as a ministry to shut-ins and those who do not belong to a church blossomed into its own type of church. Its preachers, called "televangelists," reach millions of viewers and raise millions of dollars. Some of its most famous ministries are those of Kenneth Copeland, Creflo Dollar, Benny Hinn, Eddie Long, Joyce Meyers, Joel Osteen, and Pat Robertson (the 700 Club).

The Future of Religion

Religion thrives in the most advanced scientific nations—and, as officials of Soviet Russia were disheartened to learn—even in the most ideologically hostile climate. Although the Soviet authorities threw believers into prison, people continued to practice their religions. Humans are inquiring creatures. As they reflect on life, they ask, What is the purpose of it all? Why are we born? Is there an afterlife? If so, where are we going? Out of these concerns arises this question: If there is a God, what does God want of us in this life? Does God have a preference about how we should live?

Science, including sociology, cannot answer such questions. By its very nature, science cannot tell us about four main concerns that many people have:

1. *The existence of God.* About this, science has nothing to say. No test tube has either isolated God or refuted God's existence.
2. *The purpose of life.* Although science can provide a definition of life and describe the characteristics of living organisms, it has nothing to say about ultimate purpose.

A basic principle of symbolic interactionism is that meaning is not inherent in an object or event, but is determined by people as they interpret the object or event. Does this dinosaur skeleton "prove" evolution? Does it "disprove" creation? Such "proof" and "disproof" lie in the eye of the beholder, based on the background assumptions by which it is interpreted.

3. *An afterlife.* Science can offer no information on life after death for it has no tests to prove or disprove a "hereafter."
4. *Morality.* Science can demonstrate the consequences of behavior, but not the moral superiority of one action compared with another. This means—to use an extreme example—that science cannot even prove whether loving your family and neighbor is superior to hurting and killing them.

There is no doubt that religion will last as long as humanity lasts, for what could replace it? And if something did, and answered such questions, would it not be religion under a different name?

To close this chapter, let's try to glimpse the cutting edge of religious change.

God on the Net: The Online Marketing of Religion

You want to pray here at the Holy Land, but you can't leave home? No problem. Buy our special telephone card—now available at your local 7-11. Just record your prayer, and we'll broadcast it via the Internet at the site you choose. Press 1 for the holy site of Jerusalem, press 2 for the holy site of the Sea of Galilee, press 3 for the birthplace of Jesus, press 4 for . . . (Rhoads 2007)

This service is offered by a company in Israel. No discrimination. Open to Jews and Christians alike. Maybe with expansion plans for Muslims. Maybe to anyone, as long as they can pay $10 for a two-minute card.

You left India and now live in Kansas but you want to pray in Chennai? No problem. Order your pujas (prayers), and we'll have a priest say them in the temple of your choice. Just click how many you want. Food offerings for Vishnu included in the price. All major credit cards accepted (K. Sullivan 2007).

Erin Polzin, a 20-year-old college student, listens to a Lutheran worship service on the radio, confesses online, and uses PayPal to tithe. "I don't like getting up early," she says. "This is like going to church without really having to" (Bernstein 2003).

You can go to church in your pajamas, and you don't even have to comb your hair.

Some people have begun to "attend" church as avatars.

Muslims in France download sermons and join an invisible community of worshippers at virtual mosques. Jews in Sweden type messages that fellow believers in Jerusalem download and insert in the Western Wall. Christians in the United States make digital donations to the Crystal Cathedral. Buddhists in Japan seek enlightenment online.

The Internet helps to level the pulpit: On the Net, the leader of a pagan group can compete directly with the Pope.

There are also virtual church services. Just choose an avatar, and you can walk around the virtual church. You can sing, kneel, pray, and listen to virtual sermons. You can talk to other avatars if you get bored (Feder 2004). And, of course, you can use your credit card—a real one, not the virtual kind.

Some say that the Net has put us on the verge of a religious reformation as big as the one set off by Gutenberg's invention of the printing press. This sounds like an exaggeration, but perhaps it is true. We'll see.

For Your Consideration

→ We are gazing into the future. How do you think that the Internet might change religion? Do you think it can replace the warm embrace of fellow believers? How can it bring comfort to someone who is grieving for a loved one?

By the Numbers: Changes Over Time

Percentage of U.S. population graduated from high school		Percentage of U.S. population graduated from college		SAT verbal scores, national average	
1960	**NOW**	**1960**	**NOW**	**1967**	**NOW**
42%	**87%**	**8%**	**30%**	**543**	**498**

SAT math scores, national average		Number of violent deaths at school, grades K-12		Shooting deaths at school, annual average	
1967	**NOW**	**1992**	**NOW**	**1992–2000**	**2000–2010**
516	**515**	**56**	**7**	**28**	**13**

How is technology likely to affect religion?

CHAPTER 13 Summary and Review

Education in Global Perspective

What is a credential society, and how did it develop?

A **credential society** is one in which employers use diplomas and degrees to determine who is eligible for a job. One reason that credentialism developed is that large, anonymous societies lack the personal knowledge common to smaller groups. Educational certification is taken as evidence of a person's ability. P. 382

How does education compare among the Most Industrialized, Industrializing, and Least Industrialized Nations?

In general, formal education reflects a nation's economy. Consequently, education is extensive in the Most Industrialized Nations, undergoing vast change in the Industrializing Nations, and spotty in the Least Industrialized Nations. Japan, Russia, and Egypt provide examples of education in countries at three levels of industrialization. Pp. 382–386.

The Functionalist Perspective: Providing Social Benefits

What is the functionalist perspective on education?

Among the functions of education are the teaching of knowledge and skills, providing credentials, **cultural transmission of values,** social integration, **social placement (gatekeeping),** and **mainstreaming.** Functionalists also note that education has replaced some traditional family functions. Pp. 386–388.

The Conflict Perspective: Perpetuating Social Inequality

What is the conflict perspective on education?

The basic view of conflict theorists is that *education reproduces the social class structure;* that is, through such mechanisms as unequal funding and operating different schools for the elite and for the masses, education perpetuates a society's basic social inequalities from one generation to the next. Pp. 388–391.

The Symbolic Interactionist Perspective: Teacher Expectations

What is the symbolic interactionist perspective on education?

Symbolic interactionists focus on face-to-face interaction. In examining what occurs in the classroom, they have found that student performance tends to conform to teacher expectations, whether they are high or low. Pp. 391–392.

Problems in U.S. Education— and Their Solutions

What are the chief problems that face U.S. education?

The major problems are mediocrity (low achievement as shown by SAT scores), **grade inflation, social promotion, functional illiteracy,** faked data reported by school administrators, and violence. Pp. 392–395.

What are the potential solutions to these problems?

To restore high educational standards will require that we expect more of *both* students and teachers; school administrators can be required to use a single reporting measure based on objective, verifiable data. Although we cannot prevent all school violence, for an effective learning environment we must provide basic security for students. Pp. 395–396.

What Is Religion?

Durkheim identified three essential characteristics of **religion:** beliefs that set the **sacred** apart from the **profane, rituals,** and a moral community (a **church**). P. 396.

The Functionalist Perspective

What are the functions and dysfunctions of religion?

Among the functions of religion are answering questions about ultimate meaning; providing emotional comfort, social solidarity, guidelines for everyday life, social control, and social change. Among the dysfunctions of religion are religious persecution and war and terrorism. Pp. 398–399.

The Symbolic Interactionist Perspective

What aspects of religion do symbolic interactionists study?

Symbolic interactionists focus on the meanings of religion for its followers. They examine religious symbols, **rituals,** beliefs, and **religious experiences.** Pp. 399–401; 402–403.

The Conflict Perspective

What aspects of religion do conflict theorists study?

Conflict theorists examine the relationship of religion to social inequalities, especially how religion reinforces a society's stratification system. P. 401.

Religion and the Spirit of Capitalism

What does the spirit of capitalism have to do with religion?

Max Weber saw religion as a primary source of social change. He analyzed how Calvinism gave rise to the **Protestant ethic,** which stimulated what he called the **spirit of capitalism.** The result was capitalism, which transformed society. Pp. 404–405.

Types of Religious Groups

What types of religious groups are there?

Sociologists divide religious groups into cults, sects, churches, and ecclesias. All religions began as **cults.** Those that survive tend to develop into **sects** and eventually into **churches.** Sects, often led by **charismatic leaders,** are unstable. Some are perceived as threats and are persecuted by the state. **Ecclesias,** or state religions, are rare. Pp. 405–408.

Religion in the United States

What are the main characteristics of religion in the United States?

Membership of religious groups varies by social class and race–ethnicity. Major characteristics are diversity, pluralism and freedom, tolerance, and the electronic church. Pp. 408–410.

The Future of Religion

What can we anticipate in the future?

Because science cannot answer questions about ultimate meaning, the existence of God or an afterlife, or provide guidelines for morality, the need for religion will remain. In any foreseeable future, religion will prosper. The Internet is likely to have far-reaching consequences on religion. P. 410.

Thinking Critically about Chapter 13

1. How does education in the United States compare with education in Japan, Russia, and Egypt?

2. Have your experiences in education (including teachers and assignments) influenced your goals, attitudes, and values? How have your classmates influenced you? Be specific.

3. Why is religion likely to remain a strong feature of U.S. life—and remain strong in people's lives around the globe?

CHAPTER 14

Population and Urbanization

Kenya

The image still haunts me. There stood Celia, age 30, her distended stomach visible proof that her thirteenth child was on its way. Her oldest was only 14 years old! A mere boy by our standards, he had already gone as far in school as he ever would. Each morning, he joined the men to work in the fields. Each evening around twilight, I saw him return home, exhausted from hard labor in the subtropical sun.

I was living in Colima, Mexico, and Celia and her husband Angel had invited me for dinner. Their home clearly reflected the family's poverty. A thatched hut consisting of only a single room served as home for all fourteen members of the family. At night, the parents and younger children crowded into a double bed, while the eldest boy slept in a hammock. As in many homes in the village, the other children slept on mats spread on the dirt floor—despite the crawling scorpions.

The home was meagerly furnished. It had only a gas stove, a table, and a cabinet where Celia stored her few cooking utensils and clay dishes. There were no closets; clothes hung on pegs in the walls. There also were no chairs, not even one. I was used to the poverty in the village, but this really startled me. The family was too poor to afford even a single chair.

> **"There stood Celia, age 30, her distended stomach visible proof that her thirteenth child was on its way."**

Celia beamed as she told me how much she looked forward to the birth of her next child. Could she really mean it? It was hard to imagine that any woman would want to be in her situation.

Yet Celia meant every word. She was as full of delighted anticipation as she had been with her first child—and with all the others in between.

How could Celia have wanted so many children—especially when she lived in such poverty? This question bothered me. I couldn't let it go until I understood why.

This chapter helps to provide an answer.

Population in Global Perspective

Let's look at how concern about population growth began.

A Planet with No Space for Enjoying Life?

The story begins with the lowly potato. When the Spanish *conquistadores* found that people in the Andes Mountains ate this vegetable, which was unknown in Europe, they brought some home with them. At first, Europeans viewed the potato with suspicion, but gradually it became the main food of the lower classes. With a greater abundance of food, fertility increased, and the death rate dropped. Europe's population soared, almost doubling during the 1700s (McKeown 1977; McNeill 1999).

Thomas Malthus (1766–1834), an English economist, became alarmed at this surging growth, seeing it as a sign of doom. In 1798, he wrote a book that became world famous, *An Essay on the Principle of Population* (1798). In it, Malthus proposed what became known as the **Malthus theorem.** He argued that although population grows geometrically (from 2 to 4 to 8 to 16 and so forth), the food supply increases only arithmetically (from 1 to 2 to 3 to 4 and so on). This meant, he claimed, that if births go unchecked, the population will outstrip its food supply.

The New Malthusians

Was Malthus right? This question has provoked heated debate among demographers. One group, which can be called the *New Malthusians,* is convinced that today's situation is at least as grim as—if not grimmer than—Malthus ever imagined. For example, *the world's population is growing so fast that in just the time it takes you to read this chapter, another 20,000 to 40,000 babies will be born!* By this time tomorrow, the earth will have about 228,000 more people to feed. This increase goes on hour after hour, day after day, without letup. For an illustration of this growth, see Figure 14.1.

The New Malthusians point out that the world's population is following an **exponential growth curve.** This means that if growth doubles during approximately equal intervals of time, it suddenly accelerates. To illustrate the far-reaching implications of exponential growth, sociologist William Faunce (1981) retold an old parable about a poor man who saved a rich man's life. The rich man was grateful and said that he wanted to reward the man for his heroic deed.

Large families on U.S. farms used to be common. Children helped plant and harvest crops, take care of animals, and prepare food. As the country industrialized and urbanized, children became nonproducers, making them expensive to have around. Consequently, the size of families shrank as we entered Stage 3 of the demographic transition, and today U.S. families of this size are practically nonexistent. (Note the trousers that the boy on the far left is wearing. They used to be his father's.)

What is the Malthus theorem? What is the exponential growth curve?

FIGURE 14.1   How Fast Is the World's Population Growing?

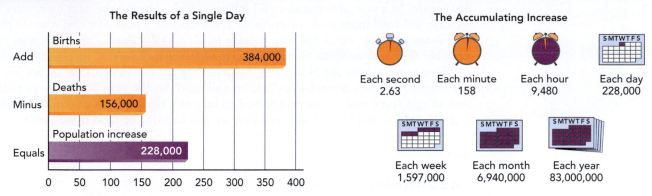

The Results of a Single Day

- Add — Births — 384,000
- Minus — Deaths — 156,000
- Equals — Population increase — 228,000

(scale: 0, 50, 100, 150, 200, 250, 300, 350, 400)

The Accumulating Increase

| Each second 2.63 | Each minute 158 | Each hour 9,480 | Each day 228,000 |
| Each week 1,597,000 | Each month 6,940,000 | Each year 83,000,000 | |

Source: By the author. Based on Haub 2011.

The man replied that he would like his reward to be spread out over a four-week period, with each day's amount being twice what he received on the preceding day. He also said he would be happy to receive only one penny on the first day. The rich man immediately handed over the penny and congratulated himself on how cheaply he had gotten by.

At the end of the first week, the rich man checked to see how much he owed and was pleased to find that the total was only $1.27. By the end of the second week he owed only $163.83. On the twenty-first day, however, the rich man was surprised to find that the total had grown to $20,971.51. When the twenty-eighth day arrived the rich man was shocked to discover that he owed $1,342,177.28 for that day alone and that the total reward had jumped to $2,684,354.56!

This is precisely what alarms the New Malthusians. They claim that humanity has just entered the "fourth week" of an exponential growth curve. Figure 14.2 shows why they think the day of reckoning is just around the corner. *It took from the beginning of time until 1800 for the world's population to reach its first billion.* It then took only 130 years (1930) to add the second billion. Just 30 years later (1960), the world population hit 3 billion. The time it took to reach the fourth billion was cut in half, to only 15 years (1975). Then just 12 years later (in 1987) the total reached 5 billion, in another 12 years it hit 6 billion (in 1999), and in yet another 12 years it hit 7 billion (in 2011).

FIGURE 14.2   World Population Growth over 2,000 Years

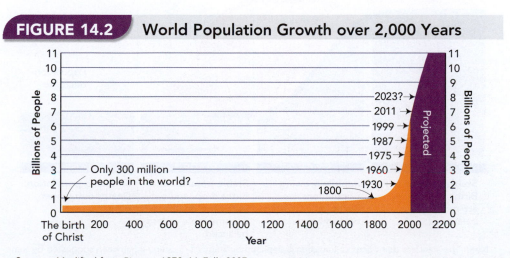

Only 300 million people in the world?

2023?
2011
1999
1987
1975
1960
1930
1800

Projected

(y-axis: Billions of People, 0–11)
(x-axis: The birth of Christ, 200, 400, 600, 800, 1000, 1200, 1400, 1600, 1800, 2000, 2200 — Year)

Sources: Modified from Piotrow 1973; McFalls 2007.

How does the exponential growth curve support the view of the New Malthusians?

On average, every minute of every day, 158 babies are born. As Figure 14.1 on the previous page shows, at each sunset the world has 228,000 more people than it did the day before. In a year, this comes to 83 million people. During the next four years, this increase will total more than the entire U.S. population. Think of it this way: *In the next dozen years, the world will add as many people as it did during the entire time from when the first humans began to walk the earth until the year 1800.*

These totals terrify the New Malthusians. They are convinced that we are headed toward a showdown between population and food. In the year 2050, the population of just India and China is expected to be more than the entire world population in 1950 (Haub 2011). It is obvious that we will run out of food if we don't curtail population growth. Soon we are going to see more televised images of pitiful, starving children.

The Anti-Malthusians

All of this seems obvious, and no one wants to live shoulder-to-shoulder and fight for scraps. How, then, can anyone argue with the New Malthusians?

To find out, let's turn to a much more optimistic group of demographers, whom we can call the *Anti-Malthusians*. For them, the future is painted in much brighter colors. They believe that Europe's **demographic transition** provides a more accurate glimpse into the future. This transition is diagrammed in Figure 14.3. During most of its history, Europe was in Stage 1. Its population remained about the same from year to year, for high death rates offset its high birth rates. Then came Stage 2, the "population explosion" that so upset Malthus. Europe's population surged because birth rates remained high while death rates went down. Finally, Europe made the transition to Stage 3: The population stabilized as people brought their birth rates into line with their lower death rates.

This, say the Anti-Malthusians, will also happen in the Least Industrialized Nations. Their current surge in population growth simply indicates that they have reached Stage 2 of the demographic transition. Hybrid seeds, medicine from the Most Industrialized Nations, and purer public drinking water have cut their death rates, while their birth rates have remained high. When they move into Stage 3, as surely they will, we will wonder what all the fuss was about. In fact, their growth is already slowing.

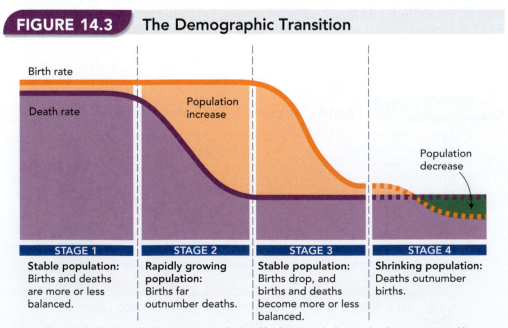

FIGURE 14.3   The Demographic Transition

Birth rate

Death rate

Population increase

Population decrease

STAGE 1	STAGE 2	STAGE 3	STAGE 4
Stable population: Births and deaths are more or less balanced.	**Rapidly growing population:** Births far outnumber deaths.	**Stable population:** Births drop, and births and deaths become more or less balanced.	**Shrinking population:** Deaths outnumber births.

Note: The standard demographic transition is depicted by Stages 1–3. Stage 4 has been suggested by some Anti-Malthusians.

What is the demographic transition? How does it support the view of the Anti-Malthusians?

Who Is Correct?

As you can see, both the New Malthusians and the Anti-Malthusians have looked at historical trends and projected them onto the future. The New Malthusians project continued world growth and are alarmed. The Anti-Malthusians project Stage 3 of the demographic transition onto the Least Industrialized Nations and are reassured.

There is no question that the Least Industrialized Nations are in Stage 2 of the demographic transition. The question is, Will these nations enter Stage 3? After World War II, the West exported its hybrid seeds, herbicides, and techniques of public hygiene around the globe. Death rates plummeted in the Least Industrialized Nations as the food supply increased and health improved. Because their birth rates stayed high, their populations mushroomed. This alarmed demographers, just as it had Malthus 200 years earlier. Some predicted worldwide catastrophe if something were not done immediately about the population explosion (Ehrlich and Ehrlich 1972, 1978).

We can use the conflict perspective to understand what happened when this message reached the leaders of the industrialized world. They saw the mushrooming populations of the Least Industrialized Nations as a threat to the global balance of power they had so carefully worked out. With swollen populations, the poorer countries might demand a larger share of Earth's resources. The leaders found the United Nations to be a willing tool, and they used it to spearhead efforts to reduce world population growth. The results have been remarkable. The annual growth of the Least Industrialized Nations has dropped 29 percent, from an average of 2.1 percent a year in the 1960s to 1.5 percent today (Haub and Yinger 1994; Haub 2011).

The New Malthusians and Anti-Malthusians have greeted this news with incompatible interpretations. For the Anti-Malthusians, this slowing of growth is the signal they had been waiting for: Stage 3 of the demographic transition has begun. First, the death rate in the Least Industrialized Nations fell—now, just as they predicted, birth rates are also falling. Did you notice, they would say if they looked at Figure 14.2, that it took twelve years to add the fifth billion to the world's population, twelve years to add the sixth billion, and twelve years to add the seventh billion? Despite the world having millions upon millions of more women of childbearing age, population growth has levelled off. The New Malthusians reply that this level growth rate still spells catastrophe—it will just take longer for it to hit.

The Anti-Malthusians also argue that our future will be the *opposite* of what the New Malthusians worry about: There are going to be too few children in the world, not too many. The world's problem will not be a population explosion, but **population shrinkage**—populations getting smaller. They point out that births in seventy-seven countries have already dropped so low that these countries no longer produce enough children to maintain their populations. If it weren't for immigration from Africa, all the countries of Europe would fill more coffins than cradles. The exception is Kosovo (Haub 2011).

Some Anti-Malthusians even predict a *demographic free fall* (Mosher 1997). As more nations enter Stage 4 of the demographic transition, the world's population will peak at about 8 or 9 billion, then begin to grow smaller. Two hundred years from now, they say, we will have a lot fewer people on Earth.

Who is right? It simply is too early to tell. Like the proverbial pessimists who see the glass of water half empty, the New Malthusians interpret changes in world population growth negatively. And like the eternal optimists who see the same glass half full, the Anti-Malthusians view the figures positively. Sometime during our lifetimes we should know the answer.

Why Are People Starving?

Pictures of starving children gnaw at our conscience. We live in such abundance, while these children and their parents starve before our very eyes. Why don't they have enough food? Is it because there are too many of them, or simply because the abundant food the world produces does not reach them?

Who is correct—the New Malthusians or the Anti-Malthusians?

Photos of starving people, such as this mother and her child, haunt Americans and other members of the Most Industrialized Nations. Many of us wonder why, when some are starving, we should live in the midst of such abundance, often overeating and even casually scraping excess food into the garbage. As in the photo on the right, which I took in San Antonio, Texas, we even have contests to see who can eat the most food in the least time. The text discusses reasons for such disparities.

The Anti-Malthusians make a point that seems irrefutable. As Figure 14.4 shows, *there is more food for each person in the world now than there was in 1950. Despite the billions of additional people who now live on this planet*, improved seeds and fertilizers have made more food available for *each* person on earth. And even more food is on the way, for bioengineers continue to make breakthroughs in agriculture. The global production of meat, fish, and cereals (grains and rice) increases each year (*State of the World* 2011).

FIGURE 14.4   **How Much Food Does the World Produce per Person?**

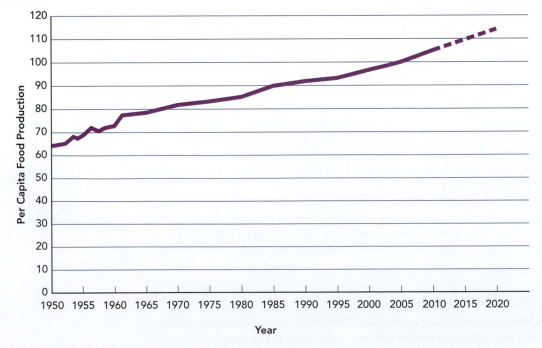

Note: 2004–2006 equals 100. Projections by the author.

Sources: By the author. *Statistical Abstract of the United States* 2010; Table 1335. Food and Agriculture Organization of the United Nations, January 27, 2012.

With the world's population growing so fast, is there less and less food for each person?

Then why do people die of hunger? From Figure 14.4, we can conclude that people don't starve because Earth produces too little food, but because particular places lack food. Droughts and wars are the main reasons. Just as droughts slow or stop food production, so does war. In nations ravaged by civil war, opposing sides either confiscate or burn crops, and farmers flee to the cities (Thurow 2005; Gettleman 2009).

The New Malthusians counter with the argument that the world's population is still growing and that we don't know how long the Earth will continue to produce enough food. They add that the recent policy of turning food (such as corn and sugar cane) into biofuels (such as gasoline and diesel) is short-sighted, posing a serious threat to the world's food supply. *A bushel of corn that goes into someone's gas tank is a bushel of corn that does not go on people's dinner plates.*

Both the New Malthusians and the Anti-Malthusians have contributed significant ideas, but theories will not eliminate famines. Starving children are going to continue to peer out at us from our televisions and magazines, their tiny, shriveled bodies and bloated stomachs nagging at our consciences, imploring us to do something. Regardless of the underlying causes of this human misery, the solution is twofold: first, to transfer food from nations that have a surplus to those that have a shortage, and second, where needed, to teach more efficient farming techniques.

These pictures of starving Africans leave the impression that Africa is overpopulated. Why else would all those people be starving? The truth, however, is far different. Africa has 23 percent of the Earth's land, but only 15 percent of the Earth's population (Haub and Kent 2008; Haub 2011). Africa even has vast areas of fertile land that have not yet been farmed. The reason for famines in Africa, then, *cannot* be too many people living on too little land.

Population Growth

Even if starvation is the result of a maldistribution of food rather than overpopulation, the Least Industrialized Nations are still growing much faster than the Most Industrialized Nations. Without immigration, it would take several hundred years for the average Most Industrialized Nation to double its population, but just forty years for the average Least Industrialized Nation to do so (Haub 2011). Figure 14.5 puts the matter in stark perspective. So does the Down-to-Earth Sociology box on the next page.

Why the Least Industrialized Nations Have So Many Children

Why do people in the countries that can least afford it have so many children? Let's go back to the chapter's opening vignette and try to figure out why Celia was so happy about having her thirteenth child. It will help if we apply the symbolic interactionist perspective. We must take the role of the other so that we can understand the world of Celia and Angel as *they* see it. As our culture does for us, their culture provides a perspective on life that guides their choices. Celia and Angel's culture tells them that twelve children are *not* enough, that they ought to have a thirteenth—as well as a fourteenth and fifteenth. How can this be? Let's consider three reasons why bearing many children is important to Celia and Angel—and to millions upon millions of poor people around the world.

First is the status of parenthood. In the Least Industrialized Nations, motherhood is the most prized status a woman can achieve. The more children a woman bears, the more she is thought to have achieved the purpose for which she was born. Similarly, a man proves his manhood by fathering children. The more children he fathers, especially sons, the better—for through them his name lives on.

FIGURE 14.5   World Population Growth, 1750–2150

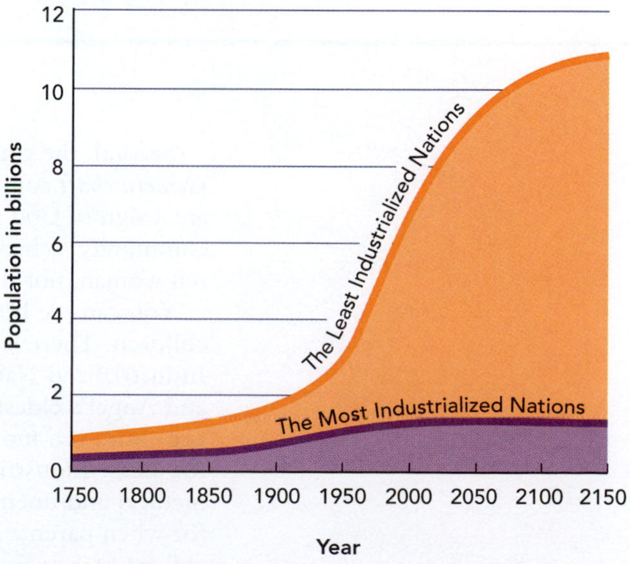

Sources: "The World of the Child 6 Billion" 2000; Haub 2011.

If there is enough food in the world to feed everyone, then why are some people starving?

Down-to-Earth Sociology

How Tsunamis Can Help Us to Understand Population Growth

On December 26, 2004, the world witnessed the worst tsunami in modern history. As the giant waves rolled over the shores of unsuspecting countries, they swept away people from all walks of life—from lowly fish peddlers to wealthy tourists visiting the fleshpots of Sri Lanka. In all, 286,000 people died.

In terms of lives lost, this was not the worst single disaster the world had seen. In 1976, several hundred thousand people were killed in China's Tangshan earthquake. In terms of geography, however, this was the broadest. It involved more countries than any other disaster in modern history.

I want to use the tsunami disaster to illustrate the incredible population growth that is taking place in the Least Industrialized Nations. My intention is not to dismiss the tragedy of these deaths, for they were horrible—as were the maimings of so many, the suffering of families, and the lost livelihoods.

Let's consider Indonesia first. With 233,000 deaths, this country was hit the hardest. At the time, Indonesia had an annual growth rate of 1.6 percent (its "rate of natural increase," as demographers call it). With a population of 220 million, Indonesia was growing by 3.3 million people each year (Haub 2004). (I'm using the totals at the time of the tsunami. As I write this in 2012, Indonesia's population has already soared to 243 million.)

This photo was snapped at Koh Raya in Thailand, just as the tsunami wave of December 26, 2004, landed.

This increase, coming to 9,041 people each day, means that it took Indonesia less than four weeks (twenty-six days) to replace the huge number of people it lost to the tsunami.

The next greatest loss of lives took place in Sri Lanka. With its lower rate of natural increase of 1.3 and its smaller population of 19 million, it took Sri Lanka a little longer to replace the 31,000 people it lost: forty-six days.

India was the third hardest hit. With India's 1 billion people and its 1.7 rate of natural increase, India was adding 17 million people to its population each year—46,575 people each day. At an increase of 1,940 people per hour, India took just 8 or 9 hours to replace the 16,000 people it lost to the tsunami.

The next hardest hit was Thailand. It took Thailand four or five days to replace the 5,000 people that it lost.

For the other countries, the losses were smaller: 298 for Somalia; 82 for the Maldives; 68 for Malaysia; 61 for Myanmar; 10 for Tanzania; 2 for Bangladesh; and 1 for Kenya ("Tsunami Deaths . . ." 2005).

Again, I don't want to detract from the horrifying tragedy of the 2004 tsunami. But by using this event as a comparative backdrop, we can gain a better grasp of the unprecedented population growth that is taking place in the Least Industrialized Nations.

Second, the community supports this view. Celia and those like her live in *Gemeinschaft* communities, where people share similar views of life. To them, children are a sign of God's blessing. By producing children, people reflect the values of their community, achieve status, and are assured that they are blessed by God. It is the barren woman, not the woman with a dozen children, who is to be pitied.

You can see how these factors provide strong motivations for bearing many children. There is also another powerful incentive: For poor people in the Least Industrialized Nations, children are *economic assets*. Look at Figure 14.6. Like Celia and Angel's eldest son, children begin contributing to the family income at a young age. But even more important: *Children are the equivalent of our Social Security*. In the Least Industrialized Nations, the government does not provide social security or medical and unemployment insurance. This motivates people to bear *more* children, for when parents become too old to work, or when no work is to be found, their children take care of them. The more children they have, the broader their base of support.

Why do women in the Least Industrialized Nations want so many children? How can a tsunami help us understand world population growth?

FIGURE 14.6   Why the Poor Need Children

Children are an economic asset in the Least Industrialized Nations. Based on a survey in Indonesia, this figure shows that boys and girls can be net income earners for their families by the age of 9 or 10.

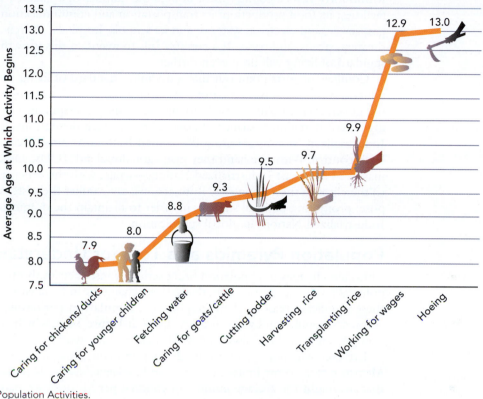

Source: U.N. Fund for Population Activities.

To those of us who live in the Most Industrialized Nations, it seems irrational to have many children. And *for us it would be.* Understanding life from the framework of people who are living it, however—the essence of the symbolic interactionist perspective—reveals how it makes perfect sense to have many children. Consider this report by a government worker in India:

Thaman Singh (a very poor man, a water carrier) . . . welcomed me inside his home, gave me a cup of tea (with milk and "market" sugar, as he proudly pointed out later), and said: "You were trying to convince me that I shouldn't have any more sons. Now, you see, I have six sons and two daughters and I sit at home in leisure. They are grown up and they bring me money. One even works outside the village as a laborer. You told me I was a poor man and couldn't support a large family. Now, you see, because of my large family I am a rich man." (Mamdani 1973)

Conflict theorists offer a different view of why women in the Least Industrialized Nations bear so many children. Feminists argue that women like Celia have internalized values that support male dominance. In Latin America, *machismo*—an emphasis on male virility and dominance—is common. To father many children, especially sons, shows that a man is sexually potent, giving him higher status in the community. From a conflict perspective, then, the reason poor people have so many children is that men control women's reproductive choices.

Consequences of Rapid Population Growth

The result of Celia and Angel's desire for many children—and of the millions of Celias and Angels like them—is that the population of the average Least

Why is having many children a reasonable choice for adults in the Least Industrialized Nations?

Industrialized Nation will double in forty years. In contrast, women in the United States are having so few children that if it weren't for immigration, the U.S. population would be shrinking.

The implications of a doubling population are mind-boggling. *Just to stay even,* within forty years a country must double the number of available jobs and housing facilities; its food production; its transportation and communication facilities; its water, gas, sewer, and electrical systems; and its schools, hospitals, churches, civic buildings, theaters, stores, and parks. If a country fails to maintain this growth, its already meager standard of living will drop even further.

Conflict theorists point out that a declining standard of living poses the threat of political instability—protests, riots, even revolution—and, in response, repression by the government. Political instability in one country can spill into others, threatening an entire region's balance of power. Fearing such disruptions, leaders of the Most Industrialized Nations are using the United Nations to direct a campaign of worldwide birth control. With one hand they give agricultural aid, IUDs, and condoms to the masses in the Least Industrialized Nations—while, with the other, they sell weapons to the elites in these countries. Both actions, say conflict theorists, serve the same purpose: promoting political stability in order to maintain the dominance of the Most Industrialized Nations in global stratification.

Population Pyramids as a Tool for Understanding

Although changes in population bring serious consequences, both on a personal and a political level, the reasons underlying these changes can be elusive. To illustrate one of these significant reasons, demographers use **population pyramids,** figures that depict a country's population by age and sex. Look at Figure 14.7, which compares the population pyramids of the United States, Mexico, and the world.

Let's see why population pyramids are important. Imagine a miracle—that overnight, Mexico is transformed into a nation as industrialized as the United States. Imagine also that overnight the average number of children per Mexican woman drops to 2.0, the same as in the United States. If this happened, it is obvious that Mexico's population would change at the same rate as that of the United States, right?

But this isn't what would happen. Instead, the population of Mexico would continue to grow rapidly. To see why, look again at the population pyramids. Notice that a

FIGURE 14.7   Three Population Pyramids

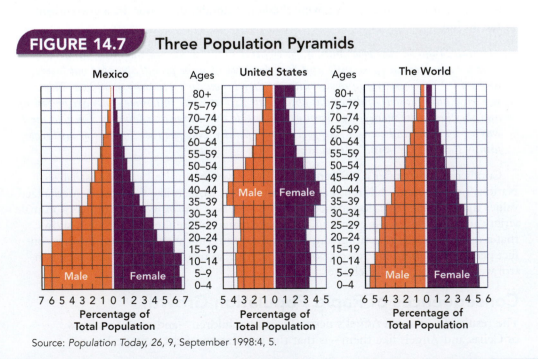

Source: *Population Today, 26, 9, September 1998:4, 5.*

What are population pyramids? How do they help us to understand population growth?

much higher percentage of Mexican women are in their childbearing years. This means that even if Mexico and the United States had the same birth rate, a larger percentage of Mexican women would be giving birth, and Mexico's population would grow rapidly while, without immigration, that of the United States would be standing still or decreasing. As demographers like to phrase this, Mexico's *age structure* gives it greater *population momentum*.

The Three Demographic Variables

How many people will live in the United States fifty years from now? What will the world's population be then? These are important questions. Educators want to know how many schools to build. Manufacturers want to anticipate changes in the market for their products. The government needs to know how many doctors, engineers, and executives to train. Politicians want to know how many people will be paying taxes—and how many young people will be available to fight their wars.

To project the future of populations, demographers use three **demographic variables:** fertility, mortality, and migration. Let's look at each.

Fertility.   The number of children that the average woman bears is called the **fertility rate.** The world's overall fertility rate is 2.5, which means that during her lifetime the average woman in the world bears 2.5 children (Haub 2011). A term that is sometimes confused with fertility is **fecundity,** the number of children that women are *capable* of bearing. This number is rather high, as some women have given birth to 30 children (McFalls 2007).

To see which countries have the highest and lowest birth rates, look at Table 14.1. You can see that three countries tie for the world's lowest fertility rate. There, the average woman gives birth to only 1.0 child. Six of the lowest-birth countries are in Europe. The other four are located in Asia. Now look at the countries with the highest birth rates. All of them are in Africa. Niger in West Africa holds the record for the world's highest birth rate. There, the average woman gives birth to 7.4 children, seven times as many children as the average woman in Macao, Hong Kong, and Taiwan.

To compute the fertility rate of a country, demographers analyze the government's records of births. From these, they figure the country's **crude birth rate,** the annual number of live births per 1,000 population. There can be considerable slippage here, of course. The birth records in many of the Least Industrialized Nations are haphazard, at best.

Mortality.   The second demographic variable is measured by the **crude death rate,** the annual number of deaths per 1,000 people. Its extremes are even higher than the extremes of the birth rate. The highest death rate is 39, a record held by Afghanistan in Asia. At 1, the world's record for the lowest death rate is held by Qatar, another Asian country (Haub 2011).

Migration.   The third demographic variable is the **net migration rate,** the difference between the number of *immigrants* (people moving into a country) and *emigrants* (people moving out of a country) per 1,000 people. Unlike fertility and mortality, migration does not affect the global population, for people are simply shifting their residence from one country or region to another.

| TABLE 14.1 | Extremes in Childbirth |

Where Do Women Give Birth to the Fewest Children?		Where Do Women Give Birth to the Most Children?	
Country	Number of Children	Country	Number of Children
Macao	1.0	Niger	7.4
Hong Kong	1.0	Mali	6.6
Taiwan	1.0	Somalia	6.5
Andorra	1.2	Uganda	6.5
Bosnia-Herzegovina	1.2	Congo, Dem. Republic	6.4
San Marino	1.2	Chad	6.2
South Korea	1.2	Zambia	6.2
Germany	1.3	Burkina Faso	6.0
Hungary	1.3	Liberia	5.8
Portugal	1.3	Angola	5.8

Note: Several other countries also average 1.3 children per woman.
Source: Haub 2011.

What are the three demographic variables? Can you explain population momentum?

Current U.S. immigration shows great diversity of origin. These individuals are taking the oath of citizenship in Washington, D.C.

What motivates people to give up the security of their family and friends to move to a country with a strange language and unfamiliar customs? To understand migration, we need to look at both push and pull factors. The *push factors* are what people want to escape: poverty, war and violence, or persecution for their religious and political ideas. The *pull factors* are the magnets that draw people to a new land, such as opportunities for education, better jobs, the freedom to worship or to discuss political ideas, and a more promising future for their children. After "migrant paths" are established, immigration often accelerates—networks of kin and friends attract more people from the same nation, even from the same villages.

Around the world, the flow of migration is from the Least Industrialized Nations to the industrialized countries. By far, the United States is the world's number one choice. The United States admits more immigrants each year than all the other nations of the world combined. Thirty-eight million residents—one of every eight Americans—were born in other countries (*Statistical Abstract* 2012:Table 41). Table 14.2 shows where recent U.S. immigrants were born. With the economic crisis, this flow has slowed. Not only are fewer migrants arriving, but many who have lost their jobs are returning to their home countries (Chishti and Bergeron 2010).

To escape grinding poverty, such as that which surrounds Celia and Angel, millions of people also enter the United States illegally. Although it may seem surprising, as Figure 14.8 shows, U.S. officials have sufficient information on these approximately 11 million people to estimate their countries of origin.

TABLE 14.2   Country of Birth of Authorized U.S. Immigrants

North America	3,269,000	Pakistan	139,000	South America	819,000
Mexico	1,554,000	Iran	112,000	Colombia	229,000
Cuba	285,000	Bangladesh	92,000	Peru	131,000
Dominican Republic	275,000	Taiwan	81,000	Brazil	112,000
El Salvador	234,000	Japan	70,000	Ecuador	102,000
Haiti	191,000	**Europe**	**1,175,000**	Venezuela	75,000
Jamaica	161,000	Ukraine	141,000	Guyana	69,000
Canada	155,000	United Kingdom	141,000	Argentina	46,000
Guatemala	150,000	Russia	133,000		
Asia	**3,363,000**	Poland	109,000	**Africa**	**759,000**
India	593,000	Bosnia and	88,000	Nigeria	98,000
China	592,000	Herzegovina		Ethiopia	96,000
Philippines	529,000	Germany	71,000	Egypt	64,000
Vietnam	276,000	Romania	50,000	Somalia	60,000
Korea	199,000	Albania	50,000	Ghana	58,000

Note: Totals are for the top countries of origin for 2001–2009, the latest years available.

Source: By the author. Based on *Statistical Abstract of the United States* 2011:Table 50.

What are the "pushes" and "pulls" behind migration?

Experts cannot agree whether immigrants are a net contributor to the U.S. economy or a drain on it. Adding what immigrants produce in jobs and taxes and subtracting what they cost in welfare and the medical and school systems, some economists conclude that immigrants produce more than they cost (Council of Economic Advisers 2007). Looking at the same data, other economists conclude that immigrants cost taxpayers billions of dollars (Davis and Weinstein 2002). Neither do economists agree whether immigrants lower or raise the income of native-born Americans (Shapiro and Vellucci 2010; Aydemir and Borjas 2011). The fairest conclusion seems to be that the more educated immigrants produce more than they cost, while the less educated cost more than they produce.

Problems in Forecasting Population Growth

"Russia's population is falling. We've got to do something. Let's give $5,000 to every woman who has a first child—and $15,000 to those who have a second child. And let men have two wives."

—*Vladimir Zhirinovsky, Russian politician, January 2010*

How politicians complicate the demographer's job. If population growth depended only on biology, making projections of the future population would be easy. Just use the **basic demographic equation.** Add and subtract the three demographic variables—fertility, mortality, and net migration—and you get a country's **growth rate,** the net change after people have been added to and subtracted from a population.

Growth rate equals births minus deaths plus net migration

Then you just project the results into the future—because current rates indicate future rates.

Or they *usually* do, and here is the rub. Some politician—maybe Zhirinovsky—comes along and pushes those rates in an unexpected direction. When Hitler decided that Germany needed more "Aryans," the government outlawed abortion and offered cash bonuses to women who gave birth. Germany's population increased.

Some politicians go in the other direction and try to slow births. The Indian government is offering $106 to each newlywed woman who waits two years to get pregnant (Yardley 2010). As you probably know, China has a "One couple, one child" policy, but you might not know how ruthlessly officials enforce this policy. Steven Mosher (2006), an anthropologist who did fieldwork in China, reports that if a woman gets pregnant without government permission (yes, you read that right!), doctors abort the fetus—even if the woman is nine months pregnant. The woman has no say in the matter. After the birth of her first child, each woman—whether she wants it or not—is fitted with an IUD (intrauterine device). If a woman has a second child, she is sterilized.

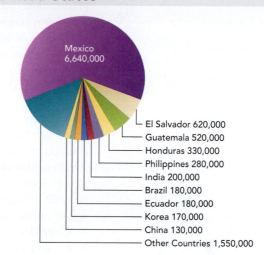

FIGURE 14.8 Countries of Origin of Unauthorized Immigrants to the United States

Mexico 6,640,000

El Salvador 620,000
Guatemala 520,000
Honduras 330,000
Philippines 280,000
India 200,000
Brazil 180,000
Ecuador 180,000
Korea 170,000
China 130,000
Other Countries 1,550,000

Source: By the author. Based on *Statistical Abstract of the United States* 2012:Table 45.

Chinese officials have become concerned about the lopsided gender ratio that their "one couple, one child" policy has produced. Their recent billboards continue to promote this policy, but by featuring a female child they are trying to reduce female infanticide.

为四化一对夫妇只生一个孩

What is the basic demographic equation? How is China's "one couple, one child" policy enforced?

Chinese officials have eased up a bit. Concerned that there will not be enough young workers to support their rapidly aging population, officials allow rural couples to have a second child—if their first one was a girl (Greenhalgh 2009). Another exception is allowing a second child if both the husband and wife are only children (LaFraniere 2011).

As you might suppose, wars, economic booms and busts, plagues, and famines also push rates of birth and death and migration up or down. As is shown in the Cultural Diversity box on the next page, even infanticide can affect population growth.

As you can see, government policies can change a country's growth rate. The main factor, though, is not the government, but industrialization. *In every country that industrializes, the birth rate declines.* Why? One reason is that industrialization makes rearing children more expensive. They require more education and remain dependent longer. Another reason is that the basis for conferring status changes—from having many children to attaining education and displaying material wealth. As people like Celia and Angel in our opening vignette begin to see life differently, their motivation to have many children drops sharply. Not knowing how rapidly industrialization will progress or how quickly changes in values and reproductive behavior will follow adds to the difficulty of making accurate projections.

Consider how difficult it is to estimate U.S. population growth. During the next fifty years, will we have **zero population growth?** (Every 1,000 women would give birth to 2,100 children, the extra 100 children making up for those who do not survive or reproduce.) Will more women go to college? (Educated women bear fewer children.) How many immigrants will we have? Will some devastating disease appear? Because of these many unknowns, demographers play it safe by making several projections of population growth, each depending on an "if" scenario. Figure 14.9 shows three projections of the U.S. population.

Let's turn to a different aspect of population, where people live. Because more and more people around the world are living in cities, let's look at urban trends and urban life.

✳ Explore
Living Data
on **mysoclab.com**

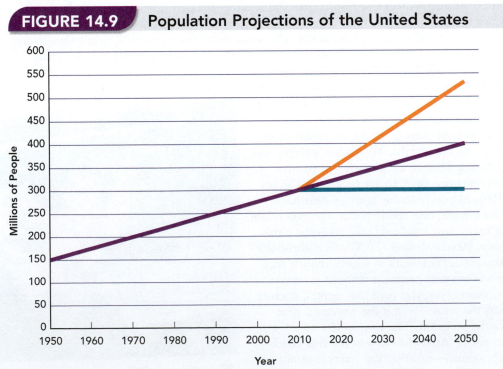

FIGURE 14.9   **Population Projections of the United States**

Note: The projections are based on different assumptions of fertility, mortality, and especially migration.

Source: By the author. Based on Day 2010.

What makes it difficult to forecast population growth accurately? What is zero population growth?

Cultural Diversity around the World

Killing Little Girls: An Ancient and Thriving Practice

"The Mysterious Case of the Missing Girls" could have been the title of this box. Around the globe, for every 100 births of girls, about 105 boys are born. In China, however, for every 100 baby girls, the total jumps to 120 baby boys. Given China's huge population, this means that China has about *30 million* more males than females under the age of 20 (Yardley 2010c). What happened to the 30 million girls?

The answer is *female infanticide,* the killing of baby girls. When a Chinese woman goes into labor, the village midwife sometimes grabs a bucket of water. If the newborn is a girl, she is plunged into the water before she can draw her first breath.

At the root of China's sexist infanticide is economics. The people are poor, and they have no pensions. When parents can no longer work, sons support them. In contrast, a daughter must be married off, at great expense, and at that point her obligations transfer to her husband and his family.

"Raising a girl is like watering someone else's plant," as they say in India, where female infanticide is also common.

In China, the past few years have brought even larger percentages of boy babies. The reason, again, is economics, but this time with a new twist. When China adopted capitalism, travel and trade opened up—but primarily to men, for it is not thought appropriate for women to travel alone. With men finding themselves in a better position to bring money home, parents have one more reason to want boys.

The gender ratio is so lopsided that for Chinese in their 20s there are six bachelors for every five potential brides. Politicians fear that the men who cannot marry—"bare branches," as they call them—will become disgruntled. Lacking the stabilizing

The sign above this couple waiting in a New Delhi doctor's office reminds patients that they should not abort fetuses just because they are female, that girls are also desirable children.

influences of marriage and children, these bare branches might become a breeding ground for political dissent. To head this off, officials have begun a campaign to stop the drowning of girl babies and the abortion of female fetuses.

Sources: Jordan 2000; Dugger 2001; Riley 2004; Sang-Hun 2007; Yardley 2007, 2009; Harney 2011.

For Your Consideration

→ What do you think can be done to reduce female infanticide? Why do you think this issue receives so little publicity and is not a priority with world leaders?

Why is the male–female ratio lopsided in China? Why do Chinese officials see this as a threat?

Urbanization

As I was climbing a steep hill in Medellin, Colombia, in a district called El Tiro, my informant, Jaro, said, "This used to be a garbage heap." I stopped to peer through the vegetation alongside the path we were on, and sure enough, I could see bits of refuse still sticking out of the dirt. The "town" had been built on top of garbage.

This was just the first of my many revelations that day. The second was that the Medellin police refused to enter El Tiro because it was so dangerous. I shuddered for a moment, but I had good reason to trust Jaro. He had been a pastor in El Tiro for several years, and he knew the people well. I was confident that if I stayed close to him I would be safe.

Actually, El Tiro was safer now than it had been. A group of young men had banded together to make it so, Jaro told me. A sort of frontier justice prevailed. The vigilantes told the prostitutes and drug dealers that there would be no prostitution or drug dealing in El Tiro and to "take it elsewhere." They killed anyone who robbed or murdered someone. And they even made families safer—they would beat up any man who got drunk and battered "his" woman. With the threat of instant justice, the area had become much safer.

Jaro then added that each household had to pay the group a monthly fee, which turned out to be less than a dollar in U.S. money. Each business had to pay a little more. For this, they received security.

As we wandered the streets of El Tiro, it did look safe—but I still stayed close to Jaro. And I wondered about this group of men who had made the area safe. What kept them from turning on the residents? Jaro had no answer. When Jaro pointed to two young men, whom he said were part of the ruling group, I asked if I could take their picture. They refused. I did not try to snap one on the sly.

My final revelation was El Tiro itself. On pages 432–433 you can see some of the things I saw that day.

Early cities were small economic centers surrounded by walls to keep out enemies. These cities had to be fortresses, for they were constantly under threat. This photo is of Ávila, Spain, whose walls date from 1090.

How did El Tiro solve its problem of urban disorder? Why is this a risky solution?

In this second part of the chapter, I will try to lay the context for understanding urban life—and El Tiro. Let's begin by first finding out how the city itself came about.

The Development of Cities

Cities are not new to the world scene. Perhaps as early as 7,000 years ago, people built small cities with massive defensive walls, such as biblically famous Jericho (Homblin 1973). Cities on a larger scale appeared about 3500 B.C., around the time that writing was invented (Chandler and Fox 1974; Hawley 1981). The earliest cities emerged in several parts of the world—in Asia (Iran, Iraq, India, China), West Africa (Egypt), Europe, and Central and South America (Fischer 1976; Flanagan 1990).

About 5,500 years ago, Norway was home to one of the first cities of Europe. The city, which had been buried under sand, was not discovered until 2010 (Goll 2010). In the Americas, the first city was Caral, in what is now Peru (Fountain 2001). It was also discovered recently, covered by jungle growth.

The key to the origin of cities is the development of more efficient agriculture (Lenski and Lenski 1987). Only when farming produces a surplus can some people stop producing food and gather in cities to spend time in other economic pursuits. A **city,** in fact, can be defined as a place in which a large number of people are permanently based and do not produce their own food. The invention of the plow about 5,000 years ago created widespread agricultural surpluses, stimulating the development of towns and cities.

Most early cities were small, merely a collection of a few thousand people in agricultural centers or on major trade routes. The most notable exceptions are two cities that reached 1 million residents for a brief period of time before they declined—Changan (Xi'an) in China about A.D. 800 and Baghdad in Persia (Iraq) about A.D. 900 (Chandler and Fox 1974). Even Athens at the height of its power in the fifth century B.C. had only about 250,000 inhabitants. Rome, at its peak, may have had a million people or more, but as the Roman Empire declined, the city of Rome became only a collection of villages (Palen 2008).

Two hundred years ago, the only city in the world that had a population of more than a million was Peking (Beijing), China (Chandler and Fox 1974). But today, as you can see from Figure 14.10, the world has about 500 cities with more than a million residents. Behind this surge lies the Industrial Revolution, which not only drew people to cities by providing work but which also stimulated rapid transportation and communication. These, in turn, allowed the efficient movement of people, resources, products, and especially today, information—essential factors (called *infrastructure*) that allow large cities to exist.

The Process of Urbanization

Although cities are not new to the world scene, **urbanization**—the movement of masses of people to cities, which then have a growing influence on society—is quite recent in world history. In 1800, only 3 percent of the world's population lived in cities (Hauser and Schnore 1965). The watershed year was 2008, when for the first time in history more people lived in cities than in rural areas. From Figure 14.11, you can see how urbanization has accelerated—and how uneven it is. Note especially the rapid increase of urbanization in the Least Industrialized Nations.

To understand the city's attraction, we need to consider the "pulls" of urban life. Because of its exquisite division of labor, the city offers incredible variety—music ranging from rap and salsa to death metal and classical, shops that feature imported delicacies from around the world and those that sell special foods for vegetarians and diabetics. Cities also offer anonymity, which so many find refreshing in light of the tighter controls of village and small-town life. And, of course, the city offers work.

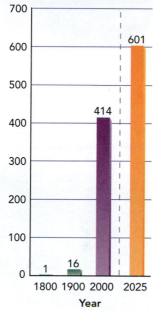

FIGURE 14.10   A Global Boom: Cities with over One Million Residents

Sources: By the author. Based on Chandler and Fox 1974; Brockerhoff 2000; United Nations 2008.

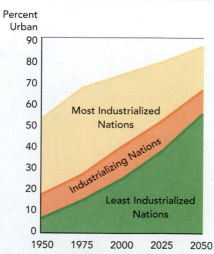

FIGURE 14.11 How the World Is Urbanizing

Percent Urban

Most Industrialized Nations

Industrializing Nations

Least Industrialized Nations

Source: By the author. Based on United Nations 2010.

What does agriculture have to do with the development of cities? What is urbanization?

Medellin, Colombia: A Walk Through El Tiro

Almost at the top of the garbage heap, I saw this boy in front of his house. His mother hung out the family's wash to dry.

Kids are kids the world over. These children don't know they are poor. They are having a great time playing on a pile of dirt in the street.

This is the "richer" area below El Tiro. As you can see, some of the residents own cars.

This is one of my favorite photos. The woman is happy that she has a home—and proud of what she has done with it. What I find remarkable is the flower garden she so carefully tends, and has taken great effort to protect from children and dogs. I can see the care she would take of a little suburban home.

The road to El Tiro. On the left, going up the hill, is a board walk. At the right of the photo is a meat market (*carnicería*). Note the structure above the meat market, where the family that runs the store lives.

It doesn't take much skill to build your own house in El Tiro. A hammer and saw, some nails, and used lumber will provide most of what you need. This man is building his house on top of another house.

El Tiro has home delivery.

An infrastructure has developed to serve El Tiro. This woman is waiting in line to use the only public telephone.

"What does an El Tiro home look like inside?," I kept wondering. Then Jaro, my guide (on the left), took me inside the home of one of his parishioners. Amelia keeps a neat house, with everything highly organized.

What do people do to make a living in El Tiro? Anything they can. This man is sharpening a saw in front of his home.

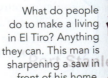

Some cities have grown so large and have so much influence over a region that the term *city* is no longer adequate to describe them. The term **metropolis** is used instead, referring to a central city surrounded by smaller cities and their suburbs. They are linked by transportation and communication and connected economically, and sometimes politically, through county boards and regional governing bodies. St. Louis is an example.

> *Although this name, St. Louis, properly refers to a city of 350,000 people in Missouri, it also refers to another 3 million people who live in more than a hundred separate towns in both Missouri and Illinois. Altogether, the region is known as the "St. Louis or Bi-State Area." Although these towns are independent politically, they form an economic unit. They are linked by work (many people in the smaller towns work in St. Louis or are served by industries from St. Louis), by communications (they share the same area newspaper and radio and television stations), and by transportation (they use the same interstate highways, the Bi-State Bus system, and international airport). As symbolic interactionists would note, shared symbols (the Arch, the Mississippi River, Busch Brewery, the Cardinals, the Rams, the Blues—both the hockey team and the music) provide the residents a common identity.*
>
> *Most of the towns run into one another, and if you were to drive through this metropolis, you would not know that you were leaving one town and entering another—unless you had lived there for some time and were aware of the fierce small-town loyalties and rivalries that coexist within this overarching identity.*

Some metropolises have grown so large and influential that the term **megalopolis** is used to describe them. This term refers to an overlapping area consisting of at least two metropolises and their many suburbs. Of the twenty or so megalopolises in the United States, the three largest are the Eastern seaboard running from Maine to Virginia, the area in Florida between Miami, Orlando, and Tampa, and California's coastal area between San Francisco and San Diego. The California megalopolis extends into Mexico and includes Tijuana and its suburbs.

This process of urban areas turning into a metropolis, and a metropolis developing into a megalopolis, is occurring worldwide. When a city's population hits 10 million, it is called a **megacity**. In 1950, New York City and Tokyo were the only megacities in the world. Today, as you can see from Figure 14.12, the world has twenty-two megacities, most of which are located in the Least Industrialized Nations. Megacities are growing so fast that by the year 2025 there are expected to be twenty-nine (United Nations 2010).

Watch
New Metropolis
on **mysoclab.com**

U.S. Urban Patterns

From Country to City.   In its early years, the United States was almost exclusively rural. In 1790, only about 5 percent of Americans lived in cities. By 1920, this figure had jumped to 50 percent. Urbanization has continued without letup, and today 80 percent of Americans live in cities.

The U.S. Census Bureau divides the country into 274 **metropolitan statistical areas (MSAs).** Each MSA consists of a central city of at least 50,000 people and the urbanized areas linked to it. About three of five Americans live in just fifty or so MSAs. As you can see from the Social Map on the next page, like our other social patterns, urbanization is uneven across the United States.

From City to City.   As Americans migrate in search of work and better lifestyles, some cities increase in population while others shrink. Table 14.3 on page 436 compares the fastest-growing U.S. cities with those that are losing people. This table reflects a major shift of people, resources, and power between regions of the United States. As you can see, five of the ten fastest-growing cities are in the West, and five are in the South. Of the ten shrinking cities, six are in the Northeast, two in the South, and two in the Midwest. New Orleans, a special case, has not yet recovered from Hurricane Katrina.

FIGURE 14.12   The World's 22 Megacities

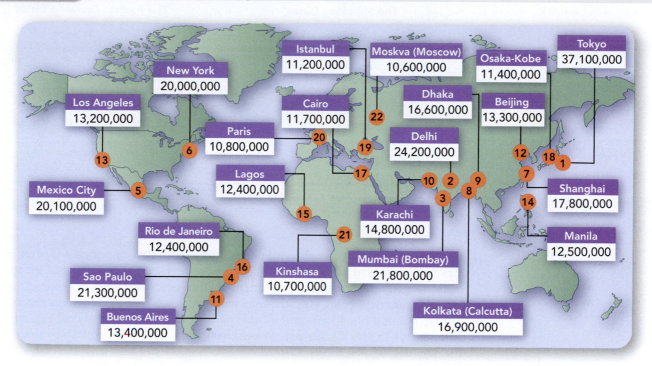

Note: Includes contiguous cities. Los Angeles, for example, includes Long Beach and Santa Ana, and New York includes Newark.

Source: By the author. Based on projected 2015 populations by United Nations.

FIGURE 14.13   How Urban Is Your State? The Rural–Urban Makeup of the United States

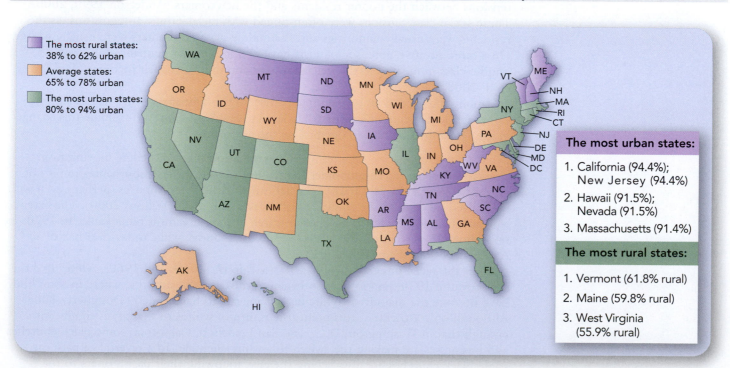

Source: By the author. Based on *Statistical Abstract of the United States* 2010:Table 29.

How many of the world's 22 megacities are in the United States? In Asia?

TABLE 14.3	The Shrinking and Fastest-Growing Cities		
The Shrinking Cities		**The Fastest-Growing Cities**	
1. −11.3%	New Orleans, LA	1. +41.8%	Las Vegas, NV
2. −6.2%	Youngstown, OH	2. +41.8%	Raleigh, NC
3. −3.5%	Detroit, MI	3. +40.3%	Cape Coral–Ft. Myers, FL
4. −3.3%	Cleveland, OH	4. +39.8%	Provo, UT
5. −3.1%	Pittsburgh, PA	5. +39.7%	Greely, CO
6. −3.0%	Buffalo–Niagara Falls, NY	6. +37.3%	Austin, TX
7. −2.4%	Flint, MI	7. +37.0%	Myrtle Beach, SC
8. −1.7%	Charleston, WV	8. +36.1%	McAllen, TX
9. −1.2%	Toledo, OH	9. +33.5%	Fayetteville, AR
10. −0.8%	Dayton, OH	10. +32.8%	Port St. Lucie, FL

Note: Population change from 2000 to 2010, the latest years available.
Source: By the author. Based on *Statistical Abstract of the United States* 2012:Table 20.

Between Cities.   As Americans migrate, **edge cities** have appeared—clusters of buildings and services near the intersections of major highways. These areas of shopping malls, hotels, office parks, and apartment complexes are not cities in the traditional sense. Rather than being political units with their own mayors or city managers, they overlap political boundaries and include parts of several cities or towns. Yet, edge cities—such as Tysons Corner near Washington, D.C., and those clustering along the LBJ Freeway near Dallas, Texas—provide a sense of place to those who live or work there.

Within the City.   Another U.S. urban pattern is **gentrification,** the movement of middle-class people into rundown areas of a city. What draws the middle class are the low prices for large houses that, although deteriorated, can be restored. With gentrification comes an improvement in the appearance of the neighborhood—freshly painted buildings, well-groomed lawns, and the absence of boarded-up windows.

Gentrification received a black eye. As a neighborhood improved, property prices would go up, driving many of the poor out of their neighborhood. This created tensions between the poorer residents and the newcomers (Anderson 1990, 2006). These social-class tensions were often tinged with racial–ethnic antagonisms, as the residents were usually minorities and the middle-class newcomers were usually whites. On a more positive note, sociologists have also found that gentrification draws middle-class minorities to the neighborhood and improves their incomes (McKinnish et al. 2008).

Among the exceptions to the usual pattern of the gentrifiers being whites and the earlier residents being minorities is Harlem in New York City. We examine this change in the Down-to-Earth Sociology box on the next page.

From City to Suburb.   The term **suburbanization** refers to people moving from cities to **suburbs,** the communities located just outside a city. Suburbanization is not new. The Mayan city of Caracol (in what is now Belize) had suburbs, perhaps even with specialized subcenters, the equivalent of today's strip malls (Wilford 2000). The extent to which people have left U.S. cities in search of their dreams is remarkable. In 1920, only about 15 percent of Americans lived in the suburbs, while today over half of all Americans live in them (Palen 2012).

After the racial integration of U.S. schools in the 1950s and 1960s, whites fled the city. Around 1970, minorities also began to move to the suburbs, where in some they have become the majority. "White flight" appears to have ended (Dougherty 2008a). Although only a trickle at this point, the return of whites to the city is significant enough that in Washington, D.C., and San Francisco, California, some black churches and businesses are making the switch to a white clientele. In a reversal of patterns, some black churches are now fleeing the city, following their parishioners to the suburbs.

What are edge cities? Gentrification? Suburbanization?

Down-to-Earth Sociology

Reclaiming Harlem: A Twist in the Invasion–Succession Cycle

The story is well known. The inner city is filled with crack, crime, and corruption. It stinks from foul, festering filth strewn on the streets and piled up around burned-out buildings. Only people who have no choice live in these desolate, despairing areas where danger lurks around every corner.

What is not so well known is that affluent African Americans are reclaiming some of these areas.

Howard Sanders was living the American Dream. After earning a degree from Harvard Business School, he took a position with a Manhattan investment firm. He lived in an exclusive apartment on Central Park West, but he missed Harlem, where he had grown up. He moved back, along with his wife and daughter.

African American lawyers, doctors, professors, and bankers are doing the same.

What's the attraction? The first is nostalgia, a cultural identification with the Harlem of legend and folklore. It was here that black writers and artists lived in the 1920s, here that the blues and jazz attracted young and accomplished musicians.

The second reason is that Harlem offers housing values, such as five-bedroom homes with 6,000 square feet, some with Honduran mahogany. Many brownstones are in good condition, although others are only shells and have to be rebuilt from the inside out.

What is happening is the rebuilding of a community. Some people who "made" it want to be role models. They want children in the community to see them going to and returning from work.

When the middle class moved out of Harlem, so did its amenities. Now that young professionals are moving back in, the amenities are returning. There were no coffee shops, restaurants, jazz clubs, florists, copy centers, dentist and optometrist offices, or art galleries—the types of things urbanites take for granted. Now there are.

The police are also helping to change the character of Harlem. No longer do they just rush in, sirens wailing and guns drawn, to confront emergencies and shootouts. Instead, the police have become a normal part of this urban scene. Not only have they shut down the open-air drug markets, but they are even enforcing laws against public urination and vagrancy. The greater safety of the area is attracting even more of the middle class.

The change is so extensive that former president Clinton chose to locate his office here, and Magic Johnson opened a Starbucks and a multiplex.

Social class preferences in music styles and volume are a source of tension between the old and new residents of Harlem. New residents have complained about these musicians at Marcus Garvey Park.

Another side of the story has emerged—tension between the people who were already living in Harlem and the newcomers. The source of irritation is often social class. The old-timers like loud music, for example, while the newcomers prefer a more sedate lifestyle. The newcomers have brought higher rents, which tenants' associations are protesting. Then there is also the old power establishment. They feel slighted if the newcomers don't ask their blessing before they open a business. The new business owners feel they don't need to get those old people's permission to open a business.

The in-fighting of this emerging drama involves African Americans. The issue is not race, but social class. The "invasion–succession cycle," as sociologists call it, is continuing, but this time with a twist—a flight back in.

Sources: Based on Leland 2003; Hyra 2006; Williams 2008; Haughney 2009; Lee 2010.

For Your Consideration

→ Would you be willing to move into an area of high crime in order to get a good housing bargain? How do you think the economic crisis—with the loss of jobs and falling real estate prices—will affect Harlem?

Smaller Centers.   Another recent trend is the development of *micropolitan areas*. A *micropolis* is a city of 10,000 to 50,000 residents that is not a suburb (McCarthy 2004), such as Gallup, New Mexico, or Carbondale, Illinois. Most micropolises are located "next to nowhere." They are fairly self-contained in terms of providing work, housing, and entertainment, and few of their residents commute to urban centers for work. Micropolises are growing, as residents of both rural and urban areas find their cultural attractions and conveniences appealing, especially less crime and pollution.

The Rural Rebound

The desire to retreat to a safe haven has led to a migration to rural areas that is without precedent in the history of the United States. Some small farming towns are making a comeback, their boarded-up stores and schools once again open for business and learning. Some towns have even become too expensive for families that had lived there for decades (Dougherty 2008b).

The "push" factors for this fundamental shift are fears of urban crime and violence. The "pull" factors are safety, lower cost of living, and more living space. Interstate highways have made airports—and the city itself—accessible from longer distances. With satellite communications, cell phones, fax machines, and the Internet, people can be "plugged in"—connected with others around the world—even though they live in what just a short time ago were remote areas.

Listen to the wife of one of my former students as she explains why she and her husband moved to a rural area, three hours from the international airport that they fly out of each week:

> *I work for a Canadian company. Paul works for a French company, with head-quarters in Paris. He flies around the country doing computer consulting. I give motivational seminars to businesses. When we can, we drive to the airport together, but we often leave on different days. I try to go with my husband to Paris once a year.*
>
> *We almost always are home together on the weekends. We often arrange three- and four-day weekends, because I can plan seminars at home, and Paul does some of his consulting from here.*
>
> *Sometimes shopping is inconvenient, but we don't have to lock our car doors when we drive, and the new Wal-Mart superstore has most of what we need. E-commerce is a big part of it. I just type in www—whatever, and they ship it right to my door. I get make-up and books online. I even bought a part for my stove.*
>
> *Why do we live here? Look at the lake. It's beautiful. We enjoy boating and swimming. We love to walk in this parklike setting. We see deer and wild turkeys. We love the sunsets over the lake. (author's files)*

Models of Urban Growth

In the 1920s, Chicago was a vivid mosaic of immigrants, gangsters, prostitutes, the homeless, the rich, and the poor—much as it is today. Sociologists at the University of Chicago studied these contrasting ways of life. One of these sociologists, Robert Park, coined the term **human ecology** to describe how people adapt to their environments (Park and Burgess 1921; Park 1936). (This concept is also known as *urban ecology*.) The process of urban growth is of special interest to sociologists. Let's look at four main models they developed.

The Concentric Zone Model

To explain how cities expand, sociologist Ernest Burgess (1925) proposed a *concentric-zone model*. As shown in part A of Figure 14.14, Burgess noted that a city expands outward from its center. Zone 1 is the central business district. Zone 2, which encircles

What is the rural rebound? What are the "pushes" and "pulls" behind it?

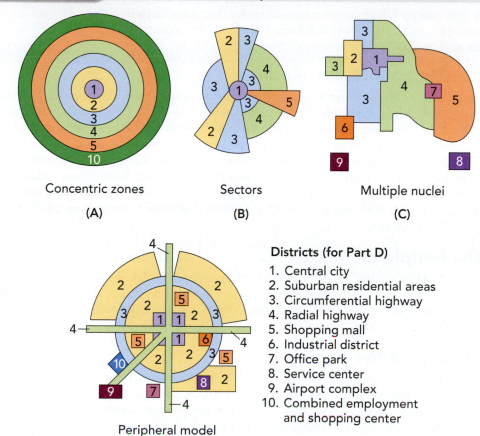

FIGURE 14.14   How Cities Develop: Models of Urban Growth

Concentric zones
(A)

Sectors
(B)

Multiple nuclei
(C)

Districts (for Parts A, B, C)

1. Central business district
2. Wholesale and light manufacturing
3. Low-class residential
4. Medium-class residential
5. High-class residential
6. Heavy manufacturing
7. Outlying business district
8. Residential suburb
9. Industrial suburb
10. Commuters' zone

Peripheral model
(D)

Districts (for Part D)

1. Central city
2. Suburban residential areas
3. Circumferential highway
4. Radial highway
5. Shopping mall
6. Industrial district
7. Office park
8. Service center
9. Airport complex
10. Combined employment and shopping center

Source: Cousins and Nagpaul 1970; Harris 1997.

the downtown area, is in transition. It contains rooming houses and deteriorating housing, which Burgess said breed poverty, disease, and vice. Zone 3 is the area to which thrifty workers have moved in order to escape the zone in transition and yet maintain easy access to their work. Zone 4 contains more expensive apartments, residential hotels, single-family homes, and exclusive areas where the wealthy live. Commuters live in Zone 5, which consists of suburbs or satellite cities that have grown up around transportation routes.

Burgess said that no "city perfectly fits this ideal scheme." Some cities have physical obstructions such as a lake, river, or railroad that cause their expansion to depart from the model. Burgess also noted another deviation from the model, that businesses were beginning to locate in outlying zones (see Zone 10). That was in 1925. Burgess didn't know it, but he was seeing the beginning of a major shift that led businesses away from downtown areas to suburban shopping malls. Today, these malls account for most of the country's retail sales.

The Sector Model

Sociologist Homer Hoyt (1939, 1971) modified Burgess' model of urban growth. As shown in part B of Figure 14.14, he noted that a concentric zone can contain several sectors—one of working-class housing, another of expensive homes, a third of businesses, and so on—all competing for the same land.

An example of this dynamic competition is what sociologists call an **invasion–succession cycle.** Poor immigrants and rural migrants settle in low-rent areas. As their numbers grow, they spill over into adjacent areas. Upset by their presence, the middle class moves out, which expands the sector of low-cost housing. The invasion–succession cycle is never complete, for later another group will replace this earlier one. The cycle, in fact, can go full circle; as discussed in the Down-to Earth Sociology box on page 437, in Harlem there has been a switch in the sequence: The "invaders" are the middle class.

The Multiple-Nuclei Model

Geographers Chauncy Harris and Edward Ullman noted that some cities have several centers or nuclei (Harris and Ullman 1945; Ullman and Harris 1970). As shown in part C of Figure 14.14, each nucleus contains some specialized activity. A familiar example is the clustering of fast-food restaurants in one area and automobile dealers in another. Sometimes similar activities are grouped together because they profit from cohesion; retail districts, for example, draw more customers if there are more stores. Other clustering occurs because some types of land use, such as factories and expensive homes, are incompatible with one another. One result is that services are not spread evenly throughout the city.

The Peripheral Model

Chauncy Harris (1997) also developed the peripheral model shown in part D of Figure 14.14. This model portrays the impact of radial highways on the movement of people and services away from the central city to the city's periphery, or outskirts. It also shows the development of industrial and office parks.

Critique of the Models

These models tell only part of the story. They are time bound, for medieval cities didn't follow these patterns (see the photo on page 430). In addition, they do not account for urban planning. Most European cities have laws that preserve green belts (trees and farmlands) around the city. This prevents urban sprawl: Wal-Mart cannot buy land outside the city and put up a store; instead, it must locate in the downtown area with the other stores. Norwich has 250,000 people—yet the city ends abruptly in a green belt where pheasants skitter across plowed fields while sheep graze in verdant meadows (Milbank 1995).

If you were to depend on these models, you would be surprised when you visit the cities of the Least Industrialized Nations. There, the wealthy often claim the inner city, where fine restaurants and other services are readily accessible. Tucked behind walls and protected from public scrutiny, they enjoy luxurious homes and gardens. The poor, in contrast, especially rural migrants, settle in areas outside the city—or, as in the case of El Tiro, featured in the photo essay on pages 432–433, on top of piles of garbage in what used to be the outskirts of a city. This topic is discussed in the Cultural Diversity box on the next page.

City Life

Life in cities is filled with contrasts. Let's look at two of those contrasts, alienation and community.

Alienation in the City

Impersonality and Self-Interest.   In a classic essay, sociologist Louis Wirth (1938) noted that urban dwellers live anonymous lives marked by segmented and superficial encounters. This type of relationship, he said, undermines kinship and neighborhood, the traditional bases of social control and feelings of solidarity. Urbanites then grow aloof and indifferent to other people's problems. In short, the price of the personal freedom that the city offers is **alienation.**

Alienation takes many forms, such as the "road rage" that makes the evening news. You can be following your routine, such as driving home from work, when the unexpected erupts (continued on page 442):

What are the multiple-nuclei and peripheral models? What are the shortcomings of the models of urban growth?

Cultural Diversity around the World

Why City Slums Are Better Than the Country: Urbanization in the Least Industrialized Nations

At the bottom of a ravine near Mexico City is a bunch of shacks. Some of the parents have 14 children. "We used to live up there," Señora Gonzalez gestured toward the mountain, "in those caves. Our only hope was one day to have a place to live. And now we do." She smiled with pride at the jerry-built shacks . . . each one had a collection of flowers planted in tin cans. "One day, we hope to extend the water pipes and drainage—perhaps even pave. . . ."

And what was the name of her community? Señora Gonzalez beamed. "Esperanza!" (McDowell 1984:172)

Esperanza means hope in Spanish.

What started as a trickle has become a torrent. In 1930, only one Latin American city had over a million people—now fifty do. The world's cities are growing by more than one million people each week (Moreno et al. 2012). The rural poor are flocking to the cities at such a rate that, as we saw in Figure 14.12 on page 435, the Least Industrialized Nations now contain most of the world's largest cities.

When migrants move to U.S. cities, they usually settle in rundown housing near the city's center. The wealthy live in suburbs and luxurious city enclaves. Migrants to cities of the Least Industrialized Nations, in contrast, establish illegal squatter settlements outside the city. There they build shacks from scrap boards, cardboard, and bits of corrugated metal. Even flattened tin cans are scavenged for building material. The squatters enjoy no city facilities—roads, public transportation, water, sewers, or garbage pickup. After thousands of squatters have settled an area, the city reluctantly acknowledges their right to live there and adds bus service and minimal water lines. Hundreds of people use a single spigot. About 5 million of Mexico City's residents live in such squalid conditions, with hundreds of thousands more pouring in each year.

It is difficult for Americans to grasp the depth of the poverty that is the everyday life of hundreds of millions of people across the globe. To understand this photo, you need to know that the "boxes" in the background are tombs. Someone is buried in each one. This girl in Manila, Philippines, lives inside a cemetery. She is frying fish on someone's coffin.

Why this rush to live in the city under such miserable conditions? On the one hand are the "push" factors that come from the breakdown of traditional rural life. More children are surviving because of a safer water supply and modern medicine. As rural populations multiply, the parents no longer have enough land to divide among their children. With neither land nor jobs, there is hunger and despair. On the other hand are the "pull" factors that draw people to the cities—jobs, schools, housing, and even a more stimulating life.

How will the Least Industrialized Nations adjust to this vast migration? Force doesn't work. Authorities in Brazil, Guatemala, Venezuela, and other countries have sent in the police and even the army to evict the settlers. After a violent dispersal, the settlers return—and others stream in. The roads, water and sewer lines, electricity, schools, and public facilities must be built. But these poor countries don't have the resources to build them. As wrenching as the adjustment will be, these countries must—and somehow will—make the transition. They have no choice.

For Your Consideration
➤ What solutions do you see for this river of migration to the cities of the Least Industrialized Nations?

What are the "pushes" and "pulls" behind the mass migration to the cities of the Least Industrialized Nations?

In crowded traffic on a bridge going into Detroit, Deletha Word bumped the car ahead of her. The damage was minor, but the driver, Martell Welch, jumped out. Cursing, he pulled Deletha from her car, pushed her onto the hood, and began beating her. Martell's friends got out to watch. One of them held Deletha down while Martell took a car jack and smashed Deletha's car. Scared for her life, Deletha broke away, fleeing to the bridge's railing. Martell and his friends taunted her, shouting, "Jump, bitch, jump!" Deletha plunged to her death. (Stokes and Zeman 1995). Welch was convicted of second degree murder and sentenced to 16 to 40 years in prison.

This certainly is not an ordinary situation, but anyone who lives in a large city knows that even a minor traffic accident can explode into road rage. And you never know who that stranger in the mall—or even next door—really is. The most common reason for impersonality and self-interest is not fear of danger, however, but the impossibility of dealing with crowds as individuals and the need to tune out many of the stimuli that come buzzing in from the bustle of the city (Berman et al. 2008).

Community in the City

Read

Death of a Neighborhood
by Rob Gurwitt
on **mysoclab.com**

I don't want to give the impression that the city is inevitably alienating. Far from it. Many people find community in the city. There are good reasons that millions around the globe are rushing to the world's cities. And there is another aspect of the attack on Deletha Word. After Deletha went over the railing, two men jumped in after her, risking injury and their own lives in a futile attempt to save her.

Sociologist Herbert Gans, a symbolic interactionist who did participant observation in the West End of Boston, was so impressed with the area's sense of community that he titled his book *The Urban Villagers* (1962). In this book, which has become a classic in sociology, Gans said:

After a few weeks of living in the West End, my observations—and my perceptions of the area—changed drastically. The search for an apartment quickly indicated that the individual units were usually in much better condition than the outside or the hallways of the buildings. Subsequently, in wandering through the West End, and in using it as a resident, I developed a kind of selective perception, in which my eye focused only on those parts of the area that were actually being used by people. Vacant buildings and boarded-up stores were no longer so visible, and the totally deserted alleys or streets were outside the set of paths normally traversed, either by myself or by the West Enders. The dirt and spilled-over garbage remained, but, since they were concentrated in street gutters and empty lots, they were not really harmful to anyone and thus were not as noticeable as during my initial observations.

Since much of the area's life took place on the street, faces became familiar very quickly. I met my neighbors on the stairs and in front of my building. And, once a shopping pattern developed, I saw the same storekeepers frequently, as well as the area's "characters" who wandered through the streets everyday on a fairly regular route and schedule. In short, the exotic quality of the stores and the residents also wore off as I became used to seeing them.

In short, Gans found a *community*, people who identified with the area and with one another. Its residents enjoyed networks of friends and acquaintances. Despite the area's substandard buildings, most West Enders had chosen to live here. *To them, this was a low-rent district, not a slum.*

Most West Enders had low-paying, insecure jobs. Other residents were elderly, living on small pensions. Unlike the middle class, these people didn't care about their "address." The area's inconveniences were something they put up with in exchange for cheap housing. In general, they were content with their neighborhood.

Who Lives in the City?

Whether people find alienation or community in the city depends on whom you are talking about. As with almost everything in life, social class is especially significant. The greater security enjoyed by the city's wealthier residents reduces alienation and increases satisfaction with city life (Santos 2009). There also are different types of urban dwellers, each with distinctive experiences. As we review the five types that Gans (1962, 1968, 1991) identified, try to see where you fit.

The Cosmopolites.   These are the intellectuals, professionals, artists, and entertainers who have been attracted to the city. They value its conveniences and cultural benefits.

The Singles.   Usually in their early 20s to early 30s, the singles have settled in the city temporarily. For them, urban life is a stage in their life course. Businesses and services, such as singles bars and apartment complexes, cater to their needs and desires. After they marry, many move to the suburbs.

The Ethnic Villagers.   Feeling a sense of identity, working-class members of the same ethnic group band together. They form tightly knit neighborhoods that resemble villages and small towns. Family- and peer-oriented, they try to isolate themselves from the dangers and problems of urban life.

Where do you think these people fit in Gans' classification of urban dwellers?

The Deprived.   Destitute, emotionally disturbed, and having little income, education, or work skills, the deprived live in neighborhoods that are more like urban jungles than urban villages. Some of them stalk those jungles in search of prey. Neither predator nor prey has much hope for anything better in life—for themselves or for their children.

The Trapped.   These people don't live in the area by choice, either. Some were trapped when an ethnic group "invaded" their neighborhood and they could not afford to move. Others found themselves trapped in a downward spiral. They started life in a higher social class, but because of personal problems—mental or physical illness or addiction to alcohol or other drugs—they drifted downward. There also are the elderly who are trapped by poverty and not wanted elsewhere. Like the deprived, the trapped suffer from high rates of assault, mugging, and rape.

In Sum: Within the city's rich mosaic of social diversity, not all urban dwellers experience the city in the same way. Each group has its own lifestyle, and each has distinct experiences. Some people welcome the city's cultural diversity and mix with several groups. Others find community by retreating into the security of ethnic enclaves. Still others feel trapped and deprived. To them, the city is an urban jungle. It poses threats to their health and safety, and their lives are filled with despair.

The Norm of Noninvolvement and the Diffusion of Responsibility

To avoid intrusions from strangers, urban dwellers follow a *norm of noninvolvement.*

> *To do this, we sometimes use props such as newspapers to shield ourselves from others and to indicate our inaccessibility for interaction. In effect, we learn to "tune others out." In this regard, we might see the [iPod] as the quintessential urban prop in that it allows us to be tuned in and tuned out at the same time. It is a device that allows us to enter our own private world and thereby effectively to close off encounters with others. The use of such devices protects our "personal space," along with our body demeanor and facial expression (the passive "mask" or even scowl that persons adopt on subways). (Karp et al. 1991)*

Social psychologists John Darley and Bibb Latané (1968) ran the series of experiments featured in Chapter 5 (p. 145). They uncovered the *diffusion of responsibility*—the more bystanders there are, the less likely people are to help. As a group grows, people's sense of responsibility becomes diffused, with each person assuming that *another* will do the responsible thing. "With these other people here, it is not *my* responsibility," they reason.

The diffusion of responsibility helps to explain why people can ignore the plight of others. Those who did nothing to intervene in the attack on Deletha Word were *not* uncaring people. Each felt that others might do something. Then, too, there was the norm of noninvolvement—helpful for getting people through everyday city life but, unfortunately, dysfunctional in some crucial situations.

As mentioned in Chapter 5, laboratory experiments can give insight into human behavior—but they can also woefully miss the mark. This classic laboratory experiment has serious flaws when it comes to real life. Recall the photo sequence I took in Vienna of the man who fell in Vienna, Austria. (See page 144.) That these people were strangers who were simply passing one another on the sidewalk didn't stop them from immediately helping the man who tripped and fell. We carry many norms within us, some of which can trump the diffusion of responsibility and norm of noninvolvement.

Urban Problems and Social Policy

To close this chapter, let's look at the primary reasons that U.S. cities have declined, and then consider how they can be revitalized.

Suburbanization

The U.S. city has been the loser in the transition to the suburbs. As people moved out of the city, businesses and jobs followed. Insurance companies and others that employed white-collar workers were the first to move their offices to the suburbs. They were soon followed by manufacturers and their blue-collar workers. This process has continued so relentlessly that today twice as many manufacturing jobs are located in the suburbs as in the city (Palen 2012). This transition hit the city's tax base hard, leaving a budget squeeze that affected not only parks, zoos, libraries, and museums, but also the city's basic services—its schools, streets, sewer and water systems, and police and fire departments.

Left behind were people who had no choice but to stay in the city. As we reviewed in Chapter 9, sociologist William Julius Wilson says that this exodus transformed the inner city into a ghetto. Individuals who lacked training and skills were trapped by poverty, unemployment, and welfare dependency. Also left behind were those who prey on others through street crime. The term *ghetto,* says Wilson, "suggests that a fundamental social transformation has taken place . . . that groups represented by this term are collectively different from and much more socially isolated from those that lived in these communities in earlier years" (quoted in Karp et al. 1991).

City versus Suburb.   Suburbanites want the city to keep its problems to itself. They reject proposals to share suburbia's revenues with the city and oppose measures that would allow urban and suburban governments joint control over what has become a contiguous mass of people and businesses. They do not mind going to the city to work, or venturing there on weekends for the diversions it offers, but they do not want to help pay the city's expenses.

It is likely that the mounting bill ultimately will come due, however, and that suburbanites will have to pay for their uncaring attitude toward the urban disadvantaged. Sociologist David Karp and colleagues (1991) put it this way:

> It may be that suburbs can insulate themselves from the problems of central cities, at least for the time being. In the long run, though, there will be a steep price to pay for the failure of those better off to care compassionately for those at the bottom of society.

Our occasional urban riots may be part of that bill—perhaps just the down payment.

Suburban Flight.   In some places, the bill is coming due quickly. As they age, some suburbs are becoming mirror images of the city that their residents so despise. Suburban crime, the flight of the middle class, a shrinking tax base, and eroding services create a spiraling sense of insecurity, stimulating more middle-class flight (Palen 2008; Katz and Bradley 2009). Figure 14.15 illustrates this process, which is new to the urban–suburban scene.

How did suburbanization contribute to the decline of U.S. cities?

FIGURE 14.15   **Urban Growth and Urban Flight**

50 years ago	25 years ago	Now
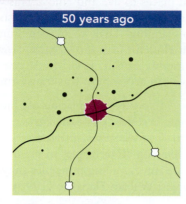	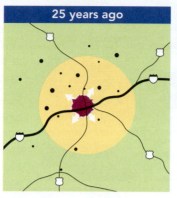	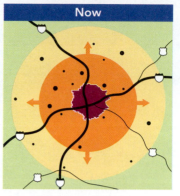
At first, the city and surrounding villages grew independently.	As city dwellers fled urban decay, they created a ring of suburbs.	As middle-class flight continues outward, urban problems are arriving in the outer rings.

Disinvestment and Deindustrialization

As the cities' tax base shrank and their services declined, neighborhoods deteriorated and banks began **redlining:** Afraid of loans going bad, bankers would draw a line around a problem area on a map and refuse to make loans for housing or businesses there. This **disinvestment** (withdrawal of investment) pushed these areas into further decline. Youth gangs, muggings, and murders are common in these areas, but good jobs are not. All are woven into this process of disinvestment.

The globalization of capitalism has also left a heavy mark on U.S. cities. As we reviewed in Chapter 11, to compete in the global market, many U.S. companies moved their factories to countries where labor costs are lower. This process, called **deindustrialization,** made U.S. industries more competitive, but it eliminated millions of U.S. manufacturing jobs. Lacking training in the new information technologies, many poor people are locked out of the benefits of the postindustrial economy that is engulfing the United States. Left behind in the inner cities, many live lives of quiet and not-so-quiet despair.

The Potential of Urban Revitalization

Social policy usually takes one of two forms. The first is to tear down and rebuild—something that is fancifully termed **urban renewal.** The result is the renewal of an area—but *not* for the benefit of its inhabitants. Stadiums, high-rise condos, luxury hotels, and boutiques replace run-down, cheap housing. Outpriced, the area's inhabitants are displaced into adjacent areas.

The second is to attract businesses to an area by offering them reduced taxes. This program, called **enterprise zones,** usually fails because most businesses refuse to locate in high-crime areas. They know that the high costs of security and the losses from crime can eat up the tax savings.

A highly promising form of the enterprise zone, called the *Federal Empowerment Zone,* is the opposite of disinvestment. It targets the redevelopment of an area by adding low-interest loans to the tax breaks. The renaissance of Harlem, featured in the Down-to-Earth Sociology box on page 437, was stimulated by designating Harlem a Federal Empowerment Zone. The low-interest loans brought grocery stores, dry cleaners, and video stores, attracting the middle class. As they moved back in, the demand for more specialty shops followed. A self-feeding cycle of investment and hope replaced the self-feeding cycle of despair and crime that had accompanied disinvestment.

As cities evolve, so does architecture. This is the second tallest communications and observation tower in the world. It is located in Guangdong, China. The tallest is located in Tokyo, Japan.

How did disinvestment and deindustrialization contribute to the decline of U.S. cities?

U.S. suburbs were once unplanned, rambling affairs that took irregular shapes as people moved away from the city. Today's suburbs are planned to precise details even before the first foundation is laid. This photo is of a suburb outside of Charlotte, North Carolina.

If they become top agenda items of the government, U.S. cities can be turned into safe and decent places to live and enjoy. This will require not just huge sums of money but also creative urban planning. That we are beginning to see success in Harlem, Chicago's North Town, and even in formerly riot-torn East Los Angeles indicates that we can accomplish this transformation.

Public Sociology.   Replacing old buildings with new ones is certainly not the answer. Instead, we need to *do public sociology* (discussed on p. 13) and apply sociological principles to build community. Here are three guiding principles suggested by sociologist William Flanagan (1990):

Scale Regional and national planning is necessary. Local jurisdictions, with their many rivalries, competing goals, and limited resources, end up with a hodgepodge of mostly unworkable solutions.

Livability Cities must be appealing and meet human needs, especially the need of community. This will attract the middle classes into the city, which will increase its tax base. In turn, this will help finance the services that make the city more livable.

Social justice In the final analysis, social policy must be evaluated by how it affects people. "Urban renewal" programs that displace the poor for the benefit of the middle class and wealthy do not pass this standard. The same would apply to solutions that create "livability" for select groups but neglect the poor and the homeless.

Most actions taken to solve urban problems are window dressings for politicians who want to *appear* as though they are doing something constructive. The solution is to avoid Band-Aids that cover up the problems that hurt our quality of life and to address their *root* causes—poverty, poor schools, crimes of violence, lack of jobs, and an inadequate tax base to provide the amenities that enhance our quality of life and attract people to the city.

By the Numbers: Changes Over Time

World population	
AT THE BIRTH OF CHRIST	NOW
300 MILLION	**7** BILLION

World per capita production of food	
1970	NOW
80 UNITS	**108** UNITS

Annual population increase of the Least Industrialized Nations	
1960s	NOW
2.1%	**1.5%**

Number of the world's cities with over 1 million residents	
1975	2025
195	**601**

Number of the world's cities with over 10 million residents	
1950	NOW
2	**22**

Percentage of the world's population that lives in cities		
1800	NOW	2050
3%	**51%**	**67%**

How can public sociology contribute to the revitalization of U.S. cities?

CHAPTER

14 Summary and Review

A Planet with No Space for Enjoying Life?

What debate did Thomas Malthus initiate?

In 1798, Thomas Malthus analyzed the surge in Europe's population. He concluded that the world's population will outstrip its food supply. The debate between today's New Malthusians and those who disagree, the Anti-Malthusians, continues. Pp. 416–419.

Why are people starving?

Starvation is not due to a lack of food in the world, for there is now *more* food for each person in the entire world than there was fifty years ago. Rather, starvation is the result of a maldistribution of food, which is primarily due to drought and civil war. Pp. 419–421.

Population Growth

Why do people in the poor nations have so many children?

In the Least Industrialized Nations, children are often viewed as gifts from God. In addition, they cost little to rear, contribute to the family income at an early age, and provide the parents' social security. These are powerful motivations to have large families. Pp. 421–425.

What are the three demographic variables?

To compute population growth, demographers use *fertility, mortality,* and *migration.* They follow the **basic demographic equation,** births minus deaths plus net migration equals the growth rate. Pp. 425–427.

Why is forecasting population difficult?

A nation's growth rate is affected by changing conditions— from economic cycles, wars, and famines to industrialization and government policies. Pp. 427–429.

Urbanization

How are cities related to farming and the Industrial Revolution?

Cities can develop only if there is an agricultural surplus large enough to free people from food production. The primary impetus to the development of cities was the invention of the plow. After the Industrial Revolution stimulated rapid transportation and communication, cities grew quickly. Today **urbanization** is so extensive that some cities have become **metropolises,** dominating the areas adjacent to them. Some metropolises spill over into each other, forming a **megalopolis.** Pp. 430–438.

What is the rural rebound?

As people flee cities and suburbs, the population of most U.S. rural counties is growing. This is a fundamental departure from a trend that had been in place for a couple of hundred years. P. 438.

Models of Urban Growth

What models of urban growth have been proposed?

The primary models are concentric zone, sector, multiple-nuclei, and peripheral. These models fail to account for ancient and medieval cities, many European cities, cities in the Least Industrialized Nations, and urban planning. Pp. 438–440.

City Life

Who lives in the city?

Some people experience **alienation** in the city; others find **community** in it. What people find depends largely on their backgrounds and urban networks. Five types of people who live in cities are cosmopolites, singles, ethnic villagers, the deprived, and the trapped. Pp. 440–443.

Urban Problems and Social Policy

Why have U.S. cities declined?

Three primary reasons for the decline of U.S. cities are **suburbanization** (as people moved to the suburbs, the tax base of cities eroded and services deteriorated), **disinvestment** (banks withdrawing their financing), and **deindustrialization** (which caused a loss of jobs). Pp. 444–445.

What social policy can salvage U.S. cities?

Three guiding principles for developing urban social policy are scale, livability, and social justice. P. 445.

Thinking Critically about Chapter 14

1. Do you think that the world is threatened by a population explosion? Use data from this chapter to support your position.

2. Why do people find alienation or community in the city?

3. What are the causes of urban problems, and what can we do to solve those problems?

Fiji

The job seemed to go on forever. Two archeologists and their team spent 25 years mapping Caracol, perhaps the oldest and largest city in the Americas. This city in Belize, which had been occupied from 600 BC to 900 AD when it was mysteriously abandoned, lay under thick jungle cover. The vegetation was so thick that the city had not been discovered until 1938 when some loggers stumbled onto it.

Year after year, the archeologists slaved away. Each year, they were able to map just a small part of the city. They knew that there were roads leading to the city, also hidden by thick jungle. And what else?

At the pace they were going, maybe archeologists would know the answer in 100 years or so.

But only if they could add more teams.

And only if they could survive the jungle's heat, insects, animals, and disease.

This is the traditional archeological way. Dig and document. What else can there be? Even attempts at using radar to map the site had failed. The jungle was too thick to penetrate.

"This is getting a little bit old," said Diane and Arlen Chase, the wife-and-husband team who for 25 years had been slogging away in the jungle. "And we aren't getting any younger either," they added. "Let's try LiDAR (light detection and ranging). And let's try it in the dry spring, when the vegetation is somewhat lighter."

> **" At the pace they were going, maybe archeologists would know the answer in 100 years or so. . . . if they could survive the jungle's heat, insects, animals, and disease. "**

For four days, a little plane flew back and forth a half-mile above the area. Everyone was curious. Would the laser beams bounced back from the ground show anything besides the vegetation? If so, what?

The results were astounding: high-quality 3-D images of what lay beneath the jungle. And not just in the area near the excavated site. LiDAR also revealed the intriguing things hidden in an *80 square mile area.* You could see crisp images of house mounds, roadways, and agricultural terraces.

In just four days, the new technology revealed more than had been discovered by slaving away for 25 years.

Based on Chase et al. 2010; Handwerk 2010; Wilford 2010.

If you want a better understanding of society—and your own life—you need to understand social change, probably the main characteristic of social life today. As we shall see in this chapter, technology, such as the laser imagery that reveals ancient cities hidden beneath the jungle, is the driving force behind this change.

Let's begin by reviewing how social change transforms social life.

How Social Change Transforms Social Life

Social change, a shift in the characteristics of culture and society, is such a vital part of social life that it has been a recurring theme throughout this book. To make this theme more explicit, let's review the main points about social change that we have looked at in the preceding chapters.

The Four Social Revolutions

Rapid social change is part of your everyday life. Why? To understand today's social change, we need to go back in history a bit. Let's start with forces that were set in motion thousands of years ago when humans domesticated plants and animals (pp. 99–101). This first social revolution allowed hunting and gathering societies to develop into horticultural and pastoral societies. The plow brought about the second social revolution, from which agricultural societies emerged. The third social revolution, prompted by the invention of the steam engine, ushered in the Industrial Revolution. Now we are in the midst of the fourth social revolution, stimulated by the invention of the microchip. The process of change has accelerated so greatly that the mapping of the human genome system could be pushing us into yet another new type of society, one based on biotechnology.

From *Gemeinschaft* to *Gesellschaft*

Although our society has changed extensively—think of how life was for your grandparents—we have seen only the tip of the iceberg. By the time this fourth—and perhaps fifth—social revolution is full-blown, little of our current way of life will remain.

Consider the change from agricultural to industrial society. It isn't just the surface that changed, such as people living in cities instead of on farms. People's lives had been built around the reciprocal obligations (such as exchanging favors) that are essential to kinship, social status, and friendship. When people moved to the city, many intimate relationships were replaced by impersonal associations built around paid work, contracts, and money. As reviewed on pages 105–106, sociologists use the terms *Gemeinschaft* and *Gesellschaft* to indicate this fundamental shift in society.

Social change comes in many forms. Shown here are students in a Fort Myer, Virginia, elementary school on the first day of desegregation in 1954. The school, operated by the military for the children of military personnel, was desegregated by order of the Defense Department.

The Industrial Revolution and Capitalism

As you can see, these are not just surface changes. The switch from *Gemeinschaft* to *Gesellschaft* society transformed people's social relationships and their orientations to life. In his analysis of this transition, Karl Marx stressed that when feudal society broke up, it threw people off the land, creating a surplus of labor. When these desperate masses moved to cities, they were exploited by capitalists, the owners of the means of production (factories, machinery, tools). This set in motion antagonistic relationships between capitalists and workers that remain today.

Max Weber traced capitalism to the Protestant Reformation (see page 404). He noted that the

What are the four social revolutions? How did society changing "from *Gemeinschaft* to *Gesellschaft*" change people's orientations to life?

Reformation stripped Protestants of the assurance that church membership saved them. As they agonized over heaven and hell, they concluded that God did not want the elect to live in uncertainty. Surely God would give a sign to assure them that they were predestined to heaven. That sign, they decided, was prosperity. An unexpected consequence of the Reformation, then, was to make Protestants hard-working and thrifty. This created an economic surplus, which stimulated capitalism. In this way, Protestantism laid the groundwork for the Industrial Revolution that transformed the world.

The sweeping changes ushered in by the Industrial Revolution, called **modernization,** are summarized in Table 15.1. The traits listed in this table are *ideal types* in Weber's sense of the term, for no society exemplifies all of them to the maximum degree. Actually, our new technology has created a remarkable unevenness in the characteristics of nations, making them a mixture of the traits shown in this table. For example, Uganda is a traditional society, but the elite have smaller families, emphasize formal education, and use computers. The characteristics shown in Table 15.1 should be interpreted as "more" or "less" rather than "either-or."

When technology changes, societies change. Consider how technology from the industrialized world transforms traditional societies. When the West exported medicine to the Least Industrialized Nations, for example, death rates dropped while birth rates remained high. As a result, the population exploded. It brought hunger, uprooting masses of people who migrate to cities that have little industrialization to support them. The photo essay on pages 432–433 and the Cultural Diversity box on page 441 focus on some of these problems.

Conflict, Power, and Global Politics

In our fast-paced world, we pay most attention to changes that directly affect our own lives or that make the headlines. But mostly out of sight is one of the most significant changes of all, the shifting arrangements of power among nations. Let's look at some of these changes.

A Brief History of Geopolitics. By the sixteenth century, global divisions of power had begun to emerge. Nations with the most advanced technology (at that time, the swiftest ships and the most powerful cannons) became wealthy through *colonialism,* conquering other nations and taking control of their resources. With the beginning of the Industrial Revolution in the eighteenth century, those nations that industrialized first exploited the resources of countries that had not yet industrialized. According to *world system theory,* this made the nonindustrialized nations dependent and unable to develop their own resources (see p. 204). The consequences of this early domination remain with us today, including the recurring conflicts over oil in the Middle East and the Arab uprisings in north Africa, but we'll get to this shortly.

G7 Plus. Since World War II, a realignment of the world's powers has created a triadic division of the globe: a Japan-centered East (soon to be dominated by China), a Germany-centered Europe, and a United States–centered western hemisphere. These

TABLE 15.1	Comparing Traditional and Industrialized (and Information) Societies	
Characteristics	**Traditional Societies**	**Industrialized (and Information) Societies**
General Characteristics		
Social change	Slow	Rapid
Size of group	Small	Large
Religious orientation	More	Less
Education	Informal	Formal
Place of residence	Rural	Urban
Family size	Larger	Smaller
Infant mortality	High	Low
Life expectancy	Short	Long
Health care	Home	Hospital
Temporal orientation	Past	Future
Demographic transition	First stage	Third stage (or Fourth)
Material Relations		
Industrialized	No	Yes
Technology	Simple	Complex
Division of labor	Simple	Complex
Income	Low	High
Material possessions	Few	Many
Social Relationships		
Basic organization	*Gemeinschaft*	*Gesellschaft*
Families	Extended	Nuclear
Respect for elders	More	Less
Social stratification	Rigid	More open
Statuses	More ascribed	More achieved
Gender equality	Less	More
Norms		
View of morals	Absolute	Relativistic
Social control	Informal	Formal
Tolerance of differences	Less	More

Source: By the author.

The Protestant Reformation ushered in not only religious change but also, as Max Weber analyzed, fundamental change in economics. This painting by Johann Zoffany from about 1775 is of Sir Lawrence Dundas, a Scottish merchant. Note the wealth that he enjoyed.

Each year, the leaders of the world's eight most powerful nations meet in a secluded place to make world-controlling decisions. And each year, protesters demonstrate near the site. This photo was taken at G8's 2009 meeting at Deauville, France.

Let them eat cake! Oxfam

three powers, along with four lesser ones—Canada, France, Great Britain, and Italy—formed G7, meaning the "Group of 7," in an effort to forge agreements on global dominance. Fear of Russia's nuclear arsenal prompted G7 to let Russia join this elite club, creating G8.

Dividing Up the World.   At their annual meetings, these world powers set policies to guide global economic affairs. Their goal is to perpetuate their global dominance. Essential to this goal is trying to maintain access to abundant, cheap oil—which requires that they dominate the Middle East, not letting it become an independent power. To the degree that these nations fail to implement policies and international relations that further their own interests, they undermine the New World Order they are trying to orchestrate.

Three Threats to This Coalition of Powers.   The global divisions that this group is trying to work out face three major threats. The first is dissension within. Currently, Russia is at the center of the intrafamilial feuding that threatens this coalition of powers (Nichol 2011). Because Russia is still stinging after losing its empire and wants a more powerful presence on the world stage, it is quick to perceive insult and threat—and to retaliate. In the dead of winter of 2006 and again in 2009, amidst a dispute with Ukraine over the price of gas, Russia turned off the pipeline that carries its gas through Ukraine to Western Europe, endangering lives in several countries (Crossland 2006; Kramer 2009). Suspicious about U.S. intentions, Russia also threatened a nuclear attack on Poland if the United States didn't back down from a plan to put missiles in Poland as part of a regional missile-defense shield (McElroy 2008). Russia and NATO continue to negotiate a mutual nuclear defense system (Nichol 2011).

The second threat is the resurgence of China. From a huge but sleepy backwater nation, China is emerging as a potential giant on the world stage of power. As China continues to develop its economic might and flex its military muscle, this country poses a threat to G8's plans, especially those concerning Asia and Africa. So far, the struggle for natural resources has been limited to bidding wars, and that for regional dominance to an occasional exchange of words. If the competition were to erupt into real war, all bets would be off concerning G8's success.

In a sign of changes to come, G8 is gradually—but with severe reluctance—bowing to the inevitable. Attempting to reduce the likelihood of conflict as China steps on turf claimed by others, G8 has allowed China to become an observer at its annual summits. As mentioned in Chapter 7, if China cooperates adequately, the next step will be to add China to this exclusive club, transforming the group into G9. It is inconceivable that China will not be incorporated into the coming New World Order.

The third threat is the resurgence of ethnic rivalries and conflicts, a menace to peace in many parts of the world—from the United States and Mexico in North America to China and Vietnam in Asia. In Europe, the Flemish defiantly proclaim that they are not Belgian, and Turks in Germany fear the young Germans who, barely held in check, threaten their lives. In Africa, violence erupts between Kenya's Kalenjin and Kikuyu, and in Nigeria the Igbo won't let the government count them because, as they say, "We are not Nigerian." We do not know how long the lid can be kept on these seemingly bottomless ethnic antagonisms or whether they will ever play

What is G7? G8? What are their significance for geopolitics?

themselves out. The end of these hostilities will certainly not come during our lifetimes.

For global control, G8 requires political and economic stability, both in its members' own backyards and in those countries that provide the raw materials that fuel its giant industrial machine. This explains why G8 cares little when African nations self-destruct in ethnic slaughter but refuses to tolerate interethnic warfare in its own neighborhoods. To allow warfare between different groups in Bosnia, Kosovo, or Georgia to go unchecked would be to tolerate conflict that could spread and engulf Europe. In contrast, the deaths of hundreds of thousands of Tutsis in Rwanda carried little or no political significance for these powerful countries.

The Emerging Relevance of Africa. No longer, however, can Africa be safely ignored. As resources grow scarcer, the connections between Africa and the interests of the Most Industrialized Nations have become more apparent. The global powers are realizing that African poverty and political corruption breed political unrest that can come back to haunt them. In addition to Africa's vast natural resources, including oil reserves that could counterbalance those of the unstable Middle East, Africa is also the world's last largely untapped market. Political stability could go a long way to transforming this continent into a giant outlet for G8's endless economic machine. This context of resources and market helps explain why the United States has raised funds for African AIDS victims and, as in Liberia, Somalia, and Darfur, has begun to intervene in African politics.

Armored vehicles blocked streets when NATO held a summit in Riga, Latvia, in 2006. Disregarding broadcast warnings to stay off the streets, I wandered around the city, taking photos. I expected to be stopped, perhaps arrested, but I was only stopped, questioned, and released.

Theories and Processes of Social Change

Social change has always fascinated theorists. Earlier in the text, we reviewed the theories of Karl Marx and Max Weber, which we just summarized. Of the many other attempts to explain why societies change, we shall consider just four: the evolution of societies, natural cycles, conflict and power, and the pioneering views of sociologist William Ogburn.

Evolution from Lower to Higher

Evolutionary theories of how societies change are of two types, unilinear and multilinear. *Unilinear* theories assume that all societies follow the same path: Each evolves from simpler to more complex forms. This journey takes each society through uniform sequences (Barnes 1935). Of the many versions of this theory, the one proposed by Lewis Morgan (1877) once dominated Western thought. Morgan said that all societies go through three stages: savagery, barbarism, and civilization. In Morgan's eyes, England, his own society, was the epitome of civilization. All other societies were destined to follow the same path.

Multilinear views of evolution replaced unilinear theories. Instead of assuming that all societies follow the same sequence, multilinear theorists proposed that different routes lead to the same stage of development. Although the paths all lead to industrialization, societies need not pass through the same sequence of stages on their journey (Sahlins and Service 1960; Lenski and Lenski 1987).

Central to all evolutionary theories, whether unilinear or multilinear, is the assumption of *cultural progress*. Tribal societies are assumed to have a primitive form of human culture. As these societies evolve, they reach a higher state—the supposedly advanced and superior form that characterizes the Western world. Growing appreciation of the rich diversity—and complexity—of tribal cultures has discredited this idea. In addition, Western culture is now in crisis (poverty, racism, war, terrorism, sexual assaults, unsafe streets) and no longer regarded as the apex

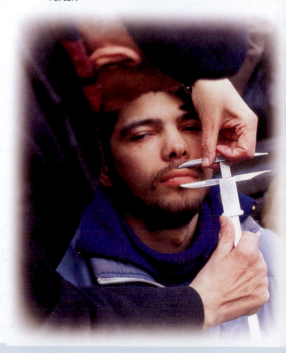

Despite the globe's vast social change, people all over the world continue to make race a fundamental distinction. Shown here is a Ukrainian being measured to see if he is really "full lipped" enough to be called a Tartar.

○⊙⌐ **Watch**

Cuba: Accidental Revolution
on **mysoclab.com**

of human civilization. Consequently, the idea of cultural progress has been cast aside, and evolutionary theories have been rejected (Eder 1990; Smart 1990).

Natural Cycles

Cyclical theories attempt to account for the rise of entire civilizations. Why, for example, did Egypt, Greece, and Rome wield such power and influence, only to crest and then decline? Cyclical theories assume that civilizations are like organisms: They are born, enjoy an exuberant youth, come to maturity, and then decline as they reach old age. Finally, they die (Hughes 1962).

The cycle does exist, but why? Historian Arnold Toynbee (1946) said that each civilization faces challenges to its existence. Groups work out solutions to these challenges, as they must if they are to continue. But these solutions are not satisfactory to all. The ruling elite manages to keep the remaining oppositional forces under control, even though they "make trouble" now and then. At a civilization's peak, however, when it has become an empire, the ruling elite loses its capacity to keep the masses in line "by charm rather than by force." Gradually, the fabric of society rips apart. Force may hold the empire together for hundreds of years, but the civilization is doomed.

In a book that provoked widespread controversy, *The Decline of the West* (1926–1928), Oswald Spengler, a high school teacher in Germany, proposed that Western civilization had passed its peak and was in decline. Although the West succeeded in overcoming the crises provoked by Hitler and Mussolini, as Toynbee noted, civilizations don't end in sudden collapse. Because the decline can last hundreds of years, perhaps the crisis in Western civilization mentioned earlier (poverty, rape, murder, and so on) indicates that Spengler was right, and we are now in decline. If so, it appears that China is waiting on the horizon to seize global power and to forge a new civilization.

Conflict over Power

Long before Toynbee, Karl Marx identified a recurring process of social change. He said that each *thesis* (a current arrangement of power) contains its own *antithesis* (contradiction or opposition). A struggle develops between the thesis and its antithesis, leading to a *synthesis* (a new arrangement of power). This new social order, in turn, becomes a thesis that will be challenged by its own antithesis, and so on. Figure 15.1 gives a visual summary of this process.

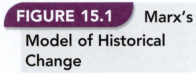

FIGURE 15.1   Marx's Model of Historical Change

According to Marx's view (called a **dialectical process of history**), each ruling group sows the seeds of its own destruction. Consider capitalism. Marx said that capitalism (the thesis) is built on the exploitation of workers (an antithesis, or built-in opposition). With workers and owners on a collision course, the dialectical process will not stop until workers establish a classless state (the synthesis).

The analysis of G7/G8 in the previous section follows conflict theory. G8's current division of the globe's resources and markets is a thesis. Resentment on the part of have-not nations is an antithesis. The demand to redistribute power and resources will come from any Least Industrialized or Industrializing Nation that gains military power. With their nuclear weapons, China, India, Pakistan, Russia, North Korea, and, soon, Iran fit this scenario. So do the efforts of al-Qaeda to change the balance of power between the Middle East and the industrialized West.

Eventually, a new arrangement of power will come. Like the old, this new synthesis will contain its own antitheses, such as ethnic hostilities or leaders who feel their countries have been denied a fair share of resources. These contradictions will haunt the new rearrangement of power, which at some point will be resolved into another synthesis. The process repeats, a continual cycle of thesis, antithesis, and synthesis.

Source: By the author.

Ogburn's Theory

Sociologist William Ogburn (1922/1938, 1961, 1964) proposed a theory of social change that is based largely on technology. As you can see from Table 15.2 on the next page, he said that technology changes society by three processes: invention, discovery, and diffusion. Let's consider each.

TABLE 15.2	Ogburn's Processes of Social Change		
Process of Change	**What It Is**	**Examples**	**Social Changes**
Invention	Combination of existing elements to form new ones	1. Cars	1. Urban sprawl and long commutes to work
		2. Microchip	2. Telecommuting and cyber warfare
		3. Graphite composites	3. New types of building construction
Discovery	New way of seeing some aspect of the world	1. Columbus—North America	1. Realignment of global power
		2. Gold in California	2. Westward expansion of the U.S.
		3. DNA	3. Positive identification of criminals
Diffusion	Spread of an invention or discovery	1. Airplanes	1. Global tourism
		2. Money	2. Global trade
		3. Condom	3. Smaller families

Note: For each example, there are many changes. For some of the changes ushered in by the microchip, see pages 457–461. You can also see that any particular change, such as global trade, depends not just on one item, but also on several preceding changes.
Source: By the author.

Invention.   Ogburn defined **invention** as a combining of existing elements and materials to form new ones. We usually think of inventions as being only material items, such as computers, but there also are *social inventions.* We have considered many social inventions in this text, including democracy and citizenship (pp. 319–320), capitalism (p. 333), socialism (p. 335), bureaucracy (pp. 133–139), and in Chapter 10, gender equality. We saw how these social inventions had far-reaching consequences on people's relationships. Material inventions can also affect social life deeply, and in this chapter we will examine how the microchip is transforming society.

Discovery.   Ogburn identified **discovery,** a new way of seeing reality, as a second process of change. The reality is already present, but people see it for the first time. An example is Columbus' "discovery" of North America, which had consequences so huge that they altered the course of human history. This example also illustrates another principle: A discovery brings extensive change only when it comes at the right time. Other groups, such as the Vikings, had already "discovered" North America in the sense of learning that a new land existed—obviously no discovery to the Native Americans already living there. Viking settlements disappeared into history, however, and Norse culture was untouched by the discovery.

Diffusion.   Ogburn stressed how **diffusion,** the spread of an invention or discovery from one area to another, can produce extensive effects on people's lives. Consider an object as simple as the axe. When missionaries introduced steel axes to the Aborigines of Australia, it upset their whole society. Before this, the men controlled axe-making. They used a special stone that was available only in a remote region, and fathers passed axe-making skills on to their sons. Women had to request permission to use the axe. When steel axes became common, women also possessed them, and the men lost both status and power (Sharp 1995).

Culture contact is the source of *diffusion*, the spread of an *invention* or *discovery* from one area to another. Shown here is a boy in a Mumbai village using a laptop provided under the "One Laptop Per Child" project. Previously, he was cut off from almost everyone except fellow villagers. How do you think modern communications will affect his orientation to life?

In Ogburn's theory, how do invention, discovery, and diffusion lead to social change? What is cultural lag?

Diffusion also includes the spread of social inventions and ideas. As we saw in Chapter 11, the idea of citizenship changed political structures around the world. It swept away monarchs as an unquestioned source of authority. The idea of gender equality is now circling the globe. To those who are used to this concept, it is surprising to think that opposition to withholding rights on the basis of someone's sex can be revolutionary. Like citizenship, gender equality is destined to transform basic human relationships and entire societies.

Cultural Lag. Ogburn coined the term **cultural lag** to refer to how some elements of culture lag behind the changes that come from invention, discovery, and diffusion. Technology, he suggested, usually changes first, with culture lagging behind. In other words, we play catch-up with changing technology, adapting our customs and ways of life to meet its needs.

How Technology Is Changing Our Lives

Extending Human Abilities. To understand what *technology* is, let's look at its three meanings. Its first meaning refers to *tools,* the items used to accomplish tasks. The tools can be as simple as a comb or as complicated as a computer. Technology's second meaning refers to the *procedures* necessary to produce tools, in this case to the ways

Do you know what that large object in the center of the photo is? In the 1920s, 30s, and 40s, middle-class families would gather in the living room after dinner and listen to the radio. (It was a sit-down dinner served by the wife and assisted by the daughters.) Can you see how technology is influencing this 1940s family? How about yourself?

we manufacture combs and computers. Technology's third meaning refers to the *skills* needed to use tools, in this case the skills we need to "produce" an acceptable hairdo or to go online.

No matter what tools, procedures, or skills we are talking about, technology always refers to *artificial means of extending human abilities*. Consider our opening vignette. The essence of the story is how greatly our new technology has extended human abilities.

All human groups make and use technology. They all have tools, procedures, and skills. The chief characteristic of technology in postindustrial societies (also called **postmodern societies**) is that it greatly extends our abilities to communicate, to travel, and to retrieve and analyze information. These *new technologies*, as they are called, extend our abilities beyond anything known in human history. We can now do what had never been done before: to transplant organs; communicate almost instantaneously anywhere on the globe; probe space; and travel greater distances faster. And, as in our opening vignette, we can produce, store, retrieve, and analyze vast amounts of information, even if we must penetrate thick jungles to do so.

The Sociological Significance of Technology.   The constant array of new devices is fascinating—from cell phones that let you to buy a Coke or catch up on the latest Hollywood gossip to satellites that help you navigate through traffic or that launch missiles. But remember that this text is not about technological devices, but about sociology. We need to keep in mind, then, *the sociological significance of technology, which is not the gadget but, rather, how technology changes our way of life*. Consider the obvious: how strikingly different our way of life would be if we had no automobiles, telephones, or televisions.

And with technology changing so rapidly, our way of life often veers into unexpected directions. Our journey to the future, then, is going to have many twists and turns. Although we don't yet know where those twists and turns will lead us, it is intriguing to try to peer over the edge of the present to at least catch a glimpse of that future.

Let's do this by focusing on the computer. We will begin with its effects on social interaction, education, business, and the waging of war. We'll then consider the computer's impact on social control and social inequality.

The Microchip and Social Life

Changes in Social Relationships.   I have stressed that technology changes our lives in fundamental ways, including the ways we interact with one another. Consider this little example.

As I work on this edition of your text, my wife and I sit at the same large dining room table that serves as our desk, each absorbed in our computers as we go about individual tasks. Although we can easily talk to one another, and do, we also send e-mails back and forth throughout the day, even though we are within arms' reach of one another. One of us finds something interesting, the latest news on Latvia or the global economic crisis, some sociological analysis, news from a friend or one of the kids, or even something humorous. By sending the message, instead of talking, we don't break the other's concentration. We attend to the message when it fits into our breaks, when we then chat with one another.

This example is how I am personally experiencing technological change, how the microchip is altering my life and relationships. Examples of how social patterns are being changed can be multiplied thousands of times over by the readers of this text. We each adapt the new technology, making it fit our particular life situation, just as the technology forces us to adapt to it. The process is a two-way street.

What is the sociological significance of technology? How are your social relationships different because of the microchip?

The microchip is transforming society, changing the way we shop, study, and relate to one another. This iPhone has more computing power than the first computers, giant hulks that filled entire rooms.

Computers in Education

Because of computers, students can take courses in Russian, German, and Spanish—even when their schools have no teachers who speak these languages. If their school also lacks sociology instructors, they can still study the sociology of gender, race, social class, or even sex, and sports. (The comma is important. It isn't sex and sports. That course isn't offered—yet.)

We've barely begun to harness the power of computers, but I imagine that the day will come when you will be able to key in the terms *social interaction* and *gender,* select your preference of historical period, geographical site, age, and ethnic group—and the computer will spew out text, maps, moving images, and sounds. You will be able to compare sexual discrimination in the military in 1985 and today, or the price of marijuana in Los Angeles and New Orleans. If you wish, the computer will give you a test—geared to the level of difficulty you choose—so that you can check your mastery of the material.

Distance learning, courses taught to students who are not physically present with their instructor, will become such a part of mainstream education that most students will take at least some of their high school, college, and graduate courses through this arrangement. Cameras in laptops allow everyone in the class to see everyone else, even though the students live in different countries. Imagine this—and likely it soon will be a reality: Your fellow students in a course on diversity in human culture will be living in Thailand, South Africa, Latvia, Egypt, China, and Australia. With zero-cost conference calls and e-mail and file exchanges, you will be able to compare your countries' customs on eating, dating, marriage, family, or burial—whatever is of interest to you. You can then write a team paper in which you compare your experiences with one another, applying the theories taught in the text, and then e-mail the paper to your mutual instructor.

Computers in Business and Finance

The advanced technology of businesses used to consist of cash registers and adding machines. Connections to the outside world were managed by telephone. Today, those same businesses are electronically "wired" to suppliers, salespeople, and clients around the country—and around the world. Computers track sales of items, tabulate inventory, and set in motion the process of reordering and restocking. Detailed reports of sales alert managers to changes in their customers' tastes or preferences. For retail giants like Wal-Mart, the computer reports regional differences in shopping patterns and preferences of products.

Technology, which drives much social change, is at the forefront of our information revolution. This revolution, based on the computer chip, allows reality to cross with fantasy, a merging that sometimes makes it difficult to tell where one ends and the other begins. A computer projects an image onto the front of the coat, making its wearer "invisible."

National borders have become meaningless as computers instantaneously transfer billions of dollars from one country to another. No "cash" changes hands in these transactions. The money consists of digits in computer memory banks. In the same day, this digitized money can be transferred from the United States to Switzerland, from there to the Grand Cayman Islands, and then to the Isle of Man. Its zigzag, instantaneous path around the globe leaves few traces for sleuths to follow. "Where's my share?" governments around the world are grumbling, as they consider how to control—and tax—this new technology.

Computers in International Conflict

Computers are also having a major impact on the international conflict. Let's look at two aspects of this significant change. First in the following Thinking Critically section, we'll look at cyber war.

THINKING CRITICALLY
Cyber War and Cyber Defense

Every country in conflict with another looks for an edge. Combining the computer's capacity to store and retrieve information with devices to monitor human activities, these same capacities can be turned into weaknesses, an Achilles heel that can bring down the powerful.

This potential of turning strength into weakness strikes fear in U.S. officials who are in charge of security and war as well as in their counterparts throughout the world (Sanger and Bumiller 2011). What if an enemy could disrupt vital communications? We could be left with a window of darkness, staring at blank screens or reading files filled with false information fed by the enemy. Military leaders would be unable to communicate with troops, while the enemy who disrupted the communications attacks. This fear pervades the military—on both sides, wherever those fluid sides line up today.

The prelude to cyber war has already begun. Thousands of attacks have been launched against the military computers of the United States, with Russia and China the suspected enemies (Sanger et al. 2009). The purpose of the attacks seems to be to find the chinks in the armor, the spots where malicious software can be installed unawares—to then be unleashed at some designated moment. Beyond the military, the targets are the nation's electrical grid, its banking system, the stock exchange, oil and gas pipelines, the air traffic control system, and Internet and cell phone communications.

Russia and China's initial cyber forays have stimulated the United States to spend billions of dollars in preparation for cyber war. We can be certain that those billions are not directed solely at defense. The United States, most assuredly, is also probing the cyber defense of its cyber enemies.

For Your Consideration
➤ Do you think that the United States should insert malicious code in Russia's and China's military and central civilian computers—just in case it needs to unleash them during some future conflict? If such a code were discovered, what do you think the consequences would be? ■

At this point these skirmishes are digital and bloodless, but this can change in the blink of an eye. Now in the Sociology and the New Technology box on the next page, let's look at a second aspect of how the microchip is changing war. By taking warfare into space, some form of Star Wars is going to become a reality.

Concerns about the Computer

Big Brother and Privacy.   Our digital society arouses deep reservations. Errors can creep into computerized records; we can be unwitting victims of phishing; cyber thieves can steal our identity. Then there is Big Brother. Increasingly, the government uses computers to monitor our lives, suspecting that we might be up to no good. Americans have been able to avoid it so far, but the Chinese authorities now issue identity cards with a chip that includes not just the individual's name and address but also education, work history, religion, ethnicity, medical insurance, police record, landlord's phone number, and—to enforce the country's "one-couple, one-child" policy—the individual's reproductive history (Bradsher 2007).

Some of us wonder if we will be next, even whether the U.S. government might outdo the Chinese in the world competition to control citizens. The Federal Drug Administration has approved an identity chip the size of a grain of rice that can be injected under the skin (Stein 2004). Designed to store a patient's medical records, the chip will also include the individual's name, address, age, weight, height, hair and skin color, and race–ethnicity. It could, of course, be programmed to include the names and addresses of our friends and associates—even any suspected acts of disloyalty. The "electronic nanny" can be activated by a scanner, so none of us would even know that we were under surveillance. It isn't difficult to jump from the capacities of this chip to Orwell's Big Brother society.

Sociology and the New Technology

The Coming Star Wars

Star Wars is on its way.

The Predator is an unmanned plane that flies thousands of feet above enemy lines. Operators at a base search the streaming video it emits, looking for targets. When they identify one, they press a button. At this signal, the Predator beams a laser onto the target and launches guided bombs. The enemy doesn't know what hit them. They see neither the Predator nor the laser. Perhaps, however, just before they are blown to bits, they do hear the sound of an incoming bomb (Barry 2001).

The Pentagon's plans to "weaponize" space go far beyond the Predator. The Pentagon has built a "space plane," the X-37B, which has an airplane's agility and a spacecraft's capacity to travel five miles per second in space (Cooper 2010). The Pentagon is also building its own Internet, the Global Information Grid (GIG), with the grandiose goal of encircling the globe to give the Pentagon a "God's eye view" of every enemy everywhere (Weiner 2004). Then they can unleash a variety of weapons: microsatellites the size of a suitcase that can pull alongside an enemy satellite and, using a microwave gun, fry its electronic system; a laser whose beam will bounce off a mirror in space, making the night battlefield visible to ground soldiers who are wearing special goggles; pyrotechnic electromagnetic pulsers; holographic decoys; oxygen suckers—and whatever else the feverish imaginations of military planners can devise.

The Air Force has nicknamed one of its space programs "Rods from God," tungsten cylinders to be hurled from space at targets on the ground. Striking at speeds of 7,000 miles an hour, the rods would have the force of a small nuclear weapon. In another program, radio waves would be directed to targets on the Earth. As the Air Force explains it, the power of the radio waves could be "just a tap on the shoulder—or they could turn you into toast" (Weiner 2005).

The Watchkeeper, a pilotless spy plane

As the United States has spent much of its national treasure on policing the world and enforcing its ideas, little nations with primitive technology have made easy targets. The Pentagon can fly the Predator over Afghanistan and Pakistan, unleashing guided bombs at will, with no fear of counter missiles being launched against the United States.

But what happens if enemy, or even rival, nations develop similar capacities—or even greater ones? We are beginning to see an ominous transition in international technological expertise. Already there is the Pterodactyl, China's answer to the Predator. To the amazement of the Pentagon, China has advanced its technology to the point that its unmanned aerial vehicles (UAVs) have begun to rival those of the United States (Page 2010; Wall 2010). China has even begun to flaunt its space weapons in the face of the Pentagon, a not-too-subtle warning not to mess with China as its leaders expand their territorial ambitions.

Weapons are made to be used—despite the constant polite rhetoric about their defensive purposes. On both sides are itchy fingers, and now that China has become an ominous threat to U.S. space superiority, the Pentagon faces a new challenge. How will it be able to contain China's political ambitions if Star Wars looms?

For Your Consideration

→ Do you think we should militarize space? What do you think of this comment, made to Congress by the head of the U.S. Air Force Space Command? "We must establish and maintain space superiority. It's the American way of fighting" (Weiner 2005). Is it rational for the United States to think that it can always maintain technological superiority? And what happens if it cannot?

Cyberspace and Social Inequality.   We've already stepped into the future. The Net gives us access to libraries of electronic information. We utilize software that sifts, sorts, and transmits text, photos, sound, and video. We zap messages and images to people on the other side of the globe—or even in our own homes, dorms, or offices. Our world has become linked by almost instantaneous communications, with information readily accessible around the globe. Few places can still be called "remote."

This new technology carries severe implications for national and global stratification. On the national level, computer technology could perpetuate present inequalities: We could end up with information have-nots, primarily inner-city residents cut off from the flow of information on which prosperity depends. Or this technology could provide an opportunity to break out of the inner city and the rural centers of poverty. On the global level, the question is similar, but on a grander scale, taking us to one of the more profound issues of this century: Will unequal access to advanced technology destine the Least Industrialized Nations to a perpetual pauper status? Or will access to this new technology be their passport to affluence?

In Sum: As technology wraps itself around us, transforming our society, our culture, and our everyday lives, we confront four primary issues: What type of future will technology lead us into? Will technology liberate us or make us slaves of Big Brother? Will the new technology perpetuate or alleviate social inequalities on both national and global levels? And finally, and perhaps most ominously, will the technology that is transforming the face of war and now being used "over there" come back to haunt us in our own land?

Social Movements as a Source of Social Change

The contradictions of social inequality that are built into arrangements of power, summarized in Figure 15.1 on page 454, create discontent. One result is **social movements,** large numbers of people who are dissatisfied about things, who organize either to promote or to resist social change. These people hold strong ideas about what is wrong with the world—or some part of it—and how to make things right. Examples include the civil rights movement, the white supremacist movement, the women's movement, the animal rights movement, and the environmental movement.

At the heart of social movements lies a sense of injustice (Klandermans 1997). Finding a particular condition of society intolerable, people join together to promote social change. Theirs is called a **proactive social movement.** Others, in contrast, feel threatened because some condition of society is changing, and they react to resist that change. Theirs is a **reactive social movement.**

To further their goals, people establish **social movement organizations.** Those who want to promote social change develop organizations such as the National Association for the Advancement of Colored People (NAACP). In contrast, those who are trying to resist these particular changes form organizations such as the Ku Klux Klan or Aryan Nations. To recruit followers and publicize their grievances, leaders of social movements use attention-getting devices, from marches and protest rallies to sit-ins and boycotts. These "media events" can be quite effective.

Social movements are like a rolling sea, observed sociologist Mayer Zald (1992). During one period, few social movements appear, but shortly afterward, a wave of them rolls in, each competing for the public's attention. Zald suggests that a *cultural crisis* can give birth to a wave of social movements. By this, he means that there are times when a society's institutions fail to keep up with social change. During these times many people's needs go unfulfilled, unrest follows, and attempting to bridge this gap, people form and become active in group campaigns.

What are social movements? What do social movements have to do with social change?

Social movements involve large numbers of people who, upset about some condition in society, organize to do something about it. An example is the "Tea Party," whose participants were upset about taxes and what they considered the leftward shift in U.S. politics.

Let's see what types of social movements there are, how they use propaganda, and the stages they go through.

Types of Social Movements

Since social change is their goal, we can classify social movements according to their *target* and the *amount of change* they seek. Look at Figure 15.2. If you read across, you will see that the first two types of social movements target *individuals*. **Alterative social movements** seek to *alter* some specific behavior. An example is the Woman's Christian Temperance Union, a powerful social movement of the early 1900s. Its goal was to get people to stop drinking alcohol. Its members were convinced that if they could shut down the saloons, such problems as poverty and wife abuse would go away. **Redemptive social movements** also target individuals, but their goal is *total* change. An example is a religious social movement that stresses conversion. In fundamentalist Christianity, for example, when someone converts to Christ, the entire person is supposed to change, not just some specific behavior. Self-centered acts are to be replaced by loving behaviors toward others as the convert becomes, in their terms, a "new creation."

The next two types of social movements target *society*. (See cells 3 and 4 of Figure 15.2.) **Reformative social movements** seek to *reform* some specific aspect of society. The animal rights movement, for example, wants to reform the ways in which society views and treats animals. **Transformative social movements,** in contrast, seek to *transform* the social order itself. Its members want to replace the social order with their vision of the good society. Revolutions, such as those in the American colonies, China, Cuba, France, and Russia, are examples.

FIGURE 15.2   **Types of Social Movements**

Amount of Change

Target of Change	Partial	Total
Individual	1 Alterative	2 Redemptive
Society	3 Reformative	4 Transformative
Global	5 Transnational	6 Metaformative

Sources: The first four types are from Aberle 1966; the last two are by the author.

What are the types of social movements? Can you explain Figure 15.2?

As Figure 15.2 indicates, some social movements have a global orientation. In our new global economy, numerous issues that concern people transcend national boundaries. Participants of **transnational social movements** (also called *new social movements*) want to change some specific condition that cuts across societies. (See cell 5 of Figure 15.2.) These social movements, which often center on improving the quality of life, are amazingly diverse, from the women's and the environmental movements to the virginity pledge and home birth movements (Walter 2001; Tilly 2004; Haenfler et al. 2012).

Cell 6 in Figure 15.2 represents a rare type of social movement. The goal of **metaformative social movements** is to change the social order itself—not just of a specific country, but of an entire civilization, or even the whole world. Their objective is to change ideas and practices of race–ethnicity, class, gender, family, religion, government, and the global stratification of nations. These were the aims of the communist social movement of the early to middle twentieth century and the fascist social movement of the 1920s to 1940s. (The fascists consisted of the Nazis in Germany, the Black Shirts of Italy, and other groups throughout Europe and the United States.)

Today, we are witnessing another metaformative social movement, that of Islamic fundamentalism. Like other social movements before it, this movement is not united, but consists of many separate groups with differing goals and tactics. Al-Qaeda, for example, would not only cleanse Islamic societies of Western influences—which they contend are demonic and degrading to men, women, and morality—but also replace Western civilization with an extremist form of Islam. This frightens both Muslims and non-Muslims, who hold sharply differing views of what constitutes quality of life. If the Islamic fundamentalists—like the communists or fascists before them—have their way, they will usher in a New World Order fashioned after their particular views of the good life.

Propaganda and the Mass Media

The leaders of social movements try to manipulate the mass media to influence **public opinion,** how people think about some issue. The right kind of publicity enables the leaders to arouse sympathy and to lay the groundwork for recruiting more members. Pictures of bloody baby seals and pitiful, cowering, abused dogs, for example, are used for this purpose by animal rights groups.

A key to understanding social movements, then, is **propaganda.** Although this word often evokes negative images, it actually is a neutral term. Propaganda is simply the presentation of information in an attempt to influence people. Its original meaning was positive. *Propaganda* referred to the name of a committee of Roman Catholic cardinals whose assignment was the care of foreign missions. (They were to *propagate*—multiply or spread—the faith.) The term has traveled a long way since then, however, and today it usually refers to one-sided information designed to distort reality.

Propaganda, in the sense of organized attempts to influence public opinion, is a part of everyday life. Our news is filled with propaganda, as various interest groups—from retailers to the government—try to manipulate our perceptions and behavior. Our movies, too, although seemingly intended simply as entertainment devices, are actually propaganda vehicles. The basic techniques that underlie propaganda are discussed in the Down-to-Earth Sociology box on the next page.

Some social movements arise quickly, recruit vast numbers of people over some specific issue, and then disappear. Shown here are hundreds of thousands of Belgians protesting their lack of government.

What is propaganda? Why is advertising propaganda? Why are movies?

Down-to-Earth Sociology

"Tricks of the Trade"—Deception and Persuasion in Propaganda

Sociologists Alfred and Elizabeth Lee (1939) found that propaganda relies on seven basic techniques, which they termed "tricks of the trade." To be effective, the techniques should be subtle, with the audience unaware that their minds and emotions are being manipulated. If propaganda is effective, people will not know why they support something, but they'll fervently defend it. Becoming familiar with these techniques can help you keep your mind and emotions from being manipulated.

Name calling. This technique aims to arouse opposition to the competing product, candidate, or policy by associating it with negative images. By comparison, one's own product, candidate, or policy is attractive. Republicans who call Democrats "soft on crime" and Democrats who call Republicans "insensitive to the poor" are using this technique.

Glittering generality. Essentially the opposite of the first technique, this one surrounds the product, candidate, or policy with images that arouse positive feelings. "She's a real Democrat" has little meaning, but people feel that something substantive has been said. "This Republican stands for individual rights" is so general that it is meaningless, yet the audience thinks that it has heard a specific message about the candidate.

Transfer. In its positive form, this technique associates the product, candidate, or policy with something the public approves of or respects. You might not be able to get by with saying, "Coors is patriotic," but surround a beer with images of the country's flag, and beer drinkers will get the idea that it is more patriotic to drink this brand of beer than some other kind. In its negative form, this technique associates the product, candidate, or policy with something generally disapproved of by the public.

Testimonials. Famous individuals endorse a product, candidate, or policy. David Beckham lends his name to Gillette, and Beyoncé tells you that L'Oréal is a great line of cosmetics. In the negative form of this

You probably know immediately why the photo on the left is propaganda, but do you know why the photo on the right is propaganda?

technique, a despised person is associated with the competing product. If propagandists (called "spin doctors" in politics) could have gotten away with it, they would have shown the president of the Islamic Republic of Iran announcing support for a candidate they oppose.

Plain folks. Sometimes it pays to associate the product, candidate, or policy with "just plain folks." "If Mary or John Q. Public likes it, you will, too." A political candidate who kisses babies, puts on a hard hat, and has lunch at McDonald's while photographers "catch him (or her) in the act" is using the "plain folks" strategy. "I'm just a regular person" is the message of the presidential candidate who poses for photographers in jeans and work shirt—while making certain that the chauffeur and Mercedes do not show up in the photo.

Card stacking. The aim of this technique is to present only positive information about what you support, and only negative information about what you oppose. The intent is to make it sound as though there is only one conclusion a rational person can draw. Falsehoods, distortions, and illogical statements are often used.

Bandwagon. "Everyone is doing it" is the idea behind this technique. Emphasizing how many other people buy the product or support the candidate or policy conveys the message that anyone who doesn't join in is on the wrong track.

The Lees (1939) added, "Once we know that a speaker or writer is using one of these propaganda devices in an attempt to convince us of an idea, we can separate the device from the idea and see what the idea amounts to on its own merits."

For Your Consideration

→ What propaganda techniques have you seen or heard recently? Recall not just product ads but also TV programs, political ads, movies, and newspaper articles. Explain why they were propaganda, not simply a source of information or entertainment.

Gatekeepers to Social Movements. The mass media play such a crucial role that we can say they are *the gatekeepers to social movements.* If those who control and work in the mass media—from owners to reporters—are sympathetic to some particular "cause," you can be sure that it will be given positive treatment. A social movement that goes against their views, however, will likely be ignored or receive unfavorable comment. If you ever get the impression that the media are trying to manipulate your opinions and attitudes—even your feelings—on some particular issue or social movement, you probably are right. Far from providing unbiased reporting, the media are under the control and influence of people who have an agenda. To the materials in the Down-to-Earth Sociology box on propaganda, then, we need to add the biases of the media establishment—the topics it chooses to publicize, those it decides to ignore, and its favorable and unfavorable treatment of issues and movements.

Multiple Realities and Social Movements

Sociology can be a liberating discipline (Berger 1963/2012). Sociology sensitizes us to *multiple realities;* that is, for any single opinion on some topic, there are competing points of view. Each represents reality as people see it, their distinctive experiences leading them to different perceptions. Consequently, different people find opposing points of view equally compelling. Although the committed members of a social movement are sincere—and perhaps even make sacrifices for "the cause"—theirs is but one view of the world. If other sides were presented, the issue would look quite different.

The Stages of Social Movements

Sociologists have identified five stages in social movements (Lang and Lang 1961; Mauss 1975; Spector and Kitsuse 1977; Jasper 1991; Tilly 2004):

1. *Initial unrest and agitation.* During this first stage, people are upset about some condition in society and want to change it. Leaders emerge who verbalize people's feelings and crystallize issues. Most social movements fail at this stage. Unable to gain enough support, after a brief flurry of activity, they fade away.
2. *Resource mobilization.* A crucial factor that enables social movements to make it past the first stage is **resource mobilization.** By this term, sociologists mean organizing and using resources—time, money, information, mailing lists, and people's skills, even their emotions (McVeigh 2009; Jasper 2012). It also includes communications

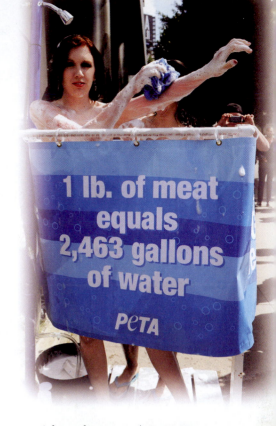

A form of propaganda is staging publicity-generating stunts to promote support for a "cause" or organization. Leaders of PETA (People for the Ethical Treatment of Animals) often choose this tactic.

To continue vigorously, a social movement needs a constant source of ideologically committed members. Shown here are such people, Minutemen volunteers who are patrolling the Arizona border with Mexico.

Why are the mass medial called gatekeepers to social movements? What do multiple realities have to do with social movements?

Watch
Crips and Bloods: Made in America
on **mysoclab.com**

technology such as cell phones, Internet sites, blogs, and tweets—and getting the attention of the mass media. For the civil rights movement, these resources included access to churches to organize protests (Mirola 2003).

In some groups, the leaders mobilize these resources from their members. Lacking capable leadership, other groups turn to "guns for hire," outside specialists who sell their services. As sociologists John McCarthy and Mayer Zald (1977; Zald and McCarthy 1987) point out, even though large numbers of people may be upset over some condition of society, without resource mobilization they are only upset people, perhaps even agitators, but they do not constitute a social movement.

3. *Organization*. A division of labor is set up. The leaders make policy decisions, and the rank and file perform the daily tasks that keep the movement going. There is still much collective excitement about the issue, the movement's focal point of concern.

4. *Institutionalization*. At this stage, the movement has developed a bureaucracy, the type of formal hierarchy described in Chapter 5. Control now lies in the hands of career officers, who may care more about their own positions in the organization than the movement for which the organization's initial leaders made sacrifices. Not much collective excitement remains.

5. *Decline and death*. During this phase, managing the day-to-day affairs of the organization dominates the leadership. Sentiment may have even shifted so greatly that there no longer is a group of committed people who share a common cause. The movement withers away, although a small staff can remain for years until the last of the funds are drained.

Resurgence

The final stage of decline and death can be postponed for decades, perhaps even for generations, as events breathe new life into a social movement and committed, fresh blood replaces faltering leaders. The outstanding example is the abortion movement, whose prochoice and prolife sides continue to energize one another. Let's look at this social movement.

THINKING CRITICALLY

Which Side of the Barricades? Prochoice and Prolife as a Social Movement

No issue so divides Americans as abortion. Despite moderate views among the majority of the population, some Americans firmly believe that abortion should be permitted at all times, even during the last month of pregnancy. They are matched by individuals on the other side who are convinced that abortion should never be allowed under any circumstance, not even in the case of rape or incest or during the first month of pregnancy. This polarization constantly breathes new life into the movement.

When the U.S. Supreme Court made its 1973 decision, *Roe v. Wade,* that states could not prohibit abortion, the prochoice side relaxed. Victory was theirs, and they thought their opponents would quietly fade away. Instead, large numbers of Americans were disturbed by what they saw as the legal right to murder unborn children.

The views of the two sides could not be more incompatible. Those who favor choice view the 1.2 million abortions that are performed annually in the United States as examples of women exercising their basic reproductive rights. Those who gather under the prolife banner see these abortions as legalized murder. To the prochoice side, those who oppose abortion are blocking women's rights—they would force women to continue pregnancies they want to terminate. To the prolife side, those who advocate choice are perceived as condoning murder—they would sacrifice their unborn children for the sake of school, career, or convenience.

There is no way to reconcile these contrary views. Each sees the other as unreasonable and extremist. And each uses propaganda by focusing on worst-case scenarios: prochoice images of young women ravished at gunpoint, forced to bear the children of rapists; prolife images of women who are nine months pregnant killing their babies instead of nurturing them.

With no middle ground, these views remain in perpetual conflict. As each side fights for what it considers to be basic rights, it reinvigorates the other. When in 1989 the U.S. Supreme Court decided in *Webster v. Reproductive Services* that states could restrict abortion, one side mourned it as a defeat and the other hailed it as a victory. Seeing the political battle going against them, the prochoice side regrouped for a bitter struggle. The prolife side, sensing judicial victory within its grasp, gathered forces for a push to complete the overthrow of *Roe v. Wade*.

In 1992, this goal of the prolife side almost became reality in *Casey v. Planned Parenthood*. In a 6–3 decision, the Supreme Court upheld the right of states to make women wait twenty-four hours between confirming their pregnancy and getting an abortion, to require girls under 18 to obtain the consent of one parent, and to specify that women be given materials describing the fetus as well as information about alternatives to abortion. In the same case, however, by a 5–4 decision, the Court ruled that a wife does not have to inform her husband if she intends to have an abortion. In 2007, in another 5–4 decision, the Court ruled a certain type of abortion procedure illegal. The names given this late-term procedure represent the ongoing struggle: One side calls it an "intact dilation and evacuation," while the other side terms it a "partial-birth abortion."

The struggle of the opposing sides is usually a quiet affair, but it makes headlines each time the Senate is asked to confirm a president's nominee to the U.S. Supreme Court. To watch these hearings is to view, in miniature, irreconcilable views of reality. This social movement also makes headlines when opposing sides confront one another in street drama, each wielding signs in the attempt to capture the attention of the mass media. There is also the rare, but more powerfully headline-grabbing assassination of doctors who perform abortions. National attention was focused briefly on Wichita, Kansas, for example, when George Tiller, who specialized in late-term abortions, was shot to death at his church, a murder disavowed by prolife organizations.

With emotions raw and convictions firm, this social movement cannot end unless an overwhelming majority of Americans commit to one side or the other. Short of this, every legislative and judicial outcome—including the extremes of a constitutional amendment that declares abortion to be either murder or a woman's right—is a victory to one and a defeat to the other. To committed activists, no battle is ever complete. Rather, each action is only one small part of a long, hard-fought, moral struggle.

Sources: Williams 1995; Douthat 2008; Forsyth 2011; *Statistical Abstract of the United States* 2012:Table 101.

With sincere people on both sides of the issue—equally committed and equally convinced that their side is right—abortion is destined to remain a controversial force in U.S. life.

For Your Consideration

➤ The last stage of a social movement is decline and death. Why hasn't this social movement died? Under what conditions do you think it will decline and die?

➤ The longer the duration of a pregnancy, the fewer the Americans who approve of abortion. How do you feel about abortion during the third month versus the seventh month? The first month versus the ninth month? What do you think about abortion in cases of rape and incest? Can you identify some of the social reasons that underlie your opinions? ■

Sumatran Tiger
Fewer than 400, Indonesia

Texas Ocelot
Fewer than 250, southern United States, northern Mexico

Mountain Bongo
About 50, Kenya

Gaur
About 36,000, Southeast Asia

Rising sea levels? No problem for the Lilypad, floating self-contained cities of 50,000 inhabitants envisioned for the future.

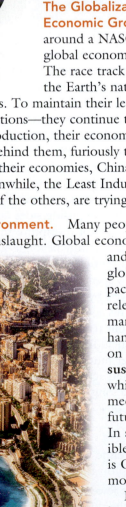

The Growth Machine versus the Earth

After a frustrating struggle of twenty years, Russian environmentalists finally won a court order to stop Baikalsk Paper Mill from dumping its wastes into Lake Baikal. When the mill filed for bankruptcy, Vladimir Putin, the prime minister of Russia, boarded a minisub and said, "I'll see if the lake has been damaged." At the bottom of Lake Baikal, Putin said, "It's clean. I can see the bottom." He then told Oleg Deripaska, the major owner of the paper mill, "You can dump your wastes in the lake." (Boudreaux 2010)

Politicians are usually more subtle than this, but befitting his power and position, Putin doesn't have to be. He can crown himself an environmental expert and give personal permission to pollute. Although the specifics differ, in country after country similar battles are being waged. While environmentalists struggle for a clean Earth, politicians fight for jobs and votes—and while doing so, line the pockets of their friends, and their own as well.

The Globalization of Capitalism and the Race for Economic Growth.   Like drivers and cars spinning around a NASCAR race track, we are in the midst of a global economic race that threatens to destroy the Earth. The race track is the Earth, and the cars and drivers are the Earth's nations. At the head of the pack are the Most Industrialized Nations. To maintain their lead—and cheered on by their sponsors, the multinational corporations—they continue to push for economic growth. Without an annual increase in production, their economic engines falter, sputtering into recession or depression. Behind them, furiously trying to catch up, are the Industrializing Nations. To develop their economies, China and the others strive for even larger percentage growth. Meanwhile, the Least Industrialized Nations, lagging even farther behind and envious of the others, are trying their best to rev up their economic engines.

A Sustainable Environment.   Many people are convinced that the Earth cannot withstand such an onslaught. Global economic production creates global pollution, and faster-paced production, which feeds the globalization of capitalism, means a faster-paced destruction of our environment. In this relentless pursuit of economic development, many animal species are gone forever. Others, hanging by a claw or a wounded wing, are on the verge of extinction. If the goal is a **sustainable environment,** a world system in which we use our physical environment to meet our needs without destroying humanity's future, we cannot continue to trash the Earth. In short, the ecological message is incompatible with an economic message that implies it is OK to rape the earth if it makes someone money.

Before looking at the social movement that has emerged about this issue, let's examine some major environmental problems.

What does "the growth machine versus the earth" mean?

Environmental Problems and Industrialization

Although even tribal groups produced pollution, the frontal assault on the natural environment did not begin in earnest until nations industrialized. Industrialization was equated with progress and prosperity. For the Most Industrialized Nations, the slogan has been "Growth at any cost."

Toxic Wastes.   Industrial growth did come, but at a high cost. Despite their harm to the environment and the dangers they pose to people's health, much toxic waste has simply been dumped onto the land, into the oceans, and with the occasional permission of Putin and other politicians, into our lakes. Formerly pristine streams have been turned into putrid sewers. The disease-ridden water supply of some cities is unfit to drink. The Social Map below shows the locations of the worst hazardous waste sites in the United States. Keep in mind that these are just the worst. There are thousands of others.

Nuclear power plants are a special problem. They produce wastes that remain lethal for thousands of years. We simply don't know what to do with these piles of deadly garbage. In addition, these nuclear factories, supposedly built with redundant safety features, are vulnerable in unexpected ways. Certainly the nuclear catastrophe at Fukushima, Japan, which continues to spew radiation, is mute testimony to nuclear folly.

We certainly can't lay the cause of our polluted Earth solely at the feet of the Most Industrialized Nations. The Industrializing Nations also do their share, with China the most striking example. This country now emits more carbon dioxide than does the United States (Rogers and Evans 2011). Of the world's forty most polluted cities, *thirty-six* are in China (World Bank 2007:Figure 5). *Nine thousand* chemical plants line the banks of China's Yangtze River, turning this major waterway into a long industrial sewer (Zakaria 2008). Like the Russians before them, authorities imprison any Chinese who dare to speak out about pollution (Larson 2011; Wong 2011). As China secures its place in the industrialized world, its leaders will inevitably place

FIGURE 15.3   The Worst Hazardous Waste Sites

Source: By the author. Based on *Statistical Abstract of the United States* 2012:Table 384.

What are some environmental problems of the Most Industrialized Nations? Of the Least Industrialized Nations?

more emphasis on controlling pollution. However, the harm done to our planet in the meantime is incalculable.

With limited space to address this issue, let's focus on fossil fuels, the energy shortage, and the rain forests.

 **Watch**
Living Data
on **mysoclab.com**

Fossil Fuels and Global Warming.   Burning fossil fuels to run motorized vehicles, factories, and power plants has been especially harmful to our Earth. Figure 15.4 illustrates how burning fossil fuels produces acid rain, which kills animal and plant life. The situation is so bad that fish can no longer survive in some lakes in Canada and the northeastern United States.

But does burning fossil fuels cause **global warming?** This question has plagued climate scientists for decades. They all are aware, as I am sure you are, that the glaciers are melting. If this continues, the seas will rise and the world's shorelines will be flooded. Some island nations will even be washed into the ocean ("Threatened Island Nations . . ." 2011).

Some scientists claim that burning fossil fuels has little or nothing to do with such events. They point out that the Earth always goes through natural cycles of warming and cooling. This one, they say, is just another in that endless cycle. This issue seemed

FIGURE 15.4   **Acid Rain**

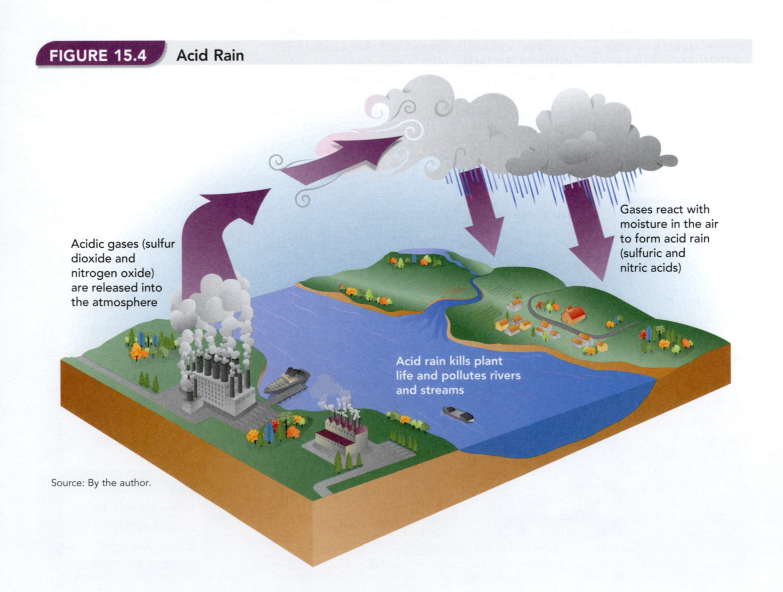

Acidic gases (sulfur dioxide and nitrogen oxide) are released into the atmosphere

Gases react with moisture in the air to form acid rain (sulfuric and nitric acids)

Acid rain kills plant life and pollutes rivers and streams

Source: By the author.

What are possible consequences of global warming?

closed when climate scientists concluded that human activity was the main driver of global warming (Rosenthal and Revkin 2007). But then climate science was rocked to its core when someone hacked into the emails of a major scientist who had been claiming that catastrophe was on its way unless we reduce carbon emissions immediately. The emails seemed to reveal that some scientists had been distorting and withholding data to fit their ideas. An investigation followed, with the conclusion that the scientists had been rude but did not distort data (Adam 2010).

The Energy Shortage and Internal Combustion Engines.   If you ever read about an energy shortage, you can be sure that what you read is false. There is no energy shortage, nor can there ever be. We can produce unlimited low-cost power, which can help to raise the living standards of humans across the globe. The sun, for example, produces more energy than humanity could ever use. Boundless energy is also available from the tides and the winds. In some cases, we need better technology to harness these sources of energy; in others, we need only to apply the technology we already have.

Burning fossil fuels in internal combustion engines is the main source of pollution in the Most Industrialized Nations. Car and truck engines that burn natural gas, a cleaner and lower-priced fossil fuel, will likely become common. Of the technologies being developed to use alternative sources of energy in vehicles, the most prominent is the gas-electric hybrid. Some of these cars are expected to eventually get several hundred miles per gallon of gasoline. The hybrid, however, is simply a bridge until vehicles powered by fuel cells become practical. With fuel cells converting hydrogen into electricity, it will be water, not carbon monoxide, coming out of a car's exhaust pipe.

The Rain Forests.   Of special concern are the world's rain forests. Although they cover just 6 percent of the Earth's land area, the rain forests are home to *one-half* of all the Earth's plant and animal species (Frommer 2007). Despite knowing their essential role for humanity's welfare, we seem bent on destroying rain forests for the sake of timber and farms. In the process, we extinguish plant and animal species, perhaps thousands a year. As biologists remind us, once a species is lost, it is gone forever.

As the rain forests disappear, so do the Indian tribes who live in them. With their extinction goes their knowledge of the environment, the topic of the Cultural Diversity box on the next page. Like Esau who traded his birthright for a bowl of porridge, we are exchanging our future for lumber, farms, and pastures.

The Environmental Movement

Concern about environmental problems has touched such a nerve that it has produced a worldwide social movement. In Europe, *green parties,* political groups whose central concern is the environment, have become a force for change. Germany's green party, for example, has won seats in the national legislature. In the United States, in contrast, green parties have had little success.

One concern of the environmental movement in the United States is **environmental injustice,** minorities and the poor being the ones who suffer the most from the effects of pollution (Lerner 2010). Industries locate where land is cheaper, which, as you know, is *not* where the wealthy live. Nor will the rich allow factories to spew pollution near their homes. As a result, pollution is more common in low-income communities. Sociologists have studied, formed, and joined *environmental justice* groups that fight to close polluting plants and block construction of polluting industries. Like the defeat at Lake Baikal that I just mentioned, this often pits environmentalists against politicians and the wealthy.

Like the members of last century's civil rights movement, environmentalists are certain that they stand for what is right and just. Most activists seek quiet solutions in politics, education, and legislation. Others, in contrast, despairing that

Why can the Earth never run out of energy? What, then, is an "energy shortage"?

Cultural Diversity **around the World**

The Rain Forests: Lost Tribes, Lost Knowledge

In the past hundred years, 90 of Brazil's 270 Indian tribes have disappeared. Other tribes have moved to villages as ranchers and gold miners have taken over their lands. Tribal knowledge is lost as a tribe's members adapt to village life.

Contrary to some stereotypes, tribal groups are not ignorant people who barely survive. On the contrary, these groups have developed intricate forms of social organization and possess knowledge that has accumulated over thousands of years. The Kayapo Indians, for example, who belong to one of the Amazon's endangered tribes, use 250 types of wild fruit and hundreds of nut and tuber species. They cultivate thirteen types of bananas, eleven kinds of manioc (cassava), sixteen strains of sweet potato, and seventeen kinds of yams. Some of these varieties are unknown to non-Indians. The Kayapo also use thousands of medicinal plants, one of which contains a drug that is effective against intestinal parasites.

Until recently, Western scientists dismissed tribal knowledge as superstitious and worthless. Now, however, some have come to realize that to lose tribes is to lose valuable knowledge.

In the Central African Republic, a man whose chest was being eaten away by an amoeboid infection lay dying because the microbes did not respond to drugs. Out of desperation, the Roman Catholic nuns who were treating him sought the advice of a native doctor. He applied crushed termites to the open wounds. To the amazement of the nuns, the man made a remarkable recovery.

I don't mean to imply that these tribes have medicine superior to ours, just that we can learn from their experience with nature. The disappearance of the rain forests means the destruction of plant species that may have healing properties. Some of the discoveries from the rain forests have been astounding. The needles from a Himalayan tree in India contain taxol, a drug that is effective against ovarian and breast

A Pishta girl of the Yine tribe in the Peruvian Amazon. The way of life of the world's few remaining rain forest tribes is threatened.

cancer. A flower from Madagascar is used in the treatment of leukemia. A frog in Peru produces a painkiller that is more powerful, but less addictive, than morphine (Wolfensohn and Fuller 1998).

On average, one tribe of Amazonian Indians has been lost each year for the past century—because of violence, greed for their lands, and exposure to infectious diseases against which these people have little resistance. Ethnocentrism underlies much of this assault. Perhaps the extreme is represented by the cattle ranchers in Colombia who killed eighteen Cueva Indians. The cattle ranchers were perplexed when they were put on trial for murder. They asked why they should be charged with a crime, since everyone knew that the Cuevas were animals, not people. They pointed out that there was even a verb in Colombian Spanish, *cuevar*, which means "to hunt Cueva Indians." So what was their crime, they asked? The jury found them not guilty because of "cultural ignorance."

Sources: Durning 1990; Gorman 1991; Linden 1991; Stipp 1992; Nabhan 1998; Simons 2006; "Last Remaining Amazon Tribes . . ." 2011.

For Your Consideration

→ What do you think we can do to stop the destruction of the rain forests?

pollution continues, that the rain forests are still being cleared, and that species continue to become extinct, are convinced that the planet is doomed unless we take immediate action. This conviction motivates some to choose a more radical course, to use extreme tactics to try to arouse indignation among the public and to force the government to act. Such activists are featured in the following Thinking Critically section.

What is happening to the rain forests? To the tribes living in them? What difference does it make?

THINKING CRITICALLY
Ecosabotage

Chaining oneself to a giant Douglas fir that is slated for cutting, tearing down power lines and ripping up survey stakes, driving spikes into redwood trees, sinking whaling vessels, and torching SUVs and Hummers—are these the acts of dangerous punks who have little understanding of the needs of modern society? Or are they the efforts of brave men and women who are willing to put their freedom, and even their lives, on the line on behalf of the Earth itself?

To understand why **ecosabotage**—actions taken to sabotage the efforts of people who are thought to be legally harming the environment—is taking place, consider the Medicine Tree, a 3,000-year-old redwood in the Sally Bell Grove near the northern California coast. Georgia Pacific, a lumber company, was determined to cut down the Medicine Tree, the oldest and largest of the region's redwoods, which rests on a sacred site of the Sinkyone Indians. Members of Earth First! chained themselves to the tree. After they were arrested, the sawing began. Other protesters jumped over the police-lined barricade and stood defiantly in the path of men wielding axes and chain saws. A logger swung an axe and barely missed a demonstrator. At that moment, the sheriff radioed a restraining order, and the cutting stopped.

Julia "Butterfly" Hill lived for two years in this 1,000-year-old redwood tree, which she named Luna. The Pacific Lumber Company finally agreed to save the tree and a 200-foot buffer zone.

How many 3,000-year-old trees remain on our planet? Does our desire for fences and picnic tables for backyard barbecues justify cutting them down? Issues like these—as well as the slaughter of seals and whales, the destruction of the rain forests, and the drowning of dolphins in mile-long drift nets—spawned Earth First! and other organizations devoted to preserving the environment, such as Greenpeace, the Rainforest Action Network, the Ruckus Society, and the Sea Shepherds.

"We feel like there are insane people who are consciously destroying our environment, and we are compelled to fight back," explains a member of one of the militant groups. "No compromise in defense of Mother Earth!" says another. "With famine and death approaching, we're in the early stages of World War III," adds another.

Radical environmentalists represent a broad range of activities and purposes. They are united neither on tactics nor on goals. Most envision a simpler lifestyle that will consume less energy and reduce pressure on the Earth's resources. Some try to stop specific activities, such as the killing of whales. The goal of others is to destroy all nuclear weapons and dismantle nuclear power plants. Some would like to see everyone become vegetarians. Still others want the Earth's population to drop to one billion, roughly what it was in 1800. Some even want humans to return to hunting and gathering societies. These groups are so splintered that Dave Foreman—the founder of Earth First!—quit his own organization when it became too confrontational for his taste.

Radical groups have had some successes. They have brought a halt to the killing of dolphins off Japan's Iki Island, achieved a ban on whaling, established trash

Read
Sixteen Impacts of Population Growth
by Brown, Gardner, and Halweil
on **mysoclab.com**

What is ecosabotage? What is radical environmentalism?

recycling programs, and saved hundreds of thousands of acres of trees, including, of course, the Medicine Tree.

Sources: Carpenter 1990; Eder 1990; Foote 1990; Parfit 1990; Reed and Benet 1990; Knickerbocker 2003; Gunther 2004; Fattig 2007; Grigoriadis 2011.

For Your Consideration

➔ Should we applaud ecosaboteurs or jail them? As symbolic interactionists stress, it all depends on how you view their actions. And as conflict theorists emphasize, your view likely depends on your social location. That is, if you own a lumber company, you will see ecosaboteurs differently than a camping enthusiast will. How does your own view of ecosaboteurs depend on your life situation? What effective alternatives to ecosabotage are there for people who are convinced that we are destroying the very life support system of our planet? ■

Environmental Sociology

A specialization within sociology, **environmental sociology** focuses on the relationship between human societies and the environment (Dunlap and Catton 1979, 1983; Bell 2009). Environmental sociology is built around these key ideas:

1. The physical environment should be a significant variable in sociological investigation.
2. Human beings are but one species among many that depend on the natural environment.
3. Human actions have unintended consequences, many of which have an impact on nature.
4. The world is finite, so there are physical limits to economic growth.
5. Economic expansion requires increased extraction of resources from the environment.
6. Increased extraction of resources leads to ecological problems.
7. These ecological problems place limits on economic expansion.
8. Governments create environmental problems by encouraging the accumulation of capital.
9. For the welfare of humanity, environmental problems must be solved.

Pollution in the Industrializing Nations has become a major problem. Shown here is a boy in Jakarta, Indonesia, scavenging paper cups from a polluted river.

The goal of environmental sociology is not to stop pollution or nuclear power but, rather, to study how humans (their cultures, values, and behavior) affect the physical environment and how the physical environment affects human activities. Not surprisingly, environmental sociology attracts environmental activists, and the Section on Environment and Technology of the American Sociological Association tries to influence governmental policies (American Sociological Association n.d.).

Technology and the Environment: The Goal of Harmony. It is inevitable that humans will continue to develop new technologies. But the abuse of our environment by those technologies is not inevitable. To understate the matter, the destruction of our planet is an unwise choice. If we are to live in a world that is worth passing on to coming generations, we must seek harmony between technology and the natural environment. This will not be easy. At one extreme are people who claim that to protect the environment we must eliminate industrialization and go back to a tribal way of life. At the other extreme

are people who are blind to the harm being done to the natural environment, who want the entire world to industrialize at full speed. Somewhere, there must be a middle ground, one that recognizes not only that industrialization is here to stay but also that we *can* control it, for it is our creation. Controlled, industrialization can enhance our quality of life; uncontrolled, it will destroy us.

It is essential, then, that we develop ways to reduce or eliminate the harm that technology does to the environment. This includes mechanisms to monitor the production and use of technology and the disposal of its wastes. The question, of course, is whether we have the resolve to take the steps necessary to preserve the environment for future generations. What is at stake is nothing less than the welfare of planet Earth. Surely this should be enough to motivate us to make wise choices.

The social movement that centers on the environment has become global. In all nations, people are concerned about the destruction of the earth's resources. This photo is a sign of changing times. Instead of jumping on this beached whale and carving it into pieces, these Brazilians are doing their best to save its life.

15 Summary and Review

How Social Change Transforms Social Life

What major trends have transformed the course of human history?

The primary changes in human history are the four social revolutions (domestication, agriculture, industrialization, and information); the change from *Gemeinschaft* to *Gesellschaft* societies; capitalism and industrialization; and global stratification. Social movements indicate cutting edges of social change. Ethnic conflicts and power rivalries threaten the global divisions that the Most Industrialized Nations have worked out. We may also be on the cutting edge of a new biotech society. Pp. 450–453.

What does "harmony of technology and the environment" mean? Is it possible to reach this goal?

Theories and Processes of Social Change

Besides technology, capitalism, industrialization, and so on, what are other theories of social change?

Evolutionary theories hold that societies move from the same starting point to some similar ending point. *Unilinear* theories assume the same evolutionary path for every society, while *multilinear* theories assume that different paths lead to the same stage of development. *Cyclical* theories view civilizations as going through a process of birth, youth, maturity, decline, and death. Conflict theorists see social change as inevitable, for each *thesis* (basically an arrangement of power) contains *antitheses* (contradictions). A new *synthesis* develops to resolve these contradictions, but it, too, contains contradictions that must be resolved, and so on. This is called a **dialectical process.** Pp. 453–454.

What is Ogburn's theory of social change?

William Ogburn identified technology as the basic cause of social change, which comes through three processes: **invention, discovery,** and **diffusion.** The term **cultural lag** refers to how symbolic culture lags behind changes in technology. Pp. 454–456.

How Technology Is Changing Our Lives

How does new technology affect society?

Because technology is an organizing force of social life, changes in technology can have profound effects. The computer was used as an extended example. The computer is changing the way we learn, work, do business, and fight wars. We don't yet know whether information technologies will help to perpetuate or to reduce social inequalities on both a national and a global level. Pp. 456–461.

Social Movements as a Source of Social Change

What types of social movements are there?

Social movements consist of large numbers of people who organize to promote or resist social change. Depending on their target (individuals or society) and the amount of social change that is desired (partial or complete), social movements can be classified as **alterative, redemptive, reformative, transformative, transnational,** and **metaformative.** Pp. 461–463.

How are the mass media related to social movements?

The mass media are gatekeepers for social movements. Because the media's favorable or unfavorable coverage affects **public opinion,** leaders choose tactics with the media in mind. Leaders also use **propaganda** to further their causes. Pp. 463–465.

What stages do social movements go through?

Sociologists have identified five stages of social movements: initial unrest and agitation, mobilization, organization, institutionalization, and decline and death. Resurgence of a declining social movement is possible. In the social movement around abortion, opposing sides revitalize one another. Pp. 465–467.

The Growth Machine versus the Earth

What are some pressing environmental problems and their cause?

Humans have always polluted, but pollution began in earnest with industrialization, which lies at the root of our environmental problems. These problems range from acid rain to **global warming** and the destruction of the rain forests. Burning fossil fuels in internal combustion engines is especially destructive. The location of factories and hazardous waste sites creates **environmental injustice,** environmental problems having a greater impact on minorities and the poor. Pp. 468–469.

Are environmental problems limited to the Most Industrialized Nations?

The rush of nations to industrialize is adding to the planet's environmental decay. The pollution in China, an Industrializing Nation, is so severe that China now emits more carbon dioxide than the United States does. Environmental activists in China are arrested and imprisoned. The world is facing a basic conflict between the lust for profits through the exploitation of the Earth's resources and the need to establish a **sustainable environment.** Pp. 469–471.

What is the environmental movement?

The environmental movement is an attempt to restore a healthy environment for the world's people. This global social movement takes many forms, from peaceful attempts to influence the political process to **ecosabotage.** Pp. 471–474.

What is environmental sociology?

Environmental sociology is not an attempt to change the environment, but, rather, a study of the relationship between humans and the environment. Environmental sociologists are generally also environmental activists. Pp. 474–475.

Thinking Critically about Chapter 15

1. How has social change affected your life? Be specific—what changes, how? Does Ogburn's theory help to explain your experiences? Why or why not?

2. Pick a social movement and analyze it according to the sociological principles and findings reviewed in this chapter.

3. Do you think that a sustainable environment should be a goal of the world's societies? Why or why not? If so, what practical steps do you think we can take to produce a sustainable environment?

As you explored social life in this text, I hope that you found yourself thinking along with me. If so, you should have gained a greater understanding of why people think, feel, and act as they do—as well as insights into why *you* view life the way you do. I sincerely hope that this book has helped you develop a sociological imagination. I really want to make sociology come alive for you.

Majoring in Sociology

If you feel a passion for peering beneath the surface—for seeking out the social influences in people's lives, and for seeing these influences in your own life—I encourage you to major in sociology. As you take more courses in sociology, you will continue this enlightening process of social discovery. Your sociological perspective will grow, and you will become increasingly aware of how social factors underlie human behavior.

In addition to people who have a strong desire to continue this fascinating process of social discovery, there is a second type of person whom I also urge to major in sociology. Let's suppose that you have a strong, almost unbridled sense of wanting to explore many aspects of life. Let's also assume that because you have so many interests, you can't make up your mind about what you want to do with your life. You can think of so many things you'd like to try, but for each one there are other possibilities that you find equally as compelling. Let me share what one student wrote me:

I'd love to say what my current major is—if only I truly knew. I know that the major you choose to study in college isn't necessarily the field of work you'll be going into. I've heard enough stories of grads who get jobs in fields that are not even related to their majors to believe it to a certain extent. My only problem is that I'm not even sure what it is I want to study, or what I truly want to be in the future for that matter.

The variety of choices I have left open for myself are very wide, which creates a big problem, because I know I have to narrow it down to just one, which isn't something easy at all for me. It's like I want to be the best and do the best (medical doctor), yet I also wanna do other things (such as being a paramedic, or a cop, or firefighter, or a pilot), but I also realize I've only got one life to live. So the big question is: What's it gonna be?

This note reminded me of myself. In my reply, I said:

You sound so much like myself when I was in college. In my senior year, I was plagued with uncertainty about what would be the right course for my life. I went to a counselor and took a vocational aptitude test. I still remember the day when I went in for the test results. I expected my future to be laid out for me, and I hung on every word. But then I heard the counselor say, "Your tests show that mortician should be one of your vocational choices."

Mortician! I almost fell off my chair. That choice was so far removed from anything that I wanted that I immediately gave up on such tests.

I like your list of possibilities: physician, cop, firefighter, and paramedic. In addition to these, mine included cowboy, hobo, and beach bum. One day, I was at the dry cleaners (end of my sophomore year in college), and the guy standing next to me was a cop. We talked about his job, and when I left the dry cleaners, I immediately went to the police station to get an application. I found out that I had to be 21, and I was just 20. I went back to college.

I'm very happy with my choice. As a sociologist, I am able to follow my interests. I was able to become a hobo (or at least a traveler and able to experience different cultural settings). As far as being a cop, I developed and taught a course in the sociology of law.

One of the many things I always wanted to be was an author. I almost skipped graduate school to move to Greenwich Village and become a novelist. The problem was that I was too timid, too scared of the unknown—and I had no support at all—to give it a try. My ultimate choice of sociologist has allowed me to fulfill this early dream.

It is sociology's breadth that is so satisfying to those of us who can't seem to find the limit to our interests, who can't pin ourselves down to just one thing in life. Sociology covers *all* of social life. Anything and everything that people do is part of sociology. For those of us who feel such broad, and perhaps changing interests, sociology is a perfect major.

But what if you already have a major picked out, yet you really like thinking sociologically? You can *minor* in sociology. Take sociology courses that continue to stimulate your sociological imagination, that keep you asking questions about social life. Then after college, continue to feed your sociological interests through your reading, including novels. This ongoing development of your sociological imagination will serve you well as you go through life.

But What Can You Do with a Sociology Major?

I can just hear someone say: "That's fine for you, since you became a sociologist. I don't want to go to graduate school, though. I just want to get my associate's degree or my bachelor's degree and get out of college and get on with life. So, if I do get a bachelor's in sociology, how can it help me?"

This is a fair question. Just what can you do with a bachelor's degree in sociology?

When my sociology department began to develop a concentration in applied sociology, I explored this very question. I was surprised at the answer: The short answer is: *Almost anything!*

Most employers don't care what you major in. (Exceptions are some highly specialized fields such as nursing, software programming, and engineering.) *Most* employers just want to make certain that you have completed college, and for most of them one degree is the same as another. *College provides the base on which the employer builds.*

If you get a bachelor's degree—no matter what it is in—employers will assume that you are a responsible person. This credential implies that you have proven yourself: You were able to stick with a four-year course, you showed up for classes, listened to lectures, took notes, passed tests, and carried out whatever assignments you were given. On top of this base of presumed responsibility, employers add the specifics necessary for you to perform their particular work, whether that be in sales or service, in insurance, banking, retailing, marketing, product development, or whatever.

If you major in sociology, you don't have to look for a job as a sociologist. If you do decide to go on for an advanced degree, that's fine. But such plans are not necessary. The bachelor's in sociology can be your passport to most types of work in society.

Final Note

I want to conclude by stressing the reason to major in sociology that goes far beyond how you are going to make a living. It is the sociological perspective itself, the way of thinking and understanding that sociology provides. Wherever your path in life may lead, the sociological perspective will accompany you.

You are going to live in a fast-paced, rapidly changing world that, with all its conflicting crosscurrents, is going to be in constant turmoil. The sociological perspective will cast a different light on life's events, allowing you to perceive them in more insightful ways. As you watch television, attend a concert, talk with a friend, listen to a boss or co-worker—you will be more aware of the social contexts that underlie such behavior. The sociological perspective that you develop as you major in sociology will equip you to view what happens in life differently from someone who does not have your sociological background. Even events in the news will look different to you.

There is one more benefit of majoring in sociology. Much of the insight and understanding that I have just described can be applied in your work setting to advance your career.

The final question that I want to leave you with, then, is, "If you enjoy sociology, why not major in it?"

With my best wishes for your success in life,

Jim Henslin

Glossary

achieved statuses positions that are earned, accomplished, or involve at least some effort or activity on the individual's part

activity theory the view that satisfaction during old age is related to a person's amount and quality of activity

age cohort people born at roughly the same time who pass through the life course together

ageism prejudice, discrimination, and hostility directed against people because of their age; can be directed against any age group, including youth

agents of socialization people or groups that affect our self-concept, attitudes, behaviors, or other orientations toward life

aggregate individuals who temporarily share the same physical space but who do not see themselves as belonging together

agricultural society a society based largely on agriculture

alienation Marx's term for workers' lack of connection to the product of their labor; caused by their being assigned repetitive tasks on a small part of a product, which leads to a sense of powerlessness and normlessness; others use the term in the general sense of not feeling a part of something

alterative social movement a social movement that seeks to alter some specific aspect of people or institutions

anarchy a condition of lawlessness or political disorder caused by the absence or collapse of governmental authority

anomie Durkheim's term for a condition of society in which people become detached from the norms that usually guide their behavior

anticipatory socialization the process of learning in advance a role or status one anticipates having

applied sociology the use of sociology to solve problems—from the micro level of classroom interaction and family relationships to the macro level of crime and pollution

ascribed status a position an individual either inherits at birth or receives involuntarily later in life

assimilation the process of being absorbed into the mainstream culture

authoritarian leader an individual who leads by giving orders

authoritarian personality Theodor Adorno's term for people who are highly prejudiced and also rank high on scales of conformity, intolerance, insecurity, respect for authority, and submissiveness to superiors

authority power that people consider legitimate, as rightly exercised over them; also called *legitimate power*

background assumption a deeply embedded common understanding of how the world operates and of how people ought to act

basic demographic equation growth rate equals births minus deaths plus net migration

basic sociology sociological research for the purpose of making discoveries about life in human groups, not for making changes in those groups; also called *pure sociology*

bilineal (system of descent) a system of reckoning descent that counts both the mother's and the father's side

biotech society a society whose economy increasingly centers on the application of genetics—human genetics for medicine, and plant and animal genetics for the production of food and materials

blended family a family whose members were once part of other families

body language the ways in which people use their bodies to give messages to others

born again a term describing Christians who have undergone a religious experience so life transforming that they feel they have become new persons

bourgeoisie Marx's term for capitalists, those who own the means of production

bureaucracy a formal organization with a hierarchy of authority and a clear division of labor; emphasis on impersonality of positions and written rules, communications, and records

capitalism an economic system characterized by the private ownership of the means of production, the pursuit of profit, and market competition

capital punishment the death penalty

case study an intensive analysis of a single event, situation, or individual

caste system a form of social stratification in which people's statuses are determined by birth and are lifelong

category people who have similar characteristics

charisma literally, an extraordinary gift from God; more commonly, an outstanding, "magnetic" personality

charismatic authority authority based on an individual's outstanding traits, which attract followers

charismatic leader literally, someone to whom God has given a gift; more commonly, someone who exerts extraordinary appeal to a group of followers

checks and balances the separation of powers among the three branches of U.S. government—legislative, executive, and judicial—so that each is able to nullify the actions of the other two, thus preventing any single branch from dominating the government

church according to Durkheim, a moral community of believers—one of the three essential elements of religion; also refers to a large, highly organized religious group that has formal, sedate worship services and little emphasis on evangelism, intense religious experience, or personal conversion

citizenship the concept that birth (and residence or naturalization) in a country imparts basic rights

city a place in which a large number of people are permanently based and do not produce their own food

city-state an independent city whose power radiates outward, bringing the adjacent area under its rule

class consciousness Marx's term for awareness of a common identity based on one's position in the means of production

class conflict Marx's term for the struggle between capitalists and workers

class system a form of social stratification based primarily on the possession of money or material items

clique a cluster of people within a larger group who choose to interact with one another

closed-ended questions questions that are followed by a list of possible answers to be selected by the respondent

coalition the alignment of some members of a group against others

coercion power that people do not accept as rightly exercised over them; also called *illegitimate power*

cohabitation unmarried couples living together in a sexual relationship

colonialism the process by which one nation takes over another nation, usually for the purpose of exploiting its labor and natural resources

compartmentalize to separate acts from feelings or attitudes

conflict theory a theoretical framework in which society is viewed as composed of groups that are competing for scarce resources

conspicuous consumption Thorstein Veblen's term for a change from the Protestant ethic to an eagerness to show off wealth by the consumption of goods

continuity theory the focus of this theory is how people adjust to retirement by continuing aspects of their earlier lives

contradictory class locations Erik Wright's term for a position in the class structure that generates contradictory interests

control group the subjects in an experiment who are not exposed to the independent variable

control theory the idea that two control systems—inner controls and outer controls—work against our tendencies to deviate

convergence theory the view that as capitalist and socialist economic systems each adopt features of the other, a hybrid (or mixed) economic system will emerge

core values the values that are central to a group, those around which it builds a common identity

corporate culture the values, norms, and other orientations that characterize corporate work settings

cosmology teachings or ideas that provide a unified picture of the world

counterculture a group whose values, beliefs, norms, and related behaviors place its members in opposition to the broader culture

credential society the use of diplomas and degrees to determine who is eligible for jobs, even though the diploma or degree may be irrelevant to the actual work

crime the violation of norms written into law

criminal justice system the system of police, courts, and prisons set up to deal with people who are accused of having committed a crime

crude birth rate the annual number of live births per 1,000 population

crude death rate the annual number of deaths per 1,000 population

cult   a new religion with few followers, whose teachings and practices put it at odds with the dominant culture and religion

cultural diffusion   the spread of cultural traits from one group to another; includes both material and nonmaterial cultural traits

cultural goals   the objectives held out as legitimate or desirable for the members of a society

cultural lag   Ogburn's term for human behavior lagging behind technological innovations

cultural leveling   the process by which cultures become similar to one another; refers especially to the process by which Western culture is being exported and diffused into other nations

cultural relativism   not judging a culture but trying to understand it on its own terms

cultural transmission of values   the process of transmitting values from one group to another; often used in reference to how cultural traits are transmitted across generations and, in education, the ways in which schools transmit a society's values

culture   the language, beliefs, values, norms, behaviors, and even material objects that characterize a group and are passed from one generation to the next

culture of poverty   the assumption that the values and behaviors of the poor make them fundamentally different from other people, that these factors are largely responsible for their poverty, and that parents perpetuate poverty across generations by passing these characteristics to their children

culture shock   the disorientation that people experience when they come in contact with a fundamentally different culture and can no longer depend on their taken-for-granted assumptions about life

degradation ceremony   a term coined by Harold Garfinkel to refer to a ritual whose goal is to remake someone's self by stripping away that individual's self-identity and stamping a new identity in its place

deindustrialization   the process of industries moving out of a country or region

democracy   a government whose authority comes from the people; the term, based on two Greek words, translates literally as "power to the people"

democratic leader   an individual who leads by trying to reach a consensus

democratic socialism   a hybrid economic system in which the individual ownership of businesses is mixed with the state ownership of industries thought essential to the public welfare, such as the postal service and the delivery of medicine and utilities

demographic transition   a three-stage historical process of population growth: first, high birth rates and high death rates; second, high birth rates and low death rates; and third, low birth rates and low death rates; a fourth stage in which deaths outnumber births has made its appearance in the Most Industrialized Nations

demographic variables   the three factors that influence population growth: fertility, mortality, and net migration

denomination   a "brand name" within a major religion; for example, Methodist or Baptist

dependent variable   a factor in an experiment that is changed by an independent variable

deviance   the violation of norms (or rules or expectations)

dialectical process (of history)   each arrangement of power (a thesis) contains contradictions

(antitheses) which make the arrangement unstable; the process continues as the new synthesis to resolve the contradictions contains its own antitheses

dictatorship   a form of government in which an individual has seized power

differential association   Edwin Sutherland's term to indicate that people who associate with some groups learn an "excess of definitions" of deviance, increasing the likelihood that they will become deviant

diffusion   the spread of an invention or a discovery from one area to another; identified by William Ogburn as one of three processes of social change

direct democracy   a form of democracy in which the eligible voters meet together to discuss issues and make their decisions

discovery   a new way of seeing reality; identified by William Ogburn as one of three processes of social change

discrimination   an act of unfair treatment directed against an individual or a group

disengagement theory   the view that society is stabilized by having the elderly retire (disengage) from their positions of responsibility so the younger generation can step into their shoes

disinvestment   the withdrawal of investments by financial institutions, which seals the fate of an urban area

divine right of kings   the idea that the king's authority comes directly from God; in an interesting gender bender, also applies to queens

division of labor   the splitting of a group's or a society's tasks into specialties

documents   in its narrow sense, written sources that provide data; in its extended sense, archival material of any sort, including photographs, movies, CDs, DVDs, and so on

dominant group   the group with the most power, greatest privileges, and highest social status

downward social mobility   movement down the social class ladder

dramaturgy   an approach, pioneered by Erving Goffman, in which social life is analyzed in terms of drama or the stage; also called *dramaturgical analysis*

dyad   the smallest possible group, consisting of two persons

ecclesia   a religious group so integrated into the dominant culture that it is difficult to tell where the one begins and the other leaves off; also called a *state religion*

economy   a system of producing and distributing goods and services

ecosabotage   actions taken to sabotage the efforts of people who are thought to be legally harming the environment

edge city   a large clustering of service facilities and residential areas near highway intersections that provides a sense of place to people who live, shop, and work there

egalitarian   authority more or less equally divided between people or groups (in marriage, for example, between husband and wife)

endogamy   the practice of marrying within one's own group

enterprise zone   the use of economic incentives in a designated area to encourage investment

environmental injustice   refers to how minorities and the poor are harmed the most by environmental pollution

environmental sociology   a specialty within sociology whose focus is how humans affect the environment and how the environment affects humans

ethnicity (and ethnic)   having distinctive cultural characteristics

ethnic work   activities designed to discover, enhance, or maintain ethnic and racial identity

ethnocentrism   the use of one's own culture as a yardstick for judging the ways of other individuals or societies, generally leading to a negative evaluation of their values, norms, and behaviors

ethnomethodology   the study of how people use background assumptions to make sense out of life

exchange mobility   about the same numbers of people moving up and down the social class ladder, such that, on balance, the social class system shows little change

exogamy   the practice of marrying outside one's group

experiment   the use of control and experimental groups and dependent and independent variables to test causation

experimental group   the group of subjects in an experiment who are exposed to the independent variable

exponential growth curve   a pattern of growth in which numbers double during approximately equal intervals, showing a steep acceleration in the later stages

expressive leader   an individual who increases harmony and minimizes conflict in a group; also known as a *socioemotional leader*

face-saving behavior   techniques used to salvage a performance (interaction) that is going sour

false class consciousness   Marx's term to refer to workers identifying with the interests of capitalists

family   two or more people who consider themselves related by blood, marriage, or adoption

family of orientation   the family in which a person grows up

family of procreation   the family formed when a couple's first child is born

fecundity   the number of children that women are capable of bearing

feminism   the philosophy that men and women should be politically, economically, and socially equal; organized activities on behalf of this principle

[the] feminization of poverty   refers to most U.S. poor families being headed by women

feral children   children assumed to have been raised by animals, in the wilderness, isolated from humans

fertility rate   the number of children that the average woman bears

fieldwork   research in which the researcher participates in a setting while observing what is happening in that setting; also called *participant observation*

folkways   norms that are not strictly enforced

functional analysis   a theoretical framework in which society is viewed as composed of various parts, each with a function that, when fulfilled, contributes to society's equilibrium; also known as *functionalism* and *structural functionalism*

functional illiterate   a high school graduate who has difficulty with basic reading and math

gatekeeping the process by which education opens and closes doors of opportunity; also called the *social placement* function of education

Gemeinschaft a type of society in which life is intimate; a community in which everyone knows everyone else and people share a sense of togetherness

gender the behaviors and attitudes that a group considers proper for its males and females; masculinity or femininity

gender socialization the ways in which society sets children on different paths in life *because* they are male or female

gender stratification males' and females' unequal access to property, power, and prestige

generalized other the norms, values, attitudes, and expectations of people "in general"; the child's ability to take the role of the generalized other is a significant step in the development of a self

genetic predisposition inborn tendencies (for example, a tendency to commit deviant acts)

genocide the systematic annihilation or attempted annihilation of a people because of their presumed race or ethnicity

gentrification middle-class people moving into a rundown area of a city, displacing the poor as they buy and restore homes

Gesellschaft a type of society that is dominated by impersonal relationships, individual accomplishments, and self-interest

gestures the ways in which people use their bodies to communicate with one another

glass ceiling the mostly invisible barrier that keeps women from advancing to the top levels at work

global superclass a small group of highly interconnected individuals in which wealth and power are so concentrated that they make the world's major decisions

global warming an increase in the earth's temperature due to the greenhouse effect

globalization of capitalism capitalism (investing to make profits within a rational system) becoming the globe's dominant economic system

goal displacement an organization replacing old goals with new ones; also known as *goal replacement*

grade inflation higher grades given for the same work; a general rise in student grades without a corresponding increase in learning

graying of America the growing percentage of older people in the U.S. population

group people who have something in common and who believe that what they have in common is significant; also called a *social group*

group dynamics the ways in which individuals affect groups and the ways in which groups influence individuals

groupthink a narrowing of thought by a group of people, leading to the perception that there is only one correct course of action, in which to even suggest alternatives becomes a sign of disloyalty

growth rate the net change in a population after adding births, subtracting deaths, and either adding or subtracting net migration

hidden curriculum the unwritten goals of schools, such as teaching obedience to authority and conformity to cultural norms

homogamy the tendency of people with similar characteristics to marry one another

Horatio Alger myth the belief that due to limitless possibilities anyone can get ahead if he or she tries hard enough

horticultural society a society based on cultivating plants by the use of hand tools

household people who occupy the same housing unit

human ecology Robert Park's term for the relationship between people and their environment (such as land and structures); also known as *urban ecology*

hunting and gathering society a human group that depends on hunting and gathering for its survival

hypothesis a statement of how variables are expected to be related to one another, often according to predictions from a theory

id Freud's term for our inborn basic drives

ideal culture a people's ideal values and norms; the goals held out for them (as opposed to *real culture*)

ideology beliefs about the way things ought to be that justify social arrangements

illegitimate opportunity structure opportunities for crimes that are woven into the texture of life

impression management people's efforts to control the impressions that others receive of them

incest sexual relations between specified relatives, such as brothers and sisters or parents and children

incest taboo the rule that prohibits sex and marriage among designated relatives

income money received, usually from a job, business, or assets

independent variable a factor that causes a change in another variable, called the *dependent variable*

individual discrimination the negative treatment of one person by another on the basis of that person's perceived characteristics

Industrial Revolution the third social revolution, occurring when machines powered by fuels replaced most animal and human power

industrial society a society based on the harnessing of machines powered by fuels

information society a society whose chief characteristic is the use of tools that extend human abilities to gather and analyze information, to communicate, and to travel; also called *postindustrial* and *postmodern society*

in-groups groups toward which one feels loyalty

institutional discrimination negative treatment of a minority group that is built into a society's institutions; also called *systemic discrimination*

institutionalized means approved ways of reaching cultural goals

instrumental leader an individual who tries to keep the group moving toward its goals; also known as a *task-oriented leader*

intergenerational mobility the change that family members make in social class from one generation to the next

internal colonialism the policy of economically exploiting minority groups

invasion–succession cycle the process of one group of people displacing a group whose racial–ethnic or social class characteristics differ from their own

invention the combination of existing elements and materials to form new ones; identified by William Ogburn as one of three processes of social change

[the] iron law of oligarchy Robert Michels' term for the tendency of formal organizations to be dominated by a small, self-perpetuating elite

labeling theory the view that the labels people are given affect their own and others' perceptions of them, thus channeling their behavior into either deviance or conformity

laissez-faire capitalism unrestrained manufacture and trade (literally, "hands off" capitalism)

laissez-faire leader an individual who leads by being highly permissive

language a system of symbols that can be combined in an infinite number of ways and can represent not only objects but also abstract thought

latent functions unintended beneficial consequences of people's actions

leader someone who influences other people

leadership styles ways in which people express their leadership

life course the stages of our life as we go from birth to death

life expectancy the number of years that an average person at any age, including newborns, can expect to live

life span the maximum length of life of a species; for humans, the longest that a human has lived

lobbyists people who influence legislation on behalf of their clients

looking-glass self a term coined by Charles Horton Cooley to refer to the process by which our self develops through internalizing others' reactions to us

macro-level analysis an examination of large-scale patterns of society

macrosociology analysis of social life that focuses on broad features of society, such as social class and the relationships of groups to one another; usually used by functionalists and conflict theorists

mainstreaming becoming part of the mainstream of society; often refers to people with disabilities

Malthus theorem an observation by Thomas Malthus that although the food supply increases arithmetically (from 1 to 2 to 3 to 4 and so on), population grows geometrically (from 2 to 4 to 8 to 16 and so forth)

manifest functions the intended beneficial consequences of people's actions

market forces the law of supply and demand

marriage a group's approved mating arrangements, usually marked by a ritual of some sort

mass media forms of communication, such as radio, newspapers, and television that are directed to mass audiences

master status a status that cuts across the other statuses that an individual occupies

material culture the material objects that distinguish a group of people, such as their art, buildings, weapons, utensils, machines, hairstyles, clothing, and jewelry

matriarchy a society in which women-as-a-group dominate men-as-a-group; authority is vested in females

matrilineal (system of descent) a system of reckoning descent that counts only the mother's side

[the] McDonaldization of society the process by which ordinary aspects of life are rationalized and efficiency comes to rule them, including such things as food preparation

means of production   the tools, factories, land, and investment capital used to produce wealth

mechanical solidarity   Durkheim's term for the unity (a shared consciousness) that people feel as a result of performing the same or similar tasks

medicalization of deviance   to make deviance a medical matter, a symptom of some underlying illness that needs to be treated by physicians

megacity   a city of 10 million or more residents

megalopolis   an urban area consisting of at least two metropolises and their many suburbs

meritocracy   a form of social stratification in which all positions are awarded on the basis of merit

metaformative social movement   a social movement that has the goal to change the social order not just of a country or two, but of a civilization, or even of the entire world

metropolis   a central city surrounded by smaller cities and their suburbs

metropolitan statistical area (MSA)   a central city and the urbanized counties adjacent to it

micro-level analysis   an analysis of small-scale patterns of society

microsociology   analysis of social life that focuses on social interaction; typically used by symbolic interactionists

minority group   people who are singled out for unequal treatment and who regard themselves as objects of collective discrimination

modernization   the transformation of traditional societies into industrial societies

monarchy   a form of government headed by a king or queen

mores (mo-rays)   norms that are strictly enforced because they are thought essential to core values or the wellbeing of the group

multiculturalism   a philosophy or social policy that permits or encourages ethnic differences; also called *pluralism*

multinational corporations   companies that operate across national boundaries; also called *transnational corporations*

negative sanction   an expression of disapproval for breaking a norm, ranging from a mild, informal reaction such as a frown to a formal reaction such as a prison sentence or an execution

neocolonialism   the economic and political dominance of the Least Industrialized Nations by the Most Industrialized Nations

net migration rate   the difference between the number of immigrants and emigrants per 1,000 population

new technology   the emerging technologies of an era that have a significant impact on social life

nonmaterial culture   a group's ways of thinking (including its beliefs, values, and other assumptions about the world) and doing (its common patterns of behavior, including language and other forms of interaction); also called *symbolic culture*

nonverbal interaction   communication without words through gestures, use of space, silence, and so on

norms   what is expected of people; the expectations (or rules) intended to guide people's behavior

nuclear family   a family consisting of a husband, wife, and child(ren)

objectivity   value neutrality in research

oligarchy   a form of government in which a small group of individuals holds power; the rule of the many by the few

open-ended questions   questions that respondents answer in their own words

operational definition   the way in which a researcher measures a variable

organic solidarity   Durkheim's term for the interdependence that results from the division of labor; people depending on others to fulfill their jobs

out-groups   groups toward which one feels antagonism

pan-Indianism   a movement that focuses on common elements in the cultures of Native Americans in order to develop a cross-tribal group identity and to work toward the welfare of all Native Americans

participant observation   research in which the researcher participates in a setting while observing what is happening in that setting; also called *fieldwork*

pastoral society   a society based on the pasturing of animals

patriarchy   a group in which men-as-a-group dominate women-as-a-group; authority is vested in males

patrilineal   (system of descent) a system of reckoning descent that counts only the father's side

patterns   recurring characteristics or events

peer group   a group of individuals of roughly the same age who are linked by common interests

personality disorders   the view that a personality disturbance of some sort causes an individual to violate social norms

Peter principle   a tongue-in-cheek observation that the members of an organization are promoted for their accomplishments until they reach their level of incompetence; there they cease to be promoted, remaining at the level at which they can no longer do good work

pluralism   the diffusion of power among many interest groups that prevents any single group from gaining control of the government

pluralistic society   a society made up of many different groups

political action committee (PAC)   a group whose purpose is to solicit and spend funds for the purpose of influencing legislation

polyandry   a form of marriage in which women have more than one husband

polygyny   a form of marriage in which men have more than one wife

population   a target group to be studied

population pyramid   a chart or graph that represents the age and sex of a population

population shrinkage   the process by which a country's population becomes smaller because its birth rate and immigration are too low to replace those who die and emigrate

population transfer   the forced relocation of a minority group

positive sanction   a reward or positive reaction for following norms, ranging from a smile to a material reward

positivism   the application of the scientific method to the social world

postindustrial society   a society based on information, services, and high technology, rather than on raw materials and manufacturing; also called *postmodern* and *information society*

postmodern society   a society in which chief characteristic is the use of tools that extend human abilities to gather and analyze information, to communicate, and to travel; also called *postindustrial* and *information society*

poverty line   the official measure of poverty; calculated to include incomes that are less than three times a low-cost food budget

power   the ability to carry out your will, even over the resistance of others

power elite   C. Wright Mills' term for the top people in U.S. corporations, military, and politics who make the nation's major decisions

prejudice   an attitude or prejudging, usually in a negative way

prestige   respect or regard

primary group   a group characterized by intimate, long-term, face-to-face association and cooperation

proactive social movement   a social movement that promotes some social change

profane   Durkheim's term for common elements of everyday life

proletariat   Marx's term for the exploited class, the mass of workers who do not own the means of production

propaganda   in its broad sense, information used to try to influence people; in its narrow sense, one-sided information used to try to influence people

property   material possessions such as animals, bank accounts, bonds, buildings, businesses, cars, furniture, land, and stocks

Protestant ethic   Weber's term to describe the ideal of a self-denying, highly moral life accompanied by hard work and frugality

public opinion   how people think about some issue

public sociology   sociology being used for the public good; especially the sociological perspective (of how things are related to one another) guiding politicians and policy makers

race   a group whose inherited physical characteristics distinguish it from other groups

racism   prejudice and discrimination on the basis of race

random sample   a sample in which everyone in the target population has the same chance of being included in the study

rapport   (ruh-POUR) a feeling of trust between researchers and the people they are studying

rational–legal authority   authority based on law or written rules and regulations; also called *bureaucratic authority*

[the] rationalization of society   a widespread acceptance of rationality (efficiency; evaluating an action according to its impact on the "bottom line") and social organizations that are built largely around this idea

reactive social movement   a social movement that resists some social change

real culture   the norms and values that people actually follow (as opposed to ideal culture)

recidivism rate   the proportion of released convicts who are rearrested

redemptive social movement   a social movement that seeks to change people and institutions totally, to redeem them

redlining   a decision by the officers of a financial institution not to make loans in a particular area

reference group   a group whose standards we refer to as we evaluate ourselves

reformative social movement   a social movement that seeks to reform some specific aspect of society

reliability   the extent to which research produces consistent or dependable results

religion   according to Durkheim, beliefs and practices that separate the profane from the sacred and unite their adherents into a moral community

religious experience   a sudden awareness of the supernatural or a feeling of coming in contact with God

replication   duplicating some research in order to test its findings

representative democracy   a form of democracy in which voters elect representatives to meet together to discuss issues and make decisions on their behalf

research method   one of six procedures that sociologists use to collect data: surveys, participant observation, secondary analysis, analysis of documents, experiments, and unobtrusive measures; also called a *research design*

reserve labor force   the unemployed; unemployed workers are thought of as being "in reserve"—capitalists take them "out of reserve" (put them back to work) during times of high production and then lay them off (put them back in reserve) when they are no longer needed

resocialization   the process of learning new norms, values, attitudes, and behaviors

resource mobilization   a theory that social movements succeed or fail based on their ability to mobilize resources such as time, money, and people's skills

respondents   people who respond to a survey, either in interviews or by self-administered questionnaires

rising expectations   the sense that better conditions are soon to follow, which, if unfulfilled, increases frustration

rituals   ceremonies or repetitive practices; in religion, often intended to evoke a sense of awe of the sacred

role   the behaviors, obligations, and privileges attached to a status

role conflict   conflicts that someone feels *between* roles because the expectations attached to one role are incompatible with the expectations of another role

role performance   the ways in which someone performs a role; showing a particular "style" or "personality"

role strain   conflicts that someone feels *within* a role

romantic love   feelings of erotic attraction accompanied by an idealization of the other

routinization of charisma   the transfer of authority from a charismatic figure to either a traditional or a rational–legal form of authority

ruling class   another term for the power elite

sacred   Durkheim's term for things set apart or forbidden, that inspire fear, awe, reverence, or deep respect

sample   the individuals intended to represent the population to be studied

sanctions   either expressions of approval given to people for upholding norms or expressions of disapproval for violating them

Sapir-Whorf hypothesis   Edward Sapir's and Benjamin Whorf 's hypothesis that language creates ways of thinking and perceiving

scapegoat   an individual or group unfairly blamed for someone else's troubles

science   the application of systematic methods to obtain knowledge and the knowledge obtained by those methods

[the] scientific method   the use of objective, systematic observations to test theories

secondary analysis   the analysis of data that have been collected by other researchers

secondary group   compared with a primary group, a larger, relatively temporary, more anonymous, formal, and impersonal group based on some interest or activity

sect   a religious group larger than a cult that still feels substantial hostility from and toward society

segregation   the policy of keeping racial–ethnic groups apart

selective perception   seeing certain features of an object or situation, but remaining blind to others

self-fulfilling prophecy   Robert Merton's term for an originally false assertion that becomes true simply because it was predicted

self-fulfilling stereotype   preconceived ideas of what someone is like that lead to the person behaving in ways that match the stereotype

serial murder   the killing of several victims in three or more separate events

sex   biological characteristics that distinguish females and males, consisting of primary and secondary sex characteristics

sexual harassment   the abuse of one's position of authority to make unwanted sexual demands on someone

shaman   the healing specialist of a tribe who attempts to control the spirits thought to cause a disease or injury; commonly called a witch doctor

significant other   an individual who significantly influences someone else's life

slavery   a form of social stratification in which some people own other people

small group   a group small enough for everyone to interact directly with all the other members

social capital   privileges accompanying a social location that help someone in life; included are more highly educated parents, from grade school through high school being pushed to bring home high grades, and enjoying cultural experiences that translate into higher test scores, better jobs, and higher earnings

social change   the alteration of culture and societies over time

social class   according to Weber, a large group of people who rank close to one another in property (wealth), power, and prestige; according to Marx, one of two groups: capitalists who own the means of production or workers who sell their labor

social construction of reality   the use of background assumptions and life experiences to define what is real

social control   a group's formal and informal means of enforcing its norms

social environment   the entire human environment, including direct contact with others

social inequality   a social condition in which privileges and obligations are given to some but denied to others

social institution   the organized, usual, or standard ways by which society meets its basic needs

social integration   the degree to which members of a group or a society are united by shared norms, values, behaviors, and other social bonds; also known as *social cohesion*

social interaction   what people do when they are in one another's presence

social location   the group memberships that people have because of their location in history and society

social mobility   movement up or down the social class ladder

social movement   a large group of people who are organized to promote or resist some social change

social movement organization   an organization founded to promote the goals of a social movement

social network   the social ties radiating outward from the self that link people together

social order   a group's usual and customary social arrangements, on which its members depend and on which they base their lives

social placement   a function of education—funneling people into a society's various positions

social promotion   passing students on to the next level even though they have not mastered basic materials

social stratification   the division of large numbers of people into layers according to their relative property, power, and prestige; applies to both nations and to people within a nation, society, or other group

social structure   the framework that surrounds us, consisting of the relationships of people and groups to one another, which gives direction to and sets limits on behavior

socialism   an economic system characterized by the public ownership of the means of production, central planning, and the distribution of goods without a profit motive

socialization   the process by which people learn the characteristics of their group—the knowledge, skills, attitudes, values, norms, and actions thought appropriate for them

society   people who share a culture and a territory

sociological perspective   understanding human behavior by placing it within its broader social context

sociology   the scientific study of society and human behavior

special-interest group   a group of people who support a particular issue and who can be mobilized for political action

spirit of capitalism   Weber's term for the desire to accumulate capital—not to spend it, but as an end in itself—and to constantly reinvest it

split labor market   workers split along racial, ethnic, gender, age, or any other lines; this split is exploited by owners to weaken the bargaining power of workers

state   a political entity that claims monopoly on the use of violence in some particular territory; commonly known as a country

status the position that someone occupies in a social group

status consistency ranking high or low on all three dimensions of social class

status inconsistency ranking high on some dimensions of social class and low on others; also called *status discrepancy*

status set all the statuses or positions that an individual occupies

stereotype an assumption of what people are like, whether true or false

stigma "blemishes" that discredit a person's claim to a "normal" identity

strain theory Robert Merton's term for the strain engendered when a society socializes large numbers of people to desire a cultural goal (such as success), but withholds from some the approved means of reaching that goal

stratified random sample a sample from selected subgroups of the target population in which everyone in those subgroups has an equal chance of being included in the research

street crime crimes such as mugging, rape, and burglary

structural mobility movement up or down the social class ladder that is due to changes in the structure of society, not to individual efforts

suburb a community adjacent to a city

suburbanization the movement from the city to the suburbs

subculture the values and related behaviors of a group that distinguish its members from the larger culture; a world within a world

subsistence economy a type of economy in which human groups live off the land and have little or no surplus

superego Freud's term for the conscience; the internalized norms and values of our social groups

survey the collection of data by having people answer a series of questions

sustainable environment a world system that takes into account the limits of the environment, produces enough material goods for everyone's needs, and leaves a sound environment for the next generation

symbol something to which people attach meanings and then use to communicate with others

symbolic culture a group's ways of thinking (including its beliefs, values, and other assumptions about the world) and doing (its common patterns of behavior, including language and other forms of interaction); also called *nonmaterial culture*

symbolic interactionism a theoretical perspective in which society is viewed as composed of symbols that people use to establish meaning, develop their views of the world, and communicate with one another

system of descent how kinship is traced over the generations

taboo a norm so strong that it often brings revulsion if violated

taking the role of the other putting oneself in someone else's shoes; understanding how someone else feels and thinks and thus anticipating how that person will act

teamwork the collaboration of two or more people to manage impressions jointly

techniques of neutralization ways of thinking or rationalizing that help people deflect (or neutralize) society's norms

technology in its narrow sense, tools; its broader sense includes the skills or procedures necessary to make and use those tools

terrorism the use of violence or the threat of violence to produce fear in order to attain political objectives

theory a general statement about how some parts of the world fit together and how they work; an explanation of how two or more facts are related to one another

Thomas theorem William I. and Dorothy S. Thomas' classic formulation of the definition of the situation: "If people define situations as real, they are real in their consequences."

total institution a place that is almost totally controlled by those who run it, in which people are cut off from the rest of society and the society is mostly cut off from them

totalitarianism a form of government that exerts almost total control over people

tracking in education, the sorting of students into different programs on the basis of real or perceived abilities

traditional authority authority based on custom

transformative social movement a social movement that seeks to change society totally, to transform it

transitional adulthood a term that refers to a period following high school (and often college), when young adults have not yet taken on the responsibilities ordinarily associated with adulthood; also called *adultolescence*

transitional older years an emerging stage of the life course between retirement and when people are considered old; approximately ages 65 to 75

transnational social movement a social movement whose goal is to change some condition around the world, not just a condition in a specific country; also known as a *new social movement*

triad a group of three people

underclass a group of people for whom poverty persists year after year and across generations

universal citizenship the idea that everyone has the same basic rights by virtue of being born in a country (or by immigrating and becoming a naturalized citizen)

unobtrusive measures ways of observing people so they do not know they are being studied

urban renewal the rehabilitation of a rundown area, which usually results in the displacement of the poor who are living in that area

urbanization the process by which an increasing proportion of a population lives in cities and those cities attaining a growing influence on the culture

validity the extent to which an operational definition measures what it is intended to measure

value cluster values that together form a larger whole

value contradiction values that contradict one another; to follow the one means to come into conflict with the other

value free the view that a sociologist's personal values or biases should not influence social research

values the standards by which people define what is desirable or undesirable, good or bad, beautiful or ugly

variable a factor thought to be significant for human behavior, which can *vary* (or change) from one case to another

voluntary association a group made up of people who voluntarily organize on the basis of some mutual interest; also known as *voluntary memberships* and *voluntary organizations*

voter apathy indifference and inaction toward politics on the part of individuals or groups

war armed conflict between nations or politically distinct groups

WASP White Anglo-Saxon Protestant; narrowly, an American of English descent; broadly, an American of Western European ancestry

wealth the total value of everything someone owns, minus the debts

white-collar crime Edwin Sutherland's term for crimes committed by people of respectable and high social status in the course of their occupations; for example, bribery of public officials, securities violations, embezzlement, false advertising, and price fixing

white ethnics white immigrants to the United States whose cultures differ from that of WASPs

world system theory economic and political connections that tie the world's countries together

zero population growth women bearing only enough children to reproduce the population

References

All new references are printed in cyan.

Chapter 1

Addams, Jane. *Twenty Years at Hull-House*. New York: Signet, 1981. First published in 1910.

American Sociological Association. "An Invitation to Public Sociology." 2004.

American Sociological Association. "Code of Ethics and Policies and Procedures of the ASA Committee on Professional Ethics." Washington, D.C.: American Sociological Association, 1999.

Aptheker, Herbert. "W. E. B. Du Bois: Struggle Not Despair." *Clinical Sociology Review, 8,* 1990:58–68.

Armstrong, David. "Hard Case: When Academics Double as Expert Witnesses." *Wall Street Journal,* June 22, 2007.

Augoustinos, Martha, Ameilia Russin, and Amanda LeCouteur. "Representations of the Stem-Cell Cloning Fraud: From Scientific Breakthrough to Managing the Stake and Interest of Science." *Public Understanding of Science, 18,* 6, 2009: 687–703.

Barnes, Fred. "How to Rig a Poll." *Wall Street Journal,* June 14, 1995:A14.

Barnes, Helen. "A Comment on Stroud and Pritchard: Child Homicide, Psychiatric Disorder and Dangerousness." *British Journal of Social Work, 31,* 3, June 2001.

Bianchi, Suzanne M., John P. Robinson, and Melissa A. Milkie. *Changing Rhythms of American Family Life*. New York: Russell Sage Foundation, 2006.

Brajuha, Mario, and Lyle Hallowell. "Legal Intrusion and the Politics of Fieldwork: The Impact of the Brajuha Case." *Urban Life, 14,* 4, January 1986:454–478.

Burawoy, Michael. "The Field of Sociology: Its Power and Its Promise." In *Public Sociology: Fifteen Eminent Sociologists Debate Politics and the Profession in the Twenty-first Century*. Berkeley: University of California Press, 2007: 241–258.

Cantoni, Davide. "The Economic Effects of the Protestant Reformation: Testing the Weber Hypothesis in the German Lands." Harvard University Job Market Paper, November 10, 2009.

Centers for Disease Control, National Center for Injury Prevention and Control Fatal Injury Data, 2011.

Coser, Lewis A. *Masters of Sociological Thought: Ideas in Historical and Social Context,* 2nd ed. New York: Harcourt Brace Jovanovich, 1977.

Crossen, Cynthia. "Margin of Error: Studies Galore Support Products and Positions, But Are They Reliable?" *Wall Street Journal,* Nov 14, 1991:A1.

Davis, R. E., M. P. Couper, N. K. Janz, C. H. Caldwell, and K. Resnicow. "Interviewer Effects in Public Health Surveys." *Health Education Research,* September 17, 2009:13–20.

DeMartini, Joseph R. "Basic and Applied Sociological Work: Divergence, Convergence, or Peaceful Co-existence?" *The Journal of Applied Behavioral Science, 18,* 2, 1982:203–215.

Dobriner, William M. *Social Structures and Systems*. Pacific Palisades, Calif. Goodyear, 1969b.

Du Bois, W. E. B. *The Souls of Black Folk: Essays and Sketches*. Chicago: McClurg, 1903.

Du Bois, W. E. B. *Black Reconstruction in America: An Essay toward a History of the Part Which Black Folk Played in the Attempt to Reconstruct Democracy in America, 1860–1880*. New York: Atheneum, 1992. Originally published 1935.

Du Bois, W. E. B. *The Autobiography of W. E. B. Du Bois: A Soliloquy on Viewing My Life from the Last Decade of Its First Century*. New York: International, 1968.

Durkheim, Emile. *Suicide: A Study in Sociology*. John A. Spaulding and George Simpson, trans. New York: Free Press, 1966. First published in 1897.

Dush, Claire M. Kamp, Catherine L. Cohan, and Paul R. Amato. "The Relationship between Cohabitation and Marital Quality and Stability: Change across Cohorts?" *Journal of Marriage and Family, 65,* 3, August 2003:539–549.

Edgerton, Robert B. *Sick Societies: Challenging the Myth of Primitive Harmony*. New York: Free Press, 1992.

Estes, Larissa J., Linda E. Lloyd, Michelle Teti, et al. "Perceptions of Audio Computer-Assisted Self-Interviewing (ACASI) among Women in an HIV-Positive Prevention Program." *PLoS ONE, 5,* 2, February 10, 2010:e9149.

Gilman, Charlotte Perkins. *The Man-Made World or, Our Androcentric Culture*. New York: 1971. Originally published 1911.

Gitlin, Todd. *The Twilight of Common Dreams: Why America Is Wracked by Culture Wars*. New York: Metropolitan Books, 1997.

Goleman, Daniel. "Pollsters Enlist Psychologists in Quest for Unbiased Results." *New York Times,* September 7, 1993:C1, C11.

Guo, Guang, Yuying Tong, and Tianji Cai. "Gene by Social Context Interactions for Number of Sexual Partners among White Male Youths: Genetics-Informed Sociology." *American Journal of Sociology, 114,* Supplement, 2008:S36–S66.

Havrilla, Karina. "A Sociological Influence in *Dora the Explorer*." ASA *Footnotes, 38,* 2, February 2010.

Henley, Nancy, Mykol Hamilton, and Barrie Thorne. "Womanspeak and Manspeak." In *Beyond Sex Roles,* Alice G. Sargent, ed. St. Paul, Minn.: West, 1985.

Humphreys, Laud. "Impersonal Sex and Perceived Satisfaction." In *Studies in the Sociology of Sex,* James M. Henslin, ed. New York: Appleton-Century-Crofts, 1971:351–374.

Humphreys, Laud. *Tearoom Trade: Impersonal Sex in Public Places,* enlarged ed. Chicago: Aldine, 1975. Originally published 1970.

Knapp, Daniel. "What Happened When I Took My Sociological Imagination to the Dump." *Footnotes,* May–June, 2005:4.

Kroeger, Brooke. "When a Dissertation Makes a Difference." *New York Times,* March 20, 2004.

Lee, Raymond M. *Unobtrusive Methods in Social Research*. Philadelphia: Open University Press, 2000.

Lengermann, Madoo, and Gillian Niebrugge. *The Women Founders: Sociology and Social Theory, 1830–1930*. Prospect Heights, Ill.: Waveland Press, 2007.

Levi, Ken. "Becoming a Hit Man." In *Exploring Social Life: Readings to Accompany Essentials of Sociology, A Down-to-Earth Approach,* 8th ed., 4th ed, James M. Henslin, ed. Boston: Allyn and Bacon, 2009. Originally published 1981.

Linz, Daniel, Paul Bryant, et al. "An Examination of the Assumption That Adult Businesses Are Associated with Crime in Surrounding Areas: A Secondary Effects Study in Charlotte, North Carolina." *Law & Society, 38,* 1, March 2004:69–104.

Manza, Jeff, and Michael A. McCarthy. "The Neo-Marxist Legacy in American Sociology." *Annual Review of Sociology, 37,* 2011:155–183.

Marx, Karl, and Friedrich Engels. *Communist Manifesto*. New York: Pantheon, 1967. First published in 1848.

McKenzie, John. "'You Don't Know How Lucky You Are to Be Here!': Reflections on Covert Practices in an Overt Participant Observation Study." *Sociological Research Online, 14,* 2, 30 May 2009.

Mills, C. Wright. *The Sociological Imagination*. New York: Oxford University Press, 1959.

National School Safety Center. "School Associated Violent Deaths." Westlake Village, Calif., 2011.

Nickel, Patricia M. "Public Sociology and the Public Turn in the Social Sciences." *Sociology Compass, 4, 9,* 2010:694–704.

O'Brien, John E. "Violence in Divorce-Prone Families." In *Violence in the Family,* Suzanne K. Steinmetz and Murray A. Straus, eds. New York: Dodd, Mead, 1975:65–75.

Osborne, Cynthia, Wendy D. Manning, and Pamela J. Smock. "Married and Cohabiting Parents' Relationship Stability: A Focus on Race and Ethnicity." *Journal of Marriage and Family,* 69, December 2007:1345–1366.

Pager, Devah. "The Mark of a Criminal Record." *American Journal of Sociology,* 108, 5, March 2003:937–975.

Pager, Devah, Bruce Western, and Bart Bonikowski. "Discrimination in a Low-Wage Labor Market: A Field Experiment." *American Sociological Review, 74,* 5, October 2009:777–799.

Park, Robert Ezra, and Ernest W. Burgess. *Human Ecology.* Chicago: University of Chicago Press, 1921.

Piven, Frances Fox. "The Neoliberal Challenge." *Contexts, 6, 3,* 2007:13–15.

Piven, Frances Fox. "Can Power from Below Change the World?" *American Sociological Review, 73,* 1, February 2008:1–14.

Resnik, David B. "Financial Interests and Research Bias." *Perspectives on Science, 8,* 3, Fall 2000:255–283.

Rosenbloom, Stephanie. "In Bid to Sway Sales, Cameras Track Shoppers." *New York Times,* March 19, 2010.

Sageman, Marc. "Explaining Terror Networks in the 21st Century." *Footnotes,* May–June 2008a:7.

Sageman, Marc. *Leaderless Jihad: Terror Networks in the Twenty-First Century.* Philadelphia: University of Pennsylvania Press, 2008b.

Schaefer, Richard T. *Sociology,* 3rd ed. New York: McGraw-Hill, 1989.

Singer, Natasha. "Shoppers Who Can't Have Secrets." *New York Times,* April 30, 2010.

Stark, Rodney. *Sociology,* 3rd ed. Belmont, Calif.: Wadsworth, 1989.

Statistical Abstract of the United States. Washington, D.C.: Bureau of the Census, published annually.

Turner, Jonathan H. *The Structure of Sociological Theory.* Homewood, Ill.: Dorsey, 1978.

Venkatesh, Sudhir. *Gang Leader for a Day: A Rogue Sociologist Takes to the Streets.* New York: Penguin, 2008.

Von Hoffman, Nicholas. "Sociological Snoopers." *Transaction 7,* May 1970:4, 6.

Wade, Nicholas. "In Dusty Archives, a Theory of Affluence." *New York Times,* August 7, 2007.

Weber, Max. *The Protestant Ethic and the Spirit of Capitalism.* New York: Scribner's, 1958. First published in 1904–1905.

Weiss, Karen G. "'Boys Will Be Boys' and Other Gendered Accounts: An Exploration of Victims' Excuses and Justifications for Unwanted Sexual Contact and Coercion." *Violence against Women, 15,* 2009:810–834.

Wimmer, Andreas, and Kevin Lewis. "Beyond and Below Racial Homophily: ERG Models of a Friendship Network Documented on Facebook." *American Journal of Sociology, 116,* 2, September 2011.

Chapter 2

Anderson, Nels. *Desert Saints: The Mormon Frontier in Utah.* Chicago: University of Chicago Press, 1966. Originally published 1942.

Bates, Marston. *Gluttons and Libertines: Human Problems of Being Natural.* New York: Vintage Books, 1967. Quoted in Crapo, Richley H. *Cultural Anthropology: Understanding Ourselves and Others,* 5th ed. Boston: McGraw Hill, 2002.

Bearak, Barry. "Dead Join the Living in a Family Celebration." *New York Times,* September 5, 2010.

Boroditsky, Lera. "Lost in Translation." *Wall Street Journal,* July 24, 2010.

Consulate General of Madagascar in Cape Town. 2012. http://www.madagascarconsulate.org.za/Madagascar_Culture.html

Cowley, Geoffrey. "Attention: Aging Men." *Newsweek,* November 16, 1996:66–75.

Dickey, Christopher, and John Barry. "Iran: A Rummy Guide." *Newsweek,* May 8, 2006.

Edgerton, Robert B. *Sick Societies: Challenging the Myth of Primitive Harmony.* New York: Free Press, 1992.

Ekman, Paul, Wallace V. Friesen, and John Bear. "The International Language of Gestures." *Psychology Today,* May 1984:64.

Fadiman, Anne. *The Spirit Catches You and You Fall Down.* Farrar, Straus and Giroux, 1997.

Gampbell, Jennifer. "In Northeast Thailand, a Cuisine Based on Bugs." *New York Times,* June 22, 2006.

Gokhale, Ketaki. "India Plans Focus on Environment." *Wall Street Journal,* August 14, 2009.

Halpern, Jack. "Iceland's Big Thaw." *New York Times,* May 13, 2011.

Katayama, Lisa. "Love in 2-D." *New York Times,* July 21, 2009.

Kent, Mary, and Robert Lalasz. "In the News: Speaking English in the United States." Population Reference Bureau, January 18, 2007.

Kingston, Maxine Hong. *The Woman Warrior.* New York: Vintage Books, 1975:108. Quoted in Frank J. Zulke and Jacqueline P. Kirley. *Through the Eyes of Social Science,* 6th ed. Prospect Heights, Ill.: Waveland Press, 2002.

Krumer-Nevo, Michal, and Orly Benjamin. "Critical Poverty Knowledge: Contesting Othering and Social Distancing." *Current Sociology, 58,* 2010:693–714.

Linton, Ralph. *The Study of Man.* New York: Appleton-Century-Crofts, 1936.

Nelson, Gary. "Hispanic-Only FIU Mayoral Debate Draws Harsh Criticism." *CBS Miami,* May 11, 2011.

Ogburn, William F. *Social Change with Respect to Culture and Human Nature.* New York: W. B. Huebsch, 1922. (Other editions by Viking in 1927, 1938, and 1950.)

Robertson, Ian. *Sociology,* 3rd ed. New York: Worth, 1987.

Salomon, Gisela, "In Miami, Spanish Is Becoming the Primary Language." Associated Press, May 29, 2008.

Sapir, Edward. *Selected Writings of Edward Sapir in Language, Culture, and Personality,* David G. Mandelbaum, ed. Berkeley: University of California Press, 1949.

Schmiddle Nicholas. "Getting Bin Laden." *The New Yorker,* August 8, 2011.

Sharp, Deborah. "Miami's Language Gap Widens." *USA Today,* April 3, 1992:A1, A3.

Sumner, William Graham. *Folkways: A Study in the Sociological Importance of Usages, Manners, Customs, Mores, and Morals.* New York: Ginn, 1906.

Usdansky, Margaret L. "English a Problem for Half of Miami." *USA Today,* April 3, 1992:A1, A3, A30.

Wakabayashi, Daisuke. "Atami Welcomes Virtual Girls, Real Boys." *Wall Street Journal,* September 1, 2010a.

Wakabayashi, Daisuke. "Only in Japan, Real Men Go to a Hotel with Virtual Girlfriends." *Wall Street Journal,* August 31, 2010b.

Whorf, Benjamin. *Language, Thought, and Reality,* J. B. Carroll, ed. Cambridge, Mass. MIT Press, 1956.

Williams, Jasmin K. "Utah—The Beehive State." *New York Post,* June 12, 2007.

Williams, Robin M., Jr. *American Society: A Sociological Interpretation,* 2nd ed. New York: Knopf, 1965.

Zellner, William W. *Countercultures: A Sociological Analysis.* New York: St. Martin's, 1995.

Zerubavel, Eviatar. *The Fine Line: Making Distinctions in Everyday Life.* New York: Free Press, 1991.

Chapter 3

Adler, Patricia A., and Peter Adler. *Peer Power: Preadolescent Culture and Identity.* New Brunswick, N.J.: Rutgers University Press, 1998.

Ariés, Philippe. *Centuries of Childhood,* R. Baldick, trans. New York: Vintage Books, 1965.

Begley, Sharon. "Twins: Nazi and Jew." *Newsweek, 94,* December 3, 1979:139.

Belsky, Jay. "Early Child Care and Early Child Development: Major Findings of the NICHD Study of Early Child Care." *European Journal of Developmental Psychology, 3,* 1, 2006:95–110.

Best, Deborah L. "The Contribution of the Whitings to the Study of the Socialization of Gender." *Journal of Cross-Cultural Psychology, 41,* 2010:534–545.

Bilefsky, Dan. "Albanian Custom Fades: Woman as Family Man." *New York Times,* June 25, 2008.

Bush, Diane Mitsch, and Robert G. Simmons. "Socialization Processes over the Life Course." In *Social Psychology: Sociological Perspectives,* Morris Rosenberger and Ralph H. Turner, eds. New Brunswick, N.J.:Transaction, 1990:133–164.

Carr, Deborah, Carol D. Ryff, Burton Singer, and William J. Magee. "Bringing the 'Life' Back into Life Course Research: A 'Person-Centered' Approach to Studying the Life Course." Paper presented at the annual meetings of the American Sociological Association, 1995.

Chauhan, Preeti, N. Dickon Reppucci, and Eric N. Turkheimer. "Racial Differences in the Associations of Neighborhood Disadvantage, Exposure to Violence, and Criminal Recidivism among Female Juvenile Offenders." *Behavioral Sciences and the Law, 27,* June 2009:531–552.

Chen, Edwin. "Twins Reared Apart: A Living Lab." *New York Times Magazine.* December 9, 1979:112.

Chodorow, Nancy J. "What Is the Relation between Psychoanalytic Feminism and the Psychoanalytic Psychology of Women?" In *Theoretical Perspectives on Sexual Difference,* Deborah L. Rhode, ed. New Haven, Conn.: Yale University Press, 1990:114–130.

Clark, Candace. *Misery and Company: Sympathy in Everyday Life.* Chicago: University of Chicago Press, 1997.

Clearfield, Melissa W., and Naree M. Nelson. "Sex Differences in Mothers' Speech and Play Behavior with 6-, 9-, and 14-Month-Old Infants." *Sex Roles, 54,* 1–2, January 2006:127–137.

Connors, L. "Gender of Infant Differences in Attachment: Associations with Temperament and Caregiving Experiences." Paper presented at the Annual Conference of the British Psychological Society, Oxford, England, 1996.

Cooley, Charles Horton. *Human Nature and the Social Order.* New York: Scribner's, 1902.

Crosnoe, Robert, Catherine Riegle-Crumb, Sam Field, Kenneth Frank, and Chandra Muller. "Peer Group Contexts of Girls' and Boys' Academic Experiences." *Child Development, 79,* 1, February 2008:139–155.

Davis, Kingsley. "Extreme Isolation." In *Down to Earth Sociology: Introductory Readings,* 15th ed., James M. Henslin, ed. New York: Free Press, 2012. Originally published as "Extreme Social Isolation of a Child." *American Journal of Sociology, 45,* January 4, 1940:554–565.

DeLuca, Stephanie, and Elizabeth Dayton. "Switching Social Contexts: The Effects of Housing Mobility and School Choice Programs on Youth Outcomes." *Annual Review of Sociology, 35,* 2009:457–491.

DeMause, Lloyd. "Our Forebears Made Childhood a Nightmare." *Psychology Today 8,* 11, April 1975:85–88.

Denzin, Norman K. *Symbolic Interactionism and Cultural Studies: The Politics of Interpretation.* Cambridge, Mass.: Blackwell 2007.

Dyer, Gwynne. "Anybody's Son Will Do." In *Down to Earth Sociology: Introductory Readings,* 14th ed., James M. Henslin, ed. New York: Free Press, 2007.

Eder, Donna. "On Becoming Female: Lessons Learned in School." In *Down to Earth Sociology: Introductory Readings,* 14th ed., James M. Henslin, ed. New York: Free Press, 2007.

Ekman, Paul. *Faces of Man: Universal Expression in a New Guinea Village.* New York: Garland Press, 1980.

Elder, Glen H., Jr. "Age Differentiation and Life Course." *Annual Review of Sociology, 1,* 1975:165–190.

Elder, Glen H., Jr. *Children of the Great Depression: Social Change in Life Experience.* Boulder, Colo. Westview Press, 1999.

Epstein, Cynthia Fuchs. *Deceptive Distinctions: Sex, Gender, and the Social Order.* New Haven, Conn.: Yale University Press, 1988.

Flavel, John H., et al. *The Development of Role-Taking and Communication Skills in Children.* New York: Wiley, 1968.

Flavel, John, Patricia H. Miller, and Scott A. Miller. *Cognitive Development,* 4th ed. Upper Saddle River, N.J.: Prentice Hall, 2002.

Furstenberg, Frank F., Jr., Sheela Kennedy, Vonnie C. McLoyd, Ruben G. Rumbaut, and Richard A. Settersten, Jr. "Growing Up Is Harder to Do." *Contexts, 3,* 3, Summer 2004:33–41.

Gallup Poll. "Very Religious Americans Lead Healthier Lives." Princeton, N.J.: Gallup Organization, December 23, 2010.

Garfinkel, Harold. "Conditions of Successful Degradation Ceremonies." *American Journal of Sociology, 61,* 2, March 1956:420–424.

Gerhard, Jane. "Revisiting 'The Myth of the Vaginal Orgasm': The Female Orgasm in American Sexual Thought and Second Wave Feminism." *Feminist Studies, 26,* 2, Fall 2000:449–477.

Gilman, Charlotte Perkins. *The Man-Made World or, Our Androcentric Culture.* New York: 1971. Originally published 1911.

Gilpatric, Katy. "Violent Female Action Characters in Contemporary American Cinema." *Sex Roles, 62,* 2010:734–746.

Goffman, Erving. *Asylums: Essays on the Social Situation of Mental Patients and Other Inmates.* Chicago: Aldine, 1961.

Goldberg, Susan, and Michael Lewis. "Play Behavior in the Year-Old Infant: Early Sex Differences." *Child Development, 40,* March 1969:21–31.

Guensburg, Carol. "Bully Factories." *American Journalism Review, 23,* 6, 2001:51–59.

Hall, G. Stanley. *Adolescence: Its Psychology and Its Relations to Physiology, Anthropology, Sociology, Sex, Crime, Religion, and Education.* New York: Appleton, 1904.

Harlow, Harry F., and Margaret K. Harlow. "Social Deprivation in Monkeys." *Scientific American, 207,* 1962:137–147.

Harlow, Harry F., and Margaret K. Harlow. "The Affectional Systems." In *Behavior of Nonhuman Primates: Modern Research Trends,* Vol. 2, Allan M. Schrier, Harry F. Harlow, and Fred Stollnitz, eds. New York: Academic Press, 1965:287–334.

Hochschild, Arlie. "Feelings around the World." *Contexts, 7,* 2, Spring 2008:80.

Horwitz, Allan V., and Jerome C. Wakefield. *The Loss of Sadness: How Psychiatry Transformed Normal Sorrow into Depressive Disorder.* New York: Oxford University Press, 2007.

Itard, Jean Marc Gospard. *The Wild Boy of Aveyron,* George and Muriel Humphrey, trans. New York: Appleton-Century-Crofts, 1962.

Jasper, James M. "Emotions and Social Movements: Twenty Years of Theory and Research." Unpublished paper, 2012.

Johnson, Wendy, Eric Turkheimer, Irving I. Gottesman, and Thomas J. Bouchard, Jr. "Beyond Heritability: Twin Studies in Behavioral Research." *Current Directions in Psychological Science, 18,* 4, 2009:217–220.

Kacen, Jacqueline J. "Advertising Effectiveness." New York: *Wiley International Encyclopedia of Marketing,* 2011.

Kagan, Jerome. "The Idea of Emotions in Human Development." In *Emotions, Cognition, and Behavior,* Carroll E. Izard, Jerome Kagan, and Robert B. Zajonc, eds. New York: Cambridge University Press, 1984:38–72.

Kahlenberg, Susan G., and Michelle M. Hein, "Progression on Nickelodeon? Gender-Role Stereotypes in Toy Commercials." *Sex Roles, 62,* 2010:830–847.

Keniston, Kenneth. *Youth and Dissent: The Rise of a New Opposition.* New York: Harcourt, Brace, Jovanovich, 1971.

Kohlberg, Lawrence, and Carol Gilligan. "The Adolescent as a Philosopher: The Discovery of the Self in a Postconventional World." *Daedalus, 100,* 1971:1051–1086.

Kohn, Melvin L. "Social Class and Parental Values." *American Journal of Sociology, 64,* 1959:337–351.

Kohn, Melvin L. "Social Class and Parent–Child Relationships: An Interpretation." *American Journal of Sociology, 68,* 1963:471–480.

Kohn, Melvin L. *Class and Conformity: A Study in Values,* 2nd ed. Homewood, Ill.: Dorsey Press, 1977.

Kohn, Melvin L. *Change and Stability: A Cross-National Analysis of Social Structure and Personality.* Boulder, Colo. Paradigm, 2006.

Kohn, Melvin L., and Carmi Schooler. "Class, Occupation, and Orientation." *American Sociological Review, 34,* 1969:659–678.

Ledger, Kate. "Sociology and the Gene." *Contexts, 8,* 3, 2009:16–20.

Levanthal, Tama, and Jeanne Brooks-Gunn. "The Neighborhood They Live In: Effects of Neighborhood Residence on Child and Adolescent Outcomes." *Psychological Bulletin, 126,* 2000:309–337.

Levine, Robert. "Planned Guns N' Roses Deal Underscores Power of Video to Sell Songs." *Wall Street Journal,* July 14, 2008.

Levinson, D. J. *The Seasons of a Man's Life.* New York: Knopf, 1978.

Matsumoto, D., and B. Willingham. "Spontaneous Facial Expressions of Emotion of Congenitally and Noncongenitally Blind Individuals." *Journal of Personality and Social Psychology, 96,* 2009:1–10.

Mead, George Herbert. *Mind, Self and Society.* Chicago: University of Chicago Press, 1934.

Meese, Ruth Lyn. "A Few New Children: Postinstitutionalized Children of Intercountry Adoption." *Journal of Special Education, 39,* 3, 2005:157–167.

Milkie, Melissa A. "Social World Approach to Cultural Studies." *Journal of Contemporary Ethnography, 23,* 3, October 1994:354–380.

National Institute of Child Health and Human Development. "Child Care and Mother–Child Interaction in the First 3 Years of Life." *Developmental Psychology, 35,* 6, November 1999:1399–1413.

Neugarten, Bernice L. "Middle Age and Aging." In *Growing Old in America,* Beth B. Hess, ed. New Brunswick, N.J.: Transaction, 1976:180–197.

Newport, Frank, Sangeeta Agrawal, and Dan Witters. "Very Religious Americans Report Less Depression, Worry." Gallup Poll, December 1, 2010.

Nordberg, Jenny. "In Afghanistan, Boys Are Prized and Girls Live the Part." *New York Times,* September 20, 2010.

Orme, Nicholas. *Medieval Children.* New Haven, Conn.: Yale University Press, 2002.

Pearlin, L. I., and Melvin L. Kohn. "Social Class, Occupation, and Parental Values: A Cross-National Study." *American Sociological Review, 31,* 1966:466–479.

Piaget, Jean. *The Psychology of Intelligence.* London: Routledge & Kegan Paul, 1950.

Piaget, Jean. *The Construction of Reality in the Child.* New York: Basic Books, 1954.

Pines, Maya. "The Civilizing of Genie." *Psychology Today, 15,* September 1981:28–34.

Quadagno, Jill. *Aging and the Life Course: An Introduction to Social Gerontology,* 5th ed. New York: McGraw-Hill, 2010.

Ricks, Thomas E. "'New' Marines Illustrate Growing Gap between Military and Society." *Wall Street Journal,* July 27, 1995:A1, A4.

Rodriguez, Richard. "The Education of Richard Rodriguez." *Saturday Review,* February 8, 1975:147–149.

Rodriguez, Richard. *Hunger of Memory: The Education of Richard Rodriguez.* Boston: Godine, 1982.

Rodriguez, Richard. "The Late Victorians: San Francisco, AIDS, and the Homosexual Stereotype." *Harper's Magazine,* October 1990:57–66.

Rodriguez, Richard. "Mixed Blood." *Harper's Magazine, 283,* November 1991:47–56.

Rodriguez, Richard. "Searching for Roots in a Changing Society." In *Down to Earth Sociology: Introductory Readings,* 8th ed., James M. Henslin, ed. New York: Free Press, 1995:486–491.

Sampson, Robert J., Jeffrey D. Morenoff, and Felton Earls. "Beyond Social Capital: Spatial Dynamics of Collective Efficacy for Children." *American Sociological Review, 64,* October 1999:633–660.

"Schwab Study Finds Four Generations of American Adults Fundamentally Rethinking Planning for Retirement." Reuters, July 15, 2008.

Segal, Nancy L. *Someone Else's Twin: The True Story of Babies Switched at Birth.* New York: Prometheus, 2011.

Segal, Nancy L., and Scott L. Hershberger. "Virtual Twins and Intelligence." *Personality and Individual Differences, 39,* 6, 2005:1061–1073.

Skeels, H. M. *Adult Status of Children with Contrasting Early Life Experiences: A Follow-up Study.* Monograph of the Society for Research in Child Development, *31,* 3, 1966.

Skeels, H. M., and H. B. Dye. "A Study of the Effects of Differential Smith, Nicola. "'Sworn Virgins' Dying Out as Albanian Girls Reject Manly Role." *Sunday Times,* January 8, 2008.

Statistical Abstract of the United States. Washington, D.C.: U.S. Census Bureau, published annually.

Suizzo, Marie-Anne. "The Social-Emotional and Cultural Contexts of Cognitive Development: Neo-Piagetian Perspectives." *Child Development, 71,* 4, August 2000:846–849.

Taneja, V., S. Sriram, R. S. Beri, V. Sreenivas, R. Aggarwal, R. Kaur, and J. M. Puliyel. "'Not by Bread Alone': Impact of a Structured 90-Minute Play Session on Development of Children in an Orphanage." *Child Care, Health & Development, 28,* 1, 2002:95–100.

Taylor, Chris. "The Man behind Lara Croft." *Time,* December 6, 1999:78.

"Top 10 Most Expensive Video Game Budgets Ever." Online Digital Battle.com. February 20, 2010.

Vandell, Deborah Lowe, Jay Belsky, Margaret Burchinal, Laurence Steinberg, and Nathan Vandergrift. "No Effects of Early Child Care Extend to Age 15 Years? Results from the NICHD Study of Early Child Care and Youth Development." *Child Development, 81,* 3, May/June 2010:737–756.

Wheaton, Blair, and Philippa Clarke. "Space Meets Time: Integrating Temporal and Contextual Influences on Mental Health in Early Adulthood." *American Sociological Review, 68,* 2003:680–706.

Williams, Dmitri, Nicole Martins, Mia Consalvo, and James D. Ivory. "The Virtual Census: Representations of Gender, Race, and Age in Video Games." *New Media & Society, 11,* 5, 2009:815–834.

Wright, Lawrence. "Double Mystery." *New Yorker,* August 7, 1995:45–62.

Zumbrun, Joshua. "The Sacrifices of Albania's 'Sworn Virgins.'" *Washington Post,* August 11, 2007.

Chapter 4

Aeppel, Timothy. "More Amish Women Are Tending to Business." *Wall Street Journal,* February 8, 1996:B1, B2.

Agins, Teri. "When to Carry a Purse to a Meeting." *Wall Street Journal,* October 1, 2009.

Alter, Alexandra. "Is This Man Cheating on His Wife?" *Wall Street Journal,* August 10, 2007.

Anderson, Elijah. *A Place on the Corner.* Chicago: University of Chicago Press, 1978.

Anderson, Elijah. *Streetwise: Race, Class, and Change in an Urban Community.* Chicago: University of Chicago Press, 1990.

Anderson, Elijah. "Streetwise." In *Exploring Social Life: Readings to Accompany Essentials of Sociology, Sixth Edition,* 2nd ed., James M. Henslin, ed. Boston: Allyn and Bacon, 2006:147–156. Originally published 1990.

Austin, S. Byrn, Jess Haines, and Paul J. Veuglers. "Body Satisfaction and Body Weight: Gender Differences and Sociodemographic Determinants." *BMC Public Health, 9,* August 2009.

Bearak, Barry. "For Some Bushmen, a Homeland Worth a Fight." *New York Times,* November 5, 2010.

Bernard, Jessie. "The Good-Provider Role." In *Marriage and Family in a Changing Society,* 4th ed., James M. Henslin, ed. New York: Free Press, 1992:275–285.

Bjerklie, David, Andrea Dorfman, Wendy Cole, et al. "Baby, It's You: And You, and You . . ." *Time,* February 19, 2001:47–57.

Brinkley, Christina. "Women in Power: Finding Balance in the Wardrobe." *Wall Street Journal,* January 24, 2008.

Buckley, Cara. "Among Victims, an Amish Farmer Quick to Adapt." *New York Times,* July 21, 2011.

Chambliss, William J. "The Saints and the Roughnecks." In *Down to Earth Sociology: Introductory Readings,* 15th ed., James M. Henslin, ed. New York: The Free Press, 2012.

Davis, Ann, Joseph Pereira, and William M. Bulkeley. "Security Concerns Bring Focus on Translating Body Language." *Wall Street Journal,* August 15, 2002.

Davis, Stan. *Lessons From the Future: Making Sense of a Blurred World.* New York: Capstone Publishers, 2001.

Dobriner, William M. "The Football Team as Social Structure and Social System." In *Social Structures and Systems: A Sociological Overview.* Pacific Palisades, Calif.: Goodyear, 1969a:116–120.

Duneier, Mitchell. *Sidewalk.* New York: Farrar, Straus and Giroux, 1999.

Durkheim, Emile. *The Division of Labor in Society,* George Simpson, trans. New York: Free Press, 1933. Originally published 1893.

Elias, Paul. "'Molecular Pharmers' Hope to Raise Human Proteins in Crop Plants." *St. Louis Post-Dispatch,* October 28, 2001:F7.

Frayer, Lauren. "Police: Baby Starved as Couple Nurtured Virtual Kid." AOL News, March 5, 2010.

Garfinkel, Harold. *Studies in Ethnomethodology.* Englewood Cliffs, N.J.: Prentice Hall, 1967.

Garfinkel, Harold. *Ethnomethodology's Program: Working Out Durkheim's Aphorism.* Lanham, Md.: Rowman & Littlefield, 2002.

Goffman, Erving. *The Presentation of Self in Everyday Life.* New York: Peter Smith, 1999. Originally published 1959.

Grabe, Shelly, L. Monique Ward, and Janet Shibley Hyde. "The Role of the Media in Body Image Concerns among Women: A Meta-Analysis of Experimental and Correlational Studies." *Psychological Bulletin, 134,* 3:2008:460–476.

Gross, Jane. "In the Quest for the Perfect Look, More Girls Choose the Scalpel." *New York Times,* November 29, 1998.

Hall, Edward T. *The Silent Language.* New York: Doubleday, 1959.

Hall, Edward T. *The Hidden Dimension.* Garden City, N.Y.: Anchor Books, 1969.

Hall, Edward T., and Mildred R. Hall. "The Sounds of Silence." In *Down to Earth Sociology: Introductory Readings,* 15th ed., James M. Henslin, ed. New York: Free Press, 2012.

Hamermesh, Daniel. *Beauty Pays: Why Attractive People Are More Successful.* Princeton, N.J. Princeton University Press, 2011.

Henslin, James M., and Mae A. Biggs. "Behavior in Pubic Places: The Sociology of the Vaginal Examination." In *Down to Earth Sociology: Introductory Readings,* 15th ed., James M. Henslin, ed. New York: Free Press, 2012. Originally published 1971.

Honeycutt, Karen. "Disgusting, Pathetic, Bizarrely Beautiful: Representations of Weight in Popular Culture." Paper presented at the 1995 meetings of the American Sociological Association.

Hughes, Kathleen A. "Even Tiki Torches Don't Guarantee a Perfect Wedding." *Wall Street Journal,* February 20, 1990:A1, A16.

Johnson-Weiner, Karen. *Train Up a Child: Old Order Amish and Mennonite Schools.* Baltimore, Md.: Johns Hopkins University Press, 2007.

Judge, Timothy A., Charlice Hurst, and Lauren S. Simon. "Does It Pay to Be Smart, Attractive, or Confident (or All Three)? Relationships among General Mental Ability, Physical Attractiveness, Core Self-Evaluations, and Income." *Journal of Applied Psychology, 94,* 3, 2009:742–755.

Kaebnick, Gregory E. "On the Sanctity of Nature." *Hastings Center Report, 30,* 5, September–October 2000:16–23.

Kanazawa, Satoshi, and Jody L. Kovar. "Why Beautiful People Are More Intelligent." *Intelligence, 32,* 2004:227–243.

Kephart, William M., and William W. Zellner. *Extraordinary Groups: An Examination of Unconventional Life-Styles,* 7th ed. New York: Worth Publishing, 2001.

Kraybill, Donald B. *The Riddle of Amish Culture,* rev. ed. Baltimore, Md.: Johns Hopkins University Press, 2002.

Kristoff, Nicholas D. "Interview with a Humanoid." *New York Times,* July 23, 2002.

Lenski, Gerhard, and Jean Lenski. *Human Societies: An Introduction to Macrosociology,* 5th ed. New York: McGraw-Hill, 1987.

Liebow, Elliott. *Tally's Corner: A Study of Negro Streetcorner Men.* Boston: Little, Brown, 1999. Originally published 1967.

Linton, Ralph. *The Study of Man.* New York: Appleton-Century-Crofts, 1936.

Marshall, Samantha. "It's So Simple: Just Lather Up, Watch the Fat Go Down the Drain." *Wall Street Journal,* November 2, 1995:B1.

McGee, Glenn. "Cloning, Sex, and New Kinds of Families." *Journal of Sex Research, 37,* 3, August 2000:266–272.

Mooallem, Jon. "Do-It-Yourself Genetic Engineering." *New York Times,* February 14, 2010.

Needham, Sarah E. "Grooming Women for the Top: Tips from Executive Coaches." *Wall Street Journal,* October 31, 2006.

Osborne, Lawrence. "Got Silk." *New York Times Magazine,* June 15, 2002.

Regalado, Antonio. "Seoul Team Creates Custom Cells from Cloned Embryos. *Wall Street Journal,* May 20, 2005.

Samor, Geraldo, Cecilie Rohwedder, and Ann Zimmerman. "Innocents Abroad?" *Wall Street Journal,* May 5, 2006.

Scolforo, Mark. "Amish Population Nearly Doubles in 16 Years." *Chicago Tribune,* August 20, 2008.

"Second Life Affair Ends in Divorce." www.cnn.com, November 15, 2008.

"Second Life Grid Survey, Region Database." January 1, 2012." http://gridsurvey.com/

Snyder, Mark. "Self-Fulfilling Stereotypes." In *Down to Earth Sociology: Introductory Readings,* 7th ed., James M. Henslin, ed. New York: Free Press, 1993:153–160.

Stiles, Daniel. "The Hunters Are the Hunted." *Geographical, 75,* June 2003:28–32.

Tönnies, Ferdinand. *Community and Society (Gemeinschaft und Gesellschaft),* with a new introduction by John Samples. New Brunswick, N.J.: Transaction, 1988. Originally published 1887.

Volti, Rudi. *Society and Technological Change,* 3rd ed. New York: St. Martin's Press, 1995.

Weiss, Rick. "Mature Human Embryos Cloned." *Washington Post,* February 12, 2004: A1.

Yager, Mark, Beret Strong, Linda Roan, Davd Matsumoto, and Kimberly A. Metcalf. "Nonverbal Communication in the Contemporary Operating Environment." United States Army Research Institute for the Behavioral and Social Sciences, Technical Report 1238, January 2009.

Zaslow, Jeffrey. "Thinness, Women, and School Girls: Body Image." *Wall Street Journal,* September 2, 2009.

Chapter 5

Albanese, Jennifer. Personal research for the author. 2010.

Asch, Solomon. "Effects of Group Pressure upon the Modification and Distortion of Judgments." In *Readings in Social Psychology,* Guy Swanson, Theodore M. Newcomb, and Eugene L. Hartley, eds. New York: Holt, Rinehart and Winston, 1952.

Bales, Robert F. *Interaction Process Analysis.* Reading, Mass.: Addison-Wesley, 1950.

Bales, Robert F. "The Equilibrium Problem in Small Groups." In *Working Papers in the Theory of Action,* Talcott Parsons et al., eds. New York: Free Press, 1953:111–115.

Bennett, Drake. "Who's Still Biased?" *Boston Globe,* March 7, 2010.

Bennett, Jeff. "Strong Demand Revs Up Ford Profit." *Wall Street Journal,* April 26, 2011.

Bond, Rod. "Group Size and Conformity." *Group Processes and Intergroup Relations, 8,* 4, 2005:331–354.

Burger, Jerry M. "Replicating Milgram: Would People Still Obey Today?" *American Psychologist, 64,* 1, January 2009:1–11.

Cartwright, Dorwin, and Alvin Zander, eds. *Group Dynamics,* 3rd ed. Evanston, Ill.: Peterson, 1968.

Cassel, Russell N. "Examining the Basic Principles for Effective Leadership." *College Student Journal, 33,* 2, June 1999:288–301.

Cooley, Charles Horton. *Social Organization.* New York: Schocken Books, 1962. Originally published by Scribner's, 1909.

Crumley, Bruce. "The Game of Death: France's Shocking TV Experiment." *Time,* March 17, 2010.

Darley, John M., and Bibb Latané. "Bystander Intervention in Emergencies: Diffusion of Responsibility." *Journal of Personality and Social Psychology, 8,* 4, 1968:377–383.

Dodds, Peter Sheridan, Roby Muhamad, and Duncan J. Watts. "An Experimental Study of Search in Global Social Networks." *Science, 301,* August 8, 2003:827–830.

Durkheim, Emile. *The Division of Labor in Society,* George Simpson, trans. New York: Free Press, 1933. Originally published 1893.

Flippen, Annette R. "Understanding Groupthink from a Self-Regulatory Perspective." *Small Group Research, 30,* 2, April 1999:139–165.

Fox, Elaine, and George E. Arquitt. "The VFW and the 'Iron Law of Oligarchy.'" In Down to *Earth Sociology,* 4th ed., James M. Henslin, ed. New York: Free Press, 1985:147–155.

Gonzales, Alberto R. "Memorandum for Albert R. Gonzales, Counsel to the President: Re: Standards of Conduct for Interrogation under *18 U.S.C. 2340–2340A.*" August 2, 2002.

Hart, Paul. "Groupthink, Risk-Taking and Recklessness: Quality of Process and Outcome in Policy Decision Making." *Politics and the Individual, 1,* 1, 1991:67–90.

Howells, Lloyd T., and Selwyn W. Becker. "Seating Arrangement and Leadership Emergence." *Journal of Abnormal and Social Psychology, 64,* February 1962:148–150.

Hughes, Everett C. "Good People and Dirty Work." In *Life in Society: Readings to Accompany Sociology: A Down-to-Earth Approach,* 7th ed. James M. Henslin, ed. Boston: Allyn and Bacon, 2005: 125–134. Article originally published 1962.

Jacobs, Margaret A. "'New Girl' Network Is Boon for Women Lawyers." *Wall Street Journal,* March 4, 1997:B1, B7.

Janis, Irving L. *Victims of Groupthink.* Boston: Houghton Mifflin, 1972.

Janis, Irving. L. *Groupthink: Psychological Studies of Policy Decisions and Fiascoes.* Boston: Houghton Mifflin, 1982.

Johnston, David, and Scott Shane. "Memo Sheds New Light on Torture Issue." *New York Times,* April 3, 2008.

Judge, Timothy A., and Daniel M. Cable. "The Effect of Physical Height on Workplace Success and Income: Preliminary Test of a Theoretical Model." *Journal of Applied Psychology, 89,* 3, 2004:428–441.

Kalev, Alexandra, Frank Dobbin, and Erin Kelly. "Assessing the Efficacy of Corporate Affirmative Action and Diversity Policies." *American Sociological Review, 71,* 2006:589–617.

Kanter, Rosabeth Moss. *Men and Women of the Corporation.* New York: Basic Books, 1977.

Kanter, Rosabeth Moss. *The Change Masters: Innovation and Entrepreneurship in the American Corporation.* New York: Simon & Schuster, 1983.

Kanter, Rosabeth Moss. *Supercorp: How Vanguard Companies Create Innovation, Profits, Growth, and Social Good.* New York: Random House, 2009.

Kantor, Jodi. "In First Family, a Nation's Many Faces." *New York Times,* January 16, 2009.

Kim, Richard. "The L Word." *The Nation,* October 19, 2004.

Kleinfeld, Judith S. "The Small World Problem." *Society,* January–February, 2002b:61–66.

Lewis, Neil A. "Justice Dept. Toughens Rules on Torture." *New York Times,* January 1, 2005.

Lippitt, Ronald, and Ralph K. White. "An Experimental Study of Leadership and Group Life." In *Readings in Social Psychology,* 3rd ed., Eleanor E. Maccoby, Theodore M. Newcomb, and Eugene L. Hartley, eds. New York: Holt, Rinehart and Winston, 1958:340–365. (As summarized in Olmsted and Hare 1978:28–31.)

Markoff, John, and Somini Sengupta. "Separating You and Me? 4.74 Degrees." *New York Times,* November 21, 2011.

Merton, Robert K. *Social Theory and Social Structure.* Glencoe, Ill.: Free Press, 1949. Enlarged ed., 1968.

Milgram, Stanley. "Behavioral Study of Obedience." *Journal of Abnormal and Social Psychology, 67,* 4, 1963:371–378.

Milgram, Stanley. "Some Conditions of Obedience and Disobedience to Authority." *Human Relations, 18,* February 1965:57–76.

Milgram, Stanley. "The Small World Problem." *Psychology Today, 1,* 1967:61–67.

Morl, Kazuo, and Miho Aral. "No Need to Fake It: Reproduction of the Ash Experiment without Confederates." *International Journal of Psychology, 45,* 5, 2010:390–397.

Muhamad, Roby. *Search in Social Networks.* Ph.D. dissertation, Columbia University, 2010.

"Mujer 'resucite blye' en España." *BBC Mundo,* February 17, 2006.

Nicholson, Ian. "'Torture at Yale': Experimental Subjects, Laboratory Torment and the 'Rehabilitation' of Milgram's 'Obedience to Authority.'" *Theory Psychology, 21, 737,* October 26, 2011.

Olmsted, Michael S., and A. Paul Hare. *The Small Group,* 2nd ed. New York: Random House, 1978.

Peter, Laurence J., and Raymond Hull. *The Peter Principle: Why Things Always Go Wrong.* New York: Morrow, 1969.

Reibstein, Larry. "Managing Diversity." *Newsweek,* January 25, 1996:50.

Ritzer, George. *The McDonaldization of Society: An Investigation into the Changing Character of Contemporary Life.* Thousand Oaks, Calif.: Pine Forge Press, 1993.

Ritzer, George. *The McDonaldization Thesis: Explorations and Extensions.* Thousand Oaks, Calif.: Sage Publications, 1998.

Ritzer, George. "The McDonaldization of Society." In *Down to Earth Sociology: Introductory Readings,* 11th ed., James M. Henslin, ed. New York: Free Press, 2001:459–471.

Russell, Nestar John Charles. "Milgram's Obedience to Authority Experiments: Origins and Early Evolution." *British Journal of Social Psychology,* 2010:1–23.

Sanchez, Juan I., and Nohora Medkik. "The Effects of Diversity Awareness Training on Differential Treatment." *Group and Organization Management, 29,* 4, August 2004:517–536.

Schulz, William F. "The Torturer's Apprentice: Civil Liberties in a Turbulent Age." *The Nation,* May 13, 2002.

Scott, Monster Cody. *Monster: The Autobiography of an L. A. Gang Member.* New York: Penguin Books, 1994.

Shane, Scott. "Report Outlines Medical Workers' Role in Torture." *New York Times,* April 6, 2009.

Shane, Scott, and Charlie Savage. "Bin Laden Raid Revives Debate on Value of Torture." *New York Times,* May 3, 2011.

Sills, David L. *The Volunteers.* Glencoe, Ill.: Free Press, 1957.

Simmel, Georg. *The Sociology of Georg Simmel,* Kurt H. Wolff, ed. and trans. Glencoe, Ill.: Free Press, 1950. Originally published between 1902 and 1917.

Statistical Abstract of the United States. Washington, D.C.: U.S. Census Bureau, published annually.

Stodgill, Ralph M. *Handbook of Leadership: A Survey of Theory and Research.* New York: Free Press, 1974.

Taylor, Howard F. "The Structure of a National Black Leadership Network: Preliminary Findings." Unpublished manuscript, 1992. (As cited in Margaret L. Andersen and Howard F. Taylor, *Sociology: Understanding a Diverse Society.* Belmont, Calif.: Wadsworth, 2000.)

Terhune, Chad. "Pepsi, Vowing Diversity Isn't Just Image Polish, Seeks Inclusive Culture." *Wall Street Journal,* April 19, 2005.

Trice, Harrison M., and Janice M. Beyer. "Cultural Leadership in Organization." *Organization Science, 2,* 2, May 1991:149–169.

Tyler, Patrick E. "A New Life for NATO? But It's Sidelined for Now." *New York Times,* November 20, 2002.

Vartabedian, Ralph, and Scott Gold. "New Questions on Shuttle Tile Safety Raised." *Los Angeles Times,* February 27, 2003.

Wald, Matthew L., and John Schwartz. "Alerts Were Lacking, NASA Shuttle Manager Says." *New York Times,* July 23, 2003.

Ward, Rose Marie, Halle C. Popson, and Donald G. DiPaolo. "Defining the Alpha Female: A Female Leadership Measure." *Journal of Leadership and Organizational Studies 17,* 3, 2010:309–320.

Weber, Max. *The Theory of Social and Economic Organization,* A. M. Henderson and Talcott Parsons, trans., Talcott Parsons, ed. Glencoe, Ill.: Free Press, 1947. Originally published 1913.

Whitehead, Tom. "Warning of New Era of Surveillance State." *The Telegraph,* November 12, 2010.

Chapter 6

Anderson, Elijah. *A Place on the Corner.* Chicago: University of Chicago Press, 1978.

Anderson, Elijah. "Streetwise." In *Exploring Social Life: Readings to Accompany Essentials of Sociology, Sixth Edition,* 2nd ed., James M. Henslin, ed. Boston: Allyn and Bacon, 2006:147–156. Originally published 1990.

Appiah, Kwame Anthony. "The Best Weapon against Honor Killers: Shame." *Wall Street Journal,* September 25, 2010.

Arlacchi, P. *Peasants and Great Estates: Society in Traditional Calabria.* Cambridge, England: Cambridge University Press, 1980.

Barnes, Helen. "A Comment on Stroud and Pritchard: Child Homicide, Psychiatric Disorder and Dangerousness." *British Journal of Social Work, 31,* 3, June 2001.

Barstow, David, and Lowell Bergman. "Death on the Job, Slaps on the Wrist." *Wall Street Journal,* January 10, 2003.

Becker, Howard S. *Outsiders: Studies in the Sociology of Deviance.* New York: Free Press, 1966.

Bhati, A. S., and Piquero, A. R. "Estimating the Impact of Incarceration on Subsequent Offending Trajectories: Deterrent, Criminogenic, or Null Effects." *Journal of Criminal Law and Criminology, 98,* 2008:207–254.

Billeaud, Jacques. "Arizona Sheriff Defends Illegal-Immigrant Sweeps." *Seattle Times,* April 26, 2008.

Catan, Thomas. "Spain's Showy Debt Collectors Wear a Tux, Collect the Bucks." *Wall Street Journal,* October 11, 2008.

Chagnon, Napoleon A. *Yanomamo: The Fierce People,* 2nd ed. New York: Holt, Rinehart and Winston, 1977.

Chambliss, William J. *Power, Politics, and Crime.* Boulder, Colo. Westview Press, 2000.

Chivers, C. J. "Officer Resigns before Hearing in D.W.I. Case." *New York Times,* August 29, 2001.

Chung, He Len, and Laurence Steinberg. "Relations between Neighborhood Factors, Parenting Behaviors, Peer Deviance, and Delinquency among Serious Juvenile Offenders." *Developmental Psychology, 42,* 2, 2006:319–331.

Church, Wesley T., II, Tracy Wharton, and Julie K. Taylor. "An Examination of Differential Association and Social Control Theory: Family Systems and Delinquency." *Youth Violence and Juvenile Justice, 7,* 1, January 2009:3–15.

Cloud, John. "For Better or Worse." *Time,* October 26, 1998:43–44.

Cloward, Richard A., and Lloyd E. Ohlin. *Delinquency and Opportunity: A Theory of Delinquent Gangs.* New York: Free Press, 1960.

Conklin, John E. *Why Crime Rates Fell.* Boston: Allyn and Bacon, 2003.

Deflem, Mathieu, ed. *Sociological Theory and Criminological Research: Views from Europe and the United States.* San Diego: JAI Press, 2006.

DeLisi, Matt, Andy Hochstetler, Gloria Jones-Johnson, Jonathan W. Caudill, and James W. Marquart. "The Road to Murder: The Enduring Criminogenic Effects of Juvenile Confinement among a Sample of Adult Career Criminals." *Youth Violence and Juvenile Justice, 9,* 2011:207–221.

Drew, Christopher. "Military Contractor Agrees to Pay $325 Million to Settle Whistle-Blower Lawsuit." *New York Times,* April 2, 2009.

Duck, W. O., and Anne W. Rawls, "Interaction Orders of Drug Dealing Spaces: Local Orders of Sensemaking in a Poor Black American Place." *Crime, Law and Social Change,* 2011.

Dunaway, Wilma A. *Women, Work, and Family in the Antebellum Mountain South.* New York: Cambridge University Press, 2008.

Durkheim, Emile. *The Division of Labor in Society,* George Simpson, trans. New York: Free Press, 1933. Originally published 1893.

Durkheim, Emile. *The Rules of Sociological Method,* Sarah A. Solovay and John H. Mueller, trans. New York: Free Press, 1938, 1958, 1964. Originally published 1895.

Edgerton, Robert B. *Deviance: A Cross-Cultural Perspective.* Menlo Park, Calif.: Benjamin/Cummings, 1976.

Gardiner, Sean, and Alison Fox. "Glance May Have Led to Murder." *New York Times,* December 6, 2010.

Garfinkel, Harold. "Conditions of Successful Degradation Ceremonies." *American Journal of Sociology, 61,* 2, March 1956:420–424.

Glaze, Lauren E., and Laura M. Maruschak. "Parents in Prison and Their Minor Children." Bureau of Justice Statistics Special Report, August 2008:1–25.

Goffman, Erving. *Stigma: Notes on the Management of Spoiled Identity.* Englewood Cliffs, N.J.: Prentice Hall, 1963.

Goozen, Stephanie H. M. van, Graeme Fairchild, Heddeke Snoek, and Gordon T. Harold. "The Evidence for a Neurobiological Model of Childhood Antisocial Behavior." *Psychological Bulletin, 133,* 1, 2007:149–182.

Gottfredson, Michael R., and Travis Hirschi. *A General Theory of Crime.* Stanford, Calif.: Stanford University Press, 1990.

Hirschi, Travis. *Causes of Delinquency.* Berkeley: University of California Press, 1969.

Hoffman, Jan. "States Struggle with Minors' Sexting." *New York Times,* March 26, 2011.

Horowitz, Ruth. *Honor and the American Dream: Culture and Identity in a Chicano Community.* New Brunswick, N.J.: Rutgers University Press, 1983.

Horowitz, Ruth. "Studying Violence among the 'Lions.'" In *Social Problems,* James M. Henslin, ed. Upper Saddle River, N.J.: Prentice Hall, 2005:135.

Jacobs, David, Zhenchao Qian, Jason T. Carmichael, and Stephanie L. Kent. "Who Survives on Death Row? An Individual and Contextual Analysis." *American Sociological Review, 72,* August 2007:610–632.

Jones, Allen. "Let Nonviolent Prisoners Out." *Los Angeles Times,* June 12, 2008.

Joyce, Theodore J. "Abortion and Crime: A Review." Cambridge, Mass.: NBER working paper 15098, 2009.

Karamouzis, Stamos T., and Dee Wood Harper. "An Artificial Intelligence System Suggests Arbitrariness of Death Penalty." *International Journal of Law and Information Technology, 16,* 1:2007.

Kontos, Louis, David Brotherton, and Luis Barrios, eds. *Gangs and Society: Alternative Perspectives.* New York: Columbia University Press, 2003.

Kubrin, Charis E., and Ronald Weitzer. "Retaliatory Homicide: Concentrated Disadvantage and Neighborhood Culture." *Social Problems, 50,* 2, May 2003:157–180.

Lombroso, Cesare. *Crime: Its Causes and Remedies,* H. P. Horton, trans. Boston: Little, Brown, 1911.

Lyall, Sarah. "Here's the Pub, Church and Field for Public Sex." *New York Times,* October 7, 2010.

Madigan, Nick. "Judge Questions Long Sentence in Drug Case." *New York Times,* November 17, 2004.

Mayer, John D. *Personality: A Systems Approach.* Boston: Allyn and Bacon, 2007.

McCarthy, Bill. "The Attitudes and Actions of Others: Tutelage and Sutherland's Theory of Differential Association." *British Journal of Criminology 36,* 1, 2011:135–147.

McCormick, John. "The Sorry Side of Sears." *Newsweek,* February 22, 1999b:36–39.

McShane, Marilyn, and Frank P. Williams, III., eds. *Criminological Theory.* Upper Saddle River, N.J.: Prentice Hall, 2007.

Merton, Robert K. "The Social-Cultural Environment and *Anomie.*" In *New Perspectives for Research on Juvenile Delinquency,* Helen L. Witmer and Ruth Kotinsky, eds. Washington, D.C.: U.S. Department of Health, Education, and Welfare, 1956:24–50.

Merton, Robert K. *Social Theory and Social Structure.* Glencoe, Ill.: Free Press, 1949. Enlarged ed., 1968.

Miller, Walter B. "Lower Class Culture as a Generating Milieu of Gang Delinquency." *Journal of Social Issues, 14,* 3, 1958:5–19.

O'Brien, Timothy L. "Fed Assesses Citigroup Unit $70 Million in Loan Abuse." *New York Times,* May 28, 2004.

Oppel, Richard A., Jr. "Steady Decline in Major Crimes Baffles Experts." *New York Times,* May 23, 2011.

Partington, Donald H. "The Incidence of the Death Penalty for Rape in Virginia." *Washington and Lee Law Review, 22,* 1965:43–75.

Read, Madlen. "Citi Pays $18M for Questioned Credit Card Practice." Associated Press, August 26, 2008.

Reckless, Walter C. *The Crime Problem,* 5th ed. New York: Appleton, 1973.

Reiman, Jeffrey, and Paul Leighton. *The Rich Get Richer and the Poor Get Prison: Ideology, Class, and Criminal Justice,* 9th ed. Boston: Allyn and Bacon, 2010.

Reuters. "Fake Tiger Woods Gets 200-Years-to-Life in Prison." April 28, 2001.

Rosenfeld, Richard. "Crime Decline in Context." *Contexts, 1,* 1, Spring 2002:25–34.

Sánchez-Jankowski, Martín. *Islands in the Street: Gangs and American Urban Society.* Berkeley: University of California Press, 1991.

Saranow, Jennifer. "The Snoop Next Door." *Wall Street Journal,* January 12, 2007.

Simon, Stephanie. "Naked Pumpkin Run." *Wall Street Journal,* October 31, 2009.

Sourcebook of Criminal Justice Statistics. Washington, D.C.: U.S. Government Printing Office, published annually.

Spitzer, Steven. "Toward a Marxian Theory of Deviance." *Social Problems, 22,* June 1975:608–619.

Statistical Abstract of the United States. Washington, D.C.: U.S. Census Bureau, published annually.

Sutherland, Edwin H. *Criminology.* Philadelphia: Lippincott, 1924.

Sutherland, Edwin H. *Principles of Criminology,* 4th ed. Philadelphia: Lippincott, 1947.

Sutherland, Edwin H. *White Collar Crime.* New York: Dryden Press, 1949.

Sykes, Gresham M., and David Matza. "Techniques of Neutralization." In *Down to Earth Sociology: Introductory Readings,* 5th ed., James M. Henslin, ed. New York: Free Press, 1988:225–231. Originally published 1957.

Szasz, Thomas S. *The Myth of Mental Illness,* rev. ed. New York: Harper & Row, 1986.

Szasz, Thomas S. "Mental Illness Is Still a Myth." In *Deviant Behavior 96/97,* Lawrence M. Salinger, ed. Guilford, Conn.: Dushkin, 1996:200–205.

Szasz, Thomas S. *Cruel Compassion: Psychiatric Control of Society's Unwanted.* Syracuse, N.Y.: Syracuse University Press, 1998.

Usher, Sebastian. "'End of Virginity' If Women Drive, Saudi Cleric Warns." *BBC News,* December 2, 2011.

Vigil, Tammy. "Boulder Police: No Full Frontal Nudity." Fox 31, Denver, Colorado, June 11, 2009.

Walsh, Anthony, and Kevin M. Beaver. "Biosocial Criminology." In *Handbook on Crime and Deviance,* M. D. Krohn et al., eds. Dordrecht, New York: Springer, 2009:79–101.

Warren, Jennifer, Adam Gelb, Jake Horowitz, and Jessica Riordan. "One in 100: Behind Bars in America 2008." Washington, D.C.: Pew Charitable Trust, February 2008.

Watson, J. Mark. "Outlaw Motorcyclists." In *Society: Readings to Accompany Sociology: A Down-to-Earth Approach, Core Concepts,* James M. Henslin ed. Boston: Allyn and Bacon, 2006:105–114. Originally published 1980 in *Deviant Behavior, 2,* 1.

"What They're Saying about Sexting," *New York Times,* March 26, 2011.

White, Joseph B., Stephen Power, and Timothy Aeppel. "Death Count Linked to Failures of Firestone Tires Rises to 203." *Wall Street Journal,* June 19, 2001:A4.

Wilson, James Q., and Richard J. Herrnstein. *Crime and Human Nature.* New York: Simon & Schuster, 1985.

Chapter 7

Akol, Jacob. "Slavery in Sudan." *New African,* September 1998.

Ayittey, George B. N. "Black Africans Are Enraged at Arabs." *Wall Street Journal,* interactive edition, September 4, 1998.

Bailey, Martha J., and Susan M. Dynarski. "Gains and Gaps: Changing Inequality in U.S. College Entry and Completion." In *Whither Opportunity?: Rising Inequality, Schools, and Children's Life Chances,* Greg J. Duncan and Richard J. Murnane, eds. Russell Sage, September 2011.

Barbassa, Juliana. "Rio Cops Use Armor to Raid Slum Where Gang Based." Associated Press, November 25, 2010.

Beckett, Paul. "Caste Away." *Wall Street Journal,* June 23, 2007.

Berger, Peter. "Invitation to Sociology." In *Down to Earth Sociology: Introductory Readings,* 15th ed., James M. Henslin, ed. New York: Free Press, 2012. Originally published 1963.

Blanchard, Ben. "China Vows No Let-Up to State Control of Internet." Reuters, June 7, 2010.

Brown, Alan S. "Mexico Redux." *Mechanical Engineering,* January 2008.

Carrington, Tim. "Developed Nations Want Poor Countries to Succeed on Trade, but Not Too Much." *Wall Street Journal,* September 20, 1993:A10.

Chandra, Vibha P. "Fragmented Identities: The Social Construction of Ethnicity, 1885–1947." Unpublished paper, 1993a.

CIA (Central Intelligence Agency). "Report of Questionable Activity in Connection with Project PBSuccess." Washington, D.C.: Central Intelligence Agency, 2003.

CIA (Central Intelligence Agency). *The World Factbook.* Washington, D.C: U.S. Government Printing Office, 2010. Published annually.

Collins, Randall. "Socially Unrecognized Cumulation." *American Sociologist, 30,* 2, Summer 1999:41–61.

Crossette, Barbara. "Caste May Be India's Moral Achilles' Heel." *New York Times,* October 20, 1996.

Davis, Kingsley, and Wilbert E. Moore. "Some Principles of Stratification." *American Sociological Review, 10,* 1945:242–249.

Davis, Kingsley, and Wilbert E. Moore. "Reply to Tumin." *American Sociological Review, 18,* 1953:394–396.

Deliege, Robert. *The Untouchables of India.* New York: Berg Publishers, 2001.

de Pastino, Blake. "Photo in the News: Robot Jockeys Race Camels in Qatar." *National Geographic,* July 15, 2005.

Du Bois, W. E. B. *Black Reconstruction in America: An Essay toward a History of the Part Which Black Folk Played in the Attempt to Reconstruct Democracy in America, 1860–1880.* New York: Atheneum, 1992. Originally published 1935.

Fraser, Graham. "Fox Denies Free Trade Exploiting the Poor in Mexico." *Toronto Star,* April 20, 2001.

Galbraith, John Kenneth. *The Nature of Mass Poverty.* Cambridge Mass.: Harvard University Press, 1979.

Gerth, H. H., and C. Wright Mills. *From Max Weber: Essays in Sociology.* New York: Galaxy, 1958.

Harrington, Michael. *The Vast Majority: A Journey to the World's Poor.* New York: Simon & Schuster, 1977.

Harris, Craig. "Fallout from Ariz. Employer Sanctions Law." *Arizona Republic,* September 15, 2008.

Harrison, Paul. *Inside the Third World: The Anatomy of Poverty,* 3rd ed. London: Penguin Books, 1993.

Hignett, Kelly. "The Changing Face of Organized Crime in Post-Communist Central and Eastern Europe." *Debatte: Journal of Contemporary Central and Eastern Europe, 18,* 1, 2010:71–88.

Huber, Joan. "Micro-Macro Links in Gender Stratification." *American Sociological Review, 55,* February 1990:1–10.

Huggins, Martha K., and Sandra Rodrigues. "Kids Working on Paulista Avenue." *Childhood, 11,* 2004:495–514.

Huggins, Martha K., Mika Haritos-Fatouros, and Philip G. Zimbardo. *Violence Workers: Police Torturers and Murderers Reconstruct Brazilian Atrocities.* Berkeley: University of California Press, 2002.

Jaffrelot, Christophe. "The Impact of Affirmative Action in India: More Political than Socioeconomic." *India Review, 5,* 2, April 2006:173–189.

Jessop, Bob, "The Return of the National State in the Current Crisis of the World Market." *Capital and Class, 34,* 1, 2010:38–43.

Kerswill, Paul. "Socio-Economic Class." In *The Routledge Companion to Sociolinguistics,* Carmen Llamas and Peter Stockwell, eds. London: Routledge, 2006.

Kifner, John. "Building Modernity on Desert Mirages." *New York Times,* February 7, 1999.

King, Eden B., Jennifer L. Knight, and Michelle R. Hebl. "The Influence of Economic Conditions on Aspects of Stigmatization." *Journal of Social Issues, 66,* 3, September 2010:446–460.

Krugman, Paul. "White Man's Burden." *New York Times,* September 24, 2002.

Kurian, George Thomas. *Encyclopedia of the First World,* Vols. 1, 2. New York: Facts on File, 1990.

Kurian, George Thomas. *Encyclopedia of the Second World.* New York: Facts on File, 1991.

Kurian, George Thomas. *Encyclopedia of the Third World,* Vols. 1, 2, 3. New York: Facts on File, 1992.

Lacey, Marc. "Tijuana Journal: Cities Mesh across Blurry Border, Despite Physical Barrier." *New York Times,* March 5, 2007.

LaFraniere, Sharon. "Views of North Korea Show How a Policy Spread Misery." *New York Times,* June 9, 2010.

Landtman, Gunnar. *The Origin of the Inequality of the Social Classes.* New York: Greenwood Press, 1968. Originally published 1938.

Lenski, Gerhard. *Power and Privilege: A Theory of Social Stratification.* New York: McGraw-Hill, 1966.

Lerner, Gerda. *Black Women in White America: A Documentary History*. New York: Pantheon Books, 1972.

Lerner, Gerda. *The Creation of Patriarchy*. New York: Oxford, 1986.

Lewis, Oscar. "The Culture of Poverty." *Scientific American, 115,* October 1966a:19–25.

Lewis, Oscar. *La Vida*. New York: Random House, 1966b.

Marx, Karl. "Contribution to the Critique of Hegel's Philosophy of Right." In *Karl Marx: Early Writings,* T. B. Bottomore, ed. New York: McGraw-Hill, 1964:45. Originally published 1844.

Marx, Karl, and Friedrich Engels. *Communist Manifesto*. New York: Pantheon, 1967. Originally published 1848.

Mende, Nazer, and Damien Lewis. *Slave: My True Story*. New York: Public Affairs, 2005.

Menzel, Peter. *Material World: A Global Family Portrait*. San Francisco: Sierra Club, 1994.

Mesure, Susie. "Newspaper Owner 'Kidnapped by Russian Mafia.'" *New Zealand Herald*, March 23, 2008.

Mosca, Gaetano. *The Ruling Class*. New York: McGraw-Hill, 1939. Originally published 1896.

Mouawad, Jad. "Saudi Officials Seek to Temper the Price of Oil." *Bloomberg News*, January 27, 2007.

Muñoz Martinez, Hepzibah. "The Double Burden on Maquila Workers: Violence and Crisis in Northern Mexico." El Colegio de la Frontera Norte, Matamoros, June 15, 2010.

Neil, Andrew. "Does a Narrow Social Elite Run the Country?" BBC, January 26, 2011.

Nelson, Dean. "Former Camel Jockeys Compensated by UAE." *Telegraph,* May 5, 2009.

Nordland, Rod. "That Joke Is a Killer." *Newsweek,* May 19, 2003:10.

Peck, Grant. "Australian Convicted of Insulting Thai Monarchy." Associated Press, January 19, 2009.

Polgreen, Lydia. "Court Rules Niger Failed by Allowing Girl's Slavery." *New York Times,* October 27, 2008.

Robertson, Ian. *Sociology,* 3rd ed. New York: Worth, 1987.

Rothkopf, David. *Superclass: The Global Power Elite and the World They Are Making*. New York: Farrar, Straus and Giroux, 2008.

Salopek, Paul. "Shattered Sudan: Drilling for Oil, Hoping for Peace." *National Geographic, 203,* 2, February 2003:30–66.

Smith, Simon C. "The Making of a Neo-Colony? Anglo-Kuwaiti Relations in the Era of Decolonization." *Middle Eastern Studies, 37,* 1, January 2001:159–173.

Stampp, Kenneth M. *The Peculiar Institution: Slavery in the Ante-Bellum South*. New York: Vintage Books, 1956.

Statistical Abstract of the United States. Washington, D.C.: U.S. Census Bureau, published annually.

Strategic Energy Policy: Challenges for the 21st Century. New York: Council on Foreign Relations, 2001.

Sullivan, Andrew. "What We Look Up to Now." *New York Times,* November 15, 1998.

Thompson, Ginger. "Chasing Mexico's Dream into Squalor." *New York Times,* February 11, 2001.

Thompson, Paul. "Pentagon Buys and Destroys 9,500 Copies of Soldier's Afghanistan Book 'to Protect Military Secrets.'" *Mail Online,* September 27, 2010.

Trafficking in Persons Report. Washington, D.C.: U.S. Department of State, June 27, 2011.

Trofimov, Yaroslav. "Brutal Attack in India Shows How Caste System Lives On." *New York Times,* December 27, 2007.

Tumin, Melvin M. "Some Principles of Social Stratification: A Critical Analysis." *American Sociological Review, 18,* August 1953:394.

UNESCO. "UNESCO Launches Global Partnership for Girls and Women's Education." June 2011.

Utar, Hale, and Luis Bernardo Torres Ruiz. "International Competition and Industrial Evolution: Evidence from the Impact of Chinese Competition on Mexican Maquiladoras." University of Colorado at Boulder and Banco de Mexico, July 2010.

Varese, Federico. *The Russian Mafia: Private Protection in a New Market Economy*. Oxford: Oxford University Press, 2005.

Wallerstein, Immanuel. *The Modern World System: Capitalist Agriculture and the Origins of the European World-Economy in the Sixteenth Century*. New York: Academic Press, 1974.

Wallerstein, Immanuel. *The Capitalist World-Economy*. New York: Cambridge University Press, 1979.

Wallerstein, Immanuel. "Culture as the Ideological Battleground of the Modern World-System." In *Global Culture: Nationalism, Globalization, and Modernity,* Mike Featherstone, ed. London: Sage, 1990:31–55.

Weber, Max. *Economy and Society,* G. Roth and C. Wittich, eds. Berkeley: University of California Press, 1978. Originally published 1922.

Wise, Raul Delgado, and James M. Cypher. "The Strategic Role of Mexican Labor under NAFTA: Critical Perspectives on Current Economic Integration." *Annals of the American Academy of Political and Social Science, 610,* March 2007:120–142.

"'You Can Die Anytime.' Death Squad Killings in Mindanao." New York: Human Rights Watch, 2009.

Chapter 8

Aldrich, Nelson W., Jr. *Old Money: The Mythology of America's Upper Class*. New York: Vintage Books, 1989.

Allegretto, Sylvia A. "The State of Working America's Wealth," Economic Policy Institute, Briefing Paper #202, March 23, 2011.

Anderson, Jenny. "She's Warm, Easy to Talk to, and a Source of Terror for Private-School Parents." *New York Times,* December 18, 2011.

Baltzell, E. Digby. *Puritan Boston and Quaker Philadelphia*. New York: Free Press, 1979.

Baltzell, E. Digby, and Howard G. Schneiderman. "Social Class in the Oval Office." *Society, 25,* September/October 1988:42–49.

Banjo, Shelly. "Prepping for the Playdate Test." *Wall Street Journal,* August 19, 2010.

Beeghley, Leonard. *The Structure of Social Stratification in the United States,* 5th ed. Boston: Allyn & Bacon, 2008.

Beller, Emily. "Bringing Intergenerational Social Mobility Research into the Twenty-First Century: Why Mothers Matter." *American Sociological Review, 74,* August 2009:507–528.

Bello, Marisol. "Poverty Affects 46 Million Americans." *USA Today,* September 30, 2011.

Bernstein, David. "The $18-Million Dollar Headache." *Chicago Magazine,* April 2007.

Blau, Peter M., and Otis Dudley Duncan. *The American Occupational Structure*. New York: John Wiley, 1967.

Braig, Stefanie, Richard Peter, Gabriele Nagel, et al. "The Impact of Social Status Inconsistency on Cardiovascular Risk Factors, Myocardial Infarction and Stroke in the EPIC-Heidelberg Cohort." *BMC Public Health, 11,* 2011:104.

"Builder Stephen Ross Buys Half of Dolphins from Huizenga." *International Herald Tribune,* February 22, 2008.

Cellini, Stephanie R., Signe-Mary McKernan, and Caroline Ratcliffe. "The Dynamics of Poverty in the United States: A Review of Data, Methods, and Findings." *Journal of Policy Analysis and Management, 27,* 2008:577–605.

Chin, Nancy P., Alicia Monroe, and Kevin Fiscella. "Social Determinants of (Un)Healthy Behaviors." *Education for Health: Change in Learning and Practice, 13,* 3, November 2000:317–328.

Cohen, Patricia. "Forget Lonely. Life Is Healthy at the Top." *New York Times,* May 15, 2004.

Cohen, Patricia. "'Culture of Poverty' Makes a Comeback." *New York Times,* October 17, 2010.

Corcoran, Mary. "Mobility, Persistence, and Consequences of Poverty for Children: Child and Adult Outcomes." In *Understanding Poverty,* Sheldon H. Danziger and Robert H. Haveman, eds. New York: Russell Sage, 2001:127–161.

Crompton, Rosemary. "Class and Employment." *Work, Employment and Society, 24,* 2010:9–26.

Dao, James. "Instant Millions Can't Halt Winners' Grim Side." *New York Times,* December 5, 2005.

Davis, Nancy J., and Robert V. Robinson. "Class Identification of Men and Women in the 1970s and 1980s." *American Sociological Review, 53,* February 1988:103–112.

DeNavas-Walt, Carmen, Bernadette D. Proctor, and Jessica C. Smith. "Income, Poverty, and Health Insurance Coverage in the United States: 2009." *Current Population Reports P60-238,* Washington, D.C.: U.S. Census Bureau, September 2010.

Dogan, Mattei. "Status Incongruence in Advanced Societies." *Societamutamentopolitica, 2,* 3, 2011:285–294.

Dolnick, Sam. "The Obesity-Hunger Paradox." *New York Times,* March 12, 2010.

Domhoff, G. William. *The Power Elite and the State: How Policy Is Made in America.* Hawthorne, N.Y.: Aldine de Gruyter, 1990.

Domhoff, G. William. "State and Ruling Class in Corporate America (1974): Reflections, Corrections, and New Directions." *Critical Sociology, 25,* 2–3, July 1999b:260–265.

Domhoff, G. William. *Who Rules America? Power, Politics, and Social Change,* 5th ed. New York: McGraw-Hill, 2006.

Domhoff, G. William. "Wealth, Income, and Power." Website: Who Rules America, September 2010. http://sociology.ucsc.edu/whorulesamerica/

Duff, Christina. "Superrich's Share of After-Tax Income Stopped Rising in Early '90s, Data Show." *Wall Street Journal,* November 22, 1995:A2.

Dye, Jane Lawler. "Fertility of American Women, June 2004." U.S. Census Bureau. *Current Population Reports,* December 2005.

Eckholm, Erik. "California's Zigzag on Welfare Rules Worries Experts." *New York Times,* October 6, 2009.

Fabrikant, Geraldine. "Old Nantucket Warily Meets the New." *New York Times,* June 5, 2005.

Faris, Robert E. L., and Warren Dunham. *Mental Disorders in Urban Areas.* Chicago: University of Chicago Press, 1939.

Featherman, David L. "Opportunities Are Expanding." *Society, 13,* 1979:4–11.

Feuer, Alan. "Accommodations for the Discreetly Superrich." *New York Times,* October 6, 2008.

Garfinkel, Irwin, Lee Rainwater, and Timothy Smeeding. *Wealth and Welfare States: Is America a Laggard or a Leader?* New York: Oxford University Press, 2010.

Geronimus, Arline T., Margaret T. Hicken, Jay A. Pearson, Sarah J. Seashols, Kelly L. Brown, and Tracy Dawson Cruz. "Do US Black Women Experience Stress-Related Accelerated Biological Aging?" *Human Nature, 21,* 2010:19–38.

Gilbert, Dennis L. *The American Class Structure in an Age of Growing Inequality,* 6th ed. Belmont, Calif.: Wadsworth Publishing, 2003.

Gilbert, Dennis L. *The American Class Structure in an Age of Growing Inequality,* 7th ed. Los Angeles: Pine Forge Press, 2008.

Gilbert, Dennis, and Joseph A. Kahl. *The American Class Structure: A New Synthesis,* 4th ed. Belmont, Calif.: Wadsworth Publishing, 1998.

Gold, Ray. "Janitors versus Tenants: A Status-Income Dilemma." *American Journal of Sociology, 58,* 1952:486–493.

Gottschalk, Peter, Sara McLanahan, and Gary Sandefur, "The Dynamics and Intergenerational Transmission of Poverty and Welfare Participation." In *Confronting Poverty: Prescriptions for Change,* Sheldon H. Danziger, Gary D. Sandefur, and Daniel H. Weinberg, eds. Cambridge, Mass.: Harvard University Press, 1994.

Haughney, Christine, and Eric Konigsberg. "Despite Tough Times, Ultrarich Keep Spending." *New York Times,* April 14, 2008.

Hellinger, Daniel, and Dennis R. Judd. *The Democratic Facade.* Pacific Grove, Calif.: Brooks/Cole, 1991.

Henslin, James M. *Social Problems: A Down-to-Earth Approach,* 10th ed. Boston: Allyn and Bacon, 2012b.

Higginbotham, Elizabeth, and Lynn Weber. "Moving with Kin and Community: Upward Social Mobility for Black and White Women." *Gender and Society, 6,* 3, September 1992:416–440.

Hofferth, Sandra. "Did Welfare Reform Work? Implications for 2002 and Beyond." *Contexts,* Spring 2002:45–51.

hooks, bell. *Where We Stand: Class Matters.* New York: Routledge, 2000.

Hout, Michael. "How Class Works: Objective and Subjective Aspects of Class since the 1970s." In *Social Class: How Does It Work?* Annette Lareau and Dalton Conley, eds. New York: Russell Sage, 2008:52–64.

Houtman, Dick. "What Exactly Is a 'Social Class'?: On the Economic Liberalism and Cultural Conservatism of the 'Working Class.'" Paper presented at the annual meetings of the American Sociological Association, 1995.

Kaufman, Joanne. "Married Maidens and Dilatory Domiciles." *Wall Street Journal,* May 7, 1996:A16.

Kefalas, Maria. "Looking for the Lower Middle Class." *City and Community, 6,* 1, March 2007:63–68.

Kennickell, Arthur B. "Tossed and Turned: Wealth Dynamics of U.S. Households 2007–2009." Washington, D.C.: Division of Research and Statistics, Board of Governors of the Federal Reserve System, November 7, 2011.

Kluegel, James R., and Eliot R. Smith. *Beliefs about Inequality: America's Views of What Is and What Ought to Be.* Hawthorne, N.Y.: Aldine de Gruyter, 1986.

Kneebone, Elizabeth, and Emily Garr. "The Suburbanization of Poverty: Trends in Metropolitan America, 2000 to 2008." Washington, D.C.: Brookings, January 2010.

Kohn, Melvin L. *Class and Conformity: A Study in Values,* 2nd ed. Homewood, Ill.: Dorsey Press, 1977.

Lacy, Karyn R. *Blue-Chip Black: Class and Status in the New Black Middle Class.* Berkeley: University of California Press, 2007.

Lacy, Karyn R., and Angel L. Harris. "Breaking the Class Monolith: Understanding Class Differences in Black Adolescents' Attachment to Racial Identity." In *Social Class: How Does It Work?* Annette Lareau and Dalton Conley, eds. New York: Russell Sage, 2008:152–178.

Landry, Bart, and Kris Marsh. "The Evolution of the New Black Middle Class." *Annual Review of Sociology, 37,* 2011:373–394.

Lareau, Annette, and Dalton Conley, eds. *Social Class: How Does It Work?* New York: Russell Sage, 2008.

Latimer, Melissa, and Rachael A. Woldoff. "Good Country Living? Exploring Four Housing Outcomes among Poor Appalachians." *Sociological Forum 25,* 2, June 2010:315–333.

Lenski, Gerhard. "Status Crystallization: A Nonvertical Dimension of Social Status." *American Sociological Review, 19,* 1954:405–413.

Lenski, Gerhard. *Power and Privilege: A Theory of Social Stratification*. New York: McGraw-Hill, 1966.

Leo, Jen. "Google's Space Explorer Sergey Brin." *Los Angeles Times*, June 12, 2008.

Lewis, Oscar. "The Culture of Poverty." *Scientific American, 115,* October 1966a:19–25.

Lichter, Daniel T., and Martha L. Crowley. "Poverty in America: Beyond Welfare Reform." *Population Bulletin, 57,* 2, June 2002:1–36.

Loprest, Pamela, and Austin Nichols. "Characteristics of Low-Income Single Mothers Disconnected from Work and Public Assistance." Low-Income Working Families Fact Sheet. Washington, D.C.: The Urban Institute, 2011.

Lublin, Joann S. "Living Well." *Wall Street Journal,* April 8, 1999.

Lublin, Joann S. "CEO Pay in 2010 Jumped 11%." *Wall Street Journal,* May 9, 2011.

Lush, Tamara. "Friend Charged with Hiding Fla. Lotto Winner Death." Associated Press, February 3, 2010.

McShane, Larry. "Abraham Shakespeare, $31M Florida Lottery Winner, Found Dead 9 Months after Disappearing." *Daily News,* January 30, 2010.

Morris, Joan M., and Michael D. Grimes. "Moving Up from the Working Class." In *Down to Earth Sociology: Introductory Readings,* 13th ed., James M. Henslin, ed. New York: Free Press, 2005:365–376.

Nakao, Keiko, and Judith Treas. "Occupational Prestige in the United States Revisited: Twenty-Five Years of Stability and Change." Paper presented at the annual meetings of the American Sociological Association, 1990. (As cited in Kerbo, Harold R. *Social Stratification and Inequality: Class Conflict in Historical and Comparative Perspective,* 2nd ed. New York: McGraw-Hill, 1991:181.)

Nakao, Keiko, and Judith Treas. "Updating Occupational Prestige and Socioeconomic Scores: How the New Measures Measure Up." *Sociological Methodology, 24,* 1994:1–72.

O'Hare, William P. "A New Look at Poverty in America." *Population Bulletin, 51,* 2, September 1996a:1–47.

O'Hare, William P. "U.S. Poverty Myths Explored: Many Poor Work Year-Round, Few Still Poor after Five Years." *Population Today: News, Numbers, and Analysis, 24,* 10, October 1996b:1–2.

"On History and Heritage: John K. Castle." *Penn Law Journal,* Fall 1999.

Peltham, Brett W. "About One in Six Americans Report History of Depression." Gallup Poll. October 20, 2009.

Peterson, Janice. "Welfare Reform and Inequality: The TANF and UI Programs." *Journal of Economic Issues, 34,* 2, June 2000:517–526.

Robinson, Gail, and Barbara Mullins Nelson. "Pursuing Upward Mobility: African American Professional Women Reflect on Their Journey." *Journal of Black Studies, 40,* 6, 2010:1168–1188.

Ruggles, Patricia. "Short and Long Term Poverty in the United States: Measuring the American 'Underclass.'" Washington, D.C.: Urban Institute, June 1989.

Samuelson, Paul Anthony, and William D. Nordhaus. *Economics,* 18th ed. New York: McGraw Hill, 2005.

Sklair, Leslie. *Globalization: Capitalism and Its Alternatives,* 3rd ed. New York: Oxford: University Press, 2001.

Srole, Leo, et al. *Mental Health in the Metropolis: The Midtown Manhattan Study.* Albany, N.Y.: New York University Press, 1978.

Statistical Abstract of the United States. Washington, D.C.: U.S. Census Bureau, published annually.

Stevens, Mitchell. *Creating a Class: College Admissions and the Education of Elites.* Cambridge, Mass.: Harvard University Press, 2009.

"Sticky Ticket: A New Jersey Mother Sues Her Son over a Lottery Jackpot She Claims Belongs to Them Both." *People Weekly,* February 9, 1998:68.

"The Wall Street Journal Survey of CEO Compensation." *Wall Street Journal,* April 2, 2009.

Treiman, Donald J. *Occupational Prestige in Comparative Perspective.* New York: Academic Press, 1977.

Tresniowski, Alex. "Payday or Mayday?" *People Weekly,* May 17, 1999:128–131.

Uchitelle, Louis. "How to Define Poverty? Let Us Count the Ways." *New York Times,* May 28, 2001.

Urban Institute. "A Decade of Welfare Reform: Facts and Figures." June 2006.

Wright, Erik Olin. *Class.* London: Verso, 1985.

Chapter 9

Adorno, Theodor W., Else Frenkel-Brunswick, D. J. Levinson, and R. N. Sanford. *The Authoritarian Personality.* New York: Harper & Row, 1950.

Alba, Richard, and Victor Nee. *Remaking the American Mainstream: Assimilation and Contemporary Immigration.* Cambridge, Mass.: Harvard University Press, 2003.

Allport, Floyd. *Social Psychology.* Boston: Houghton Mifflin, 1954.

Angler, Natalie. "Do Races Differ? Not Really, DNA Shows." *New York Times,* August 22, 2000.

Archibold, Randal C. "Arizona Enacts Stringent Law on Immigration." *New York Times,* April 23, 2010.

Archibold, Randal C., and Julia Preston. "Homeland Security Stands by Its Fence." *New York Times,* May 21, 2008.

Bartlett, Donald L., and James B. Steele. "Wheel of Misfortune." *Time,* December 16, 2002:44–58.

Bean, Frank D., Jennifer Lee, Jeanne Batalova, and Mark Leach. "Immigration and Fading Color Lines in America." Washington, D.C.: Population Reference Bureau, 2004.

Bell, David A. "An American Success Story: The Triumph of Asian-Americans." In *Sociological Footprints: Introductory Readings in Sociology,* 5th ed., Leonard Cargan and Jeanne H. Ballantine, eds. Belmont, Calif.: Wadsworth, 1991:308–316.

Bernard, Viola W., Perry Ottenberg, and Fritz Redl. "Dehumanization: A Composite Psychological Defense in Relation to Modern War." In *The Triple Revolution Emerging: Social Problems in Depth,* Robert Perucci and Marc Pilisuk, eds. Boston: Little, Brown, 1971:17–34.

Bertrand, Marianne, and Sendhil Mullainathan. "Are Emily and Brendan More Employable than Lakish and Jamal? A Field Experiment on Labor Market Discrimination." Unpublished paper, November 18, 2002.

Blee, Kathleen M. "Inside Organized Racism." In *Life in Society: Readings to Accompany Sociology: A Down-to-Earth Approach, Seventh Edition,* James M. Henslin, ed. Boston: Allyn and Bacon, 2005:46–57.

Blee, Kathleen M. "Trajectories of Ideologies and Action in US Organized Racism." In *Identity and Participation in Culturally Diverse Societies: A Multidisciplinary Perspective.* Assaad E. Azzi, Xenia Chryssochoou, Bert Klandermans, and Bernd Simon, eds. Oxford, UK: Blackwell Publishing, 2011.

Bradford, Phillips Verner, and Harvey Blume. *Ota Benga: The Pygmy in the Zoo.* New York: Delta, 1992.

Bray, Rosemary L. "Rosa Parks: A Legendary Moment, a Lifetime of Activism." *Ms., 6,* 3, November–December 1995:45–47.

Bretos, Miguel A. "Hispanics Face Institutional Exclusion." *Miami Herald,* May 22, 1994.

Browning, Christopher R. *Ordinary Men: Reserve Police Battalion 101 and the Final Solution in Poland.* New York: HarperPerennial, 1993.

Carlson, Lewis H., and George A. Colburn. *In Their Place: White America Defines Her Minorities, 1850–1950.* New York: Wiley, 1972.

Chandra, Vibha P. "The Present Moment of the Past: The Metamorphosis." Unpublished paper, 1993b.

Churchill, Ward. *A Little Matter of Genocide: Holocaust and Denial in the Americas, 1492 to the Present.* San Francisco: City Lights Books, 1997.

Cose, Ellis. "What's White Anyway?" *Newsweek,* September 18, 2000:64–65.

Cose, Ellis. "Black versus Brown." *Newsweek,* July 3, 2006:44–45.

Cowen, Emory L., Judah Landes, and Donald E. Schaet. "The Effects of Mild Frustration on the Expression of Prejudiced Attitudes." *Journal of Abnormal and Social Psychology,* January 1959:33–38.

Crosby Alex E., LaVonne Ortega, and Mark R. Stevens. "Suicide: United States, 1999–2007." *Morbidity and Mortality Weekly Report, 60, 1,* Supplements, January 4 2011:56–59.

Crossen, Cynthia. "How Pygmy Ota Benga Ended Up in Bronx Zoo as Darwinism Dawned." *Wall Street Journal,* February 6, 2006.

Dasgupta, Nilanjana, Debbie E. McGhee, Anthony G. Greenwald, and Mahzarin R. Banaji. "Automatic Preference for White Americans: Eliminating the Familiarity Explanation." *Journal of Experimental Social Psychology, 36,* 3, May 2000:316–328.

Deutscher, Irwin. *Accommodating Diversity: National Policies that Prevent Ethnic Conflict.* Lanham, Md.: Lexington Books, 2002.

DiSilvestro, Roger L. *In the Shadow of Wounded Knee: The Untold Final Chapter of the Indian Wars.* New York: Walker & Co., 2006.

Doane, Ashley W., Jr. "Dominant Group Ethnic Identity in the United States: The Role of 'Hidden' Ethnicity in Intergroup Relations." *The Sociological Quarterly, 38,* 3, Summer 1997:375–397.

Dobyns, Henry F. *Their Numbers Became Thinned: Native American Population Dynamics in Eastern North America.* Knoxville: University of Tennessee Press, 1983.

Dollard, John, et al. *Frustration and Aggression.* New Haven, Conn.: Yale University Press, 1939.

Du Bois, W. E. B. *The Souls of Black Folk: Essays and Sketches.* Chicago: McClurg, 1903.

Du Bois, W. E. B. *Black Reconstruction in America: An Essay toward a History of the Part Which Black Folk Played in the Attempt to Reconstruct Democracy in America, 1860–1880.* New York: Atheneum, 1992. Originally published 1935.

Ezekiel, Raphael S. *The Racist Mind: Portraits of American Neo-Nazis and Klansmen.* New York: Viking, 1995.

Feagin, Joe R. "The Continuing Significance of Race: Antiblack Discrimination in Public Places." In *Majority and Minority: The Dynamics of Race and Ethnicity in American Life,* 6th ed., Norman R. Yetman, ed. Boston: Allyn and Bacon, 1999:384–399.

Fish, Jefferson M. "Mixed Blood." *Psychology Today, 28,* 6, November–December 1995:55–58, 60, 61, 76, 80.

Frank, Reanne. "What to Make of It? The (Re)emergence of a Biological Conceptualization of Race in Health Disparities Research." *Social Science & Medicine, 64,* 2007:1977–1983.

Fund, John. "English-Only Showdown." *Wall Street Journal,* November 28, 2007.

Gettleman, Jeffrey, and Josh Kron, "U.N. Report on Congo Massacres Draws Anger." *New York Times,* October 1, 2010.

Greenwald, Anthony G., and Linda Hamilton Krieger. "Implicit Bias: Scientific Foundations." *California Law Review,* July 2006.

Gross, Jan T. *Neighbors.* New Haven, Conn.: Yale University Press, 2001.

Hall, Ronald E. "The Tiger Woods Phenomenon: A Note on Biracial Identity." *The Social Science Journal, 38,* 2, April 2001:333–337.

Harris, Anthony R., Gene A. Fisher, and Stephen H. Thomas. "Homicide as a Medical Outcome: Racial Disparity in Deaths from Assault in US Level I and II Trauma Centers." *Journal of Trauma: Injury, Infection, and Critical Care, 20,* 20, 2011:1–10.

Hartley, Eugene. *Problems in Prejudice.* New York: King's Crown Press, 1946.

Herring, Cedric. "Is Job Discrimination Dead?" *Contexts,* Summer 2002: 13–18.

Hill, Mark E. "Skin Color and the Perception of Attractiveness among African Americans: Does Gender Make a Difference?" *Social Psychology Quarterly, 65,* 1, 2002:77–91.

Horn, James P. *Land as God Made It: Jamestown and the Birth of America.* New York: Basic Books, 2006.

Hsu, Francis L. K. *The Challenge of the American Dream: The Chinese in the United States.* Belmont, Calif.: Wadsworth, 1971.

Hutchinson, Earl Ofari. "The Latino Challenge to Black America." *Washington Post,* January 11, 2008.

Huttenbach, Henry R. "The Roman *Porajmos:* The Nazi Genocide of Europe's Gypsies." *Nationalities Papers, 19,* 3, Winter 1991:373–394.

Jeong, Yu-Jin, and Hyun-Kyung You. "Different Historical Trajectories and Family Diversity among Chinese, Japanese, and Koreans in the United States." *Journal of Family History, 33,* 3, July 2008:346–356.

Jones, James H. *Bad Blood: The Tuskegee Syphilis Experiment,* 2nd ed. New York: Free Press, 1993.

Jones, Trina. Intra-Group Preferencing: Problems of Proof in Colorism and Identity Performance Cases. *New York University Review of Law & Social Change, 34,* 2011.

Jordan, Miriam. "Number of Immigrants Arriving from Mexico Now Equaled by Those Going Home." *Wall Street Journal,* April 23, 2012.

Kaufman, Jonathan, and Gary Fields. "Election of Obama Recasts National Conversation on Race." *Wall Street Journal,* November 10, 2008.

Kochbar, Rakesh, and Ana Gonzalez-Barrera. "Through Boom and Bust: Minorities, Immigrants and Homeownership." Washington, D.C.: Pew Hispanic Center, May 12, 2009.

Lacey, Marc. "Majestic Views, Ancient Culture, and a Profit Fight." *New York Times,* April 23, 2011.

Lee, Sharon M. "Asian Americans: Diverse and Growing." *Population Bulletin, 53,* 2, June 1998:1–39.

Leland, John, and Gregory Beals. "In Living Colors." *Newsweek,* May 5, 1997:58–60.

Lewin, Tamar. "Colleges Regroup after Voters Ban Race Preferences." *New York Times,* January 26, 2007.

Lind, Michael. *The Next American Nation: The New Nationalism and the Fourth American Revolution.* New York: Free Press, 1995.

Lynn, Michael, Michael Sturman, Christie Ganley, Elizabeth Adams, Mathew Douglas, and Jessica McNeil. "Consumer Racial Discrimination in Tipping: A Replication and Extension." *Journal of Applied Social Psychology, 38,* 4, 2008:1045–1060.

Mahoney, John S., Jr., and Paul G. Kooistra. "Policing the Races: Structural Factors Enforcing Racial Purity in Virginia (1630–1930)." Paper presented at the annual meetings of the American Sociological Association, 1995.

Marino, David. "Border Watch Group 'Techno Patriots' Still Growing." KVOA News 4, Tucson, Arizona, February 14, 2008.

McFarland, Sam. "Authoritarianism, Social Dominance, and Other Roots of Generalized Prejudice." *Political Psychology, 31,* 3, June 2010:453–477.

McLemore, S. Dale. *Racial and Ethnic Relations in America.* Boston: Allyn and Bacon, 1994.

Mohawk, John C. "Indian Economic Development: An Evolving Concept of Sovereignty." *Buffalo Law Review, 39,* 2, Spring 1991:495–503.

Montagu, M. F. Ashley. *Introduction to Physical Anthropology,* 3rd ed. Springfield, Ill.: Thomas, 1960.

Montagu, M. F. Ashley. *The Concept of Race.* New York: Free Press, 1964.

Montagu, M. F. Ashley, ed. *Race and IQ: Expanded Edition*. New York: Oxford University Press, 1999.

Murray, Christopher J. L., Sandeep C. Kulkarni, Catherine Michard, Niels Tomijima, Maria T. Bulzaccheili, Terrell J. Landiorio, and Majid Ezzati. "Eight Americas: Investigating Mortality Disparities across Races, Counties, and Race-Counties in the United States." *PLoS Medicine*, 3, 9, September 2006:1513–1524.

Navarro, Mireya. "For New York's Black Latinos, a Growing Racial Awareness." *New York Times*, April 28, 2003.

Norton, Michael I., and Samuel R. Sommers. "Whites See Racism as a Zero-Sum Game That They Are Now Losing." *Perspectives on Psychological Sciences, 6*, 2011:215–218.

Peterson, Iver. "1993 Deal for Indian Casino Is Called a Model to Avoid." *New York Times*, June 30, 2003.

Popescu, Ioana, Mary S. Vaughan-Sarrazin, and Gary E. Rosenthal. "Differences in Mortality and Use of Revascularization in Black and White Patients with Acute MI Admitted to Hospitals with and without Revascularization Services." *Journal of the American Medical Association, 297*, 22, June 13, 2007:2489–2495.

Powell, Michael, and Janet Roberts. "Minorities Hit Hardest by Foreclosures in New York." *New York Times*, May 15, 2009.

Portes, Alejandro, and Rubén G. Rumbaut. *Immigrant America*. Berkeley: University of California Press, 1990.

Powell, Michael, and Janet Roberts. "Minorities Hit Hardest by Foreclosures in New York." *New York Times*, May 15, 2009.

Pratt, Timothy. "Nevada's Gambling Revenue Rises after Two Year Slump." Reuters, February 10, 2011.

Preston, Julia. "Homeland Security Cancels 'Virtual Fence' after Billion Is Spent." *New York Times*, January 14, 2011.

Qian, Zhenchao, and Daniel T. Lichter. "Social Boundaries and Marital Assimilation: Interpreting Trends in Racial and Ethnic Intermarriage." *American Sociological Review, 72*, February 2007:68–94.

Ray, J. J. "Authoritarianism Is a Dodo: Comment on Scheepers, Felling and Peters." *European Sociological Review, 7*, 1, May 1991:73–75.

Reskin, Barbara F. *The Realities of Affirmative Action in Employment*. Washington, D.C.: American Sociological Association, 1998.

Richman, Joe. "From the Belgian Congo to the Bronx Zoo." National Public Radio, September 8, 2006.

Rivlin, Gary. "Beyond the Reservation." *New York Times*, September 22, 2007.

Roediger, David R. *Colored White: Transcending the Racial Past*. Berkeley: University of California Press, 2002.

Savage, Charlie. "Countrywide Will Settle a Bias Suit." *New York Times*, December 21, 2011.

Schaefer, Richard T. *Racial and Ethnic Groups*, 9th ed. Upper Saddle River, N.J.: Prentice Hall, 2004.

Sherif, Muzafer, and Carolyn Sherif. *Groups in Harmony and Tension*. New York: Harper & Row, 1953.

Simpson, George Eaton, and J. Milton Yinger. *Racial and Cultural Minorities: An Analysis of Prejudice and Discrimination*, 4th ed. New York: Harper & Row, 1972.

Smedley, Audrey, and Brian D. Smedley. "Race as Biology Is Fiction, Racism as a Social Problem Is Real: Anthropological and Historical Perspectives on the Social Construction of Race." *American Psychologist, 60*, 1, January 2005:16–26.

Spickard, P. R. S. *Mixed Blood: Intermarriage and Ethnic Identity in Twentieth Century America*. Madison: University of Wisconsin Press, 1989.

Statistical Abstract of the United States. Washington, D.C.: U.S. Census Bureau, published annually.

Stolberg, Sheryl Gay. "Blacks Found on Short End of Heart Attack Procedure." *New York Times*, May 10, 2001.

Suzuki, Bob H. "Asian-American Families." In *Marriage and Family in a Changing Society*, 2nd ed., James M. Henslin, ed. New York: Free Press, 1985:104–119.

Tafoya, Sonya M., Hans Johnson, and Laura E. Hill. "Who Chooses to Choose Two?" Washington, D.C.: Population Reference Bureau, 2005.

Thomas, Paulette. "U.S. Examiners Will Scrutinize Banks with Poor Minority-Lending Histories." *Wall Street Journal*, October 22, 1991:A2.

Thomas, Paulette. "Boston Fed Finds Racial Discrimination in Mortgage Lending Is Still Widespread." *Wall Street Journal*, October 9, 1992:A3.

Thomas, W. I., and Dorothy Swaine Thomas. *The Child in America: Behavior Problems and Programs*. New York: Alfred A. Knopf, 1928.

Thompson, Don. "Officials: Gang Rivalry Led to Calif. Prison Riot." Associated Press, December 10, 2009.

Thompson, Ginger. "Where Education and Assimilation Collide." *New York Times*, March 14, 2009.

Thornton, Russell. *American Indian Holocaust and Survival: A Population History since 1492*. Norman: University of Oklahoma Press, 1987.

U.S. Census Bureau, Population Division. "Percent of the Projected Population by Race and Hispanic Origin for the United States: 2010 to 2050." Constant Net International Migration Series (NP2009-T6-C):Table 6-C, December 16, 2009.

U.S. Census Bureau. "Annual Social and Economic Supplement to Current Population Survey." Washington, D.C.: U.S. Government Printing Office, 2010.

Wagley, Charles, and Marvin Harris. *Minorities in the New World*. New York: Columbia University Press, 1958.

Willie, Charles Vert. "Caste, Class, and Family Life Experiences." *Research in Race and Ethnic Relations, 6*, 1991:65–84.

Wilson, William Julius. *The Declining Significance of Race: Blacks and Changing American Institutions*. Chicago: University of Chicago Press, 1978.

Wilson, William Julius. *When Work Disappears: The World of the New Urban Poor*. Chicago: University of Chicago Press, 1996.

Wilson, William Julius. *The Bridge over the Racial Divide: Rising Inequality and Coalition Politics*. Berkeley: University of California Press, 2000.

Wilson, William Julius. "Jobless Poverty: A New Form of Social Dislocation in the Inner-City Ghetto." In *The Inequality Reader: Contemporary and Foundational Readings in Race, Class and Gender*, David B. Grusky and Szonja Szelenyi, eds. Boulder, Colo.: Westview Press, 2007:142–152.

Wirth, Louis. "The Problem of Minority Groups." In *The Science of Man in the World Crisis*, Ralph Linton, ed. New York: Columbia University Press, 1945.

Wright, Lawrence. "One Drop of Blood." *New Yorker*, July 25, 1994:46–50, 52–55.

Yinger, J. Milton. *Toward a Field Theory of Behavior: Personality and Social Structure*. New York: McGraw-Hill, 1965.

Chapter 10

Amenta, Edwin. "The Social Security Debate, Now, and Then." *Contexts, 5*, 3, Summer 2006.

Beck, Scott H., and Joe W. Page. "Involvement in Activities and the Psychological Well-Being of Retired Men." *Activities, Adaptation, & Aging, 11*, 1, 1988:31–47.

Belkin, Lisa. "The Feminine Critique." *New York Times*, November 1, 2007.

Benet, Sula. "Why They Live to Be 100, or Even Older, in Abkhasia." *New York Times Magazine, 26*, December 1971.

Bishop, Jerry E. "Study Finds Doctors Tend to Postpone Heart Surgery for Women, Raising Risk." *Wall Street Journal,* April 16, 1990:B4.

Booth, Alan, and James M. Dabbs, Jr. "Testosterone and Men's Marriages." *Social Forces, 72,* 2, December 1993:463–477.

Buchanan, Kim Shayo. "Our Prisons, Ourselves: Race, Gender and the Rule of Law." *Yale Law Review, 29,* 1, 2010:1–82.

Butler, Robert N. *Why Survive? Being Old in America.* New York: Harper & Row, 1975.

Butler, Robert N. "Ageism: Another Form of Bigotry." *Gerontologist, 9,* Winter 1980:243–246.

Carter, Nancy M. "Pipeline's Broken Promise." New York: Catalyst, 2010.

Center for American Women and Politics. "Fact Sheet: Women in Elective Office." May 2010.

Chafetz, Janet Saltzman. *Gender Equity: An Integrated Theory of Stability and Change.* Newbury Park, Calif.: Sage, 1990.

Chafetz, Janet Saltzman, and Anthony Gary Dworkin. *Female Revolt: Women's Movements in World and Historical Perspective.* Totowa, N.J.: Rowman & Allanheld, 1986.

Chalkley, Kate. "Female Genital Mutilation: New Laws, Programs Try to End Practice." *Population Today, 25,* 10, October 1997:4–5.

Choudhary, Ekta, Jeffrey Coben, and Robert M. Bossarte. "Adverse Health Outcomes, Perpetrator Characteristics, and Sexual Violence Victimization among U.S Adult Males." *Journal of Interpersonal Violence, 25,* 8, 2010: 1523–1541.

Clair, Jeffrey Michael, David A. Karp, and William C. Yoels. *Experiencing the Life Cycle: A Social Psychology of Aging,* 2nd ed. Springfield, Ill.: Thomas, 1993.

Colapinto, John. *As Nature Made Him: The Boy Who Was Raised as a Girl.* New York: HarperCollins, 2001.

Collins, Randall, Janet Saltzman Chafetz, Rae Lesser Blumberg, Scott Coltrane, and Jonathan H. Turner. "Toward an Integrated Theory of Gender Stratification." *Sociological Perspectives, 36,* 3, 1993:185–216.

Collymore, Yvette. "Conveying Concerns: Women Report on Gender-Based Violence." Washington, D.C.: Population Reference Bureau, 2000.

Costa, Stephanie. "Where's the Outrage?" *Ms Magazine Blog.* September 12, 2011.

Cowley, Joyce. *Pioneers of Women's Liberation.* New York: Merit, 1969.

Cottin, Lou. *Elders in Rebellion: A Guide to Senior Activism.* Garden City, N.Y.: Anchor Doubleday, 1979.

Cowgill, Donald. "The Aging of Populations and Societies." *Annals of the American Academy of Political and Social Science, 415,* 1974:1–18.

Crosnoe, Robert, and Glen H. Elder, Jr. "Successful Adaptation in the Later Years: A Life Course Approach to Aging." *Social Psychology Quarterly, 65,* 4, 2002:309–328.

Crossen, Cynthia. "Deja Vu." *Wall Street Journal,* March 5, 2003.

Crossen, Cynthia. "Déjà Vu." *Wall Street Journal,* February 25, 2004a.

Crossen, Cynthia. "When Worse Than a Woman Who Voted Was One Who Smoked." *Wall Street Journal,* January 7, 2008.

Cumming, Elaine, and William E. Henry. *Growing Old: The Process of Disengagement.* New York: Basic Books, 1961.

Dabbs, James M., Jr., and Robin Morris. "Testosterone, Social Class, and Antisocial Behavior in a Sample of 4,462 Men." *Psychological Science, 1,* 3, May 1990:209–211.

Dabbs, James M., Jr., Timothy S. Carr, Robert L. Frady, and Jasmin K. Riad. "Testosterone, Crime, and Misbehavior among 692 Male Prison Inmates." *Personality and Individual Differences, 18,* 1995:627–633.

Dabbs, James M., Jr., Marian F. Hargrove, and Colleen Heusel. "Testosterone Differences among College Fraternities: Well-Behaved vs. Rambunctious." *Personality and Individual Differences, 20,* 1996:157–161.

DeCrow, Karen. Foreword to *Why Men Earn More* by Warren Farrell. New York: AMACOM, 2005:xi–xii.

Diamond, Milton, and Keith Sigmundson. "Sex Reassignment at Birth: Long-term Review and Clinical Implications." *Archives of Pediatric and Adolescent Medicine, 151,* March 1997:298–304.

Digest of Education Statistics. Washington, D.C.: National Center for Education Statistics, 2007.

Domingo, Santiago, and Antonio Pellicer. "Overview of Current Trends in Hysterectomy." *Expert Review of Obstetrics and Gynecology, 4,* 6, 2009:673–685.

Donaldson, Stephen. "A Million Jockers, Punks, and Queens: Sex among American Male Prisoners and Its Implications for Concepts of Sexual Orientation." February 4, 1993. Online.

Donlon, Margie M., Ori Ash, and Becca R. Levy. "Re-Vision of Older Television Characters: A Stereotype-Awareness Intervention." *Journal of Social Issues, 61,* 2, June 2005.

England, Paula. "The Impact of Feminist Thought on Sociology." *Contemporary Sociology: A Journal of Reviews,* 2000:263–267.

Falkenberg, Katie. "Pakistani Women Victims of 'Honor.'" *Washington Times,* July 23, 2008.

Fathi, Nazila. "Starting at Home, Iran's Women Fight for Rights." *New York Times,* February 12, 2009.

Felsenthal, Edward. "Justices' Ruling Further Defines Sex Harassment." *Wall Street Journal,* March 5, 1998:B1, B2.

Fisher, Bonnie S., Francis T. Cullen, and Michael G. Turner. *The Sexual Victimization of College Women.* Washington, D.C.: U.S. Department of Justice, 2000.

Fisher, Bonnie S., Leah E. Daigle, Francis T. Cullen, and Michael G. Turner. "Reporting Sexual Victimization to the Police and Others: Results from a National-Level Study of College Women." *Criminal Justice and Behavior, 30,* 1, February 2003:6–38.

Fisher, Sue. *In the Patient's Best Interest: Women and the Politics of Medical Decisions.* New Brunswick, N.J.: Rutgers University Press, 1986.

Fleming, Kevin C., Jonathan M. Evans, and Darryl S. Chutka. "A Cultural and Economic History of Old Age in America." *Mayo Clinic Proceedings, 78,* July 2003:914–921.

Flexner, E. *Century of Struggle.* Cambridge, Mass.: Belknap, 1971. In Claire M. Renzetti and Daniel J. Curran, *Women, Men, and Society,* 4th ed. Boston: Allyn and Bacon, 1999.

Freedman, Jane. *Feminism.* Philadelphia: Open University Press, 2001.

Hacker, Helen Mayer. "Women as a Minority Group." *Social Forces, 30,* October 1951:60–69.

Hakim, Catherine. "Erotic Capital." *European Sociological Review,* 2010:499–518.

Hamid, Shadi. "Between Orientalism and Postmodernism: The Changing Nature of Western Feminist Thought towards the Middle East." *HAWWA, 4,* 1, 2006:76–92.

Hart, Charles W. M., and Arnold R. Pilling. *The Tiwi of North Australia,* Fieldwork Edition. New York: Holt, Rinehart and Winston, 1979.

Hatch, Laurie Russell. *Beyond Gender Differences: Adaptation to Aging in Life Course Perspective.* Amityville, N.Y.: Baywood Publishing Company, 2000.

Hendrix, Lewellyn. "What Is Sexual Inequality? On the Definition and Range of Variation." *Gender and Society, 28,* 3, August 1994:287–307.

Historical Statistics of the United States: From Colonial Times to the Present. New York: Basic Books, 1976.

Holtzman, Abraham. *The Townsend Movement: A Political Study.* New York: Bookman, 1963.

Huber, Joan. "Micro-Macro Links in Gender Stratification." *American Sociological Review, 55,* February 1990:1–10.

Hundley, Greg. "Why Women Earn Less Than Men in Self-Employment." *Journal of Labor Research, 22,* 4, Fall 2001:817–827.

Hunt, Stephen. *The Life Course: A Sociological Introduction.* London: Palgrave Macmillan, 2005.

Hymowitz, Carol. "Through the Glass Ceiling." *Wall Street Journal,* November 8, 2004.

Hymowitz, Carol. "Raising Women to Be Leaders." *Wall Street Journal,* February 12, 2007.

Hyse, Karin, and Lars Tornstam. "Recognizing Aspects of Oneself in the Theory of Gerotranscendence." Uppsala, Sweden: The Social Gerontology Group, 2009.

Jackson, Elizabeth A., Mauro Moscucci, Dean E. Smith, et al. "The Association of Sex with Outcomes among Patients Undergoing Primary Percutaneous Coronary Intervention for ST Elevation Myocardial Infarction in the Contemporary Era." *American Heart Journal, 161,* 2011:106–112.

Jacobs, Jerry A. "Detours on the Road to Equality: Women, Work and Higher Education." *Contexts,* Winter 2003:32–41.

Jaggar, Alison M. "Sexual Difference and Sexual Equality." In *Theoretical Perspectives on Sexual Difference,* Deborah L. Rhode, ed. New Haven, Conn.: Yale University Press, 1990:239–254.

Jerrome, Dorothy. *Good Company: An Anthropological Study of Old People in Groups.* Edinburgh, England: Edinburgh University Press, 1992.

Juncosa, Barbara. "Is 100 the New 80?: Centenarians Studied to Find the Secret of Longevity." *Scientific American,* October 28, 2008.

Keith, Jennie. *Old People, New Lives: Community Creation in a Retirement Residence,* 2nd ed. Chicago: University of Chicago Press, 1982.

Kinsella, Kevin, and David R. Phillips. "Global Aging: The Challenge of Success." Washington, D.C.: Population Reference Bureau, 2005.

Lazaro, Fred de Sam. "In Senegal, a Movement to Reject Circumcision." *PBS Hour,* August 12, 2011.

Leacock, Eleanor. *Myths of Male Dominance.* New York: Monthly Review Press, 1981.

Leopold, Evelyn. "Female Circumcision—90 Percent of Childbearing Women in Egypt?" *Huffington Post,* January 9, 2012.

Lerner, Gerda. *The Creation of Patriarchy.* New York: Oxford, 1986.

Lightfoot-Klein, A. "Rites of Purification and Their Effects: Some Psychological Aspects of Female Genital Circumcision and Infibulation (Pharaonic Circumcision) in an Afro-Arab Society (Sudan)." *Journal of Psychological Human Sexuality, 2,* 1989:61–78.

Littleton, Heather, Carmen Radecki Breitkopf, and Abbey Berenson. "Women beyond the Campus: Unacknowledged Rape among Low-Income Women." *Violence against Women, 14,* 3, March 2008:269–286.

Lurie, Nicole, Jonathan Slater, Paul McGovern, Jacqueline Ekstrum, Lois Quam, and Karen Margolis. "Preventive Care for Women: Does the Sex of the Physician Matter?" *New England Journal of Medicine, 329,* August 12, 1993:478–482.

Manheimer, Ronald J. "The Older Learner's Journey to an Ageless Society." *Journal of Transformative Education, 3,* 3, 2005.

Manpower Report to the President. Washington, D.C.: U.S. Department of Labor, Manpower Administration, April 1971.

"Melee Breaks Out at Retirement Home." *The Daily News,* March 5, 2004.

Meltzer, Scott A. "Gender, Work, and Intimate Violence: Men's Occupational Spillover and Compensatory Violence." *Journal of Marriage and the Family, 64,* 2, November 2002:820–832.

Merwine, Maynard H. "How Africa Understands Female Circumcision." *New York Times,* November 24, 1993.

Mills, Karen M., and Thomas J. Palumbo. *A Statistical Portrait of Women in the United States: 1978.* U.S. Census Bureau, *Current Population Reports,* Series P-23, Number 100, 1980.

Money, John, and Anke A. Ehrhardt. *Man and Woman, Boy and Girl.* Baltimore, Md.: Johns Hopkins University Press, 1972.

National Women's Political Caucus. "Factsheet on Women's Political Progress." Washington, D.C., June 1998.

Reiser, Christa. *Reflections on Anger: Women and Men in a Changing Society.* Westport, Conn.: Praeger Publishers, 1999.

Robbins, John. *Healthy at 100.* New York: Random House, 2006.

Rossi, Alice S. "A Biosocial Perspective on Parenting." *Daedalus, 106,* 1977:1–31.

Rossi, Alice S. "Gender and Parenthood." *American Sociological Review, 49,* 1984:1–18.

Roth, Louise Marie. "Selling Women Short: A Research Note on Gender Differences in Compensation on Wall Street." *Social Forces, 82,* 2, December 2003:783–802.

Schottland, Charles I. *The Social Security Plan in the U.S.* New York: Appleton, 1963.

Scully, Diana. "Negotiating to Do Surgery." In *Dominant Issues in Medical Sociology,* 3rd ed., Howard D. Schwartz, ed. New York: McGraw-Hill, 1994:146–152.

Semple, Kirk. "Idea of Afghan Women's Rights Starts Taking Hold." *New York Times,* March 2, 2009.

Settles, Isis H., Zaje A. T. Harrell, NiCole T. Buchanan, and Stevie C. Y. Yap. "Frightened or Bothered: Two Types of Sexual Harassment Appraisals." *Social Psychological and Personality Science,* March 29, 2011.

Slackman, Michael. "Voices Rise in Egypt to Shield Girls from an Old Tradition." *New York Times,* September 20, 2007.

Smith, Ryan A. "A Test of the Glass Ceiling and Glass Escalator Hypotheses." *Annals of the American Academy of Social Sciences, 639,* January 2012:149–172.

Smith, Stacy L., and Marc Choueiti. "Gender Disparity On Screen and Behind the Camera in Family Films: The Executive Report." Geena Davis Institute on Gender in Media, 2011.

Spivak, Gayatri Chakravorty. "Feminism 2000: One Step Beyond." *Feminist Review, 64,* Spring 2000:113.

Statistical Abstract of the United States. Washington, D.C.: U.S. Census Bureau, published annually.

Swigonski, Mary E., and Salome Raheim. "Feminist Contributions to Understanding Women's Lives and the Social Environment." *Affilia: Journal of Women and Social Work, 26,* 1, 2011:10–21.

Tuhus-Dubrow, Rebecca. "Rites and Wrongs." *Boston Globe,* February 11, 2007.

Udry, J. Richard. "Biological Limits of Gender Construction." *American Sociological Review, 65,* June 2000:443–457.

UNIFEM. *Progress of the World's Women 2008/2009.* United Nations Development Fund for Women, 2008.

U.S. Department of Education, National Center for Education Statistics. "Projections of Education Statistics to 2017," September 2008:Table 10.

U.S. Department of State. "2010 Human Rights Report: Iran." *2010 Country Reports on Human Rights Practices,* April 8, 2011.

VanderMey, Anne. "Fortune 500 Women CEOs." *CNN Money,* May 5, 2011.

Walker, Alice, and Pratibha Parmar. *Warrior Marks: Female Genital Mutilation and the Sexual Blinding of Women.* New York: Harcourt Brace, 1993.

Wang, Mo, and Kenneth S. Shultz. "Employee Retirment: A Review and Recommendations for Future Investigation." *Journal of Management, 36,* January 2010:172–206.

Weinberger, Catherine. "In Search of the Glass Ceiling: Gender and Earnings Growth among U.S. College Graduates in the 19901." *Industrial and Labor Relations Review, 64,* 5, October 2011.

Whiteman, Maura K., Susan D. Hillis, Denise J. Jamieson, Brian Morrow, Michelle N. Podgornik, Kate M. Brett, and Polly A. Marchbanks. "Inpatient Hysterectomy Surveillance in the United States, 2000–2004." *American Journal of Obstetrics and Gynecology,* January 2008:34e1–34e7.

Wilde, Elizabeth Ty, Lily Batchelder, and David T. Ellwood. "The Mommy Track Divides: The Impact of Childbearing on Wages of Women of Differing Skill Levels." NBER Working Paper N. 16582. December 2010.

Women's Bureau of the United States, Department of Labor. *Handbook on Women Workers.* Washington, D.C.: U.S. Government Printing Office, 1969.

Xie, Min, Karen Heimer, and Janet L. Lauritsen. "Violence against Women in U.S. Metropolitan Areas: Change in Women's Status and Risk, 1980–2004." *Criminology,* 2011:1–38.

Yakaboski, Tamara, and Leah Reinert. "Review of Women in Academic Leadership: Professional Strategies, Personal Choices." *Women in Higher Education, 4,* 1, 2011.

Yardley, Jim. "In India, Caste, Honor, and Killings Intertwine." *New York Times,* July 9, 2010a.

Young, Robert D., Bertrand Desjardins, Kirsten McCaughlin, Michel Poulain, and Thomas T. Perls. "Typologies of Extreme Longevity Myths." *Current Gerontology and Geriatrics Research,* 2010:1–12.

Zaslow, Jeffrey. "Will You Still Need Me When I'm … 84? More Couples Divorce after Decades." *Wall Street Journal,* June 17, 2003:D1.

Zoepf, Katherine. "A Dishonorable Affair." *New York Times,* September 23, 2007.

Chapter 11

Amnesty International. "Decades of Human Rights Abuse in Iraq." www.amnestyusa.org, 2005.

Arndt, William F., and F. Wilbur Gingrich. *A Greek-English Lexicon of the New Testament and Other Early Christian Literature.* Chicago: University of Chicago Press, 1957.

Batson, Andrew. "China Stimulus Tweaks Don't Redress Imbalances." *Wall Street Journal,* March 9, 2009.

Beah, Ishmael. *A Long Way Gone: Memoirs of a Boy Soldier.* New York: Farrar, Straus and Giroux, 2007.

Bell, Daniel. *The Coming of Post-Industrial Society: A Venture in Social Forecasting.* New York: Basic Books, 1973.

Bentley, Arthur Fisher. *The Process of Government: A Study of Social Pressures.* Chicago: University of Chicago Press, 1908.

Berger, Peter L. *Invitation to Sociology: A Humanistic Perspective.* New York: Doubleday, 1963.

Bremmer, Ian. "The Secret to China's Boom: State Capitalism." Thomson-Reuters, 2011.

Bridgwater, William, ed. *The Columbia Viking Desk Encyclopedia.* New York: Viking Press, 1953.

Burnham, Walter Dean. *Democracy in the Making: American Government and Politics.* Englewood Cliffs, N.J.: Prentice Hall, 1983.

Casper, Lynne M., and Loretta E. Bass. "Voting and Registration in the Election of November 1996."

Dahl, Robert A. *Who Governs?* New Haven, Conn.: Yale University Press, 1961.

Dahl, Robert A. *Dilemmas of Pluralist Democracy: Autonomy vs. Control.* New Haven, Conn.: Yale University Press, 1982.

Delaney, Arthur. "Revolving Door: 1447 Former Government Workers Lobby for Wall Street." *Huffington Post,* June 3, 2010.

Domhoff, G. William. *The Power Elite and the State: How Policy Is Made in America.* Hawthorne, N.Y.: Aldine de Gruyter, 1990.

Domhoff, G. William. *Who Rules America? Power and Politics in the Year 2000,* 3rd ed. Mountain View, Calif: Mayfield Publishing, 1998.

Domhoff, G. William. *Who Rules America? Power, Politics, and Social Change,* 5th ed. New York: McGraw-Hill, 2006.

Domhoff, G. William. "C. Wright Mills, Power Structure Research, and the Failures of Mainstream Political Science." *New Political Science, 29,* 2007:97–114.

File, Thom, and Sarah Crissey. "Voting and Registration in the Election of November 2008." *Current Population Reports,* May 2010.

Fischer, Claude S. *The Urban Experience.* New York: Harcourt, 1976.

Flannery, Russell. "Chinese Businessman Billionaire Days Don't Last Long." *Forbes,* June 2, 2011.

Form, William. "Comparative Industrial Sociology and the Convergence Hypothesis." *Annual Review of Sociology, 5,* 1, 1979.

Freeland, Chrystia. "The Rise of the New Global Elite." *Atlantic,* January/February 2011.

Gallup Poll. "Election Polls—Vote by Groups, 2008." Princeton, N.J.: Gallup Organization, 2008.

Guthrie, Doug. "The Great Helmsman's Cultural Death." *Contexts, 7,* 3, Summer 2008:26–31.

Hellinger, Daniel, and Dennis R. Judd. *The Democratic Facade.* Pacific Grove, Calif.: Brooks/Cole, 1991.

Hippler, Fritz. Interview in a television documentary with Bill Moyers in *Propaganda,* in the series "Walk through the 20th Century," 1987.

Hoffman, Bert. "The International Dimensions of Authoritarian Legitimation: The Impact of Regime Evolution." Leibnitz: German Institute of Global and Area Studies. Working Paper No. 182, December 2011.

Holder, Kelly. "Voting and Registration in the Election of November 2004." *Current Population Reports,* March 2006.

"It's So Much Nicer on K Street." *New York Times,* June 8, 2008.

Jamieson, Amie, Hyon B. Shin, and Jennifer Day. "Voting and Registration in the Election of November 2000." *Current Population Reports,* February 2002.

Kahn, Joseph. "China's Elite Learn to Flaunt It While the New Landless Weep." *New York Times,* December 25, 2004.

Kahn, Joseph. "Thousands Reportedly Riot in China." *International Herald-Tribune,* March 13, 2007.

Kamber, Michael. "In Afghan Kilns, a Cycle of Debt and Servitude." *New York Tmes,* March 15, 2011.

Karon, Tony. "Why China Does Capitalism Better Than the U.S." *Time,* January 20, 2011.

Kerr, Clark. *The Future of Industrialized Societies.* Cambridge, Mass.: Harvard University Press, 1983.

Kissinger, Henry A. "Avoiding a US.–China Cold War." *Washington Post,* January 14, 2011.

Lemann, Nicholas. "Conflict of Interests." *New Yorker,* August 11, 2008.

Lipset, Seymour Martin. "The Social Requisites of Democracy Revisited." Presidential address to the American Sociological Association, Boston, Massachusetts, 1993.

Liptak, Adam. "Justices, 5–4, Reject Corporate Spending Limit." *New York Times,* January 21, 2010.

Mills, C. Wright. *The Power Elite.* New York: Oxford University Press, 1956.

Mosher, Steven W. "Why Are Baby Girls Being Killed in China?" *Wall Street Journal,* July 25, 1983:9.

Mosher, Steven W. "China's One-Child Policy: Twenty-Five Years Later." *Human Life Review,* Winter 2006:76–101.

Orwell, George. *1984.* New York: Harcourt Brace, 1949.

Rothkopf, David. *Superclass: The Global Power Elite and the World They Are Making.* New York: Farrar, Straus and Giroux, 2008.

Sageman, Marc. "Explaining Terror Networks in the 21st Century." *Footnotes,* May–June 2008a:7.

Sageman, Marc. *Leaderless Jihad: Terror Networks in the Twenty-First Century.* Philadelphia: University of Pennsylvania Press, 2008b.

Sengupta, Somini. "In the Ancient Streets of Najaf, Pledges of Martyrdom for Cleric." *New York Times,* July 10, 2004.

Sheets, Lawrence Scott, and William Broad. "Georgia Says It Blocked Smuggling of Arms-Grade Uranium." *New York Times,* January 25, 2007a.

Sheets, Lawrence Scott, and William J. Broad. "Smuggler's Plot Highlights Fear Over Uranium." *New York Times,* January 25, 2007b.

Smith, Clark. "Oral History as 'Therapy': Combatants' Account of the Vietnam War." In *Strangers at Home: Vietnam Veterans Since the War,* Charles R. Figley and Seymore Leventman, eds. New York: Praeger, 1980:9–34.

Statistical Abstract of the United States. Washington, D.C.: U.S. Census Bureau, published annually.

Timasheff, Nicholas S. *War and Revolution.* Joseph F. Scheuer, ed. New York: Sheed & Ward, 1965.

Toynbee, Arnold. *A Study of History,* D. C. Somervell, abridger and ed. New York: Oxford University Press, 1946.

Veblen, Thorstein. *The Theory of the Leisure Class.* New York: Macmillan, 1912.

Vidal, Jordi Blanes, Mirko Draca, and Christian Fons-Rosen. "Revolving Door Lobbyists." Center for Economic Performance, Discussion Paper 993, August 2010.

Weber, Max. *Economy and Society,* G. Roth and C. Wittich, eds. Berkeley: University of California Press, 1978. First published in 1922.

Weber, Max. *From Max Weber: Essays in Sociology.* Hans Gerth and C. Wright Mills, trans. and ed. New York: Oxford University Press, 1946.

Weber, Max. *The Theory of Social and Economic Organization,* A. M. Henderson and Talcott Parsons, trans., Talcott Parsons, ed. Glencoe, Ill.: Free Press, 1947. Originally published 1913.

Wines, Michael. "Africa Adds to Miserable Ranks of Child Workers." *New York Times,* August 24, 2006.

Wong, Janelle, S. Karthick Ramakrishnan, Tacku Lee, and Jane Junn. *Asian American Political Participation: Emerging Constituents and Their Political Identities.* New York: Russell Sage, 2011.

Yardley, Jim. "Soaring above India's Poverty, a 27-Story Home." *New York Times,* October 28, 2010b.

Yardley, Jim, and Keith Bradsher. "China, an Engine of Growth, Faces a Global Slump." *New York Times,* October 22, 2008.

Yenfang, Qian. "Fast Growth of Economy, Fast Rise of Wealthiest." *China Daily,* March 4, 2011.

Zachary, G. Pascal. "Behind Stocks' Surge Is an Economy in Which Big U.S. Firms Thrive." *Wall Street Journal,* November 22, 1995:A1, A5.

Chapter 12

Aberg, Yvonne. *Social Interactions: Studies of Contextual Effects and Endogenous Processes.* Doctoral dissertation, Department of Sociology, Stockholm University, 2003.

Amato, Paul. "Research on Divorce: Continuing Trends and New Developments." *Journal of Marriage and Family, 72,* 3, June 2010:650–666.

Amato, Paul R., and Jacob Cheadle. "The Long Reach of Divorce: Divorce and Child Well-Being across Three Generations." *Journal of Marriage and Family, 67,* February 2005:191–206.

Amato, Paul R., and Juliana M. Sobolewski. "The Effects of Divorce and Marital Discord on Adult Children's Psychological Well-Being." *American Sociological Review, 66,* 6, December 2001:900–921.

"America's Children in Brief: Key National Indicators of Well-Being, 2010." www.childstats.gov, July 2010.

Ananat, Elizabeth O., and Guy Michaels. "The Effect of Marital Breakup on the Income Distribution of Women with Children." Centre for Economic Performance, CEP Discussion Paper dp0787, April 2007.

Belsky, Jay. "Effects of Child Care on Child Development: Give Parents Real Choice." Unpublished paper, March 2009.

Belsky, Jay. "Classroom Composition, Childcare History and Social Development: Are Childcare Effects Disappearing or Spreading?" *Social Development, 18,* 1, February 2009a:230–238.

Belsky, Jay. "Effects of Child Care on Child Development: Give Parents Real Choice." Unpublished paper, March 2009b.

Belsky, Jay, Deborah Lowe Vandell, Margaret Burchinall, K. Alison Clarke-Stewart, Kathleen McCartney, and Margaret Tresch Owen. "Are There Long-Term Effects of Early Child Care?" *Child Development, 78,* 2, March/April 2007:681–701.

Berger, Lawrence M., Maria Cancian, and Daniel R. Meyer. "Maternal Re-partnering and New-partner Fertility: Associations with Nonresident Father Investments in Children." *Children and Youth Services Review, 34,* 2012:426–436.

Bergmann, Barbara R. "The Future of Child Care." Paper presented at the annual meetings of the American Sociological Association, 1995.

Bernard, Tara Siegel. "The Key to Wedded Bliss? Money Matters." *New York Times,* September 10, 2008.

Bianchi, Suzanne M., and Lynne M. Casper. "American Families." *Population Bulletin, 55,* 4, December 2000:1–42.

Blau, David M. "The Production of Quality in Child-Care Centers: Another Look." *Applied Developmental Science, 4,* 3, 2000:136–148.

Blumstein, Philip, and Pepper Schwartz. *American Couples: Money, Work, Sex.* New York: Pocket Books, 1985.

Bronfenbrenner, Urie. "Principles for the Healthy Growth and Development of Children." In *Marriage and Family in a Changing Society,* 4th ed., James M. Henslin, ed. New York: Free Press, 1992:243–249.

Bryant, Chalandra M., Rand D. Conger, and Jennifer M. Meehan. "The Influence of In-Laws on Changes in Marital Success." *Journal of Marriage and the Family, 63, 3,* August 2001:614–626.

Bryant, Chalandra M., K. A. S. Wickrama, John Boland, et al. "Race Matters, Even in Marriage: Identifying Factors Linked to Marital Outcomes for African Americans." *Journal of Family Theory and Review, 2,* 3, September 2010:157–174.

"Career Guide to Industries: 2010–11 Edition." Washington, D.C.: Bureau of Labor Statistics 2011.

Cauce, Ana Mari, and Melanie Domenech-Rodriguez. "Latino Families: Myths and Realities." In *Latino Children and Families in the United States: Current Research and Future Directions,* Josefina M. Contreras, Kathryn A. Kerns, and Angela M. Neal-Barnett, eds. Westport, Conn.: Praeger, 2002:3–25.

Cheadle, Jacob, Paul R. Amato, and Valarie King. "Patterns of Nonresident Father Involvement." *Demography, 47* 2010: 205–226.

Cherlin, J. Andrew. "Remarriage as an Incomplete Institution." In *Marriage and Family in a Changing Society,* 3rd ed., James M. Henslin, ed. New York: Free Press, 1989:492–501.

Coleman, Marilyn, Lawrence Ganong, and Mark Fine. "Reinvestigating Remarriage: Another Decade of Progress." *Journal of Marriage and the Family, 62,* 4, November 2000:1288–1307.

Crawford, Duane W., Renate M. Houts, Ted L. Huston, and Laura J. George. "Compatibility, Leisure, and Satisfaction in Marital Relationships." *Journal of Marriage and Family, 64,* May 2002:433–449.

Crossen, Cynthia. "Déjà Vu." *Wall Street Journal,* February 25, 2004a.

Crossen, Cynthia. "Before Social Security, Most Americans Faced Very Bleak Retirement." *Wall Street Journal,* September 15, 2004b.

Cui, Ming, and Frank D. Fincham. "The Differential Effects of Parental Divorce and Marital Conflict on Young Adult Romantic Relationships." *Personal Relationships, 17,* 3, September 2010:331–343.

Dahl, Gordon B., and Enrico Moretti. "The Demand for Sons." *Review of Economic Studies, 75,* 2008:1085–1120.

Dematteis, Lou. "Same-Sex Marriages, Civil Unions, and Domestic Partnerships." *New York Times*, July 11, 2011.

Dush, Claire M. Kamp, Catherine L. Cohan, and Paul R. Amato. "The Relationship between Cohabitation and Marital Quality and Stability: Change across Cohorts?" *Journal of Marriage and Family, 65*, 3, August 2003:539–549.

Dye, Jane Lawler. "Fertility of American Women: 2006." Washington, D.C.: U.S. Census Bureau, August 2008.

Elwert, Felix, and Nicholas A. Christakis. "The Effect of Widowhood on Mortality by the Causes of Death of Both Spouses." *American Journal of Public Health, 98*, 11, November 2008:2092–2098.

Eshleman, J. Ross. *The Family*, 9th ed. Boston: Allyn and Bacon, 2000.

Falicov, Celia Jaes. "Changing Constructions of Machismo for Latino Men in Therapy: 'The Devil Never Sleeps.'" *Family Process, 49*, 3, 2010:309–329.

Farr, Rachel H., Stephen L. Forssell, and Charlotte J. Patterson. "Parenting and Child Development in Adoptive Families: Does Parental Sexual Orientation Matter?" *Applied Developmental Science, 14*, 3, 2010:164–178.

Fisher, Helen E., Lucy L. Brown, Arthur Aron, Greg Strong, and Deborah Masek. "Reward, Addiction, and Emotion Regulation Systems Associated with Rejection in Love." *Journal of Neurophysiology, 104*, 2010:51–60.

Fremson, Ruth. "Dead Bachelors in Remote China Still Find Wives." *New York Times*, October 5, 2006.

Frosch, Dan. "Its Native Tongue Facing Extinction, Arapaho Tribe Teaches the Young." *New York Times*, October 17, 2008.

Gallup Poll. "America's Preference for Smaller Families Edge Higher." Princeton, N.J.: Gallup Organization, June 30, 2011.

Gallup Poll. "Prefer Boys to Girls Just as They Did in 1941." Princeton, N.J.: The Gallup Organization, June 23, 2011.

Gartrell, Nanette, Henny Bos, Heidi Peyser, Amalia Deck, and Carla Rodas. "Family Characteristics, Custody Arrangements, and Adolescent Psychological Well-being after Lesbian Mothers Break Up." *Family Relations, 60*, December 2011:572–585.

Gatewood, Willard B. *Aristocrats of Color: The Black Elite, 1880–1920*. Bloomington, Indiana University Press, 1990.

Gelderen, Loes, Henny M. W. Bos, Nanette Gartrell, Jo Hermanns, and Ellen C. Perrin. "Quality of Life of Adolescents Raised from Birth by Lesbian Mothers: The U.S. National Longitudinal Family Study." *Journal of Developmental and Behavioral Pediatrics, 33*, 1, January 2012.

Glenn, Evelyn Nakano. "Chinese American Families." In *Minority Families in the United States: A Multicultural Perspective*, Ronald L. Taylor, ed. Englewood Cliffs, N.J.: Prentice Hall, 1994:115–145.

Glick, Paul C., and S. Lin. "More Young Adults Are Living with Their Parents: Who Are They?" *Journal of Marriage and Family, 48*, 1986:107–112.

Hall, J. Camille. "The Impact of Kin and Fictive Kin Relationships on the Mental Health of Black Adult Children of Alcoholics." *Health and Social Work, 33*, 4, November 2008:259–266.

Harford, Tim. "Why Divorce Is Good for Women." The Undercover Economist, *Slate*, January 16, 2008.

Hayashi, Gina M., and Bonnie R. Strickland. "Long-Term Effects of Parental Divorce on Love Relationships: Divorce as Attachment Disruption." *Journal of Social and Personal Relationships, 15*, 1, February 1998:23–38.

Hetherington, Mavis, and John Kelly. *For Better or for Worse: Divorce Reconsidered*. New York: W. W. Norton, 2003.

Hong, Lawrence. "Marriage in China." In *Til Death Do Us Part: A Multicultural Anthology on Marriage*, Sandra Lee Browning and R. Robin Miller, eds. Stamford, Conn.: JAI Press, 1999.

Huang, Penelope M., Pamela J. Smock, Wendy D. Manning, and Cara A. Bergstrom-Lynch. "He Says, She Says: Gender and Cohabitation." *Journal of Family Issues, 32*, February 2011.

Jeong, Yu-Jin, and Hyun-Kyung You. "Different Historical Trajectories and Family Diversity among Chinese, Japanese, and Koreans in the United States." *Journal of Family History, 33*, 3, July 2008:346–356.

Kelly, Joan B. "How Adults React to Divorce." In *Marriage and Family in a Changing Society*, 4th ed., James M. Henslin, ed. New York: Free Press, 1992:410–423.

Kennedy, Sheela, and Larry Bumpass. "Cohabitation and Trends in the Structure and Stability of Children's Family Lives." Paper presented at the annual meeting of the Population Association of America, Washington, D.C., March 31–April 2, 2011.

Kohn, Melvin L. "Social Class and Parent–Child Relationships: An Interpretation." *American Journal of Sociology, 68*, 1963:471–480.

Kohn, Melvin L. *Class and Conformity: A Study in Values*, 2nd ed. Homewood, Ill.: Dorsey Press, 1977.

Kohn, Melvin L., and Carmi Schooler. "Class, Occupation, and Orientation." *American Sociological Review, 34*, 1969:659–678.

Koropeckyj-Cox, Tanya. "Attitudes about Childlessness in the United States." *Journal of Family Issues, 28*, 8, August 2007:1054–1082.

Kreider, Rose M., and Diana B. Elliott. "America's Families and Living Arrangements: 2007." *Current Population Reports*, September 2009.

Krienert, Jessie L., and Jeffrey A. Walsh. "Characteristics and Perceptions of Child Sexual Abuse." *Journal of Child Sexual Abuse 20*, 2011:353–372.

Lareau, Annette. "Invisible Inequality: Social Class and Childrearing in Black Families and White Families." *American Sociological Review, 67*, October 2002:747–776.

Lauer, Jeanette, and Robert Lauer. "Marriages Made to Last." In *Marriage and Family in a Changing Society*, 4th ed., James M. Henslin, ed. New York: Free Press, 1992:481–486.

LeDuff, Charlie. "Handling the Meltdowns of the Nuclear Family." *New York Times*, May 28, 2003.

Letherby, Gayle. "Childless and Bereft? Stereotypes and Realities in Relation to 'Voluntary' and 'Involuntary' Childlessness and Womanhood." *Sociological Inquiry, 72*, 1, Winter 2002:7–20.

Lewin, Ellen. *Gay Fatherhood: Narratives of Family and Citizenship in America*. Chicago: University of Chicago Press, 2009.

Lichter, Daniel T., and Zhenchao Qian. "Serial Cohabitation and the Marital Life Course." *Journal of Marriage and Family, 70*, November 2008:861–878.

Livingston, Gretchen, and D'Vera Cohn. "Childlessness Up among All Women; Down among Women with Advanced Degrees." Washington, D.C.: PEW Research Center, June 25, 2010.

MacDonald, William L., and Alfred DeMaris. "Remarriage, Stepchildren, and Marital Conflict: Challenges to the Incomplete Institutionalization Hypothesis." *Journal of Marriage and the Family, 57*, May 1995:387–398.

Manning, Wendy D., and Jessica Cohen. "Premarital Cohabitation and Marital Dissolution: An examination of Recent Marriages." Bowling Green State University: The Center for Family and Demographic Research, Working Paper Series 2010–11.

"Marital History for People 15 Years Old and Over by Age, Sex, Race and Ethnicity: 2001." Annual Demographic Survey, Bureau of Labor Statistics and U.S. Census Bureau, 2004.

Masheter, Carol. "Postdivorce Relationships between Ex-Spouses: The Role of Attachment and Interpersonal Conflict." *Journal of Marriage and the Family, 53*, February 1991:103–110.

Mathews, T. J., and Brady E. Hamilton. "Delayed Childbearing: More Women Are Having Their First Child Later in Life." *NCHS Data Brief, 21*, Hyattsville, Md.: National Center for Health Statistics, August 2009:1–7.

McKinnish, Terra G. "Sexually Integrated Workplaces and Divorce: Another Form of On-the-Job Search." *Journal of Human Resources, 42,* 2, 2007:331–352.

McLanahan, Sara, and Gary Sandefur. *Growing Up with a Single Parent: What Hurts, What Helps.* Cambridge, Mass.: Harvard University Press, 1994.

McLanahan, Sara, and Dona Schwartz. "Life without Father: What Happens to the Children?" *Contexts, 1,* 1, Spring 2002:35–44.

Meyers, Laurie. "Asian-American Mental Health." *APA Online,* February 2006.

Morin, Rich, and D'Vera Cohn. "Women Call the Shots at Home; Public Mixed on Gender Roles in Jobs." Pew Research Center Publications: September 25, 2008.

Murdock, George Peter. *Social Structure.* New York: Macmillan, 1949.

Naik, Gautam. "A Baby, Please. Blond, Freckles—Hold the Colic." *Wall Street Journal,* February 12, 2009.

Osborne, Cynthia, Wendy D. Manning, and Pamela J. Smock. "Married and Cohabiting Parents' Relationship Stability: A Focus on Race and Ethnicity." *Marriage and Family, 69,* December 2007:1345–1366.

Richardson, Stacey, and Marita P. McCabe. "Parental Divorce during Adolescence and Adjustment in Early Adulthood." *Adolescence, 36,* Fall 2001:467–489.

Rosenbloom, Stephanie. "Love, Lies and What They Learned." *New York Times,* November 12, 2011.

Rubin, Zick. "The Love Research." *In Marriage and Family in a Changing Society,* 2nd ed., James M. Henslin, ed. New York: Free Press, 1985.

Russell, Diana E. H. "Preliminary Report on Some Findings Relating to the Trauma and Long-Term Effects of Intrafamily Childhood Sexual Abuse." Unpublished paper, no date.

Schmeer, Kammi K. "The Child Health Disadvantage of Parental Cohabitation." *Journal of Marriage and Family, 73,* February 2011:181–193.

Schmiege, Cynthia J., Leslie N. Richards, and Anisa M. Zvonkovic. "Remarriage: For Love or Money?" *Journal of Divorce and Remarriage,* May-June 2001:123–141.

Smith, Beverly A. "An Incest Case in an Early 20th-Century Rural Community." *Deviant Behavior, 13,* 1992:127–153.

Stack, Carol B. *All Our Kin: Strategies for Survival in a Black Community.* New York: Harper, 1974.

Staples, Brent. "Loving v. Virginia and the Secret History of Race." *New York Times,* May 14, 2008.

Statistical Abstract of the United States. Washington, D.C.: U.S. Census Bureau, published annually.

Stinnett, Nicholas. "Strong Families." In *Marriage and Family in a Changing Society,* 4th ed., James M. Henslin, ed. New York: Free Press, 1992:496–507.

Straus, Murray A. "Explaining Family Violence." In *Marriage and Family in a Changing Society,* 4th ed., James M. Henslin, ed. New York: Free Press, 1992:344–356.

Straus, Murray A. "Gender Symmetry and Mutuality in Perpetration of Clinical-level Partner Violence: Empirical Evidence and Implications for Prevention and Treatment." *Aggression and Violent Behavior, 16,* 2011:279–288.

Straus, Murray A., and Richard J. Gelles. "Violence in American Families: How Much Is There and Why Does It Occur?" In *Troubled Relationships,* Elam W. Nunnally, Catherine S. Chilman, and Fred M. Cox, eds. Newbury Park, Calif.: Sage, 1988:141–162.

Suzuki, Bob H. "Asian-American Families." In *Marriage and Family in a Changing Society,* 2nd ed., James M. Henslin, ed. New York: Free Press, 1985:104–119.

Sweeney, Megan M. "Remarriage and the Nature of Divorce: Does It Matter Which Spouse Chose to Leave?" *Journal of Family Issues, 23,* 3, April 2002:410–440.

Tasker, Fiona. "Same-Sex Parenting and Child Development: Reviewing the Contribution of Parental Gender." *Journal of Marriage and Family, 72,* 1, February 2010:35–40.

Torres, Jose B., V. Scott H. Solberg, and Aaron H. Carlstrom. "The Myth of Sameness among Latino Men and Their Machismo." *American Journal of Orthopsychiatry, 72,* 2, 2002:163–181.

U.S. Census Bureau. "50 Million Children Lived with Married Parents in 2007." Washington, D.C.: U.S. Government Printing Office, 2007.

U.S. Census Bureau. "Annual Social and Economic Supplement to Current Population Survey." Washington, D.C.: U.S. Government Printing Office, 2010

Vaughan, Diane. "Uncoupling: The Social Construction of Divorce." In *Marriage and Family in a Changing Society,* 2nd ed., James M. Henslin, ed. New York: Free Press, 1985:429–439.

Vega, William A. "Hispanic Families in the 1980s: A Decade of Research." *Journal of Marriage and the Family, 52,* November 1990:1015–1024.

Waldfogel, Jane, Terry-Ann Craigie, and Jeanne Brooks-Gunn. "Fragile Families and Child Wellbeing." In *Fragile Families, 20,* 2, Fall 2010:87–112.

Wallerstein, Judith S., Sandra Blakeslee, and Julia M. Lewis. *The Unexpected Legacy of Divorce: A 25-Year Landmark Study.* Concord, N.H.: Hyperion Press, 2001.

Wang, Hongyu, and Paul R. Amato. "Predictors of Divorce Adjustment: Stressors, Resources, and Definitions." *Journal of Marriage and the Family, 62,* 3, August 2000:655–668.

Wen, Ming. "Family Structure and Children's Health and Behavior." *Journal of Family Issues, 29,* 11, November 2008:1492–1519.

Whitehead, Barbara Dafoe, and David Popenoe. "The Marrying Kind: Which Men Marry and Why." Rutgers University: The State of Our Unions: The Social Health of Marriage in America, 2004.

Willie, Charles Vert, and Richard J. Reddick. *A New Look at Black Families,* 5th ed. Walnut Creek, Calif.: AltaMira Press, 2003.

Wilson, William Julius. "Jobless Poverty: A New Form of Social Dislocation in the Inner-City Ghetto." In *The Inequality Reader: Contemporary and Foundational Readings in Race, Class and Gender,* David B. Grusky and Szonja Szelenyi, eds. Boulder, Colo.: Westview Press, 2007:142–152.

Wolfinger, Nicholas H. "More Evidence for Trends in the Intergenerational Transmission of Divorce: A Completed Cohort Approach Using Data from the General Social Survey." *Demography, 48,* 2011:581–592.

Ying, Yu-Wen, and Meekyung Han. "Parental Contributions to Southeast Asian American Adolescents' Well-Being." *Youth and Society, 40,* 2, December 2008:289–306.

Zamiska, Nicholas. "Pressed to Do Well on Admissions Tests, Students Take Drugs." *Wall Street Journal,* November 8, 2004.

Chapter 13

ACLU. "ACLU and Asian Law Caucus Seek Records on FBI Surveillance of Mosques and Use of Informants in Northern California." ACLU Press Release, March 9, 2010.

Anderson, Philip. "God and the Swedish Immigrants." *Sweden and America,* Autumn 1995:17–20.

Associated Press. "Court Allows Priest to Sacrifice Goats in Texas Home." July 31, 2009.

Bailey, Martha J., and Susan M. Dynarski. "Gains and Gaps: Changing Inequality in U.S. College Entry and Completion." In *Whither Opportunity?: Rising Inequality, Schools, and Children's Life Chances,* Greg J. Duncan and Richard J. Murnane, eds. Russell Sage, September 2011.

Basten, Christoph, and Frank Betz. "Max Weber's Protestant Ethic in Contemporary Switzerland." Florence, Italy: European University Institute, November 2008.

Basten, Christoph, and Frank Betz. "Marx vs. Weber: Does Religion Affect Politics and the Economy?" Florence, Italy: European University Institute, 2011.

Becker, George. "The Continuing Path of Distortion: The Protestant Ethic and Max Weber's School Enrolment Statistics." *Acta Sociologica, 52, 3,* September 2009:195–212.

Benford, Robert D. "The College Sports Reform Movement: Reframing the 'Educational' Industry." *The Sociological Quarterly, 48,* 2007:1–28.

Bernstein, Elizabeth. "More Prayer, Less Hassle." *Wall Street Journal,* June 27, 2003:W3, W4.

Bosman, Julie. "New York Schools for Pregnant Girls Will Close." *New York Times,* May 24, 2007.

Bowles, Samuel. "Unequal Education and the Reproduction of the Social Division of Labor." In *Power and Ideology in Education,* J. Karabel and A. H. Halsely, eds. New York: Oxford University Press, 1977.

Bowles, Samuel, and Herbert Gintis. *Schooling in Capitalist America.* New York: Basic Books, 1976.

Bowles, Samuel, and Herbert Gintis. "*Schooling in Capitalist America* Revisited." *Sociology of Education, 75,* 2002:1–18.

Candey, Dana. "Critics of Graduation Exam Threaten Boycott in Florida." *New York Times,* May 13, 2003.

Carnevale, Anthony P., and Stephen J. Rose. "Socioeconomic Status, Race/Ethnicity, and Selective College Admissions." New York: The Century Foundation, March 2003.

Carper, James C. "Pluralism to Establishment to Dissent: The Religious and Educational Context of Home Schooling." *Peabody Journal of Education, 75,* 1–2, 2000:8–19.

Catsambis, Sophia, Anthony Buttaro, Jr., Lynn M. Mulkey, Lala Carr Steelman, and Pamela Ray Koch. "Examining Gender Differences in Ability Group Placement at the Onset of Schooling: The Role of Skills, Behavior, and Teacher Evaluation." *Journal of Educational Research, 105,* 2012:8–20.

Coleman, James S., and Thomas Hoffer. *Public and Private Schools: The Impact of Communities.* New York: Basic Books, 1987.

College Board. "College-Bound Seniors 2011," 2011a. http://www .collegeboard.com

College Board. "Improving Student Transfer from Community Colleges to Four-Year Institutions," 2011b.

Collins, Randall. *The Credential Society: An Historical Sociology of Education.* New York: Academic Press, 1979.

Davis, Kingsley, and Wilbert E. Moore. "Some Principles of Stratification." *American Sociological Review, 10,* 1945:242–249.

Deaver, Michael V. "Democratizing Russian Higher Education." *Demokratizatsiya, 9,* 3, Summer 2001:350–366.

Dillon, Sam. "States' Data Obscure How Few Finish High School." *New York Times,* March 20, 2008.

Dove, Adrian. "Soul Folk 'Chitling' Test or the Dove Counterbalance Intelligence Test." Mimeo, no date.

Douthat, Ross. "The Truth About Harvard." *Atlantic Monthly,* March 2005.

Durkheim, Emile. *The Elementary Forms of the Religious Life.* New York: Free Press, 1965. Originally published 1912.

Elinson, Elaine. "Lifting the Veil on Government Surveillance." *ACLU News,* Spring 2004.

Elliott, Joel. "Birth Control Allowed for Maine Middle Schoolers." *New York Times,* October 18, 2007.

Ernst, Eldon G. "The Baptists." In *Encyclopedia of the American Religious Experience: Studies of Traditions and Movements,* Vol. 1, Charles H. Lippy and Peter W. Williams, eds. New York: Scribners, 1988:555–577.

Farkas, George. *Human Capital or Cultural Capital?: Ethnicity and Poverty Groups in an Urban School District.* New York: Walter DeGruyter, 1996.

Farkas, George, Robert P. Grobe, Daniel Sheehan, and Yuan Shuan. "Cultural Resources and School Success: Gender, Ethnicity, and Poverty Groups within an Urban School District." *American Sociological Review, 55,* February 1990a:127–142.

Farkas, George, Daniel Sheehan, and Robert P. Grobe. "Coursework Mastery and School Success: Gender, Ethnicity, and Poverty Groups within an Urban School District." *American Educational Research Journal, 27,* 4, Winter 1990b:807–827.

Feder, Barnaby J. "Services at the First Church of Cyberspace." *New York Times,* May 15, 2004.

Fletcher, Jason. "Spillover Effects of Inclusion of Classmates with Emotional Problems on Test Scores in Early Elementary School." *Journal of Policy Analysis and Management, 29,* 1, Winter 2010:69–83.

Gabriel, Trip. "Under Pressure, Teachers Tamper with Test Scores." *New York Times,* June 10, 2010.

Gauch, Sarah. "In Egyptian Schools, a Push for Critical Thinking." *Christian Science Monitor,* February 9, 2006.

Gillum, R. F. "Frequency of Attendance at Religious Services and Smoking: The Third National Health and Nutrition Examination Survey." *Preventive Medicine, 41,* 2005:607–613.

Greeley, Andrew M. "The Protestant Ethic: Time for a Moratorium." *Sociological Analysis, 25,* Spring 1964:20–33.

Hanson, Chad. *The Community College and the Good Society.* New Brunswick, N.J.: Transaction Publishers, 2010.

Hartocollis, Anemona. "Harvary Faculty Votes to Put the Excellence Back in the A." *New York Times,* May 22, 2002.

Hellinger, Daniel, and Dennis R. Judd. *The Democratic Facade.* Pacific Grove, Calif: Brooks/Cole, 1991.

Jenkins, Philip. "The Next Christianity." *Atlantic Monthly,* October 2002:53–68.

Johnson, Benton. "On Church and Sect." *American Sociological Review, 28,* 1963:539–549.

Kelley, Tina. "In an Era of School Shootings, a New Drill." *New York Times,* March 25, 2008.

LaFraniere, Sharon. "African Crucible: Cast as Witches, Then Cast Out." *New York Times,* November 15, 2007.

"Less Rote, More Variety: Reforming Japan's Schools." *The Economist,* December 16, 2000:8.

Manzo, Kathleen Kennedy. "History in the Making." *Community College Week, 13,* 15, March 5, 2001:6–8.

Marx, Karl. "Contribution to the Critique of Hegel's Philosophy of Right." In *Karl Marx: Early Writings,* T. B. Bottomore, ed. New York: McGraw-Hill, 1964:45. Originally published 1844.

McNeill, David. "Facing Enrollment Crisis, Japanese Universities Fight to Attract Students." *Chronicle of Higher Education,* July 11, 2008.

Medina, Jennifer. "U.S. Math Tests Find Scant Gains across New York." *New York Times,* October 14, 2009.

Merton, Robert K. *Social Theory and Social Structure*. Glencoe, Ill.: Free Press, 1949. Enlarged ed., 1968.

"Mujer con cabeza humana alega religion en defensa." AOL Online News, February 14, 2006.

Nakamura, Akemi. "Abe to Play Hardball with Soft Education System." *The Japan Times*, October 27, 2006.

National Center for Education Statistics. *Digest of Education Statistics*. Washington, D.C.: U.S. Government Printing Office, 1991.

National School Safety Center. "School Associated Violent Deaths." Westlake Village, Calif., 2012.

Nauta, André. "That They All May Be One: Can Denominationalism Die?" Paper presented at the annual meetings of the American Sociological Association, 1993.

Nemtsova, Anna. "In Russia, Corruption Plagues the Higher-Education System." *Chronicle of Higher Education*, February 22, 2008.

Newport, Frank, Dan Witters, and Sangeeta Agrawal. "Religious Americans Enjoy Higher Wellbeing." Princeton, N.J.: Gallup Poll, February 16, 2012.

Osterman, Paul. "Community Colleges: Promise, Performance, and Policy." MIT Sloan School, June 2010.

Ouchi, William. "Decision-Making in Japanese Organizations." In *Down to Earth Sociology: Introductory Readings*, 7th ed., James M. Henslin, ed. New York: Free Press, 1993:503–507.

Padgett, Tim. "An Ivy Stepladder." *Time*, April 4, 2005.

Panzarella, Jamie. "Achieving the Dream: Helping Community Colleges Focus on Student Success." *Footnotes*, 36, 1, January 2008:6.

Parsons, Talcott. "An Analytic Approach to the Theory of Social Stratification." *American Journal of Sociology*, 45, 1940:841–862.

Pedersen, R. P. "How We Got Here: It's Not How You Think." *Community College Week*, 13, 15, March 15, 2001:4–5.

Pope, Liston. *Millhands and Preachers: A Study of Gastonia*. New Haven, Conn.: Yale University Press, 1942.

Rapoport, Anatoli. "Patriotic Education in Russia: Stylistic Move or a Sign of Substantive Counter-Reform." *Educational Forum*, 73, 2009:141–152.

"Reviews of National Policies for Education: Higher Education in Egypt 2010." London: Organisation for Economic Co-operation and Development, 2010.

Rhoads, Christopher. "Web Site to Holy Site: Israeli Firm Broadcasts Prayers for a Fee." *Wall Street Journal*, January 25, 2007.

Rist, Ray C. "Student Social Class and Teacher Expectations: The Self-Fulfilling Prophecy in Ghetto Education." *Harvard Educational Review*, 40, 3, August 1970:411–451.

Rist, Ray. "Student Social Class and Teacher Expectations: The Self-Fulfilling Prophecy in Ghetto Education." *Harvard Educational Review*, reprinted in *Opportunity Gap: Achievement and Inequality in Education*, Carol DeShano, James Philip Huguley, Zenub Kakli, Radhika Rao, and Ronald F. Ferguson, eds. Cambridge, MA.: Harvard Education Publishing Group, 2007:187–225.

"Russia Sets Out to Fight Corruption in Education with a New Standardized Test." Associated Press, February 2, 2007.

Schemo, Diana Jean. "Education Dept. Says States Have Lax Standard for Teachers." *New York Times*, June 13, 2002.

Stark, Rodney. *Sociology*, 3rd ed. Belmont, Calif.: Wadsworth, 1989.

Statistical Abstract of the United States. Washington, D.C.: U.S. Census Bureau, published annually.

Severson, Kim. "Systematic Cheating Is Found in Atlanta's School System." *New York Times*, July 6, 2011.

Smith, Christian, and Robert Faris. "Socioeconomic Inequality in the American Religious System: An Update and Assessment." *Journal for the Scientific Study of Religion*, 44, 1, 2005:95–104.

Sullivan, Kevin. "India Embraces Online Worship." *Washington Post*, March 15, 2007.

"Testing Times." *The Economist*, December 31, 2011.

Thompson, Ginger. "Where Education and Assimilation Collide." *New York Times*, March 14, 2009.

Tomsho, Robert, and Daniel Golden. "Educating Eric." *Wall Street Journal*, May 12, 2007.

Troeltsch, Ernst. *The Social Teachings of the Christian Churches*. New York: Macmillan, 1931.

UNESCO. "UNESCO Launches Global Partnership for Girls and Women's Education." June 2011.

Urbina, Ian. "As School Exit Tests Prove Tough, States Ease Standards." *New York Times*, January 11, 2010a.

U.S. Religious Landscape Survey. "Religious Affiliation: Diverse and Dynamic." Washington, D.C.: PEW Foundation, February 2008.

Wallace, John M., Ryoko Yamaguchi, Jerald G. Bachman, Patrick M. O'Malley, John E. Schulenberg, and Lloyd D. Johnston. "Religiosity and Adolescent Substance Use: The Role of Individual and Contextual Influences." *Social Problems*, 54, 2, 2007:308–327.

Weber, Max. *The Protestant Ethic and the Spirit of Capitalism*. New York: Scribner's, 1958. Originally published 1904–1905.

White, Jack E. "Forgive Us Our Sins." *Time*, July 3, 1995:29.

Yamamoto, Yoko, and Mary C. Brinton. "Cultural Capital in East Asian Educational Systems: The Case of Japan." *Sociology of Education*, 83, 1, 2010:67–83.

Yinger, J. Milton. *The Scientific Study of Religion*. New York: Macmillan, 1970.

Chapter 14

Aydemir, Abdurrahman, and George J. Borjas. "Attenuation Bias in Measuring the Wage Impact of Immigration." *Journal of Labor Economics*, 29, 1, 2011:69–112.

Anderson, Elijah. *Streetwise: Race, Class, and Change in an Urban Community*. Chicago: University of Chicago Press, 1990.

Anderson, Elizabeth. "Recent Thinking about Sexual Harassment: A Review Essay." *Philosophy & Public Affairs*, 34, 3, 2006:284–312.

Berman, Marc G., John Jonides, and Stephen Kaplan. "The Cognitive Benefits of Interacting with Nature." *Psychological Science*, 19, 12, 2008:1207–1212.

Brockerhoff, Martin P. "An Urbanizing World." *Population Bulletin*, 55, 3, September 2000:1–44.

Burgess, Ernest W. "The Growth of the City: An Introduction to a Research Project." In *The City*, Robert E. Park et al., eds. Chicago: University of Chicago Press, 1925:47–62.

Chandler, Tertius, and Gerald Fox. *3000 Years of Urban Growth*. New York: Academic Press, 1974.

Chishti, Muzaffar, and Claire Bergeron. "Increasing Evidence That Recession Has Caused Number of Unauthorized Immigrants in US to Drop." Washington, D.C.: Migration Policy Institute, March 15, 2010.

Council of Economic Advisers. "Immigration's Economic Impact." Washington, D.C., June 20, 2007.

Cousins, Albert N., and Hans Nagpaul. *Urban Man and Society: A Reader in Urban Sociology.* New York: McGraw-Hill, 1970.

Darley, John M., and Bibb Latané. "Bystander Intervention in Emergencies: Diffusion of Responsibility." *Journal of Personality and Social Psychology, 8,* 4, 1968:377–383.

Davis, Donald R., and David E. Weinstein. "Technological Superiority and the Losses from Migration." National Bureau of Economic Research, working paper, June 2002.

Day, Jennifer Chesseman. "Population Profile of the United States: National Population Projections." Washington, D.C.: U.S. Census Bureau, 2010.

Dougherty, Conor. "The End of White Flight." *Wall Street Journal,* July 19, 2008a.

Dougherty, Conor. "The New American Gentry." *Wall Street Journal,* January 19, 2008b.

Dugger, Celia W. "Abortion in India Is Tipping Scales Sharply against Girls." *New York Times,* April 22, 2001.

Ehrlich, Paul R., and Anne H. Ehrlich. *Population, Resources, and Environment: Issues in Human Ecology,* 2nd ed. San Francisco: Freeman, 1972.

Ehrlich, Paul R., and Anne H. Ehrlich. "Humanity at the Crossroads." *Stanford Magazine,* Spring–Summer 1978:20–23.

Faunce, William A. *Problems of an Industrial Society,* 2nd ed. New York: McGraw-Hill, 1981.

Fischer, Claude S. *The Urban Experience.* New York: Harcourt, 1976.

Flanagan, William G. *Urban Sociology: Images and Structure.* Boston: Allyn and Bacon, 1990.

Food and Agriculture Organization of the United Nations. "World and Regional Review: Facts and Figures." 2006.

Food and Agriculture Organization of the United Nations. Statistics Division, January 2012.

Fountain, Henry. "Archaeological Site in Peru is Called Oldest City in Americas." *New York Times,* April 27, 2001.

Gans, Herbert J. *The Urban Villagers.* New York: Free Press, 1962.

Gans, Herbert J. *People and Plans: Essays on Urban Problems and Solutions.* New York: Basic Books, 1968.

Gans, Herbert J. *People, Plans, and Policies: Essays on Poverty, Racism, and Other National Urban Problems.* New York: Columbia University Press, 1991.

Gettleman, Jeffrey. "Starvation and Strife Menace Torn Kenya." *New York Times,* February 28, 2009.

Goll, Sven. "Archaeologists Find 'Mini-Pompei'" *Views and News from Norway,* October 1, 2010.

Greenhalgh, Susan. "The Chinese Biopolitical: Facing the Twenty-First Century." *New Genetics and Society, 28,* 3, September 2009:205–222.

Harney, Alexandra. "The Plight of China's Favored Sons." *New York Times,* December 19, 2011.

Harris, Chauncey D. "The Nature of Cities and Urban Geography in the Last Half Century." *Urban Geography, 18,* 1997.

Harris, Chauncey D., and Edward Ullman. "The Nature of Cities." *Annals of the American Academy of Political and Social Science, 242,* 1945:7–17.

Haub, Carl. "World Population Data Sheet." Washington, D.C.: Population Reference Bureau, 2004.

Haub, Carl. "Population Data Sheet." Washington, D.C.: Population Reference Bureau, 2011.

Haub, Carl, and Mary Mederlos Kent. "World Population Data Sheet." Washington, D.C.: Population Reference Bureau, 2008.

Haub, Carl, and Nancy Yinger. "The U.N. Long-Range Population Projections: What They Tell Us." Washington, D.C.: Population Reference Bureau, 1994.

Haughney, Christine. "Harlem's Real Estate Boom Becomes a Bust." *New York Times,* July 8, 2009.

Hauser, Philip, and Leo Schnore, eds. *The Study of Urbanization.* New York: Wiley, 1965.

Hawley, Amos H. *Urban Society: An Ecological Approach.* New York: Wiley, 1981.

Homblin, Dora Jane. *The First Cities.* Boston: Little, Brown, Time-Life Books, 1973.

Hoyt, Homer. *The Structure and Growth of Residential Neighborhoods in American Cities.* Washington, D.C.: Federal Housing Administration, 1939.

Hoyt, Homer. "Recent Distortions of the Classical Models of Urban Structure." In *Internal Structure of the City: Readings on Space and Environment,* Larry S. Bourne, ed. New York: Oxford University Press, 1971:84–96.

Hyra, Derek S. "Racial Uplift? Intra-Racial Class Conflict and the Economic Revitalization of Harlem and Bronzeville." *City and Community, 5,* 1, March 2006:71–92.

Jordan, Miriam. "Among Poor Villagers, Female Infanticide Still Flourishes in India." *Wall Street Journal,* May 9, 2000:A1, A12.

Karp, David A., Gregory P. Stone, and William C. Yoels. *Being Urban: A Sociology of City Life,* 2nd ed. New York: Praeger, 1991.

Katz, Bruce, and Jennifer Bradley. "The Suburban Challenge." *Newsweek,* January 26, 2009.

LaFraniere, Sharon. "As China Ages, Birthrate Policy May Prove Difficult to Reverse." *New York Times,* April 6, 2011.

Lee, Trymaine. "In a Changing Harlem, Rift between Old and New Business Owners." *New York Times,* December 19, 2010.

Leland, John. "A New Harlem Gentry in Search of Its Latte." *New York Times,* August 7, 2003.

Lenski, Gerhard, and Jean Lenski. *Human Societies: An Introduction to Macrosociology,* 5th ed. New York: McGraw-Hill, 1987.

Malthus, Thomas Robert. *First Essay on Population 1798.* London: Macmillan, 1926. Originally published 1798.

Mamdani, Mahmood. "The Myth of Population Control: Family, Caste, and Class in an Urban Village." New York: Monthly Review Press, 1973.

McCarthy, Michael J. "Granbury, Texas, Isn't a Rural Town: It's a 'Micropolis.'" *Wall Street Journal,* June 3, 2004.

McDowell, Bart. "Mexico City: An Alarming Giant." *National Geographic, 166,* 1984:139–174.

McFalls, Joseph A., Jr. "Population: A Lively Introduction, 5th ed." *Population Bulletin, 62,* 1, March 2007:1–30.

McKeown, Thomas. *The Modern Rise of Population.* New York: Academic Press, 1977.

McKinnish, Terra, Randall Walsh, and Kirk White. "Who Gentrifies Low-Income Neighborhoods?" National Bureau of Economic Research, Working Paper 14036, May 2008.

McNeill, William H. "How the Potato Changed the World's History." *Social Research, 66,* 1, Spring 1999:67–83.

Milbank, Dana. "Guarded by Greenbelts, Europe's Town Centers Thrive." *Wall Street Journal,* May 3, 1995:B1, B4.

Moreno, Eduardo Lopez, Oyebanji Oyeyinka, and Gora Mboup. *State of the World's Cities 2010/2011: Bridging the Urban Divide.* London: UN Habitat, 2012.

Mosher, Steven W. "Too Many People? Not by a Long Shot." *Wall Street Journal,* February 10, 1997:A18.

Mosher, Steven W. "China's One-Child Policy: Twenty-Five Years Later." *Human Life Review,* Winter 2006:76–101.

Palen, J. John. *The Urban World,* 8th ed. Boulder, Colo.: Paradigm, 2008.

Palen, J. John. *The Urban World,* 9th ed. New York: Paradigm Publishers, 2012.

Park, Robert Ezra. "Human Ecology." *American Journal of Sociology, 42,* 1, July 1936:1–15.

Park, Robert Ezra, and Ernest W. Burgess. *Human Ecology.* Chicago: University of Chicago Press, 1921.

Piotrow, Phylis Tilson. *World Population Crisis: The United States' Response.* New York: Praeger, 1973.

Population Today 4, 5, September 1998.

Riley, Nancy E. "China's Population: New Trends and Challenges." *Population Bulletin, 59,* 2, June 2004:3–36.

Sang-Hun, Choe. "Where Boys Were Kings, a Shift toward Baby Girls." *New York Times,* December 23, 2007.

Santos, Fernanda. "Are New Yorkers Satisfied? That Depends." *New York Times,* March 7, 2009.

Shapiro, Robert J., and Jiwon Vellucci. "The Impact of Immigration and Immigration Reform on the Wages of American Workers." Washington, D.C.: New Policy Institute, May 2010.

"State of the World: Innovations that Nourish the Planet." Washington, D.C.: Worldwatch Institute, 2011.

Statistical Abstract of the United States. Washington, D.C.: U.S. Census Bureau, published annually.

Stokes, Myron, and David Zeman. "The Shame of the City." *Newsweek,* September 4, 1995.

Thurow, Roger. "Farms Destroyed, Stricken Sudan Faces Food Crisis." *Wall Street Journal,* February 7, 2005.

"Tsunami Deaths over 283,000." News 24.com, January 27, 2005.

Ullman, Edward, and Chauncey Harris. "The Nature of Cities." In *Urban Man and Society: A Reader in Urban Ecology,* Albert N. Cousins and Hans Nagpaul, eds. New York: Knopf, 1970:91–100.

United Nations. "An Overview of Urbanization, Internal Migration, Population Distribution and Development in the World." United Nations Population Division, January 14, 2008.

United Nations. "World Urbanizing Prospects: The 2009 Revision." U.N. Department of Economic and Social Affairs, Population Division, 2010.

United Nations. 2015 Population Projections.

Wilford, John Noble. "In Maya Ruins, Scholars See Evidence of Urban Sprawl." *New York Times,* December 19, 2000.

Williams, Timothy. "Old Sound in Harlem Draws New Neighbors' Ire." *New York Times,* July 6, 2008.

Wirth, Louis. "Urbanism as a Way of Life." *American Journal of Sociology, 44,* July 1938:1–24.

"The World of the Child 6 Billion." Population Reference Bureau, 2000.

Yardley, Jim. "Faces of Abortion in China: A Young, Single Woman." *New York Times,* May 13, 2007.

Yardley, Jim. "India Tries Using Cash Bonuses to Slow Birthrates." *New York Times,* August 21, 2010c.

Chapter 15

Aberle, David. *The Peyote Religion among the Navaho.* Chicago: Aldine, 1966.

Adam, David. "Climate: The Hottest Year." *Nature, 468,* November 15, 2010:362–364.

American Sociological Association. "Section on Environment and Technology." Pamphlet, no date.

Barnes, Harry Elmer. *The History of Western Civilization,* Vol. 1. New York: Harcourt, Brace, 1935.

Barry, John. "A New Breed of Soldier." *Newsweek,* December 10, 2001:24–31.

Bell, Michael Mayerfeld. *An Invitation to Environmental Sociology.* Los Angeles: Pine Forge Press, 2009.

Berger, Peter L. *Invitation to Sociology: A Humanistic Perspective.* New York: Doubleday, 1963.

Berger, Peter. "Invitation to Sociology." In *Down to Earth Sociology: Introductory Readings,* 15th ed., James M. Henslin, ed. New York: Free Press, 2012. Originally published 1963.

Boudreaux, Richard. "Putin Move Stirs Russian Environmentalist Row." *New York Times,* January 20, 2010.

Bradsher, Keith. "China Enacting a High-Tech Plan to Track People." *New York Times,* August 12, 2007.

Carpenter, Betsy. "Redwood Radicals." *U.S. News & World Report, 109,* 11, September 17, 1990:50–51.

Chase, Arlen F., Diane Z. Chase, and John F. Weishampel. "Lasers in the Jungle." *Archeology, 63,* 4, July/August 2010.

Cooper, Charles. "Unmanned Space Plane Opening Door to Space Weaponization?" CBS News, April 22, 2010.

Crossland, David. "Gas Dispute Has Europe Trembling." *Spiegel Online,* January 2, 2006.

Dunlap, Riley E., and William R. Catton, Jr. "Environmental Sociology." *Annual Review of Sociology, 5,* 1979:243–273.

Dunlap, Riley E., and William R. Catton, Jr. "What Environmental Sociologists Have in Common Whether Concerned with 'Built' or 'Natural' Environments." *Sociological Inquiry, 53,* 2–3, 1983:113–135.

Durning, Alan. "Cradles of Life." In *Social Problems 90/91,* LeRoy W. Barnes, ed. Guilford, Conn.: Dushkin, 1990:231–241.

Douthat, Ross. "Abortion Politics Didn't Doom the G.O.P." *New York Times,* December 7, 2008.

Eder, Klaus. "The Rise of Counter-Culture Movements against Modernity: Nature as a New Field of Class Struggle." *Theory, Culture & Society, 7,* 1990:21–47.

Fattig, Paul. "Good Intentions Gone Bad." *Mail Tribune,* June 6, 2007.

Foote, Jennifer. "Trying to Take Back the Planet." *Newsweek, 115,* 6, February 5, 1990:24–25.

Forsyth, Jim. "Proabortion Group Asks Judge to Block Texas Sonogram Law." *Reuters,* July 6, 2011.

Frommer, Arthur. *Peru.* New York: Wiley, 2007.

Gorman, Peter. "A People at Risk: Vanishing Tribes of South America." *The World & I,* December 1991:678–689.

Grigoriadis, Vanessa. "The Rise and Fall of the Eco-Radical Underground." *Rolling Stone,* June 21, 2011.

Gunther, Marc. "The Mosquito in the Tent." *Fortune, 149,* 11, May 31, 2004:158.

Handwerk, Brian. "Maya City in 3-D." *National Geographic Daily News,* May 20, 2010.

Haenfler, Ross, Brett Johnson, and Ellis Jones. "Lifestyle Movements: Exploring the Intersection of Lifestyle and Social Movements." *Social Movement Studies, iFirst,* 2012:1–20.

Hughes, H. Stuart. *Oswald Spengler: A Critical Estimate,* rev. ed. New York: Scribner's, 1962.

Jasper, James M. "Emotions and Social Movements: Twenty Years of Theory and Research." Unpublished paper, 2012.

Jasper, James M. "Moral Dimensions of Social Movements." Paper presented at the annual meetings of the American Sociological Association, 1991.

Klandermans, Bert. *The Social Psychology of Protest.* Cambridge, Mass.: Blackwell, 1997.

Knickerbocker, Brad. "Firebrands of 'Ecoterrorism' Set Sights on Urban Sprawl." *Christian Science Monitor,* August 6, 2003.

Kramer, Andrew E. "Putin's Grasp of Energy Drives Russian Agenda." *New York Times,* January 29, 2009.

Lang, Kurt, and Gladys E. Lang. *Collective Dynamics.* New York: Crowell, 1961.

Larson, Christina. "Green Activists Feel Sting of Chinese Government Crackdown." Yale e360, June 30, 2011.

"Last Remaining Amazon Tribes Nearing Extinction." *International Business Times,* June 26, 2011.

Lee, Alfred McClung, and Elizabeth Briant Lee. *The Fine Art of Propaganda: A Study of Father Coughlin's Speeches.* New York: Harcourt Brace, 1939.

Lenski, Gerhard, and Jean Lenski. *Human Societies: An Introduction to Macrosociology,* 5th ed. New York: McGraw-Hill, 1987.

Lerner, Steve. *Sacrifice Zones: The Front Lines of Toxic Chemical Exposure in the United States.* Cambridge, Mass.: MIT Press, 2010.

Linden, Eugene. "Lost Tribes, Lost Knowledge." *Time,* September 23, 1991:46, 48, 50, 52, 54, 56.

Mauss, Armand. *Social Problems as Social Movements.* Philadelphia: Lippincott, 1975.

McCarthy, John D., and Mayer N. Zald. "Resource Mobilization and Social Movements: A Partial Theory." *American Journal of Sociology, 82,* 6, 1977:1212–1241.

McElroy, Damien. "Russian General Says Poland a Nuclear 'Target.'" *Telegraph,* August 15, 2008.

McVeigh, Rory. *The Rise of the Klu Klux Klan: Right-Wing Movements and National Politics.* Minneapolis: University of Minnesota Press, 2009.

Mirola, William A. "Asking for Bread, Receiving a Stone: The Rise and Fall of Religious Ideologies in Chicago's Eight-Hour Movement." *Social Problems, 50,* 2, May 2003:273–293.

Morgan, Lewis Henry. *Ancient Society.* New York: Holt, 1877.

Nabhan, Gary Paul. *Cultures in Habitat: On Nature, Culture, and Story.* New York: Counterpoint, 1998.

Nichol, Jim. "Russian Political, Economic, and Security Issues and U.S. Interests." Washington, D.C.: Congressional Research Service, November 4, 2011.

Ogburn, William F. *Social Change with Respect to Culture and Human Nature.* New York: W. B. Huebsch, 1922. (Other editions by Viking in 1927, 1938, and 1950.)

Ogburn, William F. "The Hypothesis of Cultural Lag." In *Theories of Society: Foundations of Modern Sociological Theory,* Vol. 2, Talcott Parsons, Edward Shils, Kaspar D. Naegele, and Jesse R. Pitts, eds. New York: Free Press, 1961:1270–1273.

Ogburn, William F. *On Culture and Social Change: Selected Papers,* Otis Dudley Duncan, ed. Chicago: University of Chicago Press, 1964.

Page, Jeremy. "China's New Drones Raise Eyebrows." *Wall Street Journal,* November 18, 2010.

Parfit, Michael, "Earth First!ers Wield a Mean Monkey Wrench." *Smithsonian, 21,* 1, April 1990:184–204.

Reed, Susan, and Lorenzo Benet. "Ecowarrior Dave Foreman Will Do Whatever It Takes in His Fight to Save Mother Earth." *People Weekly, 33,* 15, April 16, 1990:113–116.

Rogers, Simon, and Lisa Evans. "World Carbon Dioxide Emissions Data by Country: China Speeds Ahead of the Rest." *Guardian,* January 31, 2011.

Rosenthal, Elisabeth, and Andrew C. Revkin. "Science Panel Calls Global Warming 'Unequivocal.'" *New York Times,* February 2, 2007.

Sahlins, Marshall D., and Elman R. Service. *Evolution and Culture.* Ann Arbor: University of Michigan Press, 1960.

Sanger, David E., and Elizabeth Bumiller. "Pentagon to Consider Cyberattacks Acts of War." *New York Times,* May 31, 2011.

Sanger, David E., John Markoff, and Thom Shanker. "U.S. Plans Attack and Defense in Cyberspace Warfare." *New York Times,* April 27, 2009.

Sharp, Lauriston. "Steel Axes for Stone-Age Australians." In *Down to Earth Sociology: Introductory Readings,* 8th ed., James M. Henslin, ed. New York: Free Press, 1995:453–462.

Simons, Marlise. "Social Change and Amazon Indians." In *Exploring Social Life: Readings to Accompany Essentials of Sociology: A Down-to-Earth Approach, Sixth Edition,* 2nd edition, James M. Henslin, ed. Boston: Allyn and Bacon, 2006:157–165.

Smart, Barry. "On the Disorder of Things: Sociology, Postmodernity and the 'End of the Social.'" *Sociology, 24,* 3, August 1990:397–416.

Spector, Malcolm, and John Kitsuse. *Constructing Social Problems.* Menlo Park, Calif.: Cummings, 1977.

Statistical Abstract of the United States. Washington, D.C.: U.S. Census Bureau, published annually.

Stein, Rob. "FDA Approves Implantable Identity Chip." *Washington Post,* October 14, 2004.

Stipp, David. "Himalayan Tree Could Serve as Source of Anti-Cancer Drug Taxol, Team Says." *Wall Street Journal,* April 20, 1992:B4.

"Threatened Island Nations: Legal Implications of Rising Seas and a Changing Climate." New York: Columbia University, Conference at Columbia Law School, May 23–25, 2011.

Tilly, Charles. *Social Movements, 1768–2004.* Boulder, Colo.: Paradigm Publishers, 2004.

Toynbee, Arnold. *A Study of History,* D. C. Somervell, abridger and ed. New York: Oxford University Press, 1946.

Wall, Robert. "China's Armed Predator." *Aviation Week,* November 17, 2010.

Walter, Lynn. *Women's Rights: A Global View.* Westport, Conn.: Greenwood Press, 2001.

Weiner, Tim. "Pentagon Envisioning a Costly Internet for War." *New York Times,* November 13, 2004.

Weiner, Tim. "Air Force Seeks Bush's Approval for Space Weapons Programs." *New York Times,* May 18, 2005.

Wilford, John Noble. "Mapping Ancient Civilization, in a Matter of Days." *New York Times,* May 10, 2010.

Williams, Rhys H. "Constructing the Public Good: Social Movements and Cultural Resources." *Social Problems, 42,* 1, February 1995:124–144.

Wolfensohn, James D., and Kathryn S. Fuller. "Making Common Cause: Seeing the Forest for the Trees." *International Herald Tribune,* May 27, 1998:11.

Wong, Gillian. "Wife Visits Jailed China Activist Ahead of Release." Associated Press, June 20, 2011.

World Bank. "Cost of Pollution in China: Economic Estimates of Physical Damages." Washington, D.C: World Bank, February 2007.

Zakaria, Fareed. *The Post-American World*. New York: W. W. Norton, 2008.

Zald, Mayer N. "Looking Backward to Look Forward: Reflections on the Past and the Future of the Resource Mobilization Research Program." In *Frontiers in Social Movement Theory*, Aldon D. Morris and Carol McClurg Mueller, eds. New Haven, Conn.: Yale University Press, 1992:326–348.

Zald, Mayer N., and John D. McCarthy, eds. *Social Movements in an Organizational Society*. New Brunswick, N.J.: Transaction, 1987.

Name Index

Subject Index

Credits

Photo Credits

Chapter 1: pp. 2–3 Paul Mathews/Reuters/Landov pp. 5 Paul Emile Boutigny/The Bridgeman Art Library/Getty Images pp. **top:** 6 Roger-Viollet/The Image Works **middle:** Hulton-Deutsch Collection/Corbis **bottom:** Bettmann/Corbis pp. 7 **top:** Bettmann/Corbis **middle:** Joanne Ciccarello/Christian Science Monitor/The Image Works **bottom:** Jamie Carstairs/Impact/HIP/The Image Works pp. 8 The Granger Collection, NYC pp. 10 **clockwise from time:** Mary Evans Picture Library/The Image Works, University of Chicago Library, The Granger Collection, NYC, Bettmann/Corbis, The Granger Collection, NYC, The Granger Collection, NYC, Wellesley College Library, University of Chicago Library, Bettmann/Corbis, Bettmann/Corbis pp. 11 Everett Collection/SuperStock pp. 12 **top:** National Portrait Gallery, Smithsonian Institution/Art Resource, NY **middle:** The Granger Collection, NYC **bottom:** Yaroslava Mills pp. 13 Nickelodeon/Everett Collection pp. 16 University of Chicago Library pp. Pictorial Parade/Archive Photos/Getty Images pp. 19 Bettmann/Corbis pp. 22 Biel Alino/epa/Corbis pp. 25 Cartoonbank.com pp. 27 Gaetan Bally/Keystone/Corbis pp. 28 G. B. Trudeau/Universal Uclick pp. 29 Pearson pp. 30 **top:** Dinodia/The Image Works **bottom:** Dinodia/The Image Works pp. 31 Stephen Lovekin/WireImage/Getty Images pp. 33 ilian casino/Alamy pp. 34 Zoriah/EyePress EyePress/Newscom

Chapter 2: pp. 38–39 David Young-Wolff/PhotoEdit pp. 41 Karim Sahib/AFP/Newscom pp. 43 Jesus Diges/EPA/Landov pp. 44 Mariana Bazo/Reuters/Landov pp. 45 (clockwise) Pearson, Pearson, Pearson, Pearson, James Henslin, Steve Hamblin/Alamy pp. 46 **second row left:** Jean-Pierre Lescourret/Corbis **second row middle:** Panorama/The Image Works **second row right:** Piers Cavendish/Impact/HIP/The Image Works **bottom left:** ilse schrama/Alamy **bottom right:** Pacific Stock/SuperStock pp. 48 Pearson pp. 49 Chris Graythen/Getty Images pp. 50 Owen Franken/Corbis pp. 51 Dan Riedlhuber/Reuters/Landov pp. 52 John Raoux/AP Photos pp. 53 Seto Masato pp. 54 **top:** Ali Jarekji/Reuters/Landov **bottom:** Peter Morgan/Reuters/Landov pp. 55 **top left:** Pearson **top right:** Nicky Loh/Reuters/Landov **middle left:** Don Mason/Alamy **middle right:** Todd Glaser/Aurora Photos **bottom left:** Jeff Haynes/Reuters/Landov **bottom right:** Timothy a. Clary/Afp/Getty Images/Newscom pp. 58 Clarke Historical Museum pp. 59 **top:** Oliver Berg/EPA/Landov **bottom:** Carpenter, Dave/CartoonStock Ltd pp. 61 Paulo Santos/Reuters/Corbis

Chapter 3: pp. 64–65 Kymri Wilt/Danita Delimont Photography/Newscom pp. 66 Thomas Wanstall/The Image Works pp. 67 James Henslin pp. 68 Elise Jacob - UNEP/Still Pictures/The Image Works pp. 69 Nina Leen/Time & Life Pictures/Getty Images pp. 70 BE&W/SuperStock pp. Ariel Skelley/Corbis pp. 72 Bill Anderson/Photo Researchers, Inc. pp. 73 AP Photos pp. 74 **left to right:** Gary Hershorn/Reuters/Corbis, Lynne Fernandes/The Image Works, Matt York/AP Photos, Pool/Tim Graham Picture Library/Getty Images, Aaron Kehoe/Upi/Landov, pp. 76 TON KOENE/dpa/Landov pp. 77 Ben Speck/Getty Images News/Getty Images pp. 78 Frank and Ernest used with the permission of the Thaves and the Cartoonist Group. All rights reserved. pp. Harry Briggs/Cherry/Corbis pp. 80 **left:** Marcus Brandt/dpa/Landov **right:** SHNS photo/Eido/Newscom pp. 81 Post Stock/The Palm Beach Post pp. 82 Pearson pp. 83 George Doyle/Stockbyte/GettyImages pp. 84 Bill Aron/PhotoEdit pp. 86 moodboard/Corbis pp. 87 **left:** Oasis/Photos 12/Alamy **right:** Bob Adelman/Corbis pp. 88 Eye Ubiquitous/Glow Images pp. 89 AP Photos

Chapter 4: pp. 92–93 Dallas and John Heaton/Free Agents Limited/Corbis pp. 94 Doug Mills/AP Photos pp. 97 Arko Datta/Reuters/Landov pp. 98 Sheryl Nadler/Reuters/Landov pp. 98 Tobias Schwarz/Reuters/Corbis pp. 101 Frans Lanting/Corbis pp. 103 Linden/SIPA/Newscom pp. 105 George Doyle/Getty Images pp. 106 **left:** Scott Dalton/AP Photos **right:** Piotr Redlinski/The New York Times/Redux pp. 107 Landis Tim/SIPA/Newscom pp. 108 **vintage postcard:** Stephen Mulcahey/Alamy **stamp:** Stamp Collection/Alamy **camera lens:** Ingvar Björk/Alamy **world political map:** Topography Resources/Alamy

middle left, right, bottom: James Henslin pp. 109 **all images:** James Henslin pp. 110 **left:** Ng Han Gua/AP Photos **right:** Exactostock/SuperStock pp. 111 **left:** Pearson **right:** Plush Studios/Getty Images pp. 112 **top:** Ali Haider/EPA/Newscom **bottom:** Comedy Central/Everett Collection pp. 114 Creators Syndicate, Inc. pp. 115 **left:** Ian West/PA Photos/Landov **right:** FRED PROUSER/Reuters/Corbis pp. 116 Robert Galbraith/Reuters/Landov pp. 120 **all photos:** James Henslin **US postage stamp:** Blinow61/Shutterstock **camera lens:** Ingvar Björk/Alamy pp. 121 **all photos:** James Henslin pp. 122 **all photos:** James Henslin

Chapter 5: pp. 124–125 Andy Clark/Reuters/Landov pp. 127 **top left (left to right):** John Birdsall/The Image Works, Konstantin Sutyagin/Shutterstock, Veer Incorporated **top right:** Brand X Pictures/JupiterImages **bottom left:** Reuters/Landov **bottom right:** Alex Segre/Alamy pp. 129 Robert Weber/Cartoonbank.com pp. 130 David J. Phillip/AP Photos pp. 131 **left:** bad/ZUMA Press/Newscom **right:** Scott Houston/Sygma/Corbis pp. 133 ZUMA Press/Newscom pp. 134 North Wind Picture Archives/Alamy pp. 136 Danny Lehman/Corbis pp. 137 **top left:** March of Dimes Foundation **top right:** March of Dimes Foundation **bottom:** SuperStock/SuperStock pp. 138 **top:** Tom Cheney/Cartoonbank.com **bottom:** Pearson pp. 140 ColorBlind Images/Blend/AP Photos pp. 142 Kazuhiro Nogi/AFP/Getty Images/Newscom pp. 143 Pearson pp. 146 Pictorial Press Ltd/Alamy pp.148 Milgram shock experiment

Chapter 6: pp. 152–153 Matt York/AP Photos pp. 154 Shower in India pp. 155 Nigel Pavitt/John Warburton-Lee Photography/Alamy pp. 156 Babu/Reuters/Landov pp. 157 Rick Madonik/Toronto Star/ZUMA Press/Corbis pp. 158 SuperStock pp. 159 **top:** Chris Matula/Palm Beach Post/ZUMA Press/Newscom **bottom:** Lucy Nicholson/AFP/Getty Images/Newscom pp. 160 Bill Higgins pp. 161 Wolfgang Rattay/Reuters/Landov pp. 165 Rick Wilking/Reuters/Landov pp. 166 A. Ramey/PhotoEdit pp. 167 Pam Francis/Getty Images pp. 169 Underwood Photo Archives/SuperStock pp. 170 Leo Cullum/Cartoonbank.com pp. 173 Mike Twohy/Cartoonbank.com pp. 175 Pool/AP Photos pp. 178 AP Photos pp. 179 Pearson

Chapter 7: pp. 183–183 Philippe Huguen/AFP/Getty Images/Newscom pp. 184 Shawn G. Henry pp. 185 The Granger Collection, NYC pp. 186 James Henslin pp. 187 Alain Morvan pp. 188 James Henslin pp. 189 Topham/The Image Works pp. 190 **left:** Jacob August Riis/Bettmann/Corbis **right:** Bettmann/Corbis pp. 192 Jose Perez/Splash News/Newscom pp. 193 Adam Davy/PA Photos/Landov pp. 194 World History Archive World History Archive/Newscom pp. 197 James Henslin pp. 201 James Henslin pp. 202 **all photos:** James Henslin **postage stamp:** Ivan Vdovin/Alamy **camera lens:** Ingvar Björk/Alamy **world map:** Topography Resources/Alamy pp. 203 **all photos:** James Henslin pp. 205 **top:** Bob Daemmrich/The Image Works **bottom:** David Bacon/The Image Works pp. 206 Mohamed Nureldin Abdallah/Reuters/Landov

Chapter 8: pp. 210–211 Jeff Greenberg/The Image Works pp. 212 Mario Anzuoni/Reuters/Landov pp. 215 Splash News/Newscom pp. 218 Karim Sahib/AFP/Getty Images/Newscom pp. 219 Orlin Wagner/AP Photos pp. 221 John Van Hasselt/Corbis pp. 222 **left to right:** LTA WENN Photos/Newscom, Hans Deryk/Reuters/Landov, Everett Collection, Martin Bureau/AFP/Getty Images/Newscom pp. 223 Boris Drucker pp. 224 James Henslin pp. 226 **left:** Danny Lawson/EPA/Landov **right:** David Bacon/The Image Works pp. 227 Bob Daemmrich/The Image Works pp. 228 Bettmann/Corbis pp. 229 Corbis/SuperStock pp. 230 The Library of Congress pp. 232 Jean-Yves Rabeuf/The Image Works pp. 236 James Henslin

Chapter 9: pp. 238–239 Warren Morgan/Corbis pp. 240 John Stillwell/PA Photos/Landov pp. 241 Toru Hanai/Reuters/Landov

Text Credits

Ch. 1, pp. 15 Figure 1.4 Figure from "The Mark of a Criminal Record" by Devah Pager, from AMERICAN JOURNAL OF SOCIOLOGY, March 2003. Volume 108(5). Copyright © 2003 by Devah Pager. Reprinted with permission by University of Chicago Press.

Ch. 2, pp. 44 excerpt: Excerpt from GLUTTONS AND LIBERTINES: HUMAN PROBLEMS OF BEING NATURAL by Marston Bates, January 16, 1968. Copyright © 1968 by Marston Bates. Reprinted with permission of Russell & Volkening as agents for the author **pp. 52 excerpt:** Excerpt from COUNTERCULTURES: A SOCIOLOGICAL ANALYSIS by William W. Zellner, 1995. Copyright © 1995 by St. Martins Press. Reprinted with permission of Worth Publishers.

Ch. 3, pp. 65 excerpt: Excerpt from "Extreme Isolation of a Child" by Kingsley Davis, from AMERICAN JOURNAL OF SOCIOLOGY, January 4, 1940, Volume 45. Copyright © 1940 by the Kingsley David Estate. Reprinted with permission. **pp. 68 excerpt:** Excerpt from "A Study of the Effects of Differential Stimulation on Mentally Retarded Children" by H.M. Skeels and H.B. Dye, from PROCEEDINGS AND ADDRESSES OF THE AMERICAN ASSOCIATION ON MENTAL DEFICIENCY, 1939, Volume 44. Copyright © 1939 by the AAID. Reprinted with permission. **pp. 78 excerpt:** Excerpt from SCHOOL TALK: GENDER AND